P9-ARP-306

MEXICO
A Country Guide

MEXICO
A Country Guide

Contributors

Barbara Belejack
David Brooks
Elaine Burns
Laura Carlsen
Erika Harding
Luis Hernández
Joe Keenan
Felipe Montoya
Talli Nauman
Beth Sims

Edited by Tom Barry

The Inter-Hemispheric Education Resource Center
Albuquerque, New Mexico

LIBRARY
COLBY-SAWYER COLLEGE
NEW LONDON, NH 03257

F
1208
.M58275
1992

7/92

Copyright © 1992 by the Inter-Hemispheric Education Resource Center

First Edition, January 1992

Cover photo © Debra Preusch/Resource Center

No part of this book may be reproduced, stored in a retrieval system, or trans-
mitted in any form, by any means, including mechanical, electronic, photocop-
ying, recording, or otherwise, without prior written permission of the
publisher.

Published by the Inter-Hemispheric Education Resource Center

ISBN: 0-911213-35-X

Library of Congress Catalog Card Number: 91-076168

The Inter-Hemispheric Education Resource Center
Box 4506 Albuquerque, New Mexico 87196-4506

108833

Contributors

Tom Barry, editor of the book, is a research associate at the Resource Center. He wrote all sections of the book except for those listed below with their authors.

Barbara Belejack, a Mexico City journalist: Health and Welfare, Education and Student Organizing, and Other Foreign Interests.

David Brooks, the director of Mexico-U.S. Diálogos: Popular Organizing.

Elaine Burns, an organizer for Mujer a Mujer (MAM): Women and Feminism.

Laura Carlsen, a *Business Mexico* editor: Mexican Labor and Unions, Native People, and Nongovernmental Organizations (along with Luis Hernández).

Erika Harding, an editor for the Latin American Data Base: Human Rights.

Luis Hernández, Mexico City writer and organizer: Nongovernmental Organizations (with Laura Carlsen).

Joe Keenan, editor of *El Financiero International*: Political Parties and Elections (pages 24 to 29).

Felipe Montoya, a Resource Center research assistant, coauthored with Tom Barry: Agriculture and the Agrarian Crisis, and the Environment.

Talli Nauman, an Associated Press correspondent: Immigration and Refugees, and Communications Media.

Beth Sims, a Resource Center research associate: U.S. Foreign Policy, U.S. Economic Programs, and U.S. Security Assistance.

Acknowledgments

After more than 12 years of concentrating almost exclusively on Central America and the Caribbean, the Resource Center has again included Mexico in its research priorities. A Spanish-language information booklet for undocumented Mexican workers in the United States and an audiovisual entitled *La Frontera* were among the earliest resource materials produced by the center. With the publication of *Mexico: A Country Guide*, the Resource Center initiates a new series of publications and audiovisuals about Mexico.

The book represents the concerted effort of the entire staff. With her considerable organizing skills, Debra Preusch, the center's administrator and executive director, kept the staff working as a tight team and guided the research, writing, and production work to their successful conclusion. Besides her own contributions as an analyst and writer, Beth Sims also edited the entire manuscript. Nancy Guinn and John Hawley managed the design and production of the book. Research assistance came from Marisa Barrera, Hugh Bartling, Harry Browne, Colin Forsyth, Jodi Gibson, Claudia Medina, Felipe Montoya, Suzanne Stamatov, Trudy Wood-Foucar, and Beth Wood. The book was indexed by John Hawley, and LaDonna Kutz proofread it. Special thanks to John Hawley, whose care for detail and language, together with many long nights, brought the book to its successful conclusion.

The book benefited from the comments on various sections by the following experts and scholars: Miguel Alvarez, Cindy Anders, George Baker, David Barkin, Vivian Brochet, Roderic Camp, Víctor Clark Alfaro, Maria Cook, James Cypher, Roxanne Dunbar Ortiz, Bill Frelick, Paul Ganster, Michael Foley, Jonathan Fox, Carlos Heredia, Claudia Isaac, Dick Kamp, Mary Kelly, Karen Kovacs, Gilda Larrios, Kevin Middlebrook, Mario Monroy, Gray Newman, Andrew Reding, Primitivo Rodríguez, David Ronfeldt, Cristina Safa, Roberto Sánchez, David Stoll, Eduardo Valle, Ramón Vería, Steven Wager, Sidney Weintraub, and Matt Witt.

Finally, this book and the Resource Center's Mexico Project would not have been possible without the generous support of the John D. and Catharine T. MacArthur Foundation, North Shore Unitarian Universalist Veatch Program, Threshold Foundation, Max and Anna Levinson Foundation, Presbyterian Hunger Program, United Church Board for Homeland Ministries, Congregation of the Sisters of Divine Providence, Mennonite Central Committee, Christian Church and United Church of Christ. The Resource Center has also received general support from the Evangelical Lutheran Church in America; Dominican Sisters Poverty, Justice and Peace Fund; Sunflower Foundation; National Community Funds; Samuel Rubin Foundation; Maryknoll Fathers and Brothers; and United Methodist Office for the United Nations.

Tom Barry
Albuquerque, New Mexico
December 15, 1991

Table of Contents

List of Tables

The Resource Center

The Inter-Hemispheric Education Resource Center is a private non-profit research and policy institute located in Albuquerque, New Mexico. Founded in 1979, the Resource Center produces books, policy reports, audiovisuals, and other educational materials about U.S. foreign policy, as well as sponsoring popular education projects. For more information and a catalog of publications, please write to the Resource Center, Box 4506, Albuquerque, New Mexico 87196.

Board of Directors

Toney Anaya, *Former Governor of New Mexico*; Tom Barry, *Resource Center*; Blase Bonpane, *Office of the Americas*; Fred Bronkema, *Human Rights Office, National Council of the Churches of Christ*; Ann Mari Buitrago, *Center for Constitutional Rights*; Noam Chomsky, *Massachusetts Institute of Technology*; Dr. Charles Clements, *SatelLife*; Dr. Wallace Ford, *New Mexico Conference of Churches*; Antonio González, *Southwest Voter Research Institute*; Don Hancock, *Southwest Research and Information Center*; Patricia Hynds, *Maryknoll Lay Missioner*; Mary MacArthur, *Peace Brigades International*; Jennifer Manríquez, *Community Activist*; John Nichols, *Author*; Debra Preusch, *Resource Center*; Thomas E. Quigley, *U.S. Catholic Conference*; Margaret Randall, *Writer and Photographer*; Frank I. Sánchez, *Partnership for Democracy*; Peter Schey, *Center for Human Rights and Constitutional Law*; Beth Wood, *Central America Information Center*.

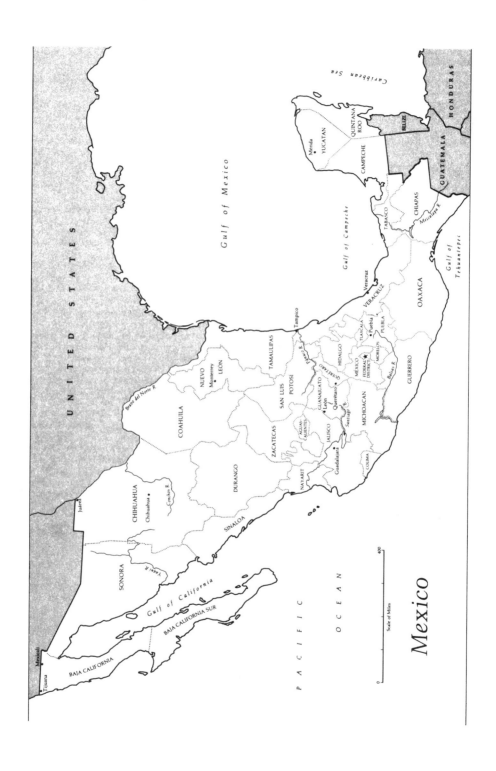

Mexico

Introduction

More than a hundred years before the U.S. eastern seaboard was colonized, Mexico City was a thriving colonial capital of the Spanish Empire. And for many centuries previous to the Spanish conquest, what is now called Mexico was home to several of the world's most advanced civilizations.

This early lead on development in the New World was soon lost. Economic and political progress in the United States and Canada quickly outstripped the pace of development in Mexico. The Mexican Revolution (1910-17) established a new foundation for the country's political and economic progress. The centralized political institutions and the new economic development strategies ushered in by the revolution gave Mexico a degree of political stability and economic growth that was the envy of other developing nations.

By the early 1970s, however, Mexico was again clearly slipping behind. As the economy stagnated, the country's political institutions and development strategies seemed increasingly outdated and inappropriate for modern times. The 1982 debt crisis and economic decline made reform urgent. Major changes were clearly needed to avoid political turmoil and to get the economy growing again. Many observers, however, considered Mexico too attached to old economic structures and its traditional style of one-party politics to undertake the needed reforms. But the speed with which the Mexican government moved to restructure the country's political and economic life surprised both its right- and leftwing critics.

The economic restructuring cautiously begun by President Miguel de la Madrid and later embraced by President Carlos Salinas put Mexico in the forefront of countries moving away from protected economies and toward free trade. In the early 1970s Mexico had been a leading voice among third world countries calling for a new international economic order to include a readjustment of North-South trading relations so as to correct imbalances favoring the industrial world. By the late 1980s Mexico had become a leading advocate of free market economics and neoliberal restructuring. Throwing off its third world label, Mexico under Salinas seeks to integrate itself into the developed world. To do so, the Mexican government has removed barriers to foreign investment and imports, promoted export production, and reduced its own direct participation in the economy. To cement this

radical economic restructuring, Mexico in 1991 entered into free trade negotiations with Canada and the United States as a partner in the economic integration of North America.

The overhaul of the political system in Mexico has been less dramatic.
Responding to its critics, the Salinas government instituted a new election-
reform package, created a human rights commission, and reduced the level
of obvious election fraud. Despite these and other reforms, Mexico's more
than six-decade history as an essentially one-party state continues. The
symbiotic relationship between the Institutional Revolutionary Party (PRI)
and the government still largely defines political life in Mexico.

Although the structure of politics remains much the same, the character
of the state and the ruling party are rapidly changing. The populist and nationalist rhetoric that formerly framed official discourse has been quietly
abandoned. Instead, the new catch words of government officials are economic integration, productivity, exports, privatization, and free trade. For a
strategic few of those not immediately benefiting from this capitalist modernization, the government offers its "solidarity" in the form of a new presidential social-welfare program called Pronasol. In its drive to modernize, the
Mexican state is reforming its corporatist networks of peasant and worker organizations at the same time it solicits new ties with the business elite, the middle classes, foreign investors, the Catholic church, and Washington. No longer
is membership in one of PRI's corporatist organizations necessary for party
membership. Instead of organizing by popular sectors, PRI is now open to individuals and it is beginning to organize by neighborhood and area.

By midterm in the Salinas administration there was little doubt that the
country was in the process of rapid change. Although there is little disagreement that major changes are needed to move the country forward, not
all Mexicans agree on the direction of the government's restructuring program. Many among the country's poor, workers, and peasants—the so-
called popular sectors—feel left out and victimized by the free market
economic reforms. There is also widespread skepticism that these reforms
will lead to long-term economic stability and growth. Another concern is
that, by dropping the revolution's nationalist and populist traditions, the
country will regress to the polarized social conditions that characterized life
in pre-revolutionary Mexico.

Whereas the major criticisms of economic modernization come from the
left and refer mainly to its neoliberal character and its rapid pace, the
government's political modernization program is criticized from both the
left and the right for its slow progress and narrow reach. Fraud remains
widespread in Mexican elections, and PRI's ready access to television and
state financial resources also works against meaningful democratization.
Human rights abuses remain pervasive, and the government has repeatedly
relied on its security forces to enforce its new economic and political order.
Instead of truly opening the democratic process, the government seems
more intent on consolidating PRI control.

The Changing Face of Mexico

The radical economic restructuring that is sweeping Mexico is taking place against a background of dramatic changes in Mexican society and in global trading and investment. Mexico since World War II has become a decidedly urban society, with the percentage of the population living in urban areas rising from about 40 percent in 1950 to 72 percent in 1990 (Table a). Agriculture, which traditionally formed the foundation of the economy, has been far surpassed in importance by services, commerce, manufacturing, and the petroleum industry.

Mexico's population has exploded. After World War II the country had fewer than 25 million people. By the early 1990s the population had increased to near 90 million, and by the year 2000 Mexico is expected to have well over 100 million people. Since the early 1970s government population-control programs have worked to slow down the rate of population growth, which had risen to nearly 3.5 percent a year in the 1960s. Today, that figure is down to almost 2 percent and is expected to continue dropping (Table b). Unfortunately, this decreasing rate of population growth has not yet significantly lowered the numbers of young women and men entering the work force for the first time. The annual increase in the number of Mexicans looking for jobs stands at about 3.5 percent, which means that as many as a million new jobs have to be created each year—far beyond the capacity of the Mexican economy.

Since the early 1980s there has been a growing awareness of the environmental consequences of uncontrolled economic development and population growth. Urban pollution has been the best consciousness-raiser. A

Table a
Urbanization of Mexico, 1950-90

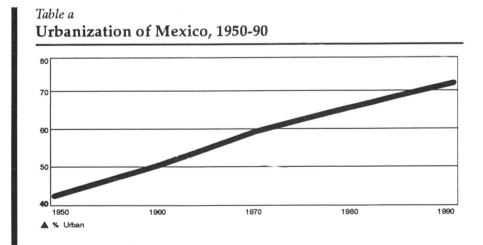

▲ % Urban

SOURCE: Inter-American Development Bank, *Social and Economic Progress 1990.*

permanent pall of pollution hangs over the Mexico City metropolitan area, the home of more than a quarter of the country's population. Living in the city means accepting a daily assault on one's health from dangerous levels of ozone, nitrogen oxide, sulphur, and other poisons. Many think that the city is already unlivable, but some public health experts predict that Mexico City may be virtually uninhabitable in another two or three decades. Nonetheless the city continues to expand, its outskirts filling up with squatters driven by desperation out of the depressed countryside.

Mexico City is the exaggerated case of a national phenomenon. The two other largest cities, Guadalajara and Monterrey, are also smothering in smog; yet even the smaller cities are clogged with traffic and choked by poisonous air. The automobile explosion is the main culprit of urban air pollution, but the dimensions of the country's environmental crisis extend far beyond the problem of smog. In the rush to industrialize and boost agroexports, Mexico's water, air, plants, and all living things have been treated as expendable resources.

The environmental and human costs resulting from such unregulated development are only now being tallied. Declining fishing yields, polluted tourist spots, salinated croplands, contaminated water supplies, desertified pastures, and deforested watersheds are just several aspects of the environmental nightmare facing Mexico. Although the country's industrialists, agribusinesses, and state enterprises are mainly responsible for ecological imbalances, the problem also stems from the uneven distribution of wealth and resources in Mexico. Even if the government were strictly to enforce environmental regulations, the assault on Mexico's environment would continue. In their fight for subsistence, the poor often recklessly exploit the country's natural resources, clearing jungle land for their small plots, cutting down trees for firewood, farming on slopes that are already eroded. This ecocide of poverty has long constituted the dark underside of Mexico's economic development.

Along with environmental destruction, modernization has brought consumerism to Mexico. Like many other poor nations, the country has fallen into the trap of consuming like a first-class industrial power. The effort to provide goods to middle-class consumers has been an important part of the country's economic development policies, first in the form of import-substitution and more recently in opening up its borders to foreign goods. In the 1960s, for example, the government encouraged the creation of an automobile industry as a foundation for wider industrial development, even though only a small portion of the Mexican populace could afford to buy a car.

The prospect of a free trade agreement has attracted new U.S. retailers, like Price Club and Wal-Mart, to Mexico. But even before the initiation of free trade negotiations the Mexican market was filling up with imported consumer goods. There has long been a thriving business in smuggled imports, especially electronic goods, from the United States. With the dramatic lowering of import barriers in the mid-1980s, Mexicans have seen their options as consumers multiply as a flood of foreign goods entered the market. Everything from Snickers, Pampers, and U.S. breakfast cereals now tempt Mexican consumers.

Since the early 1980s—when the country was bankrupt, inflation soaring, and the economy contracting—the international image of Mexico has dramatically improved. By 1991 the economy was experiencing steady per capita growth, investment was increasing, and the government's own finances were in good order. It remains to be seen if this economic stability will endure and if the benefits of this invigorated economy eventually trickle down to the popular sectors.

Table b
Population Growth, 1950-2000

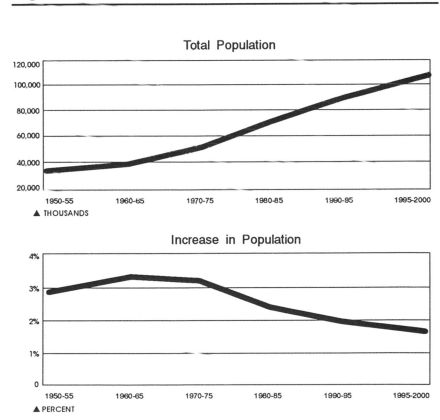

Total Population

▲ THOUSANDS

Increase in Population

▲ PERCENT

SOURCE: CEPAL, *Notas sobre la economía y el desarrollo,* July 1991.

The economic recovery during the first three years of the Salinas administration is undeniable. But it is also true that most Mexicans have yet to see the benefits of this recuperation of economic growth. Instead, Mexicans have seen the purchasing power of their wages cut at least in half since 1980. At the same time, the price of basic goods has risen faster than the inflation rate, and government support for education and other social services has diminished. To survive, all family members, including young children, are forced to find jobs, most of them on city streets as part of Mexico's booming informal sector of vendors and micro-entrepreneurs. Economic restructuring and liberalization are aggravating the already pronounced geographical divisions of wealth in Mexico, as the border states benefit from new investment and trade while the southern states just get poorer.

Unless the Mexican government acts to ensure that the country's wealth is more equitably shared, the country faces the real danger of returning to the conditions of the *porfiriato* (1876-1910), the dark period in Mexican history presided over by Porfirio Díaz. Already the country's increasingly skewed pattern of income distribution closely resembles that period. But there are other parallels, particularly the importance and privileged place being given to foreign investors, industrialists, and agroexporters. The distancing of the country's political elite from the popular sectors is another similarity. The populist and nationalist stances that emerged from the Mexican Revolution were a reaction to the *porfiriato*'s alliances with industrial barons, landed aristocrats, and foreign financiers. It was a period of sustained economic growth, infrastructure expansion, and relative political stability, but it was also a time of deepening misery among the country's poor and workers.

One sector of the Mexican population that has seen little change in the 20th century is the country's indigenous people. Although post-revolutionary governments gave long overdue recognition to the wonders of pre-Columbian Indian civilizations, the native population has remained at the lowest level of Mexican society. Admired in the abstract, in practice Indians are disdained and relegated to the worst-paid, hardest jobs, including maids and migrant farm laborers. Pushed off the best land and into the southern highlands, many Indian communities today find they can no longer subsist on eroded plots, forcing them to seek work in the strawberry and tomato fields of Baja California and southern California.

The Future of Mexico

Mexico is a country that demands attention. Its nearly 2,000-mile border with the United States is the only place in the world where a major third world nation adjoins a major industrial power. Here the North and the South meet, and their common futures are being shaped. For its part, Mexico hopes to erase the geographic and economic divisions that have kept it poor and undeveloped. The United States hopes that pushing aside trade and investment barriers will bolster its position as a global power with the opening of new markets and as the competitiveness of its capitalist class increases.

One danger is that Mexico will become another Puerto Rico, completely dependent on U.S.-owned export production. Mexico is becoming ever more dependent on U.S. trade and investment. Economic integration, if not properly guided, might also turn Mexico into a cheap imitation of an industrialized country, with a small elite that shares the consumption habits of an industrial giant but without its technological know-how, productivity capacity, and domestic investment capital. Another obvious danger is that increased dependence on the U.S. market will make Mexico particularly vulnerable to downturns in the U.S. economy and changes in U.S. economic policies, such as renewed protectionism or reduced enthusiasm for free trade.

What is so striking about Mexico is the rapidity with which its political elite has dropped its nationalist and populist postures. Substituting for them have been real commitments to neoliberal reforms that open up the country to the international market and that work against the immediate interests of Mexico's popular sectors. Internal factors have played a part in setting this new direction. But just as important has been the process of global integration of finances, trade, and production—a trend that has made old economic strategies unviable. The forces of global capitalism give no support to and have little tolerance for nationalist and populist approaches to economic development.

Mexico, however, confounds most predictions. Pragmatism rather than ideology guides most policymaking and individual decisions. What one year is done in the interest of economic stability, can be completely undone soon thereafter for the same reasons, as was the case with the bank nationalization. Few could have predicted the speed with which the government moved to restructure its economy. Similarly, the meteoric rise of Cuauhtémoc Cárdenas in the 1988 presidential elections and the subsequent rebound of President Salinas and PRI were completely unexpected. Also surprising was the speed with which Salinas moved to renovate the PRI and undermine its old guard.

Although the future may be uncertain, the issues facing Mexicans in the 1990s are becoming clearer. In politics, the continued allegiance (or at least acquiescence) of the Mexican people to a PRI government and the country's strong presidency is at the heart of the internal debate. In economic matters, the ability of such measures as privatization, free trade, and export promotion to spark new broad economic development is being put to the test. Mexicans will also have to decide whether it is necessary to leave many of the values and traditions of the Mexican Revolution behind them as the country lurches toward economic modernization and the 21st century.

PART ONE

Government and Politics

"Mexicans do not live but only imagine democracy."
—*Lorenzo Meyer, Mexican historian, 1991.*[1]

© Merideth McGregor/Impact Visuals

The Legacy of Revolution

Government in Mexico is more than the workings of political institutions and the interplay of political parties. It is also about the Mexican Revolution—that set of political and armed struggles that ended the Porfirio Díaz regime (1876-1910), known as the *porfiriato*, and established a new constitution and government. In Mexico the revolution has never been allowed to pass into history. It has been kept alive in the rhetoric of the politicians and in the patriotic propaganda of the public education system. The hopes and demands of the poor are inevitably framed in the language of the revolution, as are government decrees on everything from social welfare to economic policy and foreign affairs.

The ruling political party and the center-left opposition party both want to be regarded as the one true heir of the revolution. As such, the government party calls itself the Institutional Revolutionary Party (PRI) while its center-left opponent named itself the Party of the Democratic Revolution (PRD). In contrast, the National Action Party (PAN), the country's other major party, developed as part of a citizens' movement opposed to the social reforms resulting from the revolution.

With the momentous changes under way in the country's political and economic structures, reflections about the origins, objectives, and final disposition of the Mexican Revolution are increasingly relevant. On the one hand, the technocratic Salinas government may be relegating the revolution to the pages of history, where it belongs, making room for a more modern society. On the other, Salinas may simply be continuing the time-honored practice of making the pragmatic reforms needed to maintain Mexico's vaunted stability. Then again, instead of renouncing the revolution or continuing its most cynical legacies, perhaps what Mexico needs is a dramatic reaffirmation of its social and political objectives along the nationalist and populist lines advocated by the PRD's Cuauhtémoc Cárdenas.

The Revolution in Retrospect

The Mexican Revolution did not begin with a bloody revolt of exploited peasants and workers, as one might imagine. Although there was indeed growing rebelliousness among Mexico's exploited classes, the revolution was launched as a constitutional challenge: a progressive sector of the country's bourgeoisie wanted political reform not radical economic restructuring. The first slogan of the revolution was not *"tierra o muerte"* (land or death) but "effective suffrage, no reelection." It was only after the *porfiriato* gave way, with little loss of blood, to a more liberal regime headed by Francisco Madero that demands mounted for fundamental socioeconomic change. As political scientists Daniel Levy and Gabriel Székely wrote, "A form of political liberty, not political equality, and certainly not economic equality, was Madero's abiding principle."[2]

With the stability of the *porfiriato* shattered, Mexico descended into chaos. The changes Madero instituted—including press freedom, free elections, and new guarantees of the right to private property—were not the revolutionary changes for which many Mexicans were hoping. In fact, life seemed much the same, except for the absence of the autocratic Porfirio Díaz. Politicians and the civil service easily adapted to the new government. The army and the Catholic church continued to dominate rural society, and foreign investors and Mexico's own oligarchy kept the exploitative economic structures firmly in place.

Madero was assassinated in 1913 in a military coup—backed covertly by Washington—led by General Victoriano Huerta. As army commander, Huerta had personally directed operations to crush the peasant rebellion led by Emiliano Zapata in the state of Morelos. The overthrow of the constitutional government of Madero by the brutal Huerta gave rise to three distinct revolutionary armies determined to unseat Huerta. Zapata, who had withdrawn his conditional support of Madero for his failure to order the return of communal landholdings to the peasant communities, directed the rebellion from the south.

From the north came the Chihuahua-based popular forces of Francisco "Pancho" Villa. Also marching on the Huerta army from the north were the troops of Venustiano Carranza, governor of Coahuila, who had proclaimed himself the first chief of the Constitutionalist Army of the North. No military man himself, Carranza came to rely on three military officers from Sonora (Alvaro Obregón, Adolfo de la Huerta, and Plutarco Elías Calles) for the successful campaign against President Huerta. The eruption from the north of a new generation of outsiders to the country's political and economic elite pushed the revolution to the right. The aim of these northerners, later known as the "revolutionary millionaires," was not to destroy the economic elite but to join it.

Huerta fled into exile in 1914, but peace did not return to Mexico. All three armies (those of Carranza, Zapata, and Villa) agreed that the country needed to return to constitutional rule. Zapata and Villa had been fighting primarily not for legalistic principles but for a revolutionary agrarian reform program to establish a degree of economic equality in the countryside. The *villista* and *zapatista* forces proved incapable of forming a government, however, allowing Carranza to take control of the nation in 1916. Although a conservative himself, Carranza knew that political flexibility and a measure of social reform were needed to consolidate his regime. Unlike Madero, Carranza also opened up government and politics to the intellectuals, professionals, labor leaders, and elements of the business and rural elites who had been left out of the *porfiriato*.

In 1917 a constitutional convention ratified Mexico's third *magna carta* (succeeding the constitutions of 1824 and 1857, resulting respectively from independence and the Liberal reform movement), which challenged society's feudal and colonial structures. The 1917 document went far beyond the reforms instituted by the 1857 constitution.[3] In many ways it was a revolutionary document which incorporated many of the most progressive social demands of the time, including extensive labor rights, such as an eight-hour day, worker's compensation, a minimum wage, the right to form a union, and the responsibility of companies to provide for health, education, and housing opportunities. Although the *zapatistas* and *villistas* were considered enemies of the government, the constitutional convention did incorporate demands for land reform, including the revival of the *ejido* system of communal landholdings. The constitution was also a strong nationalist proclamation, establishing the government's control over natural resources. Although not representative of Carranza's own conservative views, the constitution did reflect his realization that a certain degree of reform was necessary, at least on paper, to stabilize his regime.

Various opinions exist about the dates defining the Mexican Revolution. Whereas most historians place the start of the revolution in October-November 1910 when Madero published his Plan of San Luis Potosí proclaiming that he was the rightful president and calling for a popular uprising against Díaz, the end of the revolution is the subject of debate. Although most scholars mark the revolution's end with the signing of the new constitution in 1917, violent political turmoil continued into the 1920s, shaping the ultimate character of the post-revolutionary state.

Carranza made the fatal error of trying to avoid free elections by installing a puppet successor in 1920. This attempt to perpetuate himself in power precipitated a coup by the Northwest Group and its leader Obregón. As an authoritarian reformer, Obregón helped stabilize the country, establishing himself as an astute statesman and politician. In 1923 Obregón chose as his successor Plutarco Elías Calles, his right-hand man and a member of the original Northwest Group. Calles did succeed Obregón in 1924, but his hold on power was briefly contested by a military rebellion led by de la Huerta.

The no-reelection issue surfaced again in 1928 when Calles attempted to reinstall Obregón. But a few days after his new election, President Obregón was murdered by a disgruntled newspaper cartoonist and fervent Catholic. Some suspected that Calles himself was behind the murder, after which he ruled the country until 1934 from his mansion in Cuernavaca. This period in Mexican history is known as the *maximato*, and Calles was referred to as the *Jefe Máximo*.[4] Along with Obregón, Calles succeeded in eliminating military challenges to the central government from dissident army officers. His regime, however, was stained in blood by the Cristero Rebellion (1926-29), set off by attempts of the president to enforce the anti-clerical provisions of the constitution (see Church and Religion, Part 4). Calles called for creation of the National Revolutionary Party (PNR), which was founded in 1929 as a vehicle to propagate his personal influence. This laid the foundation for the country's single ruling party, which has functioned for more than six decades as an extension of presidential power. In 1934 Calles appointed Lázaro Cárdenas as his successor.

In the two decades that followed Madero's call for a popular uprising, an estimated one in ten Mexicans died in revolutionary and counterrevolutionary turmoil. The nation had a new pantheon of revolutionary heroes, ranging from the liberal Madero to the revolutionary Zapata and the *caudillo* Obregón, and the new constitution enshrined the dreams of the most progressive reformists and revolutionaries. There was real social progress: a limited land-distribution program, timid labor reforms, and the creation of public-education and social-security systems. The ranks of the aristocratic oligarchy that had prospered during the *porfiriato* were forced open to encompass a business elite that included self-made ranchers and entrepreneurs. The Mexican Revolution also opened up government and business to the country's *mestizo* population. The years of conflict finally ensured respect for the doctrine of no reelection and created a common yearning for political stability and economic development.

Noteworthy as these accomplishments were, they were hardly revolutionary. Conservative fears that the revolution was an attack on capitalism proved unwarranted.[5] Most large landowners and industrialists survived the upheaval with their property intact. Similarly, the political elite that emerged was as intent as Porfirio Díaz had been on demobilizing the masses and fortifying the central government. In addition, the revolution's *caudillos* moved to subordinate the army and the Catholic church to the centralized political institutions, thus ensuring the future of a strong centralized state.

Reviving Revolutionary Dreams

If the Mexican Revolution means the commitment to greater social justice, economic equality, popular participation, and economic nationalism, all principles enshrined in the 1917 constitution, then Lázaro Cárdenas was Mexico's first and last truly revolutionary president. Cárdenas, who had previously served as the governor of Michoacán, revived the dreams of the revolution. Twice as much land was distributed during his tenure (1934-40) as had been since the start of the agrarian reform program in 1915. Rather than using the security forces to stamp out labor agitation, the president encouraged union organizing and supported demands for higher pay and the enforcement of a minimum-wage law.

The Cárdenas government unleashed the country's popular forces, promoting their organization and participation in government. He temporarily displaced the conservative alliance, also called the bankers' alliance, that had dominated economic policy since the beginning of the revolution.[6] The progressive alliance led by Cárdenas was not socialist, but it did believe that a modern Mexico could not be constructed if workers' rights were denied and the peasants remained landless. In the interests of political stability Cárdenas laid the foundation for Mexico's corporatist state.

Rather than leaving the new popular organizations to function independently of the state, a network of officially licensed organizations and associations was created. The National Peasant Confederation (CNC) was formed to represent peasant interests, and the Mexican Workers Confederation (CTM) was founded to represent the new union movement. In 1938 the PNR was renamed the Party of the Mexican Revolution (PRM), giving it a new vitality by directly incorporating within the structure of the party the official organizations of the trade unions, peasant associations, and popular organizations (mainly consisting of civil servants). Crowning the legacy of Cárdenas was his nationalization of foreign oil interests in 1938 after British and U.S. firms declined to meet worker demands.

It was Cárdenas who established the principle that the state should be the *rector* of society, the guiding force and arbiter that acts as a buffer between labor and capital while actively promoting economic development in the common interest. He believed that popular support was needed for a stable state where capitalism could flourish.[7] With his labor and land reforms he sought to expand the domestic market by increasing consumption. By making large public-sector investments in basic infrastructure (roads, irrigation projects, electricity) and strengthening the country's financial system, Cárdenas also laid the foundations for the more than three decades of steady economic growth that followed his administration.[8]

For the popular sectors, Cárdenas became the main symbol of the Mexican Revolution, despite having come to power nearly two decades after the revolution ended. It was Cárdenas who gave *zapatista* dreams a living form. Revolutionary rhetoric became reality under Cárdenas. And it was the revered Cárdenas who in his bold move to nationalize oil production finally stood up to the *gringos*—and won. By promoting mass-based popular organizations, Cárdenas increased nonelite participation in the country's political and economic structures. Peasants and workers were being heard by government officials for the first time. But policymaking and the appointment of leaders remained a top-down process. Corporatism resulted in a broader social consensus, especially among workers and peasants, but at the same time it served to alienate the middle classes from the government. Although corporatism did increase popular participation in the official party, it served more to legitimize than to democratize government in Mexico.

Economic Growth and Political Stability

Mexico has had ten presidents from Lázaro Cárdenas through Carlos Salinas de Gortari. Post-Cárdenas governments embellished the populist and nationalist rhetoric of the Cárdenas era. Although for the most part this has been mere posturing and empty gestures, the Mexican government has sought, in the interests of its own stability, to attend at least to some degree to the demands of the country's major popular sectors. Beginning with the Miguel Alemán administration (1946-52), the conservative alliance regained dominance over policymaking. In 1946 the PRM was renamed the Institutional Revolutionary Party (PRI), and its corporatist sectors degenerated into instruments of state control. Concern for the country's poor became overshadowed by the drive to industrialize and modernize.

It was not until 1968, on the eve of the Olympics to be held in Mexico City, that the political stability achieved by four decades of one-party rule was endangered. The "revolutionary family," so often hailed by PRI, was breaking apart. Not all its members were given shares in the country's economic progress, and many Mexicans found that they were left out of "family" decisions. In the 1960s workers, peasants, students, and slum dwellers began forming organizations independent of PRI's corporatist structures. They demanded social justice and democratization. The consensus born in the Cárdenas years was disintegrating, dissidence was on the rise, and an independent civil movement was emerging in Mexican society (see Popular Organizing, Part 3).

Co-option and corruption were (and still are) the usual instruments of social control in Mexico. But at its heart Mexico is governed by an authoritarian state that clamps down hard on effective dissent, whether it be from the media, opposition parties, or popular organizations. Worried that an independent and grassroots popular movement was beginning to undermine its credibility and control, the government cracked down on October 2, 1968, when hundreds of protesters, mostly students, were killed by army troops in the Tlatelolco plaza.

In 1970 the government moved slightly to the left. At home, President Luis Echeverría announced that economic policy would stress "shared development" rather than the "stabilizing development" of previous administrations. It was, however, largely in the foreign policy arena that Echeverría flaunted his progressive agenda. An independent civil movement continued to gestate, but its leaders were routinely co-opted by government initiatives and offers. In the late 1970s the government's credibility was boosted by an electoral reform and a political-amnesty decree, and as a result of the oil boom. Mexico's economic pie was suddenly expanding again, and everyone sought a bigger piece.

Political stability in Mexico since 1940 has been bolstered by economic progress. Although the wealth was not evenly distributed, large sectors of the Mexican population did see real benefits of the economic growth. The advancing economy, together with the increasing influx of foreign loans, enabled PRI to distribute material rewards among its supporters and affiliated corporatist structures.

But the country's economic crisis (erupting first in 1976 and then again in 1982 and 1985-86) gave a new dimension to the country's political crisis, which had been brewing since the late 1960s. Domestically and internationally, the Mexican government was increasingly assessed as being authoritarian and unresponsive to the socioeconomic plight of the country's poor majority. Designed to channel dissent rather than to offer opposition groups a true chance at power, the electoral reform of 1977 did little to alter the political system's undemocratic character. With the debt crisis and the crash of oil prices in 1982, popular frustration with the deteriorating economic conditions in the country increased, adding to the already considerable popular dissatisfaction with the government.

Desperate to regain control of the country's skidding economy and to regain popular support, President López Portillo nationalized the domestically owned banks. This bold step was greeted with wide acclaim by a public tired of having the country's wealth drained off by the major financial/industrial conglomerates. But the bank nationalization proved to be half-hearted, leaving the country's financiers wounded but still at the top of Mexico's economic power structure. At first it appeared that bank nationalization might signal the rebound of PRI's progressive wing, but it was quickly apparent that the conservative coalition that had dominated Mexico since the Alemán administration still retained a strong upper hand.

A string of PAN victories in the municipal elections of 1983 signaled a new era of politics in Mexico, in which a clean sweep (*"carro completo"*) by PRI candidates could no longer be assumed. Economic reforms designed to move Mexico toward a neoliberal model of development picked up pace in the 1980s, particularly after the 1985-86 economic crisis. Whereas economic reform moved quickly forward, PRI adopted a low-risk, gradualist approach to political reform.[9] By no means, however, would political reform and the opening of the country's electoral system be allowed to endanger PRI's control of government or the process of neoliberal modernization.[10]

The Crisis of Legitimacy

The Mexican government has honed its adaptive skills over six decades. In recent years, this ability to adapt and manipulate to its advantage has surprised even longtime observers of Mexico's unique political system. Since 1982 it has proved to be extraordinarily resilient. The economic policies that guided the country's development for more than four decades have been tossed aside in favor of radical strategies that have won the nation praise from politicians, investors, and academics around the world. From a party whose candidates were virtually assured of election, PRI now regularly does battle with two major opposition parties.

Since 1982 the government has won high marks both at home and abroad for its ability to negotiate an innovative solution to the debt crisis. President Salinas won respect for his willingness to go after corrupt union leaders, PRI politicians, police officials, and even members of the business elite. For the first time, the government acknowledged that human rights abuses were a serious problem in Mexico and even set up a commission to investigate these violations (see Human Rights). President Salinas also sponsored an electoral reform that eventually received the backing of all the opposition parties with the exception of the PRD.

For all its achievements the government still cannot shake its crisis of legitimacy. Over the decades its credibility has rested on its revolutionary origins and on its successful direction of the country's economic development. The fraudulent character of the country's democracy has been generally accepted, and Mexican voters have been often described as "system loyalists." In the past the government has faced several major crises, including internal dissidence within PRI in the early 1950s, labor turmoil in the late 1950s, and the student protests of the late 1960s. But it was not until the economic crisis of 1976 that the state faced a generalized crisis affecting the entire system.[11] Increased oil revenues in the 1978-81 period temporarily allayed this system crisis. However, the new economic downturn in 1982, followed by the earthquake of 1985 and the economic crisis of 1985-86, combined to shake the Mexican system to its core. As the system broke down (manifested by economic crisis, fewer material rewards, and more of the population outside corporatist structures) political discontent increased (see Popular Organizing, Part 3). Its democratic, popular, and revolutionary credentials have been increasingly questioned.

The Mexican government has carefully honored the no-reelection principle, but Madero's demand for effective suffrage has never been met. Government in Mexico is self-perpetuating, as each president still chooses PRI's nominee for the next president. PRI thus serves as an instrument of government rather than as an independent influence on government policy. PRI's extensive patronage system and its control over the media (particularly television), along with the government's refusal to host international election observers, undermine effective democratization.[12] The Salinas administration did move to open up the political process, although still practicing "electoral engineering" when necessary to secure strategic election victories. In the 1989-90 state elections, the government also resorted to "selective democracy," permitting gains by satellite parties and the center-right opposition while seeking to destroy center-left forces.

In the long term, however, the stability of the Mexican government may be more threatened by its violation of the social contract of the revolution than by popular frustration with political fraud and manipulation. From a state built on progressive social guarantees, it has been quickly evolving into one driven purely by neoliberal principles and the financial bottom line.[13]

The constitution's Article 3 states that the Mexican state is democratic, "considering democracy not only as a legal structure and a political regime but also as a system of life founded on a constant economic, social, and cultural betterment of the people." The concentration of wealth in today's Mexico is not unlike that of Mexican society at the turn of the century. Unless current trends are reversed, the economic reforms being pushed through by the Salinas government will likely lead to further impoverishment of the popular sectors while accelerating the concentration of national wealth by large domestic and foreign investors.

Nationalism, long a prominent feature of Mexican politics and the government's foreign policy, has been reinterpreted by the Salinas government to mean accepting international economic integration and neoliberal modernization (see Foreign Policy). Nationalist sentiments, however, may again be stirred by the increasing predominance of U.S. economic and foreign policy interests in Mexico's domestic affairs.

Mexico's transition toward democracy, understood in its simplest sense of allowing free and secret balloting for public officials, promises to be a delicate process, not without the potential for widespread social unrest and violence. Previous reports of PRI's demise, however, have been exaggerated, and it is certainly possible that this most flexible and adaptive of political organisms will defeat the current challenge to its control. The stability of its control, and of the Mexican nation, depends ultimately, however, not only on accurate ballot counting. It also depends on PRI's ability to win and maintain popular support for the dramatic economic-modernization project now under way.

Structure of Government

Like many countries in Latin America, Mexico can pride itself on a long history of civilian-controlled government. For nearly seven decades the country has had the same political system, making it one of the most stable countries in the world.

The United Mexican States is guided by the precepts of the Constitution of 1917, the country's third constitution and the one that incorporates the principles of the Mexican Revolution. The constitution has been called the world's first modern socialist constitution, preceding the Soviet Union's, because of its commitment to agrarian reform, labor rights, and national control over natural resources. Like Mexico's 1857 document, the 1917 constitution incorporates the major features of representative democracy, including federalism, separation of powers, a bicameral congress, and a Bill of Rights.[1] The constitution is a living document that is frequently amended to include current matters of public policy.[2]

Government in Mexico is partitioned constitutionally into independent executive, legislative, and judicial branches. An effective system of checks and balances is lacking, however, because of the pervasive power of the executive branch. The centralized character of the Mexican state and the extensive appointment power of the president create a strong presidency. For the past six decades the presidency has been controlled by just one party, which has also dominated the legislative branch.

Every six years a new president is directly elected for a six-year term, called a *sexenio*. There is no vice president. In the case of the removal or death of the president, a provisional president is elected by congress to govern until new elections are held. The president, who cannot stand for reelection, is at once chief of state, chief of government, and chief of the armed forces. The constitution also gives the president direct control over the Federal District (approximately Mexico City), the federal attorney general's office, and numerous parastatal enterprises and agencies. There are 22 officers in the president's cabinet, including 17 ministries or secretariats, four presidential assistants, and the governor of the Federal District. The most powerful of the cabinet ministers are those of finance, interior (*gobernación*), commerce and industry, and planning and budget. There are also what are known as subcabinets, the most important of which is the economic cabinet, which includes those ministers responsible for economic policy. The entire cabinet rarely meets as a unit and derives its influence from the president's interests and priorities. Since the 1930s all nominated presidential candidates have come directly from the cabinet. According to tradition, the president names the next PRI presidential candidate. Among the extensive nominating powers of the president are the appointment of the governor (more commonly called regent) and other administrators of the Federal District, removing state governors, and the naming and removal of cabinet heads and other federal employees.

The Congress of the Union, which holds two regular sessions a year, includes a lower house, or Chamber of Deputies, and an upper house, or Senate.[3] Neither deputies nor senators can stand for consecutive reelection. The Chamber of Deputies has 500 members, 300 of whom are directly elected in legislative districts, while the remaining 200 are distributed among the parties according to proportional representation.[4] The deputies serve for three-year terms corresponding to the two halves of the presidential *sexenio*. The Senate consists of 64 senators—two from each state and two from the Federal District. The senators serve six-year terms, with half the Senate renewed by direct election every three years.[5]

By virtue of his position as head of state and "supreme head" of PRI, the president dominates the Congress. Although directly elected, PRI deputies and senators owe their nominations to the president. This dependency, together with the prohibition on reelection, serves to obstruct the development of an independent legislative branch. Congress has never failed to pass a bill proposed by the president and has never overridden a presidential veto or passed a bill opposed by the president. In 1989 President Salinas initiated more than 90 percent of the legislation considered by congress. In the 1988-91 period, however, the Congress became increasingly important as a forum for the opposition. A two-thirds majority of each house is needed to approve constitutional amendments, something that President Salinas was able to achieve in the 1988-91 period on two occasions by relying on the support of some PAN deputies.

Mexico's judicial system includes local and federal courts based on Roman civil law. At the highest level of the federal court system is the Supreme Court. The president submits to the Senate for its *pro forma* confirmation the names of the 26 judges of the Supreme Court. The Supreme Court, in turn, appoints circuit and district judges and magistrates. Each year the Supreme Court judges elect a president of the court, usually the one among them who is closest to the president of the nation. The country's president names the attorney general, as well as other officials of the prosecutor's office.

Political power is highly centralized in the executive branch and the presidency in Mexico City, but certain residual government functions are the responsibility of state and municipal officials. The 31 states can make their own laws, as long as those laws do not contravene the federal constitution. Like the federal government, states have three branches of government, and the principle of no consecutive reelection applies to both the governors, who serve six-year terms, and the members of the Chambers of Deputies, who serve three-year terms. The states have no upper house. States are subdivided into *municipios* ("municipalities," roughly equivalent to U.S. counties), which have their own elected *ayuntamientos* (town councils) and council presidents, all of whom serve three-year terms. Throughout Mexico there are nearly 2,400 municipalities, each including several towns.

The free municipality (*libre municipio*) of Mexico City was abolished in 1928 by President Obregón, leaving the country's largest city completely subject to federal administration. Until 1989 Mexico City, the nation's capital, had no representative body. In November of that year, pursuant to a 1986 presidential decree and the 1988 elections, the Assembly of Representatives met for the first time. It is made up of 40 members directly elected from voting districts and 26 plurinominal seats distributed among the parties on the basis of the number of votes each receives in direct balloting. The assembly can post notices and make regulations in Mexico City, but it cannot make laws. It can only recommend that congressional delegates propose them. The city's regent is a cabinet member (known officially as Governor of the Federal District) appointed by the president.

Carlos Salinas de Gortari was elected president in July 1988 and inaugurated in December of that year. He received the presidential sash from Miguel de la Madrid, who had named him the PRI presidential candidate in October 1987. Scheduled to serve as president until December 1994, Salinas was elected by a narrow majority (50.7 percent according to official figures), although the election results were hotly contested by both major opposition parties.[6] The 1988 election placed a substantial non-PRI representation (240 of the 500 seats) in the Chamber of Deputies for the first time and four opposition candidates became members of the Senate. After the midterm elections in August 1991, in which PRI candidates received (according to official figures) about 61.4 percent of the vote, PRI controlled 320 seats in the Chamber of Deputies, 61 seats in the Senate, and all but three of the governorships.[7] Like the 1988 elections, the midterm elections were marred by widespread fraud and irregularities.

How Government Functions

Nominally a federalist system, government in Mexico is actually highly centralized with nearly absolute power concentrated in the office of the president. Upon assuming office, Mexican presidents regularly vow to fight centralism but then proceed to explore the full extent of their authoritarian powers. Since 1929 presidential power has been framed and supported by a single ruling party. Speaking to a neoliberal forum on democratization in Mexico City, Peruvian novelist Mario Vargas Llosa described the Mexican government as the "perfect dictatorship." To the consternation of his Mexican hosts, he continued expounding on the unusual qualities of authoritarianism in Mexico: "It may not seem to be a dictatorship, but has all the characteristics of dictatorship: the perpetuation, not of one person, but of an irremovable party, a party that allows sufficient space for criticism, provided such criticism serves to maintain the appearance of a democratic party, but which suppresses by all means, including the worst, whatever criticism may threaten its perpetuation in power."[8]

The centralization of political power in the hands of the president, *presidencialismo*, and a one-party state have been the main instruments of authoritarian rule in Mexico. But dictatorial rule has been masked and modified by its populist posturing and its corporatist structures. The government seeks to co-opt and incorporate dissidents rather than resort to official violence. Unlike many authoritarian regimes that act virtually independently from society's civil sectors, the Mexican government has established itself, through its corporatist and bureaucratic structures, as the representative of a coalition of civil interests. Repression has been used selectively to silence those that it cannot otherwise persuade or corrupt.

Through the corporatist and patronage networks of PRI, the government has insinuated itself into every nook and cranny of society, using a many-branched corporatist network. In the process, the regime has come to be known as the "PRI government," with the implicit assumption that, at least in the short run, it will remain just that way. So close is the identification of the PRI with the government that it uses the same green, white, and red colors as the Mexican flag.[9]

PRI, however, is an appendage of government, not an independent policymaking organization. It is a vote-getting machine with few ideological principles other than holding on to state power. As the tool of a highly vertical and centralized power structure, its job is to mobilize the population behind the president and to rationalize his policies to the party's main pillars of support. Only since the late 1970s have opposition parties succeeded in winning significant percentages of the votes, and it was not until 1988 that the party faced the risk that its presidential or gubernatorial candidates would not be elected.

Political power in Mexico is concentrated in a political elite headed by the president in office. It is the president, in consultation with members of this political elite (many of whom are not even active in PRI), who chooses the PRI president and most of the country's important officials. The task of the party is to ensure that polling results in elections show the PRI nominees as winners. The Senate must approve the appointments of judges and military chiefs, but approval has always been a mere formality since all but a thimbleful of senators have been loyal members of the president's party. Before 1988 there were in effect no opposition members of the Senate. Similarly, the executive is mandated to carry out laws enacted by the full Congress. In practice, however, the president has proposed the laws and members of Congress, the majority of whom are loyalists in the lower house as in the Senate, have rubber-stamped them.

The Supreme Court rarely makes the news. Most legal cases are resolved outside the court system, which is not only bound by bureaucratic red tape but is also fettered with corruption. Trial witnesses, for example, are commonly paid, professional liars, and it is not unusual for judges who make unpopular decisions to receive death threats.

PRI candidates in the capital and in state and local elections are usually handpicked by the party, just as they are at the national level. As the party has moved to democratize and establish closer communications with its voting base, it has sought to nominate candidates who are better known and more respected by local voters. Especially since 1988 this attempt to field candidates with more vote appeal has helped PRI secure a more solid base of popular support in some parts of the country.

Federal Congress members normally make lists of candidates for all the mayors' offices in their respective districts. They then get the approval of the governor and pass the names along to PRI local committees, who announce the nominees.[10] State and local governments are strongly subordinated to the federal bureaucracy in Mexico City, which has been the seat of power from pre-colonial times through the present—for more than five centuries. This centralism in Mexican politics is seen in the rising proportion of Mexico City residents in the presidential cabinet. Whereas only about 5 percent of the cabinet members in the late 1930s were from Mexico City and 40 percent during the López Portillo administration, nearly 60 percent of the first Salinas cabinet were *chilangos* or Mexico City residents.[11]

In modern history, the federal government has controlled about 85 percent of public funds, leaving states less than 12 percent and *municipios* a skimpy 3 percent. As a result of recent reforms, the share of the *municipios* has risen to about 5-7 percent of total public spending. Moreover, most *municipios* get 80 percent of their revenues from federal and state governments and only 20 percent from local sources.[12] When an opposition party wins in a local election, it can find itself suddenly shut off from this important source of financing. Centralism in Mexico also manifests itself in the disproportionate amount of public funding received by the Federal District, which is allocated about half of total federal government expenditures although it includes only one-sixth of the country's population.

Centralized power in Mexico has been augmented by the state's activist role in the economy. Not only has the state provided the basic infrastructure for economic development (such as irrigation systems, ports, and railroads), but it has also provided direct backing to the capitalist class through subsidies, protectionist policies, and lax tax collection. The Mexican state has also assumed a direct role in the economy, with state corporations regularly accounting for 40 percent or more of capital formation. Another dimension of government has been its role as social benefactor. In recent years, state enterprises have been sold off and the state's social budget cut.

There remains a strong sense, however, that state intervention is essential for economic growth and development, as seen in the government's deepening commitment to promote exports and private investment with government funds, as well as in the "*solidaridad*" campaign of Pronasol (see The Underside of Modernization, Part 2).

Presidencialismo

The president in Mexico is a mythical figure with absolutist powers. He has been regarded as the embodiment of the Mexican nation, the defender of the revolution, and the protector of the popular classes. Although no longer called "*El Jefe Máximo*," as was President Calles, the president is still seen as the nation's chief *patrón*, the one person who has the power to alter the forces of fate. He is Mexico's chief patriot, the first to defend the nation against foreign intervention. Notwithstanding the constitutionally mandated division of powers, the president has dictatorial authority.

In the first few decades after the revolution, presidential power was more limited by the role of the legislature. The power of the Congress began to decline with the institution of the "no-reelection" principle in 1933 and its extension to deputies and senators. This has restricted the ability of legislators to develop local bases of support apart from the party and made their political careers more dependent on party allegiance. Also limiting the role of Congress in Mexico's federalist system was the creation of corporatist structures, along with their extensive bureaucracy. It was not until 1988 that the Chamber of Deputies again presented an obstacle to presidential power. But rather than acknowledging this as a major landmark in the return to a more democratic federalist structure of government, President Salinas reacted by seeking to reinforce and expand *presidencialismo*.

The president appoints and removes governors at will, completely disregarding the voters who put the state leaders in place. The president also installs and dismisses leaders of Congress, the Supreme Court, PRI, public-sector labor unions, and midlevel administrators through staged elections, rubber-stamped ratifications, and letters of "resignation."[13] It was more than coincidence that all three of PRI's leading precandidates for the presidential nomination in 1988 were the offspring of major political figures—as was Cuauhtémoc Cárdenas.[14] As if to compensate for being unable to run for a second term, the president traditionally names his successor in a practice known as the "*dedazo*" or "fingering." This authoritarian idiosyncrasy gives rise to a unique political vocabulary and a barrage of political cartoons of obscene fingers every presidential election year, as speculation builds over which of the outgoing president's close collaborators will be "*destapado*" or "uncovered." The "*tapado*" or "covered one" is revealed at a "*destape*" or "uncovering," conducted by the head of one of the corporatist organizations that form the skeleton of PRI.

His almost papal stature has made criticism of the president a matter of sacrilege. In the past, to criticize the president was to criticize the entire Mexican system. Since the October massacre of 1968, however, direct criticism of a sitting president has become increasingly common. The exuberant booing of President de la Madrid by the spectators of the World Cup soccer games in 1986 demonstrated that the taboo had been broken.

Although the president enjoys extraordinary powers, these are limited by tradition and a sense of what the public will tolerate. Government in Mexico has never been constrained by a rigid ideology but the myth of the Mexican Revolution does persist and still guides the system of governance. Most prominent is the principle of "effective suffrage, no reelection" that has historical resonance, dating back to the attempt by Porfirio Díaz to perpetuate his dictatorship and the successful campaign of Francisco Madero in 1910 to replace him. The subordination of the church to the state is another revolutionary principle that has guided government in Mexico. And the Mexican president is expected to rule the country while keeping the revolutionary goals of social justice and economic nationalism firmly in place, at least as part of official rhetoric.

More than a head of state, the president is also the chief of government. In essence, rule is by executive decree. Congressional ratification of the budget and legislative reforms is virtually guaranteed, although the president has at times made modifications to ensure full public and legislative support. The Supreme Court has never found a presidential decree, law, or proposed constitutional amendment to be unconstitutional or otherwise unlawful. By practice, the court reviews individual cases rather than providing judicial review of the laws themselves.

Salinas and a Strengthened Presidency

At the same time that the almost dictatorial powers of the president were being questioned and challenged as never before, the presidency became stronger and more influential during the first three years of the Salinas *sexenio*. The 1988 electoral fraud that placed Salinas in office further tarnished the integrity of the presidency and opened the way for opposition charges that Mexico's president was indeed a dictator. To a remarkable degree, however, President Salinas managed to refurbish the image of the presidency during his first three years, restoring its credibility and in the process emerging as a respected, indeed heroic figure for many Mexicans (Table 1a).

Instead of reducing the powers of the presidency, as advocated by democratic reformers, Salinas increased the centralization of power in Mexico.[15] As one critic noted, the president's decisionmaking style contradicted his own definition of political modernization.[16] Electoral reforms were pushed through that only heighten the power of the presidency, a record number of governors were dismissed, and Salinas showed himself quite ready to apply the "*mano dura*" (iron hand) in repressing political opposition and rank-and-file labor struggles. Moreover, Salinas has been willing to use his presidential powers to strike against the country's revolutionary ideology in such issues as church-state relations, national control over the economy, and the central place of social justice in economic policymaking. With the strong showing of PRI in the 1991 midterm elections, there was even widespread talk that Salinas might maneuver to seek reelection.

Mexico's political stability has been at least partially attributable to the tendency of incoming presidents to correct imbalances left by previous administrations. While one president might stress the importance of social welfare, another might emphasize the importance of the financial bottom line. In this way, the presidency has oscillated between progressives and conservatives since 1929, with Lázaro Cárdenas being the prototype of a progressive president and Miguel Alemán being the historical standard of a conservative, probusiness president.[17]

Although this "pendulum theory" does describe the nature of the evolution of the presidency, it tends to mask the larger truth that since 1940 the populist element in Mexican government has been dominated by the state's commitment to the advance of capitalism, albeit commonly framed in progressive rhetoric. During the Salinas administration the pendulum swung toward the right extreme, particularly in economic policy, raising some fears that the equilibrium that historically stabilized Mexico might be irrevocably lost, at least in the short and medium terms.

Table 1a
Carlos Salinas de Gortari

President of Mexico (1988-94).

Minister of Planning and Budget (1982-88).

Director, Institute of Political, Economic, and Social Studies (IEPES), PRI's think tank (1981-82).

Director General of Economic and Social Policy, Ministry of Planning and Budget (1979-81).

Ministry of Finance, various posts (1974-79).

Postgraduate studies at Harvard (1972-74), receiving two master's degree in public administration and a Ph.D. in political economy (completing his doctoral dissertation in 1978).

Born April 3, 1948 in Mexico City, son of Raúl Salinas Lozano, secretary of industry and commerce under President López Mateos (1958-64), senator (1982-88).

Corporatism Crumbling

Mexico both delights and confounds political scientists for its special mix of authoritarianism and democratic freedoms, centralism and consensus rule.[18] There are numerous historical and cultural explanations of the country's unique system of governance, but the most common refers to the post-revolutionary government's need to rein in centrifugal and dissident forces by establishing a strong central government headed by a president with near-dictatorial authority. At the same time, to maintain the stability of the country the new government had to include within its goals the demands of the various popular sectors, as well as ensuring that both the military and the Catholic church remained subservient to the nation's political leadership.

Aside from the formation of PRI itself, probably the single most important factor contributing to political stability in Mexico was development of the party's, and therefore the government's, corporatist structure. Corporatism has been defined as "a system of interest representation linking associations of civil society with decisional structures of the state."[19] An organization of corporations is the dictionary definition of the term. State corporatism (as contrasted with the social corporatism seen in West Germany) is often associated with fascism (as in Italy under Mussolini) or with authoritarian populist regimes (such as Juan Perón's in Argentina). In Mexico, corporatism has had a populist character as well, ensuring that the government, at least to some degree, considers the needs of the incorporated sectors in its economic and social policies.[20]

The first two sectors to be incorporated into the ruling party were the government-organized peasant associations and labor unions. Later a third sector, popular organizations, was added to the corporatist structure. Merchants and small businessmen of the informal sector as well as the military (after 1940) were included in PRI's popular sector, which also comprises professionals, community organizations, teachers, and government bureaucrats.[21] The government obligated the private sector to form its own licensed associations, organized by the nature of the business. The official organizations of the peasantry, labor, and the popular sector have enjoyed their own place in the party, along with the allocation of a set of seats in the Chamber of Deputies. In contrast, the business organizations have functioned more like lobbying organizations that present their demands directly to the executive branch and through the media (see The Private Sector and Its Organizations, Part 3).

State corporatism in Mexico has functioned to keep the incorporated sectors pacified and aligned with PRI. Two main social institutions, the military and the Catholic church, have been excluded from the corporatist structure, although they, like the foreign and domestic business sectors, do communicate their concerns directly to the president and his cabinet officers.

The successful incorporation of different sectors directly into the political process in Mexico has been called inclusionary authoritarianism. The massive student-led demonstrations in 1968 were the first obvious signs that the consensus on which the government based its authority was breaking down. And the emergence of hundreds of independent citizen groups in the 1970s—from new labor unions to squatters' groups and community organizations—demonstrated the degree to which the state did not represent the interests of large sections of civil society. Nevertheless, the government and PRI have demonstrated amazing political adeptness in their ability to co-opt many of the new citizens' organizations that have emerged.

The old corporatist structure that has a sustained the Mexican state and ruling party is disintegrating. The ongoing economic crisis and the declining ability of the state to award favors to the official sectors are the leading factors behind the corporatist crisis. The incompatibility of corporatist structures with the forces of economic and political modernization is also a major factor. Finally, the development of strong, independent civil organizations with their own social agendas and bases of popular support highlights the increasingly dysfunctional character of Mexico's corporatist institutions.

Patrones and Camarillas

Pervading the entire political system in Mexico are patron-client relationships. The *patrones*, people with relative political clout, provide protection and support in power struggles. They also provide upward mobility, in the form of financing, to clients. The clients, people with relatively less standing, return loyalty and votes.[22] In this top-down system, a *patrón* can be anyone from the president down to a congressman, a union boss, or a self-appointed rural power broker, known as a *cacique*. The clients are lesser politicians, rank-and-file unionists, struggling businesspeople, and poor farmers.

A closely related aspect of this importance of personal influence, sometimes known as *personalismo*, is the existence of *camarillas* or cliques that revolve around one central political figure. To climb through the governmental and political bureaucracy, aspirants to higher positions attach themselves to individuals with greater influence. As the head of the *camarilla* rises, so do all its members. The essential virtue is loyalty not to particular policies or ideologies but to the leaders of the *camarillas*, and the key to mobility is association with the right group.[23] As an example, Carlos Salinas attached himself to the clique headed by Miguel de la Madrid and rose with him in the executive branch.[24]

So exaggerated is this reliance on personal connections in Mexico that it must be regarded as one of the largest obstacles to further social, political, and economic development. It places the emphasis on individualistic solutions rather than on institutional reforms and social mobilization. Clientelism forces individuals to compete among themselves for favors selectively distributed by *patrones*. So ingrained is this system that those who fail to win patronage blame themselves for not making the right connection. These patron-client relationships shape society into top-down social structures that in turn form the pillars of the regime.

Such social welfare initiatives as the National Solidarity Program (Pronasol) are the institutional expression of the patron-client relationship. Typical of Mexico's approach to social welfare, Pronasol offers short-term palliatives to communities the government hopes to integrate more fully into its system of patronage and political loyalty. The system of clientelism functions best when the economy is advancing and there is more to hand out. Clientelism, like the closely related system of corporatism, loses its social control capability when there are fewer jobs and social welfare benefits to distribute.[25] The advantage of Pronasol in this regard has been that it bypasses the usual bureaucratic obstacles to target more effectively and efficiently those communities and areas deemed most important.

The Takeover by Technocrats

Mexico is no longer run by career politicians. Rather it is in the hands of *técnicos* or *tecnócratas* (technocrats), who generally have little personal connection with either the electoral system or party politics. Over the past two decades the executive branch has increasingly become the domain of the *técnicos* or modernizers, while the traditional *políticos* or dinosaurs, have been left on the sidelines. Emblematic of this change is the fact that none of the four presidents, from Echeverría to Salinas, held any elective office before being nominated for president.[26]

Typically, executive officers do not rise through the ranks of PRI but are professionals who have made their careers in the federal bureaucracy. Unlike the *políticos*, they often come from wealthy families, have attended private schools, and have received advanced degrees, usually in economics or public administration, from foreign universities.[27] As a result, a division of labor began to define itself in Mexico between the technocrats who make policy and the politicians who implement it. As Wayne Cornelius and Ann Craig observed, "The technocrats in high places concern themselves with economic problem-solving, while the career politicians concentrated in the PRI, the state governorships, and the municipalities are responsible for winning elections, orchestrating popular and congressional support for government decisions, and maintaining the regime's ties with leaders of traditional support groups."[28]

This is not to say that the *técnicos* are not politically adept but simply that they usually have had no direct contact with the population. Like the *científicos* of the Porfirio Díaz dictatorship, their decisions are often influenced by foreign models of modernizing development, sometimes ignoring the social and political realities at home.[29] With the advent of the Salinas administration, the *técnicos* gained unprecedented control and influence. But as a result of their uncompromising neoliberalism, this technocratic elite has angered some traditional politicians and historical allies of PRI who warn that the new economic policies will lead to economic and political chaos in Mexico. The electoral rebound of PRI under Salinas, however, served to undermine and marginalize these critics.

It would be a mistake, however, to overemphasize the difference between the technocrats and the traditional politicians. Although the *técnicos* are pushing forward a rationalization or modernization of the state bureaucracy, they are proving at least as corrupt and clientelistic as their predecessors. Also blurring the distinction between the modernizers and the dinosaurs has been the modernization of political fraud by the *técnicos*, who in addition to playing computer tricks with voter registration rolls have had no qualms in calling in the troops to crush dissidence.

Political Parties and Elections

The Mexican political system has always been a source of fascination for students of government and political science. While the rest of Latin America was in the hands of military governments, Mexico managed to maintain a stable, relatively democratic, and at least formally multiparty electoral system. When many Latin governments collapsed in the aftermath of the foreign debt crisis and subsequent austerity campaigns, the Mexican ruling party muddled through. With the emergence of democracies in much of Latin America and the demise of one-party states in Eastern Europe and beyond, Mexico found itself out of step again. Its traditional one-party "democracy," once popular as a model for other developing countries to follow, is viewed by many as an anachronism at best, an autocratic holdover at worst.

Comparisons with other countries are inevitable when trying to find an explanation for the ruling Institutional Revolutionary Party's unusual longevity. PRI has been compared to Mayor Daley's political machine in Chicago; both excelled in preventing the emergence of an independent opposition and in winning elections with promises of patronage, airtight control of the voting system, and outright corruption and fraud.

PRI's tenure has also been equated with the Communist Party's longtime one-party rule in the Soviet Union. Like the Soviet Communists, PRI has controlled the economic as well as the political course of the nation, has co-opted or crushed opposition movements, and has channeled all political activity through the party bureaucracy. The often inscrutable ebbs and flows of power in the Mexican system, combined with the "punishment" and "rehabilitation" of key political actors, have also been cited by those favoring this comparison.

PRI and its apologists, meanwhile, sometimes point to such systems as Japan's Liberal Democratic Party as proof that a one-party system is not necessarily synonymous with an absence of democracy.[1] More often, though, *priístas* defend Mexico's system as a unique brand of democracy—"*democracia a la mexicana*"—that has been adapted to the needs of a still-rural, poor, and underdeveloped nation. With more than a hint of nationalistic sentiment, they argue that PRI need not be identical to the United States or other "Western" democracies to be considered democratic. Indeed, even in official PRI rhetoric Mexico's democracy is not considered perfect but "perfectible" or "in the process of being perfected," a tacit recognition not only of the system's peculiarities but also of its shortcomings.

Beginning in the 1960s the fraudulent character of Mexico's "democracy" came under increased questioning by the country's intellectuals and popular movements.[2] The failure of the country's development model in the 1970s and the deepening economic crisis of the 1980s strengthened popular sentiment for true democracy. By the mid-1980s a diverse group of Mexican intellectuals began to speak out loudly for a reform, or a "democracy without adjectives," in the words of one of these critics.[3] This loud speaking had become a shout by the end of the 1980s, both before the fateful July 1988 federal elections when a group of PRI dissidents calling itself the Democratic Current tried to open up PRI's internal candidate selection processes, and afterwards when Carlos Salinas de Gortari's electoral victory was attacked by a broad cross section of opposition voices as the product of a crude electoral fraud.

Like all comparisons, those measuring the Mexican system by yardsticks from other societies are severely limited. The Mexican system was forged in the aftermath of a bloody social revolution. This experience led to the creation of political institutions that put a higher premium on the avoidance of sectarian strife and on ending revolutionary violence than on other considerations. Likewise, Mexico's proximity to and long, porous border with the United States has certainly been a factor in Mexican political developments. Stability, once again, has been prized and rewarded, while radical tendencies have been rooted out or co-opted before they could pose a threat to stability and present a pretext and opportunity for foreign intervention.

Thus, on many different fronts the Mexican political system has been molded by factors and events that its neighbors have felt not as strongly or at all. A common saying in Mexico holds that *"como México no hay dos."* Given the country's unique historical, political, and geographical situation, a slightly modified version of this maxim could serve as an excellent guide to students of the PRI and its strategies of control and survival: "Like the Mexican political system, there is no other."

Outsiders arriving on the scene in Mexico frequently make some erroneous assumptions about the way politics works in the country. One such mistake is the supposition that PRI has won all of its electoral victories by fraud. In fact, until the 1980s, PRI faced little opposition and probably would have won most elections cleanly. Only in the last half of the 1980s did PRI encounter real opposition capable of defeating it at the polls, and that opposition was mostly local (the National Action Party in certain northern strongholds) or spontaneous (the surprising showing of Cuauhtémoc Cárdenas in the Mexico City area and several western states in 1988). No long-term, well-established opposition to the ruling party exists. Both major opposition parties are splintered by factions. Whereas PAN has a more developed party structure than the PRD (which remains largely a one-man party), it has a more narrow social base than the PRD, which limited its potential to replace PRI as a majority party.

Many Mexicans continue to tolerate PRI, perhaps not voting for it (or not voting at all) but not actively opposing it either. The reasons range from self-interest (because of the PRI's well-greased patronage mechanisms) to habit and indoctrination, instilled by PRI's mighty propaganda apparatus and that of its private-sector allies in the media. Some of this lingering tolerance—maybe most of it—can be summed up in another popular Mexican saying: *"Más vale malo conocido que bueno por conocer"* ("Better a known evil than an uncertain good"). How long this tolerance will last, and what will be needed to bring it to an end, is one of the great unanswered questions of Mexico's immediate political future.

Another common assumption is that PRI's stranglehold on power is demonstrated solely through ballot box stuffing and the doctoring of results behind closed doors. Although these do occur, especially in tight races where all stops are pulled out, the true extent of PRI's influence on the voting public and on the entire electoral process is far broader, deeper, and subtler.

Mysterious "helping hands" materialize to push pro-PRI initiatives and trip up opposition challenges at every stage of the political process. When Cárdenas ally Porfirio Muñoz Ledo tried to run for governor from Guanajuato in early 1991, his path was blocked by a state court ruling declaring him to be a nonresident of the state. The PRI candidate had his candidacy instantly approved by the same court, though he had spent the previous six years as mayor of Mexico City. After several weeks of legal haggling Muñoz Ledo was mysteriously granted permission to run by another state court. His PRI opponent was already off and running, his campaign in full swing, and Muñoz Ledo was left looking as if he had struck a deal with PRI to get his candidacy approved. Such discretionary treatment and arbitrariness, invariably operating in PRI's favor, pervade the Mexican electoral system.

Byzantine Voting

Nowhere is the discretionary treatment more obvious, or more notorious, than in the voting process itself. What in most countries is a fairly straightforward procedure of casting ballots, collecting them, and counting them, in Mexico is a Byzantine, at times incomprehensible maze of manipulation and intrigue. Those most adept at influencing the vote count through surreptitious means have been dubbed "alchemists," in part for their mysterious ways, in part for their ability to extract electoral gold from a pile of common rocks.

In theory, votes are counted first at the *casilla* where they are cast and in the presence of opposition representatives. Copies of the public *actas* that result are posted at the *casilla*, and the originals are sent to a regional headquarters, where they are added to *actas* from other districts. From there, in the case of a national election, the results are phoned or cabled in to the Federal Electoral Commission's main computer banks, where the nationwide results are tabulated and winners and losers declared. The local *actas*, all of them, are sealed and sent along to the central headquarters as well. The whole process is allowed one week—plenty of time for the results to be altered.

The course Salinas followed through this process in 1988 is instructive. Instead of electoral results being released immediately, as had been promised, the final results were held by the governmental electoral commission for eight days following the elections. This, however, did not stop Salinas from declaring himself the "indisputable" victor on election night. Computer failure was blamed for the delay in releasing results. When results finally were released only about half of the "public" *actas* were made public by the electoral commission, and a 50.7 to 31.1 percent victory was declared for Salinas. In the polling-booth documents made public, Cárdenas held a slim 39 to 34 percent lead over Salinas; in the unpublished *actas*, Salinas was said to be ahead 67 to 20 percent. The unpublished *actas*, some 25,000 of them, remain under around-the-clock army guard in the basement of the Congress building.

That there was massive fraud in the 1988 federal elections is almost pointless to deny. Even the untrained eye, looking at the statistical results of the polling, can find anomalies and oddities that no amount of statistical theory can explain. Abstention rates in areas of strong opposition support, for instance, were generally far higher than in areas of PRI support; abstention in isolated rural regions was surprisingly much lower than in urban centers of greater political awareness. Entire regional districts of strong PRI support showed voter turnouts in numbers greater than the total number of registered voters in the area.

The conclusion of many opposition supporters and independent analysts was that many ballots marked for opposition candidates, and particularly those marked for Cárdenas, were "lost," discarded, or burned in the week following the elections. Massive quantities of pro-Salinas votes, meanwhile, were "found" or supplied in the days following the elections and attributed to rural areas where opposition vigilance of the voting process was slight or nonexistent. Not surprisingly, many observers and millions of citizens reached the conclusion that Cárdenas had won the election, and that Salinas and PRI had subsequently stolen it from him. In the end Salinas was certified as president by the Mexican Congress, although not a single opposition member backed his confirmation.

While more obvious in the intense scrutiny that followed the 1988 elections, the majority of the dirty tricks used by the government in support of the ruling party at that time had been in use for decades in support of the PRI machine. Indeed many of them have reappeared and played a prominent role in state and local elections since July of 1988. The lasting impact of the 1988 elections was the blow, potentially fatal, to the credibility of the democratic process, and the subsequent delegitimization of the country's elected officials.

Beyond the relatively crude mechanisms for altering the final vote count directly, PRI has other means of control of the electoral process that continue to elude all efforts at reform. The use of public funds to benefit PRI candidates is presumed to be widespread and is almost impossible to prove or control from the outside. Control of the news media, both locally (in state and municipal elections) and nationally, is also pervasive, and often used to defame opposition candidates. Finally, unpunished violence against opposition figures is a haphazard but nonetheless consistent feature of PRI control. In the 1988 elections the most notorious case of violence was the gangland-style slaying of a top Cárdenas aide and his assistant on the eve of the elections. Although no hard evidence was presented linking the ruling party (or anyone else) with the killings, many blamed reactionary elements within or associated with PRI for the murders. On a less dramatic scale, the government also controls think tanks, access to government information, and, to some extent, the privileges of academia, thereby limiting its opponents' ability to formulate policies and platforms to challenge its own.

As noted previously, electoral fraud has also been included in the "modernization" craze that has swept Salinas-era Mexico. In more recent elections the electoral commission charged with drawing up new voter rolls has been accused of manipulating these lists to PRI's benefit through a high-tech, "cybernetic" fraud. Districts and even select neighborhoods with a history of strong support for the opposition have had their voter rolls "shaved," the opposition charges, with new names of unknown residents (the vote brigade to be brought in from outside on election day) added every tenth or twentieth name. Many registered voters in local elections in the late 1980s and early 1990s went to the polls on election day only to find their names missing from the list of registered voters. Furthermore, the opposition charges, efforts to register voters in opposition areas have been half-hearted, whereas voter registration of 85 to 90 percent of eligible voters is common in rural areas and PRI strongholds.

Voter disillusionment with the electoral system is blamed for high rates of abstention, which is one of the toughest problems for those hoping to out-ballot PRI. In a typically Mexican twist, PRI has even been accused of promoting stories about possible fraud before election day in an effort to keep voter turnout low. In general, however, abstention has resisted most attempts at serious study, since the numbers all appear to be skewed by a long history of fraud. Voter turnout among eligible voters in the hotly contested 1988 presidential elections, for example, was 49 percent, while turnout in 1982, when Miguel de la Madrid ran a traditionally ho-hum campaign and won easily, was 66 percent. The problem for students of Mexico's abstention rate is that no one knows whether the 1982 turnout was inflated with widespread fraud, whether the 1988 turnout was low because so many votes for the opposition were disqualified or simply "lost," or both. Even establishing what happened, moreover, would shed little light on the quantitative effects of fraud, leaving abstention a mostly unstudied, though extremely important, component of the current political scene.

The 1991 voter turnout was surprisingly high (66 percent of eligible voters) considering that it was a midterm election. The officially reported turnout for the elections of 1991 was the highest ever for a midterm election. PRI's major get-out-the-vote drive among its supporters and beneficiaries was probably one explanation for the larger than expected turnout, but vote inflation and fraud by the government were certainly also factors.

Electoral Reform

Electoral reform has long been a demand of the opposition parties, but the various reforms instituted since 1963 by the government served mainly to perpetuate the system of one-party rule.[4] In times of economic and social crisis PRI has announced reforms of the electoral system that help channel dissent into the electoral system (and away from more confrontational tactics). With the expanded credibility of electoral politics and the consequent increase in the participation of opposition parties, the democratic credentials of the ruling party are reinforced.

The appearance of independent candidates challenging PRI's monopoly on power gave rise to the first electoral reform in 1946. The federal reform law included provisions that ensured PRI's grip on political power, including a Federal Electoral Commission controlled by the party. In 1954 women were finally granted the right to vote. In its first few decades the federal government was sensitive to all challenges to the one-party state. By the early 1960s, however, government leaders realized that the existence of an electoral opposition fortified rather than undermined Mexico's status as a "one-party democracy." A 1963 reform guaranteed the opposition minimum representation in the Chamber of Deputies. Just as the 1963 reform was probably sparked by the 1958-59 labor upheaval, the 1969 reform that lowered the minimum voting age to 18 years was the result of the 1968 student protests.

The next electoral reform came close on the heels of the 1976 economic crisis. This was another attempt to give opposition parties a larger stake in the electoral process. Increasing voter abstention and apathy were undermining the government's claim to legitimacy. The reform was also widely regarded as a strategy to provide a counterweight to the rising popularity of the conservative PAN by giving a new electoral opening to the country's numerous left parties. The reform added 100 seats to the Chamber of Deputies for distribution on the basis of proportional representation, thereby giving even the smallest parties a chance for a seat in Congress.

The next electoral reform came almost ten years later in 1986, at a time when the country was facing a political crisis of unprecedented proportions. The previous reform had failed to catalyze the formation of a viable left opposition, and voter abstention remained high, with the exception of the 1982 presidential election. PAN, however, continued to gain strength (having won five municipalities in 1983), and demands were escalating, at home and abroad, that election fraud be terminated.

The 1986 reform did not, however, represent a major step toward democratization. The number of seats allocated for proportional representation was increased to 200. But this seemed to guarantee PRI control of the majority of congressional seats, even if it were to win less than half the vote. The government, through the creation of a new election tribunal, promised to announce election results more promptly. More important than the conservative character of the 1986 electoral reform was PRI's continued practice of widespread fraud, which denied PAN a string of congressional and municipal victories and probably two governorships in 1986.

To address nationwide disillusionment with the electoral system, and in some respects to compensate for the dubiousness of his own victory, Salinas promised and delivered an electoral reform package at the end of his first year in office. In an alliance with a segment of PAN's congressional delegation, the government gained two-thirds approval for a constitutional amendment, which paved the way for the codification of electoral reform and its approval by Congress. The 1989 reform overhauled a large part of the electoral system, resulting in some important advances. But there were also some steps backward, and such important issues as the appointed government in the Federal District were ignored.

The new electoral code, called the Federal Code of Electoral Procedures and Institutions (Cofipe), was approved by more than four-fifths of the Chamber of Deputies, with the only significant opposition coming from the Party of the Democratic Revolution (PRD). Among some of its features were the creation of a Federal Electoral Institute (IFE) to organize and validate election procedures, the establishment of a new Federal Electoral Tribunal to mediate federal electoral disputes, the overhaul of the voter list and the distribution of new voter registration cards, and the encouragement of more democratic practices at polling stations.

Nevertheless, the PRD and other members of the opposition charged that the reform was merely cosmetic, saying that the ruling party's control of the electoral apparatus was not loosened in any significant form and may even have been strengthened. Elections, they pointed out, continue to be administered by the Ministry of the Interior, the department that was also responsible for the country's internal security. The reform effectively increased the number of PRI-controlled votes in the electoral institute (charged with running the elections) and left the interior minister as institute chairman. At the time of this reform, the position was held by Fernando Gutiérrez Barrios, the man who directed the feared Directorate of Federal Security during the 1968 student massacre.[5]

Another major concern was the perpetuation of the so-called "governability clause" in place since 1986.[6] The reform not only kept this measure but it modified in a way that increases the overrepresentation of the dominant party. The clause guarantees a majority of congressional seats to the party that wins more than a 35-percent plurality. This makes control of the congress by opposition coalitions virtually impossible, leaving the dominant party in control of the Chamber of Deputies as long as it outpolls each of the opposition parties individually. The governability clause also negates the potential role of small parties as power brokers and kingmakers.

The PRD also objected to the new prohibition on coalition presidential candidates, such as the National Democratic Front (FDN) had in 1988. The reform outlaws the nomination of one presidential candidate by parties whose slates of deputies and senators are different. Other demands of the opposition, such as a guarantee of equal television time, went unheeded in the final elaboration of the reforms. In public statements, PAN members who voted to approve the reform considered it an improvement, the best reform possible under the circumstances.

One of the primary concessions to the opposition in the reform was the revision of the voter rolls, which had been discredited as being stacked with PRI faithfuls, including the dead (the so-called cemetery vote), in previous elections. Yet through the cybernetic "shaving" of these rolls, this concession rapidly suffered a discrediting of its own. The new voter rolls were used for the first time in federal elections in August 1991, which the PRD's Cárdenas contended were even more fraudulent than those held in 1988. According to Cárdenas, "Before election day, these elections were already corrupted by 'original sins' like the manipulations of the voter enrollment lists and retention of registration cards."

Proponents of expanded democratization in Mexico say that political modernization has to extend beyond the absence of fraud and a more balanced electoral reform. Chief among their demands are the end of *presidencialismo* and the institution of an effective system of checks and balances, especially a more active role for the Congress in lawmaking. In addition to these demands for a true separation of powers, reformers continue to demand that an independent electoral authority be created, that the government promote a genuine multiparty system, and that internationally recognized standards of human rights be enforced. To ensure that democratic modernization is more than just ongoing official manipulation, reformers advocate the presence of independent foreign election observers—a demand categorically rejected by government officials as an infringement of Mexico's national sovereignty.

There are other models Mexico could have chosen to guarantee the "electoral transparency" that President Salinas has repeatedly promised. Perhaps the most pertinent example and one of the best alternatives comes from Nicaragua, where a ruling party (the Sandinistas) created an independent electoral system. The Electoral Tribunal that presided over the 1990 elections in Nicaragua is, in effect, a fourth branch of government, with two of its five members drawn from the party in office, another two from opposition parties, and the fifth being a respected citizen independent of all parties. Andrew Reding of the World Policy Institute concluded, "The problem

with such systems is that they work. That makes them appealing to the opposition but unthinkable to the Mexican government."[7]

The Political Parties

Although Mexico has long been a "one-party" state, it also has a solid
history of opposition parties. Some of these opposition parties resulted
from schisms within PRI (such as the one that gave rise to the PRD) while
others emerged as leftist or rightist opposition parties. But the effectiveness
of these parties has been limited. Instead of threatening the stability of the
political system, they have been its escape valves. Instead of highlighting
the undemocratic character of Mexican politics, their existence has been evidence of Mexico's pluralism (Table 1b). Opposition parties have also
served to channel political dissent into a forum controlled and manipulated
by the government. They have offered an outlet for anti-PRI politicians and
a way for the electorate to express a "no" vote. This stabilizing and legitimizing
function of opposition parties was captured in the oft-repeated phrase by political analyst Jesús Reyes Heroles: "He who resists, supports."[8]

In the late 1970s mushrooming popular support for PAN began to
change this dynamic. A large portion of this support came from voters
wishing to protest PRI's grasp on power, but it was also speculated that the
conservative party's expanded backing may have also come from new public sentiment for private-sector solutions to the country's economic problems.[9] A new electoral reform law and increased electoral participation by
leftist parties did little to halt PAN's momentum. Although at first—especially in the 1983 municipal elections—the government decided to recognize the conservative party's local victories, it later resorted to repression to
defend PRI victories in gubernatorial and mayoral contests against strong
PAN candidates in the northern border states.

As it turned out, however, it was not from the right but from the left
that the government faced its greatest challenge in the 1988 presidential contest. The National Democratic Front (FDN), led by Cuauhtémoc Cárdenas,
grew out of a PRI faction known as the Democratic Current (CD).[10] The CD
called for greater internal democracy within PRI and challenged the neoliberal
direction the party leadership was taking under the de la Madrid administration. Instead it advocated a return to the revolution's ideals of economic
nationalism and social justice. The 1987 "unveiling" of the technocrat Carlos Salinas de Gortari as PRI's presidential candidate resulted in the departure of Cárdenas, Porfirio Muñoz Ledo, and other CD proponents. These
former *priistas* went on to form an electoral coalition with three small parties—PARM, PPS, and PFCRN—that in the past had mainly supported the
PRI's presidential candidate. Joining the coalition later was the Mexican Socialist Party (PMS), whose own presidential candidate Heberto Castillo
dropped out of the race. Support for the FDN, however, went far beyond
the popular bases of each of the coalition members. As the 1988 elections

demonstrated, the FDN attracted widespread support from most sectors of Mexican society.

It probably will never be known how close Cárdenas came to beating Salinas in 1988, or if he actually did win. Following the election, though, it did seem certain that electoral politics in Mexico would never be the same. The political escape valves—both to the left and the right of the PRI—had proved to be genuine threats to PRI's longevity as the ruling party.

The 1988 election precipitated a crisis of legitimacy and raised hopes that the one-party system was on its way out. But subsequent interim elections proved the staying power of PRI and highlighted the difficulties of forming a national party capable of challenging its pervasive influence. Recovering from the trauma of 1988, PRI in subsequent elections and other

Table 1b

Party Election Results, 1970-91[1]

(in percentages)

PARTY	1970	1973	1976	1979	1982	1985	1988	1991
PRI	80.0	69.8	80.3	69.8	69.4	65.0	51.1	61.4
PAN	13.6	14.7	8.5	10.8	17.6	15.5	18.0	17.7
PDM	0.0	0.0	0.0	2.1	2.3	2.7	1.3	1.1**
PSUM/PMS[2]	0.0	0.0	0.0	5.0	4.4	3.2	4.4*	0.0
PMT/PMS	0.0	0.0	0.0	0.0	0.0	1.5	0.0*	0.0
PRT	0.0	0.0	0.0	0.0	1.3	1.3	0.5	0.6**
PST/PFCRN[3]	0.0	0.0	0.0	2.1	1.8	2.5	9.3*	4.4
PPS	1.4	3.6	3.0	2.6	1.9	2.0	9.2*	1.8
PARM	0.8	1.8	2.5	1.8	1.4	1.7	6.1*	2.1
PRD	0.0	0.0	0.0	0.0	0.0	0.0	0.0	8.6
PEM	0.0	0.0	0.0	0.0	0.0	0.0	0.0	1.4**
PT	0.0	0.0	0.0	0.0	0.0	0.0	0.0	1.1**
Annulled	4.2	10.0	5.7	5.9	0.0	4.7	0.0[4]	4.2
Abstained	35.8	39.8	38.2	50.7	34.4	49.5	52.6	34.0

Figures may not add to 100 percent due to rounding.

*Members of FDN

**These parties lost their electoral registration because they did not obtain 1.5 percent of vote.

[1]These figures represent votes for political parties and do not necessarily correspond to the votes for presidential cadidates.

[2]The PSUM and the PMT merged in 1987 to form the PMS.

[3]PST renamed the PFCRN in 1988.

[4]There were 695,042 annulled ballots in the 1988 election, but the government did not officially acknowledge these in the final vote tallies since doing so would have meant that for the first time a Mexican president had been elected with less than half of the votes cast.

SOURCE: Figures from the Federal Electoral Commission, Mexico City.

LIBRARY
COLBY-SAWYER COLLEGE
NEW LONDON, NH 03257

108833

face-offs with opposition parties demonstrated its old skills of political manipulation and fraud. It alone would establish the rule of the political game in Mexico, and despite vociferous protest it would set the pace of economic and political modernization. Electoral fraud was harder than ever to prove. To undermine opposition complaints, it was the government itself that occasionally recognized opposition complaints about fraudulent elections, thereby underlining its own legitimacy.

Once again, particularly after the 1991 midterm elections, Mexico seemed to be returning to the old scenario where opposition parties served to stabilize and legitimize the country's political system. The time-tested strategy "to carry a big stick and offer small carrots" was again proving successful in keeping the opposition parties divided and sustaining several satellite parties attracted by PRI favors.[11] The old axiom of Mexican politics that the only way to power is through negotiation, not confrontation, with the government seemed confirmed by political events during the first three years of the Salinas *sexenio*.

The Institutional Revolutionary Party (PRI)

On the Mexican political spectrum, PRI is generally defined as "centrist," meaning essentially that it positions itself between opponents on the right and on the left, while adhering more or less to the principles that were the basis for its formation. A great deal of PRI's ideology and political leanings at any given moment, however, depend on the president in power. At the midpoint in his administration, Salinas could already be considered an aberration to the "pendulum theory" of Mexican politics, by which more "conservative" presidents are followed by more "progressive" presidents, and vice versa. His predecessor, Miguel de la Madrid, was one of the most conservative presidents in recent history, yet Salinas pursued the same conservative economic policies as, and in some cases with more zeal than, his predecessor. Some have argued that it was de la Madrid's failure to respect the unwritten "pendulum" law of Mexican politics that led to the schism in PRI and prompted its progressive wing to form a new party.

PRI's principles have traditionally been populist and paternalistic, with considerable money (and far more rhetoric) spent on public works. This rhetoric was toned down and the paternalism and public works cut back in the de la Madrid and Salinas administrations, partly for ideological reasons and partly because of the economic crisis. In their stead has come an emphasis on private investment and free market "neoliberalism." Salinas has greatly accelerated these trends, speeding up Mexico's integration into the U.S. economy at the same time.

In these about-faces on economic policy alone it is easy to see why generalizations about PRI are dangerous, and why its monolithic image should be propagated with great care, if at all. It was *priistas* who nationalized the banks in 1982, and it was *priistas*, nine years later, who reprivatized them. In more than a few cases, it was the same individuals enacting and justifying both policies. As Lorenzo Meyer observed, "It is PRI that now condemns its own past, but it is PRI that proposes to save the country."[12] Perhaps the greatest irony during the Salinas administration was that the most serious threat to PRI was made up of former *priistas*, including many who once served as PRI officials. And the leader of the opposition to PRI, Cuauhtémoc Cárdenas, was a party *cachorro* (cub)—the son of the man who more than any other is credited with consolidating the ruling party's hold on power.

It is easy to mistake PRI for a monolithic structure, bent solely on self-preservation, but that would be to overlook the internal diversity and opportunism that, over the years, may have been its greatest strength. This diversity has exhibited itself in ongoing debates about party reform. Internal party reform has been on the agenda since the early 1980s when the government began to realize that electoral reform alone would not restore the credibility of the one-party system: PRI itself needed a major overhaul.

In the past PRI relied on its ability to co-opt and incorporate to ensure that new social forces, such as the environmentalists or squatter groups, did not acquire too much independent stature outside the party. But the inclusionary capabilities of its corporatist structures were becoming increasingly ineffectual—a fact brought home to party leaders by the 1988 elections. During that election PAN was able to hold on to its segment of mainly middle-class, urban voters, and the FDN made considerable inroads into rural voting blocks—the longtime stronghold of PRI support—as well as capturing a large sector of urban voters.

Not since 1929, the year the party was born as the National Revolutionary Party, had a PRI national assembly been so anxiously anticipated as the 14th National Assembly held in August 1990. Reform was in the air at that assembly, and the reform measures debated in 1990 remain major—and potentially very divisive—issues within the party.[13]

The party leadership, answerable to President Salinas himself, came to the 1990 assembly with a package of reforms that aimed to inject a degree of democratic participation into candidate selection. The party hierarchy led by PRI chief Luis Donaldo Colosio and the Federal District's regent Manuel Camacho also hoped to free the party from its formal commitment to the social goals of the Mexican Revolution and to institute neoliberal philosophy as the party's new model of development. An attempt to undermine the old corporatist structures was the third element of the *salinista* reform package.

Objections came from diverse factions of the party. Two reform movements within the party—the Critical Current headed by Rodolfo González Guevara and the Movement for Democratic Change (MCD) spearheaded by Julio Hernández López—lobbied for more democracy within the party.[14] The vaguely worded reform that candidates be approved "in consultation with the bases" was unacceptable to some democratization critics who instead lobbied for the effective participation of the rank and file in candidate selection from the bottom up—all the way to the nomination and approval of the presidential nominee. In contrast, the so-called "dinosaurs" of the party fought many of the reform proposals, partly to protect their own vested interest in the old style of running PRI and partly out of the real concern that too much reform would destabilize the party, and hence the government.

The national assembly ended without having endorsed the ideological reforms that President Salinas and his collaborators desired. It also failed to endorse the neoliberal project of Salinas and declined to erase from party documents PRI's commitment to the Mexican Revolution's objectives of social justice, economic nationalism, and the central role of the state.

Internal democracy was incorporated into the party statutes, but the autocratic power of the presidency remained essentially intact. As a concession to the critics of *tapadismo*, PRI's candidate will no longer be "unveiled." The nominee, who will likely still be handpicked by the outgoing president, will now be required to win majority support from the party's national political council of senior party officials. Although undoubtedly an improvement from the clandestine rituals of the past, the new method will not create the open nominating process that critics had demanded, since the council was likely to be packed with members loyal to the outgoing president.

Clearly, a few small steps toward internal democratization were taken by the 1990 party congress, but most decision making remained the domain of the party's National Executive Council (CEN), the size of which was slashed from 22 to 9 members at the 1990 party congress. Despite the modest gains the few democratization measures were rarely honored in the 1991 midterm elections. Although some primary-style runoff elections were held and other "consultations" by the PRI leadership with the party bases were conducted, most candidates were simply announced in Mexico City as "unity candidates."

The traditional corporatist pillars of the party remain in place, but new party structures are being built up around them and will probably displace them before the end of the decade. Party modernizers set out to dismantle the corporatist system of quotas for the three sectors—labor, peasantry, and popular groups/government employees—after the failure of these sectors to deliver their constituencies in the 1988 elections. But fearing a new party schism, the unofficial quota system was allowed to persist, although party activists can now join PRI as individuals and fewer PRI candidates will be designated by sectoral organizations. Another important change in the party structure is the increased emphasis on party organizing by locality rather than by sector. This is an explicit recognition that most Mexicans no longer fit into the old corporatist categories and that where a person lives is probably the most important element in successful political mobilization (see The Underside of Modernization, Part 2).[15]

PRI, the self-described "party of the revolution," campaigned in 1991 as the party of innovation. Party posters emblazoned with its new slogan,

"Vote PRI: So that change may continue," were plastered throughout the country. Mexican television viewers watched slick prime-time promotional ads for the party. At least for the poor, probably the most effective vote-getting strategy was Pronasol, a government pork barrel used as a negotiable fund available to popular organizations willing to steer clear of "*cardenismo.*"[16]

Building on its resounding, albeit fraud-filled, election victories of 1989-90 (in which it won about 75 percent of the votes in local contests), PRI solidified its stature as the ruling party in the 1991 midterm elections.[17] According to official results, the party attracted 61.4 percent of the vote and directly won 290 of the 300 electoral districts for congressional deputies (PAN won the other 10 seats that are directly elected, with the remaining seats distributed proportionately among the other parties that attracted at least 1.5 percent of the vote). In addition, PRI won 31 of the contested 32 seats in the Senate, as well as winning all six of the governorships on the ballot. Although the official results showed clear PRI victories in the gubernatorial races in Guanajuato and San Luis Potosí, the newly elected PRI governors in those two states resigned in the face of popular protests and new elections were scheduled. PRI also secured 40 of the 40 directly elected seats in the Representative Assembly of the Federal District (Table 1c). The ruling party also widened its base in the state chambers, winning about 80 percent of the state deputy seats.

For those who had thought that the times of the *carro completo* or clean sweep were over, the resounding 1991 victory by the PRI slate was a shocking setback. The victory represented a personal triumph for President Salinas and presented the possibility that he will use the party's new power to deepen the neoliberal economic restructuring already under way. Instead of

Table 1c
Political Party Power, 1991

Office	PRI	PAN	PRD	Fringe[1]	Total Seats
Deputy	320	89	41	50	500
Senator	61	1	2	0	64
Governor[2]	29	2	0	0	31
Mexico City Assembly	40	10	6	10	66

[1]These are the PFCRN, PARM, and PPS, respectively winning 23, 15, and 12 national chamber seats. In the case of the Assembly of Representatives of the Federal District, PEM also won proportional representation.

[2]PAN won the governorship of Baja California in 1989. In 1991, after protests led mainly by PAN, the newly elected PRI governors in Guanajuato and San Luis Potosí resigned to allow new elections in 1992. A PAN politician was appointed interim governor of Guanajuato, while a PRI official was named interim governor of San Luis Potosí.

SOURCE: Figures from the Federal Electoral Commission, Mexico City.

arising through administrative reforms and presidential decrees, neoliberal changes may be incorporated directly into the constitution. Although PRI fell just short of obtaining a two-thirds majority in congress, having won just 64 percent of the seats, it could count on functional two-thirds control, when including the votes of satellite parties (mainly the PFCRN) and those of PAN on many issues. Soon after the election President Salinas announced that he would act to allow the privatization of the *ejidos* (communal landholding). Salinas might also choose to push through such controversial measures as changes in the federal labor law and opening up the oil industry to direct foreign investment. There was also speculation that Salinas might attempt to change the prohibition against reelection.

Ironically, PRI's overwhelming victories in the interim elections cast doubt on the 1988 assertion of President Salinas himself that "the era of the virtual one-party system has ended."[18] In the first three years of the Salinas *sexenio*, the entire state apparatus had been mobilized to ensure the triumph of PRI candidates in the off-year elections and to pave the way for a large margin of victory for PRI in the upcoming 1994 presidential contest.

But so enormous was the party's engineered victory in 1991 that it raised new questions about the viability of pluralism and democracy under a PRI government. The party's electoral sweep reflected the popularity of Salinas among the voting population, which will make it even more difficult for party dissidents to resist the advance of what detractors call *salinismo*—meaning the deepening of presidential power, the replacement of revolutionary principles by neoliberalism, and the transformation of traditional corporatist structures.

The National Action Party (PAN)

Since its inception in 1939 PAN has been linked to traditional Latin American conservative thought. It was founded to protest the social policies of the Lázaro Cárdenas era and to fight the continued subordination of the Catholic church to an increasingly powerful centralized and secular state government. The oldest of the opposition parties, PAN has a righteous history of protesting PRI fraud. The dominant philosophy of the party is conservative christian-democratic, although PAN has also encompassed social-democratic political leanings. Its current principles include an expanded role for the private sector, less centralization, more separation of powers, and a reduced public sector. Its economic platform differs little from that of the Salinas government, although the party says that the pace of political reform should match that of economic reform.

With its strongest support found in the northern border states, Yucatán, Jalisco, Guanajuato, and in Mexico City, PAN showed itself to be a formidable opponent to PRI in the 1980s. So substantial was its support that the government recognized its victories in a half-dozen municipal elections in 1983, and by 1989 it was forced to acknowledge the PAN gubernatorial victory in Baja California. This was the first time an opposition candidate had been allowed to win a statehouse since PRI was formed.

Since 1982 PAN has experienced major changes in its composition and in its relations with PRI. Although PAN was always regarded as a conservative party to the right of PRI, it was not until 1982 that it became the chosen (although temporary) vehicle of a vocal sector of the country's business elite. Reacting to the bank nationalization by López Portillo, many of the country's financiers and investors backed the PAN campaign against statism. Although PAN's stand against PRI fraud and the one-party state were still the principles that attracted most voter support, the party became increasingly known for its support of privatization of state enterprises and other neoliberal reforms. The *neopanistas*, as the post-bank nationalization party affiliates were known, found in wealthy businessman Manuel Clouthier the ideal party leader and presidential candidate.

In the 1980s PAN succeeded in establishing a de facto two-party system in the northern states, although PAN's local election victories were not always recognized by the government. Over the decades the party developed strong cadre structures, but it has never become a mass party. PAN is most successful in urban areas among middle-class, well-educated voters. Its inability to draw support in the countryside or among urban workers has been its outstanding weakness.

Over the years PAN's enemies accused it of being servile to the interests of North American business and affiliated in various ways with the U.S. Republican Party.[19] PAN has also been dubbed the "party of the rich" within Mexico, because of the support it enjoyed from a number of successful business figures, especially in the country's north. Such name-calling served PRI's interests by bolstering the contention that PRI is a centrist and populist party under attack from the rich and right wing.

The emergence in 1988 of the National Democratic Front broke PAN's forward momentum and undermined its claim to be the only viable opposition. It did, however, still succeed in winning a sizable portion of the 1988 vote, 17 percent, becoming the best-represented opposition party in the national Congress. Future prospects of the party were clouded by its lack of nationally recognized leaders (Clouthier died in a 1989 car crash) and the absence of a social program that would appeal to the country's poor majority. In many ways, PRI has moved to the right of PAN with its own conservative economic-modernization program, thereby taking over PAN's own banner. Not only did PRI appropriate PAN's economic platform, but the Salinas government also assumed as its own the concept of *"solidaridad,"* which had long been PAN's philosophical response to class conflict. As PRI continues to shift to the right, PAN finds itself without a distinctive identity.

Since 1988 two factions have emerged in the National Action Party. There are the traditionalists who uphold the party's history of principled opposition to the one-party state. Viewing themselves as the champions of the small businessman, the farmer, and other individual citizens unfairly treated by the state, they refuse to negotiate or compromise with the government. The 1990 founding of the Doctrinal and Democratic Forum as a faction of PAN reflected member discontent with PAN's transformation into a party of the loyal opposition.

With the advent of the Salinas government, the traditionalists lost control of the party to the gradualists or accommodationists. This faction, led by PAN president Luis Alvarez and backed by wealthy business interests in the northern border states, views negotiation as the quicker path to power. In the 1991 midterm elections the party increased by 1 percent its vote total. Because of the poor showing of the PRD, the PAN regained its place as the nation's second largest party. The 1991 elections, in which PAN won 17.7 percent of the vote, demonstrated that PAN was becoming more of a national party and less of a strictly regional party. Its proportion of the vote declined in many districts where it had traditionally been strong but increased in many others where it had fared poorly in previous elections. Although PRI officially won the governorships in Guanajuato and San Luis Potosí, new elections scheduled because of popular protests might lead to two other PAN governor seats in 1992.

The Party of the Democratic Revolution (PRD)

As expected, the FDN coalition disintegrated following the 1988 presidential election. Intent on finding a new political vehicle for the tremendous popular support shown for the Cárdenas candidacy, the former *priistas* of the Democratic Current moved quickly to form a new party called the Party of the Democratic Revolution (PRD). Of the constituent parties of the FDN coalition, only the Mexican Socialist Party (PMS) merged into the new party.[20] Support for the party is found throughout the country but is concentrated in Mexico City and in the states of Michoacán, Oaxaca, and Guerrero.

The PRD is an eclectic and unprecedented joining of Mexico's progressive parties, embracing positions from PRI's left wing to those of now-defunct socialist and communist parties. This merging of former *priistas* with social-democratic leanings and the socialist PMS led some to characterize the PRD as "two parties in one." The PMS itself represented the fusion of two leftist parties: the Unified Socialist Party of Mexico (PSUM), which itself was an outgrowth of the Mexican Communist Party (PCM), and the Mexican Workers Party (PMT), the party headed by Heberto Castillo. Upon merging, the two parties exchanged the hammer and sickle, and even the designation "communist," for the Mexican tricolor and the concept of Mexican socialism.[21] Although the Democratic Current and the socialist party constituted the two main pillars of the PRD, the new party could also count on the support of many of the country's grassroots community organizations, many of which had previously distanced themselves from electoral politics.[22]

More than anything, though, the PRD is the party of engineer and politician Cuauhtémoc Cárdenas, and his moderate progressive positions hold sway despite the presence of more radical elements (whose radicalism was tempered in light of international developments). The main appeal of Cárdenas has been moral, as he presented himself and his party as the honest, democratic, and peaceful option to PRI's high-handed and undemocratic processes and policies. He has refused to enter into negotiations with the ruling party, which has won Cárdenas much public sympathy.

The PRD has explicitly defined itself as pluralistic, inviting into its ranks "democrats and nationalists, socialists and Christians, liberals and ecologists."[23] This pluralism and its dominant social-democratic ideology have been criticized by the marxist left. They categorize the PRD as a liberal, reformist party, not a revolutionary one while charging that the principal promoters of PRD have not broken with their *priista* past.[24] Membership in the PRD is individual, not by organization, thereby breaking the corporatist mold set in place by Cuauhtémoc's father in the 1930s. Founded in protest of PRI's undemocratic practices, the PRD has also attempted to distinguish itself from other parties by its internal democracy.

Within the PRD factional struggles have been loud and public, with some elements criticizing its "PRI-like" hierarchy. The party apparatus is controlled largely by former *priistas*, while its rank and file is often more militant and more closely aligned with the traditional left opposition. A hard-fought primary campaign to select the candidate for the Mexico City Senate seat in 1991 left some scars, and evoked very low voter turnout, but was hailed outside the party (and accepted inside of it) as fair and democratic—a considerable advance in Mexican politics.

As of late 1991 none of the infighting had erupted into large-scale or significant divisions within the party. Major figures, however, like leftist intellectual Jorge Alcocer, left the party complaining that Cárdenas ran the party, despite his democratic pretensions.[25] The Alcocer resignation in early 1991 also brought to light another major issue of contention within the party—whether or not to negotiate (and thereby compromise party principles) with PRI. Alcocer accused Cárdenas of "fundamentalism" for his unwillingness to recognize the legitimacy of the Salinas government. It was the position of Cárdenas that any accommodation with the Salinas administration would reinforce absolutist rule in Mexico by restoring its democratic face. This factionalism between the reformists who argue for the need to reach out to progressive elements within PRI and to the government itself in some cases and those anti-accommodationists or *rupturistas* who demand that the PRD stay clear of the tentacles of officialdom will likely continue to rock the party in the years to come.

By midterm in the Salinas administration the PRD was still more of a political front than a strong party with a national infrastructure. Squabbling and debate among the party leadership, although a sign of the party's democratic foundations, inhibited effective party organization and outreach. The growth of the party was further obstructed by an obvious government campaign to undermine the PRD. Whereas some PAN victories were recognized, clear PRD victories in local and state elections in 1989 and 1990 (Michoacán, Guerrero, and possibly Tabasco) were suppressed by fraud and repression. The PRD chose the path of "permanent confrontation" with Salinas, and the government responded in the same way it has always treated those who refuse to be pacified: isolating, repressing, and seeking to divide and discredit the guilty party.

It was the hope of the Cárdenas coalition that the surge in popular support seen in the 1988 presidential election would solidify into strong voter identification with the PRD in the 1991 midterm elections. Instead, it saw its support plunge from the officially recognized 31 percent in 1988 for the FDN's Cárdenas to 8.6 percent for the PRD in 1991. According to official results, it won a plurality in not a single electoral district, and the party lost two of its four senate seats. Like PAN, the PRD protested that the election results were tainted by fraud. So overwhelming was its loss, however, that the party also had to acknowledge that weaknesses in the internal structure of the party contributed to its poor showing. Moreover, the electoral defeat underlined the necessity of developing a political institution not dependent on having the revered Cárdenas name on the ballot. In the wake of the devastating election, PRD leaders said they would consider forming an electoral alliance with PAN to challenge the one-party state in the 1994 presidential contest.

The Political Fringe

The rest of Mexico's political parties are primarily fringe parties, representing traditional and recent factions of the left or right. They have served mainly to legitimize the government by demonstrating its pluralism. In practice, many of the fringe parties actually have functioned as PRI "satellites," throwing their support to PRI presidential candidates in return for certain privileges.

Since the merging of the PMS—which had represented the country's largest socialist alliance—with the PRD in 1989, Mexico has had no viable left opposition party. Electoral politics have long been a source of differences and infighting among the Mexican left. The decision whether to cooperate with the government or to work outside governmental structures to effect change has historically haunted the left, and is one that the PRD itself faced at the beginning of the decade.[26]

On one side there are those interested in using the electoral opening to push forward their own progressive agendas while keeping rightist elements, namely PAN, at bay. The more radical left insist that participation in electoral politics does nothing but fortify the one-party state and the capitalist economic system. In the past, the radicals have included those who broke away from the Mexican Communist Party and other leftist organizations to support the guerrilla movements of the post-1968 era. Much more numerous have been the grassroots community groups concentrated in

Mexico City, Durango, Monterrey, and Chihuahua, which have advocated direct-action tactics over electoral participation. With the real hope of an electoral victory by the National Democratic Front in 1988, many of these groups offered at least tactical support for the Cárdenas campaign.

Most of the fringe parties—with the exception of the PDM on the right and the PRT on the left—joined the FDN coalition in 1988, hoping to ride Cárdenas's coattails into the Chamber of Deputies. The gamble proved exceedingly successful for the PPS, PARM, and the PFCRN. In contrast, the trotskyite PRT, which ran independently of the PRD, lost its electoral registration for failing to win the required 1.5 percent of the 1988 vote. Now standing apart from the PRD, these three parties—PPS, PFCRN, and PARM—have served PRI's purposes in splitting the PRD vote. In the words of one observer, the three have wanted "to have one foot with Cárdenas and the other with the government."[27] As Mexico moved toward a three-party electoral system in the 1990s (and especially considering the new prohibition against coalition candidates), the fringe parties seem destined to descend further into insignificance. They are still artificially sustained, however, by federal funds and large public-works projects, and their continued survival might well prove necessary to guarantee the president a two-thirds majority in Congress.

The following are brief profiles of Mexico's fringe parties, listed in order of their showing in the 1991 midterm elections:

Party of Cárdenas Front for National Reconstruction (PFCRN):

The PFCRN was formed as the Socialist Workers Party (PST) in 1975 and was renamed the PFCRN in 1988 upon joining the FDN.[28] Its opportunistic adoption of the Cárdenas name has successfully confused voters into thinking that it is the party of Cuauhtémoc Cárdenas. It declined to join the PRD and won 4.4 percent of the 1991 vote, based almost solely on the strength of its name. The PFCRN, directed by Rafael Aguilar Talamantes, has been labeled *marxista-salinista* by its critics for being an unabashed ally of the government while at the same time maintaining its populist image.

Authentic Party of the Mexican Revolution (PARM):

The PARM was founded in 1954 by army officers as a result of their declining influence within PRI. Known first as the "Hombres de la Revolución," they were conservative PRI dissidents who were opposed to the expansion of the Mexican state. PARM supported PRI in presidential elections until 1988 when it joined the FDN coalition. It broke off from the FDN following the election and retained its electoral registry in the 1991 elections, winning 2.1 percent of the vote. PARM has strongholds in a few scattered areas of the nation but cannot be considered a national force of any importance.

Popular Socialist Party (PPS):

The PPS was founded in 1948 and backed the candidacy of socialist labor leader Vicente Lombardo Toledano in the 1952 elections. Originally called the Popular Party (PP), it took its present name in 1960. The PPS still considers itself a marxist-leninist party, although it traditionally supported PRI until 1988 when it joined the FDN coalition. It failed to join the PRD and campaigned independently in 1991, capturing 1.8 percent of the vote.

Mexican Ecologist Party (PEM):

The PEM emerged in 1987 from the Ecologist Alliance, which was formed in 1984. Originally named the Mexican Green Party, the PEM won only 1.4 percent of the 1991 vote thus failing to obtain registry as a legal party. Following the midterm elections PEM underwent a severe internal crisis during which the party's president removed its directors in Mexico City.

Labor Party (PT):

The PT was founded in 1991, although it evolved from the Organization of the Revolutionary Left—Mass Tendency (OIR-LM), the Popular Defense Committees (CDP) of Chihuahua and Durango, Land and Liberty of Monterrey, and other socialist popular organizations characterized by their maoist orientation. By associating with the PMS and the FDN in the 1988 contest, these popular organizations received two congressional seats. The PT calls for the construction of a humanistic socialist society as an alternative to the vision of the dogmatic left. It captured only 1.1 percent of the 1991 vote thereby failing to win its electoral registry. The PT has also been labeled a *marxista-salinista* party because of the connections of some party leaders with the Salinas administration, links between party supporters and the Pronasol program, and its financial potential to reduce support for the PRD.

Mexican Democratic Party (PDM):

The PDM was founded in 1972 in Guanajuato by rightist Catholics with *cristero* and *sinarquista* leanings.[29] It has advocated the implementation of a social-christian philosophy. A regional party based primarily in the Bajío and in the Jalisco highlands, the PDM won just 1.1 percent of the 1991 vote, thereby failing to gain registry as a legal party.

Revolutionary Workers Party (PRT):

The PRT emerged from the 1968 student movement; in 1976, activists of the International Communist Group and the Socialist League founded the party, which has had a trotskyite socialist philosophy. The PRT did not join the FDN coalition and has been critical of the PRD's reformist approach. In 1990 the party allied itself with former members of the stalinist faction of the PCM. It won only 0.6 percent of the 1991 vote, thus failing to earn electoral registry.

Social Democratic Party (PSD):

The PSD, founded to participate in the 1982 elections, has been directed by the brothers Luis and Ernesto Sánchez Aguilar, and has provided strong backing to the Assembly in Defense of Democratic Suffrage (ADESE). Not legally registered.

Authentic Party of the Socialist Left (PAIS):

The PAIS, founded in 1990, is the creation of ex-PMS leader Manuel Terrazas, who was previously the chief of the United Communist Left (UIC). Through its association with the PMS in 1988 it obtained one congressional seat. Not legally registered.

The Future of Political Modernization

Mexico is undergoing a period of rapid transition—a time when old structures and styles are being dropped in favor of ones deemed more modern and effective. Many antigovernment critics of this modernization drive complain that economic modernization is far outpacing political modernization. The government, in other words, has embraced *perestroika* but has been more timid about *glasnost*.[30]

Political parties on both the left and right in Mexico share the view that the government has failed to promote true political modernization by creating the conditions that would finally allow the Mexican people to choose its leaders. Although the main opposition parties are both critical of the narrow reach of the government-sponsored political modernization, they each have their own concept of democratization. While the PRD stresses the fundamental importance of free elections, it also holds forth a social-democratic vision that includes the principles of social justice and popular participation. In contrast, PAN's view of democratization is limited to the more narrow but better defined principles of representative democracy.

There is, however, even less agreement about the character and pace of economic modernization. The government's conversion to neoliberalism in the 1980s pleased many of its conservative and business critics. At the same time, however, the government's new economic policies sparked new antigovernment sentiment among the country's lower classes and among intellectuals and professionals of leftist and nationalist tendencies. Whereas President Salinas argues that economic modernization forms the foundation for democratization, his left and center-left critics insist that democracy cannot wait and that broad-scale democratization is an essential first step toward choosing a new economic model for Mexico.[31]

In the electoral arena, the depth of popular concern about the spurious character of Mexican democracy first became evident in the rising support for PAN candidates. Although PAN remained a serious contender for political power in Mexico, it was the emergence of Cuauhtémoc Cárdenas and the forces of *neocardenismo* in 1988 that opened up the political debate in Mexico. The result has been a broader and more serious discussion about Mexico's political and economic future.[32]

Neocardenismo vs. the State

What began as a schism in the revolutionary family—the emergence of the dissident Democratic Current—gave life to a new dynamic in Mexican politics, namely the standoff between the conservative modernization strategy of the PRI government and the *neocardenista* movement led by Cuauhtémoc Cárdenas. At issue in this political clash are the populist and nationalist objectives of the Mexican Revolution as well as the quality and character of Mexican democracy.

Radical leftist change is not in the political cards for Mexico. The country has moved sharply to the right, especially in the realm of economics but also with respect to the ruling party's choice of allies and the government's foreign policy. Having appropriated the free market banner of its longtime critics on the right, the government found that the main obstacle to its brand of economic modernization was to its left. The FDN's impressive showing in 1988 not only raised speculation about the possibility of a left-of-center victory in 1994, but it also encouraged local activists and supporters to initiate their own electoral challenges on the municipal level.

After 1988, the PRD stood at the front of the *neocardenista* opposition, but the party and the movement have not been one and the same. Included in the ranks of the *neocardenista*s are hundreds, indeed thousands, of popular organizations that have risen up on local, regional, and national levels to struggle for rights to land, better wages, and improved living standards. Although not actually unified around any specific goals, they commonly identify with the principles of social justice, economic nationalism, and popular participation as represented by the policies of Cuauhtémoc Cárdenas. And while most have not belonged to any popular organization, the millions of Mexicans who have seen their wages fall and their standard of living erode represent potential supporters of *neocardenismo*.[33]

In many obvious ways, *neocardenismo* represents a return to the past. As Carlos Monsiváis observed, the PRD's Cárdenas "is the candidate of a historical memory and the emotions associated with it."[34] *Neocardenismo* is, in good part, an effort to recover the values of the Mexican Revolution as put into practice by Mexico's populist hero, Lázaro Cárdenas. Those objectives, as enshrined in the constitution, have been referred to with respect during all successive *sexenios* but have been largely ignored or defied in practice. This process of displacing populist and nationalist policy orientations began with the probusiness administration of Miguel Alemán and reached new heights under the de la Madrid and Salinas administrations.

The demands of the *neocardenistas* for sovereign control of national wealth and social justice are echoes of the Mexican Revolution. Cárdenas seeks popular recognition for the PRD as the true heir of the country's revolutionary and populist past. At the same time he is pushing forward a program of democratization. According to Cárdenas, "The economic modernization that Mexico needs cannot be carried out without a thorough democratization of the country's politics and society."[35]

Democratization was the PRD's main organizing strategy in the 1988-91 period. Challenging the legitimacy and authoritarianism of the PRI government were seen as the best route to power. According to this strategy, true democratization in Mexico would precipitate the disintegration of PRI—in the manner of the communist parties of the old socialist bloc—thereby making room for the country's purported majority, the *neocardenistas*. In this effort the PRD sought to build multiparty coalitions and multiclass alliances. The attention given to the abuses of the electoral system struck a strong chord of support among Mexicans grown tired and angry with one-party rule. But the government proved unexpectedly adept at manipulating the democratization issue—partly by artifice but also through reforms that have gained some popular respect.

In 1990 Jorge Alcocer (who left the PRD in January 1991) remarked that the PRD's future success would depend on its ability to awaken citizen interest in the electoral system and raise popular concern about electoral fraud.[36] This protest strategy proved inadequate, though, as subsequent events demonstrated. With its electoral-reform initiative, which received important support from members of all opposition parties except those of the PRD, PRI was able to regain a significant degree of democratic legitimacy. In the face of the demonstrable progress of political modernization, the PRD appeared to be intransigent and unreasonably confrontative to many Mexicans pleased with this progress, limited as it might be. Furthermore, like PAN, the PRD proved unable to offer an adequate response to electoral fraud, mainly because of the legal difficulties of documenting it.

PRI was also able to turn the tables on the PRD's confrontative stance following evidently fraudulent elections in Michoacán and Guerrero. Photos and film clips of purported PRD activists with machetes and shotguns were widely circulated, with the apparent purpose of creating the impression that the PRD challenge would lead to widespread violence and dangerous political instability. In its campaign to discredit the PRD, PRI circulated rumors that PRD activists were communists with strong links to regional drug mafias.[37] At the same time, President Salinas shielded himself from PRD attacks by successfully cultivating a reformist image. He cast the blame of fraud and human rights violations on lower ranks in the party, government, and police, all the while broadening the already powerful system of *presidencialismo*.

At least initially, the building of a national party with an infrastructure and organizers that would extend into every municipality proved far beyond the PRD's capabilities. Lacking this organizational base, the party has resorted to the kind of campaign tactics that typify the PRI: the vertical imposition of candidates unfamiliar to the local population and the wholesale plastering of party propaganda on walls, telephone polls, and any other available space. Internal squabbling and well-publicized factionalism and desertions from the PRD (as well as PAN) contrasted sharply with the unified image presented by PRI.

But even more problematic has been the inability to formulate a coherent and credible economic alternative to the PRI government. Instead, the PRD has mainly protested the failings, injustices, and probable consequences of PRI's generally successful initiatives, such as Pronasol, the free trade agreement, privatization, deregulation, and even the anti-inflationary Pact for Economic Recovery and Stability. In doing so, the PRD offered a critique of neoliberal modernization, not an alternative to it. This problem is not peculiar to the PRD and Mexico's *neocardenistas*, it is one that is shared by leftists, social-democrats, and popular movements throughout the world. In the face of the rapid internationalization of capital and the predominance of conservative political regimes in the industrial world, it remains a formidable challenge for progressive politicians and activists to formulate credible nationalist alternatives.

The PRD and Cárdenas have an economic platform, but it is vague and not well developed. One problem is the perceived restorationist character of the PRD's program of social change. Voters are told that the populist pact that guided the country since the revolution will be restored. But that pact is largely mythical, and is remembered mostly as empty government rhetoric. This position has failed to engender broad support among Mexicans, who after decades of statist solutions and leftist rhetoric by opposition politicians were cynical about economic alternatives that have the ring of populism, nationalism, and socialism.

Aware that propagating old populist solutions was not enough, after the 1988 election Cárdenas did begin searching for up-to-date formulas to deal with old economic problems. According to Cárdenas, "The issue is not whether the economy should be modernized and opened up, nor whether many of the costlier programs of the Mexican welfare state should be made more cost-effective and efficient. . . . The real issue is at what speed, how deeply, and under what conditions these changes should be undertaken . . . [and] who should pay the unavoidable costs that a program of economic restructuring entails."[38]

Although Cárdenas has an economic vision, it is one that is diametrically opposed to the version of economic modernization being pushed by Salinas. Instead of strictly honoring debt service schedules, for example, he called for limiting debt payments to a small percentage of export earnings or the gross domestic product (GDP). Rather than putting the state's weight behind programs to increase foreign investment, Cárdenas emphasizes job creation and the development of the domestic market by increasing purchasing power. Although he does not oppose increased foreign investment, the PRD leader insists on stricter controls on foreign investment and on the cross-border flow of foreign exchange. A heretic in the circles of modern economic reformers, Cárdenas calls for a mixed economy, believing that state intervention is needed to spread the benefits of economic growth to all social classes and to ensure sovereign national control of the economy.

The strong showing Cárdenas made in 1988 gave rise to a new progressive political party in Mexico and held forth the possibility that, for the first time since the 1930s, there would be a joining of political and social move-ments. Cárdenas himself defined his political challenge in that manner. As the FDN presidential candidate, he asserted that "Our struggle is a perma-nent, long-term endeavor to bring about the changes we think our country needs."[39] But bridging the gap between popular movements and demo-cratic political contests is a difficult one, and one with few modern prece-dents. If the PRD is to succeed, it will have to find ways to create a national political party that extends beyond the Cárdenas name and which repre-sents the aspirations of peasants, workers, underpaid bureaucrats and teachers, urban squatters, and all those being pushed to the side by free market modernization.

PRI's landslide victory in 1991 dampened, at least temporarily, hopes that a *cardenista* coalition could sweep aside the ruling party in the electoral arena. Those midterm elections demonstrated not only the resourcefulness and resiliency of the government but also the serious failing of the incipient coalition to develop a strong organizational structure and a popular plat-form. Most discouraging to PRD supporters was evidence that voters actu-ally supported PRI's brand of economic and political modernization. Future efforts to revive the neocardinista coalition will require a strong party-building program, the development of a credible economic platform, and a renewal of the kind of social mobilization that led to the impressive Cárdenas showing in 1988.

Redefining the State and the Party

During the de la Madrid and Salinas *sexenios* the Mexican government repeatedly exhibited its still considerable capacity for adaptive change. Over the years its policies and rhetoric have changed from conservative to progressive and back again in the interests of ensuring the nation's political and economic stability. Since 1982 the government has labored to adapt it-self, and its associated political party, to dramatic changes in Mexico's so-cial, economic, and political climates.

The spectacular successes of PAN in the early 1980s followed by the FDN's unprecedented popular challenge in 1988 seemed to indicate that the "one-party democracy" was nearing its end. There could no longer be "business as usual" in Mexico. But President Salinas quickly proved that as-sessment to be wrong. Subsequent PRI landslides, the popularity of Salinas, and the failings of the two major opposition parties to develop credible al-ternatives demonstrated the staying power of the ruling party. Events in the 1988-91 period tended to reinforce the widely accepted belief that PRI and government in Mexico are two sides of the same coin.

Many of the usual instruments of control—corruption, electoral fraud, corporatism, co-option—remained part of the manipulative political system in Mexico. But in its drive to adapt to the changing climate, the government also found new ways to strengthen and extend the structures of inclusion-

ary authoritarianism, which have long distinguished politics and government in the country. Mexican observers have called these later adaptations
"*neocorporativismo*."[40]

At the 1990 party congress, President Salinas did not equivocate about
his intentions to transform PRI. He told the gathered delegates that the
challenge before them was to build "a new political party." This party's
mission was to transform the state and economy while maintaining its lock
on political power. The challenge was to reform the party without tearing it
apart, and during his first three years Salinas proved quite successful in
holding the party together at the same time its structures and very principles were being radically altered.

The Salinas government did not move to expand the old corporatist
components. Instead it has let them slowly crumble. The PRI government
did, however, begin redefining its corporatist strategy while searching for
new allies and reformulating old alliances. PRI itself was submitted to restructuring process—evolving from a party formally identified with the
workers, peasants, and popular classes to one that is open to the whole of
civil society. Its former class-linked identity—the "party of the workers," as
it was known in the Cárdenas era—is quietly being dropped in the attempt
to attract the middle classes, entrepreneurs, and financial elite into the active ranks of the party. The idea is to restore legitimacy by finding new
bases of support among the social forces that may previously have been
marginalized by outdated corporatist structures.

This is not to say that the lower classes are being pushed out of the
party. But the new style of corporatism stresses productivity over patronage—although clientelism and electoral quotas remain part of the government's
political arsenal. It seeks alliances with small-farmer organizations that produce cash crops, preferably for export. With respect to labor organizations,
the PRI government is promoting worker *solidaridad* with the productivity
goals of the company, rather than encouraging class confrontation. Independent peasant and worker organizations are not encouraged, while those
willing to cooperate with PRI benefit from government credit, technical assistance, and official recognition.

The neoliberalized government promises to incorporate willing workers and peasants into the country's push toward economic modernization.
For the poor, with little productive potential in this economic restructuring,
the government has extended its "*solidaridad*" and charity through the Pronasol program. The Mexican government no longer aspires to be a welfare
state in the old tradition of bureaucratic social welfare agencies. Rather it
has assumed the role of the philanthropist, handing out funds and projects
directly to beneficiaries. In that way, not only is there less waste but the
government also polishes its own image and widens its base of support (see
The Underside of Modernization, Part 2).

To broaden the base of the party, government officials have shown a
willingness—in the Echeverría tradition of incorporating leftist dissidents—

to reach out to popular organizations and negotiate differences. And to bolster the credibility of corporatist organizations like the National Peasant Confederation (CNC), PRI encourages the formation of grassroots Peasant Solidarity Base Committees.

The Salinas administration has also demonstrated its willingness to include more old-style *políticos* in the bureaucracy and cabinet than were seen in the de la Madrid years.[41] At the 1990 party congress President Salinas made a point of welcoming the party's left wing, and the party leadership was willing to incorporate into the party statutes numerous reforms proposed by dissident groups. At the same time, however, Salinas made it clear to party members that there was a line that dissidents, either inside or outside the party, should not cross. At the 1990 party congress he charged that "those of the opposition who insult the party here at home and have no shame in criticizing PRI and the government abroad" had, in effect, become "allies of those who seek to subvert our national sovereignty."[42]

As part of the government's search for new allies, it has opened its arms to Washington and the Catholic church—in open defiance of the deeply rooted conventions of the Mexican Revolution. Rapid economic modernization along the neoliberal lines recommended by Washington, together with the sudden emergence of a strong center-left contender in Mexican politics, have resulted in a marked decline in U.S. concern over the dubious state of political modernization in Mexico.[43] Although the economy began moving forward under Salinas, the benefits of this growth have not yet trickled down below the business community. But the promise that free trade, new foreign investment, and amicable relations with Washington will lead to socioeconomic progress development has won Salinas, and by association PRI, a new measure of popular support.

On the electoral stage, neocorporatism in Mexico means a system of selective democracy. Electoral reforms have been accompanied by a modernization of vote manipulation. Recognition of the victories by PAN paralleled a campaign to discredit, isolate, and crush the PRD, regarded to be the greater threat. But PRI also committed itself to adopting new party organizing and campaign tactics. Counting on its multitude of party functionaries, PRI has been able to reach into every electoral district, knocking on doors and making the personal contact that wins elections. As yet the party has been unable to present voters with a record of improved socioeconomic conditions. It has shown, however, its willingness to spend an impressive amount of its resources on community development projects through Pronasol. It can also point to some progress in reducing corruption and increasing efficiency of state agencies. Evidence of major economic reforms also serves to raise voter expectations and ensure support, at least in the short term.

During the Salinas administration the government demonstrated its knack for outmaneuvering political opponents by appropriating their platforms. Its support for the private sector and rapprochement with the Cath-

olic church, for example, undermined PAN's raison d'être. Its electoral reforms, creation of a human rights commission, recognition of vote fraud,
and campaign against corruption all made it more difficult for opposition
parties to claim the mantle of democratic reform.

For the time being, a gradualist approach to political modernization
and *neocorporativismo* appears to be serving the government well. The
strategy's ultimate success, however, will probably depend more on the
strength and dimensions of Mexico's economic recovery than on the integrity of its political modernization project.

Security Forces

The Mexican military is a product of the Mexican Revolution. The pre-revolutionary army disintegrated, and the old regime's network of *rurales* (irregular rural police) virtually disappeared. The new army that emerged was steeped in revolutionary mythology, with its generals serving as the leaders of the new state.

Concerned for the stability of the revolutionary regime, the general-presidents that ruled the country until 1946 established the principle that military threats would be brutally suppressed and military loyalty would be richly rewarded.[1] They also began the process of subjecting the army to the country's emerging political institutions. In the 1920s, under President Plutarco Elías Calles, the army gradually began losing its central place in politics and government. The formation of an official political party by Calles in 1929 served to keep the armed forces subordinate to political control.

Calles' successor, General Lázaro Cárdenas, incorporated the army as an official sector of the ruling party in 1938, thereby further ensuring the loyalty of the armed forces to the central government. At the same time, however, Cárdenas moved to limit the power of regional military chieftains by establishing a system of regular rotation of zone commanders. President Cárdenas moved to professionalize the army, reduce strength, and retire old revolutionary generals. The taming of the military continued under President Avila Camacho, who soon after taking office in 1940 dissolved the "military sector" of the ruling party and its quota of congressional seats.[2]

The election of Miguel Alemán in 1946 began Mexico's uninterrupted history of civilian rule. To further limit the army's power and reduce the threat of provincial uprisings, Alemán placed the fuel and food supplies of the military garrisons under civilian control—a practice that continues today. The taming of the armed forces—a process that began under Calles and was completed during the Alemán presidency—has been one of the most remarkable achievements of Mexico's political system. This decline in the military's political power is evident throughout the political system. Between 1929 and 1946 eight military officers held nondefense-related cabinet positions, whereas only one military official has held a cabinet post other than secretary of defense and secretary of the navy since 1946. Fifteen states had military governors in 1948, but since then there have been, at most, only one or two officers serving as governor at any one time. Although the political quota for the military has decreased significantly, it still appears to exist in the form of having at least one military officer as governor. Military officers are also found sprinkled through the lower and middle levels of the government bureaucracy, another indicator of military-government deal making.

Unlike its counterparts in other Latin American countries, Mexico's military has stayed in its barracks, leaving politics to the politicians. Remarkably, Mexico has not experienced military rebellions or coups since the late 1920s—a record unmatched elsewhere in Latin America. The emergence of a dominant political party and its corporatist structure helped ensure the military's subservient role in Mexico. Without foreign enemies, there has been little need to mobilize for national defense, which is another reason the armed forces have remained on the sidelines in Mexican politics.

On its southern border, the tiny Central American republics represent no threat to the country's territorial sovereignty. On the northern border, there exists no feasible defense against the superior might of the United States.[3] As a result, Mexico maintains only a minimal national defense capability. Beginning in the late 1960s and continuing into the 1970s, isolated leftist guerrilla and terrorist groups did pose a challenge to internal security for the first time since the *Cristero* Rebellion of the 1920s, but these challenges were crushed without the necessity of full-scale military mobilizations.[4]

The Military in Profile

A wall of silence and secrecy surrounds and protects the Mexican military. It is a closed institution, whose members are discouraged from speaking to outsiders about its internal workings. Other than federal budget figures, there is no public record about the armed forces. Even major essays and books addressing the question of national security in Mexico only touch lightly on the internal workings of the armed forces. Academics and journalists have learned that research and reporting on the military is extremely difficult because of the hermetic nature of the institution. Researchers have also found that questions about the military may not be looked upon favorably. As a result, foreign observers have provided much of the available information on and analysis of the security forces.[5] Even within the country's political elite and in the government bureaucracy that reviews budget requests there is little knowledge of the military internal affairs.[6]

The Mexican government's expenditures on its armed forces generally represent about 0.5 percent of the GNP, one of the lowest ratios in the hemisphere—about the same level as Costa Rica (Table 1d). Mexico exports no arms, and arms imports are rarely higher than 1 percent of total imports.[7] Regular armed forces number about 150,000 members, more than double the size in the late 1960s.[8] The official military budget does not represent the totality of the military's financial resources. Discretionary funds that are sometimes passed to the military are not included in the official budget. Although most of this discretionary funding covers small to medium expenditures, the president occasionally approves larger off-budget funding requests, as was the case in government funding for the purchase of U.S. fighter jets in the early 1980s. According to one study, income from the military commissaries is another important source of revenue for the armed forces.[9]

The army and air force are organized under the authority of the minister of national defense, while the navy has its own cabinet minister. With some 105,000 members, the army is the dominant military service. The army administers 36 zones (covered by ten military regions), with the zones roughly corresponding to state boundaries and the federal district. The exceptions are Chiapas, Guerrero, and Veracruz, each of which has two army zones.[10] A plan is under way to convert the army's organizational structure into one of corps, organized along tactical lines. The air force, which holds a semi-autonomous position within the Ministry of National Defense, has 8,000 members, including 1,500 in an airborne brigade. Mexico's air force is entirely subordinate to the army and the Ministry of National Defense. The navy has 35,500 members, including its naval air force and marine force. The principal naval installations are found in Veracruz, the country's major port; and there are four naval districts on each coast.[11]

Mexico also has a volunteer rural guard, sometimes called the *rurales*, with some 60,000 members. Drawing their troops almost exclusively from the *ejidos* (communal landholdings), these militias answer to the local army commander. Armed with old carbines, militia members are expected to maintain public order and are said to serve as "the eyes and ears of the government in outlying rural areas."[12]

All males are required to register for military service after reaching 18 years of age. In turn they receive an identification card, called a *cartilla*, which has to be renewed every five years until the men turn 40. A small number of these men are selected for an active reserve of some 250,000 personnel. Enlistment in the military service, however, is entirely voluntary. New recruits generally come from rural areas and are often indigents who

Table 1d

A Comparison of Military Expenditures, 1989

	%GNP	%Budget	$ Per Capita	Soldiers per 1000 People
Mexico	0.6	2.2	$12.0	1.8
Costa Rica	0.5	3.1	7.0	2.8
El Salvador	3.8	34.9	39.0	8.4
United States	6.3	27.5	1250.0	9.1

SOURCE: U.S. Arms Control and Disarmament Agency, *World Military Expenditures*, 1989.

see the military as their only hope for social mobility. They serve a three-year tour of duty, and those who reenlist commonly become noncommissioned officers by the end of their second tour of duty.[13]

Whereas the troops and noncommissioned officers are drawn from the rural poor, military officers usually have lower-middle-class backgrounds. To become a commissioned officer, a candidate has to pass through one of three officer schools, the largest being the Heroic Military College, in Mexico City. Besides this first level of "formative" academies, the Mexican military has three higher tiers in its educational structure: technical training schools, higher command and staff studies at the Higher War College (ESG), and the National Defense College.

As defined by the organic statutes of the armed forces, the military has three main missions: to defend Mexico's sovereignty and independence, to maintain the rule of the constitution and the law, and to preserve internal order. By their own statutes, the armed forces are also obligated to participate in civic-action projects and to provide assistance in the case of natural disasters.

Since the 1940s the preservation of Mexico's domestic order has been the military's main concern, aside from its considerable civic-action operations. Because Mexico has faced no territorial threats since 1916, when General John J. Pershing led a U.S. Army invasion to seek out Pancho Villa, national defense has required little vigilance. For the military, preserving internal order has meant everything from running state enterprises (as was the case during the 1958-59 railroad strike) and responding to natural disasters to suppressing antigovernment political protests and hunting down guerrillas. At least 25,000 of Mexico's troops are assigned to anti-narcotics operations. Civic-action projects such as cleaning up after floods and immunization programs, have long been part of the army's work, and this extends to natural conservation activities, including extensive tree planting—all of which have helped the military to retain the public's goodwill.

As in other sectors, corruption exists in the top ranks, although it is largely confined to manipulations of the military's own budget. Some observers, however, assert that senior officers are sometimes allowed to enrich themselves with assorted and mostly illegal business activities like drug trafficking because corruption keeps the military subservient to the civilian regime.[14] In keeping with the terms of an unstated agreement between the government and the military, military officers are not prosecuted by civilian authorities for their illegal or extra-official activities. There does exist, however, a tradition of strict discipline within the armed forces. This discipline, as well as the degree of security and comfort that the military provides, serve to keep the lower ranks fairly content. Steady meals, expanding benefits, regular pay raises, and the hope for social mobility help maintain the loyalty of the troops, most of whom come from society's lower strata.

The Modernization of the Military

In the 1960s the Mexican military became afflicted with an image problem. The army's 1968 massacre of protesting students in the Tlatelolco plaza tarnished the military's reputation as a member of Mexico's revolutionary family. Due to its lack of modern equipment and uniforms, the military's own self-image has also been a problem. The Mexican military used to look like a remnant of another era. Its World War I helmets, single-shot carbines, and equestrian cavalry gave the impression that it was stuck in time. Starting in the early 1970s the armed forces have slowly become unstuck, benefiting from a modernization effort that has given them new uniforms, a stock of modern weaponry, and even a squadron of jet fighters.

The government's decision to modernize the military probably dates back to the social turmoil that surrounded the 1968 massacre. The subsequent rise of guerrilla movements and the increasing military participation in anti-narcotics operations reinforced the initial determination to modernize the military by increasing its size, streamlining its organizational structure, upgrading equipment, and improving the education of the officer corps.[15] The oil boom of the late 1970s gave the government the funds to pay for this modernization effort, while at the same time pointing to the rising need to protect the industry's expanding production facilities. The 1982 economic crisis forced the government to scale down the military's modernization plans and to rein in its budget, although the military budget was not as drastically affected as other parts of the public sector.

Modernization has helped improved the image of the Mexican military. Horses have been sold off in exchange for jeeps, and outdated weaponry has been junked in favor of modern varieties. One of the most dramatic upgrades was the purchase during the first Reagan administration of a dozen F5-E supersonic fighters. New destroyers also came from the United States, while Mexico bought armored vehicles from France and transport aircraft from Switzerland. Mexico does have a small domestic military industry which manufactures G-3 automatic rifles (under a West German license), medium-range rockets, and armored personnel carriers, while the navy produces its own patrol boats.[16] With the injection of oil monies into the economy in the 1970s, the military saw the opportunity to become more high-tech. Even though those hopes have not been entirely fulfilled due to subsequent budget cutbacks, military officials are generally proud of their institutions. Increasing military and anti-narcotics assistance from the United States in the 1980s has furthered military modernization while at the same time cementing a closer relationship between the armed forces of the two countries (see U.S. Security Assistance, Part 6).

Until 1981 the Higher War College was the highest military academy. Its graduates have been regarded as general staff officers, virtually guaranteed to become colonels, about half of whom eventually become generals. The opening of the National Defense College added yet another tier to

Mexico's military education system. This is a policy center for the top brass to study and formulate national-defense strategy as well as to discuss international affairs and national resource management. It is expected that the associates of the National Defense College will also formulate, for the first time, a national security policy. Along with the founding of the National Defense College, the government also authorized the creation of another study center called the navy's Center for Higher Command Studies and National Security.

Previously, military education was almost exclusively limited to military subjects and to military instructors. As part of the modernization of educational structure, however, civilian lecturers and subjects formerly regarded as the exclusive terrain of civilians, including social, economic, and political issues, became part of the military curriculum at the National Defense College.

The military modernization project has continued, although the lack of budgetary resources has slowed its advance. It had been expected that the armed forces would reach 220,000 by the early 1990s, but the economic crisis put a halt to this ambitious plan. Nevertheless, the military has made substantial advances, most notably in terms of new equipment and weaponry and improved education and living conditions. The Social Security Institute for the Mexican Armed Forces (ISSFAM) has made considerable benefits available to its members, and housing has been steadily improved.

Keeping the Peace

As part of its mission to preserve internal order, the military frequently serves as a quasi-police force. Army officials often serve as the chiefs of judicial police, security police, district police, riot police, and other police units. This interweaving of military and police functions is most apparent in cases when the military is called in to maintain order during strikes and political disturbances. The blurring of distinctions is also apparent in the extensive involvement of the armed forces in anti-narcotics operations. The army is primarily responsible for the eradication of illegal crops, while the navy interdicts drug-transporting vessels.[17] In recent years, however, the army has also directly pursued leading drug traffickers and even apprehended state and municipal police officials suspected of collaborating with narcotics smugglers.

Still remembering Tlatelolco, the military is wary about intervening in local political and social clashes, preferring instead to intercede in potential problems before they threaten internal security.[18] Despite this reluctance the armed forces have become increasingly involved in internal security matters, no longer simply supplementing the police but assuming a principal role in maintaining public order.

The armed forces have long played a role in preserving order and suppressing political opposition during elections.[19] As political conflict expanded in the 1980s, so did the military's presence during the electoral process. The government commonly sends in heavy military patrols prior to elections in strongly contested areas, the idea being to forestall protests through intimidation. As was the case in Guerrero in 1990, army troops have been used to dislodge opposition groups from town halls.

Army troops frequently find themselves serving as the government's gendarmes in support of its economic restructuring policies. The military played a role in suppressing worker struggles at the Ford plant in Cuautitlán, the Modelo Brewery in Mexico City, and the country's largest copper mine, in Cananea, Sonora. Usually, the mere presence of the army is enough to quiet protests.[20] Similarly, in rural struggles the military regularly sides with the landowners rather than the peasants. Troops removed antigovernment demonstrators from municipal palaces in Juchitán, Oaxaca, Piedras Negras, Coahuila, and in various municipalities in Michoacán. Despite the government continued efforts to suppress opposition through the deployment of the armed forces, the military is generally respected by the Mexican people.

The military has proved itself capable of dealing with small guerrilla challenges—although it committed extensive human rights violations while seeking out these independent forces—and it has also proved its ability to handle tactical police-like operations in the case of labor and political strife.[21] It is unlikely, however, that the armed forces would be able to cope with widespread social disruption if political protests were to occur simultaneously throughout the nation.[22]

A military-led coup or the militarization of politics in Mexico are unlikely scenarios in a country where there is deep support on the part of the armed forces for the civilian regime. Although there is a certain sense of moral superiority among the armed forces, there is also a recognition of the immense political and economic problems they would be forced to manage if they seized power. This realization has been continually reinforced by the failed experiences of military rule elsewhere in Latin America. Moreover, there is a deep sense of patriotism and loyalty to the Mexican Revolution and the political system it engendered. To maintain the loyalty of the armed forces, the president regularly praises the military in national addresses, and on trips throughout the country he rarely fails to visit the local zone commander.

The armed forces have served as the guardians for the country's political elite and the enforcers of its policies. In return, the civilian government does not interfere in the military's internal affairs. The president is supreme commander of the military, according to the constitution and the military's own organic laws. Not only does he appoint the ministers of navy and national defense but he also names other military officials such as the judges of the high courts, inspector general, and the attorney general of military justice. However, because Mexico's political elite has little knowledge of the military, these and other appointments come largely at the recommendation of the military hierarchy itself.

Political ambitions are not encouraged within the military, which requires its members to be loyal to the president and nonpartisan. At least among the troops, this does not mean automatic support for PRI, as demonstrated by the strong showing of Cárdenas in 1988 in areas of high troop concentrations. There was some trembling in high government circles when Cárdenas called upon the army to intervene to ensure a clean electoral process during the 1988 national elections.

Although the military does not participate directly in politics, its influence is growing. The Ministry of National Defense, for example, has become a primary actor in internal security matters. According to Roderic A. Camp, "The increasing role of the military, primarily focusing on internal security, legitimizes its potential for a larger voice, not just in the execution of policy decisions but more importantly in the formulation of those policies."[23]

The Meaning of National Security

It has only been since the late 1970s that the concept of national security has been discussed and debated within Mexico.[24] Unlike national defense, which refers to the defense of territorial borders, the term "national security" has been used to include mainly internal factors, such as threats from leftist dissidents or from social disintegration. In Latin America, the concept of national security, as promoted by U.S. military strategists and embraced by military officials in Central America and in the Southern Cone nations, has served to rationalize military intervention in national political affairs under the justification of protecting the nation's security against usually exaggerated local threats. In Mexico, numerous political leaders and intellectuals consider the term to be part of a dangerous language that leads to the militarization of politics. For this reason, the military has been discouraged from developing a national-security doctrine.

Both military and political leaders have increasingly referred to the concept of national security.[25] Concern about protecting Mexico's newfound oil wealth and fears that the increasing social turmoil on the country's southern border would spill over into Mexico were the leading factors sparking the discussion about national security.[26] In 1980 Felix Galván, defense minister during the López Portillo administration, broadly defined national security as "maintaining a social, economic, political equilibrium that is guaranteed by the armed forces."[27]

The National Development Plan, issued in 1983 by President de la Madrid, took the concept out of the exclusive domain of the military, defining national security as "the integral development of the nation, and an instrument to maintain the condition of liberty, peace, and justice within the framework of the constitution." According to the plan, the military's role is to contribute and collaborate to ensure national security.[28] This definition of national security continues to run through government documents, although beginning in 1987 drug trafficking has been defined as the principal threat to the nation's security. Concerned about new formulations of the definitions of national security and internal security, Mexican intellectuals addressing these issues have argued for security policies that are more closely linked to supporting the principles of the national constitution, democratization, and social justice.[29] Although the Mexican government regularly includes the "integral development of the nation" in its concept of national security, no development-related officials have been included in the national security cabinet that was established in 1989 by President Salinas. The cabinet includes the attorney general and the ministers of the interior, national defense, and foreign relations.

The Police

Whereas the armed forces are regarded with some respect in Mexico, the police are uniformly hated. A 1990 report by the Ministry of the Interior, which oversees all police activity, concluded that Mexicans fear the police because of their corrupt and criminal behavior.[30] As Mexicans say, "If you see a cop coming on your left and a thief coming on your right, it's better to go with the latter."

Low pay, inadequate training, and a long tradition of corruption within the regular police forces propagate the famous system of "*mordidas*" (bribes) that officers extort from the people they detain. This system converts the average traffic cop into an habitual lawbreaker. The role of the Mexican police may best be understood when taken in historical context. Porfirio Díaz, who ruled the country for three decades before the Mexican Revolution, created the first official police force out of the country's most dangerous criminals.

There are dozens of police units in Mexico, including the Federal Judicial Police, State Judicial Police, Federal District Judicial Police, Preventive Police, Auxiliary Police, National Security Directorate Police, Municipal Police, Riot Police, Bank Police, Customs Police, Subway Police, Highway Police, Forest Police, Rural Police, Riot Corps, Grupo Zorros, and the Inspectors' Corps. Among the most notorious of the police units was the anti-narcotics unit of the Federal Judicial Police (PJF) and the Grupo Tiburón of the Office of the Attorney General, both of which were reorganized by Salinas in 1990 in response to rising human rights complaints. The PJF and its agents, commonly called *madrinas* (godmothers), remain the most frightening force in the land.

Besides the official police, there are hundreds of private police units working for companies, growers, and ranchers. Those paramilitary forces working for rural political bosses and large landlords are known as "*guardias blancas*," or white guards. There are also clandestine police units working for official agencies, like "*Los Intocables*" or "The Untouchables," a group of fiscal auditors and federal police that work for the Treasury Department's Income Division. Rural *caciques* operate death squads to terrorize communities seeking land reform, and the *charros* of the official unions form goon squads to quell dissidents.

Both the police and military have justified violent repression of civilians by their fears of the reemergence of armed leftist insurgency in Mexico. But the victims of these attacks claim they are being targeted simply because they have spoken out against PRI or defending constitutional rights. In its report on human rights violations in Mexico, subtitled *A Policy of Impunity*, Americas Watch concluded: "The far greater threat to Mexico's national security is the undisciplined, corrupt, and violent practices of elements of its police and security forces. Systematic reform of these forces is needed immediately."[31]

Human Rights

The abuse of human rights is institutionalized in Mexico, a situation that has remained largely unchanged since the Mexican Revolution. Mexico's authoritarian political system has fueled human rights abuses and shielded the perpetrators from prosecution. Public servants are often underpaid, undereducated, and undertrained, making them more susceptible to general corruption and the use of excess force. The power structure developed since the revolution is based on co-option and clientelism, rather than on true merit and fair public competition. Loyalty to the system and PRI is rewarded with posts in government and other political and economic favors, and often confers immunity from prosecution for criminal acts.[1]

Torture, arbitrary detention, imprisonment on political grounds, disappearances, abysmal prison conditions, repression of the labor movement, censorship, electoral fraud, and abuse of indigenous and rural populations are persistent human rights violations within the Mexican system. Generally, these abuses are committed by various police organizations and rural bosses or their hired thugs, who are often off-duty or retired members of the police or military. These groups have established a reign of violent corruption generally ignored and sometimes explicitly protected by low-level state and federal government representatives.

During the first half of the Salinas administration, the human rights situation reflected old patterns while showing some new twists. Past forms of abuse continued unabated while measures against the drug trade and PRI's struggle to maintain its monopoly on political power added new strains to the system and resulted in additional human rights violations.

Salinas showed himself to be an active proponent of the U.S. "war on drugs." Increased pressures to stop the drug traffic stimulated human rights violations, as well as corruption and ungovernability in the various national-security forces. In return for large amounts of financial aid, high-tech equipment, and special police training, Salinas permitted a constant U.S. Drug Enforcement Administration (DEA) presence in Mexico (see U.S. Security Assistance, Part 6). He also created an anti-narcotics division within the Federal Judicial Police (PJF), a highly autonomous drug-fighting force that is responsible for a large part of the abuses committed under Salinas. The Mexican press reports daily on abuses resulting from the drug

war, ranging from unlawful arrest, harassment, and illegal search and sei-
zure, to brutal torture resulting in death.

Another major cause of the increased violence in the 1988-91 period
was the government's drive to destroy and discredit the political opposition, particularly the PRD. The government resorted to increased fraud and
repression to protect its monopoly on political power. In defense, the PRD
formed its own human rights office, which recorded a total of 97 deaths of
PRD leaders, members, and sympathizers by the end of 1990. These reported deaths steadily increased under Salinas: 13 in 1988, 25 in 1989, and
59 (with six disappeared) in 1990.[2]

It would be difficult to compare the extent of human rights abuses before
and after 1988, but most human rights leaders and independent human rights
organizations believe that the situation is at least as bad as it was before the
Salinas administration. Although Mexico has repeatedly rejected petitions to
allow foreign election observers, the government has permitted international
human rights observers to enter the country and conduct investigations. Various municipal, state, and federal agencies generally cooperate with international monitoring groups gathering data for their reports on rural abuse and
the state of the prisons, although human rights research teams are commonly
denied access to certain government facilities and documents.

The National Human Rights Commission (CNDH), formed by the government in 1990, established a policy of cooperation with independent national and international organizations. Any criticism by the U.S.
government on such official agencies as the Inter-American Human Rights
Commission (CIDH), of the Organization of American States, however, has
been repeatedly rejected outright as an infringement upon Mexico's sovereignty and interference in domestic policy. The Mexican government stated
that the CIDH must abstain from considering petitions to investigate electoral fraud made by the PRD and PAN. Similarly, the CIDH is prohibited
from looking into human rights complaints presented by domestic human
rights organizations not affiliated with the government.

Human rights abuses, although long a serious problem in Mexico, gained
international attention with the 1990 publication of reports by Americas Watch
and Amnesty International. The Americas Watch report called the human
rights situation in Mexico a "policy of impunity," and Amnesty International
warned that a "human rights emergency" existed in Mexico.[3] Media coverage of violations dramatically increased following the release of the reports.
The presence of an increasingly vocal and well-publicized human rights
movement in Mexico also sparked a growing national interest in such issues. The movement put direct pressure on the government and kept international attention on the human rights climate in Mexico.

It would be incorrect to imply that journalists and human rights activists have complete freedom to report on abuses. A number of members of
the press and activists who have implicated the PJF and government representatives in human rights abuses, corruption, and involvement with drug

trafficking have received death threats or been assassinated. In May 1990, for instance, Norma Corona Sapién, the leader of a prominent Sinaloa human rights organization who denounced abuses by the PJF, was gunned down in the street near the university where she taught.[4]

Human rights abuses by the country's security forces and rural vigilantes have long been tolerated by the Mexican government. Violations of the rights of Mexico's native population, prisoners, and peasants have received little national attention. In the 1960s public complaints about the government's human rights violations increased in the face of the official crackdown on political dissidents, many of whom were from the middle and upper classes. Suspected members of leftist student organizations and armed revolutionary groups were tortured, assassinated, and "disappeared" by the armed forces and police. Rising concern about official abuses in the 1980s was not necessarily a reflection of an actual deterioration of the human rights climate. Abuses such as police torture and the violent suppression of peasants had become almost the accepted norm in Mexican society. But the escalation of the anti-narcotics campaign and new political challenges to one-party government resulted in a rash of high-profile human rights violations that affected prominent citizens as well as the traditional lower-class victims of officially sanctioned violence.

At the same time Mexico came under increased international scrutiny, especially by the United States, due to its highly acclaimed economic successes and the free trade initiative. Following the controversial 1988 presidential elections, Salinas came under fire for the country's sluggish movement toward democratic reforms—which stood in stark contrast to the whirlwind pace of economic change. Testimony in the U.S. Congress in September 1990 motivated Representative Doug Bereuter (R-NE) to request that the State Department consider a travel advisory for Mexico's west coast.[5] Additional criticism emerged through the debate on granting fast-track authorization for negotiating of the free trade agreement. International human rights agencies and various groups opposed to the free trade agreement pressed for the inclusion of democratic and human rights standards in the proposed agreement.

In response to such criticisms, the Mexican government instituted a number of legal reforms intended to reduce abuses, removed controversial personnel from government and law-enforcement positions, and took various other steps in a bid to improve the nation's image abroad. But government critics greeted these reforms with skepticism, saying that they did little more than reiterate existing legal guarantees. Although Mexico's carefully groomed human rights image took a beating in the late 1980s, the U.S. government generally ignored the human rights situation in Mexico, apparently for political and economic reasons. Whereas the State Department's annual human rights reports for 1989 and 1990 portrayed relatively accurately the very serious problems in Mexico, the Bush administration began negotiating a free trade agreement without exerting any significant pressure for democratic reform or improvement of the human rights situation.[6] Washington also backed away from previous criticisms of the police and the government, and it has cooperated with the Mexican government in turning the focus from such abuses to the country's economic condition and liberal reforms. While political opposition parties and domestic human rights groups were charging the government with massive political fraud and the increased use of repressive force, Washington was hailing President Salinas for making Mexico into one of the most open economies in the world.

Some Ongoing Forms of Abuse

Torture, usually combined with arbitrary detention, was commonly inflicted on political prisoners in the late 1960s and early 1970s and has become more widespread since then.[7] A 1991 report by Americas Watch found that the Mexican prison system is "characterized by massive overcrowding, deteriorating physical facilities, poorly trained and vastly underpaid guards and other prison officials, a system-wide culture of corruption, and lack of adequate funding."[8] Arbitrary arrest, torture, and extrajudicial killings do occur as a result of election violence and rural land conflicts, but more often such abuses take place in the context of routine law enforcement, especially in drug-related cases.[9]

The Binational Human Rights Center (CBDH) in Tijuana reported in 1991 that 99 percent of those held in the state's prisons had been tortured.[10] Torture of minors is not uncommon in Mexico; the CBDH documented 75 cases of minors being tortured by members of the Tijuana-area security forces in 1990. According to Amnesty International, approximately 80 percent of all prisoners are victims of torture.[11]

The CBDH listed 50 different methods of torture used on prisoners in the state's jails and prisons. The most common methods were beatings, suffocation with a plastic bag, submersion in a tank of water or forcing carbonated mineral water (sometimes laced with chile peppers) into the nose, and electrical shocks to extremely sensitive parts of the body. Psychological torture, threats to family members, and extortion are also common in Mexico.[12]

According to Americas Watch, torture "occurs in all parts of the country and is practiced by most if not all branches of the federal and state police, as well as by the armed forces."[13] The PJF, and particularly its antinarcotics division, were implicated in a large majority of the reports of torture, extrajudicial killings, and other forms of "abuse of authority," including robbery and intimidation of subjects. Some of the most flagrant of these abuses occur in the northern states of Sinaloa, Durango, and Chihuahua, where drug trafficking is reportedly most common.[14] Other federal police forces, including the Federal Highway Police and the Intelligence Division of the Ministry of Protection and Highways, and such state divisions as the State Judicial Police, the State Highway Police, and the State Preventive Police, have been implicated in the full range of human rights abuses

abuses across the country.[15] Although reports of violations by members of the military are less frequent than in the past, the recurrence of these abuses suggests that torture and extrajudicial assassination remain "institutionalized techniques" used by the armed forces.[16]

Another human rights issue still prominent in Mexico is "disappearance." During the 1970s Mexico's army and police, with the support of U.S. advisers, engaged in counterinsurgency operations to eliminate several small leftist guerrilla movements. According to Mexican human rights organizations, more than 500 people disappeared during that period, and their whereabouts are still unknown.[17] Disappearances have continued, although on a smaller scale, into the 1990s.[18] A troubling phenomenon is the disappearance of people following election or land-related violence. The PRD reported six party militants missing as of year-end 1990, although most rural disappearances, as with other abuses against isolated rural and indigenous populations, are not officially reported.[19] Armed civilians and plainclothes officials are generally responsible for "disappearances," and the lack of municipal, state, and federal government investigation and response indicates official acquiescence, if not actual involvement.

Rural violence is another long-standing element of the Mexican human rights scene and continued to be a major problem during the Salinas *sexenio*. During the first 15 months of his administration, approximately 60 indigenous and *campesino* leaders were murdered, not including those killed in electoral violence.[20] Rural human rights abuses include land and property seizures, destruction of property, intimidation, disappearances, and killings. The government has consistently failed to detain and prosecute those responsible.[21] Americas Watch has called rural violence an "unabating problem" in Mexico. "It grows out of long-standing disputes over land and out of frustrations by peasants and members of Indian communities over the inadequacies of Mexico's land reform program. The Mexican government responds as though the violence were an inevitable by-product of land-related tensions in the countryside, and rarely intervenes."[22]

The Decrepit Legal System

Mexico's human rights legislation is exemplary, and the country is a signatory to various important international human rights declarations.[23] Nevertheless, the government fails to enforce these laws and protections. Moreover, the legal system is notoriously slow. The law requires that judges issue an order of imprisonment within 72 hours of an arrest and that the prisoner be tried within minimum time periods—up to one year—depending on the crime. One investigation showed, however, that six of every ten inmates, many of whom had waited much longer than a year, were still awaiting sentencing.[24]

The horrors of Mexican prisons have been well-documented by Americas Watch, religious organizations, and articles in both the national and international press. As of September 1989, the nation's prisons held 80,000 inmates in space designed for 55,000.[25] Moreover—as in Sinaloa—"space" does not guarantee a prisoner a bunk or a cell, which are bought and sold among prisoners for between $300 and $10,000, but rather the right to sleep on a concrete slab or the floor.[26]

The wealthy can live very well in prison, as in the case of drug traffickers Rafael Caro Quintero and Ernesto Fonseca Carrillo. They occupied luxurious private suites within the Western Penitentiary. Quintero reported that his jailers attempted to extort $1 million from him, which resulted in the revelation of his living conditions to the press.[27] Extortion and corruption are standard procedures in the understaffed, underfinanced, and overcrowded institutions. Guards and prison officials are severely underpaid, which contributes to the cycle of corruption.

Poor prisoners, often indigenous people who do not speak Spanish, are forced to labor for their survival, and families are charged outrageous fees to visit the inmates or to bring them the necessities that the prison does not provide.[28] The Ministry of the Interior (*Gobernación*) acknowledged that there were approximately 8,000 indigenous prisoners in the system "who don't even know why they are there."[29]

Besides these problems, prison facilities are old, in disrepair, and often unsafe; medical and mental-health care are inadequate; and in many cases there is no separation of the sexes or of dangerous and nondangerous prisoners. There are few rehabilitation programs outside of some independent church-sponsored Bible and literacy groups, and prison job programs are rare and extremely limited. It is not uncommon for children to be incarcerated. Mexico's penal system has been commended, however, for allowing the children of female inmates to remain with their mothers, and for its less-structured atmosphere that provides inmates with some level of personal freedom.

Human Rights Organizations

One of the initiatives taken by the Salinas administration to improve Mexico's human rights image was the June 1990 creation of the National Human Rights Commission (CNDH). The move was warily applauded by the national and international human rights communities, which saw the CNDH both as a major opportunity and as a potential means of government control over the burgeoning human rights movement. The CNDH is severely limited in its powers because it is not legally independent, but was created by and reports directly to the president. It has no means of enforcing its recommendations. Instead, its power rests on the moral integrity and reputation of its members, as well as on its ability to publicize abuses and recommendations.[30] A report issued by Americas Watch in September 1990 concluded, however, that despite official statements and an increase in human rights monitoring, the number and seriousness of the abuses committed by Mexican authorities had not diminished.[31] Most nongovernmental human rights groups believe that human rights can be permanently guaranteed only if the government gives the judicial system and the legislature the independence they need to scrutinize the executive branch and its functionaries.

In its first year, the CNDH made some 84 recommendations, 36 of which were accepted by the appropriate authorities. However, the commission had major confrontations with the Office of the Attorney General (PGR), which failed to comply with most of the CNDH's recommendations.[32] The PGR denied any conflict with the CNDH, but it quickly became evident that the government had created an agency that was attempting to overcome its legal and operative limitations. The CNDH, in its attempts to improve the country's human rights climate, has come into conflict with Mexico's leading security officials. Commission complaints apparently resulted in the replacement of Javier Coello Trejo, the head of the anti-narcotics division of the Federal Judicial Police and the revamping of this notorious security force. His personal bodyguards had been accused of gang rape and Coello Trejo was himself implicated in the cover-up of that abuse and others by his forces. Likewise, Federal Attorney General Enrique Alvarez del Castillo was replaced, in a surprise move by Salinas in May 1991, following his refusal to comply with certain CNDH recommendations. But considering that these two men were simply transferred to other government posts, their removal seemed more like a public-relations ploy and underscored Americas Watch charges of "a policy of impunity."

In addition to the government's own CNDH there are many other human rights groups around the country. Estimates of their numbers range from 75 to over 100. Most of these groups by far are nongovernmental, but an increasing number of states are creating their own human rights offices. Concern about human rights violations has increased dramatically since the mid-1980s, and especially after the 1985 earthquake. Among the early torchbearers of the human rights movement were two women: Mariclaire Acosta who founded the Mexico chapter of Amnesty International, and Rosario Ibarra de Piedra of the Eureka Committee for the Defense of Prisoners, the Persecuted, Disappeared Persons, and Political Exiles (EUREKA) and the National Front Against Repression. As a result of the massive destruction caused by the 1985 earthquake and because of the government's ineffective and fraudulent response to the crisis, an entire network of social organizations sprang up. Following the disaster several of these organizations specialized in human rights monitoring and helped spearhead the growing movement. The movement also benefited from the international attention Mexico received during and after the earthquake.[33]

The major national nongovernmental human rights organizations in Mexico City are: the Mexican Commission for the Defense and Protection of Human Rights led by Mariclaire Acosta; EUREKA; the Fray Bartolomé de Las Casas Human Rights Center; the Miguel Agustín Pro-Human Rights Center; and the academically oriented Mexican Human Rights Academy, directed by Sergio Aguayo. The first four have responded directly to complaints and have been considered highly credible. EUREKA focuses on the issue of the disappeared, while the Academy functions more as a think tank. In addition, the PRD's Human Rights Secretariat has been a very active proponent of human rights, especially in areas it controls or where it has heavy support. Some of the most active and effective groups, however, are the independent human rights organizations that have emerged in various states or along the border. These are usually the first to respond to a complaint by an individual or one presented in the press; they are also the ones most vulnerable to intimidation tactics.

Foreign Policy

Mexico's foreign policy has been largely a product of the country's own revolutionary history and its geographical proximity to the United States.[1] Both factors help explain Mexico's historic commitment, as incorporated into the constitution, to nonintervention in the internal affairs of other nations, self-determination of peoples, international cooperation for development, nonmilitary conflict resolution between governments, and the search for international peace and security.[2] Another tenet of Mexican foreign policy has been the diplomatic recognition of all governments, based on the principle that no country has the right to judge the internal business of another.[3]

Historically, Mexico's foreign policy has slanted to the left. It was, for example, the only Latin American nation not to break diplomatic and business relations with Cuba. Mexico also gave strong support to the Allende government in Chile; and later—in violation of its own principle of nondiscriminatory diplomatic recognition of foreign governments—declined to recognize the Pinochet government. More recently, Mexico stood behind the Sandinista guerrillas in their bid to overthrow the Somoza regime in Nicaragua, and in 1980-81 provided significant diplomatic backing for the leftist guerrillas in El Salvador.

The government's revolutionary and nationalistic traditions have contributed to this foreign policy leftism. Leftist positions in the foreign policy arena have also served to pacify and manipulate Mexico's own leftists. By siding with progressive social movements outside the country, the Mexican government has skillfully diverted attention from conservative and repressive policies at home. Such positions have also served to declare its independence from U.S. hegemony.[4]

Before the 1970s Mexico's foreign policy had a largely defensive character (in relation to the United States) and was limited geographically.[5] Under Echeverría the country's foreign policy became markedly more assertive, especially in seeking leadership in the third world.[6] Mexico championed third world positions, such as pushing forward the Charter of Economic Rights and Duties of States.[7] Its aggressive leftism was toned down during the López Portillo *sexenio*, but the country's assertive posture in foreign policy continued and was bolstered by its newfound oil wealth. Leftism was not abandoned, however, as shown by López Portillo's support for the Sandinistas and the Salvadoran guerrillas.

Mexico's noninterventionist, progressive foreign policy has been described as "one of the grand national traditions, sustained and upheld throughout the country's history in the most trying of circumstances."[8] These principles made the country a haven for exiles and asylum seekers of all political stripes, vaulted Mexico into the midst of international antinuclear campaigns, and served as a basis for the country's efforts to achieve peace and stability in Central America. In a 1983 effort that contributed to pacification in the region of Central America, Mexico, along with Colombia, Panama, and Venezuela, launched the Contadora initiative, proposing a negotiated solution to the Nicaraguan conflict in opposition to U.S. military intervention.

Over the years Mexico became known as a safe haven for political refugees. Thousands of exiles from the Spanish Civil War and from the Chilean dictatorship of Augusto Pinochet took asylum in Mexico. In 1988 the government granted safe passage out of the country to Puerto Rican independence fighter Guillermo Morales, against U.S. demands for his extradition. It granted asylum in 1991 to Panamanian banker Rafael Arosemena, accused of pilfering money from the National Bank of Panama under the regime of Manuel Antonio Noriega. The Salinas government inaugurated the Asylum Rights and Public Freedom Institute on the grounds of the home of one of its most famous haven seekers, former Soviet revolutionary leader Leon Trotsky.

Mexico's high-minded foreign policy principles, not always strictly adhered to, have been more a matter of pragmatism than idealism. They are based, on one hand, on the need to avoid direct confrontation with the United States. On the other, they are aimed at maintaining legitimacy and political stability at home. The absence of a military component or threat of the use of force in foreign policy are obvious concessions to U.S. military supremacy.[9] Meanwhile, the anti-yankee tone in political rhetoric has served as a consensus-gathering device on the domestic front, playing on collective resentments derived from the memory of the 1914-16 U.S. invasions and the loss of nearly half the national territory to the United States in 1848 as a result of the Mexican-American War.

The Merger of Economic and Foreign Policies

By the late 1980s the anti-imperialist political rhetoric had been scrubbed out of most of Mexico's foreign policy positions, to be replaced with an approach based strictly on economic concerns. Leaving the third-worldism of the Echeverría administration far behind, Mexico, beginning with the de la Madrid *sexenio*, has sought primarily to maintain better relations with the highly developed nations—the countries that are its main source of credit, trade, and investment. This shift was chiefly a result of the 1982 crisis and the collapse of the country's development model. It occurred in the context of foreign debt renegotiation, the globalization of the economy, the shattering of barriers between Eastern and Western Europe, the end of the Cold War, and the formation of new economic blocs. "The accords between the two superpowers that mean the end of the Cold War, as well as the integration process of the great political and economic blocs, represented by the European Community, the Pacific Rim, and the U.S.-Canada free trade agreement, are the most significant expressions of the new geopolitical reality we are experiencing," said Foreign Minister Fernando Solana in 1989. "They are the concerns that regulate our foreign policy actions."[10]

The change in approach began in the late 1970s and early 1980s, but was firmly established in the administration of President Carlos Salinas de Gortari. In his campaign speeches, Salinas made it clear that efforts to boost foreign trade and investment in Mexico by all economic blocs, but especially with the United States, were to become the main thrust of foreign policy. "In the matter of debt, we shall always place firm negotiation before open confrontation," Salinas said in a campaign speech dedicated to foreign policy.[11] In his administration, Mexico's interest in defending Central America from U.S. intervention began to take a back seat, as a kid-glove approach came into play in bilateral relations between Mexico and the United States. After a 1989 debt renegotiation considered successful by his administration, Salinas went on to push for a free trade agreement between Mexico, the United States, and Canada, an achievement that U.S. Ambassador John Negroponte said would "institutionalize acceptance of a North American orientation to Mexico's foreign relations." Negroponte, the former U.S. ambassador to Honduras who directed the "secret war" against Nicaragua, wrote that Mexico "is in the process of dramatically changing the substance and image of its foreign policy . . . from an ideological, nationalistic, and protectionist vision to a more pragmatic, competitive, and outward-looking view of world problems."[12]

But even before free trade negotiations began the new orientation was plainly evident, as seen in Mexico's willingness to condemn General Noriega before the U.S. invasion, its initial offer to send troops to the Persian Gulf, a subsequent agreement to increase oil exports to the United States, its abstention from the United Nations vote to send human rights observers to Cuba, and its marked reluctance to back attempts to find independent and Latin American solutions to North-South conflicts.

President Salinas put a new spin on the nationalist and progressive principles of Mexican foreign policy. According to Salinas, the country's process of opening up to the world economy is based on the principle of "progressive nationalism," meaning that Mexico will seek to modernize its economy and to revitalize its international standing.[13] And "the modern exercise of sovereignty demands an efficacious insertion in international markets."

Since the 1982 crisis Mexican foreign policy has become increasingly aligned with its economic policy. This shift has been "a necessary condition for the preservation of Mexico's sovereignty and promotion of its national interests," according to the Salinas administration.[14] Former and present members of the country's diplomatic corps complain that the country no longer has a clear foreign policy, apart from the government's newly adopted economic policy. Reflecting this change, foreign policy matters like the free trade negotiations are managed more than ever by the president's own advisers and his economic cabinet rather than the Ministry of Foreign Relations.[15] An underlying concern of many Mexicans is that just as Mexico's economic policy increasingly resembles that of the United States, so too will Mexican foreign policy follow the U.S. model.

PART TWO

The Economy

"The only thing that is not negotiable [in the free trade agreement] is the virginity of the Virgin of Guadalupe. That stays. Everything else is on the table."

—*Senior Ministry of Finance official, 1990*[1]

© Cindy Reiman/Impact Visuals

Economy: a chronology

1965 Import-substitution industrialization peaks as the economy enjoys growth rates 6 percent or higher, but the agricultural sector falters turning the country into a net food importer. The Border Industrialization Program opens the northern border to foreign-owned assembly plants called *maquiladoras*.

1975-1976 The economy slows to zero growth as the industrialization process falters and the development model that guided Mexico through its "miracle years" proves faulty. Capital flight aggravates the economic crisis, and the *peso* suffers a major devaluation.

1977 Suddenly Mexico's future looks bright as the result of the oil boom, and foreign creditors rush in to bankroll the expansive government.

1981-1982 Oil prices slip, capital flight accelerates, and foreign capital dries up as the oil-fueled economic boom (1977-1981) goes bust. The *peso* falls sharply and austerity measures are imposed in the face of the government's inability to pay its external debt. In a desperate move to control capital flight, President López Portillo nationalizes the banking system as relations between government and business become increasingly hostile.

1985-1986 Under pressure from international lenders and the newly organized private sector, the de la Madrid government begins the disincorporation or privatization process. The country's neoliberal direction becomes increasingly apparent, especially with its entry to the worldwide GATT trade agreement. But the economic crisis worsens as oil prices again plummet and the domestic market shrivels. The restructuring of the economy begins in earnest.

1988-1989 The economy stabilizes as nonpetroleum exports rise and the economy shows per capita economic growth for the first time since 1981. President Salinas throws the country wide open to foreign trade and investment as part of the neoliberal overhaul of the economy.

1990-1991 Economic growth continues, but the trade balance turns sharply negative and inflation persists. Foreign investment and the repatriation of flight capital are encouraging, however. But economic recovery is endangered by the weakness of domestic market and steady decline of wages and living standards. The proposed free-trade accord will ensure further economic liberalization and place new exphasis on export promotion and attracting foreign investments.

Restructuring and Modernization

You do not have to look far to see that the Mexican economy is modernizing. Credit-card phone booths, a bustling stock market, supermarket shelves laden with imports, and a diversified, increasingly high-tech export sector are just a few of the signs that Mexico is moving fast-forward toward economic modernity. But modernizing means more than adapting to the faster paced world of fax machines and computers. For Mexico, going modern also means tossing out the economic structures and development strategies that have shaped the country since the Mexican Revolution. Replacing them are new structures and strategies considered by Mexico's policymakers to be more compatible with a rapidly evolving world economy.

In the 1980s Mexico adopted as its own an economic development strategy that stresses integration with the world market. Rather than resisting the global integration of trade and capital, Mexico has embraced it. Known in the past for its protective and nationalist economic policies, the country has opened its borders to the unrestricted flow of trade and investment. For the government, modernization has also meant reordering its own house. Budget deficits have been narrowed, social services cut, state subsidies for public utilities and basic goods reduced, and hundreds of government-owned companies eliminated or sold to private investors.

Two basic principles have guided recent economic policy: economic stabilization and comparative-advantage growth. Economic stabilization refers to a program to resolve the country's main financial problems, including budget deficits, persistent inflation, a destabilized *peso*, and the balance-of-payments crisis (mainly due to the external debt and capital flight). As practiced in Mexico, economic stabilization rests on the assumptions of monetarist economic theory. Monetarism essentially holds that economic crisis and declining capital accumulation originate in an imbalance between public-sector spending and revenues. Excessive state intervention through social services, employment creation, minimum-wage regulation, and parastatal enterprises, along with the borrowing to support such intervention, receive the major blame for the lack of equilibrium in the national economy.

Once the economy is stabilized—through austerity measures, privatization, and liberalization of trade and investment—new economic growth will result from private investment in export-oriented businesses that take advantage of Mexico's comparative advantages in the world economy. Chief among these advantages is cheap labor. Proximity to the U.S. market and the country's many natural resources also give Mexico a competitive edge. This focus on foreign markets and low-wage export production contrasts with now unpopular economic development theories that stress the need to broaden the national market and increase domestic demand—goals that can only be achieved by reducing unemployment, keeping wages above inflation rates, and protecting society against the wealth-concentrating tendencies of private capital.

Together the economic policies of the Mexican government—beginning with the de la Madrid administration and increasingly during the Salinas years—belong to the neoliberal school of economic thought. In the tradition of classic economic liberalism, the neoliberal economists of today's global economy advocate the greatest possible reliance on world markets and the forces of international competition to coordinate economic activity.[2] To make this possible, they insist on the removal of government controls on foreign trade and investment.

Neoliberal economists contend that economic growth can be spurred by the "liberalization" of both the domestic and external sectors. Once foreign trade and investment are liberalized, or opened up, the country can benefit from the dynamic of global integration of markets and production. On the domestic level, neoliberals reject the intervention of the state in the economy—except in those activities necessary to establish a framework in which the private sector can prosper. In economic terms, then, liberalization refers to all market-enhancing mechanisms, both in the domestic and external sectors.

All this is not to say that a decade ago Mexico's political elite had a clear vision of where it was taking Mexico. Actually the Mexican government has resorted to much ad hoc policymaking. Although it is certainly true that a neoliberal and monetarist vision of economic management was gaining force in the early 1980s, policymaking was still more pragmatic and incremental than doctrinaire—as it has been throughout Mexico's post-revolutionary history. Austerity measures, budget cutting, high interest rates, a return to monetarism, and other features of its economic stabilization evolved over the decade into a full-blown neoliberal project by the end of the 1980s.[3]

Escalating capital flight, the flattening out of oil prices, the debt crisis, the devalued *peso*, and a rapidly integrating global economy in the 1980s established the economic context in which new policy directions were set. Also important were internal political and social factors, including the widening split between the neoliberal technocrats and the nationalists/populists within elite political circles, the anti-statist challenge from PAN conservatives, and the subsequent rise of the center-left forces led by Cuauhtémoc Cárdenas.

This political upheaval in Mexico during the 1980s was closely related to what progressives called the "dispute for the nation," meaning the assault on the social-justice, nationalist, and populist values of the Mexican

Revolution by the "neoliberal project."[4] The jockeying for a dominant position between progressives and conservatives in the 1980s was another manifestation of the long-running friction between what have been the two main influences on government policy since the 1930s. These are the conservative bankers' alliance and the populist Cárdenas coalition (named after President Lázaro Cárdenas).[5] On the international level, increasing pressures from Washington, the International Monetary Fund (IMF), and the World Bank also shaped and guided the turns in Mexican economic policy.

One Step Forward, Two Steps Back

Liberalization represents a move away from an inward-oriented economy, with a high degree of state intervention, toward outward-oriented development and capitalist modernization. Hailed as a step toward a bright future, economic liberalization constitutes, in at least some important ways, a return to the country's pre-revolutionary past. The Mexican Revolution brought to a violent close three decades of dictatorial rule by Porfirio Díaz. This was an era characterized by its openness to foreign investment, its dependence on the external sector, and the free rein given to capitalist forces. The *porfiriato* (1877-1910) was a time of economic growth and political stability, albeit at the cost of an exploited and repressed peasantry and working class.

Guiding economic policy during the *porfiriato* was a group of planners called *los científicos* (the scientists). Under their supervision the economy appeared to flourish. New ports and railroads were built, and foreign investment—particularly in agriculture and mining—flowed into the country. But little of this wealth trickled down to the *campesinos* and the workers.

Like the *científicos*, the planners and technocrats of the de la Madrid and Salinas administrations (mainly educated at Yale and Harvard), sometimes known as *técnicos*, place their faith in the forces of the private sector and international capitalism. This new breed of economic liberals expresses confidence, however, that the dual policies of economic stabilization and comparative-advantage development will eventually lead not only to stability and economic growth but also to improved social welfare without government intervention.[6]

Mexico Turns Inward and Industrializes

The ouster of President Díaz threw the country into economic and political chaos. It then took more than two decades for the nationalist and populist character of the new revolutionary state to take shape. The new direction appeared in the 1917 constitution, which reassigned to the government the ownership of the country's subsurface mineral resources. The revolution's novel character was, however, most clearly defined by an aggressive agrarian-reform program and the nationalization of the oil industry, both implemented during the Lázaro Cárdenas government (1934-40).

More than its populism or nationalism, however, it was the government's dedication to modernization through industrialization that defined the economic direction of Mexico until 1982. At the end of the *porfiriato* Mexico had only a thin industrial base and only an incipient capitalist class. Most foreign investment was extractive and export-oriented, while a rising flow of imports satisfied the consumer needs of the wealthy and the slowly expanding middle class.

To advance beyond the feudal and neocolonial economic structures of the pre-revolutionary era, the Mexican government recognized the need to encourage the development of an indigenous capitalist sector. This domestic bourgeoisie would become a partner with the state in its industrialization and agricultural-modernization projects.

At least during the Cárdenas years, certain parameters of this capitalist development were set forth. Although the state subsidized and otherwise facilitated the growth of domestic capitalism, it was concerned that the advance of capitalism not upset the country's delicate social and political balance. The state became the *rector* (regulator, or arbiter) that controlled and guided the economy for the common good. At the same time it was boosting business, the state recognized the need to protect the society as a whole, particularly the interests of workers and peasants.[7]

By the 1960s Mexico had become a model for state-led industrial development in the third world. In the space of several decades, the country had evolved from a mainly rural, agricultural nation to an industrializing and increasingly urban society. As a percentage of national production, the manufacturing sector's contribution increased from 18 percent to 24 percent between 1950 and 1980.

The first spurt of post-revolutionary industrialization began in response to the Great Depression of 1929. As the economy of the industrial world shut down, small Mexican industries emerged to supply the local market. Later, when the industrial powers were caught up in World War II, this phenomenon of import substitution occurred to an even greater degree. It was not until the postwar period, however, that the Mexican government implemented specific policies to encourage the substitution of foreign goods with local ones. Such import-substitution industrialization characterized economic planning in Mexico until the early 1980s.

The nationalist approach to economic development followed by Mexico until the 1980s regarded industrialization as the essential foundation for the development of a modern economy. Obviously, government policies that promote import substitution—including import licensing, subsidies for infant industries, and high tariffs—run directly against the grain of economic liberalism. Instead of relying on comparative advantage in the international market, domestic industries are protected and fostered by the government.

Theoretically, at least, import substitution saves the industrializing country foreign exchange by reducing imports while fostering the expansion of the domestic market through the creation of new industries and a new class of wage workers. During the initial stages of industrialization, the cheap food produced by the country's small farm sector allows industrialists to keep wages low. Capitalist agriculture also benefits under this scenario, because it gradually modernizes with the help of inputs like machinery and fertilizer supplied by local industries.

Both in terms of broadening the domestic market and in lowering the import share of manufactured products, import substitution in Mexico proved enormously successful until the early 1970s. The economy expanded at a brisk pace, and Mexico was able to meet more of its consumer needs with domestic manufactures. Whereas imports represented more than half of the total supply of manufactured products in 1929, by 1970 imports accounted for only one-fifth of this supply.[8]

Import-substitution as a development strategy began to stagnate in the early 1970s, and by the end of the decade the import share of manufactured goods was rapidly rising. The flaws of import substitution as a principal path to development are now apparent. But during the heady days of strong economic growth (1940-70) Mexico was widely regarded as a model developing nation. Many academics studying Mexico termed those three decades of more than 6 percent annual growth the "miracle years."

The pre-1970 years of economic growth, particularly the period from 1954 to 1970, were also called the era of "stabilizing development." Working closely with the country's financial elite, the government maintained a monetarist policy that gave a high priority to stable domestic prices and stable foreign exchange rates. This stability worked well for the country's emerging industrial conglomerates and financiers but worked against the interests of the poor majority, who saw their share of national income decline. Another fundamental weakness of "stabilizing development" was that economic growth came to rely more on foreign borrowing than on internal savings—a practice that assumed new dimensions in later years.

The Mexican Miracle Goes Bankrupt

By the mid-1970s the signs that the Mexican growth model was disintegrating were widespread. Although the industrial sector kept expanding, it also became increasingly import-dependent. Mexico had succeeded in creating a relatively self-sufficient consumer goods industry. But it proved less successful in developing an industrial base for intermediate and capital goods that required higher technology. Besides becoming increasingly dependent on imported technology, the industrial sector had grown more inefficient. Not having to worry about imports except for those smuggled into the country, Mexican industrialists produced goods that were more expensive and of lesser quality than similar products available on the world market. Protectionism allowed an industrial sector to develop, but after three decades of doing business with government subsidies and protective tariffs, Mexican industries grew inefficient and uncompetitive. As one Mexican scholar observed, the government never stopped babying the country's infant industries which, as a result, had grown senile.

Another ominous sign for the Mexican miracle was the decline in the country's food self-sufficiency. Agrarian reform and other government policies to support the small-farm sector resulted in expanding per capita basic-grains production until the mid-1960s. In terms of government resources, even more attention was given the export-oriented capitalist sector, which benefited from state-financed irrigation projects and technical assistance. Vegetable and fruit exports to the United States boomed, and the extension of the country's livestock industry displaced food crops. As per capita food production fell, agricultural imports began to rise.

Serious structural deficiencies in the industrial and agricultural sectors were compounded by a raft of financial problems. These included a widening budget deficit, an overvalued *peso*, double-digit inflation, a dangerous dependence on foreign loans, rising capital flight, and an increasing import bill. At least some of these financial problems arose from President Echeverría's attempt to move the country away from "stabilizing development" toward a policy of "shared development," which aimed to slow the pace of capital concentration and broaden the benefits of economic growth. Adding to the country's accumulating financial difficulties, Mexican oil reserves could no longer satisfy domestic demand, forcing the country to import oil at the very time that international prices were on the upswing.

By mid-1976 the country faced an economic crisis of huge proportions. To keep the Echeverría government afloat financially, the U.S. Federal Reserve Board authorized $800 million in emergency credit for Mexico. Later that year the new López Portillo administration imposed an austerity program in connection with an emergency loan from the International Monetary Fund. For a short while it appeared that the government was embarking on a conservative economic stabilization program to address the country's financial imbalances. Real wages began to decline, for example, and social services stagnated. A major stabilization program would not, however, be implemented until 1983. Austerity fell aside when Mexico struck it rich in 1977 with the development of newfound oil reserves.

With the exploitation of massive oil fields in the Bay of Campeche, worries about the country's deep structural weaknesses and shaky finances slid aside. Confidence in the country's newfound economic strength pervaded both the government and the private sector. The international financial community shared and encouraged this optimism in Mexico's economic future. Representatives of foreign banks, flush with petrodollars (recycled oil profits, mainly from the Mideast) lined up in front of government offices to lend virtually unlimited sums to oil-rich Mexico.

The flood of foreign credit into Mexico encouraged the government to go on a wild spending spree. Predictably, the government's fiscal budget deficit widened and inflation soared. High inflation and an unstable *peso* undermined private-sector confidence in the economy, causing unprecedented capital flight to the United States and other countries where more stable currencies and higher interest rates prevailed. It was not until oil prices began falling in mid-1981, however, that the instability of the Mexican economy became obvious to all. The government soon found that it was unable to cover its budget and could not meet the annual payments on its external debt—which by 1982 was one of the largest in the developing world.

The 1978-81 oil boom had given the "Mexican miracle" a second life. But at the outset of the de la Madrid *sexenio*, there existed no doubt that the miracle years were over. Mexico had sunk into a deep economic crisis with no easy solutions. The immense and unpayable external debt symbolized the crisis, but behind the debt problem lingered long-ignored structural deficiencies that also needed immediate attention.

Although the escalating debt-service burden certainly was the main symptom of the government's financial instability, the outflow of debt payments was actually considerably lower than the draining of the country's foreign exchange reserves through private capital flight. It was this rising capital flight that actually precipitated the debt crisis. It also led to the government's decision in late 1982 to institute foreign exchange controls and to nationalize the banking system.[9]

On the brink of financial collapse, Mexico appealed to the World Bank, the IMF, and Washington for emergency assistance. The aid came in 1982 and throughout the 1980s, although not without a price. The international financial community, led by Washington, demanded that Mexico restructure its economy along neoliberal lines. On hand to direct this restructuring was a new crop of PRI politicians and bureaucrats, educated in the United States and themselves proponents of neoliberal economics.

The Debt Crisis 1982-91

Until the mid-1970s there was little public discussion of Mexico's deepening indebtedness. During the economic crisis of 1976 there was a brief surge of concern about the country's debt burden and its dependency on foreign lenders. But the euphoria produced by the 1978-81 oil boom washed away those concerns. They arose again in 1981-82, however, when sinking oil prices and rising interest rates pushed Mexico to the edge of bankruptcy. In August 1982 Mexico announced that it would be unable to pay the $24 billion in debt servicing (principal and interest payments) due by the end of 1984. Suddenly the severity of Mexico's debt predicament became a major international concern and the symbol of the country's weak financial situation.[10]

The enormity of the debt burden was shocking. In 1970 Mexico had an external debt of $6 billion. By 1982 the external debt had risen to $86 billion.

Between 1978 and 1982 the country's total external debt jumped 255 percent; in 1981 alone Mexico borrowed more than $24 billion. And yet it was not the actual size of the debt that precipitated the crisis. The problem facing Mexico in 1982 was that foreign lending was drying up at the same time that export revenues were falling and interest rates were soaring. Capital inflows (either from new loans, investment, or exports) were no longer sufficient to cover the rising debt-service payments. Interest payments alone represented more than 50 percent of export income.[11]

Total external debt comprises both public-sector and private-sector foreign borrowing. At the start of the 1970s, nearly 70 percent of the debt belonged to the public sector, a proportion that rose to nearly 80 percent by 1978. During the oil boom the rate of private-sector borrowing exceeded that of the government, rising from 21 percent in 1978 to 31 percent of the total external debt in 1982. Because of the subsequent government assumption of portions of the private-sector debt and a dramatic decrease in private borrowing, the private-sector debt dropped from $24 billion in 1982 to $4 billion in 1989. By late 1991, as a result of a flurry of new private borrowing on external markets, Mexico's private-sector debt had risen to nearly $7 billion—or about 7 percent of total foreign debt.

Approximately three-quarters of the external debt was owed to commercial banks in 1982, with the balance belonging to multilateral banks and foreign governments. The largest chunk of commercial credit—about one-third—came from U.S. banks.[12] In the early stages of debt renegotiations, the commercial banks insisted on maintaining high interest rates and short-term payback periods. By the end of the decade, however, the private banks yielded to pressure from Washington and the multilateral institutions to reduce their interest rates and soften their terms on new loans.

Borrow Today, Pay Tomorrow

Having long prided itself on its political and economic independence, Mexico now found that it was beholden to the likes of Citibank and J.P. Morgan. How could the country have allowed itself to become so indebted and dependent? Overconfidence that oil prices would continue to rise was the major factor for the debt buildup during the years of fastest debt accumulation (1978-82). Mexico's large oil reserves served as a guarantee that the debt could easily be paid off. During the height of the oil boom, the government—and almost everyone else—ignored the doomsaying of socialist Heberto Castillo, who, among others, warned that the rapid development of the country's oil reserves would result in dangerous levels of foreign dependence.[13] But it should be remembered that Mexico was not alone in thinking that oil was the ticket to the future. When trying to assign blame for the debt crisis, it is also worth remembering that the IMF and the World Bank encouraged Mexico to increase its commercial borrowing during those heady years when oil prices were high.

It would be a mistake, however, to attribute the debt crisis solely to oil fever. Actually the country had since the 1950s been relying on foreign borrowing to push forward its economy. The government's traditionally unrealistic and unstable development plans had long since opened the door to the current debt crisis. From the beginning Mexico had not insisted that the industrialization process should pay its own way, nor did it ever seriously seek to generate development capital by revamping its tax system. Private wealth was virtually exempt from taxation. Capitalist accumulation was, in a sense, underwritten by the state. But capitalists were not the only ones who benefited from the government's deficit spending. Expensive public-sector investment projects were launched, wages raised, and the social-service budget increased, all using foreign capital. Borrowed funds rushed into the government's coffers—and rushed out again to pay for grandiose investment schemes dreamt up by cabinet ministers.

As in other countries experiencing economic crisis, wealthy Mexicans began pulling their money out of the country when their confidence in the economy and government management faltered. This capital flight further weakened the economy and hastened the debt crisis. Of course no direct correlation exists between the inflow of foreign loans and the flight of capital. But it is well known that in Mexico and other countries the increase in foreign debt has facilitated private capital accumulation. At the same time that Mexico was accumulating debt, capital flight accelerated. One estimate indicates that during the period from 1971 to 1985 Mexico lost $56 billion in capital flight, a figure that represents 60 percent of the external debt accumulated during that period.[14]

It would also be unfair to pin the debt crisis solely on a spendthrift public sector. The private sector also caught the borrowing fever. When the crisis broke in 1982, private borrowers owed foreign creditors more than $26 billion. One-third of the private-sector debt was found in nine industrial groups.[15] When the economy stopped growing and the *peso* was devalued, many heavily indebted private companies were forced to divest. To prevent a total collapse of private investment, the government came to the rescue of the private sector. It created a special agency that helped private debtors obtain dollars to pay their debts.[16] In 1983 the government assumed $11 billion in private liabilities and then put its own bargaining power behind the renegotiation of the entire private-sector debt during subsequent debt talks.[17] In spite of its claims of bankruptcy and its rhetorical commitment to "free market" solutions, the Mexican state managed to come up with the financing to subsidize the country's wealthy industrialists.

Dealing with the Debt

When confronted by his government's financial crisis, López Portillo frantically began printing and buying *pesos* to convert into dollars to make the debt payments. But this only compounded the crisis by fueling inflation and capital flight, as the value of the *peso* plummeted. Desperate to regain hold of the country's economy, the government nationalized the banks in late 1982, accusing the previous owners of decapitalizing the nation. Although the nationalization won popular approval, it did nothing to improve the business climate in Mexico. Nor was it ever fully implemented, leaving the state still without the means to regulate the flow of capital.

Mexico was on the verge of economic collapse. But the foreign lending community, afraid that a breakdown in debt servicing in Mexico would endanger the increasingly precarious international financial system, was not about to let the country default on its debt. Washington came through with a bridge loan until refinancing of the debt could be arranged by the multilateral banks and commercial creditors. At first the international financial community regarded Mexico's debt crisis as a short-term liquidity problem that could be solved with emergency loans, austerity measures, and currency devaluation. The lenders rejected pleas for lower interest rates, postponement of principal payments, and other debt-relief measures. The debt was refinanced, but not on softer terms. In return Mexico was obligated to undertake a harsh financial restructuring program that would balance its books even as the flow of foreign credits dried up. The economy was to be "shocked" back to stability.

Mexico proved to be the model debtor during the first few years of the stabilization program, following through with recommended financial adjustments and austerity measures while keeping its debt payments on track. But the debt crisis would not go away, and in 1985 Mexico was again asking for emergency loans. This time the creditors, led increasingly by the World Bank, responded with more money and better refinancing terms. In line with the new position taken by U.S. Secretary of the Treasury James Baker, the lending community saw the need to promote economic growth in addition to austerity. For the next four years debt renegotiations followed this pattern of softened refinancing terms and new capital inflows.

At the same time the demands for economic restructuring hardened. As a condition of the new credit deal in 1986, Mexico agreed to a major restructuring of its economic policies, including reductions in tariffs and other restrictions on trade, the liberalization of foreign investment, more reductions in public spending, tax reform, the divestiture of state-owned enterprises, and the reform of domestic price controls.

Still the debt crisis persisted. By 1987 the external debt had risen to a peak of $107 billion. Once on the debt train it was hard for either debtor or creditor to get off. With little new investment and insignificant economic growth, Mexico depended on new foreign loans to pay its interest payments. And the creditors felt they had to lend more money to ensure payment of past debts. But debt renegotiations took an encouraging turn at the start of the Salinas *sexenio*. For the first time international creditors seemed to recognize that economic stability in Mexico would not be achieved without a strong dose of investment and growth. To make this possible the IMF, together with the World Bank, agreed to lend Mexico nearly $8 billion by 1994. More important than this 1989 agreement with the multilateral lenders was the agreement signed in early 1990 with the commercial banks. In a complicated deal worked out among Washington, the commercial banks, and the IMF and World Bank, the commercial debt was substantially reduced and the debt-service schedule eased.

The 1990 agreement, based on the so-called Brady plan (named after the U.S. Secretary of Treasury), also reinitiated the debt-for-equity program first instituted in 1985. Called the Program of Exchange of Public Debt for Investment, this program allowed foreign investors to buy discounted debt and then sell it to the Bank of Mexico. These investors were then paid in *pesos* to be used for investment in the country. Chrysler, for example, bought $100 million in Mexican debt for about $65 million and then exchanged that debt for *pesos* worth the full $100 million, which it invested in Mexico. The 1985 program did decrease the debt by $3.8 billion and encouraged foreign investment, but it was not looked on favorably by the government, because other foreign investors, like Chrysler, used *pesos* rather than dollars for their expansion projects in Mexico. In late 1987 the government suspended debt-for-equity swaps, claiming that the program was inflationary (because it injected large sums of *pesos* into the economy). Then in 1990

Table 2a
Mexico: Total Foreign Debt, 1970-91

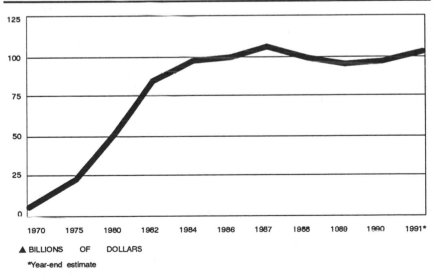

▲ BILLIONS   OF   DOLLARS

*Year-end estimate

SOURCES: U.S. Department of State, *Economic Trends Report: Mexico*, August 1991; World Bank, *External Debt of Developing Countries, World Debt Tables 1990-91*.

the Salinas government acceded to the demands of bankers and foreign investors that the program be renewed.[18]

As a result of the 1989-90 negotiations, Mexico's accumulated debt and its debt-servicing burden were substantially lightened for the first time since the debt crisis exploded.[19] As a result of all the restructuring, swaps, bond guarantees, and discount selling in 1989-90, the external debt dropped to $93 billion by early 1990. The agreement and talk of a free trade deal with the United States, however, opened the way for new borrowing, and by late 1990 total foreign debt was back up to $98 billion and projected to rise to $102 billion by January 1992 (Table 2a).[20]

After signing the debt agreement in 1990, President Salinas said Mexico had achieved what it wanted and no further refinancing agreements would be necessary. According to Citibank President John Reed, the deal was the "cheapest that can be made in the market."[21] Although the Salinas and Bush administrations hailed the agreement as a major breakthrough, many observers of the debt crisis were more skeptical. In a *New York Times* opinion piece entitled "It's a Bad Deal for the Model Debtor," an analyst at the Council on Foreign Relations said that the restructuring of the commercial debt did not go far enough and would still require Mexico to use at least 20 percent of its export earnings to cover annual interest payments.[22] According to economist John Kenneth Galbraith, the Baker and Brady plans simply disguised that the creditors were not being paid and would never be paid. "We have to let the past be history," asserted Galbraith, "admit that the debts are not payable, and strike them from the books."[23]

Annual debt payments have been extracted from the Mexican population, in large part, in terms of unemployment, reduced social services, lower wages, higher-priced public utilities, and the rising cost of basic goods. There existed a widespread sentiment in Mexico, and with good reason, that the Mexican poor were making foreign creditors rich. This conviction translated into strong support for political positions demanding a moratorium on debt payments. Nationalist resentment against foreign lenders and their imposition of economic restructuring was not discouraged by the government, in its effort to transfer the blame for worsening social conditions away from itself. Public focus on the foreign debt also shifted attention away from the enormity of the domestic debt owed to Mexico's own financiers.

In the early 1980s Mexico, as one of the developing world's largest debtors, had been in the position to push forward the issue of debt relief. But instead of joining a debtors' cartel or unilaterally declaring a debt moratorium, Mexico chose to remain safely inside the world financial community. In return for playing by the rules set down by the IMF, the World Bank, Washington, and the commercial banks, Mexico received relatively favorable treatment. It gained access to new loans and in doing so attracted increased foreign investment. These benefits, however, must be weighed against the combined economic and political costs of being such a model debtor.

The Debt Crisis Is Not Over

Nearly ten years after the debt crisis erupted, Mexico remained burdened with an external debt of $100 billion by late 1991. The debt crisis was far from resolved. Even after the 1989 debt restructuring Mexico was paying foreign creditors some $10-13 billion a year in debt servicing. Except for a short period in the mid-1980s, Mexico proved to be a model debtor—pushing through recommended financial restructuring and promptly meeting its payment schedule. Between 1982 and 1991 more than $125 billion flowed out of Mexico in debt servicing—about two-thirds of which was in the form of interest payments.

The Salinas government, echoing the assertions of Washington, insisted that Mexico could grow out of this debt burden. To do this it counted on increased flows of repatriated capital, foreign investment, and export revenues. But as noted elsewhere, an increasingly negative trade balance and less-than-expected inflows of direct investment jeopardized the government's optimistic projections. Also worrisome was the highly liquid nature of much of the incoming capital. Placed in the stock market and bonds—rather than in plants and equipment— this private capital inflow could leave the country just as quickly as it came in.

Meanwhile the foreign debt continued to climb and will likely surpass the previous high of $107 million within a year or two if current upward

---

Table 2b
Total Debt, 1990

Total External Debt[1]	**$98.2 billion**
Public Sector	$77.8 billion
Banks	$7.8 billion
Bank of Mexico (Central Bank)	$6.5 billion
Private Sector	$6.1 billion
Total Debt/GDP	42.6%
Debt Service[2]/Exports	49.0%
Debt Service/GDP	5.0%
Total Domestic Debt	**$54.0 billion**

[1]Public Sector debt in 1990 was held by commercial banks (44.1%), World Bank and IDB (14.7%), official bilateral (11.5%), and other (4.5%), while the IMF held the Bank of Mexico's debt.
[2]Based on 1990 debt service of $13.1 billion. Debt service includes interest payments and amortization (payments on the principal).

SOURCES: U.S. Department of State, *Economic Trends Report: Mexico*, August 1991; Inter-American Development Bank (IDB), *Economic and Social Progress in Latin America 1991*.

trends persist. Official optimism about the country's ability to pay the accumulating debt appeared unwarranted, just as the faith in debt-led growth had been a decade before. As a popular refrain has it, *"ya viene la fiesta otra vez,"* or "here we go again."

Debt Not Just a Foreign Problem

The foreign debt is by no means the only part of Mexico's debt burden. Just as the government looks to foreign capital markets and lenders for funds to keep its books balanced, so it has raised revenues from domestic financial markets. To attract these funds, the government offered bonds with interest rates much higher than international rates. In fact, Mexican financiers made it clear that they would refuse to lend the government money except at what amounted to be extortionate rates. In 1990 the domestic debt was $54 billion; by mid-1991 it had risen to $57 billion (Table 2b). To service this debt—owed mainly to the country's oligarchs—the Salinas government had to pay more than $10-13 billion annually to private creditors. By 1990 domestic debt service stood at about the same level as the foreign debt service.

This represents an extraordinary transfer of Mexico's national wealth into the hands of its financial elite. In a very real sense it was the country's lower classes that were making the richest much richer. The increased tax burden to pay for this debt fell disproportionately on the country's workers. At the same time, the government essentially refused to tax the capitalist class for fear of scaring off capital and endangering the newly constructed tripartite alliance among the state, the national business elite, and foreign investors. In other words, the poor paid most of the taxes while the oligarchy owned the internal debt.[24]

Together the foreign and domestic debt-service payments have put broad economic development designed to improve the welfare of the entire society beyond the government's financial capabilities. Indebted to international and national creditors for its tenuous stability, the government also found them to be its major associates in economic planning.

Turning the Economy Around

The economic crises of 1982 and 1986 marked the onset of a new era in Mexico's economic development. No longer could the government continue—at least under the old formulas—with its policies of state-led economic growth. The capital and revenues required for such development simply were no longer there. Foreign loans had dried up, and capital flight was rampant. The policies that promoted import-substitution industrialization were proving a drain on the economy. As the economy sank into a recession, the government found itself without the revenues to pursue populist programs.

Sentiment grew that the country's recovery would largely be dependent on the willingness of foreign capitalists to pump up the economy with billions of dollars in new investment. Although nationalism still found a place in the government's political rhetoric, the government increasingly looked outside the country for economic salvation. During successive debt renegotiations, the government essentially handed over its economic policy to foreign lenders, hoping to restimulate growth through a radical restructuring of the economy.

Before the economy could grow, however, it had to be stabilized. To this end the de la Madrid and Salinas governments implemented an economic stabilization program that relied primarily on orthodox structural adjustment measures (austerity, currency devaluation, trade liberalization, tax reform, and privatization) advocated by the IMF, the World Bank, and Washington. In addition, beginning in 1988 the government instituted its own program of wage and price controls. Unlike the earlier focus on inward-oriented development, the new emphasis was placed on export-oriented growth.

Clearly the Mexican economy was due for an exhaustive overhaul. Foreign loans and the oil boom had allowed the government to postpone this renovation, but declining oil prices and the debt crisis finally made it unavoidable. By the decade's end most of the main goals of the restructuring—a more balanced budget, trade and investment liberalization, restoration of business confidence, reduced inflation, and renewed economic growth—had largely been achieved.

Economic growth rates, inflation figures, trade and capital balances, investment flows, and the government's budget balance are the commonly cited figures used to evaluate economic performance and stability. For the most part it appeared that the economy had stabilized and was inching forward. Mainly as the result of draconian cuts in social services, government payroll, and public-sector investment, the government's financial deficit dropped from 17 percent of the GDP in 1982 to 3.5 percent in 1990. Although it was true that government finances improved during those years, the budget-deficit figures were the result of a new formula that conveniently left out annual interest payments. If they had been included, the government's budget deficit would have approximately matched that of 1982. The government's improved financial state was also attributed to multibillion-dollar influx from the sales of major parastatal enterprises and the national banks—a quick source of revenues that future governments will not be able to count on. Still, the de la Madrid and Salinas administrations did bring a new level of stability to government finances.

Debt renegotiations in the late 1980s succeeded in lowering the debt-service burden, and Mexico delighted international creditors with its strict adherence to its schedule of debt payments. Most encouraging was a steady increase in exports—the combined result of the government's export-promotion policies, currency devaluation, and the restructuring of the industrial sector. Mexico never experienced the continuing extreme hyperinflation that has plagued other third world nations, although inflation rates occasionally reached 160 percent or more during the de la Madrid administration. Anti-inflationary policies were somewhat successful, but the goal of single-digit inflation remained beyond reach. By 1989 government could, however, point to increased flows of foreign capital into the country. Foreign investment was increasing, capital that had left Mexico during the height of the crisis was returning, and foreign loans and credits were once again on the rise.

Beginning in 1989 the economy experienced small but sustained per capita growth. Growth rates in the period from 1989 to 1991 were slightly higher than the estimated 2-2.5 percent annual rate of population growth. In 1988 the economy grew 1.4 percent, then 3.1 percent in 1989, 3.9 percent in 1990, and an estimated 4-5 percent in 1991. Nonetheless, because of the sharp drop in per capita income—about 15 percent—in the 1982-88 crisis period, the Mexican economy still had a long way to go before recovering pre-crisis income levels. To return the economy to the pre-1982 per capita income levels, the economy would have to expand at the rate of 6.5 percent or more for at least four years. Assuming this happens, the Mexican economy would still have lost a decade or more of economic development.

The rosy economic indicators paraded around by the Salinas government—narrowing budget deficit, lower inflation, renewed economic growth—could not disguise the essentially weak state of the Mexican economy at midterm in the Salinas *sexenio*. For the first time since 1982 the economy was experiencing steady growth in the 3-4 percent range. But this was anemic, especially considering that the economically active population was growing at about the same rate. Neither did the new economic growth the tremendous backlog of under- and unemployed workers left without decent jobs by the crisis of the 1980s.

The 1989-90 debt renegotiation package was greeted with a great ballyhoo. Mexico did enjoy some debt relief, but the massive debt burden did not go away. In fact, the country owed at least $16 billion more by late 1991 than it did in 1982 when the crisis exploded. Moreover it faced the 1990s with an internal debt that had also mortgaged away any possibility for the kind of economic development that would bring along the poor majority.

Mexico's budget deficit did shrink. Yet the tightening of the budget came at the cost of reduced public-sector investment, layoffs of government employees, reduced social services, higher taxes on the working class, and the transferral of state enterprises, often at fire-sale prices, to the business elite.

Meanwhile economic-restructuring initiatives, debt renegotiations, and free trade discussions created new interest in Mexico among foreign investors and lenders, and contributed to capital-flight repatriation. But even this encouraging inflow of foreign capital had a dark side, since most of it went into indirect investment in the stock market and into services rather than into productive investment. The renewed flow of foreign lending from the World Bank, the Inter-American Development Bank (IDB), and commercial banks, while temporarily pulling the economy out of its crisis, raised concerns about Mexico's future ability to meet its debt-service payments.

Heightening these concerns was the country's rapidly deteriorating trade balance. As Mexico opened up its borders to foreign trade, its domestic farm and industrial sectors found they could not compete against cheap imports and began shutting down production. Stagnant investment in production for the domestic market, then, is yet another sign of the economic malaise underlying the official optimism in Mexico.

The Underside of Modernization

A recitation of the usual economic indicators gives only a partial view of the impacts of the restructuring Mexico has undergone since 1982. An assessment of other factors—such as the welfare of the citizenry, the distribution of wealth, and the condition of the domestic business sector—reveals an even more disturbing scenario. Beneath the surface of Mexico's apparent recovery, potential economic problems and their political offspring are being spawned by the government's current economic policies.

Broad-based development paralleled economic growth to a remarkable degree during Mexico's miracle years. These three decades of economic modernization gave rise to an extensive middle class of professionals and bureaucrats. Industrialization brought with it a new proletariat that enjoyed increasing wage levels. Income also steadily increased in the rural sector as a result of the opening of new lands, rising productivity, and government-sponsored irrigation projects.[25]

The country's inward-looking and state-led model of development facilitated this conversion of economic growth into widespread development. Income did not automatically trickle down. Tripartite negotiations with the PRI-associated labor and peasant organizations ensured that a portion of the expanding national wealth would be shared with the lower classes. When concessions were not granted automatically by the state, popular mobilizations extracted them. The government itself was responsible for improving social welfare, through an aggressive extension of educational and medical services. Called "stabilizing development" by some scholars, the Mexican model of growth resulted in enviable political and economic stability.

The model did have its share of fatal flaws, including technological dependence, increasing reliance on foreign capital, and widespread inefficiency. Although the benefits of development were relatively widespread, poverty was still the lot of the majority. Substandard housing, malnutrition, ill health, and underemployment were the norm, especially among the isolated and marginalized rural poor. The expansion of the proletariat and middle class had given Mexico "the facade of a modern, industrializing power," as economist David Barkin observed.[26] Industrialization resulted in rapidly changing consumption patterns, but most Mexicans could not afford the consumer goods being churned out by the manufacturing sector.

This facade began to crumble in the 1970s, and the development model was increasingly called into question. These were years of transition, in which the gains of the peasants and workers were rolled back at the same time that the capitalist class became ever more concentrated. In the 1980s Mexico again began modernizing, but the focus was on internationalization, not internal industrialization.

This time there was little concern for spreading out the benefits of economic advances. And the government made little effort to hide the fact that this new style of modernization was taking place on the backs of the country's poor majority. To keep manufacturing internationally competitive, wages were held below subsistence level. To balance the budget, social services were cut. To replenish a treasury depleted by debt payments, public utility rates were raised. And to keep inflation down, wage increases were kept well below price increases. As a result of restructuring, Mexico became an increasingly polarized society. Many were driven into the informal economy, while others joined the migratory flow north. In contrast to the spreading impoverishment of Mexico, wealth grew increasingly concentrated among a small oligarchy.

The State of Poverty

For most of its history the Mexican government can point to a constantly expanding economy. Much of the credit for the country's economic development belongs to the state itself, which pushed the economy forward with its extensive public-investment program and its support for capital accumulation by the country's weak capitalist sector. Although Mexico has historically enjoyed one of the world's highest growth rates, the government has a poor record in ensuring that this increased wealth is equitably distributed. As the World Bank reported in 1980, Mexico has "one of the worst profiles of income distribution of any nation on earth."[27]

During the years of steady economic growth from 1940 to 1976 most Mexicans did experience improved socioeconomic conditions. Some of the new wealth did trickle down, and new government education and health programs also benefited the poor. Nonetheless at the end of this period the poorest sectors found themselves worse off in relation to other economic groups. Income distribution statistics are notoriously difficult to track over long periods. According to one such study, the concentration of income in the mid-1970s in Mexico was higher than it had been in 1910, the year the revolution broke out.[28]

Between 1950 and 1977 (the year after Mexico's first major economic crisis), the lowest 40 percent of the population saw their share of the country's personal income drop from 12.6 percent to 11.8 percent. The share of the bottom 10 percent dropped from 2.3 percent to 1.2 percent.[29] In the period from 1950 to 1977 the share of the top 10 percent also declined. The most substantial relative gains in income share went to the expanding middle

Table 2c
Social Indicators

Housing

Deficit	6,000,000+ homes
Substandard	40 %
Shortfall in Mexico City	800,000 homes

Health

Life Expectancy 1991	69
Infant Mortality 1990 (per 1,000 births)	36
No access to health facilities 1985-88	15%
No access to safe water 1985-88	11%
Rural with no access to safe water	53%

Nutrition

Extreme malnutrition 1974	8%
Extreme malnutrition 1989	15%
Rural children malnourished	50%
Decline in per capita beef and pork consumption 1980-90	50%
Per capita milk consumption in 1980	125 liters
in 1990	74 liters
Average calorie and protein intake per day in 1987	1653 calories
in 1990	1431 calories

Living Conditions

Rural household income as percent of agricultural sector GDP in 1980	36%
in 1990	25%
Rural household income as % of total GDP in 1980	36%
Rural homes under poverty line	43%
Urban homes under poverty line	23%
Homes in all of country under poverty line	30%
Unemployment in 1990	18%

SOURCES: Bread for the World, *Hunger 1992, Second Annual Report on the State of World Hunger,* 1991; CEPAL, *Notas sobre el desarollo social in América Latina,* July 1991; U.S. Department of Commerce, *Business America,* April 8, 1991. Also figures from National Nutrition Institute and Ministry of Agriculture (SARH), 1991.

class of bureaucrats, professionals, and industrial workers—a sector that had grown to include nearly 30 percent of Mexican society.

Due to the "shared development" policies of President Echeverría and the massive public-sector job increases during the oil boom years, economic growth appears to have been more broadly distributed through 1983, when the government's new austerity program took effect. The post-1982 crisis, however, aggravated long-term trends toward high overall income concentration and the impoverishment of the poor majority (Table 2c).

A 1984 survey conducted by the Economic Commission for Latin America and the Caribbean (ECLA) of the United Nations estimated that 28 million Mexicans were unable to meet their basic needs. Some 10 million fell into the category of "extreme poverty." By 1990, however, the government reported that 41 million (or nearly half) of the population fell below the poverty line, with 17 million living in conditions of extreme poverty.[30] According to this estimate, one of every five Mexicans is living in conditions of absolute poverty—without access to adequate nutrition, housing, or health care.[31] Making matters worse, the cost of basic goods has been rising faster than the overall inflation rate.

The World Bank, which called poverty in Mexico a "structural problem," estimated in 1990 that one-sixth of Latin America's poverty-stricken population lives in Mexico. It singled out four states where the problem is most serious: Oaxaca, Chiapas, and Guerrero, in the south, and Hidalgo, in east-central Mexico. Seventy percent of the combined population of these states lives below the poverty line. About half the population has not finished primary school, and in many isolated towns the illiteracy rate is 50 percent—4 times greater than in regions with better economic conditions. Between 30 and 40 percent of the population lack access to health services, and 80 percent are without potable water.[32] Between 60 and 70 percent lack acceptable housing in these four states. Expressed in other terms, all of the state of Oaxaca eats as much as the wealthy Mexico City neighborhood of Lomas de Chapultepec does.[33] This disparity is not peculiar to the four states mentioned above. In general, rural residents suffer disproportionately from unemployment, infant mortality, and lack of government services.

Wages and Unemployment

Another way to measure poverty and income distribution in Mexico is to look at the purchasing power of the minimum wage. Until the 1976 crisis real minimum salaries had been rising steadily since the mid-1940s. But currency devaluations and reduced government backing for the demands of organized labor translated into a drop in real wages after 1976. Wages briefly recuperated at the height of the oil boom in 1982, but the purchasing power of Mexican workers subsequently declined each year through 1991.

According to Mexico's constitution, "the minimum wage should be sufficient to satisfy the normal material, social, and cultural needs of the head of household and to provide for the education of his children." Prior to the

1982 crisis, one minimum wage could be stretched to cover the most basic needs of a family of four. By 1991 a family needed more than two minimum wage salaries to meet the same fundamental needs.[34]

The minimum wage (about $3.90 a day by 1991) is increased every year or two, but these raises regularly fall below the rate of inflation. Since 1982 the purchasing power of the minimum wage has dropped an average of 12 percent annually, with the rate of decline reaching 14 percent in the period from 1988 to 1991. Between 1982 and mid-1991 the purchasing power of the minimum wage dropped 66 percent (Table 2d). According to a report by the national university's economics department, by 1991 the purchasing power of the minimum wage had been reduced to just half of that enjoyed by workers in the period between 1936 and 1938.[35]

In 1987 the government instituted a tripartite national economic pact between business, the official labor unions, and itself, designed to reduce inflation through wage and price controls. Due to expire at the end of 1991, the economic pact was disastrous for the country's working class. Minimum wages increased about 80 percent during this period, but the price of

Table 2d
Minimum Wage in Mexico, 1978-91

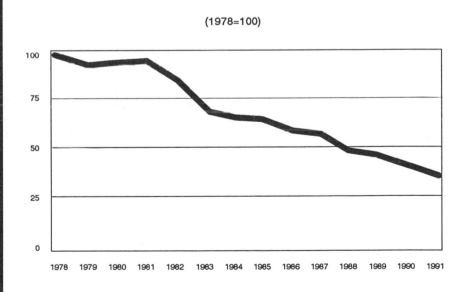

(1978=100)

SOURCE: Department of Economic Research, Banamex. Based on data from the Nation Institute of Statistics, Geography and Information (INEGI) of the Ministry of Programming and the Budget (SPP), the Banco de México, and the National Commission on Minimum Wages.

basic goods increased 250 percent. Another way to measure the rapid decline in real minimum wages in Mexico is to compare what one wage could buy in 1981 as compared to 1991. In 1981 one day's minimum wage could buy about 18 pounds of beans; by 1991 it represented only 5.5 pounds.

Mexico has one of the lowest minimum wages in the world—about one-tenth of that in the United States, one-fourth of South Korea's, and two-fifths of Singapore's. According to ECLA the real minimum wage in countries at similar levels of development in Latin America—Argentina, Brazil, Colombia, Chile, Venezuela, Uruguay, and Costa Rica—all outranked that of Mexico.[36]

To survive, most families had several members working, either as wage laborers or in the expanding informal sector. The National Minimum Wage Commission saw no need to raise the minimum wage to make up for the two-thirds drop in purchasing power over the past ten years, arguing that most workers receive more than the minimum and that moonlighting is common. An estimated 10-20 percent of the urban work force receives the minimum or less, while the other 80 percent or more earn an average of 2.5 minimum wages.[37] But according to ECLA, nearly 60 percent of workers in rural areas earn no more than the minimum wage—when they can find work.

Continuing economic difficulties and the ongoing restructuring of the economy combined to increase the concentration of wealth in Mexico. This was apparent in the decreasing share of national income received by workers. Wages and salaries in 1976 represented 45 percent of the national income, declining to 37 percent in 1981 and falling to 28 percent by 1989.[38] By contrast, the share received by capital steadily increased during the 1980s, rising from 54 percent in 1981 to 62 percent.[39]

Unemployment in Mexico is commonly estimated at about 18 percent, although the government itself regularly reports urban unemployment at under 3 percent—a discrepancy at least partially accounted for by the fact that the government considers a person employed even if she or he works only an hour per week. Government figures also measure only urban unemployment. Economic growth since 1988 brought new jobs, but this increase in private-sector employment was paralleled by widespread job losses in the public sector.

Underemployment affects 25-40 percent of the population, rising to higher levels in rural areas. Perhaps the best indicator of the declining ability of the Mexican economy to provide employment was the startling growth of the informal sector. Between 1982 and 1990 the number of Mexicans working outside the formal economy, mostly as street vendors, jumped by more than 80 percent.[40]

Since 1974, when President Echeverría instituted a government-sponsored family-planning program, Mexico has made dramatic strides in reducing its fertility rate and population growth. The rate of population growth fell from 3.5 percent in 1970s to about 2 percent by 1990. This decrease was not yet reflected in the growth of the economically active population, however, which was still increasing at nearly 3.5 percent annually because of the high birth rates in the late 1960s and early 1970s.[41] It has been estimated that the Mexican economy would have to grow at the per capita rate of at least 7 percent a year to provide jobs for new workers entering the work force and to accommodate the many who have lost jobs due to the economic crisis and restructuring. Looking at this problem another way, the Mexican economy would have to create 1.5 million jobs annually through the year 2000 to approach the desired objective of near full employment.[42]

Budget Cuts and Solidarity

The Mexican constitution goes beyond the vague formula of guaranteeing the right to "life, liberty, and the pursuit of happiness" to state specifically that government has the obligation to provide for the health, education, housing, and economic survival of the population.[43] Never have these obligations been fully met but the Mexican state has sustained numerous institutions, like the Social Security Institute, which have provided a modicum of social services. Perhaps more importantly, the government has offered some protection for the working class through the federal labor law.

Beginning in the early 1980s, however, the government's social programs were cut back. By 1990 budget allocations for social services such as health and education were down 10 percent below the level of social expenditures in 1980.[44] Deregulation, austerity measures, and privatization cut bigger holes in the already tattered welfare net existing in Mexico. Recognizing that its own social-service programs were deteriorating, the government encouraged private entrepreneurs to begin filling the large gaps in education, housing, health, and other social services.[45]

Although the overall budget figures showed a sharp cut in expenditures for social services, the Salinas government loudly proclaimed its dedication to combating poverty. In 1989 it created an entirely new program, the National Solidarity Program (Pronasol), to direct the fight against poverty.[46] The program is run out of the Office of the Presidency and the Ministry of Planning and Budget (SPP), the old stomping grounds of Salinas himself before becoming president. Most branches of government, however, channel resources to the program. The public budget of Pronasol comes largely from the sale of the parastatal enterprises such as Telmex (the Mexican Telephone Company).[47] The U.S. embassy estimated that more than 50 percent of the public sector's capital expenditures were channeled through Pronasol in 1990.[48]

The creation of Pronasol was an apparent reaction to the 1988 national elections when the popular dissatisfaction with the PRI government was made clear by the opposition vote and the social mobilization behind the populist candidate Cárdenas. In response, President Salinas launched an alternative populist program, a kind of neoliberal populism that selectively distributes state resources to diffuse social discontent, undermine the opposition, and build support for the ruling party. Contrasting Pronasol with the spendthrift populism of past administrations, Salinas claims that this social program represents a fiscally responsible and selective approach to relieving poverty. The program carefully chooses its beneficiaries, and rather than simply handing out funds Pronasol stresses "co-participation" or solidarity between the government and recipients.

Pronasol funds flow to Solidarity Committees established at the local level to sponsor food-aid programs, production projects, social-services programs, and infrastructure projects. By 1991 there were approximately 28,000 Solidarity Committees scattered throughout the country.[49] Pronasol's food programs have been channeled through Conasupo and the National System for the Integral Development of the Family (DIF). To increase production by poor communities, Pronasol established the Solidarity Funds for Production for small farmers, Solidarity Funds for Indigenous Communities for ethnic groups, and Women in Solidarity to provide credit for the establishment of microenterprises for women. Through its Solidarity Health Program, more than 700 health clinics were established or rehabilitated by 1991 and 26 hospitals expanded.

In education, Pronasol created the Solidarity for a Dignified School Program, which improved 34,000 schools and provided over 100,000 scholarships to university students. Its infrastructure programs are channeled through the Municipal Solidarity Funds program, which claimed to have provided electricity to five million homes and improved water supplies to 700 urban communities. In addition, Pronasol moved to present property titles to 450,000 families previously living as urban squatters.

Pronasol advocates proclaimed the program a new form of providing assistance that avoids bureaucratic red tape and corruption that characterizes other social welfare programs. In addition, the program has attempted to work directly with community groups and grassroots leaders rather than relying on the established *cacique*-type patrons. But the program has been criticized as simply a token measure to calm the rising expectations of those living in extreme poverty while the nation waits for the trickle-down benefits of foreign investment and an export-based economy.[50] All agree, however, that Pronasol serves as a highly successful public-relations program for PRI and President Salinas.

During the 1989-91 period Mexicans were bombarded with solidarity propaganda, especially in the electronic media. One of the most played tunes on the radio was the rendition of the "Hymn of Solidarity" by Mexico pop artists. About the only time Televisa viewers saw brown *mestizo* faces was when watching the frequent Pronasol television spots. The "country of the revolution," as historian Enrique Krauze once called Mexico, had become the country of Solidarity.[51]

Despite government insistence that Pronasol is nonpartisan, the program frequently looks and sounds like an old-fashioned PRI patronage campaign. Like PRI itself, Pronasol sports the colors of the national flag.

President Salinas regularly storms the country on "solidarity" tours, initiating projects to bring electricity and water to poor neighborhoods or to legalize the property rights of longtime "*paracaidistas*," or squatters. Meanwhile his critics have compared Pronasol to "the wife of the factory owner who used to organize charitable breakfasts to benefit the poor who were made so by her husband."[52]

At first glance the welfare-state nature of Pronasol seems to be at odds with the privatizing, neoliberal logic of the Salinas government. In fact the solidarity campaign in Mexico closely resembles antipoverty programs sponsored by neoliberal administrations in other Latin America countries. In El Salvador, Nicaragua, and Guatemala, neoliberal policymakers have instituted "social investment funds" as part of half-hearted efforts to soften the impact of neoliberal reforms on the country's poorest sectors. In Mexico and in other countries affected by structural adjustment, international lenders and donors such as the World Bank and the U.S. Agency for International Development (AID) have insisted that the government cut social services and payroll while at the same time funding (directly or indirectly) band-aid programs such as Pronasol that help stabilize the government.[53]

The underlying logic is that while economic reforms establish free market mechanisms by which society competes for its well-being, there are inevitably inefficient and backward members who are left behind. To guarantee their subsistence and to preempt their social mobilization, specially targeted welfare and community development programs are necessary for the stability of the state.

In Mexico this social investment fund is also being used for explicitly political purposes. Areas of the greatest need are not necessarily Pronasol's top priorities. Immediately after its founding the program began targeting *neocardenista* strongholds and began signing funding agreements with numerous independent popular organizations outside PRI's corporatist tentacles, including the National Union of Regional Peasant Organizations (Unorca), Democratic Peasant Front of Chihuahua, Plan de Ayala National Coordinator, Popular Defense Committees (CDP), and elements of the National Coordinator of Urban Popular Movements (Conamup).[54] Government funding obviously works to undermine the autonomy of these and other groups, but it also weakens their internal cohesion and sense of purpose. Pronasol also channeled funds to Solidarity Committees in all but a few of the municipalities held by the PRD in an obvious attempt to divide the opposition's base of support. As for those communities or groups that decline to associate with Pronasol and PRI, they often must pay the material price of being denied access to community development funds.

A manifestation of the government's neocorporatist strategy, Pronasol has bypassed the old corporatist networks and established new and innovative forms of PRI patronage and clientelism. In fact, some speculate that the Solidarity Committees may be the grassroots base of a reconstituted PRI. Through these committees, the government has created a patronage infrastructure where party loyalty is returned for material rewards. The modernizing wing of PRI has taken to calling PRI the "Party of Solidarity," and PRI even has its own Program of Social Solidarity designed to organize party loyalists around social demands that are met by Pronasol.[55] Solidarity funds are also manipulated to reward the "modernizers" of the party, while the denial of these resources serves to punish PRI politicians who do not fall in line with the *salinista* wing of the party. As Denise Dresser observed: "The 'solidarity' discourse, imagery, and selective resource allocation are playing a crucial role in . . . neutralizing the opposition as well as creating a base for a refurbished PRI."[56]

As the 1991 midterm elections amply demonstrated, Pronasol has served the government well in bolstering its legitimacy and winning support for PRI candidates. The extraordinary flow of resources through this presidential initiative creates the impression that the government is indeed concerned about social justice, even though its economic policies may be aggravating social inequities. At least initially this poverty program has helped create a new social consensus for the PRI government, allowing it to proceed with its economic restructuring while offering only limited democratization.

Rather than tackling the deep structural problems leading to skewed income and resource distribution in Mexico, Pronasol is a compensatory program designed to pacify and provide temporary relief. An obvious problem with this strategy is that the funds to back this social investment fund are not built into the budget but come from the contingency fund created by the sale of state enterprises. If these funds dry up and Pronasol slows down, PRI loyalty among the popular sectors, which the government has engendered through its distributive capabilities, may also sharply decline.[57]

The Informal Sector Out of Control

Mexico has always had an informal economic sector of vendors and laborers whose activities are untaxed, unregulated, and—in a legal sense—unauthorized. In the course of the 1980s this informal sector mushroomed as a result of the economic crisis. Estimates of its size range from 25 percent to 40 percent of the official GDP, having increased more than 80 percent between 1982 and 1990.[58] One study estimated that more than one-quarter of the economically active population participated in the informal sector in 1989, up from just 4.4 percent in 1980.[59]

At the low end of the informal sector are those who have taken to the streets to sell Chiclets, shine shoes, or wipe car windows. Many find that they can easily earn more than the minimum wage selling trinkets and candies.[60]

Others with enough *pesos* to invest have set up stalls along busy streets and outside the metro stations. At the high end are those entrepreneurs involved in the smuggling and sale of electronics and household appliances, such as those in the famous Tepito market in downtown Mexico City. Here consumers can even flip through catalogs to order a desired stereo system or VCR, which is then smuggled in from California the following week.

As wage rates continue to sink below inflation and peasant farmers are forced out of the market, millions of Mexicans find that only in the informal sector can they keep up with the cost of living. A study by the National Consumer Institute found that workers in the informal economy were more successful in protecting their income than were wage workers.

The explosion of the informal sector threatens the formal business community, especially small-business owners. Because they are not taxed and have little overhead, street vendors can sell at 10 to 40 percent below the prices charged by legal shopkeepers. And with small inventories, street vendors can easily change products to match changing consumer interests. Businesses have insisted that the government restrain the informal sector, claiming it represents unfair competition. The government itself is concerned because of all the taxes it loses.

But attempts to control the informal sector are handicapped by its size and its political clout. As part of its vote-getting machine, PRI has incorporated street vendors into merchant associations and poor people's organizations that are affiliated with the party.[61] Not only is the government reluctant to stamp down on a base of political support, but it is also concerned that a campaign to eliminate the informal sector would cut off an important safety valve for the poor.

Investing in Mexico

Reflecting the acute lack of confidence in the stability of the Mexican economy, private investment—both domestic and foreign—weakened noticeably beginning in 1983. The drop in private investment was paralleled by a dramatic decrease in public-sector investment. As a result, economic growth came to a standstill. By 1988 the government's economic-stabilization and restructuring programs had succeeded in renewing investor confidence in the economy, and private investment slowly began to increase. Capital that had left Mexico began to repatriate, and industries started to reinvest in plants and equipment. Foreign investment also began flowing into the country in the late 1980s and shows no signs of letting up. Nonetheless, the levels of recent private investment still fall short of those enjoyed during the boom years.[62]

Compared with the pre-crisis era, public-sector investment played a reduced role in pushing the economy forward. In recent years private-sector investment expanded at a faster pace than government investment, and in 1990 it accounted for more than 70 percent of total investment.[63] For the most part, those able to invest have been the owners of large export-oriented industries or agribusinesses. The small- and medium-scale firms serving the tight domestic market do not have the resources to invest in the equipment and machinery needed for restructuring. Confronted by cheaper imports, many industries, particularly in the textile, shoe, and clothing sectors, have been divested.

A rapid increase in foreign investment formed the cornerstone of the government's stabilization plans. Before the 1982 crisis the government relied on heavy foreign borrowing to cover trade gaps and government deficits. No longer able to count on such major inflows of foreign loans, the government then turned its attention toward foreign investors as its principal source of foreign exchange. To make the country more attractive to foreign capitalists, many of the earlier restrictions on foreign investment were erased from the books. Instead of restricting foreign investors, the government began openly courting them.

Behind the new drive to attract foreign investments is a long history of ambivalence and conflict. One of the sparks that ignited the 1910 revolution was the 1906 miners' strike at the U.S.-owned Cananea copper mine. Also imprinted deep in the memory of the Mexican people—and of prospective foreign investors—is the nationalization of the petroleum industry in 1938. As uneasy as this relationship sometimes has been, foreign investors generally have found Mexico a hospitable and profitable place to do business. To further its own development objectives, however, the Mexican government has traditionally excluded foreign investment from certain "strategic" sectors and restricted its full participation in other "priority" areas. Under Mexican law the state has the exclusive right to develop petroleum, other hydrocarbons, and 19 basic petrochemicals. Other strategic sectors reserved to the state include electricity, railroads, nuclear energy, telegraphic communications, and the mining of radioactive minerals. Activities that have been reserved exclusively for Mexican companies include radio and television, exchange houses, fishing cooperatives, and credit unions.

During the 1960s and 1970s, for example, the government enacted a series of decrees and laws that redirected foreign investment from its traditional areas (agriculture, transportation, public utilities, and mining) into manufacturing.[64] But the changing nature of foreign investment in Mexico was not simply the result of government edict. It also corresponded to the rise of transnational corporations in the post-World War II era and their drive to dominate foreign markets.

As the Mexican economy expanded so did foreign investment, especially in the fastest-growing areas of manufacturing such as food processing. Occasionally the Mexican government angered certain foreign investors by instituting new restrictions. Such was the case with the Mining Law of 1961, which forced foreign mining firms like Amax to expand their corporate structures to include 51-percent Mexican ownership. The limitation to 49-percent ownership was extended to all areas of foreign investment by the 1973 Foreign Investment Law. Exceptions to this rule were the *maquiladoras* (where 100-percent foreign ownership was permitted) and to those investments where 100-percent foreign ownership would be deemed in Mexico's best interests. This comprehensive new law was consistent with the government's commitment to promote the growth of a domestically based industrial sector. Besides the restrictive foreign-investment law, as part of his effort to boost national sovereignty President Echeverría pushed through the Transfer of Technology Law and the Law on Patents and Trademarks, both of which restricted the ability of foreign companies to limit the use of their technology. Nonetheless, Mexico still ranked as one of the leading recipients of new foreign investment in the third world in the 1970s.

In response to the crisis Mexico gradually began reversing its restrictive foreign-investment policies. More exceptions were made to the 49-percent limitation, most notably the permission granted to IBM in 1986 to operate a wholly owned subsidiary. Another landmark in this new opening for foreign investment came as part of the 1985 debt renegotiations that allowed foreign firms to purchase government debt obligations and convert them into investment capital (debt-equity swaps). Most sweeping, however, were the 1989 administrative changes in the regulations of the Foreign Investment Law, making 100-percent foreign ownership possible without prior government approval in most industries.

The opening for foreign investment only grew wider after 1989 as the Salinas government showed every indication of meeting most of the demands of Washington and foreign business interests for unrestricted foreign investment. President Salinas even indicated that Mexico would soon welcome foreign investment or co-investment in such "strategic" areas of the economy as ports, roads, power generation, oil, and railways. Another sign of the government's willingness to meet foreign investors' demands was the replacement of the old Law on Patents and Trademarks with a new law modeled on international standards.

The government rolled out the red carpet for prospective foreign investors, who benefit from new tax incentives, subsidies, and promotion programs designed to attract export-oriented foreign investment. As part of the its efforts to woo foreign investors, the government began revamping the country's communications and transportation infrastructure. The result was a marked upgrading of the country's telecommunications capabilities and the deregulation of the transportation industry. In addition the government hopes that the proposed free trade agreement will serve as an incentive for producers to locate to Mexico as a tariff-free springboard into the U.S. market.

These and other changes contributed to substantially increased inflows of foreign investment. With the continuing progress toward a free trade accord, this trend should continue, although the rate will have to quicken to meet the Salinas administration's goal of $25 billion in new foreign investment by the end of the president's *sexenio* in 1994.[65]

But even with the added investment, there is reason to question whether Mexico's long-term development needs will be advanced by this effort to attract foreign capital. Not all new foreign investment has flowed into new productive activities. In the case of the debt-equity swaps, foreign investors are merely buying into the country's existing productive capacity. The same was true in the case of foreign involvement in the newly privatized public-sector corporations. In addition much of the investment has gone into commerce and services, especially tourism. Another factor in measuring the impact of foreign investment is the high concentration in the automobile industry, with companies like Nissan and Ford making investments of up to a billion dollars. In contrast to the 1960s and 1970s, when most foreign investment went into industries producing for the local market, the new money coming into Mexico flowed into export-oriented industries that rely mostly on foreign-made inputs.

Although the scenario is questionable from the Mexican standpoint, the prospects look bright for foreign investors. *Fortune* magazine called Mexico the best bet for new foreign investment in Latin America. Cheap labor, proximity to the U.S. market, and a booming stock market have been the main reasons for this judgment.

Trade Imbalances

As in most developing countries, trade deficits have been the norm in Mexico. This imbalance in the current account was covered easily by surpluses in the capital account until 1982. Until the economic crash, new foreign investment, loans, and credit flowing into the country usually covered the annual deficits in trade, while financing the government's widening budget deficits. As the debt crisis illustrated, this was a precarious way to run an economy.

Although pre-1982 trade deficits were easily balanced by capital inflows, the weakening of Mexico's trade sector during the 1970s pointed out the increasing instability of the Mexican economy. On the agricultural front, food imports were rising while the value and volume of the country's traditional exports (coffee, sugar, cotton, and minerals) were dropping. In the industrial sector, import-substitution development was proving counterproductive because of the continuing large imports of intermediate and capital goods needed to turn the cogs of the country's technology-dependent manufacturing plants.

With respect to the oil industry, Mexico's petroleum trade balance suddenly turned negative in the early 1970s. With the development of vast reserves in 1977, the problem reversed itself, and Mexico became overdependent on its oil exports. By 1982 these constituted 78 percent of all exports. Yet even with the income of oil exports, overall trade deficits persisted. Nonetheless during this heyday of high oil prices and a steady influx of foreign loans, few were worried about the country's feeble external sector.

The debt crisis and the sudden drying up of capital inflows forced Mexico to look to the export sector as its main source of new foreign capital. Beginning with the de la Madrid administration, the government's entire economic policy was premised on exporting Mexico out of the crisis. In large part this new attention given to export promotion was the result of conditions laid down by Washington, the IMF, and the World Bank. It also represented the ascendancy of the neoliberal technocratic faction of the country's political elite.

Export-promotion policies implemented during the de la Madrid administration succeeded in moving Mexico away from its dangerous dependence on oil exports. Manufactured exports gained unprecedented

Table 2e
Mexico's External Sector, 1990-91

	1990	1991*
Current Account[1]	-$5.3billion	-$10.0 billion
Trade Balance	-3.0	-8.0
Exports	26.8	30.0
Imports	29.8	38.0
% Composition of Exports[2]		
Petroleum	31%	30%
Crude Petroleum	27%	26%
Other	4%	4%
Non-Petroleum[3]	69%	70%
Agriculture	14%	12%
Mining	2%	2%
Manufacturing	53%	55%
% Composition of Imports[4]		
Consumer	15%	14%
Intermediate	62%	63%
Capital Goods	23%	22%
Mexico-U.S. Trade Balance	2.5 billion	$0.0
Capital Account	$8.8 billion	$14.0

* Estimated.

[1]Includes exchange of Services and Unrequited Transfers, as well as merchandise trade.
[2]Based on January-May figures for 1990 and 1991. Figures do not add to 100 percent due to rounding and unspecified production activities.
[3]In 1990 agriculture, mining and manufacturing accounted, respectively, for 20 percent, 4 percent and 76 percent of nonpetroleum exports, changing to 19 percent, 3 percent, and 78 percent in 1991.
[4]Intermediate goods are those like steel or wood used in the production process of other goods, while capital goods include machinery and plant.

SOURCE: U.S. Department of State, *Economic Trends Report: Mexico*, August 1991.

prominence in the 1980s—mainly as the result of *maquila*-type production—rising from 18 percent in 1980 to 55 percent of export income by 1991.
At the same time, oil slipped to one-third or less of the country's export offering—largely the result of sinking oil prices (Table 2e).

Mexico enjoyed trade surpluses during the years of economic stagnation (1983-88). New export-promotion policies (including government subsidies and incentives) played an important role in this positive trade
balance, but also responsible were the country's undervalued currency and
a shrinking domestic market, which had caused Mexico's imports to drop
sharply. The devalued *peso* and the impoverishment of the society made
imports a luxury few could afford. And as the internal market constricted,
many larger manufacturers began focusing on the export market. Positive
trade balances during the de la Madrid *sexenio*, then, were at least as much
a sign of a recessionary economy as an indicator of a dynamic export sector.

The trade balance turned negative again with the Salinas administration. Manufactured imports continued to increase, but at a slower pace. The
problem was that imports were rising more than twice as fast as exports in
the 1989-91 period. For some observers the 1990 trade deficit of $3 billion—
with projections of an $8 billion trade deficit in 1991—indicated a danger-
ously unbalanced economy. Widening trade deficits once again placed
Mexico in the shaky position of depending on foreign capital inflows to
cover trade imbalances and deficits in the current account (Table 2f).

Government representatives, however, asserted that increased imports
were a sure sign of expanding confidence in the economy. For the most part
that appeared to be true, since most of the increased import costs were from
the purchase of intermediate and capital goods for business. Yet the rise in
intermediate and capital imports, while certainly a sign that investors were
more optimistic about economic growth, highlighted the country's longtime inability to create its own capital-goods sector. It underlined Mexico's
technological dependence and its failure to support its own research and
development sector.[66] This absence of technological development has long
represented a major obstacle to the country's modernization and industrialization plans. Even more worrisome than this dependency on foreign-made
equipment and machinery were the expanding agricultural imports and the
influx of foreign consumer goods.

In the past, one either had to travel abroad or go to the Tepito smuggler's
market in Mexico City to purchase foreign-made goods. Since 1986, however, foreign products have flooded the domestic market. Everything from
Italian pasta and Diet Coke to European cookies and Italian loafers is now
available. Mexicans are now washing their dishes with Joy detergent and
their hands with Dove soap. In many cases local manufacturers have closed
down because imports are cheaper and better made. Finding that they
could not compete with cheap Asian goods, many Mexican companies shut
down their factories and became distributors of imported shoes, clothes,
toys, and other consumer goods. Although most of the affected manufac-

turers were Mexican, transnational corporations that had been producing uncompetitive goods behind the country's import barriers were also adversely affected by trade liberalization.[67]

Price and quality were the main factors behind the import boom, but foreign products also conveyed a desirable sense of status. In the subways, hawkers attract customers with the claim that the toenail clippers, candies, and other little goodies they are selling are *"importados."* In the richer neighborhoods boutiques such as the *Super Americano* are cashing in on this new craving for anything foreign.[68]

When the trade liberalization process that began in 1986 started to take full effect in 1988, the resulting trade deficits shattered Mexico's dreams of exporting its way out of crisis and toward economic development. In the short term a trade deficit is not necessarily the sign of a weakening economy. As long as new capital flows cover the foreign exchange costs of these imports, the economy will remain stabilized. In recent years this has been the case with Mexico, which has benefited from increased foreign investment, a reduced debt-service burden, and new foreign loans and credit.

Given Mexico's agricultural crisis, its dependency on foreign inputs for manufacturing, and its uncompetitive business community, the country's trade problems appear to be more than a passing economic occurrence. If

Table 2f
Mexican GDP, Exports and Imports

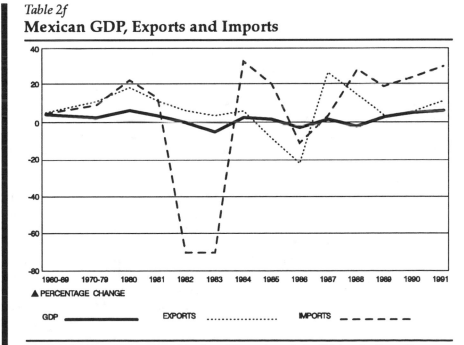

SOURCES: Sidney Weintraub, *A Marriage of Convenience*, Oxford University Press, New York, 1990; U.S. Department of State, *Economic Trends Report: Mexico*, August 1991.

the trade deficits persist over the next few years, a new round of economic instability may result, particularly if foreign capital flows diminish. The main challenge facing the government is to make certain that increased imports, loan capital, and investment flows become the foundation of a dynamic export sector. Otherwise Mexico may once again be confronting the fallacy of debt-led growth—and facing high import and debt-service bills it cannot pay.

Terms of Trade and Trading Partners

Mexico's trade problems cannot be separated from the general condition of deteriorating terms of trade affecting most third world nations.[69] Export prices for unprocessed commodities, in particular, have been falling, while the prices of imports from industrialized countries have been steadily rising. During the 1980s Mexico was the Latin American nation most disadvantaged by the terms-of-trade crisis.[70] The sharp drop in oil prices was the major factor, but the prices of other major exports, including sugar and coffee, also fell dramatically. Declining terms of trade continue to be a problem of the early 1990s. In the first half of 1991, for example, the country's terms of trade declined by about 20 percent.

Perhaps the most salient feature of Mexico's external sector is its increasing dependence on the United States. About 65 percent of the country's imports come from the United States, and about 70 percent of its exports go to the U.S. market.[71] This market dependence is either a blessing or a curse, depending on how well the U.S. economy is doing. When it is booming, the U.S. economy can absorb virtually all that Mexico can export. But when it turns recessionary (as it did in 1974 and 1982), economic crisis in Mexico often follows.[72] The 1990-91 U.S. recession, at least initially, did not precipitate an economic crisis in Mexico, although it did result in a slow down in Mexico's exports to the shrinking U.S. market.

During the Salinas administration Mexico mounted an aggressive campaign to expand trade and investment with Europe and Asia and entered into free trade negotiations with the Central American nations, Chile, Venezuela, and Colombia. Nevertheless the main focus of Mexico's trade initiatives remains on the United States. Increasing integration of trade and investment with the United States, spurred by the General Agreement on Tariffs and Trade (GATT) agreement and encouraged further by free trade negotiations with Washington, only increased the country's dependence on the U.S. market. In Latin America there arose some concern that Mexico, previously a leading advocate of increased intraregional trade, was turning its back on the south. Even before the free trade negotiations, Latin America accounted for only 4 percent of Mexico's trade (see Other Foreign Interests, Part 6).[73]

The Big Move into GATT

Liberalizing trade has been on the government's agenda since the 1976 economic crisis, when the shortcomings of Mexico's protectionist policies and debt-led growth first became obvious. In the late 1970s López Portillo raised the possibility of Mexico's joining the GATT, a multilateral accord setting standards for trade relations among its members. The proposal faced strong opposition from members of the president's cabinet, who were unwilling to toss out the nationalist/populist principles of governance. Opposition also came from the country's intellectual community as well as its peasant and labor organizations. The critics asserted that joining GATT would mean pushing to the side the country's nationalism and its commitment to re-forming North-South economic relations.[74] At the time a chief concern was that accession to GATT would give the United States a mechanism to control Mexico's oil wealth.[75]

When the 1982 debt crisis and collapse of oil prices again forced Mexico to reevaluate its economic model, the question of the country's accession to GATT was reopened. In the face of the sharp economic downturn and the fading faith in third world internationalism, opposition to the government's move toward free trade dissipated. The onset of another economic crisis in 1985-86, precipitated by a new drop in oil prices and continuing capital flight, hurried Mexico along its path toward trade liberalization. When Mexico finally joined GATT in 1986, public opposition was minimal.

By eliminating import quotas and licenses and by slashing tariffs, Mexico aimed to create the kind of business climate that would attract foreign investors, reverse capital flight, and open up new export opportunities. Mexico had been one of the most protected economies in the world; by the close of the decade it had become one of the most open.[76]

Summing up the four years of liberalization following Mexico's GATT agreement, the U.S. International Trade Commission (ITC) noted in 1990 that "based on the premise that excessive and obsolete regulations were largely responsible for inefficiency in the use of Mexican resources, Mexico has implemented a far-reaching program of deregulation." Besides praising Mexico's privatization initiatives and its lowering of trade barriers, the ITC also reported that more than 25 sectors of the economy had been deregulated or were under review for further deregulation, including trucking, telecommunications, petrochemicals, the financial system, insurance, technology transfer, trade secrets, food production, and export commodities such as sugar, cacao, and coffee.[77]

The Push toward a Free Trade Agreement

When President Reagan in 1980 suggested the possibility of a free trade zone "from the Yukon to the Yucatán," the López Portillo government was not interested.[78] By the end of the decade Mexico not only had joined GATT but was eagerly pursuing a free trade agreement with the United States and Canada. Why the dramatic change?

The reasons behind Mexico's decision to join GATT in 1986 largely explain the urgency with which it later sought a free trade pact with its northern neighbors. Concluding that it was time to discard its inward-oriented development model, Mexico saw adopting GATT trading guidelines as the first step toward building a new and vigorous export-oriented economy. As the 1980s drew to a close, the stepped-up pace of global integration encouraged Mexico to consider the advantages of further integration with its most important trading partner. There was also increased regionalism to consider. As Europe moved toward an integrated market and as Canada and the United States moved closer to signing a free trade accord, Mexico became worried that it might be left out in the cold.

Entering a regional trading bloc with the United States would ensure that the U.S. market would stay open to Mexico-based exporters.[79] Besides increased trade with the United States, the continued growth of the *maquiladora* sector and the recent expansion of a high-tech, export-oriented automobile industry highlighted the strong potential for increased U.S. investment in Mexico. A free trade accord would make investing in Mexico even more attractive while guaranteeing Mexico access to the world's largest market at a time when protectionist sentiment was rising in the United States.[80]

Since entering GATT the de la Madrid and Salinas governments continued to push trade liberalization with all Mexico's trading partners, although the most dramatic opening has been with the United States. Several bilateral accords with Washington were signed in the late 1980s, and then in August 1990 President Salinas formally requested to enter into free trade negotiations with the United States.[81] Six months later President Bush announced that Canada would join the negotiations for a trilateral trade accord. Upon becoming president, Salinas said he was not interested in entering into a free trade agreement with the United States. But the government's failure to get the debt deal it wanted from Washington and the deepening realization that little trade and investment would be coming from the unifying Europe made a free trade agreement with the United States look more attractive.

There are two ways to look at a North American FTA. On the one hand, it will have little significance, given the integration that has already occurred, particularly between the United States and Mexico. An FTA would formalize and perhaps accelerate the ongoing integration process in North America. On the other hand, the FTA will be of great significance as a signal of the start of a new era in economic and political relations. An FTA will help lock into place the liberalization measures taken by the de la Madrid and Salinas governments, making it difficult for future governments to change the market orientation of Mexico's economic policies. The integration of the Mexican economy with that of the United States will also mean that Mexico's foreign policy will be formulated in the shadow of the FTA. A representative of the Canadian Labor Congress observed, "The FTA is fundamentally about power. It shifts power from governments (federal and provincial) to the corporate sector. It entrenches that power beyond the reach of future governments. And it limits governmental capacity to define and pursue national development goals."[82]

In many ways a free trade agreement with the United States and Canada will be just another step in the liberalization of the Mexican economy. Mexico had already lowered most of its import barriers even before negotiations started.[83] But more than a commercial opening, an FTA between Mexico and the United States will open a new chapter in the history of two neighbors who in the past have often viewed each other with mistrust and suspicion. In Mexico approval of an FTA is virtually assured, given the lack of popular opposition and the executive branch's tight control of the legislative and judicial branches of government. Big labor and big business in Mexico have expressed their support, although there has been widespread fear among small farmers and small manufacturers that they will be smothered by imports.

What Mexico Wants

With two-thirds of Mexican trade and foreign investment tied to the United States, de facto integration—with or without an FTA—already exists. In a certain sense all Mexico wants is to guarantee this access to an economy 25 times as large as its own. It wants this badly, and needs it with equal urgency.

In a country where association with the United States has always been a political liability, President Salinas staked the success of his administration on the progress of the proposed FTA. Rapid approval of a free trade agreement might mean that the expected increase in trade and investment would be felt before the end of his *sexenio*. Any delay in its approval would threaten the entire neoliberal experiment, while giving more opportunity for the coalescence of anti-FTA forces and PRI's political opposition.

A North American free trade agreement will, according to the Salinas government, pull Mexico out of the stagnation of the third world and place it firmly in the realm of the first world. In theory at least the agreement will not only give Mexico privileged access to trade and investment but also to first world technology and services. Along with U.S. and Canadian proponents of the treaty, the government argued that close association with the rest of North America would create jobs and raise productivity levels in Mexico, with a corresponding boost in wages.

The Mexican government recognizes that some sectors will inevitably suffer as its borders open further to U.S. trade. In general it will be the small- and medium-size firms that will be least able to compete. Specific sectors that are especially vulnerable to increased competition include steel, automobile parts, food processing, paper, electronics, and portions of the pharmaceuticals and petrochemicals industries. Of special concern is the agricultural sector. In early 1991 Mexico's agriculture minister warned that grain producers would be wiped out if U.S. farm commodities were allowed to enter Mexico freely. Increased U.S. food imports would raise the already substantial trade deficit. A flood of U.S. agricultural commodities would lead to severe social dislocation in the countryside and raise the level of rural political unrest. As FTA negotiations progress, therefore, Mexico will likely press for long phase-in periods for free trade in its weakest industries.

About 95 percent of the value of Mexican exports to the United States encounter a tariff of 10 percent or less. However, certain goods face U.S. tariffs of 30 percent or more. Among Mexican exports burdened with protectionist tariffs are footwear (73 percent tariff), brandy (66 percent), and textiles (37 percent). Although these goods facing tariffs of 30 percent or more comprise less than 1 percent of the country's exports to the United States, Mexico wants these tariff barriers torn down.

Also of major concern are nontariff barriers such as import quotas, antidumping quotas, health and sanitary restrictions, prohibitive technical standards, and voluntary restraint agreements that obstruct exports to the United States. Quotas for example protect the U.S. sugar industry against competition from cheaper Mexican sugar. Industrialized nations like the United States have been particularly innovative in protecting domestic industries using nontariff barriers. Mexico hopes that a free trade accord will also knock down import restrictions that are plainly protectionist but are disguised as antidumping, environmental, or health-related restrictions. The prohibition against Mexican avocados is often cited as an example of a nontariff barrier erected to protect U.S. producers in the name of dubious health standards.[84]

A distinctive feature of a free trade accord involving Mexico and the United States is the sharp disparity between the respective economic positions of the two countries. Mexico would like this asymmetry to be recognized in the FTA negotiations. Its representatives at the preliminary talks called for faster tariff reductions by the United States and a clear acknowledgment of Mexico's less-developed status in the final agreement. But Mexico soon found that, like it or not, it was in the big leagues and could expect no special treatment from the other players. From the beginning U.S. negotiators have insisted on complete reciprocity. "We must approach these negotiations as equals," said Robert Pastorino, deputy chief of mission at the U.S. embassy in Mexico.[85]

Mexico has repeatedly declared that oil would not be included in an FTA and that the agreement would be in strict accordance with the constitution. Going into FTA negotiations with the United States, the Canadian government had also reassured voters that its energy sector would not be covered by the agreement. As finally negotiated, however, the FTA states that Canada can reduce oil and gas supplies to the United States only in proportion to domestic cutbacks.[86] It is likely that Mexican oil will not be di-

Table 2g
United States, Mexico, and Canada, 1990

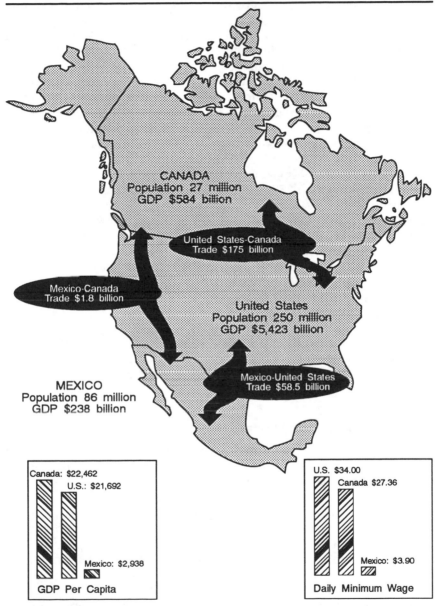

CANADA
Population 27 million
GDP $584 billion

United States-Canada
Trade $175 billion

Mexico-Canada
Trade $1.8 billion

United States
Population 250 million
GDP $5,423 billion

MEXICO
Population 86 million
GDP $238 billion

Mexico-United States
Trade $58.5 billion

Canada: $22,462
U.S.: $21,692
Mexico: $2,938
GDP Per Capita

U.S. $34.00
Canada $27.36
Mexico: $3.90
Daily Minimum Wage

SOURCES: U.S. Department of State, *Economic Trends Report: Mexico*, August 1991; International Monetary Fund, *International Financial Statistics*, August 1991; International Monetary Fund, *Direction of Trade Statistics*, June 1991; U.S. Department of Commerce, *Survey of Current Business*, June 1991; U.S. Department of Commerce, *Business America*, April 8, 1991.

rectly included in the final trilateral FTA because of the political sensitivity of the issue in Mexico. Although it was not initially part of the formal FTA talks, the opening of the oil industry was being discussed in backroom sessions (see Pemex and the Oil Industry).

The FTA negotiations among the three countries of North America are about much more than trade. Reduction of tariffs and nontariff barriers will certainly constitute a major part of an FTA, but also important will be agreements concerning investment, services, and technology transfer. A chief objective of the Mexican negotiators is to attract more foreign investment, not only because the country desperately needs more capital, but also because it realizes that investment produces trade. As it is, an estimated 60 percent of Mexican manufactured exports are produced by subsidiaries of U.S. corporations.[87] Norms for technology transfer, intellectual property (copyrights and patents, for instance), and the flow of services will also be high on the agenda.[88] Although an FTA will clearly encompass more than just trade, it will likely be limited to issues defined strictly as business. Washington has declined to discuss labor mobility as part of the accord, for example, arguing that immigration has nothing to do with trade. Unlike preparations for the expanded European Community, in 1992, which includes the movement of people among its "four freedoms," the North American agreement will limit itself to three freedoms: the free movement of goods, investment, and services.

In approaching an FTA, Mexico has dreams that integration of the North American market will allow its economy to take off in the same manner as the economies of the "four tigers" of Asia. The country's superior natural resources, its cheap labor, and its proximity to the United States, together with the advantages of a trilateral FTA, supposedly will set the stage for this take-off. Following this line of reasoning, *Business Week* called Mexico "the young jaguar."[89]

Disparity and Complementarity

The signing of a North American free trade agreement would create, as its supporters often note, the "biggest free trade zone in the world." It would bring together 362 million people (compared with 326 million in Europe) and a combined GDP of $6.3 trillion (Table 2g).

Of course, there will be tremendous disparities among the three partners. Mexico's GDP for instance has been just 4 percent of that of the United States, and there exist striking imbalances in the degree of dependence among the three partners (Table 2h). Advocates of a trilateral accord see many such disparities as potential sources of complementarity. By combining the technology and capital of the United States (and secondarily Canada) with Mexico's cheap and readily trained work force, they say, the region's exports will gain a competitive edge. This complementarity between labor and capital, along with the expansion of markets, is where the proposed FTA represents a convergence of interests among the three countries.

Proponents of the accord argue that wage rates in Mexico will remain depressed until productivity increases. The injection of capital and technology as a result of the FTA will boost productivity and eventually wage rates. It is true that Mexican productivity (output per worker) is about one-sixth that of the United States; it does not necessarily hold, however, that wages increase as productivity increases. On an economy-wide scale, the use of highly productive, capital-intensive manufacturing technologies may help to depress wages by failing to provide jobs for the unemployed.

The high productivity enjoyed by much of the auto industry in Mexico is not reflected in significantly higher wage rates. And certainly the first 25 years of the *maquiladora* program did not lead to increased wage levels. An abundant labor supply and the lack of a strong labor movement tend to keep wages low even in times of rising productivity. Furthermore, if the disparity between wage rates diminishes, the complementarity between

Table 2h

Trilateral Trade, 1990

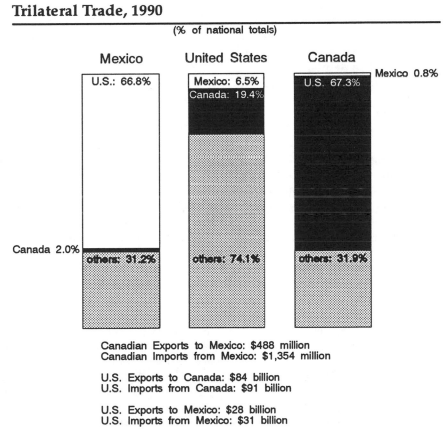

(% of national totals)

| Mexico | United States | Canada |

U.S.: 66.8% — Mexico: 6.5% / Canada: 19.4% — U.S. 67.3% / Mexico 0.8%

Canada 2.0% — others: 31.2% / others: 74.1% / others: 31.9%

Canadian Exports to Mexico: $488 million
Canadian Imports from Mexico: $1,354 million

U.S. Exports to Canada: $84 billion
U.S. Imports from Canada: $91 billion

U.S. Exports to Mexico: $28 billion
U.S. Imports from Mexico: $31 billion

SOURCE: International Monetary Fund, *Direction of Trade Statistics Yearbook 1991.*

economies also decreases. Capital that is now attracted to Mexico would probably look to other countries if Mexican wages rose appreciably.

Three's a Crowd

In early 1991 Canada officially joined the FTA talks. Reactions were mixed in Mexico. The expansion of negotiations to include Canada were, in several ways, a setback for Mexico. Adding another member raised the risk of slowing down the talks and thereby threatening Mexico's economic and political stability. Although Canada does represent a potential source of new investment and trade, it is also seen as a competitor with Mexico for the U.S. market. The export offering of the two countries is competitive, especially in auto parts and to a lesser extent in furniture, clothing, and telecommunications equipment.

Like the United States, Canada hopes to expand exports to Mexico and to give its corporations better access to Mexico's cheap labor supply.[90] But the Canadian population is not so keen on the idea of entering into another free trade accord, particularly since the FTA with the United States failed to produce either jobs or investment in Canada. The country's manufacturing work force contracted, foreign control of the economy increased, and the U.S. market remained protected by numerous nontariff barriers. Some Canadian companies moved to the United States where, particularly in the sunbelt states, wages are lower, unions nonexistent, and social benefits minimal. Manufacturing workers in Canada also saw companies migrate to Mexico and fear that more will run away if a trilateral FTA is signed. In 1990 Electrowire Inc., a subsidiary of a U.S. firm that manufactures auto parts in Ontario, warned workers that it would move to Mexico if they did not accept a three-year wage freeze. Workers were shown a study that praised the advantages of "cooperative workers that follow your instructions" and "hourly costs including bonuses, space and utilities from $2.95 to $4.50 compared with a Canadian average of $12 that does not include these extras."[91]

Although there existed strong support for a trilateral FTA in the conservative government of Brian Mulroney and among the large corporations, Canada joined the talks mostly as a defensive measure. Acknowledging widespread popular opposition to the FTA at home, Mulroney argued that joining the free trade talks between Mexico and the United States is essential to protect Canadian interests. The Canadian government was apparently more concerned about the negative consequences of staying out of a new accord than convinced of the positive effects of becoming part of a North American free trade zone. Because of the increasing resemblance between Mexican and Canadian exports to the United States, the government felt there could be some diversion of U.S. trade away from Canada if it stayed outside the FTA.

The Canadian government thus decided that it would be better to participate as an equal member in the FTA negotiations, rather than to remain as an observer and not be able to defend its interests. As a condition for full participation at the bargaining table, Canada agreed not to slow down the talks.

An Alternative Development and Trade Proposal

In 1990-91 the proposed FTA faced little public opposition in Mexico. In fact there was widespread agreement with the position of the government that economic salvation lay to the north. Even among the incipient opposition to the accord, there existed general acceptance of increased economic integration with the United States. Like FTA opponents in the United States, those in Mexico, however, would like to include a social charter within the final FTA.

The general position of the North American FTA opposition is that trade must be viewed as an instrument for broad development, and that any free trade accord must include a social charter that provides for standards for human rights, environmental protection, and labor rights. The main concern of the PRD opposition party is that the proposed free trade agreement would reduce Mexico to the status of a permanent supplier of cheap labor for the industrialized north.

As the PRD's Cárdenas stated, "The exploitation of cheap labor, energy, and raw materials, technological dependency and lax environmental protection should not be the premises upon which Mexico establishes links with the United States, Canada, and the world economy." Instead Cárdenas called for the creation of a Continental Development and Trade Initiative, which would explicitly recognize Mexico's unequal status and would include a broad social charter. In sharp contrast to the agreement being negotiated, such an initiative would also guarantee labor mobility, giving Mexican workers legal and broad access to the U.S. job market. In addition, Mexico would receive compensatory financing in recognition of the fundamental disparities of the three economies and the fact that the disadvantaged country would have to make more and costlier adjustments to facilitate a free trade environment.[92]

One sign of emerging popular opposition to the FTA in Mexico was the founding in early 1991 of the Mexican Action Network on Free Trade. This coalition of independent unions, environmental groups, and popular organizations expressed their concern that the FTA will subvert national sovereignty. It warned that the FTA is about more than trade but "gives a legal and permanent status to the subordination of national needs to the interests of large corporations and to the neoliberal policies which have already cost our people so much."[93]

The Privatization of the Mexican State

The pervasive presence of the state has been one of the most prominent features of Mexico's post-revolutionary economy. This participation assumed diverse forms, ranging from price controls, protectionist tariffs, and subsidized supply services to direct involvement in productive activities. Dominating of the parastatal economy were the decentralized agencies like Pemex and the Federal Electricity Commission (CFE), although this expansive state-controlled sector also included mixed private and public companies and trust funds.

With the advent of the de la Madrid administration the role of the state in the economy started to shrink. At first the cutbacks in government spending and the shedding of parastatal corporations were mostly austerity measures designed to improve government finances and make it more efficient. Gradually, however, the reduction of the state's economic presence and influence became part of a radical economic restructuring process fueled by neoliberal imperatives.

Deregulation of the internal market and the opening up of the economy's external sector formed part of this restructuring. But it was the privatization of government-owned corporations that provided the most dramatic evidence that the state's function in Mexican society was being reshaped. At issue is the degree of autonomy of the state in its relations with the private sector and its ability to manage the economy in the best interests of the entire society.

By defining certain "strategic" sectors for exclusive state control, the 1917 constitution opened the doors for major government participation in the economy. During the first few decades after the Mexican Revolution, however, state intervention in the economy was more pragmatic than visionary or ideological. The first state corporations (including the Bank of Mexico, the national development bank Nafinsa, and the CFE) emerged as a result of the government's efforts to reconstruct the economy after the many years of armed struggle.[94] The rebuilding of a strong centralized state met little resistance from the business community, which stood to benefit from a stronger state infrastructure of services and finance.

Beginning in the *sexenio* of Lázaro Cárdenas, the government assumed for itself the role of *rector* of the economy. More than simply a guide and regulator of the country's economic development, the state has also been a major actor in many industries. In addition, the government has put its own revenues and institutions at the explicit service of the private sector through the provision of infrastructure and subsidies.

In 1938 the nationalization of the oil industry heightened state intervention in the economy. This bold move also set the stage for the government's central role in the import-substitution industrialization process and the three-decade "miracle" growth of the economy (1940-70). Before 1940 the public sector was largely confined to areas of strategic interest such as transportation, finance, communications, oil, electricity, and various other infrastructure sectors. As the industrialization process unfolded, the public sector expanded, actively promoting the development of national industries (which it subsidized with cheap oil) and taking over bankrupt enterprises.

There was little opposition on the part of Mexican capitalists either to the *rectoría* of the state or to its active participation in the economy. On the contrary a close alliance existed between the private and public sectors during the period from 1940 to 1970. The parastatal sector had increased from 12 firms in 1930 to 57 in 1940, 158 in 1950, 259 in 1960, and 491 by 1970.[95] Cracks in this relationship began to appear under the presidency of Luis Echeverría (1970-76), when the government began to move away from the conservative monetarist economic policies that had guided development since the 1940s.

Until the 1970s the partnership between state and capital had functioned within a corporatist framework that, for the most part, left politics to the ruling party and business to the capitalists.[96] The state's participation in the economy included subsidizing business activity, promoting industrialization, constructing infrastructure, providing credit, and participating directly in certain strategic sectors. Some Mexican presidents were regarded as being more probusiness than others, but there was general agreement that state participation in the economy was good for business.

Under Echeverría state interventionism increased in the belief that an expanded development state would reinforce national sovereignty while increasing economic independence and guaranteeing a more equitable distribution of wealth. The participation of the state in new productive activities and the creation of hundreds of new state enterprises during the 1970s severely strained the state-business alliance. The private-sector elite feared that state policymaking was becoming too autonomous. As a result a new independent business organization called the Businessmen's Coordinating Council (CCE) was formed in 1975, and an important sector of businessmen lent their support to the conservative opposition party, PAN.[97]

The oil boom and the flood of foreign loans into Mexico temporarily allayed these tensions. But López Portillo's inability to manage the economy—as seen in rising inflation, an overvalued *peso*, widening budget deficits, and the debt crisis—fueled a new round of private-sector opposition to the government. This opposition was aggravated by the ever-expanding role of the state in the economy. In fact between 1972 and 1982 the number of majority-owned state enterprises more than tripled.[98] The dramatic decision of López Portillo to nationalize the banks in September 1982 precipitated a new standoff between the state and the capitalist elite.

No longer was the private sector content with a return to the corporatist past; it demanded that the rules of the game be radically revised, to put the business elite in the driver's seat of economic policymaking.[99] As the 1980s progressed, the Mexican business community added its voice to the international chorus calling for the liberalization of the economy. The public sector was blamed for all the country's economic woes. Coparmex (the Mexican Employers Confederation) and other business organizations, together with Washington and other foreign lenders, demanded that state enterprises be privatized.

The tremendous growth of the state since 1960 was at least partly due to the government's acquisition of bankrupt private firms. A 1988 study found that 53 percent of the parastatal firms originated in private-sector bankruptcies.[100] Some critics of privatization say that the program is simply a revolving door that allows the same companies and conglomerates that managed their businesses badly in the 1960s and 1970s to purchase parastatals that have been restored to financial health by the government. According to Gustavo Rodríguez, a high public official during the Echeverría administration, "If you look at the history of parastatals, you see that the sector grew from the bad administration of the private sector, from fraudulent bankruptcies, from a whole series of processes that have made this a country of rich businessmen and poor businesses."[101]

State participation in the economy reached its apex in 1983. Public-sector income accounted for as much as a third of the GDP; public-sector investment accounted for 46 percent of gross capital formation, with state enterprises alone constituting nearly 20 percent of the GDP and 28 percent of gross capital formation.[102] Even these figures do not fully represent the enormity of Mexico's public sector since they do not include subsidies of Conasupo (National Staple Products Company) and other parastatals, nor do they reflect the monopoly status enjoyed by the state in certain sectors. The complete picture of the role of the public sector in the Mexican economy would also have to include an estimate of the impact of price controls, state regulations, and subsidized supplies and services.[103]

Paring Down the State

The public sector has been shrinking since 1983 as state enterprises have been sold off, merged, or dissolved and as the government has cut social services and subsidies. At first the constriction of the public sector was mainly the result of the government's frantic attempts to stabilize state finances in response to the debt crisis and the gaping budget deficit (which reached 17 percent of the GDP in 1982). Although the government recognized the need to modernize state enterprises for the purposes of costcutting and efficiency, it did not initially contemplate privatizing these entities or radically restructuring the state. In fact, de la Madrid reaffirmed the *rectoría* of the state in his inaugural address, declaring that: "To direct the process of development is the fundamental role of the Mexican state. . . . Its obligations in this regard cannot be renounced and are necessary to fulfill the constitutional project of nationalism, plural democracy, and a mixed economy."

It was not until early 1985 that a combination of domestic political troubles, international pressure, and the deepening of the economic crisis obligated the government to begin a process of *descorporación* (literally "disincorporation"). Disincorporation included the dissolution, liquidation, transfer, and sale of public entities.[104] The latter included decentralized agencies, mixed public and private firms, and trust funds controlled by the federal government. By the time Salinas took office, the vague term "disincorporation" had given way to the more accurate term "privatization" to refer to the dismantling of the state economic sector. The sale or liquidation of parastatals continued through the end of the de la Madrid *sexenio*, by which time the government had ordered the privatization or liquidation of nearly 750 parastatals.

Disincorporation Accelerates

President Salinas, who as de la Madrid's planning minister had directed the 1982-88 disincorporation program, brought new vigor to what was now called privatization. Upon assuming the presidency, Salinas announced that he was seeking nothing less than the "redefinition of the role of the state."[105]

More than simply a pragmatic response to the economic crisis, the ideological character of the privatization process under Salinas became clearer. According to the new president, "The postwar orthodoxy in which many of my generation were educated associated more state property with more justice. But in time the overbearing presence of the state ceased to promote growth and gradually became one of the obstacles [to growth]. A bigger state is not a more capable nor a more just state."[106] According to Salinas privatization was the cornerstone of the structural reform whose objective was not "having a state which is larger but, rather, democratically stronger and more efficient."[107]

Pressure to privatize came from the local business elite and from international lenders. Aware that to be successful the privatization process needed wide political backing, Salinas also sought to create a popular base of support for dismantling state enterprises. Suddenly privatization became a "social demand" to which government was responding.[108] Salinas justified his increasingly aggressive privatization program to the public by arguing that state resources are better spent on education and other social services than on the modernization of the phone company or banking system. In his first state of the union address, Salinas presented this new social justification for an expanded disincorporation program. "As the public sector's productive activities grew," he said, "its attention to potable water supply, health, rural investment and food supply, housing, the environment, and justice decreased."

In 1990 Salinas responded to mounting criticism that disincorporation affected only small and relatively unimportant enterprises by announcing the privatization of the national banking system and the national phone company (Telmex). These two measures sent a clear message to the international financial community and foreign investors that Mexico was indeed serious about privatization. It also demonstrated that even sectors previously regarded as untouchable or "strategic" would not necessarily remain exempt from privatization. Unlike some other state enterprises that had been privatized, both the telecommunications company and the banking system were highly profitable ventures.[109] But both needed large injections of capital for modernization. Lacking this investment capital, the government decided to privatize its interests and thereby raise billions of dollars for its cash-starved treasury.[110]

In the first three years of the Salinas administration, privatization went further and faster than most observers originally believed possible.[111] Besides the national banking system and Telmex, Salinas ordered the privatization of the highly profitable companies in the steel, mining, and airline industries. By mid-1991 the state was left with about 260 firms, down from the 1,155 it controlled in 1982.[112] Plans were under way to sell off as many as a hundred or more additional parastatals.[113] Excluding the ongoing bank privatization, the Salinas government brought $5.5 billion into state coffers from privatization deals in its first two and one-half years.

In the 1985-91 period the participation of the federal government had been eliminated in 26 areas of economic activity.[114] The government insisted that privatization did have limits, however, and that it had no intention of selling off Pemex, the electricity company, the railroads, or the social-security institutes.[115] The government promised to retain control of eleven "strategic" industries as well as institutions in such social sectors as education, health, and regional development.[116] But seeing how far the privatizing zeal of Salinas already pushed the privatization process, even these symbols of the Mexican state might eventually be sold to the highest bidder or dismantled.

The streamlining of the public sector, while appreciated by the private sector and improving government short-term finances, has not been entirely positive for the country's economic stability. In the last half of the 1980s more than 110,000 jobs were lost because of austerity measures at the four largest public enterprises.[117] And the government repeatedly demonstrated its readiness to use privatization or the threat of privatization to break unions. In the cases of Fundidora Monterrey, the Cananea copper mine, and Aeroméxico, the government declared the firms bankrupt and subject to liquidation, thereby canceling existing labor contracts and making the firms more attractive to private buyers.[118]

Private-sector investment did not compensate for public-sector cutbacks, meaning that those dropped from the government payroll generally entered the expanding ranks of the unemployed. Neither did new private investment made up for declining public-sector investment. The sharp drop in public-sector capital formation raised concerns among such private-sector organizations as the Confederation of Industrial Chambers (Concamin), which blamed declining public-sector investment for economic stagnation, decapitalization, and the decline of living standards.[119] Concamin and other business organizations complained that government borrowing was not being used for capital formation but rather to cover debt payments and budget deficits. At the same time that the private sector called for an accelerated rate of privatization, it advocated increased capital investment by the public sector as a way to push the economy forward.

The Size and Nature of the Public Sector

Public-sector participation in the GDP had climbed from 15 percent in 1975 to as much as 25 percent in 1983, not counting oil revenues. Since then the government's presence in the economy has been on a steady decline, dropping to 17 percent by 1990.[120] Changes in the composition of the external sector also indicated rising private-sector participation in the economy.

In 1990 private enterprise accounted for 85 percent of all import spending (up from 60 percent in 1981) and 60 percent of exports (up from 18 percent in 1981). In 1990 the private sector supplied 80 percent of the employment and 75 percent of production in Mexico.[121] For the same year, private-sector investment represented 72 percent of total investment, with the public sector accounting for the balance.[122]

The privatization of state enterprises formed one part of the government's program to promote private business. Other measures included the withdrawing of state monopoly rights to such sectors as the paper industry, communications, and road construction. In addition the state deregulated agricultural commodities, petrochemicals, and trucking. While applauding these market-oriented reforms, rightwing critics charged that Salinas did not go far enough to rid Mexico of the development state and open the way for a totally market-based economy.[123] They lobbied for the substantial modification of Articles 25 through 28 of the constitution, which define the state's role in "strategic" and "primary" industries. Also enshrined in the constitution is the concept of *rectoría*, which obligates the state to "plan, conduct, coordinate, and orient all national economic activity."

State-run firms received nearly $3.3 billion in government subsidies in 1990. More than 90 percent of these subsidies were concentrated in just five companies: the National Staple Products Company (Conasupo), the Federal Electricity Commission (CFE), the Mexican Institute of Social Security (IMSS), the Mexican National Railroads (Ferronales), and the Mexican Fertilizer Company (Fertimex). It would be unfair, however, to call state enterprises inefficient simply because they are not profitable and drain the government's budget. Conasupo was established not to make a profit but to distribute food at subsidized prices to the poor and to buy from small farmers at guaranteed prices. Similarly the electricity company has a history of extending electric wires into rural areas, not because it is profitable but as a public service.

Privatization and the Concentration of Capital

When López Portillo nationalized the banking system, during the final days of his administration, the already rocky public-private partnership fell apart. Both Echeverría and López Portillo had tried at various phases of their administrations to restore private-sector confidence in the government, but their populist rhetoric and failure to rein in the public sector alienated and frustrated members of the business community. Beginning with the austerity measures undertaken at the start of the de la Madrid administration, the public-private partnership was gradually renewed after 1982. It was the government's ad hoc adoption of neoliberalism in the last half of the decade, however, that cemented the relationship. Suddenly the private sector was thrust into center stage in the reworking of the Mexican economy.

Mexico of course never was the socialist state that its rightwing critics claimed. Soon after the revolution the state began fostering the development and reconstitution of the national bourgeoisie, and Mexican capitalists came to rely on the collaboration of the government in their drive for capital accumulation. The conflicts that did arise mainly resulted from the government's attempts to maintain political stability by responding to the demands of the country's workers and peasants. What is different today is that the government has largely assumed the logic of the private sector in defining the good of the entire population in terms of what benefits business.

Obviously privatization bolsters the private sector. The main problem here is not that state assets are being privatized, but that this wealth is contributing to a dangerous concentration of capital. Within Mexico the privatization program has come under increasing criticism for its tendency to reinforce the power of the major capitalist groups. For the most part the only bidders for state enterprises on the auction block have been the country's huge conglomerates.[124] Privatization allowed private purchasers to gain dominant or monopoly control in the following industries: copper, soft drinks, sugar and syrups, transport services, buses, diesel motors, trucks, appliance manufacturing, lumber and paper, and telecommunications.[125] As of mid-1991 just 17 enterprises and individuals had purchased 96 companies sold to the private sector.[126]

Of major concern to those following decreasing state autonomy in economic decisionmaking is the sale of the national banking system, which will inevitably bolster the already considerable power of the country's major investment groups and create new financial oligopolies.[127] After the banks were nationalized the government allowed 34 percent of their stock to be returned to private owners. A 1990 constitutional amendment deleted reference to banking services among the strategic sectors, thus paving the way for the complete reprivatization of the 18 state-owned banks.[128]

Both the left and the right criticized the privatization process for furthering "crony capitalism" in Mexico. Several of the largest companies, such as the Cananea copper mine, were sold behind closed doors to those close to the PRI elite rather than to the highest bidder. A precedent for these secret sales was set in 1987 when minority shares in the nation's banks were sold to a select clientele in an arrangement that one analyst called "high-tech political patronage."[129]

Critics charged that the government was not pursuing its privatization program to "democratize" capital and promote "popular capitalism," as it claimed. The Salinas government could have done this by promoting more stock offerings or by transferring at least partial ownership to company workers. Small business owners and investors complained that the government should give them more opportunity to acquire state property. For the most part the Salinas administration preferred to ignore these criticisms, making it clear that its true priority was to make Mexican business competitive, not to make it more democratic—despite all the official rhetoric linking privatization and democratization.[130] In his first annual report, Salinas put it clearly: "In today's competitive world, what are required are great consortia that can face the great multinationals."

Privatization also opened the door for expanded foreign control over the Mexican economy.[131] The domestic private sector, while eager to snap up state assets, does not have the capital needed for the modernization of many of the industries being privatized. Foreign capital will be used to upgrade the privatized telecommunications, mining, and banking sectors. Initially, at least, foreign ownership in Mexico's banks will be limited to 30 percent (10 percent for individuals). It is expected that Washington will use the FTA negotiations to exert increased pressure for a wider opening for foreign investment in the banking sector.[132]

But Salinas argued that the domestic banking industry needed more time before it will be ready to compete with international banks. It is feared that if the banking sector is completely liberalized it will be dominated by such banks as Citibank and Bank of America. There was growing concern in Mexico that privatization, particularly when it involves the largest parastatals, constituted a national giveaway program allowing foreign investors to increase their stake in the economy at fire-sale prices.

In the end, the promised benefits of the privatization program will have to be weighed against the likely dangers of dismantling the state corporations. The possible benefits included increased efficiency, reduced state control, increased private-sector investment, a short-term injection of funds, more government money for social services, and smaller budget deficits.

Among the hazards of privatization are increased concentration of private wealth, increased foreign control, and reduced government ability to manage the economy for the common good. Although privatization injected large sums of sale revenues into the government budget, the absence of many parastatals will increasingly deprive the state of annual revenues and force the government to raise taxes. Privatization constituted an assault upon the remaining populist and nationalist dimensions of the Mexican state. Without the framework of a parastatal sector, particularly in strategic industries, the government's ability to ensure that economic development results in equitable wealth distribution and improved social welfare is much reduced.[133]

Even when considering Mexico's long-term economic growth, the wholesale dismantling of the public sector represents certain dangers. In the past the state played a critical role in fostering private capital accumulation, building key industries, and providing the supplies and services needed for industrialization and economic modernization. Taken in that context it would be hard to measure the efficiency and productivity of the parastatals by typical profit/loss accounting. After all, Mexican industries and agribusinesses have grown rich from cheap electricity, oil, fertilizer, irrigation, and credit provided by state-owned enterprises.[134]

The facile "let the market do it" philosophy so prevalent in policymaking circles remains essentially untested in Mexico. And there is little evidence in the country's history to suggest that its private sector—accustomed to high profit levels, risk-free investments, and high levels of government protection—will be capable of providing the catalytic development role Mexico needs.[135] Finally, it will have to be the Mexican people themselves who will have to judge whether privatization has made their phones work any better, sparked economic development, or improved their standard of living.

Mixed Economic Prospects

By 1989 the Mexican economy had turned around according to most economic indicators. After a long period of negative economic growth (1983-88), the economy enjoyed three years of positive per capita growth. Finally *la crisis* seemed to be over, at least in the view of most economic analysts.

This apparently bright economic picture sparked a mood change among domestic capitalists, foreign investors, and international creditors, who greeted the country's radical economic restructuring with effusive praise. Because of his commitment to economic liberalization, President Salinas has been called the "Margaret Thatcher of Mexico." The IMF's managing director called Mexico a "lighthouse" on the debt issue and "an example to the world" for its economic management.[136] Although support for the Salinas administration was stronger outside Mexico, the neoliberal reformers of the Salinas government also counted on the enthusiastic backing of the country's own capitalist elite and considerable popular support as well.

Nevertheless, the government's economic program was not entirely on track by midterm in the Salinas *sexenio*. The major issues and concerns about the Mexican economy included the following:

Trade Balance: Economic stabilization measures, particularly austerity measures and major currency devaluations, contributed to trade surpluses from 1982 to 1988, but after 1989 Mexico suffered from expanding trade deficits. The deficit was projected to rise to $8-10 billion in 1991. The problem was not that exports stagnated, but that imports rose much faster than exports.[137] As the growth rate of exports slowed, import growth has accelerated.

Export Promotion: The government's entire economic development strategy was premised on the growth of consumer demand in the United States and rising Mexican exports to satisfy that demand. A stagnating U.S. economy depressed these hopes, and Mexico found that it faced stiff competition from the Asian nations and other countries turning to export-led development. Moreover the country's need to import most of the inputs for export production and the control of this sector by foreign investors undermined the benefits of increased Mexican exports.

Foreign Investment: The flow of foreign capital to Mexico since June 1988, although higher than traditional rates, fell considerably short of government projections. The relative lack of direct investment in productive activities and the disproportionate investment in financial and commercial services reduced the impact of this new foreign investment. Instead of expanding business, foreign investment often bought into pre-existing enterprises through debt swaps and privatization deals. Although increased foreign investment is critical to government stabilization and growth projections, critics of the focus on attracting foreign investors charged that the Mexican economy is being denationalized.

Capital Formation: Between 1983 and 1988 gross investment fell an average of more than 4 percent annually. Private-sector investment rose sharply after 1988 but not enough to compensate for reduced public-sector investment. Investment has for the last few years stood at 17-19 percent of the GDP. Although a major improvement, this rate of capital formation still fell short of the government's goal of 26 percent. One problem has been that repatriated flight capital went mostly into short-term and high-yield bank deposits and government debt instruments rather than into productive investments.

Economic Growth: During the period from 1983 to 1988 Mexico experienced zero economic growth. Since then Mexico has experienced slightly positive per capita growth, and the government projected a 6-percent economic growth rate by 1994. Although an important step forward, recent growth rates of 3-4 percent were only narrowly above the rate of population increase. Substantially higher rates of growth will be needed if the economy is to recover the per capita income levels seen before the crisis broke out in 1982.

Sectoral Growth: The contribution of the productive sectors (manufacturing, agriculture, and mining) has steadily dropped as a percentage of the GDP, while the contribution of all types of services has risen sharply in recent years. The startling growth of the informal sector, which employs more than a fifth of the work force, was the most striking example of this increase in the service economy, although other service sectors such as banking, real estate, and tourism were also expanding faster than the productive sectors.

Agriculture: Since the 1960s the agricultural sector has taken a back seat to industrialization. Consistent with this history, the health of the country's agricultural economy and its rural population were adversely affected by Salinas's restructuring of the economy. As a result of the government's export-oriented policies, the food-crop sector was increasingly unable to satisfy domestic food needs. Falling per capita production of basic foodstuffs was the major reason for increasing food imports—led by maize, soybeans, and milk—and contributed to the country's increasing agricultural trade imbalance. Exports have proved unable to outdistance increasing imports, as the government had hoped.

Manufacturing: Although manufactured exports have increased steadily since 1983, the sector remains unbalanced. Only about 15 percent of the manufacturing industry was internationally competitive, and in 1990 it suffered an $8 billion deficit—the largest since 1982. Trade liberalization forced many manufacturers out of business, and reduced consumer demand has meant that large factories are operating at 70 percent of capacity, while small- and medium-size plants are functioning at less than 50 percent of capacity.

Domestic Market: The country's own market received scant attention from the government's economic planners. With the main concern being to promote exports and attract foreign investors, farmers and manufacturers producing for Mexican consumption face hard times. The government's policy of restraining wages to combat inflation and to keep exports cheap meant that consumption of even the most basic goods declined. The government has rejected the strategy of demand stimulus to revive the domestic market and reverse the country's deteriorating social conditions. Since there existed little linkage between the export sector and domestic production (most inputs being imported), the prospects for trickle-down growth of the domestic sector appeared grim. Basically, the government was telling domestic producers that to survive they had to match both the efficiency and the low cost of the international market—meaning competing against industrial technology and the most depressed wage rates of the underdeveloped world.

Infrastructure Deficiencies: A poor transportation network has constituted a major obstacle to the kind of "take-off" of economic development Mexico seeks. Railroads remain in poor condition and undependable. Similarly, the nation's highway grid is poorly maintained and needs to be greatly expanded. There has been a critical shortage of maritime transport, with Mexico servicing less than 10 percent of its maritime trade.[138] To improve its roads, rail system, and ports, the government sought joint ventures with private investors.

Debt Crisis: The 1989-90 restructuring of the external debt alleviated the crisis but did not solve it. The external debt was once again rising rapidly, the result of increased external borrowing. Of at least equal concern was the $57 billion internal debt that because of high interest rates kept domestic debt-service payments at approximately the same level of the external debt-servicing costs. Payments to internal creditors drained the treasury of some $12 billion a year in the 1989-91 period.

Public-Sector Budget Deficits: The government made great strides in reducing its financial deficit, down to 3.5 percent in 1990 and a projected 1.9 percent in 1991, from 17 percent in 1982. By clamping down on tax evasion and broadening the tax base, the government increased its revenues while austerity measures cut expenditures. The biggest drain on the federal budget was debt service, with combined payments on external and domestic debt representing 45 percent of all expenditures. The government's financial deficit, especially when interest payments are included in the calculations, was still larger than such international creditors as the IMF and World Bank recommend, since the federal government continued to depend on extensive borrowing. The government persisted in its attempts to reduce its borrowing requirement through new austerity measures, elimination of consumer subsidies, and new rounds of price increases for public utilities and basic food goods. But these financial reforms only contributed to the further impoverishment of the Mexican population and the further constriction of the domestic consumer market.

Privatization: The government's privatization program moved rapidly to transfer state enterprises to the private sector. The program was justified to the Mexican people as an effort to direct state resources toward social services rather than toward the modernization of state corporations. In fact the income from liquidating and selling parastatal firms went to pay the government's foreign and domestic debt more than to increase social welfare. Some likened the privatization of profitable enterprises such as the banks and Telmex to selling the family jewels to pay off a debt incurred by a family member.[139] Critics argued that by selling these profitable firms the government lost a steady source of revenue while reducing its ability to regulate the economy for the common good. Thus far the privatization program has not sparked much organized popular opposition. If the government should extend privatization to such "strategic" sectors as Pemex (the Mexican Petroleum Company) and the CFE, the political risks of the program may become more apparent.

Inflation: A low rate of inflation in line with that of Mexico's major trading partners, mainly the United States, is essential for long-term economic stability. But inflation rates of 20 percent or more continue to undermine the government's economic-stabilization program. The fear is that inflation would rapidly rise again if wage and price controls are eliminated.

Exchange Rate Fluctuation: With a regularly paced devaluation of the *peso*, Mexico sought to restore confidence in the national currency. Its stated objective was to stabilize the *peso* with the dollar once the economy had fully recovered. But as inflation caused havoc with real wages and domestic prices, the government faced pressure to slow down or freeze the pace of devaluation. There is growing concern among export-oriented businesses, however, that the *peso* is becoming overvalued, thereby slowing the growth of exports. A major devaluation could boost exports, but it would also exert inflationary pressure and likely increase political discontent. As long as the country enjoys a surplus in capital accounts, a major devaluation will likely be postponed.

Uneasy Social Pact: The social pact between government, business, and labor unions had been extended three times since it was first concluded in 1987.

Inflation dropped from the 100-160 percent rates that plagued the de la Madrid government as a result of wage and price freezes but nonetheless continued to be a major economic concern. Fear of uncontrolled inflation and currency speculation kept the social pact in force through December 1991, and will likely serve as justification for continued repression of wage demands. The mainstay of the social pact has been strict wage controls, while the price freeze has been less strictly enforced. Consequently, the poor and working class were hardest hit by the successive agreements. Although the pacts supposedly included labor, they represented the official labor confederation and not independent unions or poor peoples' organizations.

Employment: The economy is expanding, but not fast enough to supply employment to all the one million Mexicans entering the work force every year. This work force is increasing at an average rate of 3.5 percent, substantially higher than the birth rate. Official unemployment declined from the height of the crisis, but underemployment and participation in the informal sector markedly increased. Especially serious was the labor situation in rural areas, where nearly 50 percent of the work force has remained unemployed or underemployed.

Concentration of Wealth: Based on long experience of high economic growth rates, it has become a truism in Mexico that economic growth does not necessarily translate into improved social welfare. The economic elite and a small but growing middle class were always the prime beneficiaries of economic growth. In the past, however, the lower classes did see small socioeconomic gains as a result of their own struggles and because of the corporatist nature of the Mexican state. In recent years, wealth has become increasingly concentrated in Mexico. Corporatist labor and peasant organizations no longer even minimally defend the interests of their constituencies, and the government's neoliberal policies tend to concentrate wealth within the elite business community and among foreign investors. One telling indicator of the increasingly skewed distribution of income was that real wages dropped at least 50 percent during the 1980s, while per capita income fell 12 percent— meaning that wage earners saw their incomes drop 4 times as fast as the general rate of economic decline. If the Mexican economy is to stabilize and develop over the long term, it is generally agreed that income must be more broadly distributed and the relative decline of wages reversed.

Internationalization of Capital: With the transborder flow of capital more rapid and mobile than ever before, the Mexican government faced increasing obstacles to regulating and directing its own financial wealth. Channeling capital and credit into broad national development plans, long-range industrial development, and job-creation projects became more difficult. Seeing the possibilities of populist, nationalist, and socialist economic-development strategies narrowed by global capital integration, the adoption of neoliberal reforms appeared to be the most expedient solution to the country's economic crisis.

Free Trade Agreement: Even before free trade negotiations began with the United States, Mexico was well on its way toward liberalizing most aspects of its economic life. A free trade accord will reinforce the neoliberal restructuring previously undertaken and deepen the already heavy dependence on the U.S. market. Like other liberalization initiatives, an FTA is a gamble that the private sector, both domestic and foreign, will pull the nation out of economic crisis and place it firmly among the ranks of the newly industrializing nations. The obvious danger is that asymmetry of international trade will serve to maintain Mexico as a provider of cheap labor and transform it into an appendage of the U.S. economy. By giving private capital new privileges and prominence, further trade liberalization will leave large sectors of the population out of the development process. A final danger is that free trade and liberalization will be seen as a panacea for the country's economic ills and an excuse for not formulating coherent industrial and agricultural strategies for Mexico's large domestic market.

Structure of the Economy

Mexico, the world's 11th most populated country and the 13th largest in land area, ranks 15th in the size of its gross domestic product (GDP). It has the second largest economy in Latin America after Brazil. Mexico's economic size places it among what are variously called intermediate, middle-income, or advanced developing nations. In 1990 its GDP stood at $238 billion, with a per capita GDP of $2,938.

Extractive or primary industries, including agriculture and mining, represent a declining percentage of the GDP. In the 1950s those sectors accounted for nearly a quarter of the GDP, but in 1990 constituted about 11 percent. Manufacturing, which accounted for 18 percent of the national product in the 1950s, rose to a nearly 25 percent share in the 1980s. The largest economic sectors are commerce, including restaurants and hotels, and services (Table 2i).

Worker productivity—measuring total sectoral employment against total output—is lowest in the agricultural sector, which except for services is the largest source of employment in Mexico. Productivity in the manufacturing sector, which employs about half as much as agriculture, is about 5 times higher than that of the farm sector. Worker output is highest in mining and financial sectors.[1]

There exist sharp regional differences in the concentration of economic activity in Mexico. The Federal District alone accounts for 27 percent of the GDP, and the state of Mexico for another 11 percent. Among the other most important states economically are Jalisco, Nuevo León, and Veracruz, each of which accounts for more than a 5-percent share of the nation's GDP.[2] Also striking are the wide differences between the states of the northern border region (including Baja California, Sonora, Chihuahua, Coahuila, Nuevo León, and Tamaulipas) and those of the southeast (Campeche, Chiapas, Oaxaca, Quintana Roo, Tabasco, and Yucatán). The number of workers per business in the northern states is 7 times higher than that in the southeastern states. In the southeastern states 55 percent of the population is rural and 70 percent lack electricity and sewage services. In contrast, 75 percent of the population in the northern border states is urban and 30 percent lack basic services.[3]

During the 1980s Mexico experienced major changes in its economic structure. Between 1981 and 1989 per capita income fell at an average annual rate of more than 1 percent. During the same period the value of exports rose at an annual rate of 7 percent. Most of this export growth was in the manufacturing sector, which increased its share of export income from 21 percent in 1981 to 49 percent by 1990. Productivity in the manufacturing sector increased by 30 percent during the 1980s, while the costs of labor dropped by nearly 30 percent, mainly because of declining wages. The rise in manufacturing exports has not been reflected in an increase in employment in that sector, which had 15 percent fewer workers by the decade's end. Export growth is led by the country's largest firms, mainly subsidiaries of foreign corporations.[4]

Large firms dominate the manufacturing sector in terms of contribution to the GDP and the country's export income, but those firms that employ fewer than 250 workers (the micro-, small-, and medium-scale industries) represent a full 98 percent of Mexico's total number of manufacturing companies. Despite their numbers, these businesses account for only about half of manufacturing employment and less than 40 percent of the sector's contribution to the GDP.[5]

Since the early 1980s government economic policy has increasingly focused on those industries and sectors capable of increasing exports and for-

Table 2i

Mexico: Leading Economic Sectors, 1990

Commerce, Restaurants, Hotels 25.5%

Financial Services 27.9%

Manufacturing 22.6%

Agriculture 7.4%

Transportation, Communications 6.6%

Mining 3.5%

Electricity 1.4%

Construction 5.1%

SOURCE: Department of State, *Foreign Investment Climate Statement*, August 16, 1991.

eign exchange earnings. Most important in this regard are the oil, *maquiladora*, automotive, and tourism industries. Outside the *maquila* plants, the automotive industry is the leading source of export earnings in the manufacturing sector. This chapter examines these leading industries, along with the mining and agricultural sectors.

Pemex and the Oil Industry

When Mexican motorists buy their gas, there is only one brand and one price. Since 1938 the government has controlled all aspects of the country's petroleum industry—from exploration and production to refining and distribution. Frustrated by the arrogance and profiteering of the U.S. and British oil companies, President Lázaro Cárdenas nationalized their operations on March 18, 1938. Cárdenas was immediately promoted to the pantheon of national heros, and Mexicans still celebrate March 18 as a "day of national dignity."

Today Mexico's oil industry is not only a major player in the nation's economy but also a prime source of government revenues. Petróleos Mexicanos (Pemex), the state-owned enterprise that emerged from the 17 expropriated companies, is the world's fourth largest petroleum company and the largest corporation in Latin America.[6] Pemex has 50 percent more sales than the country's six most important private corporations combined. Known as the government's "cash cow," as much as 60 percent of the income from Pemex is turned over to the government in the form of fees and taxes, which account for about a third of the federal government's budgetary receipts.[7] Oil and gas sales represent about one-third of Mexico's export income.[8]

Since its nationalization more than 50 years ago the oil industry has been a key factor in the country's economic development. In 1990 Pemex operations accounted for 13 percent of the country's GDP. Providing oil at subsidized prices, the oil giant, whose motto is "At the service of the nation," fueled Mexico's industrial development. At first the new state enterprise was unable to match the production levels of the foreign firms, but it soon proved capable of meeting the expanding economy's demand for petroleum. Throughout the third world the Mexican government's strategic use of this state enterprise to boost economic expansion was seen as a model for state-led development.

Since the 1970s, however, the Mexican oil industry has alternated between periods of boom and crisis. The first crisis came in the early 1970s when oil production fell short of domestic needs. From 1971 to 1974 Mexico became a net importer of petroleum for the first time since the revolution. Forced to import oil, Mexico also began increasing exploration operations, resulting in the discovery of the Tabasco-Chiapas fields in 1972 and the Campeche reserves in 1976. By the end of the decade production had increased 6 times. Not only did Mexico suddenly enjoy vastly expanded oil reserves, it also was benefiting from rising world oil prices. By 1980 more than 75 percent of the country's export revenue came from the sale of this one commodity. But the boom was short-lived. Prices began sliding in 1981 and then crashed in 1986, falling from $33 a barrel in 1981 to $12 a barrel in 1986.

After the frantic push to expand production and exports during the 1970s, the 1980s were a period of stagnation. Squeezed by the external debt, the government was unable to spend the money Pemex needed to increase exploration and drilling and to recapitalize its industrial plant.[9] Instead, oil revenues were used for debt payments and to pay the government's operating expenses.

With domestic demand increasing, production declining, and reserves dwindling, the need to expand exploration and production operations became increasingly urgent. Experts predicted that if current consumption rates continued without the discovery of new reserves or major new investment in the industry, Mexico would be forced to begin importing as early as the late 1990s.[10] The Salinas administration promised to capitalize Pemex to head off this crisis. Cash-poor itself, the government sought out private capital—both domestic and foreign—to finance new exploration, production, and refining operations. The president ruled out equity participation in the industry, however, something that foreign investors and Washington are advocating as the only long-term solution to the country's capital-short and technology-dependent oil industry.

The lack of capital has not been the only problem facing Pemex. One of the world's largest firms, it has also been one of the least efficient. So embarrassingly high are its production costs that Pemex has refused to reveal what it costs to produce one barrel of crude oil. A corrupt union and the absence of cost accounting have contributed to the company's weak financial state. The arrest and ouster of union chief Joaquín Hernández Galicia ("La Quina") curtailed the union's power, allowing the government to begin slashing the Pemex payroll. New management that instituted standard accounting practices and a degree of market discipline have also strengthened the financial position of Pemex. According to Pemex chairman Francisco Rojas, "Pemex has had the hard task of functioning as an integrated oil company and an instrument of the government's economic policy."[11]

The old strategy of producing refined oil for the domestic market and exporting crude clearly needs revision. "Pemex has failed to become a modern and aggressive trading agent in world markets commensurate with the size of its oil reserves [and] its assets," observed Mexican analyst Gabriel Székely.[12] Like development, modernization presupposes capital and technology—both of which Mexico sorely lacks but which foreign investors and creditors are eager to provide.[13]

By midterm in the Salinas administration the Mexican government was clearly interested in increased foreign participation in the oil industry, but it balked at opening up the sector to direct foreign investment in production. Declining to offer the risk contracts that many foreign investors wanted, the government did allow foreign companies to assume a major role in exploration and refining. By securing new foreign financing from the export-import banks of the United States, Japan, and Canada, Pemex plans to increase its service contracts with foreign firms from those countries. Two early cases of this in 1991 were a drilling contract with Triton Industries of Houston and a contract with Diamond Shamrock for the construction of an oil refinery.

Few Energy Alternatives

Other than petroleum, Mexico is energy poor. During the 1980s only 1.5 percent of the country's energy needs came from coal, 3.5 percent from hydroelectric and geothermal power, and less than 5 percent from firewood. The balance was generated from crude oil and gas supplied by Pemex. In Mexico, natural gas production is largely ancillary to crude oil exploration and production. Only 15 percent of the country's natural gas comes from nonassociated wells. Rather than being gathered for productive use, most natural gas is flared in Mexico, although this practice is changing. After declining from 1982 to 1986, natural gas production is currently increasing, albeit at a slow rate. Because production increases are falling far short of rising consumer demand, imports of natural gas, mainly from Texas, have been increasing rapidly. Not only is imported natural gas often less expensive than domestically produced fuel, it is also cleaner. With natural gas imports in 1991 more than 6 times those of 1990, Pemex is seeking to develop its own gas fields in the country's southeast and north.

The country's electricity sector has faced its own problems. More than 90 percent of the country's electricity is supplied by the Federal Electricity Commission (CFE). To avoid the electricity shortfalls projected for the near future, the CFE in 1991 began discussions with the U.S. Department of Energy to open up Mexico to foreign investment in the construction and operation of electricity generation plants. Popular opposition, as well as technical and financial obstacles, delayed operations at the nuclear power station at Laguna Verde in the state of Veracruz. When the plant finally began to generate electricity commercially in 1990, it was 14 years behind schedule. Continuing protests by a strong antinuclear coalition led by the National Coordinator against Laguna Verde (Conclave) and serious technical difficulties jeopardize the profitable operation of this controversial power plant.[14]

Proven petroleum reserves are estimated at 65 billion barrels, down from 72 billion barrels in 1983.[15] Mexico's reserves are the seventh largest in the world. Pemex has a refining capacity of 1.5 million barrels per day, but its lack of capital has meant that Mexico is now forced to import refined products to meet domestic demand. In coming years the country's crude oil exports are expected to drop steadily as domestic demand increases due to population and economic growth.[16] Not only is Pemex financially strapped but it also lacks the necessary technology and equipment needed to drill in the oil-rich Bay of Campeche.[17] Pemex has begun mapping plans for a second oil boom fueled by increased exploration. Lacking the capital to do it alone, the state oil company has negotiated new foreign loans and opened up the business to private companies.

The government is seeking $15-20 billion in the next several years for the oil industry. Critics fear that the ambitious development program announced by the government will result in increased dependency on the United States as a result of new foreign investment in the oil industry and heavy foreign borrowing by Pemex. Besides renewed oil exploration, the Mexican government would like to meet increasing domestic demand for energy (expected to rise by a third between 1988 and 1994) through expanded use of other energy sources, mainly coal, and through increased efficiency and conservation.

The business of exporting Mexican energy reserves has long been at the heart of the debate about the future of the country's petroleum industry. Oil is emotion in Mexico, observed one international petroleum expert.[18] In the 1960s vehement opposition arose—mainly from the intellectual and leftist communities—over plans to build a pipeline to export natural gas to the United States. Critics argued that Mexico should retain its reserves for future use. To ensure that Mexico would not become dependent on one foreign market, the government in 1980 stipulated that no more than 50 percent of its exports would go to any one country.

Mexico regularly exports about half of its production, with an increasing percentage going to the United States.[19] At first, exports to the United States dropped from 70 percent to 50 percent of the total export offering. In violation of its own guidelines, approximately 60 percent of the country's exports now go to the United States.[20] The willingness of the government to increase exports during the Persian Gulf crisis raised new concerns in Mexico that the country's oil industry was at the service of Washington.[21] It also underscored the country's position as a stable and close source of crude oil for the United States.[22] As Mexico begins to incur new foreign debt to boost production, the country will come under new pressure to increase exports, particularly to the United States, which is the principal source of the new funds.

Pemex for Sale

The gap between the government's rhetoric and its actions was stretched new distances in 1990-91 as the government began gradually opening the oil industry to private investors and financiers while at the same time proclaiming that the national patrimony of oil resources would neither be privatized nor included in the free trade negotiations. But government initiatives to attract foreign capital have belied its nationalistic rhetoric.

Setting the stage for the gradual dismantling of Pemex was the decapitalization of the company beginning with the 1981-82 financial crisis. During the 1980s the government, desperate for cash to meet its debt payments and cover fiscal deficits, drained Pemex of the capital necessary to increase exploration and production operations.

The Salinas government has insisted that it will abide by Article 27 of the national constitution, which makes the state the owner of the country's petroleum resources. But rather than openly contravening the constitution by inviting foreign investors to participate in oil production, the government has been opening the doors wider to increased foreign participation in drilling, refining, transportation, distribution, and petrochemical production. Also being negotiated with foreign partners are loans, credit guarantees, commercial transactions, and economic-aid agreements that will greatly increase foreign involvement in Mexico's oil industry.

One of the first signs of the changes under way was the creation in 1987 of Pemex-associated holding companies that would include private capital and would administer the company's international operations.[23] As the dismemberment of Pemex proceeds through the 1990s, it is likely that Pemex will be divided into affiliated subsidiary corporations, which will facilitate the privatization process while allowing a core company to remain in state hands.

The crushing of the powerful Petroleum Workers Union of the Mexican Republic (STPRM) in 1989 by the newly inaugurated Salinas may also have been related to PRI's long-term intentions to reduce state control of the oil industry. After jailing the corrupt union patriarch whose power base challenged PRI's leadership, the government installed union leaders it could manipulate and who would not have the power to block government plans to trim and privatize Pemex.[24]

It is unclear to what extent Mexico's oil industry will be included in a free trade agreement with the country's two northern neighbors. Publicly, U.S. trade negotiators have declared that Washington will not insist on any agreement that violates the Mexican constitution, and the Salinas government has repeatedly insisted that economic integration will not extend as far as Pemex.

As talk of free trade continues, however, the debate over the inclusion of Pemex has intensified. In the United States, pressure has mounted within the business community to further open up Mexico's oil and petrochemical industry to U.S. investment. Representatives of U.S. chemical companies have even suggested that U.S. trade negotiators insist that new foreign investment in Mexican petrochemical production be exclusively from Canada and the United States. California oilmen let it be known that they were not interested in "drill for hire" accords but wanted a piece of the pie—what they call risk contracts. And Dow Chemical officials asserted that they would oppose a free trade agreement if further guarantees for foreign investment in the petrochemical industry were not included.[25]

Clearly, the United States is interested in opening up Mexico's oil industry to U.S. investors and in winning new assurances that the United States will enjoy favored access to the country's sizable reserves. But the pressure to privatize Pemex is not all one-sided. To pursue its stabilization and modernization plans, the Salinas government recognizes that it needs to open up the oil industry to the flow of foreign capital.[26] Whether or not Mexico's oil industry is specifically included in a free trade agreement will probably have more to do with the political sensitivity of the issue than with the real intentions of the two countries. Meanwhile, the Mexican government is searching for innovative ways to skirt constitutional restrictions on foreign involvement.[27]

Petrochemicals Go Private

It was not until the late 1950s that the government took steps to develop a domestic petrochemicals industry.[28] By instructing Pemex to invest in petrochemical production the country successfully sought to reduce chemical imports. The new petrochemicals industry was also able to contribute to the country's broader industrialization strategy through the subsidized production of such petrochemicals as ethylene and benzene. Mexico today is a major petrochemicals producer—the 15th largest in the world—but even so suffers from a widening trade deficit in petrochemicals.[29] Thirty percent of the basic chemicals used by domestic industries are imported. The United States supplies more than 90 percent of its imported natural gas and nearly half of its imported refined petroleum products.[30]

Although a major petrochemicals industry was created, the industry failed to develop a competitive edge in the international market because it focused too narrowly on meeting domestic demand. State control over the industry also resulted in inefficient production and distribution practices. The lack of government investment in the industry since the early 1980s further debilitated petrochemical production in Mexico. The industry's research arm, the Mexican Petroleum Institute, has been unable to compete with the technology, engineering, and research capacity of foreign firms. As a result, the petrochemicals industry, like the entire petroleum sector, has become ever more dependent on foreign technology.

Until recently, petrochemical production was strictly regulated. Pemex has maintained a monopoly over what the government has called "basic" petrochemicals, while production of "secondary" petrochemicals has required state permits and has restricted foreign ownership to 40 percent. All petrochemicals not included in these two categories are unregulated and therefore open to 100 percent private and foreign ownership. In line with the government's privatization and modernization programs, Pemex's involvement in petrochemicals has been sharply reduced.[31]

Foreign investment in Mexico's petrochemical industry was substantial even before the recent deregulation. At least 30 transnational corporations, including Allied Chemical, BASF, Celanese, Du Pont, Monsanto, and Union Carbide, had a stake in the industry. Foreign investment in petrochemicals will increase dramatically as the government further loosens restrictions.

Besides direct ownership, the government will likely permit foreign financing of Pemex-owned refineries and may enable foreign firms to invest in basic petrochemicals through the purchase of automatically renewable government bonds or *fideicomisos*. Whereas the original goal of the petrochemicals industry was to make Mexico self-sufficient in petrochemicals, privatization and exports became the new focus.

Maquila Manufacturing

At first glance, the move toward economic liberalization would seem to be a complete break with the country's traditional economic policies. Opening the borders to the free flow of trade and investment certainly represents the end of Mexico's longtime adherence to the principles of import-substitution industrialization. Yet this new liberalization is in many ways merely an extension of the country's *maquiladora* program, which since 1965 has nurtured a foreign-owned manufacturing enclave along the U.S. border. Unlike the domestic focus of import-substitution industrialization, *maquila* manufacturing is export-oriented.

Three factors intersected to stimulate the creation of Mexico's *maquila* sector. Setting the stage were the 1962 changes in U.S. customs regulations that permitted (under tariff items 806.30 and 807.00) the duty-free import of U.S. components sent abroad for processing or assembly.[32] This broad revision of U.S. tariffs has meant that manufacturers importing goods into the United States pay duties only on the value added during those portions of the production process that take place outside U.S. borders.[33] Another major factor behind the creation of the *maquila* industry was the end in 1964 of the U.S. *bracero* program. Since 1951 the program had authorized U.S. growers to contract temporary farm labor from Mexico. The end of the program resulted in a sudden increase in unemployment along Mexico's northern border.

The globalization of capitalist production was a third important stimulus to the *maquila* industry. Beginning in the 1950s labor-intensive phases of the production process were being gradually transferred from industrialized countries to places such as Hong Kong, Korea, and Taiwan. By the mid-1960s Mexico wanted to find a place for itself in this new international division of labor.

Responding to these three factors, the Mexican government in 1965 instituted the Border Industrialization Program. The program opened up a 20-kilometer strip along the northern border to labor-intensive, export-oriented assembly plants. These plants are commonly known as *maquiladoras*.[34] They are also referred to in English as "drawback industries," "export-processing plants," or "in-bond" industries (in reference to the bond registered in lieu of Mexican import duties).

Since the early years of the Border Industrialization Program the *maquiladoras* have been exempt from the Mexicanization laws that required majority Mexican ownership for most investments. Neither have the *maquiladoras* been subject to protectionist tariff barriers. Until 1972 the border industrialization program did, however, limit these export-processing plants to the border region. For the past 20 years, though, *maquiladoras* have been permitted in all parts of Mexico, although approximately 80 percent are still located along the Mexico-U.S. border and are concentrated in the five cities of Tijuana, Mexicali, Nogales, Ciudad Juárez, and Matamoros.[35]

Initially it was thought that this program would give rise to "twin plants" along the border, with the labor-intensive operations handled in Mexico and the more capital-intensive work done on the U.S. side. The program sparked the establishment of hundreds of assembly plants on the Mexican side of the border, but most investors preferred to supply them from their home factories rather than setting up new factories in border cities such as San Diego or Brownsville. At first only smaller companies took advantage of Mexican tariff provisions that allowed the duty-free import of U.S. components into Mexico on the condition that the finished products be exported. Gradually, however, more Fortune 500 companies began opening plants south of the border.

During the 1980s and especially after the 1982 devaluation that made Mexican wage rates among the cheapest in the world, the assembly business boomed. During this period, the *peso* dropped from about four U.S. cents to less than 0.04 cents, bringing large wage savings to foreign employers. Whereas the *maquila* industry constituted less than 3 percent of total manufacturing sales in 1980, the sector represented nearly 11 percent by 1989. *Maquila* production increased 350 percent while other manufacturing industries expanded by only 10 percent between 1981 and 1990.[36]

Unsophisticated assembly operations characterized the early years of the Border Industrialization Program. Such easy-to-assemble products as gloves, toys, and dolls were typical of the first *maquiladoras*. As electronics, machinery, and automobile firms began shifting their assembly operations to Mexico in the 1970s, *maquiladora* manufacturing became increasingly sophisticated. Today, high-tech operations make up more than three-quarters of *maquiladora* production.[37] Electric and electronic goods account for more than 40 percent of the value-added production while garments and textiles account for only 6 percent.[38]

Costs and Benefits

After the oil industry, the *maquila* sector is the leading source of foreign exchange. Since 1980 the number of *maquiladoras* has quadrupled, rising to some 2,000 assembly plants employing more than 450,000 workers and netting some $3.5 billion in foreign exchange. The sector's value-added represents 1.5 percent of the GDP, 13 percent of total exports, and 24 percent of manufacturing exports.[39]

Maquiladoras have proved to be a major source of employment in border cities. But it was not the unemployed *braceros* who found jobs in the assembly plants that began locating along the border in the late 1960s. Until the 1980s more than 80 percent of *maquiladora* employees were women, usually between the ages of 17 and 24. The reputed manual dexterity and passivity of females were cited as the reasons for the discriminatory hiring practices. Lately, however, male hiring has markedly increased, with men now constituting about 35 percent of total *maquiladora* employment. The tendency toward hiring more males has paralleled the rise of high-tech manufacturing operations, including robotics, in the industry.

The increasing male work force also reflects the industry's search for steady workers. Reflecting the general dissatisfaction with work conditions, the industry is subject to extraordinary turnover rates, which are commonly as high as 15 percent monthly and in some cases rise to 200 percent annually or higher.[40] Not uncommon are absentee rates of 10-15 percent. Low wages and poor work conditions are the leading reasons for the high turnover rates, although many also seek employment on a temporary basis. Because of the rapid and repetitive nature of most *maquila* operations, health and safety problems are widespread. At the Foster Grant plant, for instance, a worker handles 7,200 sunglasses a day by repeating the same operation every five seconds.[41] Among the most common problems are deterioration of eyesight, ulcers, and nervous disorders, as well as puncture wounds, chemical burns, and electric shocks.[42] A 1990 survey found that 81 percent of the *maquila* workers questioned in the Matamoros and Reynosa plants were suffering from musculoskeletal disorders related to working conditions.[43]

For foreign investors, the main advantages of the *maquiladora* program have been easy access to the U.S. market and the low wages paid to Mexican workers. Mexican wages have always undercut those paid to U.S. workers, but since the early 1980s the wages paid Mexican workers have been among the lowest in the world. Although wage rates in the *maquila* industry are higher than the national minimum wage, *peso* devaluations and wage freezes have kept Mexican wages well under the levels paid in Hong Kong, Korea, Singapore, and Taiwan. Including benefits, *maquila* workers in 1990 received the equivalent of $1.30 to $1.60 an hour.[44] To cash in on these savings, dozens of U.S. firms have closed plants in the United States and established *maquiladoras*. General Motors, which has nearly 50 assembly plants in Mexico, opened up 12 new plants in 1987 while at the same time closing 11 plants in the Midwest and laying off 29,000 U.S. workers.[45]

The employment and foreign exchange benefits of the *maquiladora* program are considerable, but one has only to pass through the shopping districts in the U.S. border towns to see that U.S. merchants are benefiting from the spending habits of *maquiladora* employees just as U.S. manufacturers are benefiting from their low-paid labor. It has been estimated that 30-50 percent of the wages of the country's nearly half million maquiladora workers are spent in the U.S. shopping districts catering to Mexicans. To reverse this money drain, the Mexican government has backed the construction of fancy shopping malls in the major Mexican border cities.[46]

The benefits of the *maquiladora* sector must also be measured against the cost to the Mexican government in constructing and maintaining infrastructure. To attract foreign investment, the government has built new roads, bridges, and even the industrial parks themselves. While the government has jumped to provide the infrastructure needed by the assembly plants, it has failed to provide services to the workers. In Nogales and other border cities, industrial parks that host the *maquiladoras* are surrounded by squatter communities where workers live in makeshift huts without running water or sewage disposal. There is little public transportation and the streets are unpaved. In Ciudad Juárez, some of the city's industrial work force even live in caves.

Along with these other costs, in many ways the *maquiladoras* function on the margins of the Mexican economy. Less than 2 percent of the inputs used in the *maquiladora* sector come from local sources, with the balance coming from the United States and the Far East.[47] Rather than increasing the local content, the *maquila* sector has tended to decrease reliance on local suppliers and depend more on "just-in-time" foreign supply lines. By exempting Mexican suppliers from sales taxes and reducing the taxes on foreign companies that use local suppliers, the Mexican government hopes to raise local content to 4 percent by 1994.[48] The enclave nature of the

Table 2j
Investment in Mexican Maquiladoras, 1991

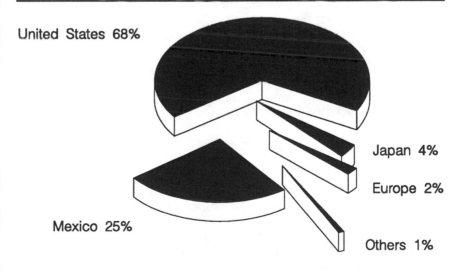

United States 68%

Japan 4%

Europe 2%

Mexico 25%

Others 1%

SOURCE: American Chamber of Commerce, Mexico City, 1991.

maquiladora industry is also seen in its lack of technology transfer. Most of the jobs, even those in the high-tech industries, require little training (usually less than three days) and involve repetitive actions. Rarely do workers understand the technology they use every day.

The export-oriented automotive industry has a better record, with car manufacturers reporting 15-30 percent local content and engine manufacturers registering 40-50 percent local content. But the benefits of this backward linkage are less than they appear since many of the suppliers that surround Ford and other auto factories are subsidiaries of other U.S. firms, like Goodyear.

The *maquiladora* sector is the province of foreign capital, which directly controls about 75 percent of the assembly plants, with the Mexican plants being mostly small sweatshops and subcontractors (Table 2j). More than 90 percent of the foreign-owned *maquila* sector is in the hands of U.S. investors, although Japanese investment has risen sharply since the mid-1980s. There were only five Japanese *maquiladoras* in 1985; by 1991 there were nearly 50 with many others planned. Like the U.S. firms, such Japanese corporations as Sony, Hitachi, and Toshiba see border *maquila* production as way to increase their global competitiveness. It is also a way to avoid U.S. quotas and other protectionist barriers raised by the United States against Japanese imports.

Mexican entrepreneurs have found a place in the *maquiladora* industry by offering broad services to foreign investors. Mexican firms do everything from constructing industrial parks and contracting the work force to supplying transportation, negotiating with customs authorities, and managing the factories. In addition to joint ventures with foreign capital, Mexican entrepreneurs act as subcontractors for U.S. firms. These subcontractors produce to the specifications of the U.S. investor using the inputs and raw materials provided by the foreign firm. A variation of this contracting arrangement is the "shelter program," under which a Mexican company is created solely to manufacture and assemble for foreign investors. Unlike the subcontracting arrangement, where the Mexican investor manages the plant, *maquiladoras* operating under the shelter program generally have a full-time manager from the foreign firm.

Free Trade and the Maquila Industry

Critics of the proposed NAFTA say that free trade will generalize *maquila*-style manufacturing throughout Mexico. As production-sharing arrangements increase, manufacturing employment is also likely to rise. But there is little reason to believe that this new NAFTA-related investment will do much better than the *maquila* sector in facilitating technology transfer and increasing linkages with the Mexican economy.

The two features that have distinguished the *maquiladora* program—no restriction on foreign ownership and the tax-free import of materials and equipment—are no longer unique. Recent changes in the investment laws have opened the way for 100-percent foreign ownership throughout the country, and government decrees have extended import concessions to all export-oriented firms. This liberalization of investment and trade will be reinforced by a FTA, which will further loosen investment rules and tariff barriers.[49]

In recognition of these changes, *maquiladoras* are no longer being called "in-bond" industries. Instead the term "production sharing" is becoming more common. The definition of a *maquiladora* is becoming less clear, but the basic concept of cheap labor as a complement to foreign capital remains the same. While it seems certain that production-sharing industries will continue to target foreign markets, there is increasing interest in selling some of the assembled products in Mexico. New regulations now permit selling as much as 50 percent of the finished products on the domestic market. Nonetheless, more than 95 percent of *maquiladora* products were still exported in 1990, although this opening to the domestic market will likely become more important to investors if they see an increased pace of domestic consumption in future years.

The status of Japanese and other non-U.S. companies in the *maquiladora* sector is certain to be a matter of contention during the NAFTA negotiations. Congressional members have already expressed their concern that a NAFTA with Mexico could open another beachhead for foreign producers eager to enter the U.S. market. It is likely that the FTA will establish strict rules-of-origin to prevent foreign producers from using Mexico as an export platform to the United States. It may be, however, that most Japanese companies will be able to comply with these rules since virtually all the Japanese firms in the *maquila* sector belong to parent companies legally registered in the United States, like the California-based Sanyo North America. In recent years, the rising value of the yen has also encouraged Japanese *maquilas* to decrease input purchasing from Japan and increase U.S. purchases. Sanyo and other firms have also begun to enter joint ventures with Mexican firms to increase local content.[50]

Auto Industry: Center Place in Industrialization

Contrary to what is commonly believed, the export-oriented manufacturing sector in Mexico consists of more than low-technology and labor-intensive assembly plants scattered along the northern border. The early *maquiladoras*, mainly unsophisticated assembly operations, comprised the first wave of export-oriented industrialization in Mexico. Since the mid-1970s a second wave of high-technology, export-driven industrialization has been sweeping the country.

Today Mexico is an export platform for many high-tech goods. Many of the country's new manufacturing plants are among the most sophisticated in the world, employing the latest technology and work-organization systems. Sanyo televisions, Whirlpool appliances, IBM computers, Caterpillar

forklift trucks, and Kodak cameras are among the products being manufactured in these high-technology factories. Since the mid-1980s the automotive industry has ridden the crest of this second wave of industrialization.

Automobile manufacturing in Mexico is nothing new. The Ford Motor
Company set up its first plant in Mexico in 1925. Before Mexico embarked
on its import-substitution industrialization program, the automobile industry assembled most vehicles from imported kits.[51] With the emergence of
the import-substitution strategy of industrialization in the 1960s, the proportion of imported inputs dropped sharply as independent Mexican companies began to supply parts. To satisfy the requirement that assembled
vehicles have a domestic content of at least 60 percent, an extensive engine
and auto-parts manufacturing sector emerged alongside the assembly
plants concentrated in south-central Mexico.

The original goal of the country's industrial planners to have a car with
100-percent domestic content (the fabled Mex-car) was abandoned by 1980.
As initially conceived, however, the automobile industry was to be the center of a modern industrial complex in Mexico that would reduce the
country's dependence on foreign-made capital and consumer goods. Mexico did attract major car companies like Nissan and Volkswagen to produce
for the local market, but the country's market for cars was never large
enough to support a modern and self-sufficient vehicle industry. The automotive sector did foster related domestic industries, but like other Mexican
industries the automotive sector was still heavily dependent on foreign-
made intermediate and capital goods.

In the late 1970s the country's automotive industry gained a new dimension. The major automobile companies began setting up *maquiladoras* for the
purpose of supplying their U.S. factories with cheap parts.[52] It was not, however, until General Motors and Ford opened engine factories in northern Mexico in 1982-83 that this high-technology, export-oriented industrialization
really took off. Nissan, Volkswagen, and Chrysler soon followed Ford's lead in
engine manufacturing. Ford's $800 million investment in the car-manufactur-
ing plant in Hermosillo took the industry a step farther.

Instead of producing the Mex-car, Mexico has lately become a major
player in the manufacture of what is known as the "world car." The world
car is an automobile whose nationality is difficult to identify because it is manufactured using components, capital, and labor from several nations. The Trac-
ers and Escorts produced at the new Ford plant in Hermosillo (opened in 1986)
are prototypes of the new world car: 15 percent of the components are supplied from Mexico, 20 percent from Japan, and 60 percent from the United
States.[53] According to the chief of an engine-manufacturing factory in Mexico,
the plant brought together "U.S. managers, European technology, Japanese
manufacturing systems, and Mexican workers."[54]

In 1980 the automotive industry suffered a $1.5 billion deficit. Ten years
later the country was enjoying an industry trade surplus of about the same
magnitude. The automotive industry, which exported nearly 300,000 cars in

1991, accounts for nearly 10 percent of the country's manufactured exports. Between 1985 and 1990 U.S. imports of autos from Mexico rose at an average annual rate of about 35 percent, making Mexico the fourth-largest supplier of vehicles to the United States. Major new investments by most of the major car companies mean that automobile and engine exports to the United States will probably more than double by 1995, although the 1990-91 recession in the United States slightly slowed projected growth. Five companies control the export market. In order of sales, they are Ford, General Motors, Chrysler, Volkswagen, and Nissan.

The meteoric rise of the export-oriented auto industry in Mexico put to rest the theory that only the most labor-intensive phases of the manufacturing process can be transferred to nonindustrialized nations like Mexico. Corporations have found that even the most advanced production processes can be successfully transferred to Mexico without loss in quality or productivity—and with considerable savings in wage costs. Harley Shaiken, an economist at the University of California-San Diego, recently conducted a study of five high-tech manufacturing plants in Mexico. He found that productivity and quality in the Mexican factories were comparable to or better than those of similar U.S. plants operated by the same parent company. In the case of the automobile plant studied, the training time for skilled workers in Mexico was considerably shorter than in the United States.[55]

The high-tech companies have discovered a vast labor pool of semi-skilled workers who have graduated from Mexico's technical and vocational schools. In addition, the firms have also been able to pick among the graduates of the Monterrey Institute of Technology and other private schools for their technicians and managers.

Although these industries are highly automated and roboticized, they still employ large numbers of workers. The savings in wages at a factory like Ford in Hermosillo, which employs more than 2,000 workers, can be considerable. According to Shaiken's calculations, an auto company like Ford can save $672 per vehicle in labor costs alone. If management costs are also included in a comparison of U.S. and Mexican production costs, the savings are even greater.[56] As well as providing cheap labor (about $3 an hour including benefits) for auto and engine manufacturers, workers in such northern cities as Hermosillo and Chihuahua have proved to be more easily integrated into innovative work-organization systems than their U.S. or Canadian counterparts. With no history of union organizing, they are also less resistant to flexible contracts that allow workers to be switched from job to job as needed.

The boom in the export-oriented automotive industry has spurred the creation of an industrial zone spreading across northern Mexico. Before the late 1970s there was no auto industry found in the northern region, but this area now accounts for 65 percent of Mexico's engine production and 30 percent of automobile production. Auto manufacturers have been attracted to northern Mexico because of its proximity to the United States, the presence of a low-cost and unorganized work force, the easy accessibility of technical assistance, and the many incentives offered by the local and federal governments. Some predict that this zone, already known as Little Detroit, might some day rival industrial production in South Korea, Taiwan, or even the U.S. Midwest.[57]

The growth of the export-oriented automotive industry in Mexico illustrates the broad dimensions of global economic integration. Although labor costs do represent a declining percentage of overall production costs for most high-tech industries, transnational corporations have found that significant savings result from transferring production to low-wage sites overseas. Moreover, the automotive and other high-tech industries are concluding that cheap foreign labor is not only capable of simple assembly operations but can also be inexpensively trained to become a highly skilled and flexible work force.[58] Free trade advocates argue that the integration of the U.S., Canadian, and Mexican automotive sectors—like other manufacturing industries—may actually save Canadian and U.S. jobs by keeping automobile companies from searching for low-cost production alternatives outside North America. Canadian and U.S. manufacturing workers put little stock in this argument, given their experience of a steady downward pull of wage levels and a southward flow of jobs. Those companies that keep all or part of their operations at home have used the threat of plant transfer to force major wage reductions from besieged unions.

Like the automotive export market, the domestic automobile market in Mexico is also booming. Despite its severe pollution problems, the Mexican government is encouraging increased auto sales as a way to push industrialization forward. Falling consumer demand in Mexico pushed the domestically oriented vehicle industry into a recession in the 1980s. With the economy picking up beginning in 1988, so did auto sales. Vehicle sales on the domestic market jumped from about 200,000 cars sold in 1983 to more than 450,000 by 1990. Vehicle manufacturers see an expanding car market in Mexico if the economy continues to grow.[59]

Five foreign firms with manufacturing plants in Mexico account for more than 95 percent of total domestic sales. In order of sales, they are Volkswagen, Nissan, Ford Motor Company, General Motors, and Chrysler. The domestic auto industry has been protected by local-content rules (36 percent) and tough government restrictions against the importation of foreign-made cars. In 1991 the car market squeaked open as a result of a new arrangement with the industry that allows companies to import the equivalent of 10 percent of their exports. About 20,000 cars per year, mainly luxury models, are now being imported from the United States. By 1994 all restrictions against vehicle imports are scheduled to be lifted.

Tourism

In Mazatlán you can dance world-class at a $6-million discothèque at the El Cid Mega Resort. The new vacation resort is one of 13 tourism "megaprojects" sponsored by the Mexican government in its ambitious drive to double the number of tourists visiting the country by the year 2000. Nearly 7 million tourists now visit Mexico every year, more than 85 percent of them from the United States.[60] Tourism is already big business in Mexico—the third largest source of foreign exchange after the oil industry and the *maquiladora* industry. The tourism sector accounts for more than 6 percent of the GDP, produces nearly 20 percent of the country's nonpetroleum foreign exchange, and employs about 1.8 million people.[61] Although the number of tourists coming to Mexico is rising, the rate of increase is considerably lower than government projections.[62] About 30 percent of the tourism business goes to planned megaprojects such as Cancún, while 27 percent goes to the traditional beach resorts like Acapulco, and another 24 percent goes to Mexico's major cities.[63]

Acapulco was the government's first major success in tourism. Since the 1920s this beautiful harbor town has served as the favored resort for vacationers from Mexico City, but in the 1950s it became a popular destination for foreign tourists as well. Acapulco was Mexico's first tourism megaproject. In the late 1940s President Alemán, eager to cash in on the post-war travel boom, told government engineers to upgrade and expand Acapulco with the infrastructure necessary to convert it into a luxury tourist spot. Both Mexico and Alemán benefited. In a few years foreign exchange from tourism had tripled and the value of the property that Alemán had quietly purchased soared.[64]

Megaproject planning in tourism received a new boost in the 1960s when the Bank of Mexico planners suggested "the building of complete tourist cities from the ground up."[65] The country's 6,000 miles of coastline were closely studied for average weekly hours of sunshine, tidal patterns, and possible supply routes. In 1969 government planners began work on "integral tourist resorts." Leading the list was the uninhabited island of Cancún, followed by Ixtapa in Guerrero, Los Cabos and Loreto in Baja California Sur, and finally the Bahías de Huatulco gracing the harsh Oaxacan coastline.

The Huatulco project is well under way. The government removed the several thousand peasant and fishing families that lived near the site of the project, and the new airport is bringing in planeloads of tourists to the Sheraton and other posh resorts that continue to rise up along the coastline. The tourism invasion and the appropriation of land and water rights have met some local resistance at Huatulco and other megaproject locations. In the face of federal backing for these billion-dollar projects and in the absence of meaningful local government, those adversely affected by the tourism complexes have little recourse but to join the industry as waiters, guides, and handicraft vendors.

The National Fund for Tourism Development (Fonatur), the government agency that plans resort complexes and encourages private investment in these projects, has 13 tourism megaprojects planned or in progress.[66] From Baja California to the Caribbean coast, more than $3.5 billion in state and private funds are currently being invested in new or expanded tourism enclaves. This drive to double the size of the tourism industry also counts on loans from the Inter-American Development Bank and is being accompanied by a $30 million annual advertising campaign by the Ministry of Tourism. The government has attracted foreign and private investors into the tourism industry through the use of debt swaps, whereby investors buy a portion of the country's external debt at a discounted rate in exchange for local investments.[67]

With the changes in the foreign investment law that permit 100-percent foreign investment in tourism projects, the government successfully attracted the interest of such major hotel firms as Westin, Stouffer, Nikko, Club Med, Marriott, and Sheraton. Hilton, which had left Mexico after its adoption in 1973 of new restrictions on foreign investment, came back to the country, encouraged by changes that now permit foreign firms to invest in coastal properties.

The government's thirst for foreign exchange resulted in the creation of hundreds of thousands of jobs and billions of dollars in investment and tourist dollars. But the megaprojects of the tourism industry have often had serious human and environmental costs. Entire communities have been removed to make way for the tourist centers. Although the industry creates jobs, it is mostly seasonal, low-paid, and unskilled employment. In addition, as the industry becomes increasingly dominated by transnationals, profit repatriation and expensive imports reduce the direct financial benefits of the tourism boom. Little of the wealth from the industry actually trickles down to spur the economic development of local communities.

Since the first projects to expand Acapulco, Mexico's planners have learned few environmental lessons. Over the decades the waste from the tourism industry contaminated the formerly pristine Acapulco Bay, and the same process of despoliation is now under way from small tourist spots like San Angel to Cancún and other megaprojects. Ecotourism—or low impact, nature-oriented tourism—has not yet caught on in Mexico, as it has, for example, in Costa Rica. For the government, the focus is still mainly on big bucks and a quick return.

The Mining Industry

Dating back to the early Spanish silver mines near Guanajuato, mining has been the foundation of the country's industrial sector. Although the importance of mining in the national economy has been steadily declining since World War II, the country's mining industry still accounts for nearly 3 percent of the GDP and employs more than 230,000 workers. Mexico ranks

15th among the world's mineral producers. It is the world's largest producer of silver, and is among the top five producers of lead, mercury, zinc, bismuth, graphite, antimony, molybdenum, sulfur, fluorspar, and sodium sulfate. It ranks number seven among copper producers. It is one of the few Latin American countries to have coal reserves, but further development of its reserves is not considered commercially viable. Mining exports increased nearly 40 percent in the 1980s and accounted for 10 percent of the country's nonpetroleum exports.[68] About two-thirds of Mexico's mining exports go to the United States.

Three-fourths of the Mexican land mass exhibits geological characteristics indicating mineral deposits. But the government says that only 20 percent of this has been explored in detail. To tap this wealth the Salinas government cut taxes on mining operations, sold off state-owned mines, and encouraged foreign investment.[69] It also launched a new program of regional mapping to pinpoint mineral reserves.[70]

Before the Mexican Revolution the country's mines were run almost exclusively by foreign concessions. The revolution and the country's restrictive foreign investment laws resulted in increased domestic investment, including substantial public-sector investment (rising to 40 percent of the industry by 1982) in the mining sector. Economic modernization during the 1980s resulted in the divestiture of many state-owned mining companies and a rapid increase in foreign investment.[71] So intent is the government on attracting foreign investment that it offers dollar credits to new private investment in the mining sector. Among the foreign corporations that now have interests in Mexico's mines are Phelps Dodge, Du Pont, Asarco, Amax, and Standard Oil (United States); Placer, Cominco (Canada); Metal Gesellschaft (Germany); and Sumitomo (Japan).[72]

Grupo Industrial Minera México (IMMSA) is the largest mining company in the country, controlling much of the silver mining and 95 percent of the country's copper production. IMMSA, in which Asarco has a minority interest, acquired the Cananea copper mine in northern Sonora in 1990. The mining company had been acquired from Asarco by the government as part of the "Mexicanization" process in the early 1970s. Before selling Cananea, the largest open-pit copper mine in the world, the government closed it down to break a strike and called in the army to squash labor protests. It thereby paved the way for the sale of the mine to a private investor. The government's sale of Cananea at a bargain price to Jorge Larrea of IMMSA was another step in a privatization process that, in the name of modernization, has pushed aside the interests of workers while contributing to the monopolization of Mexican industry by a small circle of Mexican capitalists financed by foreign investors.[73]

Agriculture and the Agrarian Crisis

The future of the agricultural sector has been the subject of heated discussion among Mexicans at least since their revolution, and the debate continues today with no sign of resolution. At issue is the agricultural sector's function in the country's economy and society.

On one side of the debate are those who say that agriculture should continue its historical function of providing dignity, jobs, and sustenance to Mexican peasants, who have been called the heart and soul of the Mexican Revolution. Closely related to this concern for the welfare of the nation's peasantry is the argument that the fundamental purpose of the agricultural sector is to feed the Mexican nation. Farm policy, it is said, should give Mexico food security by making it self-sufficient in basic food commodities. Both as a way to aid the peasantry and to promote adequate food production, proponents advocate agrarian programs that reach out to *campesinos* with credit and technical assistance while continuing the country's land-distribution program. It is argued that agricultural development in Mexico should be more balanced, rather than prioritizing export production.

Others consider these views to be a vain nostalgia for a bygone era long since eclipsed by a world that is economically integrated, with prices and supply determined by the international market. Rather than continuing to protect and subsidize Mexico's farm community, they say that the agricultural sector is long overdue for a serious transformation that puts a premium on productivity and the ability to compete in the global marketplace. Instead of propping up hopelessly backward sectors, the state should direct its limited resources to those farmers and investors that are commercially viable. Those proposing the neoliberal modernization of the agricultural sector commonly hold that the *ejido* (a communal landholding system) should be abolished to open the way for the full-scale capitalist transformation of Mexican agriculture.[74]

A Fading Tradition of Agrarian Populism

By 1910 at the end of nearly 40 years of dictatorship under Porfirio Díaz, 70 percent of Mexico's arable land was held by one percent of the population.[75] Discontent among the northern growers and the industrialists with the inefficiency of the country's large estates together with massive peasant unrest provided an agrarian base for the revolutionary upheaval. But apart from the rhetoric of the new rulers and the promises contained in the 1917 constitution, the peasantry made few gains during the first decades of the revolutionary state. In 1930 President Calles declared the agrarian reform a "failure," even though most of the country's large estates or *latifundios* continued to exist and millions of peasants remained landless. Not until the Lázaro Cárdenas *sexenio* (1934-40) did Mexico's *campesinos* see a substantial state commitment to bettering their conditions.

Upon taking over the reins of the state in 1934, Cárdenas gave the government's half-hearted agrarian reform program new life. Traditional communal holdings were recognized and 45 million acres were distributed in the form of *ejidos*. Cárdenas distributed 3 times as much land as had been previously handed out and more irrigated land than any other president before or after him. More than simply passing out parcels of land, President Cárdenas also encouraged peasant mobilization to pursue their demands and created the National Peasant Confederation (CNC) as part of the state's new corporatist structure.

More than simply a measure to calm rural tensions and increase political support among the peasantry, the agrarian reform under Cárdenas was regarded as a way to increase agricultural production and form a foundation for the industrialization of Mexico. To pursue this development strategy, the Ejido Credit Bank was created and technical assistance was extended to the beneficiaries of the reform. Although Cárdenas himself encouraged the collective or cooperative management of the *ejidos*, most of the beneficiaries of Mexico's land distribution program chose to farm individual plots, which later, as the population grew and land distribution decreased, gave rise to the *minifundio* (small subsistence or below-subsistence farms) sector in the south and central regions of the country.

Although the country's land distribution program continued into the 1980s, the main focus of Mexican policymakers after 1940 was to shift national resources toward large-scale, privately owned commercial agriculture. Under Cárdenas the agrarian reform had played out in the context of a class struggle that pitted landless peasants and reform beneficiaries against large landowners and other opponents of the state's populist programs. Agrarian populism persisted in the official rhetoric after 1940, but the state's agrarian policies were pursued more to pacify the rural population than to promote social justice or increase agricultural production.

The turn away from the aggressive agrarian populism of the Cárdenas era became most clear during the Miguel Alemán administration (1946-52). President Alemán introduced the concept of *amparo agrario* (agrarian protection), which was effectively a counterreform. The definition of a small landholder—not subject to expropriation—was expanded to mean 100 hectares of irrigated land, 200 hectares of rain-fed land, 300 hectares of orchards, 400 hectares of good-quality grazing land, 800 hectares of scrub lands, and, in desert regions, enough land to graze 500 head of cattle, which could mean as much as 50,000 hectares.[76] Not content with those limits, large landholders, many of them politicians, commonly placed the title of additional lands in the names of hired help and family members.

Although the main focus of the state's agricultural policies was the promotion of large commercial ventures in the north and northwest, each president in his turn announced that more land would be redistributed into *ejidos* for landless peasants. Never was all this land actually distributed, and most of it was worthless for cultivation. Approximately 85 percent of the land distributed between 1952 and 1982 was not arable. During the Echeverría *sexenio* (1970-76) the agrarian reform briefly regained its former vigor. But rather than any serious attempt to resolve the country's worsening agrarian problems, the land distribution program under Echeverría, who handed out more land than any president since Cárdenas, was a political maneuver to reduce the power of the large landholders of the north while strengthening the ties between the peasants and the government. The *campesinos* were once again the pawns of national politics.

Starting with López Portillo (1976-82), the Mexican government has attempted to redefine its agrarian policies, talking less about social justice and more about the need for social-welfare programs in the countryside, less about landlessness and more about the need to increase productivity. Like López Portillo himself, his two successors declared that the land distribution program was at its end because there was no more land to hand out.

Among the concrete manifestations of this new direction was the introduction by López Portillo of a new Agricultural Development Law that encouraged association between the *ejidos* and private "small landholders." Concerned about the rising imports of basic grains, the López Portillo administration also launched the Mexican Food System (SAM) in 1980 with the objective of regaining food self-sufficiency by 1985.[77] Flush with revenues from the oil boom and foreign loans, the government threw money at the basic grains sector. A combination of large subsidies and heavy rains resulted in a sharp increase in grain production in 1981.

Despite its apparent success in increasing food production, SAM was short-lived. In response to the debt crisis, massive capital flight, and plummeting oil revenues in 1981-82, the government assumed an economic stabilization program that required sharp cutbacks in government services and subsidies. Programs aimed at improving the welfare of the peasantry were among the first to suffer from the austerity measures. Recognizing that the problems that gave rise to SAM still existed, the de la Madrid administration came up with another plan to improve domestic food production. Called the National Food Program (Pronal), it faded quickly for lack of resources and the absence of a viable strategy to reverse the decline in the country's agricultural sector.

From Austerity to Neoliberal Restructuring

The de la Madrid administration stumbled along without a clearly defined agricultural policy. There was no mistaking, however, that the government was determined to bury the agrarian reform. Like López Portillo before him, President de la Madrid stressed the need to reorganize the *ejidos* and the privately owned *minifundios* into "efficient and productive units" that could absorb modern technology and farm commercially.[78] He reiterated López Portillo's claim that there was no more land to distribute— the agrarian reform having established 28,000 *ejidos* covering more than two-fifths of the national territory and benefiting nearly three million families. Although clearly indicating that the *ejidos* should be more closely integrated into capitalist agribusiness, the president was reluctant to call for the outright privatization of the *ejidos*, knowing that such a proposal would spark a firestorm of rural protests.

Beginning in 1985 it became apparent that the costcutting of the government's economic stabilization program was evolving into a restructuring of the agricultural sector. Not only was the government slashing its agricultural budget and rural infrastructure projects, it was also gradually reducing the state's regulatory role and its direct financial involvement in the farm sector. Slowly at first, and then picking up speed in the Salinas administration, the government liberalized domestic and international commerce in agricultural commodities. Neoliberal restructuring superseded the politics of austerity.

The elimination of most import licenses (meaning that the government no longer had to approve the purchase of foreign commodities) has been the most significant step toward the complete liberalization of foreign agricultural trade.[79] On the domestic side, the announcement that there would be no more land distributed and the termination of price guarantees for all but a few basic goods—including dry edible beans and corn—indicated that the government was indeed serious about leaving behind its traditional agrarian populism.

As with its other economic policies, the government's new approach to the agricultural sector was the product of both international and domestic factors. Upon joining the multilateral GATT trade accord in 1986, Mexico accelerated its liberalization policies, opening up its international trade far beyond the terms of the agreement. As the decade progressed, foreign lenders, particularly Washington and the World Bank, stepped up their pressure for a radical restructuring of the agricultural sector. In its *Agriculture Sector Report* on Mexico at the start of the Salinas administration, the World Bank called upon the new government "to liberalize agriculture and . . . produce products of commercial value instead of basic food crops." Furthermore, the World Bank observed that "if agriculture is to contribute to the increase in the Mexican economy's rate of growth it is essential that . . . subsidies for fertilizers, fuel, credit, water, seeds, and crop insurance be reduced even more, at a gradual but drastic pace."[80]

The Salinas administration was as committed to neoliberal restructuring as its foreign lenders. Like the de la Madrid administration, the Salinas government downplayed former promises that Mexico would achieve food self-sufficiency while declaring that it was committed to "food sovereignty." Although never fully explained by government officials, food sovereignty apparently did not refer to the country's ability to produce its own food but to maintain its capacity to purchase on the international market the foodstuffs needed to supplement domestic production.

In 1990 President Salinas released the government's "National Program of Modernization of the Countryside, 1990-94." The program clearly outlined the private-sector focus of the new agricultural policy in Mexico. In a dramatic turnaround from previous policies of increased state intervention in the agricultural sector, the new modernization program stressed the privatization of state agricultural enterprises.

Even before the program was announced, the government had been moving to sell off its various firms and agencies. The restructuring of Conasupo, the state food distribution agency, and Inmecafe, the coffee-marketing board, had already begun. True to its promises to dismantle the parastatals, the government sold various sugar mills to the Mexican branches of PepsiCo and Coca-Cola. Several of Conasupo's food-processing plants were sold to Anderson-Clayton, one of the oldest U.S. agribusinesses in Mexico and now a subsidiary of the food giant Unilever. Further privatization of Conasupo and the projected sale of Fertimex, the parastatal that produces pesticides and fertilizers, will further reduce the state's direct participation in the agricultural sector.[81]

Instead of pushing forward an agrarian reform program, the agricultural plan expressed the government's commitment to provide greater land-tenure security by stepping up efforts to give all landholders clear title to their property. Other measures detailed in the modernization plan included the replacement of generalized subsidies with specific subsidies targeting certain producers and regions, the reduction of tariffs on agricultural inputs, and the channeling of credit from the National Rural Credit Bank (Banrural) only to those producers capable of producing commercially. In line with other government programs to promote export production, the 1990 modernization plan also committed the government to establish "agroindustrial corridors" to link cropland, processing plants, and transportation infrastructure.

By midterm in the Salinas administration the government's commitment to the economics of comparative advantage and privatization in the farm sector was quite evident. Still to be resolved, however, was the status of the *ejidos*, which were widely considered to be the main obstacles to future agricultural growth. During his election campaign Salinas promised repeatedly that the *ejido* would remain a constitutionally protected form of landholding, but future policies of the Salinas administration pointed to the effective dismantling of the sector.

Rather than directly eliminating the *ejido*, the Salinas government moved toward the "modernization and transformation" of the *ejido* by encouraging the wedding of the communal subsistence sector with the private agroindustrial sector. In practice, this meant an association between *ejidos* and capitalist firms. The willingness of the Salinas administration to back a joint venture between Gamesa (a PepsiCo subsidiary), the country's largest cookie and pasta maker, and an *ejido* in northern Mexico demonstrated the government's support for partnerships between *ejiditarios* and agribusinesses. In a 1981 reform to the Agrarian Reform Law, the government permitted various types of association between *ejiditarios* and private interests, although not the outright renting of *ejido* lands to private agribusiness. The regulations were broadened in 1990, and there are new government proposals to liberalize still further the use and rental of *ejidos*.

Private investors, both local and foreign, have constantly complained that the government must do more than encourage joint ventures with *ejidos*. The legal obstacles to renting *ejido* land and to the private ownership of large estates must also be removed if agribusiness is to expand in Mexico.[82] "The best way to compete is through high efficiency and economies of scale," stated a representative of Del Monte Foods, which already has operations in the country.[83] Standing directly in the way of the economies of the scale that Del Monte and other U.S. investors want are the *ejidos*, which cannot legally be rented out, sold off, or managed by capitalist enterprises. In November 1991, bolstered by the ruling party's landslide victory in the August midterm elections, Salinas announced his intention of seeking constitutional changes that will allow *ejiditarios* to receive individual land titles, enabling them to do what they please with their property, including renting and selling it to agribusinesses and other capitalist ventures.

The Lay of the Land

Mexico's mountainous terrain and its arid climate make it less than ideal for agriculture. Two mountain ranges run through the country, the north is largely desert, tropical jungles cover the south, and the soil of the Yucatán peninsula is paper thin. About half the country is considered too steep to cultivate, and more than 50 percent of the territory is arid, with another 20-35 percent considered semi-arid. Only about 15 percent of Mexico's 487 million acres are considered arable. Some 55 million acres are under cultivation, while 184 million acres are dedicated to grazing.[84]

The lack of water is the main impediment to intensive cultivation in Mexico. To remedy this problem, the government sponsored massive irrigation projects, mainly in the country's north and northwest. As a result, Mexico enjoys one of the world's highest proportions of irrigated arable land, with about one-quarter of its cultivated land under irrigation.[85]

One of the most striking changes in the Mexican landscape over the past thirty years has been the expansion of the livestock industry. In the 1970s alone, grazing lands in the central and northern regions increased by 50 percent while in the southeastern tropical lowlands grazing lands tripled. Not only have cattle directly replaced basic grains in many areas, but croplands were increasingly turned over to the cultivation of animal feed, including sorghum, oats, and alfalfa. Although per capita consumption of meat in the late 1980s was about 60 kilos a year, government figures showed that more than a third of the population rarely eat meat or drink milk.[86]

Land tenure, although more equitable than in most other Latin American nations, remains skewed. Officially all private landowners are called "small landholders." In fact, there are numerous large "small landholders," some of whom control as much as 2.5 million acres. Despite their unconstitutionality, these "concealed" *latifundios* are again being consolidated throughout Mexico.[87] At the other pole, there exist more than 400,000 subsistence farmers on small private plots. According to Banrural, *minifundios* (5 hectares or less) account for nearly 60 percent of all farms in Mexico.

Ejidos occupy 43 percent of Mexican farmland and comprise well over 60 percent of the nation's farmers. Yet they produce less than 10 percent of the country's agricultural output.[88] This low productivity is not necessarily inherent in the structure of the *ejido* but rather is largely due to the fact that the land distributed to the *ejidos* was the most marginal of Mexico's cropland. The low productivity of the *ejido* sector is also the result of its abandonment by the state virtually from the moment the *ejidos* were established. The common political wisdom in Mexico is that the *ejido* was created and has been protected by politicians not for production but for electoral votes; that land was distributed simply to pacify the revolutionary peasantry. The intended beneficiary of Mexico's agrarian populism was not the nation's *campesinos*—ironically termed "the chosen children of the regime" by one of Mexico's eminent scholars—but the state itself.[89]

Monocultural production is a major economic and environmental problem in the *ejido* sector. According to Banrural, about two-thirds of the *ejidos* produce corn and little else. And while 85 percent of the *ejidos* report agriculture as the principal activity, only 12 percent of *ejido* land is arable.[90]

The real efforts at increasing productivity since the end of World War II have been directed at the expanding large-scale agroexport sector. After the Cárdenas *sexenio*, not only did the "communist threat" of the communal nature of the *ejido* target it for destruction, but the dream of industrialization drained it of any support. The policies that prevailed then, and which have continued into the present, are policies oriented toward industry and agribusiness.[91]

Crisis Indicators

Like the rest of the economy Mexico's agricultural sector experienced sustained per capita economic growth in the 1940-70 period known as the "miracle years." The agrarian reform, although never fully implemented, did serve to increase grain production while reducing peasant unrest. The Green Revolution, sponsored by international donors such as the Rockefeller and Ford foundations, introduced the extensive use of chemical fertilizers and pesticides and increased reliance on agricultural machinery. Traditional agroexports, mainly coffee and sugar, provided some of the capital needed for Mexico's industrialization, while the country's *ejiditarios* and small farmers kept the growing urban population and industrial work force supplied with cheap food.

About the same time that the flaws of the country's industrialization strategy were becoming apparent, the weaknesses of the agricultural sector also showed themselves. After having achieved self-sufficiency and demonstrating sustained increases in per capita grain production, Mexico became a net importer of basic grains in the 1970s. After the initial gains from opening up of frontier lands for cultivation and productivity gains resulting from the increased use of agricultural inputs, per capita farm production began to fall. Another problem was the exhaustion of traditional agroexport production. This decline in traditional exports was largely offset by the rapid rise of such nontraditional agroexports as tomatoes and strawberries, which benefited from government programs to irrigate the northern flatlands. But the problem of declining per capita grain production was never adequately addressed.

The contribution of agriculture to the Mexican economy has been steadily diminishing despite the country's continued need for high productivity in the sector. Agricultural output as a portion of the GDP fell from 16 percent in 1960 to 7 percent in 1990. In the 1960s the agricultural sector experienced an average annual growth rate of 4 percent. This fell to 3.3 percent in the 1970s and just 1.3 percent in the 1980s. The decline of the agricultural sector relative to industry is not of course a sign of economic weakness, but indicates normal development. The problem is that the productivity of the agricultural sector has also declined and that other sectors of the economy have not been able to provide adequate sources of employment for the many displaced farm families.

The starkest indicators of agriculture's fundamental weakness come from the external sector. During the 1980s imports of basic grains—mainly corn, sorghum, and soybeans—rose sharply. By 1990 the country was also facing rising imports of wheat and rice, as the government reduced its subsidies for these and other crops. Despite Mexico's increasing agroexports, the need for huge purchases of grains constitutes a serious drain on the country's foreign exchange reserves. Overall, Mexico is suffering from major agricultural deficits. In 1990 Mexico's total agricultural deficit was $1.4 billion.[92]

At least part of the decline in agricultural production was the result of reduced government support for agriculture. The government's agricultural and food-support budget dropped from more than $8 billion in 1981 to about $3 billion in 1988.[93] Most severely affected has been the country's peasantry. Government credit, always difficult to get, fell by half in the 1980s. At the same time prices of inputs shot up while the government held farm prices down.

While the Salinas government was sounding the bells of agricultural "transformation and modernization," the country's small-farm sector was undergoing a demodernizing process. For lack of credit and capital, farmers were forced to abandon new technologies and reduce their use of improved seeds and chemical inputs. Many subsistence farmers began producing only for their own consumption, while others abandoned farming to join the migrant stream or to find work in the cities.

Two Views on Agricultural Modernization

Agricultural crisis in Mexico has resulted in increasing polarization between rural and urban Mexico and between the capitalized and undercapitalized growers. Summing up the dualistic and polarized character of the agricultural sector, one scholar of agrarian policies described Mexico in 1991 as the "land of runaway urbanization, impoverished *ejidos*, and prosperous *latifundistas*."[94] The duality of Mexican agriculture, however, is not so much a product of recent modernization strategies as a deep-rooted, historical reality.

Since the 1940s the Mexican government has favored large private landholders with major irrigation projects and has promoted commercial cash crops. Over time the two sectors—the large agribusinesses and small subsistence sector predominantly on *ejido* lands—continued to grow apart. Agricultural production and land ownership became increasingly concentrated in the hands of an agricultural elite, with the subsistence sector becoming less productive and more marginalized.

The duality in Mexican agriculture is not simply a division between export-oriented and domestic food production. The polarization in Mexican agriculture has resulted from longtime government policies not only to increase exports but also to modernize commercial agriculture with the objective of providing cheap food for the cities and grains for the livestock sector. The beneficiaries of this policy and associated Green Revolution were largely commercial wheat growers, but also commercial-level producers of maize and rice.

Closely related to this cheap-food policy that characterized Mexican agriculture since the 1940s has been the leveling off of support prices for basic grains since the mid-1960s. Pressed by the political imperative to keep urban residents supplied with cheap food (and thereby supporting industrialization by serving to keep wage levels down), the government squeezed basic grains farmers, particularly the small-farm sector that produced most of the country's maize. At the same time the rising demand of the middle class for beef, pork, and poultry was met by government policies encouraging the production of feed grains. Commercial producers responded by turning to more capital-intensive (more farm machinery) production methods and to less labor-intensive crops, such as sorghum. Many small maize farmers also turned to sorghum production to supply the expanding market for cattle feed. With the 1989-90 opening of the northern border to sorghum imports, these growers were ruined.

The dual structure of Mexican agriculture produces, on the one hand, an upward spiral in which larger, wealthier farms have ready access to capital and agricultural inputs to increase their productivity. Agricultural research and development programs also tend to meet the needs of agribusiness.[95] These investments stimulate further productivity in the agribusiness sector, which, in turn, prompts still more capital investment, research, and development programs. On the other hand, the small landholder and *ejido* sector are victims of a downward spiral of decapitalization and decreasing productivity.

The backwardness of the rain-fed or dryland agriculture in Mexico, especially among subsistence farmers, is not the result of the peasantry's resistance to modernization. On the contrary, numerous studies have demonstrated that small farmers are as interested as large farmers in increasing productivity and in growing the most profitable product.[96] They do not, however, have equal access to the resources needed to stimulate such productivity.

This duality between capitalists and peasants and between large cash-crop farmers and small producers of basic grains accounts in large part for the often contradictory characterization of the agricultural sector's health. Proponents of agroindustrial strategies and export-oriented agricultural policies applaud the movement toward capital-intensive, large-scale agriculture. They see the changes under way in Mexican agriculture as a much-needed modernization and perceive a new vigor in the agricultural sector. But those who look at the conditions of small farmers who produce for the domestic market are deeply critical of current trends. They point to rising food imports, agricultural trade imbalances, declining per capita food production, increasing landlessness, and rural poverty as evidence of an acute agricultural crisis.

Rising food imports is one indicator of uncertainty in the agricultural sector. Mexico now ranks among the world's four largest importers of grain.[97] The country has to import a quarter of its corn and is the world's largest importer of powdered milk.[98]

Corn or maize, a grain whose ancient origins were in the mountains of Mexico, is the staple for millions of poor Mexicans. During the past 20 years, while Mexico's population has exploded, maize production has slumped. In 1970, maize was cultivated over 18.3 million acres. Ten years later that area had decreased to 16.8 million acres. In 1990, despite major new cultivation as a result of government incentives, the area cultivated with maize remained below the 1970 acreage dedicated to that grain.

Not only is per capita food production declining in Mexico, so is per capita food consumption. During the 1980s per capita consumption of such basic products as meat, milk, and corn dropped sharply. Per capita meat consumption fell by 40 percent between 1984 and 1989, according to the Mexican government.[99] A 1991 report by the National Chamber of Hospitals concluded that nearly half of all children residing in rural Mexico suffered from malnutrition, rising to 75 percent in the southern states of Chiapas, Oaxaca, and Guerrero.[100]

Prevailing trends in rural production, including the expansion of the livestock industry, mechanization, and the cultivation of capital-intensive agricultural products for export, have interacted to bring about massive rural unemployment. With the trend toward capital-intensive exploitation in agriculture as a whole, permanent employees have been replaced by machinery and by temporary and migratory laborers whose employment is guaranteed only on a day-to-day basis.[101] Even the employment generated by the emerging agroindustrial plants, touted as the solution to rural unemployment, is minimal. During harvest time a substantial number of workers are hired, but this employment is highly seasonal, leaving the majority of the region's workers unemployed for most of the year. Today 80 percent of the rural population is without steady work.[102] Moreover, employers rarely meet the legal minimum wage or allow workers the required rest periods, much less pay overtime or provide other benefits required under Mexico's labor laws.[103]

For the Mexican rural population, government neglect of the *campesino* sector, low standards of living in the countryside, high food prices, and the expanding power of landowners at the expense of peasants were factors that helped spark the Mexican Revolution.[104] Today, the conditions of poverty, malnutrition, unemployment, landlessness, and the lack of basic services continue to fuel rural dissatisfaction with the government. Although the rural population constitutes a diminishing portion of total Mexican population, their actual numbers continue to increase. By the year 2000 an estimated 35 million people will be living in rural Mexico—more than the country's total population at the time of the Mexican Revolution.[105]

At the same time that agricultural modernization has marginalized the Mexican peasantry, it has also injected a new dynamism in other areas. Between 1940 and 1990 the land under cultivation tripled.[106] Over the past two decades the amount of land irrigated increased by over 20 percent.[107] The area cultivated with fruits and vegetables, as well as with commercial crops such as coffee, cotton, and tobacco, also expanded, a process that was further stimulated by new agroindustrial investment. This expansion, especially in the last five years, stimulated increases in productivity and exports. Measured in terms of hours of labor per ton produced, such crops as barley, garlic, onions, tomatoes, and wheat have all increased in terms of productivity. In some cases productivity has increased by as much as 80 percent because of labor-saving technological changes.[108] Between 1985 and 1990 the value of agricultural exports increased by 50 percent.[109]

By 1991 there were signs that the government's agricultural policies might be stimulating new growth, not only in export production but also in domestic food production. By eliminating price lids for some products and raising the guaranteed price for others, the government encouraged new cultivation of basic grains. Through the National Solidarity Program (Pronasol), government credit and other assistance was directed to the small-farm sector. The rebound of the agricultural sector in 1990, while important, fell far short of recuperating the lost ground in per capita production experienced over the previous two decades. Heavy rains that year and the political character of the increased government attention to the small-farm sector just prior to midterm elections also qualified the significance of the 4-percent growth in the agricultural GDP experienced in 1990.

Clearly the liberalization of the domestic agricultural market could benefit the entire agricultural sector. Peasant and commercial farmers alike have been affected by policies that maintain low prices for basic foodstuffs in the interest of keeping the population supplied with cheap food and meats. By raising prices to levels that guarantee adequate profits, the government could encourage increased basic-grain production by both peasants and larger growers. The problem is that international agricultural trade is being liberalized at the same time the domestic market is being deregulated. International price and productivity levels, not the free trade on the domestic market, will then determine whether Mexican farmers can profitably produce basic grains and all other commodities.

The Agroexport Boom

Whereas the domestic agricultural sector stagnated during the 1980s, the export sector boomed, increasing at an average annual rate of nearly 10 percent. Ninety percent of the country's agricultural exports go to the United States, and Mexico is the second largest supplier of agricultural products to the United States after Canada. Between 1982 and 1990 Mexican agricultural exports to the United States more than doubled.

Horticultural exports (mainly fruits and vegetables) fueled this export growth. As the U.S. vegetable market expanded and the costs of Mexican labor decreased in the 1980s, there was increased investment in horticultural production by both foreign and domestic agribusinesses. Mexico is by far the largest source of U.S. horticultural imports, supplying more than 50 percent of the winter vegetables imported into the United States.

Coffee, however, is Mexico's single largest agricultural export to the United States. Mexico is the world's fourth largest coffee producer, and its coffee exports to the United States constitute more than a third of the country's total agricultural exports.[110] Unlike other export crops, coffee in Mexico is produced mainly by small growers, with 70 percent of the growers owning less than 5 acres.

Mexico is the largest foreign supplier of feeder cattle to the U.S. market. Whereas the United States imports cattle on the hoof from Mexico, Mexico is the second largest export market for U.S. meats. Imported meat from the United States, which accounts for about 2 percent of total Mexican meat consumption, steadily increased during the 1980s due to greatly expanded promotional and credit programs sponsored by the U.S. government.[111] During the 1980s Mexico became an important supplier of processed foods to the United States. These included tomato sauce and paste, fruit juices, and beer.[112]

Horticultural production in Mexico depends almost exclusively on the U.S. market, which is not only fickle economically but often hostile politically. When nontariff barriers in the United States block exports, and when plant disease, excess pesticide usage, or low market prices make it difficult for exporters to market their produce profitably, they face heavy losses. Because there is no effective domestic market for horticultural products, growers are forced to dump their harvest. At the same time, horticultural growers are among the most privileged in the country. They have been the privileged targets for credit, technical assistance, and input subsidies. They also occupy the best land, employ the poorest migrant laborers, and generally violate government labor and land-tenure regulations.[113]

About a quarter of Mexico's agricultural exports do not compete with U.S. products. Such Mexican exports as coffee, cacao, and tropical fruits, for example, are not cultivated in the United States. Although many of the fresh horticultural commodities exported by Mexico are also produced in the United States, they supplement low U.S. production during the winter months and do not directly compete with U.S. growers. These winter vegetables and fruits provide U.S. consumers greater year-round selection and lower prices. Such products as cantaloupes, watermelons, and asparagus have complementary production seasons with the United States, thereby again providing no direct competition with U.S.-based growers. Other Mexican exports such as strawberries, tomatoes, and cucumbers may compete directly with U.S. products, although Florida growers are often unable to supply the U.S. winter market with the quantity and quality consumers demand. Besides its climate, cheap land and labor are Mexico's main advantages in undercutting U.S. growers. Even with rising Mexican exports, however, U.S. production of most horticultural commodities increased during the 1980s, benefiting from increasing U.S. consumer demand and advances in agricultural technology.[114]

Foreign firms have generally stayed away from direct investment in agricultural cultivation in Mexico, preferring instead to invest in food processing for the Mexican market. As horticultural export production increased, foreign firms jumped into the business but rarely in direct production. Instead companies such as Heinz, United Brands, and Castle & Cooke contracted farm production while others set up fruit- and vegetable-processing plants for the export market. In many sectors of agroindustry in Mexico, foreign control exceeds 50 percent, rising to 75 percent in some businesses. Among the most important foreign food-processing corporations in Mexico are PepsiCo, Ralston Purina, Campbell's, General Foods, Del Monte, Beatrice Food, Gerber, Kellogg, Kraft, and Nestlé.[115]

A new twist in the agroindustry sector is the plan to use Mexico as a base for exporting processed foods to the United States. PepsiCo, for example, announced in 1991 its plan to export snack foods to the United States. In the late 1980s major agribusiness firms, including Kraft and Campbell's, and dozens of smaller investors established *maquiladoras* to assemble agricultural components into finished goods for the export market. Everything from geraniums to sushi and lemon wedges are processed by these agro-*maquilas*. Stock geranium plants, for example, are shipped to Mexico where they are inserted into a synthetic rooting material by Mexican workers.[116]

The Threat of Free Trade

The proposed free trade agreement represents another step toward the full insertion of the Mexican economy into the international market. Even before the free trade negotiations opened, Mexico had greatly liberalized its agricultural trade. By 1991 few import licenses remained and tariffs were reduced to a trade-weighted average of 11 percent (compared to a 7-percent U.S. average). One example of this pre-NAFTA liberalization was the dramatic surge—increasing nearly 50 times—in U.S. exports to Mexico of processed cereal products, primarily breakfast cereals and breads, after Mexico eliminated its import-license requirement.

Mexican agricultural exporters stand to gain by a free trade agreement. It is unlikely, however, that a free trade accord would result in dramatic increases in agricultural exports to the United States. Already 40 percent of Mexico's exports enter the United States duty free under the Generalized System of Preferences (GSP) and other trade agreements. Even if all tariff barriers were torn down, exporters in Mexico would still face stiff nontariff barriers in the form of health, safety, and quality regulations, which are often used in a discriminatory manner to keep out competitive products.

Trade negotiators were immediately faced with deciding how much to liberalize the agricultural sector. The technological superiority of U.S. agricultural production and the substantial government support U.S. growers receive—from disaster relief to the funding of agricultural research and development—would put Mexican growers at a profound disadvantage in a completely liberalized trade environment. Even if U.S. government subsidies were completely eliminated, which is highly unlikely, the U.S. farm sector enjoys such a tremendous head start that Mexican growers would be hard put ever to catch up.

Mexican corn production, for example, is not likely to be competitive with U.S. or Canadian producers, at least in the foreseeable future. According to one estimate, Mexican corn production per hectare averaged 1.7 metric tons (MT) in a recent five-year period—compared to a 7-MT average in the United States and 6.2 MT in Canada. Still more striking is the labor-intensive nature of Mexican corn production. Labor time per ton of corn in Mexico was estimated at 17.8 days, while it was only 1.2 hours in the United States.[117] In another example, Mexico produces 542 kilos of beans per hectare compared to 1,661 in the United States. The per hectare rice yield in Mexico is 3.3 MT compared to 6.2 MT in the United States. Another indicator of the wide production gap that exists between Mexico and its prospective free trade partners is the measure of gross agricultural output per worker. In 1988 this stood at $1,799 in Mexico, $45,052 in the United States, and $36,617 in Canada.[118]

Production of basic grains is not the only area of agricultural production that would be threatened by free trade. Growers of potatoes, apples, pears, and many other agricultural commodities will likely be pushed out of the market trade if completely regionalized. Even with products in which Mexico enjoys a strong comparative advantage because of labor-intensive cultivation or climate, free trade might not be entirely positive in the long run. As more growers switch to these crops, not only in Mexico but elsewhere throughout the world, prices will likely plummet as the U.S. market becomes saturated. Especially the small commercial farmers will likely have a difficult time switching crops back and forth in response to changes in U.S. market prices and demand.

In no other sector is Mexico so vulnerable to the undermining of domestic business as in agriculture. In resisting U.S. pressure to open its agricultural market, Mexico of course would not be alone. As it is, even the multilateral GATT agreement retains strong protections for national agricultural and livestock industries. GATT allows tariffs of up to 50 percent on agricultural commodities as well as the setting of import licenses for nearly all agricultural products.

The Peasant Response

Although Mexico's agrarian-reform program failed to end the problem of landlessness in Mexico, it largely succeeded in pacifying the peasant population and keeping it close to the ruling political party. Demands for social justice and land were effectively channeled into the Ministry of Agrarian Reform instead of sparking widespread rural revolt. Also instrumental in controlling the peasantry has been the CNC, the corporatist peasant confederation established during the Cárdenas *sexenio*.

As an official organization the CNC has been able to offer *campesinos* expedited attention to demands. This very link with PRI has compromised the CNC's resolve to side with the peasantry in confrontations with the state. In the first three years of the Salinas administration, this proclivity to back the government's position was seen clearly in the CNC's support for the economic pact which kept a lid on farm prices. This inability to represent peasant interests led to the creation of numerous independent organizations. These range from *zapatista* groups demanding a renewal of agrarian reforms, to sectorial associations fighting for their specialized economic interests, to local groups fighting for higher prices and better access to credit and technology.

When the López Portillo administration attempted to put a new spin on agrarian populism by focusing on the social welfare of the peasantry rather than on the problem of landlessness, the country's poor rural residents responded with new cries of "Land to those who work it." By the late 1980s, however, peasant demands for land distribution had subsided. Independent peasant groups recognized that even a renewed agrarian reform would not resolve the structural problems of the countryside. Instead, they echoed the government's own discourse on the importance of productivity. But rather than simply accepting the government's position, these organizations stepped up their demands for increased credit, public-sector investment in small-scale irrigation projects, and more control over the commercialization of their produce—all seen as essential for better productivity.[119]

The incorporation of production-related demands into the agenda of independent peasant organizations has not excluded the voicing of other noneconomic demands, such as calls to end government corruption and repression by private and public security forces. Other common demands relate to the defense of local natural resources, the need for higher prices, and the autonomy of the *ejidos*.[120] As free trade negotiations opened, Mexican peasant and farm organizations began to demand that protections against international competition, particularly in the basic-grain sector, remain in place.

Challenges Facing Mexican Agriculture

Mexico's neoliberal economic policies and its embrace of global market integration will face their hardest test in the country's agricultural sector. If these policies are to succeed, they will have to prove that increased export production based on Mexico's comparative advantages (mainly cheap labor and climate) can earn enough foreign exchange to cover the increase in food imports resulting from liberalization.[121] This new modernization will have to confront the country's huge food-import bills, tackle the failings of the country's dual agricultural structures, and be willing to leave behind the political heritage of the government's cheap-food policies.[122]

Even if the modernization of the agricultural sector addresses these challenges, Mexico will likely still face the problem of underutilization of rural labor. Most export production and commercial production of grain crops are considerably less labor-intensive than traditional rain-fed domestic food production in Mexico. Although the old *zapatista* slogan "Land to those who work it" may no longer be a reasonable solution to Mexico's agrarian problems, the old problems of landlessness and rural poverty continue to plague Mexico and demand new solutions.

PART THREE

Social Forces

"The revolution has not triumphed. In your hands is the will and the power to save it; but if, unfortunately, you do not, the shades of Cuauhtémoc, Hidalgo, and Juárez and the heroes of all time will stir in their tombs to ask: What have you done with the blood of your brothers?"

—*Emiliano Zapata*[1]

© Cindy Reiman/Impact Visuals

The Private Sector and its Organizations

The separation of state and private capital is a half-truth that has served to stabilize the modern Mexican nation. In keeping with its populist pretensions, the ruling party incorporated labor unions, peasant associations, and popular organizations into its corporatist structure. However, no official role was ever given to business. Along with the Roman Catholic Church and the military, the private sector has been one of the powerful but "invisible" sectors in Mexican society.[2] The idea was that business and politics should not mix, at least not in any public or official way.

Until the 1980s direct participation in party politics by the business community was rare. Politics was considered a dirty, small-time affair, beneath the dignity of businessmen. Moreover direct politicking by business leaders was unnecessary. The business community influenced economic policymaking not through partisan politics but by way of behind-the-door deals with the president's economic cabinet negotiated for the most part by the leading business organizations. In addition, there has been a revolving door between the business community and positions in the various economic ministries, such as treasury, planning and budget, and the central bank.[3]

Immediately after the adoption of the constitution in 1917 the government established the first obligatory business chamber, the Confederation of Chambers of Commerce (Concanaco). A year later a counterpart chamber, the Confederation of Industrial Chambers (Concamin), was formed to incorporate the country's manufacturers and industrialists. The most important member of Concamin has been the National Chamber of Manufacturing Industries (Canacintra), which historically has been more representative of small- and medium-scale manufacturers than of large industrialists. All local, state, and national chambers of commerce are required to associate with these two confederations.

Initially, these obligatory chambers received a degree of direct government support, but this fell off as the business associations became more autonomous. Other business groups emerged that were not chartered by government statute and were more independent. The oldest of these is the Mexican Employers Confederation (Coparmex), which from its founding in 1929 has been explicitly antisocialist—its early doctrine being "not class struggle but class collaboration."[4]

Business and the State

The private sector has never been completely united. Size, type of business, and geographical location have created differences and divisions within the country's business community. Differing perspectives about the role of the state have raised another obstacle to private-sector unity.

Ideological opposition to the Mexican state arose during the Cárdenas *sexenio* as the result of the government's populist policies. Between 1940 and the early 1970s, however, there existed an unofficial political pact between business and government. For the most part, business leaders recognized the strategic role played by the state in expanding the country's economic base. The Mexican government synthesized and gave cohesion to Mexico's drive toward industrialization.[5] With steady economic growth rates, a protected market, and state subsidies, there was little substantial argument with the state's role in managing the economy.

Nevertheless, since the Mexican Revolution there has always existed a tug-of-war between two sets of actors who have aimed to shape state policy.[6] On the one side has been a loosely defined coalition of nationalists and populists, which reached its height of influence during the Cárdenas presidency. Called the "Cárdenas coalition" by some, this leftward pull on state policy visibly lost most of its strength with the advent of the administration of Miguel Alemán. Although never completely disappearing as a policy influence, the progressive coalition did not again exercise a decisive role in government decisionmaking until the Echeverría administration's adoption of a "shared-development" strategy of economic growth. The 1982 nationalization of the banking system could also be attributed to the weight of the progressives within Mexico's political elite.

The more dominant influence on policy has been variously described as the "bankers' alliance," "conservative coalition," and the "neoliberal project." Since the early days of the revolution this competing alliance has held control of the government's financial policy. At the center of this conservative private-sector coalition have been the country's private financiers, bankers, and associated industrialists. Largely due to the clout wielded by this alliance, the Mexican government historically has exercised little control over domestic financial markets. This policy has allowed wealth and financial resources to become increasingly concentrated in the hands of a small number of conglomerates, or *grupos*.[7]

This ongoing but uneven competition between progressive and conservative forces has been called the "fight for the nation" by some Mexican analysts.[8] Between 1940 and 1970, however, there really was not much of a fight. The influence exercised by peasant and worker organizations, together with their progressive allies in the intellectual, business, and political communities, gradually faded in the halls of government. With the loss of that source of support, the state's autonomy vis-à-vis its capitalists diminished. The country experienced a progressive subordination of the state to private capital.[9]

Nevertheless, in the early 1970s the pact between business and government began to break down. The change from the "stabilizing development" financial policies of the previous three decades to the "shared-development" proclamations of the Echeverría administration established the context for the rupture. The private sector's successful opposition to the administration's proposed tax reform and the establishment of a 40-hour work week (down from 48) were symptomatic of the new confrontative posture of Mexican business.[10] Rising private-sector anger with the direction of government policy was also apparent following the 1973 kidnapping and murder of Monterrey oligarch Enrique Garza Sada by suspected leftist terrorists. The death of Garza Sada radicalized many businessmen, who charged that the government's populist policies fomented attacks on the private sector. Yet another concern was that the government was breaking its alliance with the country's financial elite by turning to foreign instead of domestic financing.[11]

Another factor in the emergence of an organized business opposition was the expansion of the state's direct participation in the economy. In the view of the business community, state economic intervention, particularly through the increasing number of parastatals, had become excessive. Also important was the deteriorating health of the economy. Stabilizing development had reached its limits by the mid-1970s, and business proved to be the government's fair-weather friend. For the first time since the 1930s, the country experienced no per capita economic growth. As the economy slid into crisis, capital flight soared and business opposition deepened.

Symbolic of this new hostile stance of business was the 1975 creation of the Businessmen's Coordinating Council (CCE).[12] For at least three decades, the state had nurtured the country's bourgeoisie, but its progeny—no longer content with subordinate status—set out to redefine state-capital relations.[13] The CCE was a new kind of creature since it grouped together both registered business associations such as Concanaco and independent groups like Coparmex. It aimed to present a united front against what were regarded as populist and economically unsound practices of the government.

The oil boom (1978-81) eased tensions between the public and private sectors, but the lax fiscal management of López Portillo, symbolized by his dogged determination to defend the overvalued *peso*, resulted in massive capital flight and declining business confidence. The loss of as much as $20 billion through capital flight in 1981-82, combined with a sharp drop in oil prices, finally forced the president to devalue the *peso*.

In a desperate attempt to regain control of the economy and win popular support, López Portillo in September 1982 shocked the business community by announcing the nationalization of domestic banks and the imposition of foreign-exchange controls. Explaining the dramatic move in his September 1982 State of the Nation address, López Portillo said, "In the last two or three years . . . a group of Mexicans . . . supported and advised by the private banks has stolen more money from our country than the empires which have exploited us since the beginning of history. They've robbed us . . . but they won't rob us again."

The Bank Nationalization and Its Repercussions

Instead of signaling the triumph of the progressive coalition, the bank nationalization signaled the beginning of the ascendancy of the neoliberal project. As a strike against the country's financial oligarchy, the nationalization was widely applauded by leftist intellectuals and worker and peasant organizations. It also received the support of many of the country's small- and medium-scale businesses. For the most part, however, Mexico's private sector vehemently opposed the bank nationalization.

Effective national control over foreign exchange flows and the national financial system was never achieved. The bank nationalization unleased a new wave of private-sector opposition to state intervention in the economy and sparked unprecedented political activity by elements within the business community. The new political aggressiveness of portions of the business community bolstered the strength of those factions within PRI that wanted the government to revamp its relations with the private sector. Although President de la Madrid was quick to declare the "irreversibility" of the bank nationalization, he also moved rapidly to make amends with the business community. One of his first acts as president was to invite members of the Mexican Council of Businessmen (CMHN), an exclusive association that draws together the country's richest businessmen, to join him for a breakfast meeting at the presidential mansion of Los Pinos. Bankers were fully compensated for their expropriated interests. Also to placate the alienated financial community, President de la Madrid fostered the creation of a parallel banking system that opened the way for the reconstitution of the country's financial oligarchy.

Stiff austerity measures, including an effective freeze on wage increases, pleased the business community but it demanded more. It wanted the corporatist, populist state completely dismantled. In its place the business elite wanted a state that would promote the private sector as the true and only instrument of economic development. Slowly at first but then more rapidly as the decade progressed, the private sector saw its wishes come true. Among the signs of this restructuring of government-business relations were the increasing liberalization of trade and investment (marked in 1986 by the GATT accession), accelerating privatization, and wage and price policies that tended to concentrate wealth.

For Mexican businessmen, the September 1982 bank nationalization marked the beginning of a new era in government-business relations. No longer simply defending their consultative role in the government's policymaking process, they went on the offensive with the objective of establishing a new and superior place for the private sector in Mexican politics. No longer would they be the "invisible sector"; no longer would they be treated as "second-class citizens." In immediate reaction to the bank nationalization, former CCE President Manuel J. Clouthier, together with other anti-PRI business leaders, sponsored a series of political forums that warned of the spread of socialism in Mexico. Shedding their previous reluctance to participate in partisan politics, many of the country's major business figures began to participate openly in the electoral process.

Particularly in northern Mexico, many entrepreneurs began publicly supporting the country's two major conservative parties, the National Action Party (PAN) and the smaller Mexican Democratic Party (PDM), as a way to promote a more pronounced private-sector focus in government. At the same, however, other prominent businessmen, such as Gamesa owner Alberto Santo de Hoyos, were welcomed into the folds of the ruling party. Still others waffled between supporting PAN and working for change within the PRI government.

The association between sectors of the business community and PAN crested in the 1985 midterm elections. But as the *técnicos* and neoliberals gained strength within PRI, a new alliance between state and capital began to emerge. Besides adopting market-oriented policies, the ruling party solicited the participation of leading moderate business leaders, both as candidates and as directors of policymaking commissions within the party. In the tradition of government-business dealings in Mexico and throughout the world, this alliance came with immediate financial rewards. Investors close to PRI were given privileged access to state enterprises, as was the case in the privatization of Mexicana Airlines (bought in part by Pablo Bréner, member of PRI's fundraising committee), Telmex (bought in part by Carlos Slim, also a member of the fundraising committee), and the Cananea copper mine (bought by Jorge Larrea, a personal friend of President Salinas).

The signing of the tripartite Economic Solidarity Pact in 1987 by labor, business, and government representatives demonstrated how much relations between the private and public sectors had improved since the dark days following the bank nationalization. Augustín Legorreta, former owner of Banamex and president of the CCE, signed the unprecedented accord concerning price and wage freezes. Only five years before, Legorreta and the CCE had led the private-sector opposition to the bank nationalization.

Since 1987 relations between business and government have improved steadily as a result of a stream of state initiatives to promote private business interests. Even so, Mexico's business organizations continually prod the government to further liberalize the economy. Leading this attack have been the sectors most radically committed to the free market, but they generally count on at least tacit support from most of the business community. The chief demand is the reform of federal labor law, which organizations such as Coparmex say must be modernized to reflect the central place of the private sector.

Business would like to abolish collective labor contracts, replacing them with contracts between employers and individual workers. In the state of Nuevo León this has already been accomplished, with the official unions being replaced by company unions or no unions at all. If "modernized," the federal law would restrict the right to strike and would virtually eliminate federal protections of the work force. Business organizations are also calling for the *flexibilización* of wage laws to allow employers to pay and hire by the hour (rather than at a salaried rate) and to reassign workers to different jobs as they see fit. The part-time hiring practices of such transnational fast-food firms as McDonald's are seen as the model for more flexible worker-employer relations in Mexico. Essentially, the business sector is demanding that the forces of the market substitute for state regulation of employment practices.[14] The Salinas government, although in essential agreement with the proposed changes to the labor law, seemed reluctant to introduce a reform bill in Congress for fear of generating popular opposition. Instead, it simply declined to enforce the existing law and sought to "modernize" employer-worker relations through extra-official economic pacts.

Divisions within Business

The populist rhetoric of Echeverría and the bank nationalization by López Portillo served to rally the business community around a common program demanding that the private sector be given a central place in directing the country's development. Nonetheless, political and strategic differences prevented the effective unity of the private sector, as did long-running variations in the size, type, and geographical base of the country's businesses.[15]

Historically there has been a rift in the business community between the "radicals" and the "moderates," with the radicals taking a more uncompromising posture on such matters as the country's mixed economy and the corporatism of the one-party state. Based largely in the north, the radicals constitute the private sector's right wing and are the most ideologically committed. In general, the moderates are less ideological and more pragmatic. With their strongest base in the Mexico City metropolitan area, the moderates are oriented more toward the national market and as such to the regulation and protection of the state. Rather than supporting an independent political posture for the business community, this faction favors working within PRI to formulate economic and social policies.

As the business-government alliance began to disintegrate in the early 1970s, the radicals became the dominant voice in the emerging debate over the respective roles of government and capital. The radicals, too, led the assault against bank nationalization. As the government moved ever closer to the neoliberal project, however, the moderates resumed their place as the leading voice of the business elite. This evolution was particularly evident in the less confrontative stance of the CCE, but was also seen in even more traditionally hard-line organizations like Coparmex.

The friction between radicals and moderates has aggravated traditional divisions between the commercial, industrial, and financial communities, as well as accentuating north-south differences. One of the main forums for these conflicts has been the CCE, which has moved from being an opposition group to one that offers strong backing for the government's economic policies.[16] Largely responsible for this turn toward the government has been CMHN, which succeeded in isolating the radicals of the CCE. Because of this willingness to defend the government and to enter into joint economic pacts, radicals within the CCE regarded members of the progovernment business faction as "conservatives," who were being used by the governments as instruments of a private-sector *charrismo* to maintain state control over the business community.[17]

Questions about the nature of the reconstituted business-government alliance were not the only divisive issues facing the CCE midway through the Salinas *sexenio*. There was also rising concern about the elite control of the country's main business alliance by a small group of industrialists and financiers. Within the CCE, this small oligarchic circle includes the Mexican Council of Businessmen (CMHN), Mexican Investors Association (AMCB), and the Mexican Association of Insurance Institutions (AMIS). But the CCE is not the only business organization vulnerable to charges of anti-democratic procedures. All but the smallest of the national, state, and municipal business associations are top-down organizations controlled by the business elite. Small- and medium-scale firms are generally excluded from the hierarchy of the main business associations.

Since the outbreak of the 1982 crisis the gap between large and small businesses has widened, as the country's biggest capitalists tended to take advantage of the recession to buy up smaller enterprises. It was also the larger investors who benefited from fluctuating currency exchanges, capital flight, and Mexico's new financial market. Perhaps the most significant difference, though, has been the ability of the larger firms to reorient themselves to the export market, while the smaller companies have found that they are unable to compete with the flood of cheap imports.

Initially the entire business community stood behind the demands for less state interventionism. As neoliberal reforms progressed, however, many Mexican businesses, particularly those in the manufacturing sector, feared that liberalization was threatening their very survival. Whereas big business organizations stand solidly behind the market openings, many smaller enterprises tremble in the face of a free trade agreement with Canada and the United States. Seeing that their interests are not represented by the CCE and other national business associations, small- and medium-scale firms have sponsored the creation of new business chambers more concerned with the state of the domestic market.[18]

Just as the rules of the economy are changing so is the Mexican oligarchy. Its relationship to the state and to the international market is being redefined and reshaped. Increasing economic integration and emphasis on export production are pushing other business organizations to the foreground. These include the National Import-Export Association (ANIERM), the National Foreign Trade Council (CEMAI), and the Coordinator of Foreign Trade Groups (COECE). Established at the initiative of the Salinas administration, COECE was immediately drawn into the government's free trade policymaking. Alongside these Mexican business organizations stand those associations representing the interests of foreign corporations, particularly those from the United States. The government's initiative in the late 1980s to increase exports through new financial instruments and to promote key industrial sectors like the auto industry also served to increase the importance of export-oriented business associations.[19] For example, the American Chamber of Commerce of Mexico (Amcham), which has always been a strong voice for U.S. investors, has become more influential with the steady transnationalization of the Mexican economy.[20] Also important are such transnational groups as the U.S. Council of the Mexico-U.S. Business Committee, which is jointly sponsored by the U.S. Chamber of Commerce, the Council of the Americas, and Amcham.

The Rich and Famous

Geographically, private wealth is concentrated in the Mexico City metropolitan area, Monterrey, and Guadalajara. The leading families from these three cities, primarily Mexico City and Monterrey, control the country's main business associations. Other geographic concentrations of wealth are found in such secondary cities as Puebla and Chihuahua.

Increasingly the term "oligarchy" is being used to describe the wealthiest Mexican families. This elite is also known as "the 300" and the "Senate." Estimates of the number of members of the inner economic circle in Mexico have ranged from 30 to a thousand or more. However, it was the widely reported statement of oligarch Augustín Legorreta in 1988 that a "very comfortable little group of 300 people make all the economically important decisions in Mexico" that has made 300 the most common estimate.[21]

The 300 families include the old aristocracy (including such family names as Garza Sada, Sánchez Navarro, Iturbide, and Arango) as well as the rich of the "miracle" years (1940-70), including the Alemán, Azcárraga, O'Farrill, Ruíz Galindo, and Legorreta families. The turbulent 1970s and 1980s produced new members of the oligarchy whose wealth flows from financial speculation, the stock market, the oil boom, and lately, the government's privatization program (including Slim, Bréner, Saba, and Hank).[22]

Besides this regional and familial concentration of wealth, economic power in Mexico tends to concentrate in major investment groups. The integration of financiers and industrialists into *grupos* dates back to the Porfirio

Díaz regime. Mexico's corporate wealth is still mainly found in the country's leading investment groups or conglomerates. The most famous of these investment groups is the so-called Monterrey Group, which is divided into four different industrial conglomerates: Alfa, Visa, Cydsa, and Vitro. Other major groups include Grupo Chihuahua, Grupo Peñoles, Grupo Bimbo, Grupo Condumex, Grupo Minera México, Grupo Sabre, Grupo Televisa, and Grupo Hermes.[23] During the 1980s many of the leading holding companies were forced to restructure because of their large foreign debt, with some of their corporate holdings passing into foreign hands. The overly indebted state of some groups, notably the Alfa Group, also resulted in government bailouts.

Before the bank nationalization, Mexico's major investment groups were closely linked with the country's leading private banks, with each bank essentially acting as the financial arm of a different industry. More than any other economic sector, the financial industry also had close associations with the government, with a revolving door between leadership levels of the Mexican Bankers Association and public offices.[24] The bank nationalization temporarily disrupted the linkage between banks and industry. Subsequent financial reforms, however, opened the way for the creation of a parallel financial system that gave rise to new oligarchs and the reshaping of older financial groups.

In large part the wealth that had previously been concentrated in the private banks was found later in the Bolsa Mexicana de Valores (stock market) and new financial institutions that arose after the bank nationalization. By 1987 it was said that just ten *casas de bolsa* (stock brokerage firms) controlled 80 percent of the stock and speculative activity in the country. The four dominant *casas de bolsa* are Inverlat, Operadora de Bolsa, Acciones y Valores de México, and Probursa. Some of the leading brokerage firms are direct descendants of the prenationalized banks while others represent new financial wealth. Judged to be among the most profitable stock markets in the world during the 1980s, the Bolsa Mexicana de Valores was the source of spectacular speculative wealth during and after the 1987 crash, when stocks plummeted.

President de la Madrid did not reverse the nationalization order of his predecessor, but he did foster the rise of a reconstituted financial elite. Besides permitting the previous owners to own up to 34 percent of the nationalized banks, he allowed private investors to serve as managers of the nationalized banks and authorized former owners to buy back from the government all nationalized property except regular savings banks. As a result, new investment banks, also called nonbank financial intermediaries, became the foundation of an emerging network of private financing.

Ironically, a principal source of investment profit for the parallel financial system has been the government itself. The banks were nationalized in a desperate attempt to obstruct capital flight. To attract this capital back into the country, the government allowed high interest rates to prevail. But the main victim of this high-interest policy has been the government, whose debt-service payments on its domestic debt (loaned by private financiers) rose to double the rate paid on its external debt.[25]

The New Mix of Politics and Business

The PAN opposition has been more critical of the increasing monopolization of wealth in Mexico than has PRI. Leaders of PAN have complained that the reconstitution of the financial conglomerates and the resurgence of speculative investment endanger the country's economic stability. With this same indignation, the *panistas* criticized business radicals for wanting to turn the party into a businessmen's organization. One PAN leader in Mexico City accused this faction of trying to convince the Mexican people that "what is good for Kimberly Clark [a major multinational corporation] is good for Mexico."[26]

Bank reprivatization, which began in 1991, will likely serve to reestablish the close linkage between industrial and financial sectors in Mexico, while further empowering the country's oligarchy and its bankers' alliance. This is only one element, however, in the emergence of a new political and economic order in Mexico. Politically, the business community is no longer one of the "invisible sectors" in the country's policymaking and politicking. Both PAN and PRI compete to sponsor the same businessmen as candidates, and the Salinas administration threw open the doors of the ruling party to the business sector.

The economic order is characterized by the increased concentration of wealth, a government wedded to the interests of an export-oriented private sector, and the expanded presence of foreign capital. More than ever before, the country's popular forces are being isolated. Instead, a mutually beneficial tripartite coalition is forming between the state, the country's oligarchy, and foreign investors and traders.

It is a dynamic but fragile order. The fragility comes largely from the essentially weak nature of the Mexican private sector. Economists have long described the capitalist class in Mexico as a "rentier" class used to easy income and reluctant to risk capital in a competitive market. It has traditionally depended on the state for protection and patronage. Even while pushing for a leaner state, Mexican businesses remain overly dependent on the government for riskless income, special contracts, and support services. The opening up of Mexico to the international market may force Mexican capitalists to become more competitive. However, a rise in business foreclosures, especially among small- and medium-scale firms, is more likely. As is already the case, many of the country's largest corporations will seek to find some niche in the export market or will instead choose to sell out to foreign capital.

Mexican Labor and Unions

In many respects Mexico has one of the most advanced labor laws on the continent, largely as a result of the Mexican Revolution. The Constitution of 1917 and federal labor laws guarantee a minimum wage, the eight-hour day, the right to strike, severance pay, overtime pay, workers' compensation, and liberal maternity-leave benefits.[1] Current labor practices, however, often violate both the intent and the letter of the law. Many Mexican unions serve to filter and control workers' demands, prevent the entrance of more militant unions, negotiate political power for their leaders, and garner votes for PRI through coercive measures—anything but represent worker interests.

When the 1985 earthquake struck Mexico City, it revealed the fact that thousands of "contracts of protection" existed in the numerous small shops destroyed. In those contracts, the unions holding collective bargaining rights had neither a presence in the workplace nor contracts with the workers. The contracts had been signed between management and corrupt union leaders. The workers did not even know of the existence of the unions that supposedly represented them. Along with contracts of protection, workers also work under "company contracts" forged with management-invented unions and contracts between official unions and management, whose terms are never put to a democratic vote by the rank and file. Both governmental labor authorities and official unions themselves consistently deny workers the freedom to choose representation—sometimes at the cost of worker bloodshed and death. The reasons for these distortions of Mexican unionism lie in the country's peculiar labor history and the nature of the Mexican state.

History of the Mexican Labor Movement

The history of Mexican labor follows closely the evolution of the Mexican state. Since the establishment of the one-party government in 1929, the organized labor movement has been largely defined by its relation to the government and the ruling party. As a prominent labor researcher put it, labor history has posed a serious question: "To what extent [is] the fate of

Mexican unionism . . . sealed by the political system, instead of being an element in the transformation of that system?"[2]

The Mexican Revolution, which began in 1910 and culminated in the Constitution of 1917, generally serves as a starting point for a review of organized labor in the country. Some important struggles did take place before then, however. The infamous Cananea Copper Mine strike of 1906—broken by the Mexican army and the Arizona Rangers in the interests of its U.S. owner—presaged the outbreak of the revolution and is remembered in ballads. But labor conflicts during the *porfiriato* remained largely isolated incidents because the dictatorship prohibited the growth and consolidation of a militant labor movement.

Although industrial workers played a relatively minor role in the revolution, they became a key element in strengthening the new government in the shaky post-revolutionary period. Strong leaders abetted by the revolutionary ideology of the times were able to win important legal guarantees in the construction of a new social pact.

The first national union to build a corporate alliance with the government was the Revolutionary Confederation of Mexican Workers (CROM), which threw its support behind President Alvaro Obregón. When the strongman of that confederation, Luis Morones, was discredited, union leaders began to split from the federation. Two powerful former CROM leaders, Vicente Lombardo Toledano and Fidel Velázquez, left to constitute the Mexican Workers Confederation (CTM) in February 1936. The CTM became the largest and most politically influential group in organized labor.

The CTM attained its privileged position under the aegis of President Lázaro Cárdenas. When Cárdenas assumed the presidency in 1934, he set about institutionalizing the already strong relations between organized labor and the state. In fact, the corporatist structures that characterize contemporary Mexican politics have their roots in that era. Historian Lorenzo Meyer described *cardenista* corporatism as "a complex combination of modern elements with strong roots in the past . . . that resulted in an authoritarian system but one that tended to be inclusive."[3] Cárdenas supported many labor struggles against capital, particularly nationalist conflicts with international capital.

The corporatist unions saw a steady growth in both their political strength and economic gains for organized workers over the next decades. With corporatist unions firmly in place, however, relatively little progress was made in developing real representation or internal democratic structures. Nonetheless, several democratic movements—such as the railroad workers' movement that struck in 1958—left an indelible mark on future generations of workers.

By the early 1970s the clout of the labor sector (especially that of Fidel Velázquez, the leader of the CTM beginning in 1941) in PRI corporatist infrastructure had grown to the point of being perceived as disproportionate by President Luis Echeverría. To counterbalance the CTM, he permitted the official registration of a number of independent unions, a practice which had traditionally been strictly limited. The newly formed unions arose from renewed grassroots activity, spurred in large part by activists from the 1968 student movement. These experienced organizers reacted to the repression of the student movement by seeking new terrain on which to organize for social change. Feeding into these new unions were many activists who drew their inspiration from or were aligned with the 1968 student movement. They dedicated their work to creating democratic rank-and-file labor currents that pressured the government to grant them official recognition. The independents enjoyed considerable strength in the 1970s, but as the new unions began to mount a militant challenge in the factories and in the streets Echeverría quickly closed the door. Since then the federal labor authorities have consistently denied petitions for registration by independent unions.[4]

Mexican labor entered into a major crisis with the economic downturn of 1982. The IMF-modeled austerity politics of the de la Madrid and Salinas administrations placed mere survival in jeopardy for thousands of workers and their families, as real wages plummeted and government services and benefits were cut back.[5] Corporatist unions suffered since the heavily indebted government no longer had any plums to hand out in exchange for political allegiance, and unions of all types were sapped of their bargaining power as national industry began to close shops or go underground.[6]

In December 1987 President de la Madrid signed the first of what would be a series of economic pacts between government, labor, and business. The Solidarity Pact was designed to stem the alarming 160-percent inflation of that year. It froze both prices and wages, actually doing a much more effective job of the latter than of the former, as demonstrated by the accelerated decline of workers' buying power. The agreement also froze workers' hopes of recovering a portion of their losses since the 1982 crisis.[7]

Salinas continued the anti-inflation, anti-worker policies of his predecessor. The pacts, which have been consistently renewed, granted a nominal wage hike that served as a ceiling not only for the government-established minimum wage but also for most government wages. Private businessmen also reported receiving heavy pressures from the administration to keep within range of the ceiling in their contract revisions. Official unions acquiesced in this process with some grumbling but no concrete action in defense of the standard of living of their members. Independent coalitions to protest the pacts at times mobilized large numbers of people but were short-lived.

The Official Labor Confederations

Mexican labor unions are typically divided into three major categories: official (or corporatist) unions; the newer, self-described modernizing unions; and independent unions.[8]

The first group includes most members of the Labor Congress (CT), as well as the CTM, which claims to represent 5.5 million workers in 14,000 unions. These unions, which include the mighty oil-workers' union—part of the CTM—and several other confederations, actually include a clause in their collective contracts that requires workers to affiliate with PRI. Decisions are made within the elite union leadership with very little decisionmaking power on the rank-and-file level.

Corporatist unions serve to block workers' demands or independent representation in many industries. Since the onset of the economic crisis, leaders have consistently backed down on labor demands for wage hikes and benefits. In a classic example of how real representation is bypassed in the corporatist system, Fidel Velázquez, acting as the representative of all Mexican workers, signed the solidarity pacts despite the fact that the agreements compromised even Velázquez with their blatantly antilabor content. Even so, the internal organization of the CTM assures that its secretary general, "don Fidel," maintains iron control over the confederation.

Corporatist unions hold many strings enabling them to dominate organized labor. Foremost among them is their relation to federal, state, and local labor authorities. Besides having the power to deny registration to independent unions, labor authorities may declare strikes "nonexistent" on supposed technicalities, control ratification of union elections through the Boards of Arbitration and Conciliation, and participate in national policymaking as the labor representatives on regulatory and policy commissions. Given the agreement between corporatist unions and the Mexican government, and particularly their usefulness in stemming workers' demands and harvesting their votes, these unions constitute a critical part of the system of rule in Mexico.

The June 1991 vote at the Ford Motor Company plant in Cuautitlán on whether to retain CTM representation or change unions illustrated how close this government-union relationship can be. A letter from Secretary of Labor Arsenio Farrell to Secretary of Trade and Development Jaime Serra Puche was leaked to the press several days before the vote. The letter referred to conversations with Ford in which the Ministry of Labor urged management to coordinate election preparations with the CTM.[9] The case of Ford highlighted another timeworn method of enforcing discipline in corporatist unions—violence. When workers began to make independent demands, armed CTM thugs infiltrated the plant and killed a worker in January 1990.[10] Thugs often arrive in force at union elections to coerce votes for official unions.[11]

Other unions and federations in the corporatist camp include the CROM, formed in 1918 and the predecessor of the CTM. The second largest industrial federation is the Revolutionary Confederation of Workers and Peasants (CROC), formed in 1952. Although also affiliated with PRI, some of the territorial feuds between CROC and the CTM have been bloody, such as the famous shoot-out in the Hotel Presidente Chapúltepec in 1989. Included among other smaller corporatist unions are the Confederation of

Workers and Peasants (CTC) and the Revolutionary Workers Confederation (COR).[12]

Modernizing and Independent Unions

Two other huge unions round out a general picture of official unionism. The first, the oil-workers' union, previously had tremendous economic power in the country. In February 1989 President Salinas decided to put an end to the largely autonomous control that union leader Joaquín Hernández Galicia ("La Quina") wielded over Petroleos de Mexico. In a predawn raid, federal agents arrested Hernández Galicia on arms and other charges. The government immediately replaced him with the more docile Sebastián Guzmán, who was more amenable to the privatization of large parts of the Pemex empire. While Salinas received kudos for his daring move to put an end to La Quina's tyranny, his gangland methods were nearly identical to La Quina's. When a new leader was imposed on the union, hopes were dashed that the move was a signal of the new administration's willingness to open spaces for more democratic representation for the 25,000 oil workers.

The largest official federation is the Federation of State Employees Unions (FSTSE), with nearly 2 million members. This federation is considered a "dinosaur" by the business association Coparmex because of its archaic tactics for controlling workers and the hardline corporatist attitudes of its leaders.

The official unions joined in an umbrella organization, the Labor Congress (CT), in 1966. The CT's rotating leadership has been handpicked, or at least approved, by Fidel Velázquez, and the CTM is the most influential presence within it. Tensions have arisen within the CT as some members have insisted that the organization take a more active stance in defense of workers' rights. Nonetheless, in August 1990 the CT reaffirmed its direct relation with PRI in a document called the "Political Pact of PRI and the Organizations of the Labor Congress." The stated purpose of the pact was "to preserve the joint action that [PRI and the CT] have maintained for over four decades."[13]

The "modernizing" unions are those that recognize a need to update the government-labor pact and promote demands through negotiation. They view themselves as an alternative current to the *charros* (imposed labor leaders), without breaking fully from the corporatist fold. Within this group two powerful unions that share a long history of democratizing tendencies have taken the lead: the Union of Telephone Workers of the Republic of Mexico (STRM) and the Mexican Electricians Union (SME).[14] The SME convoked a march of thousands to support a strike in February 1987. Despite the public support, the government intervened to run the national electricity company and declared the strike illegal. The electrical workers' gains fell far short of their demands. Nonetheless, the union's head, Jorge

Sánchez, has maintained a high profile for his leadership in the creation of this new current.

The telephone workers under Secretary General Francisco Hernández Juárez, who rose to power in 1976 as a leader of the union's democratic current and was recently re-elected to a fifth term, have found themselves at the center of some of Mexico's most pressing labor questions. The telephone company faces the need to modernize equipment, improve services, and restructure its operations after being privatized. Through these changes the union has sought to participate in decisionmaking and productivity plans, with mixed results.[15] The close relationship of Hernández Juárez and President Salinas enabled the union to negotiate some concessions from the company and government. These included a 4.4-percent share of ownership in the privatized company and representation on the committee charged with formulating recommendations regarding the communications sector for the team negotiating the North American Free Trade Agreement (NAFTA). However, some sectors within the union argued that this political affiliation has prohibited the union from taking positions overtly critical of Salinas administration policies.

In general the stance of the "modernizing unions" has been to defend sectoral interests while not taking up the defense of broader workers' rights that could conflict more directly with the administration's economic policies. The telephone-workers' and electrical-workers' unions joined with the pilots' association and others to form a new umbrella organization called the Union Federation of Goods and Services Providers (Fesebes). This current is considered closest to the Salinas administration's economic reforms.

Independent unions play an important role in the labor movement despite their small numbers. These unions are not affiliated with PRI and often wage battle against government labor policy and the official unions. Independent unions include workers at the National Autonomous University (UNAM) and several other national and regional universities, unions of the Authentic Labor Front (FAT), the September 19 Garment Workers Union, unions at some automobile factories, and others. The membership of independent unions has been slashed in recent years through the combination of workplace closures in national industry, privatization, and repression from the government and official unions.

A more recent strategy among democratic union activists has been to create rank-and-file movements within official unions. Due to the impossibility of registering independent unions with the government and their often marginalized position within the labor movement, workers in the National Education Workers Union created a democratic organization within the union in 1979. At its height, the National Coordinator of Education Workers (CNTE) included about 150,000 members of the union's estimated 800,000 total membership. In addition, it maintained a significant presence in several Mexico City locals, as well as in locals in various Mexican states. The CNTE's demands have centered on pay raises, but its insistence on democratic forms of union representation enabled it to bring down one of the most infamous *charro* leaders, Carlos Jonguitud, who had ruled over the union with a combination of repression and violence. A successful national strike led by the CNTE in 1989 ended Jonguitud's reign and put a brake on the violence that was commonplace under his leadership.

Current Trends

There exists a broad consensus that the Mexican labor movement is currently in crisis. That crisis is seen both in workers' economic conditions and the relationship between corporatist labor and the government. The minimum wage has fallen a full 60 percent over the past ten years. Although nearly one-third of the country's approximately 31 million economically active citizens are unionized, unions have been unwilling or unable to defend workers' interests since the crisis in 1982.[16] After that time, union membership has not made any difference in wage protection.

The figures translate into poverty, even for those fortunate enough to have a full-time job. The 1991 minimum wage of 11,900 pesos (less than four dollars) per day in Mexico City failed to cover even basic necessities. All major indices of social well-being reflect worker losses—drops in food consumption, increases in poverty-related diseases, and terrible living conditions.

For the estimated 40 percent of the work force that is unemployed or underemployed, things are worse. While government figures cite open unemployment at 3 percent, independent estimates range between 13 percent and 25 percent. Both the widely hailed industrial reconversion project and the privatization of state-owned enterprises have sent thousands of Mexican workers out into the streets, and new job creation has not been able to absorb the estimated one million people a year entering the work force. Privatizations alone have left over 200,000 workers without jobs, with no retraining or placement provisions.[17] Almost the only significant job creation is taking place in the informal sector, where workers face uncertainty, government harassment, and low incomes.

While workers and their families have lost, so have the official unions that failed to represent them. It is now commonplace to refer to a "crisis in corporatism" in Mexico. The Salinas administration's model of economic development, based on exports and global integration, has presented a new series of challenges and problems to Mexican labor that the old-style unions have been unable to address.

At the root of the problem is the changing relation between economic policy and labor organization. Corrupt unions run against the grain of new productive criteria. As Lorenzo Meyer put it, "The project to open the economy that was closed for 40 years is incompatible with a corporatist structure of the work force—if the Mexican government has destroyed barriers that protected its inefficient business members, it is also logical to suppose that it should destroy the corporatist protections that defend workers and employees who receive salaries and benefits not justified by the logic of competitiveness and efficiency."[18]

Although broad sectors of society agree that the old *charro* unions should soon become a thing of the past, the question of union democracy remains absent in governmental discourse. The Salinas administration finds itself between a rock and a hard place on the issue. Productivity concerns impel a revamping of the labor arm of the party, but the highly efficient— and coercive—electoral services of the unions are still indispensable to the party. Given the contradiction, the administration has made few moves to dismantle the official unions' control over the rank and file, while at the same time cutting down labor's role in national decisionmaking.

Elected posts have always been one of the most important rewards the government can grant loyal labor leaders. PRI allots a certain number of candidacies to each of the corporatist sectors and traditionally a large proportion has gone to labor. In the 1988 federal elections, 18 of the 66 PRI labor candidates for Congress were defeated—a shocking humiliation. The results were both a statement on the real rank-and-file popularity of the official labor leaders and an embarrassment to official labor. Labor journalist Sara Lovera noted that for the 1991 congressional elections, labor was given 53.5 percent fewer candidacies in the party.[19] This was seen in part as a punishment for labor's previous poor showing and a reflection of the diminishing importance of labor as a pillar of the party. The party leadership still depends on affiliated unions to bring in the votes, but it no longer feels obliged to assure political careers to PRI labor leaders.

"The crisis of corporatism stems from the incapacity of unions to develop an alternative project to that of the state and big capital, one that goes beyond simply resisting change and seeks to take into their hands an alternative to resolve the economic crisis," according to labor researcher Enrique de la Garza.[20] Democratic unions and movements want to take up that challenge in the context of protecting workers' rights and raising their standards of living. The government and business is looking more toward plans that would abolish collective bargaining in favor of individual contracts, piecework and job flexibility. Meanwhile the official unions—assigned the role of being labor's public voice—do not seem to have much of a plan at all. For this reason, the big issues such as the proposed National Productivity Pact (agreed to in principle by official labor, government, and business representatives in June 1990) and changes to the federal labor law are temporarily dead in the water.

The crumbling condition of official labor does not necessarily herald better times for workers because management is simply more able to impose its alternative than is democratic unionism. Labor expert Alberto Anguiano summed up the dangers: "The possible end to corporatism, with the crisis and decomposition of official labor and its apparatus of control over workers, does not seem to presage more but rather less democracy, not more but less autonomy of unions, not stronger unions but the perversion of real worker representation."[21]

International Division of Labor

Cheap labor that is held under tight control is one of Mexico's primary comparative advantage in the process of opening its economy, attracting foreign investment to pay off its foreign debt, and luring transnational production. Therefore, the government is not granting any major concessions to labor's wage demands, nor is it likely to do so in the near future.

The *maquiladoras* are often looked to as a sign of things to come. Wage levels in the plants tend to be only very slightly above minimum wage. On the border, the level and type of unionization varies more based on industry and region than on whether a company is national or international. For example, Tijuana plants show an organization rate of 10-15 percent, Ciudad Juárez 40-50 percent and Tamaulipas 100 percent.[22] The variations in the different regions are due to the strength of the CTM and, to a lesser degree, CROC. In Tamaulipas the CTM has such a strong presence that new plants must sign a collective bargaining agreement before construction, leading to the perverse situation of choosing a union for workers who have not yet been hired. Recent trends indicate that new plants seek to locate in less-organized regions.[23] Apparel, chemical, and automotive plants tend to have a higher rate of unionization, while organizing in electronics plants is low. In any event, many of the labor "agreements" are protective contracts.

Unions of all types are striving to define a position in the face of Mexico's headlong rush toward economic integration in a North American economic bloc. The issue is creating even sharper divisions between the different union currents. Official unions have endorsed NAFTA as a direct result of their subordination to the administration and business interests, now more closely allied than ever. It is likely that these unions will lose significant membership in formerly national industries reeling under the blow of free trade. Some of the hardest hit by trade liberalization include the garment industry, the already defunct toy and electronic-appliance industries, and other industries that grew up within a protected and growing domestic market.[24] These unions have steered clear of the U.S. and Canadian opposition and have kept silent on issues of wage differentials and occupational safety and health.

The modernizing unions have demanded a say in the negotiations, primarily to voice their concerns about the possible adverse effects on specific industries. They tend to support the process of integration as inevitable and, in the long run, desirable for Mexican workers. The independent unions and currents have been most outspoken in criticizing the NAFTA process and making direct links with unions in the United States and Canada that oppose the agreement. Although most of these unions also agree that the process is irreversible, they have actively sought to protect workers' rights in negotiations.

Popular Organizing

After the violent repression of the student movement in 1968, popular organizing efforts in Mexico multiplied and diversified. Pressed by economic necessity and hamstrung by the PRI-dominated political system, Mexico's popular forces created independent labor organizations, urban and peasant movements, and even guerrilla forces to advance their demands. They were joined by organizations infused with the new social consciousness of the Catholic church and linked to the "popular church" and its Christian base communities. The fortunes of these organizations ebbed and flowed, and some—like the guerrilla movements—folded due to repression, co-option, or their own strategic failures. But the intensification of the economic crisis in the 1980s set off a burst of organizing that spawned or reinvigorated popular movements throughout the country.

Members of the "popular classes," that is, peasants and small rural producers, poor urban dwellers, students, and workers, make up the organizations in these movements. Compelled primarily by the needs of their own constituency or sector, the popular organizations tend to focus on collective projects and initiatives designed to solve immediate problems. Until the late 1980s, most of these movements maintained their organizational independence from electoral parties. Because of this, they are often referred to as the "social left" as opposed to the "electoral left."

Many of the leaders and organizers of these new movements trace their activist roots to 1968. Their organizing strategies, however, are based in diverse political visions. In addition to the legacy of past Mexican revolutionaries like Emiliano Zapata and Rubén Jaramillo, Mexico's contemporary popular leaders have been influenced by the Cuban revolution, maoist movements, Ché Guevara, and other national liberation movement leaders. The Solidarity movement in Poland has also motivated Mexican popular organizers.

Organizing in the 1970s

The economic crisis of the 1970s—rescued only briefly by the oil boom—stimulated organizing activities among workers, peasants, and others who found their economic positions eroding steadily. State-controlled unions and peasant organizations were ineffective instruments for pressing demands that conflicted with the development models and economic strategies of the government. Instead, these official organizations controlled their members through a combination of patronage and repression, a situation that had existed since the 1940s. As a consequence, these sectors created new organizations, independent of the state and PRI's corporatist structures, to fight for their interests.

Several organizations stood at the vanguard of these new endeavors. The democratic currents within the electrical workers and the emerging university workers were two of the earliest and most important, although the democratic faction of the electrical union was ultimately defeated.[1] In the countryside, the *zapatista* ideals of the south once again stimulated movements that demanded "land for those who work it." In the state of Guerrero, as well as in some parts of the north, a guerrilla movement led by a former schoolteacher and an agricultural worker posed another form of resistance. Workers, students, and peasants also experimented with grassroots, multifront coalitions in their attempts to wrestle for regional power. The Student-Worker-Peasant Coalition of the Isthmus (COCEI) in the isthmus region of Oaxaca is an important example of such a coalition.[2]

At the end of the 1970s and in the first years of the 1980s, efforts to build national coordinating bodies for labor, peasant, and popular urban movements began to bear fruit. Three mass-based coordinating committees were established. Called *coordinadoras*, these committees brought together disparate local groups into common fronts at the national level. They were the National Coordinator of Education Workers (CNTE), the National Coordinator/Plan of Ayala (CNPA), and the National Coordinator of the Urban Popular Movement (Conamup).

Experiments with National Coordination

CNTE: The National Coordinator of Education Workers is the democratic current that emerged within the national teachers union (SNTE), Latin America's largest trade union. Founded in 1979, the CNTE became the protagonist of the most important Mexican labor mobilization of the 1980s. Its two major demands were the democratization of the union and the defense of living standards. The CNTE organized tens of thousands of teachers and supporters in unprecedented mobilizations in various central and southern states. It effectively challenged the power of the corrupt PRI-allied leadership of the SNTE and gained control of various locals in Oaxaca, Morelos, Chiapas, and the state of México.

This movement, with roots in the democratic teachers' struggles of the 1950s and early 1960s, has been subject to extreme repression by both government authorities and the national leadership of the union. As of 1991, CNTE members continue to be assassinated, intimidated, tortured, and assaulted. Their threat to the Mexican government lay not only in the demand for union democracy but also in their natural role as community leaders in the countryside and in the *barrios* (neighborhoods) of the cities. The CNTE is also exceptional because it directly links the countryside and the urban centers through its membership. It thus challenges the regime's ability to maintain divisions among social sectors. At its height, 150,000 members belonged to the CNTE. During mobilizations, hundreds of thousands more have joined them, including students and parents who march side by side with teachers, a result of the movement's solid links with local communities.[3]

CNPA: The National Coordinator/Plan of Ayala was established in 1979 with Emiliano Zapata's son, Mateo, as one of the co-founders. The CNPA was composed primarily of local and regional peasant organizations that were formed to demand their right to work the land.[4] Named after the *Plan de Ayala*, Emiliano Zapata's decree on peasant rights and land reform, the CNPA sought access to land and the implementation of the agrarian reform demanded during the revolution. The CNPA flourished in the early part of the 1980s as it manifested its strength through mass mobilizations and civil-resistance actions.

Mexico's rural population diminished in proportion to its urban population—from 65 percent of the country's population in 1940 to 35 percent in 1980. In absolute terms, however, it doubled from 13 million to 27 million. These figures indicate the continued importance of access to land, despite Mexico's increasingly urban nature. As Arturo Warman, social historian and director of the National Indigenous Institute, pointed out, "in all Mexican history . . . never have there been more *campesinos* without land; or so many without sufficient land for sustained production."[5]

Despite the significance of the issue, the CNPA faltered by the mid-1980s as a result of new government policies and a fair dose of repression. The government stymied the demand for land by announcing that agrarian reform had come to an end and that there would be no further land redistribution. Although some organizations within the CNPA are still active in the early 1990s, the CNPA itself is a shadow of what it was at its height.

Conamup: The National Coordinator of Urban Popular Movements includes community organizations, neighborhood associations, and citywide coalitions from Mexico's vast urban slums. Founded in 1981, Conamup became the most dynamic of the mass movements. Rather than organize people in the workplace, where they were likely to be controlled by an official union or government organization, Conamup focused on the *barrio* as a more fertile arena in which to develop an independent popular movement.[6]

Conamup linked the local demands of community organizations with a national agenda of housing and community issues. In so doing, the organization challenged the status quo administration of resources and planning for urban areas. Conamup pressured the government to satisfy basic community needs (housing, lighting, sewage, schools, subsistence food distribution, and transportation). It also promoted training to help communities organize themselves and develop skills to meet community needs. For instance, Conamup helped set up popular collective kitchens and promoted training in areas such as construction, literacy, and nutrition.

These *coordinadoras* challenged the government constantly. They demanded the resolution of specific problems, such as potable water systems, land claims, and respect for local union elections. In a broader arena, the popular movements called for democratization. In Mexico, where the state has dominated decisionmaking since the revolution, just fomenting the *autogestación*, or self-organization, of popular forces was tantamount to creating autonomous spaces for popular experiments with democracy. The *coordinadoras* created a place in which to define and articulate the demands of a mass base that was loosely coordinated at a national level. In addition, the decentralized leadership in these organizations made them difficult to threaten or buy off.

Yet with the possible exception of the CNTE, the *coordinadoras* began to lose momentum in the mid-1980s. Ultimately the multiclass electoral front that erupted in 1987 and 1988 surpassed the *coordinadoras* as a representative of the broader "civic movement." A number of factors contributed to this decline. By instituting a "neocorporatist" strategy, through which it offered tacit support to organizations that cooperated with its policies, the government limited the effectiveness of autonomous groups. In addition, the very nature of the work of the *coordinadoras*—organizing to resolve immediate demands—impeded the creation of structures through which to respond to larger political issues. Likewise, the immediate character of the struggle hampered the development of long-term strategic programs. The difficulties of creating internal democratic structures in an undemocratic national context also weakened these organizations.

Economic Crash, Organizing Surge

Mexico's economic crash in 1982 set the stage for a wave of popular organizing. As social conditions worsened, costing the nation 20 years of development (living standards and income levels declined to 1960s levels in many cases), popular forces in addition to the *coordinadoras* emerged to fight back.[7] The 1985 earthquake, as well as the dislocations caused by austerity measures and economic restructuring, accelerated this process. Feeding into the popular movements and, consequently, transforming them were a number of groups representing specific sectors or interests. These influences included the "people's church," the human rights movement, women's organizations within the movements, and "cultural workers" such as artists and poets.

On September 19, 1985, Mexico City was hit by an earthquake that prompted an upswelling of popular organizing. During the first days after the disaster the government insisted that the situation was under control but took no action. There was, however, a spontaneous yet organized popular response. City dwellers formed brigades and coordinated rescue and relief efforts without the participation of authorities. For those few days the city was essentially run by its people. Students met poor city dwellers and newly arrived migrants met professionals as everybody joined together in the emergency. From these meetings grew an unprecedented solidarity and the formation of new alliances in the face of disaster.

The physical earthquake was followed by a political one. It provoked a consciousness that remains as constant a point of reference as 1968 does for the popular movements. For years afterward it would be said that "Aún tiembla" ("it still trembles"). The phrase expressed the understanding that popular forces could organize themselves and create structures to solve their own problems without the government brokering the social deal.

A number of new popular urban organizations were created because of the earthquake. They first responded to the immediate demands of thousands of affected inhabitants. Later they began to take on broader, longer-range objectives. The Coordinator of Victims (CUD), among others, organized people affected by the earthquake so they could effectively pressure the government for assistance. A number of other popular groups, many with links to Conamup, also worked with earthquake victims but focused on a wider range of long-term problems.

One of the most dynamic of the new groups was the Neighborhood Assembly (*Asamblea de Barrios*). The Neighborhood Assembly first came together to demand new housing for earthquake victims. After successfully negotiating these demands, the organization's base expanded to include various neighborhoods that had acute housing problems. Among the problems the organization confronted were buildings owned by absentee landlords, one-family apartments occupied by several families, and abuse and eviction by landlords with powerful links to local authorities.

The Neighborhood Assembly's strategy of finding collective solutions to common problems has inspired some unusual approaches to mobilizing popular forces. At a mass rally in 1986, for instance, a new folk hero took the stage. Super Barrio is promoted as the representative of the urban poor and of their struggle. The character, said to be many people, wears the costume of a professional wrestler—full-body tights of flaming red, gold lamé trunks, and a full-head mask with an "SB" emblazoned on his chest. Super Barrio said he decided to "step down from the wrestling ring and join the struggle in the social ring." He remains incognito in order to emphasize the need for collective action in seeking social change. "I am not an individual to defend their rights, that is my power. We are all Super Barrio."[8]

The Neighborhood Assembly has proved to be a forceful and innovative representative of the urban popular movement. Rather than organize dreary protest rallies and marches, for instance, the group uses humor as a political weapon and sponsors upbeat celebrations that challenge government bureaucrats. These methods have attracted a substantial following, and officials have had to negotiate with Super Barrio and his colleagues simply because of the mass base they represent. When the authorities move to evict someone in an organized neighborhood, the threatened tenant will set off three firecrackers as a signal for the community, frequently accompanied by Super Barrio, to come block the action. To institute collective power in the organization itself, the members of the group practice "assembly democracy," holding mass, open-air meetings to discuss and decide on issues affecting their communities.

In the countryside, organizations of small producers have replaced the CNPA as the most active force in the rural sector. While the landless peasants that formed the core constituency of the CNPA fought for access to land, Mexico's small producers seek guaranteed prices, subsidies, credits, and market access. Among the groups representing these forces is the National Union of Regional Peasant Organizations (Unorca) at the national level and product-specific organizations such as the National Coordinator of Organizations of Coffee-Growers (CNOC). The tactics used by these groups, including entering into direct negotiations with government authorities, mark a new approach to popular organizing. The challenge to independent organizations, as they are invited to enter into discussions with the government and official peasant bodies, is to maintain their autonomy while attempting to resolve immediate demands.

The Mobilization of Other Sectors

In 1987 the Mexican government presented a plan to reform the national university which stimulated a wave of student organizing in the country. Affecting some 350,000 students, the plan proposed to restrict the open admissions policy, increase fees, and streamline services. Angry students organized massive marches of hundreds of thousands of supporters. The protestors rejected the plan for what they characterized as "an elite university" that would no longer serve the popular classes for which it was originally founded. At its height, the movement filled the Zócalo, Mexico City's historic central square. As the movement grew, its members expanded their targets to include the very premises of the government's economic and political project. In many cases, alliances that were first made during the earthquake blossomed as parts of the popular urban movement and other sectors moved to support the students. Even youth gangs and other marginalized sectors joined the students.

Another sector that fed into the popular movements in the 1980s was the "popular church." Liberation theology provided the popular movements with an analytical approach to political and social organizing rooted in a moral framework. Identifying the status quo as "systemic sin," religious workers who held these beliefs interpreted contemporary Mexican reality through a mix of the Bible and Marx. To communicate their views and encourage social activism, they organized study groups and held community education activities. These programs simultaneously advanced popular understanding of social critiques based in liberation theology and mobilized community members to solve common problems.

The role of the popular church within the urban and rural movements, although not pervasive, had an extraordinary impact. The Christian base communities (claiming some 150,000 members coordinated in nine regions throughout Mexico) viewed grassroots organizations as "the seed, strength and base for a new society that is being born." These communities also expressed their own commitment to working toward the development of that new society.[9] In addition, their perspectives on human rights, social justice, and international solidarity increasingly became integrated with those of the popular movements, providing a vision rooted in the Catholic traditions of the nation. Two outstanding leaders of the popular church—Bishop Samuel Ruíz of San Cristóbal de las Casas and former Archbishop Sergio Méndez Arceo of Cuernavaca—have contributed immeasurably to consciousness-raising and organizing among workers, peasants, the urban poor, Indians, and refugees.

Organizations in defense of human rights represent a relatively new area of work among popular movements. The growing number of human rights groups throughout the nation trace their origins to popular reaction against the crackdown on students in 1968 and the activities of relatives of political prisoners and the disappeared. Those early efforts spread as dozens of local human rights groups came together to protest the violence against their communities and popular movements. As the movement grew in force and number, the National Front against Repression was organized to spearhead actions in a more coordinated fashion. More recently, the Mexican Commission for the Defense and Promotion of Human Rights, along with religious-based organizations, have promoted human rights work in local communities and provided relentless criticism of the government's human rights performance.

Women play an increasingly pivotal role in the popular movement. They make up the majority of the membership in the popular urban organizations, but it took the pressure of women activists to get the male-dominated leadership of those organizations to add gender-based issues to the popular agenda (see Women and Feminism, Part 4). In 1983, for example, women formed their own group within Conamup to address their own particular needs and concerns. There has been some movement toward including progress on women's issues such as abortion, domestic violence, rape, child care, women's health concerns, and women's employment among the objectives of popular organizations, but the effort is far from complete.

As spaces for social dialogue are forced open in the country, Mexico's popular movements are creating cultural expressions that reflect the conditions faced by *los de abajo*. Independent journalism, social history projects, journals for chronicling the movement, ballads, poems and slogans, murals and cartoons have all provoked an exchange of ideas that reflect popular consciousness of contemporary national reality. Radio programs open the airwaves to discussions about the problems shared by city dwellers. Cartoons openly challenge the rhetoric of the country's political and economic elite.[10] Murals depict the new heroes of the movement. Detective stories are written about independent union strikes, whether Zapata is still alive, and the corruption of the government.[11] Super Barrio himself is a popular cultural expression.

Political Awakening

As the economic crisis deepened, the organizations representing Mexico's popular sectors realized that the specific demands of each constituency were in fact intertwined. The interests of the majority were being violated by *la crisis*, and the government's economic reforms made it increasingly clear that the costs of stabilization and restructuring would be borne disproportionately by the country's poor.

With the emergence of Cuauhtémoc Cárdenas and the National Democratic Front, the popular movements found a national figure who expressed this consciousness (see Political Parties and Elections, Part 1). A symbiotic relationship grew between a society in movement—much of it not linked with any electoral party—and the rise of Cárdenas. On July 6, 1988, the majority of voters of Mexico, by many accounts, voted against PRI and for the coalition led by Cárdenas.[12]

The 1988 electoral insurgency shocked PRI, but the opposition parties were also surprised. In large part, the strong showing by Cárdenas was the result of the many decades of popular organizing in Mexico. Not just a protest vote against PRI, a vote for Cárdenas was for many Mexicans a vote in favor of a more just and participatory society. Through their history of organizing outside the government's corporatist structures, the popular organizations had opened up a space in Mexican society for independent and populist candidates like Cárdenas. During the 1988 campaign there was an unprecedented merging of the popular movement and electoral politics. Cuauhtémoc Cárdenas reached out to the popular organizations for electoral support. At the same time, the country's independent labor unions, peasant associations, student organizations, and urban groups welcomed Cárdenas into what was regarded as their common struggle for democracy and justice.

Despite being blocked in his election bid, Cárdenas remains the major democratic opposition leader in Mexico and, as of 1991, still enjoys broad support among the popular sectors. His candidacy and the experience of the 1988 elections marked a turning point in contemporary Mexican history. For the popular movement it raised a basic question. As "civil society" and the issue of political democracy at a national level become ever more central to Mexico's future, should the popular movement, collectively referred to as the "social left," rethink its relationship to the "electoral left"?

Strategy and Options

During the last decade, the debate on strategy among various popular movements centered on two key issues. The first question—whether to participate in electoral politics through coalitions with the electoral left—was brought to a head by the 1988 elections. The second problem had even broader implications for the autonomy and long-term viability of the organizations: how to respond to the government's carrot-and-stick approach of repression coupled with offers of negotiation and patronage.

For most of the 1980s popular organizations expressly rejected any formal relationship with an opposition party. They argued that past experiences showed that these efforts almost always led to electoral defeat, manipulation of the movement for the party's own ends, and ultimately to a weakening, if not complete destruction, of the participating social organizations. A notable exception was the COCEI, which gained political power in the town of Juchitán in Oaxaca by joining with a national opposition party earlier in the decade.[13]

With the rise of Cárdenas, however, the debate deepened. Most of the popular movement was not opposed to its members participating in political parties, but formal organizational links were avoided. Yet with the *cardenista* movement gaining momentum among their ranks, some organizations, such as the Neighborhood Assembly, decided to enter the campaign and join the electoral front on a formal basis. Others did not. Among the organizations that stayed clear of the campaign was Conamup, although most of its members probably considered themselves *cardenistas*. In fact, this decision was one of the factors that contributed to the decline of Conamup as a national actor.

Following the elections the debate continued to evolve, and those organizations that chose to enter the electoral arena faced practical choices about philosophy and institution building. Various *cardenista* factions, for instance, clashed during the difficult process of building a party out of the diverse coalition that supported Cárdenas in 1988. In the same vein, mass-based popular organizations struggled with the unfamiliar tasks of building a political party.

The government's *concertación* strategy presented another controversial issue for the popular movements. In essence, this strategy was designed to develop consensus and harmony among opposing social sectors. The government offered to negotiate specific demands if the popular organizations agreed to stay within certain parameters for the negotiation. The move toward *concertación* became coupled with Pronasol, a presidential initiative to draw local communities into relief and development activities (see The Underside of Modernization, Part 2). Through tactics such as these, the government asked popular organizations to shift from an oppositional position to a partnership of sorts.

Many activists argued that engaging in actions under the auspices of the Pronasol initiative or participating in negotiations within government-drawn limits inevitably led to co-option. But proponents asserted that if specific popular demands could be resolved through such activities, it would be irresponsible for popular leaders to reject the opportunity. This debate has continued as groups attempt to combine tactics that can be seen as cooperative with more confrontational tactics—such as occupying government offices, blocking highways, and mounting hunger strikes—designed to keep pressure on the government.

Pronasol and *concertación* served to weaken the autonomy of those organizations that took part in the government's programs. Through Pronasol came some striking improvements, especially in communities that previously lacked almost everything. But political opponents maintained that Pronasol was essentially a permanent PRI political campaign. The program was advertised everywhere—on television, in movie theaters, on billboards, and in the print media. Many argued that the program targeted areas where there were strong opposition forces in the 1988 elections and that it was specifically devised to recoup the losses of the ruling party. Even so, its programs challenged popular movements that wished to remain independent of the government yet were primarily organized to resolve immediate needs.

A new discussion began to unfold within the popular movements as the process of economic integration with the United States accelerated through the negotiation of a North American Free Trade Agreement. In the past there were attempts to forge links to the south—through solidarity work with Central America, for instance. But relations with counterparts to the north have only recently been explored.

Some popular labor, peasant, and urban organizations began to incorporate binational issues into their agendas. They participated in an expanding number of forums with counterpart organizations in the United States and Canada. Super Barrio, for example, made appearances in California and Texas, and Conamup sent a delegation in 1987 to join U.S. housing groups in forging joint demands. Representatives of the National Union of Regional Peasant Organizations and the National Coordinator of Organizations of Coffee Growers, among others, met with farmers' organizations, while the CNTE and other independent labor organizations developed contacts with U.S. unions. In addition, exchanges took place among progressive church sectors, human rights groups, and cultural organizations on both sides of the border. As the future of Mexico became ever more intertwined with that of the United States, social-justice activists saw an extraordinary opportunity for popular cooperation. As Super Barrio said, "there is no border among the people."[14]

Issues for the Future

Mexico, according to a prominent Mexican analyst, is increasingly "a society that organizes itself."[15] Popular social movements are coming together to build a space for independent action within a decades-old centralized, corporatist political structure. In this effort they are similar to those nongovernmental organizations, business associations, and other elements of civil society that do not share an official relationship with the state. As Mexico's economy and political system are transformed, each of these sectors is hoping to shape the transition in its own favor.

Multiple challenges face the popular movements in this task. In addition to coming to terms with the government's co-option strategies, the popular movements must decide how to respond to government "modernization" policies that are presented as prerequisites for long-term economic growth but that carry immediate devastation for the popular sectors. The implications of further integration with the United States is another key question. The proposed free trade agreement, while hastening integration along lines favored by elite business and government interests, might offer popular forces a chance to help shape the outcome. Popular organizations must decide whether to oppose the accord or to try to influence its contents, and in what direction.

Democratization continues to be the fundamental issue in Mexico's political debate. The country's popular movements have not stood outside the political arena but have increasingly linked the struggle for justice with the fight for political democracy. As they decide how to participate in this battle, Mexico's popular organizations have been obligated to re-examine their organizing strategies. In this process they are weighing the benefits and costs of moving beyond the day-to-day pursuit of sectoral interests to work more directly for political change. Building multiclass coalitions will be key to successful electoral challenges. Joining in such an electoral enterprise holds the old danger, however, of being absorbed in the corporatist structure of a political party.

The popular movements form an activist electorate with a wide social agenda. Besides being important players in the democratization drama sweeping Mexico, the country's popular organizations also serve as living models of a more participatory society. Through their own struggles to represent popular interests, these groups have helped redefine politics in Mexico. With a large part of the society organized on the grassroots level, the elite and corporatist style of traditional politics becomes less viable. At the same time, the existence of a strong and independent popular movement makes the transition to a democratic Mexico more likely.

Nongovernmental Organizations

As in many other Latin American countries, Mexican nongovernmental organizations (NGOs) were born out of the charity and development work of the Catholic church, business groups, and university students. The Catholic church and other private institutions have carried out programs aimed at the poor, sick, and disabled since the time of the Spanish conquest. With the passage of time, however, a range of other social sectors including political parties and non-Catholic churches also began to form NGOs. "Traditional" NGOs that conduct relief, development, educational, or social-service operations now stand alongside similar institutions set up by popular organizations affiliated with Mexico's grassroots movements.

The ambiguity of the term "nongovernmental organization" makes it hard to quantify the presence of NGOs in Mexico. A private hospital is as nongovernmental as a popular health clinic operated in a poor *barrio* of the city. Several authors, however, have made an effort to catalog these institutions using different criteria.[1] Research indicates that there are more than 500 NGOs in Mexico. Of these, more than half have their offices and conduct operations in Mexico City, but their scale varies from local groups to national programs. Not even the largest, however, operate in all regions of the country.

A Weak Sector

Compared to other Latin American countries where NGOs play a major role in local development, Mexican NGOs are generally weak and only moderately influential. This is the result of a complicated mix of elements that interact to undermine the position of NGOs vis-à-vis other sectors of the society. Such factors include the omnipresence of the Mexican state in the economy and society, Mexico's low priority as an aid recipient among the international development agencies, the role played by national universities in social service and development activities, the strength of popular organizations, and the characteristics of the NGOs themselves.

For decades the Mexican state has maintained a strong presence in the economy and the society at large. The party-state system and Mexico's top-down corporatism have imposed authoritarian models on civil society that have made autonomous organizing the exception rather than the rule. In addition, the high level of state involvement in economic, health, education, and social-service fields has circumscribed independent citizen participation in these areas. Given this context, NGOs have had great difficulty finding social niches in which to function that are not already dominated by the Mexican government and its agencies.

Mexican NGOs have also had limited support from international development agencies, most of which never saw Mexico as a priority. Mexico, from their point of view, was an industrializing country that did not need financial aid. They considered Mexico a "developing," not underdeveloped, country that was democratic, oil-rich, and attending to its poor. As a result, donations from large foreign agencies were most often limited in amount and scope. The situation changed somewhat after the 1985 earthquake, when dozens of new financing agencies came to Mexico for the first time to participate in disaster relief programs. Along with international NGOs already working in the country, the newcomers encountered a Mexico that differed greatly from the stereotypes. They also found Mexican counterparts with whom to establish ties of economic cooperation. Some of these projects were only temporary. In other cases, the international organizations set up their own offices or worked directly with urban grassroots organizations that were establishing their own infrastructure, rather than channel funds through the weak Mexican NGO network. As a consequence, Mexican nongovernmental organizations remained relatively marginal.

Like the Mexican state, the country's universities have performed functions played by NGOs in other countries. In the mid-1960s, public universities went through a convulsive process of democratic reform in their internal governing structures. They also began to question and reformulate their curricula and social work programs. This process gathered steam with the 1968 student movement. Thousands of students and professionals eventually left academia, at least temporarily, to link up with "the people." Departments in various disciplines developed programs of grassroots participation and technical assistance. These trends continued until the economic crisis of 1982, when plummeting salaries began to constrain university-sponsored projects devoted to social service and development.

Popular organizations have also competed with NGOs. In the 1970s regional grassroots organizations sprang up throughout the country to mobilize communities around economic, political, and social issues. In many cases these organizations later evolved into small rural and urban development agencies, creating their own technical teams and conducting activities apart from the NGOs. In the process many of the latter were displaced.

Their own weaknesses accelerated the displacement of many of these organizations. This was especially the case when projects supported by NGOs failed and their small, isolated groups of beneficiaries were incapable of articulating a broader social and economic agenda. In addition, inadequate communication, as well as problems of accountability and paternalism, hounded many of these organizations and exacerbated the image of *padrinos* (godparents) of the poor. That NGOs receiving foreign funding had to follow international development aid "fads" in designing and conducting projects also appeared as a threat to their autonomy and diminished their status in Mexican communities.

Moreover, tension between grassroots organizations and NGOs arose to a point that continues to cause friction. Popular organizations resented the fact that the NGOs working on behalf of the poor held the purse strings to foreign funding; many movements that sprang from the poor and represented them had to rely on those NGOs as their links to foreign funding. The fact that almost no NGOs made serious attempts to develop ties directly between such popular movements and international funding agencies compounded the problem.

The Expansion and Diversification of NGOs

Both domestic and international influences have shaped the modern face of Mexico's NGOs.[2] In the early 1960s, for instance, many groups associated with the Catholic church broke away to start their own programs, prompted by the Cuban revolution and the progressive institutional changes then sweeping the Roman Catholic Church. Similarly, new development approaches spurred the creation of a network of credit and savings cooperatives and technical training centers during the 1960s.

In the 1970s one sector of NGOs became much more radical as it responded to the triple impact of the student grassroots movement of 1968, national liberation struggles in many countries of Latin America, and liberation theology. Working to varying degrees outside the church hierarchy, religious workers and lay persons applied liberation theology's social-action component directly to work with the poor. They concentrated on popular education in fields such as literacy, health, and technical training—all with the objective of *concientización* (consciousness-raising) to prepare the poor for "structural change." These NGOs also funded and developed the projects that grew out of the numerous Christian base communities throughout the country. They supported many small-scale economic projects designed to relieve poverty and raise consciousness simultaneously.

At the same time, members of the business community inspired by Catholic reformism took another route. They formed the Mexican Foundation for Rural Development, a network of more than 38 centers, to provide credit, technical assistance, and organizational assistance to middle-level *campesinos*. The foundation refers to its targeted sector as the "promotable stratum," small rural producers without high incomes but not the poorest of the poor. Other groups that were neither business nor religious began to promote development strategies emphasizing self-management and sustainability. One prominent example was the creation of Anadeges, a rural NGO with projects nationwide.

Mexico experienced a rapid expansion of NGOs in the 1980s, a time of deepening economic crisis. The U.S. Agency for International Development, an arm of the State Department that provides international development aid, began funneling larger amounts of assistance to Mexican NGOs during the decade. The crucial stimulus to the NGO expansion was the 1985 earthquake. Even traditional foreign aid agencies began to seek nongovernmental channels for their relief assistance when international journalists exposed the ineptness and corruption of government relief activities. Private organizations both foreign and domestic came into the limelight as viable options for spearheading reconstruction activities. Although the government continued to play a prominent role, NGOs participated in building housing projects and at the same time gave impetus to emerging grassroots organizations of the urban poor. Many of these organizations discovered the world of international funding through the NGOs in this period.

The institutional proliferation caused the formation of networks based on regional coordination, fields of action (such as health, popular education, ecology, and women's issues), or development approaches (including such NGOs as Anadeges and Interinstitucional). Some of the emerging grassroots movements formed their own NGOs and challenged the already established NGOs to build their own direct links to international donor agencies.

The State of NGOs in the 1990s

The vast majority of the international funding organizations concentrate their funding in the southern part of the country, where the most widespread and extreme poverty exists. The projects supported vary, although they tend to follow the changing patterns of emphasis laid out by the international aid community. Their focuses consequently include women's issues, ecology, the condition of indigenous peoples, and microbusinesses. With the exception of some European donors, the majority of the international agencies prefer to back specific projects rather than to provide institutional support for the Mexican NGOs themselves.

NGOs working in rural development have found a fertile field for involvement simply because the need is great. Two major tendencies exist. One cluster of NGOs includes groups that formerly emphasized small-scale self-help projects but which have begun to link community projects with the autonomous *campesino* movement and to coordinate demands for alternative development programs. Adult Education Services (Sedac), active in the state of Hidalgo, has effectively made this transition in its work.

The other tendency includes NGOs that target their support to the specific demands of the *campesinos* in very specialized areas such as credit, marketing, and technical assistance. These NGOs are often regional organizations that can study and respond to needs based on geographical and socioeconomic factors. The Center for Support to the Oaxacan Popular Movement (CAMPO) is a successful example of this. Formed in the late 1980s, CAMPO provides consultants and organizing assistance in the areas of coffee production and marketing, as well as food distribution.

Environmental NGOs are the latest on the scene. Environmental groups have moved from being basically middle-class membership organizations to becoming institutionalized NGOs, although the majority are still limited in base and scope. Those environmental groups with closest ties to grassroots organizations tend to work in the fields of sustainable rural development. An example is Rural Studies and Consulting (ERA), which works with communities in the highlands of Oaxaca to develop a program of indigenous control over local forestry resources.

There are few NGOs that work exclusively with women's issues, although many have programs specifically targeting women. One exception—and one of the oldest NGOs in Mexico—is CIDHAL, with offices in Mexico City and Cuernavaca. CIDHAL provides women's health and sexuality classes, leadership training for women in the urban poor movement, and support for the national network against rape and violence against women.

Groups of business leaders with religious affiliations have formed some of the most influential and well-financed development NGOs. In addition to the Mexican Foundation for Rural Development, there has been a proliferation of groups that support microenterprises. One of these is the Microenterprise Development Foundation (ADMIC). Located in the heavily industrial Monterrey region, ADMIC provides credit and technical assistance to low-income microenterprises.

Moving into the 1990s, Mexican NGOs are not only continuing their traditional service and development activities; they are reconceptualizing their role in society and developing new methods and organizational structures. For example, progressive NGOs responded to a June 1990 meeting of Catholic church and private-sector NGOs by holding their own conference. At the June meeting, mainstream NGO representatives discussed issues such as tax exemption and access to funding through debt swaps, indicating an increasing level of collaboration among the church hierarchy, the private sector, and the government. This potential for increased coordination among three powerful sectors of Mexican society sounded a warning to more independent NGOs that did not share the same perspectives on issues and that had much less political clout with which to advance alternative views. In response, the progressive groups formed the "Convergence of Civic Organizations for Democracy."

NGOs changing history and the expanding needs of the country and its people have caused shifts in NGO programming. Providing technical advice from teams of specialists in areas such as accounting, agronomy, regional development, and popular education has, for example, become a major focus of many of these organizations.

The friction between grassroots beneficiaries and the NGOs is still an unresolved problem that some grassroots organizations are handling by forming their own NGOs to develop direct links with funding agencies. Meanwhile, as the popular movements have taken another turn, this time toward participation in electoral politics, some NGOs are taking a more specifically partisan perspective toward their work, although with mixed results.

A discussion very much on the front burner concerns whether NGOs should act "at the service of the poor" or as independent protagonists of social change. Proponents of the first position argue that funds destined to alleviate poverty and strengthen grassroots organizations should be channeled to those projects with as little deviation as possible. Proponents of the latter view, however, take a longer-term perspective. They argue that NGOs are in a position to become popular "think tanks," using their resources to articulate popular positions and demands while directly influencing policymaking.

PART FOUR

Social Sectors and Institutions

"My administration has carried out its constitutional and political commitment with enthusiasm and conviction. I have accepted from the people a mandate for change that is designed to set Mexico on the way to achieving its historical goals. We have our own path to follow in forging a more prosperous, freer and fairer country, not only for ourselves, but also for building up the heritage of efforts and solidarity that we will pass on to future generations."

—President Carlos Salinas de Gortari, 1990[1]

© San Diego Union/Michael Franklin

The Situation of Women in Mexico in the 1990s

Education:

The illiteracy rate for adult women is 20%, compared to 14% for men.

Half of all elementary students are female and two-thirds of all students in vocational training are women, but women represent only 4 of 10 university students.

Employment:

The number of women in the workforce grew 21% during the 1960s, and then jumped 150% during the 1970s (corresponding data for the 1980s unavailable).

The proportion of women in the workforce climbed from 19% in 1970, to 28% in 1980, to an estimated 34% in 1989.

As of 1980, 24% of women who worked outside the home were employed in the informal sector, 19% were office workers, 17% were domestic workers, 15% were craft or factory workers, and 12% were farmworkers.

31% of all salaried men and 52% of all salaried women receive less than the minimum wage.

Politics:

Women represent 63% of all registered ·voters.
Only 269 women have occupied major political posts since the Mexican Revolution. Only two women have served as governors.

In 1991, 10% of the Chamber of Deputies were women, and women held 12% of the seats in the Senate.

Marital Status:

51% of all women between 15 and 50 are married; 32% are single; 9% live with their unmarried partners, 1% are divorced, 2% widowed, and 4% separated.

SOURCES: Mexico: Sistema Nacional de Salud, *La Salud de la Mujer en México: Cifras Comentadas*, 1990. Additional figures from Mujer a Mujer, Mexico City.

Women and Feminism

In downtown Mexico City, former center of the Aztec empire, construction workers in 1978 unearthed an eight-ton icon of the dismembered moon goddess Coyolxauhqui. According to Aztec mythology, Coyolxauhqui had been decapitated and thrown down the temple steps by her newborn brother Huitzlipochtli, god of war. When the Spanish arrived, they built their own version of gender domination on the ruins of the Mexica world. Women historians are only now beginning to uncover the artifacts of centuries of women's everyday lives and unrecorded struggle in Mexico. And in their efforts to unravel the system that has perpetuated women's subordination, modern-day Mexican feminists have reclaimed the image of Coyolxauhqui as a potent symbol in their own work.

Despite oppressive attitudes and institutional limits, women played an important role in the creation of modern Mexico. They formed a major part of the work force in the earliest stages of Mexico's industrialization—particularly in tobacco and textile factories. Likewise, women were key players in the strikes that swept the country in the 1880s. In the following years, women unionists, teachers, and professionals formed groups to denounce the Díaz dictatorship and demand women's civil rights and suffrage. Among the most influential of these organizations were Las Hijas de Cuauhtémoc, the Women's Political Propaganda League, and the Society to Protect Women Political Prisoners.

Countless ballads testify to women's participation in the Mexican Revolution. They served not only as *soldaderas* and *Adelitas*, whose labor made the prolonged war possible, but as officers and combatants—including a battalion of women whose husbands and brothers had been killed in the *magonista* insurrection of 1908.

Other activists took part in political efforts to ensure that women as a whole—and not just as members of a particular social class—benefited from revolutionary gains. At Mexico's First Feminist Congress, held in the Yucatán in 1916, some 700 women, mostly rural teachers, questioned traditions and promoted women's political leadership. Despite such activism, the Constitution of 1917 denied women political equality. It did, however, recognize certain labor and individual rights, including the right to divorce.

Building and Pacifying the Movement

Women's political activity intensified over the next two decades. In 1922 prostitutes in Veracruz sparked the country's first urban movement with marches against police violence and a citywide rent strike. The 1930s brought a period of tremendous organizing, in which rural teachers of the Mexican Communist Party and the National Revolutionary Party (PNR) played a major role. From its inception in 1929, the PNR looked to women as key agents for combatting *cristero* "religious fanaticism" and for converting leftover revolutionary fervor into rural and community development projects of the new government. Communist women, meanwhile, secretly organized *campesinas* and women factory workers for class struggle.

The National Women Peasants and Workers' Conferences of the early 1930s brought together local leadership from both the PNR and the Communist Party from across the country. At each conference conflicts between the two camps occupied center stage. Communist women were pilloried as *Malinches* from Russia because they opposed women's autonomous organizing as "a deviation from the class struggle," while women of the PNR were branded as "bourgeois" and "anti-men."[2] Even so, the two groups developed joint platforms against sexual abuse and domestic violence and in favor of suffrage and economic support for single mothers.

In the spirit of the broad antifascist coalitions of the day, a truce was called in 1935, and the major women's organizations came together to form the United Front for Women's Rights. With demands that included the vote, maternity leave, women's access to land, the eight-hour day, and condemnation of the foreign debt and U.S. intervention, the United Front rapidly swelled to over 50,000 members. It successfully organized for women's unionization, workplace child-care centers, and women's hospitals.

When President Lázaro Cárdenas nationalized the oil industry, local committees of the Front raised 7 percent of the payment to foreign companies through sales of jewelry, chickens, piggy banks, and sewing machines. Two weeks after the expropriation Cárdenas announced the transformation of the PNR into a party of mass organizations (the PRM), and invited the United Front to take part. Believing their participation would soon bring the vote, women from the front declared that "Women's unity within the new party . . . will bring the solution of our demands." As the women from the United Front turned to organizing within the PRM, autonomous forms of women's organization disappeared. The vote, however, was not granted to women until 1954.

The Second Time Around

Mexico's second round of feminism was touched off in 1970 when women academics and journalists supported demonstrations by U.S. feminists. Over the next years, through articles, forums, and documentaries,

Mexican feminists brought to light issues such as sexual and domestic violence, lesbian rights, and abortion. In the late 1970s, feminists launched projects such as Colectivo Cine Mujer and *FEM*, one of the first feminist journals in Latin America.

But the movement remained limited to small groups of women within the middle class. On the one hand, access to domestic workers spared most professional women from the double day. On the other, popular organizations growing out of the left and the progressive church considered women's issues secondary, divisive, or nonexistent.

In 1979, however, women from leftist parties, unions, and feminist organizations formed the National Front for Women's Rights and Liberation (FNALIDM). Heir to the United Front of the 1930s, FNALIDM organized marches, forums, and demonstrations for International Women's Day, for "voluntary motherhood" on Mothers' Day, and against violence against women. That year the National Front proposed legislation for a Law for Voluntary Motherhood to legalize abortion. Presented by the congressional Left Coalition to the Chamber of Deputies, the bill was roundly defeated through what feminist activist Amalia García described as "an anticommunist, antifeminist witch-hunt."

Although FNALDIM lasted only two years, it allowed women grassroots and political activists to integrate a feminist perspective into their work. Just as important, it provided feminists a first contact with the popular movement, an experience that led to new forms of organizing. In 1980 for instance, three feminist groups that had initiated work with women from the popular sectors organized the First National Conference of Grassroots Women. The conference brought together women peasants, workers, and neighborhood activists from across the country. This historic conference planted the seeds of what has come to be known as "grassroots feminism."

The Emergence of Grassroots Feminism

Women have been particularly affected by austerity measures and the economic restructuring undertaken by recent Mexican administrations. Traditionally considered responsible for family survival, women have had to work even harder and longer to make up for cutbacks in food subsidies, public services, and the calamitous drop in the buying power of wages. The survival crisis has converted the *colonias populares* into centers of new forms of organization, with women at the hub.

In 1983, three years after the founding of the National Coordinator of the Urban Popular Movement (Conamup), women organized their first nationwide conference to reflect on the urban movement—composed almost 90 percent of women, but led by men. Women began organizing their own groups within the movement. They learned to speak in public, run meetings, negotiate with government officials, administer community programs, and plan and evaluate their own political work. They developed their own structures locally, regionally, and nationally within the urban movement and fought for access to leadership posts on all levels.

The Conamup organizations took root primarily in the settlement areas on the edges of major cities. When the 1985 earthquake "tore down the walls of women's domestic confinement" in the capital's inner city tenements, a new generation of urban grassroots women's organizations emerged.[3] Through the use of popular education methodology, women from the urban movement integrated organizing around economic survival demands with consciousness-raising and action regarding the sexual division of labor and violence against women. They are now working to take these issues to the movement as a whole.

Campesina organizing has developed primarily out of the Christian base communities and is strongest in the southeast, where seven regional conferences are held annually. Women's organizing in the countryside focuses on labor-saving projects (such as corn mills and tortilla machines), food production (community gardens, chickens), and income-generating projects (crafts, cheese). Other focuses include literacy and health—the latter ranging from traditional healing practices to women's sexuality and violence against women.

Women in the Urban Work Force

Women's labor is playing an increasingly important role in the restructuring of Mexico's economy. Under the pressures of privatization and free trade, state-owned national industries where unionized male workers earned a "family wage" are being dismantled. Meanwhile, tremendous growth is taking place in the *maquiladoras*, the service sector, and the informal sector, including sweatshops, "home work," and street vending. These sectors are beyond the pale of such hard-won guarantees as minimum wage, job security, union representation, seniority rights, and labor law protection. Forced there by survival needs, women comprise the major work force in each of these areas.

Since the establishment of the Border Industrialization Program in 1965—supposedly to employ male migrant workers displaced by the termination of the *bracero* program—the *maquila* industry has depended primarily on women's labor. The composition of the work force is changing, however, as the industry expands beyond the garment and electronics industries into those that traditionally employ men, such as automobile and furniture manufacturing. As a result, the percentage of women *maquila* workers has fallen from 85 percent in 1975 to about two-thirds of the labor force in 1990. Even though women's participation in this labor force is declining proportionately, the actual number of women working in *maquilas* is increasing due to the rapid growth of the entire sector (see Maquila Manufacturing, Part 2). The *maquila* industry has considered women particularly suitable for the labor relations being introduced through the industry.

Generally, women are also considered more adaptable to new management techniques in which a "family atmosphere" replaces the former model of worker-management antagonism.

Factors such as these, plus the inherent difficulties of organizing a work force with the high turnover rate common to the *maquilas*, has made unionizing women workers in this sector particularly difficult. In addition, the corporatist union old guard and male-dominated left have virtually ignored this mushrooming sector of workers. In the border towns, however, women in the *maquiladoras* are slowly and carefully exploring new forms of labor-community organizing. Typically low-profile and informal, these efforts bring women together in networks of neighborhood-based mutual support groups where they reflect on and confront problems at home, work, and in the community.

A key catalyst to women's unionism has been the September 19 Garment Workers Union. Within hours of the 1985 earthquake, feminists, union organizers, and women garment workers who had long been seeking a form of independent organization, came together in the rubble of Mexico City's two largest garment districts. Through the clarity and courage of these women, the garment workers successfully demanded that the government allow them to form an independent union. The union has since served as a center of support for grassroots women's organizing and for the independent union movement in general. It has, however, been greatly weakened by the transnationalization of the garment industry, government repression, and internal conflicts.

Other unions have also been important to women's organizing. Telephone operators have formed the basis for the struggle in telecommunications since 1915. They now face technological changes that imply greater management control over the work process and the likely layoff of some 10,000 operators, mostly women. Unions in the education sector have also been significant in terms of women's unionizing efforts. For example, the first unions to incorporate feminist demands were the independent university workers' unions that emerged during the 1970s. Likewise, elementary school teachers—almost all of whom are women—form the core of the democratic teachers' movement in Mexico City.

According to the official census, some 719,000 women were working as domestic workers in 1980—up 50 percent from 1970. Domestic workers represent a major portion of rural-to-urban migration. They work under conditions of extreme isolation, exploitation, and abuse. Beginning in the late 1970s with the support of churches and feminists, domestic workers have formed unions, cooperative employment agencies, child-care centers, legal services programs, adult literacy courses, and consciousness-raising groups.

The Birth Pains of Popular Feminism

Hoping to convert feminism into a mass movement, most feminist organizations since 1980 have focused on working with women from the popular sectors. In pursuit of this objective, the mostly middle-class activists in feminist groups have supported organizers in the popular movements who promote consciousness-raising around women's issues. Projects have included workshops and campaigns focusing literacy, women's identity, legal rights, sexuality, maternal mortality, and domestic and sexual violence.

This cross-class relationship has been an uneasy one. Women from the popular movements have accused middle-class feminists of not respecting the internal processes of their mixed grassroots organizations, while feminists have felt used by male-dominated popular organizations. Nevertheless, these relationships are bearing fruit. A strong grassroots feminist presence in the Fourth Latin American and Caribbean Feminist Conference held in Mexico in 1987 was one sign of this collaboration between the country's feminist and popular sectors. The formation of the Benita Galeana Women's Coalition in 1988 and the large, energetic International Women's Day Marches in 1989 and 1990 also pointed to the success of these endeavors.

Mexican feminists have joined in activities to combat AIDS in the country. In 1989 current and former female and male prostitutes came together to form Cuilotzín, from the Nahuatl word for sex workers. According to the government anti-AIDS project, ConaSIDA, Cuilotzín's "safer sex" workshops and condom-promotion campaigns have been partially responsible for the exceptionally low incidence of AIDS among prostitutes in Mexico. The group has organized forums and demonstrations against police abuse at the Mexico City council and recently began organizing among gangs and street children.

Although homosexuality is not expressly prohibited by law, lesbians and gays are targets of legal, employment, and social discrimination. Lesbian and gay organizing erupted in Mexico in 1979 with large marches and the formation of groups such as GOHL, Oikabeth, and Lambda, whose work around homosexual liberation was linked to the left. In 1987 Mexico hosted the First Latin American and Caribbean Conference of Lesbian Feminists, at which some 250 women founded the Latin American Network. Similarly, the National Coordinating Council of Lesbians, founded in 1987, organizes annual conferences. Its member organizations have sponsored film series, speakers bureaus, theater groups, and forums on human rights in eight states throughout the country. In June 1991 Mexico hosted the conference of the International Lesbian and Gay Association.

Sexuality and Violence

Mexico's government targets the country's "fertile-age" women for an assortment of family-planning programs (Table 4a). Initiated in 1974, these programs have lowered the country's birth rate from 38 to 26 per 1000 inhabitants. Women's sterilization has risen from fifth to first place as a contraceptive method in little more than 15 years. The practice of involuntary and coerced sterilization has been well-documented, especially among indigenous and poor urban women, but little progress has been made toward halting this activity.

Abortion is illegal in Mexico, except in cases of rape, severe genetic anomalies, and endangerment of the mother's life. In December 1990, in a surprise move, the legislature of the state of Chiapas decriminalized abor-

---

Table 4a

Women's Sexuality and Reproductive Health, 1990

In Mexico City, half of all women become sexually active before they are 17; 90% before they are 21; 71% do so outside of marriage.

47% of all hospitalizations are due to normal births; another 10% are due to "other obstetrical problems," and "abortion" (including miscarriage) accounts for 9% more.

Officially, there are 64 maternal deaths for every 100,000 live births, although Yolanda Senties, head of the government's maternal-child health program writes that "insufficiencies in data registry . . . suggest that the panorama could be much worse."

52% of all women living with male partners use some form of birth control. The primary form of birth control is female sterilization (accounting for 36% of all women who use birth control and 66% of women users served by the country's public health services). The next most common methods are the IUD (19%), the pill (18%), rhythm (8%), withdrawal (6%), and the Depo Provera injection (5%).

For every 100 women who have been sterilized, only 11 men use condoms or have had vasectomies.

The cancer rate for women is twice that of men. Uterine cancer is the principal cause of cancer death in women, causing 12 deaths a day. According to official figures, government health services have equipment and personnel to provide regular pap smears for only 20% of women over age 25.

* Note: Official policy regarding women is reflected in the type of statistics available. While annual surveys detail the heterosexual practices of "fertile-aged" women—a factor in population-control policies—data on women's employment is sketchy. In fact, in 1987 the national economic employment survey ceased to separate data by gender. Until 1989, there was no official documentation on the incidence of domestic and sexual violence, and then only in the Mexico City metropolitan area.

SOURCES: Mexico: Sistema Nacional de Salud, *La Salud de la Mujer en México: Cifras Comentadas*, 1990. Additional figures from Mujer a Mujer, Mexico City.

tion "for reasons of family planning." As a result, the issue rose from a 10-year dormancy to take center stage in a struggle led on the one side by Pro-vida and the Catholic hierarchy, and on the other by a coalition of some 60 union, artist, urban popular, feminist, student, indigenous, and citizen organizations. The Chiapas reform has since been suspended pending a ruling by the National Commission on Human Rights. Meanwhile, anti-abortion forces succeeded in removing the provision for abortions in the case of genetic defects, rape, and incest in the Federal District of Mexico.

The antirape center in Mexico (*Centro de Apoyo a la Mujer Violada*) was formed in 1981. It focuses primarily on educating health workers, criminal justice professionals, and the general public about rape. Groups that have attempted to provide direct services have suffered both repression and a demand which far outstrips their limited resources.

When Carlos Salinas became president he called for the formation of government centers to prosecute perpetrators and tend to the victims of sexual violence. He also invited feminists to take part. After heated discussion the newly formed feminist National Network against Violence against Women decided to support the government programs and organized independent citizens' committees to monitor their functioning.

In 1990 the feminist movement developed a working relationship with all congresswomen from every political party to successfully sponsor a "Sex Crimes" bill. The bill redefined rape and, for the first time, penalized anyone who "uses their power derived from labor, teaching, domestic or any other subordinating relationship" to commit sexual harassment.

Women and Democracy

Immediately after the "electoral earthquake" in 1988, when the end of PRI's one-party monopoly appeared in sight, prominent feminists organized Women in the Struggle for Democracy. Simultaneously, women from political parties, grassroots organizations, and the feminist movement formed the Benita Galeana Women's Coalition to struggle for democracy and economic survival, and against violence against women.

Months before the 1991 federal elections, women from these and other coalitions joined to hold a "Women's Convention for Democracy." Twenty candidates were selected to represent various women's organizations and sectors, including the urban movement, prostitutes, and lesbians. Their candidacies were negotiated with the various opposition parties, and they supported each others' campaigns across party lines.

Activists, theorists, and academics came together to develop a common "women's platform" for use in the campaigns and for future legislation. Among the topics included were sexuality and reproductive rights, violence issues, and women's rights to land and housing. According to Women's Convention candidate Patricia Mercado, the campaigns allowed feminists to "break with the former small spaces of the movement." As the activists canvassed Mexico City, Mercado observed, they discovered "women at the point of explosion behind every door."

As women's organizing takes root within the popular movements, and as the feminist movement enters into traditionally male-dominated spheres of action, Mexico's political culture is slowly being transformed. Women are promoting the use of more participatory methodologies instead of speech-filled plenary sessions. For the first time contradictions within the personal and domestic spheres are being taken seriously, along with class issues and other areas more commonly treated in Mexican politics. Just as important, the marginalization of women is coming to be understood as a basic obstacle to democracy.

Native People

Mesoamerica is the seat of some of the greatest cultures in the history of humanity. Vestiges of the Olmec culture, beginning nearly 4,000 years ago, form part of the Mexican heritage. The centuries preceding the Spanish conquest in 1521, divided into the pre-classic and post-classic periods, saw the rise of Indian civilizations that not only left their marks on Mexican culture but also made important contributions to the development of human knowledge and art.

Like the Olmecs, the Mayan, Zapotec, Mixtec, Toltec, and later Aztec civilizations reached high levels of artistic and scientific achievement. Among the more momentous and well-known contributions of these societies were the Maya discovery of the concept of zero and the Aztec calendar, but advanced medical, astronomical, and mathematical knowledge formed part of daily life as well. By the time the Spanish conqueror Hernán Cortez landed in 1519, Mesoamerica had a population of an estimated 25 million Indians, with the Aztecs ruling over an extensive and highly stratified empire.

Through their myths and visions of the cosmos there existed a kind of unity throughout what is now known as Mesoamerica—a region extending from the south of the United States to Nicaragua. This Mesoamerican religious tradition is not so much a crystallized set of beliefs as a dynamic philosophy that survived the disruption produced by the European invasion. From the remote past to the present, this tradition continues to evolve. Many aspects have been lost, but significant myths and rituals still form an important part of community life in rural and even urban Mexico.[1]

Allied with Indian groups who were already resisting Aztec dominance, Cortez overthrew the empire led by the Aztec Montezuma. He then began the task of killing or enslaving the conquered peoples, as well as his former allies. Years of colonization, advanced both militarily and through the Catholic church, soon changed the face of what is now Mexico. Disease, war, and slavery wiped out huge numbers of Indian people.

But it was much easier to build a cathedral atop an ancient temple and obliterate its physical traits than to impose a culture, religion, and government upon a civilization that predated the Spanish by centuries. Indian culture and resistance continues to the present as a vital force in Mexican society.

A Multi-Ethnic Nation

The National Indigenous Institute (INI) puts the official estimate of Mexico's indigenous population at seven million—about 9 percent of the population.[2] To reach this number, it counts all persons over five who speak an indigenous language. In contrast to the genocide and isolation of native groups in the United States and Canada, generations of intermarriage occurred in Mexico, leading to the birth of the mestizo race. Partly for this reason, the National Institute of Statistics, Geography, and Information (INEGI) in charge of the national census uses language to measure indigenous population.

Although language can be one good measure for inclusion in the category of Indians, other considerations should be incorporated in defining the subtle frontier between Indians and non-Indians in Mexico. Many Mexicans consider themselves members of indigenous groups but no longer speak their native language due to influences such as out-migration and educational practices that emphasize assimilation. Following traditions and obeying indigenous ways of going about daily life can be a more inclusive indicator of "indigenousness" than language. If these criteria were applied, the figures for Mexico's Indian population would rise dramatically.

Thirteen Mexican states are designated as "eminently indigenous" according to the 1980 census, which provides the latest comprehensive data available. These states are: Oaxaca, Chiapas, Quintana Roo, Campeche, Guerrero, Hidalgo, Nayarit, Puebla, San Luis Potosí, Veracruz, Yucatán, the state of Mexico, and Michoacán. Throughout these states and, indeed, throughout all the states of the republic, some 56 different ethnic and language groups have been identified. Among the most important of these groups are the Tarahumaras, Nahuas, Huicholes, Purépechas, Mixtecos, Zapotecas, Otomís, Totonacas, and Mayas.[3]

With about 1.4 million people, the Nahuas are the largest language group, and Nahuatl is spoken in the states of Veracruz, Hidalgo, San Luis Potosí, Guerrero, Oaxaca, and Puebla.[4] Like the Nahuas, the members of other large Indian groups—including the Mayas, Zapotecs, and Mixtecs— are so numerous that they dominate certain regions of the country. The Mayas, for instance, pervade the southeastern states of Quintana Roo, Campeche, and Yucatán. The Yokolatanes (Chontales) who live in Tabasco and part of Oaxaca are also Mayan in origin, but are counted as a separate group. Although their numbers are harder to come by, the steady flow of migrants from Guatemala has significantly increased the Mayan population in Mexico, especially in Chiapas.

Like the Mayas, groups like the Nahuas, Otomís, and Mazahuas of the central highlands, as well as the Zapotecs and Mixtecs of Oaxaca, are too large and their members too dispersed to remain isolated from outside influences.[5] On the other hand, there are a number of tiny indigenous ethnic and language groups, such as the Kiliwas and Cucapas, that live in pockets throughout the country. Even larger groups such as the Tarahumara Indians of the mountain forests of Chihuahua existed in relative isolation until recently.

High rates of migration to the cities and the United States encouraged the use of Spanish and English and changed many Indian customs. But proof of the strength of indigenous identity among Mexicans can be found in the surprising levels of cultural identification and community cohesion maintained by members of different ethnic groups in their new surroundings. Organizations of Mixtecs have formed in California, for instance. Likewise, it is not unusual for migrants to return faithfully each year to their communities for the festival of the village saint or to fulfill traditional community work or leadership obligations.[6]

Indigenous populations in Mexico face the same problems as indigenous populations throughout the continent. Their communities tend to be among the poorest, their cultures are besieged by outside influences, and their land and labor are "permanent targets" of exploitation.[7] Agricultural activities—whether raising crops for family consumption or commercial crops such as coffee—continue to form the backbone of economic activity in indigenous communities. Increasingly, however, these traditional occupations are being supplemented or replaced by other means of making a living. Among these are migrant farming within Mexico or in the United States and commercial activities, especially in the informal sector of the cities.

In addition, land struggles that have persisted for centuries are far from resolved in many indigenous zones. In many areas, *caciques* or rural bosses not only control land use but also monopolize the marketing of nearly all regional production and the local food supply.[8] In Chiapas, for example, the Tzeltales, Tzotziles, Tojolabales, Chamulas, and others have been pushed off their land and are now forced to provide cheap labor on large cotton and coffee plantations.

Indian Activism

The ways that Indians in Mexico work to defend their cultures, communities, and livelihoods are rich and varied, adding a crucial dimension to popular organizing in Mexico. From the time of Mexico's war of independence to the numerous peasant movements calling for "land and liberty," indigenous groups have participated actively in national movements. Hundreds of local, state, and regional indigenous organizations exist that combine broad-based economic demands with those specific to the needs of indigenous people. Two national organizations with a presence in several regions exist: the National Front of Indian Peoples (FIPI) and, to a lesser degree, the National Coordinator of Indian Peoples (CNPI).

Indian activism is changing Mexican society. At the beginning of the 1990s five main areas of organizing activity are proving most fruitful. Among these are a number of movements to promote local and regional economic development, human rights, sound ecological practices, and indigenous culture. Likewise, the approach of the quincentennial anniversary of the landing of Christopher Columbus in the Americas prompted a variety of organizing efforts as part of the pan-American protest campaign, "500 Years of Indigenous and Popular Resistance."

Most development projects in indigenous zones face the dual challenge of getting out from under the *caciques* and creating economic alternatives. The Union of Indigenous Communities-100 Years of Solitude in Oaxaca unites mostly Zapotec communities that include fishermen, subsistence and corn farmers, coffee growers, and day laborers. With the objective of building an alternative food-distribution system, the union now independently administers several government-funded warehouses of basic commodities. It has also set up a network to market the commodities produced by its members.[9] Another example is the State Coordinator of Coffee Producers of Oaxaca. Among its members are Zapotecs, Mazatecs, Mixtecs, Triquis, and several other ethnic groups found in Oaxaca. The organization has created marketing links for small producers so that more of the proceeds from exports remain in the communities and are not siphoned off by intermediaries.[10]

Although the human rights of Mexico's indigenous people have been regularly violated since the conquest, there has been increased activism around the issue over the past few years. Human rights violations in modern Indian communities include assassinations—usually by *caciques* or their henchmen—eviction from their land, illegal imprisonment, beatings, and harassment. Human rights violations increased with the drug war, leading to harassment and imprisonment of indigenous leaders.[11] In October 1989 Indian groups gathered at the first forum on Human Rights of Indian Peoples.[12] Scores of statements testified to the violation of basic human rights of Indians and called for protection. A special meeting on indigenous women focused on violations suffered especially by women: rape, forced sterilization, and discrimination.[13] A second forum extended the process, and a growing network of local grassroots human rights organizations is working to expose and eliminate human rights violations in the villages.

As global ecological consciousness grows, so does a recognition that traditional indigenous land-use patterns teach much about sustainable and organic agriculture. Coffee growers in the highlands of Chiapas are successfully growing and exporting organic coffee, for example.[14] In Chihuahua, opposition to a new World Bank project galvanized Tarahumara resistance to clearcutting their forests. Mayan groups have also participated actively in the creation of Biosphere Reserves to protect their native rainforests.

One of the newly endangered zones is the Guerrero area called "La Ruta de los Santos" (the Route of the Saints). This area is one of the most important Nahua population centers in the country. The Alto Balsas region where the Nahua communities are located is being considered by economic planners as the site for an enormous dam. If approved, the flooded region would wipe out ancient archaeological sites and disrupt the life of 17 productive communities that have maintained traditional ways. The communities have organized in the Council of Nahua Peoples of Alto Balsas to fight the dam construction.

With varied success, the Indians of Mexico have devised ways to preserve their cultures from the imposition of European culture since the conquest. In addition to making sure that children learn to speak the ethnic language, the different Indian groups continue their traditional practices in areas such as religion, crafts, music, and dance. Herbalists and *curanderos* or shamans still practice in villages throughout the nation and even in the streets of Mexico City. In another example, the community museums of Oaxaca illustrate how communities participate actively in preserving their cultures. In one town, villagers brought an 800-pound sacred stone down from the mountains by hand to install in their community museum. This Zapotec group also recreated the traditional dance of the feather that portrays the conquest and was banned centuries ago.[15]

Mexican indigenous groups also began planning an alternative commemoration for the 500th anniversary of the landing of Columbus. The Mexican Council "500 Years of Indian and Popular Resistance" has linked up with indigenous and grassroots organizations of the poor in other countries to protest the mainstream celebrations of the conquest. Since its inception the council has also worked to expand representation and participation to Indian groups from all parts of the country and to establish connections among regions and organizations. More than 80 organizations belong to the council. Its principles and objectives include the right to self-determination and equality in economic, political, and civil rights. Looking to the future, the council is forging links with Indian organizations in other countries to carry on community action projects after 1992.

An amendment to the Mexican constitution was passed in July 1991 that defines the nation as "multi-ethnic" and protects the right to preserve indigenous languages and cultural practices. While heralded as a long-needed recognition, some Indian groups criticized the amendment, saying that it is too general to be applied effectively. They also objected to the fact that Indian organizations were not sufficiently consulted in its drafting.

The government's formal recognition of the rich racial and cultural diversity that exists in Mexico is a step forward. But racism continues to permeate daily life in the country. Even rights that are assured theoretically are violated in practice. As a result, the denial of self-determination, democracy, and dignified working and living conditions for Mexico's first inhabitants continues to be the rule rather than the exception throughout the country.

Immigration and Refugees

Burgeoning migration to the United States is one of the best-known social phenomena of Mexico, but its true nature is shrouded in misconceptions. Millions of Mexicans are migrants at some point in their lives. Lured by the demand for labor north of the border, they are simultaneously driven by limited opportunities at home.[1]

Migration from Mexico to the United States has been a fact of life since the mid-1800s, and U.S. policy has alternated between encouraging Mexican immigration and restricting it.[2] Over the years legal immigration to the United States has gone hand-in-hand with continuous flows of undocumented Mexican migrants. Because they are admitted officially, it is easy to measure trends in the annual migration of legal immigrants. From a low of about 500 in 1901, their numbers climbed to 405,172 in 1989.[3] More than three-quarters of those admitted in 1989, however, were previously undocumented entrants who were legalized under provisions of the 1986 Immigration Reform and Control Act.

Getting an accurate count of the numbers of Mexicans who come to the United States without official permission is a tricky proposition.[4] Estimates used by the U.S. government, however, suggest that the total number of undocumented Mexicans in the United States falls between 1 million and 2 million.[5] The number of migrants who move to the United States to stay is mounting, but annual net migration is expected to reach no more than 200,000 by the year 2000.[6] Contrary to popular belief, only a small percentage of migrants move permanently. The rest return home after stints of several months. About half of those who migrate on a temporary basis only make the trip once, although several members of the same family may take turns at working in the United States in what is known as relay migration.

Conventional wisdom dictates that the migrants drawn to work and live in the United States are jobless illiterates—a perception that feeds racist stereotypes. But numerous studies have established that most migrants hail from families with a modicum of formal schooling. Nearly 20 percent of all migrants have studied to the secondary school level, while between 80 and 90 percent are literate.[7] And at least 90 percent are employed before leaving Mexico.[8] But these resources no longer translate into job or income opportunities in their own country. As a result, many of the most resourceful and enterprising opt for migration as a means to supplement family income.

One of the recent U.S. efforts to put a brake on the flow of undocumented migrants to the United States was the Immigration Reform and Control Act (IRCA). Enacted in 1986, the IRCA combined penalties for employers who hired undocumented workers with various amnesty and temporary-worker provisions. The latter allowed qualified migrants who were previously undocumented to obtain legal status, either as U.S. residents or as temporary workers. The new law led to an initial drop in the estimated number of undocumented Mexicans who entered the United States. But the hard economic situation in Mexico, combined with continued U.S. interest in hiring low-paid Mexican labor, frustrated the purpose of the IRCA. By 1991 the number of migrants crossing the border without authorization had climbed back to the level reached in 1985, before the law was enacted.[9] Studies by the investigatory arm of the U.S. Congress discovered that U.S. employers had reacted to the IRCA by discriminating against people who looked Hispanic, despite their country of origin or their visa status in the United States.[10]

Economic Factors

The declining rate of population growth in Mexico does not seem to affect the number of migrants to the United States.[11] A much more important factor in the size and composition of Mexico's migrant flow is the country's economic situation. The crash in 1982 and the subsequent years of austerity and restructuring pushed even middle-class Mexicans and midlevel *campesinos* to the edge of economic disaster. The precarious situation prompted changes in the composition of the migrant population. Many families adopted household "survival strategies" that included increased reliance on income from family members sent to work in the United States.

Thus, in comparison to those who migrated before 1982, the class range of post-crisis migrants is much greater. As professionals and other members of the formal working class got pushed out of their jobs or saw their employment and income opportunities shrivel, many of them joined the migrant flow. The crisis also stimulated a growing number of women and children to make the trip that at one time was predominantly undertaken by young men. In addition, more people age 45 and over are joining migrant ranks, and the flow from industrial areas, such as Mexico City and the states of Mexico and Puebla, is increasing.[12]

In the past the bulk of migrants toiled in the fields. Now undocumented workers are spreading out into various sectors. Seasonal agricultural work still employs more than 40 percent of Mexico's migrants, according to some sources.[13] But jobs in construction and manufacturing are common as well. More and more migrants are finding employment in service jobs such as gardening, domestic work, auto repair, waiting tables, and other restaurant work. At least one study found that more than 50 percent of new migrants were seeking work in services.[14]

Decades of migration from rural pockets have left indelible marks on the small towns that traditionally have been the source of nearly three-quarters of the migrant work force. Eight states that claim 26 percent of the national population contribute the vast majority of migrant workers. These are Baja California, Chihuahua, Durango, Guanajuato, Jalisco, Michoacán, San Luis Potosí, and Zacatecas. At certain times of the year, these tiny communities may lose large numbers of the working-age male population to employment in the United States.[15] But the remittances sent home by these and other migrant workers often fuel a boom in the local economy, as new and better homes, satellite dishes, stores, school buses, banks, and community buildings spring up, paid for with money earned to the north.

No official figures are available on the amount of money migrants funnel into the Mexican economy. The quantity fluctuates based on the number of migrants at any given time, how much they earn in the United States, and what they spend in Mexico. But researchers at El Colegio de México estimated that undocumented workers residing in the United States injected $2 billion into Mexico in 1984. That would mean their contributions constituted the fourth largest source of foreign exchange for the country.[16]

In addition to helping families make ends meet in the troubled Mexican economy, a large portion of the money a migrant takes back to Mexico goes for improvements on a home. Construction steps up dramatically after holiday vacation visits by migrants. And the money spent in town on such occasions has a multiplier effect, giving a punch to the local economy. No official statistics exist for how much of the money goes into savings. But the fact that banks operate in some tiny towns characterized by high levels of migration is cited as an indicator that at least some migrant money goes into deposits for future use.

In some cases the funds go into community projects, such as church renovation, construction of recreation halls and schools, and establishment of ambulance services. By funding improvements such as drinking water and drainage systems, they also help to modernize community infrastructure. In Ecuandureo, Michoacán, where the community organizes twelve days of Christmas festivities, migrants in Chicago pool resources to fund one of the days' observances and those in California underwrite another. In Cupareo, Guanajuato, residents have used migrant money to organize a funeral committee for returning bodies of migrants who die in the United States.[17]

Central American Refugees

In the early 1980s a leap in the number of migrants to Mexico from Central America added a new dimension to the migration trends in the country. Fleeing war, poverty, and mistreatment, Central Americans of all educational levels and all social strata—farmers, laborers, professionals, and deserting soldiers—began heading north. Most of them have used Mexico as a springboard for journeys to the United States.[18]

Although the numbers are difficult to pin down, estimates put Mexico's Central American refugee population at about 400,000. Of the total, about 85 percent crossed into the country without authorization. Reliable figures are difficult to get, but estimates suggest that about 45 percent of the undocumented entrants are Guatemalan. Another 34 percent are Salvadoran, 13.7 percent Honduran, and 6 percent Nicaraguan. The rest come from other countries.[19]

Some 43,000 legally recognized Guatemalans live in refugee camps that dot the southern and eastern states of Mexico.[20] But more than 100,000 undocumented Guatemalans are also in Mexico, fleeing the turmoil in their homeland but unable to gain legal recognition and protection in their northern neighbor.[21] Another 40,000 to 60,000 Guatemalans cross Mexico's southern border every fall to harvest coffee. Many also work in banana and sugar plantations in Mexico, where the pay is higher than in Guatemala. Like their Mexican counterparts in the United States, Guatemalans who migrate to work in their neighboring country take the most back-breaking, low-paying jobs and often suffer discrimination.[22] Like Mexican migrants, they usually return home after working seasonal or temporary jobs.

The remaining hundreds of thousands of Central Americans in Mexico are mostly just passing through on their way north. Their numbers reached as high as 18,000 a month during the late 1980s. The most numerous group is Salvadoran, followed by Guatemalans, Hondurans, and Nicaraguans.[23] They walk, hitch rides with truckers, take buses, trains, and sometimes even planes over a honeycomb of routes leading to the United States. Traffickers make thousands of dollars off Central Americans who need guides along their way. The migrants find they must fork out additional money to corrupt officials. Mexican migrants face similar shakedowns. "Migrants have become a lucrative business, being prime victims in an extortion industry that has reached millions of dollars," says Víctor Clark, a founder of the Tijuana-based Binational Center for Human Rights.[24]

The Mexican constitution provides for the protection of political exiles and freedom of movement within the country for citizens and foreigners alike. Authorities occasionally stress that position as a matter of policy. In practice, however, there is a high degree of official corruption, as well as coordination with U.S. agencies bent on eradicating the flow of undocumented entrants. The sad result is a high degree of officially sanctioned violence and harassment directed at both Mexican and Central American migrants. Lacking official protection, migrants also fall prey to common criminals.[25]

Abuse of migrant populations is widespread throughout Mexico's security forces. Violations by officials are rarely denounced. But a sampling of 83 human rights violations against Central Americans in Tijuana in 1988 and early 1989 revealed accounts of robberies, rape, destruction of documents, and murders at the hands of officers.[26] According to the study, extortion was the most frequent migrant rights abuse. A full 95 percent of complaints charged that verbal or physical threats were made to force payments of bribes. Mexican migrants who reported extortion in 1988 were robbed of an average of $62 each, while Central American migrants lost an average of $171.[27] In addition, Central American migrants are often separated from their family members, jailed without due process, and deported.[28]

In an effort aimed at preventing undocumented Central American migrants from entering the United States, Mexico's interior minister joined in "Operation Hold the Line" with the INS, the Drug Enforcement Administration, and the CIA.[29] The operation employed undercover agents to infiltrate the clandestine network that helps migrants enter the United States. The INS reallocated $700,000 of its budget to pay Mexico to cooperate in the project.[30]

Mexican officials deny any formal ties to the operation, but internal memoranda of the INS from 1988 and 1989 document the specifics of the plan and Mexico's involvement.[31] Moreover, a 1989 INS newsletter reported the success of the operation, citing the "cooperation [of] the Government of Mexico . . . including the establishment of checkpoints along transit corridors and the deportation of intercepted Central Americans."[32] Deportations of Central Americans from Mexico jumped 500 percent from 1988 to 1989 and another 30 percent from 1989 to 1990. In 1990, more than 110,000 Central Americans were arrested in Mexico and dumped across the border in Guatemala.[33]

Uncertain Future

Pressure from independent human rights advocates in Mexico and the United States has forced Mexican leaders to embark on a campaign promoting the defense of migrants. In an unprecedented move, the Ministry of the Interior and the Ministry of Foreign Relations offered to extend identification cards to the Catholic church for distribution among Central American refugees. The cards were designed to prevent continuing abuses, detentions, and deportations.[34]

President Salinas in 1989 urged the U.S. Congress to modify American immigration laws and regulations to protect the human rights of migrants. In addition, he pressed Mexican consulates in the United States to take a more aggressive stance in confronting INS human rights abuses.[35] The interior minister instituted a project called Programa Paisano, a highly publicized effort to clean up the practices of Mexican migration and customs officials. A new money transfer system was also announced in 1990, after studies showed that Mexican police and customs officials pocketed about $200 million or 40 percent of the earnings that legal Mexican migrants tried to send to their families over a three-month period.[36]

Even more optimistic for Central American migrants were the July 1990 additions to Mexico's General Population Law. Until that time Mexico's legal code included no reference to, definition of, or provisions for refugees.

Because of that hole in the country's legal fabric, refugees in Mexico had to request other visa statuses in order to avoid being deported. Their only other recourse was to remain undocumented and hidden. Surprisingly, the changes to the law included an extraordinarily broad definition of refugees by international standards.[37] It also obligated Mexico not to return them to their countries of origin—or to send them to a third country—if their "life, liberty, or security would be threatened."[38]

But a full year later the law had yet to be implemented. While Salinas has publicly championed the cause of migrant defense, little progress has been made on ensuring better treatment of migrants either in Mexico or in the United States. In late 1990 Salinas announced a meeting in Tijuana of supposedly singular importance to migrant defense. He ended up spending a rushed twenty-five minutes on the presidential bus in Mexicali discussing the topic with a handful of people. At that meeting Salinas told listeners he wanted the INS brought to task for abuses. He was reminded in turn that Mexican authorities themselves continue to follow a pattern of abuse of migrants.[39]

Despite his public proclamations Salinas clearly relegated the issue of migrant rights to the back seat in relation to other issues involving the United States. Mexico's U.S. consulates, for example, have no coordinated system in place to document, analyze, or respond to the treatment of Mexican migrants in the United States. The consulates therefore mostly operate on an ad hoc basis, squandering resources that could be used to secure a significant place for migration issues in bilateral discussions.

Salinas agreed to exclude the migrant problem from negotiations for a trilateral free trade agreement (NAFTA) that will institutionalize economic relations with the United States and Canada. Pumping up the economy, raising living standards, and stimulating job creation in Mexico are the major reasons given in the country for support for NAFTA. Given the economic impetus for migration, supporters of the agreement argue that its salutory effects—if they are borne out—should slow the movement of Mexico's workers to the United States in search of employment. In the short run, however, the opposite may well be the case. For one thing, the areas that are providing increasing numbers of migrants, including places like Oaxaca and Mexico City, are not likely to be the main recipients of new investment. In addition, low-wage service jobs in the United States are becoming more numerous as a result of structural shifts in the U.S. economy. These are precisely the types of occupations that are drawing increasing numbers of Mexican workers. Furthermore, the gap between earning power in the United States and that in Mexico is very wide and is not expected to narrow, at least in the near future. Thus the factors that pull Mexicans to the United States for employment are likely to remain in place.

Likewise, the Commission on International Migration and Cooperative Economic Development (Asencio Commission) concluded that the initial stages of economic development frequently increase migration out of the country. The commission observed that the creation of low-paying jobs in

Mexico, which plans to use its cheap labor as an important source of comparative advantage in regional trade relations, may well provide more people with the resources needed to go north in search of better-paid jobs. Even if Mexico's economy does become more robust as a result of NAFTA, the commission predicted that it would take at least five years for wages and living standards to rise high enough to stem the northward flow.

Health and Welfare

In Mexico the pathologies of the first and third worlds combine to tax a health care system that must deal with the "chronic" diseases of the industrialized world—cardiovascular disease and cancer—while coping with infectious diseases produced by inadequate housing, water, drainage, and the cumulative effects of malnutrition and lack of prenatal care.[1] In addition to the classic mix of diseases of progress and poverty, Mexico has the second highest incidence of AIDS in Latin America. The spread of cholera is another major health concern.

Although the general rule of thumb holds that statistics are unreliable in Mexico, health statistics are especially unreliable. Traditionally births and deaths are underreported in rural areas; many people lack birth certificates. Researchers must also contend with the severely flawed 1990 census and the undercount of several sectors of the population. Finally, as described by a leading social policy analyst who asked to remain unnamed, the Salinas administration "has a bad habit of censorship on health. They don't talk about AIDS. They don't talk about measles. They don't talk about cholera."[2]

Although serious problems persist, Mexico has steadily expanded its health services over the years, stimulating marked improvement in overall health conditions. From 1930 to 1989 life expectancy increased from 37.5 years to 67, and total death rates declined from 26 per 1,000 in 1930 to 5 per 1,000 in 1986.[3] The drop in death rates resulted from dramatic progress in health care and immunization, but also reflects the history of urban migration and consequent improved access to medical facilities and treatment.

Since 1983, Article 4 of the constitution has guaranteed public-health protection as a basic human right. The public health-care system that is charged with ensuring that right dates back several decades, beginning with the creation of the Mexican Social Security Institute (IMSS) in 1943. Traditionally the IMSS—financed by employee, employer, and government contributions—has been the largest part of the health-care bureaucracy and has insured the greatest number of workers and their families. Government workers have their own social security institute, the Social Security Institute of State Workers (ISSSTE). Pemex also operates its own health-care system.

Despite the large numbers of the population that are covered by the social security institutes, more than 35 percent of the country's people fall outside their purview.[4] For major health problems, most of those not covered by the institutes resort to general care facilities operated by the Ministry of Health (SSA) or private charities such as the Red Cross.[5] An estimated 5 to 10 percent of the population relies on private health care, which varies from the simple office front of an individual practitioner to highly specialized private facilities.

Inequities in the Health Care System

In his 1990 state of the nation report President Salinas indicated that 94 percent of the population had access to some form of health care. The assumption that virtually everyone has health care, however, is misleading. Nowhere are the massive inequities in Mexican society so blatantly revealed as they are in its public-health statistics—which in all likelihood far underestimate the problems. The government's own analysis indicates that poor and rural populations will increasingly be unable to compete for scarce health resources with urban populations suffering from degenerative diseases.[6] That same study also indicates that if present trends continue, by the year 2000 there will be 66,000 deaths from preventable infectious diseases every year. The National Solidarity Program (Pronasol) reports that more than half of the deaths of children under four are related to malnutrition; in rural areas only one in four children under four have normal height and weight.

As these statistics suggest, health-care services are unequally distributed throughout the country.[7] The central valley of Mexico, which includes the Federal District and the state of Mexico, has approximately 50 percent more doctors than needed. Although many are private specialists and thus not needed by or available to the bulk of the population, residents of Mexico City have more access to health care than people in other regions. Likewise, the government spends far more proportionally on health services in the Federal District than elsewhere. For different reasons a lucrative strip of health-care providers has sprung up along the Mexican side of the border with the United States. Based in cities like Tijuana, these doctors include dentists, plastic surgeons, and other specialists who cater to the U.S. public at prices one-third to one-half of those in the United States.[8]

In contrast the poorest rural states such as Chiapas and Oaxaca, as well as more impoverished sections of large urban centers, have a shortage of doctors and hospital beds. These inadequate services compound health problems resulting from poor sanitation and poverty. A federal epidemiologist working in Chiapas, for instance, described areas where more than 75 percent of the population lacked access to potable water and almost 90 percent of children were malnourished.[9] Deaths of infants ranging in age from two to 12 months were more than 3 times the national infant mortality rate, and census studies in the region found that the average mother delivered seven children but lost two of them before their second birthdays.[10] In Oaxaca maternal mortality rate is twice that of the national average.[11]

The financial crisis of the 1980s and the economic reforms enacted by the government in response undermined the country's health care system and left those most at risk even more vulnerable. From 1980 to 1989 the government's IMSS budget was reduced by 44 percent; that of the ISSSTE dropped 61 percent.[12] SSA facilities, which are entirely dependent on the federal government, suffered 50-percent cuts.[13] Nutrition for the population on the whole also worsened after 1981. Between 1981 and 1987, for instance, there was a sharp decline in the per capita consumption of such important foods as fresh milk (21.8 percent), beans (29.7 percent), and corn (10.3 percent). Per capita consumption of beef, pork, and fish declined even more.[14]

These negative symptoms of the financial crisis combine with intransigent problems in the Mexican health-care system to aggravate health conditions in the country. One example is the death toll in the 1989-90 measles epidemic. Governmental bungling, coupled with the long-term effects of malnutrition, resulted in over 900 deaths from measles in 1989.[15] In the rural highlands of Chiapas alone, there were over 500 deaths reported from measles in the first seven months of 1990.[16] As the correspondent for the Mexico City newspaper *El Universal* wrote, "Forgotten for ages, beaten down by alcoholism, malnutrition and a shameful misery that contrasts with the agricultural wealth and the wealth of the surrounding forests, [the dead] . . . are victims not so much of a disease as of official lack of concern and of the inefficiency of [the public health agencies.]"[17]

Health Hazards Multiply

AIDS statistics date from 1982. Statistics about the actual number of people infected with the AIDS virus or of those who have developed full-blown cases of the disease fluctuate from source to source. The number of cases officially reported—3,944 AIDS cases in 1990—and an estimated 200,000 to 400,000 people infected with the virus place Mexico second in Latin America and 11th in the world in terms of incidence.[18] Despite initial attempts at aggressive public education campaigns, the government's agency on AIDS, ConaSIDA, has increasingly been influenced by the Catholic church and has backed away from its original, more candid approach.

Inadequate health care confronts AIDS patients in Mexico. As a result, the estimated life expectancy is less than one year, as compared to three years in countries such as Spain and the United States.[19] In order to remedy these conditions and confront prejudice, private AIDS and gay-activist groups have been working to educate the public and the medical communities, prevent the spread of AIDS, protect the rights of those afflicted with the disease, and lobby for better care for AIDS patients.

Pollution-related illnesses are another manifestation of Mexico's contradictory status as an industrializing country still hampered by the features of lagging development. For myriad reasons, both air and water pollution are problems throughout the country (see Environment, Part 5). The disastrous air quality in most urban centers—Mexico City being the most infamous—has led to a variety of illnesses. Chronic bronchitis and pulmonary emphysema, as well as asthma and bronchial cancer, are the most commonly treated diseases at public health-care institutes.[20] In addition, some 70 percent of Mexico City's inhabitants are reported to have pollution-related visual problems ranging from eye irritations to severe conjunctivitis.[21] There are also indications that the city's residents suffer from dangerous levels of lead exposure. Disorders resulting from high blood levels of lead contamination range from insomnia and irritability, to motor skill problems, convulsions, and even death.

Water pollution from industrial and human waste also causes health problems in the country. Along some parts of the border, for instance, health experts have found viruses such as polio, typhoid, and salmonella contaminating the water. Human feces and carcinogenic chemicals also pollute Mexican water supplies, with hazardous results for nearby inhabitants.

A Time Bomb

Traditionally the Mexican health-care system has suffered from an emphasis on individual curative medicine at the expense of public-health initiatives and prevention.[22] Of course, Mexico is not the only country guilty of such an emphasis, which in fact is the demon of western medicine. But in Mexico, as in most developing countries, many of the principal causes of death—respiratory disease, infectious intestinal disorders, and other contagious disease such as typhus—could be eliminated or reduced dramatically with improved sanitation and waste disposal, housing, nutrition, and personal hygiene. Even heart disease and cancer, which assume top places in Mexico's list of killer diseases, are highly responsive to diet and other preventive and primary-care interventions.

Mexico produces more doctors than the country can absorb given current social, political and economic arrangements. The bulk of these physicians tend to locate in urban areas, glutting the market there while leaving large swaths of countryside with only minimal public services. Doctors in the rural areas are typically young medical school graduates performing their year of *servicio social*, the required public service internship. In recent years the nation's public universities have been ordered to cut back on the number of medical graduates they turn out each year—a policy that some charge leads to an inadequate supply of medical school graduates to staff the rural clinics.

Despite the low percentage of Mexicans who reportedly depend on the private sector, the private health-care sector has grown consistently and is one of the most viable sectors of the economy. To some researchers, this indicates that Mexico is headed toward a greater privatization of medical care and a system in which employers will increasingly turn to private insurance corporations to meet the needs of their employees. This trend is stimulated by public-health budget cuts that have led to deterioration of the quality of service and lack of confidence in public medical institutions. Bank workers, Mexico City subway workers, and employees of several universities and Monterrey Group corporations are among the increasing number of Mexicans who receive private health-care insurance.[23]

Another sector of Mexico's health-care system is the government's Pronasol program. Traditionally, public-health services in Mexico have served more than a medical function; they also generated payoffs for the political system. By supplementing poor wages and defusing discontent, these medical services helped undercut opposition forces. Pronasol continues to serve that function, operating as a limited poverty program and political slush fund to boost PRI support and douse the potential for radical protest in impoverished areas. Critics charge that it has the potential to serve as the blueprint for a "radical departure from a social policy based on universal social security benefits" to one based on "public charity and philanthropy."[24] The current IMSS-Solidarity programs have their origins in previous programs designed to extend medical coverage to marginal areas. During the oil boom years, for instance, the government's IMSS-Coplamar program set up an extensive network of small rural clinics in areas that had never before had health care.

A government study projecting the nation's health needs into the 21st century described the current public-health system as a "time bomb," predicting that "the incapacity of the health sector to attend the public in a few years will be alarming."[25] As Mexico moves toward greater integration with the U.S. economy, it is possible that it will try to meet future needs by importing the U.S medical care/insurance complex, a solution which it can ill afford. An expanded private medical-care system in Mexico would be expensive and exclusive. As noted by researchers at the Autonomous University of Mexico's Social Medicine Program, "The limitations are obvious in a country like Mexico if we consider that half of the population lives in conditions of extreme poverty. The only way to make private medical care extensively available is if it is paid for by the state through a universal medical insurance."[26] But such systems have their own limitations, and at any rate, it is just such state intervention that Mexico has been abandoning with its economic liberalization programs.

Education and Student Organizing

On paper Mexico has a well-developed and equitable educational system. In reality, the system is as flawed and uneven as other social, political, and economic institutions in the country. Noteworthy achievements such as the reduction of illiteracy and the establishment of a national public-education system stand alongside glaring inefficiencies and shortcomings. The Mexican constitution, for instance, guarantees the right to a free, secular education to all children from six to 14. It also requires parents to educate children under the age of 15. The obligation is virtually never enforced, however, and even education officials occasionally admit that many parents take their children out of school for economic reasons.

Throughout much of its modern history Mexico has attempted to expand educational services to reach greater segments of the population. In many ways it has been successful in this endeavor. As of 1990, the official literacy rate is 92 percent, compared to 36 percent in 1934. Similarly, average years of schooling increased from 1.5 years in 1934 to slightly more than six years in 1990. Total matriculation increased from 1.4 million (one in every 12 Mexicans) in 1934, to 25.4 million (one in three) in 1987.[1]

In part these numbers reflect the increase in educational demand caused by the demographic explosion that began in the 1940s. Nevertheless, for many years school expansion far outpaced population growth. In fact, from 1930 to 1980 school enrollment increased 12 times while the population increased only 4 times.[2] Still, it was not until his last state of the nation report, in 1988, that President Miguel de la Madrid could announce that Mexico had met "100 percent of the effective demand" for primary education, an admittedly dubious achievement on the eve of the 21st century.

Foundations of the System

The first three decades following the Mexican Revolution established the relationship between the players in a highly centralized, nationalistic, and secular educational system. The Ministry of Public Education (SEP) has dominated the educational sector since it was created in 1921, and decisions about education at the local level have traditionally been made in Mexico

City. The close ties of the education ministry to PRI and to the country's political system mean that educational plans and programs change totally every six years, following the rhythm of the presidential *sexenio*. Curriculum innovations and reforms introduced in one period are changed almost totally in the next, often without an evaluation of the plans previously implemented.[3]

Although efforts began in 1979 to decentralize the decisionmaking process, the change has been slow going for political, technical, and economic reasons. Initiatives of the Salinas administration were aimed at further decentralizing the sector, but as of 1991, education was still controlled by the national government. Even the official teachers union, the National Union of Education Workers (SNTE), was tied to the center. Incorporated into PRI's popular sector in 1944, the SNTE is the largest union in Latin America.

Mexico's first education minister, José Vasconcelos, personified the country's nationalist approach to its educational curriculum. A controversial philosopher and politician, Vasconcelos established libraries and rural schools and distributed books throughout the population. But he is perhaps best known for his writings on the Mexican identity, defining the mestizo as the "cosmic race." Textbooks, dating from the 1970s, still emphasize nationalism. Future revisions, however, can be expected to reduce nationalist rhetoric in favor of general ideals of national identity, democracy, and independence.[4]

Despite the constitutional requirement that schools be secular, church-run institutions continued to exist after the revolution. Following the Cristero Rebellion the relationship between the main protagonists in educational policy was settled; the church was formally excluded, but tolerated in practice.[5] Private religious-run schools continue to be a popular alternative to public education for middle- and upper-class families, along with private bilingual institutions.

The 1960s and 1970s were characterized by the massive expansion of higher education.[6] In response to the 1968 student movement, which ended in the massacre of more than 300 students and others at the Tlatelolco plaza in Mexico City, the Echeverría administration poured tremendous resources into the educational system. As part of this initiative the government created additional institutions such as universities, university preparatory schools, and vocational institutes. This effort to contain dissidence by co-opting it—a typical PRI maneuver—was quite successful. By expanding higher education the government also partially resolved or postponed the problem of finding jobs for an expanding pool of young people entering the job market.

A Revolution Derailed

The economic crisis of the 1980s and the realization that the quality of a Mexican education had not kept pace with the increase in educational institutions put an end to the sector's headlong expansion. President Miguel de la Madrid responded by announcing a "Revolution in Education." The plan was designed to decentralize education, transfer resources and responsibilities to the states, and revise teacher training methods. The plan also aimed to shrink the bureaucracy of the education ministry, a haven for the state-controlled SNTE.

The results were limited. The government was unable to deal with the union bureaucracy, dominated by Carlos Jonguitud, the *cacique*-style boss who came to power in 1972 after ousting the SNTE's leaders during an armed assault on the union's Mexico City headquarters. The SNTE "leader for life" also served as governor and later senator of his home state of San Luis Potosí, while suppressing union dissidents. Jonguitud and the SNTE upper echelon saw decentralization as a threat to their power, and the government was dependent on the SNTE for electoral purposes. By the end of the *sexenio*, therefore, the education revolution was over. As a matter of fact, secret negotiations between SEP and the SNTE actually helped reverse the process. Such an outcome is not surprising. As a leading educational researcher in Mexico has written, "a true educational revolution would require profound transformations in state-societal relations that respond to wider economic and political changes. No amount of techno-rationalization can substitute for those changes."[7]

Jonguitud's ultimate ouster reflected the fact that these changes had not yet occurred by the end of the decade. In 1989, following weeks of protest marches and a national strike called by dissident teachers, Jonguitud was finally removed from his union post—but not from his Senate seat. His removal did not herald a change in business-as-usual, however, since he was replaced by a protégé.[8]

The economic crisis also helped to derail the educational revolution. Between 1982 and 1990 overall public expenditures devoted to education declined almost 21 percent.[9] Despite budget increases, Mexico spends far less than the 8 percent of gross national product that the United Nations recommends developing countries allot for education, a share that declined from 5.5 percent in 1982 to 2.5 percent in 1990.[10] The crisis was also felt in the pocketbooks of those most responsible for educating Mexico's population. In 1982 a teacher earned the equivalent of 3.5 minimum wage salaries; by 1990 a teacher earned 1.5 minimum salaries. Similarly, in 1990 the purchasing power of a university professor's salary was worth only 25 percent of its 1980 value. In real terms the total budget for the nation's largest public university, the National Autonomous University of Mexico in Mexico City, decreased by 44 percent from 1981 to 1986. As a result of all these factors, teaching has become less a profession than one of several part-time jobs.

Dashed Hopes and New Plans

Teacher attrition, student dropout rates, severe budget cuts, an unwieldy bureaucracy, and the corporatist political role of the official teachers' union continue to compromise the quality of education in Mexico.

In addition, the system suffers from serious attrition problems: currently slightly more than half of the children who begin primary school finish, while 25 percent of those who enter secondary school never finish. The attrition rate at the nation's public universities is estimated at 50 to 70 percent.

Also disturbing is the system's failure to provide an educational avenue to a better life for many sectors of the population. The middle class has largely disowned the public-school system, and education no longer provides a ticket to upward mobility for the poor. Moreover the system has failed most miserably where it is most needed. Despite an official national literacy rate of 92 percent, illiteracy rates in poorer areas like Chiapas and Oaxaca far outpace those in Mexico City or the northern border states, and 80 percent of the children of campesinos or indigenous families do not complete primary school.[11]

Meanwhile there has been a dramatic increase in the number of private educational institutions, particularly at the university level. Although a relatively low percentage of students in higher education attend private institutions—20 percent—the figure underestimates the change in the composition of this sector. The number of private schools for higher education nearly doubled between 1980 and 1990, rising from 97 to 190. Among the most important private institutions are the Iberoamericana, founded in 1943 in response to the "growing secularization of society"; the radically rightwing University of Guadalajara, founded in 1935; the Autonomous Technical Institute (ITAM) in Mexico City, founded in 1946; and the Monterrey Institute of Technology (ITESM), inspired by the Massachusetts Institute of Technology (MIT) in the United States and founded by the Monterrey Group in 1943.[12] Moreover, President Salinas and members of his "economic cabinet" all hold advanced degrees from elite U.S. universities—the implied prerequisite for the young and politically ambitious.

The shift toward private education has profound effects on business-government-society relationships in Mexico. Government officials have traditionally taught classes at UNAM, which has served as a recruiting ground for students with political ambitions. Increasingly both students and the politician-teacher are bypassing the public system and the egalitarian ideals which it has imperfectly fostered.

Soon after taking office President Salinas delivered a speech addressing the problems with the nation's educational system, noting the high attrition rate, regional disparities, and "dashed hopes" that plagued the system. SEP responded with a theoretical model prepared by an interdisciplinary group of specialists. The new model is designed to promote greater teacher flexibility, parental involvement, and regional differences in curriculum. The education ministry also hopes to deemphasize rote learning. The long-range plan is to foster the decentralization of education, with SEP ensuring that adequate resources are allotted to poorer states.

But there is little real incentive for state governments to assume the burden of public education. Another obstacle is the less than enthusiastic reaction of the teachers' union, which argues that more teacher input is needed in the reshaping of the educational system. At best the educational modernization announced by Salinas remains a promise, one which will not be realized without real decentralization and a major change in the country's political realities.

Student Movements

In 1968 students from UNAM, the National Polytechnic Institute in Mexico City, and thousands of secondary and preparatory students presented the Mexican political system with its most serious challenge since it was founded. As the summer progressed, hundreds of thousands of students took to the streets, the army fired upon and occupied schools, and thousands were arrested. On the eve of the Mexico City Olympics, the nation's image as a stable bureaucracy in Latin America was shattered.

The administration charged that foreign subversives were directing and financing the students. Student leaders denied the charges and put forth a platform demanding the release of political prisoners, the abolition of a constitutional provision that gave free rein to arbitrary arrest and imprisonment, and the reformation of law-enforcement agencies. "We weren't extremists. If the students' petitions had been resolved by Díaz Ordaz, the democratization would have been accelerated," a student leader recalled 20 years later.[13]

Instead, on the afternoon of October 2, 1968, helicopters buzzed over a middle-class housing project at Tlatelolco, a historic site in Mexico City where several thousand students had gathered for a meeting. Suddenly plainclothes police and soldiers began firing on the crowd, leaving hundreds dead.

The massacre effectively ended the movement. Although students had marched through the capital streets to the cheers of local residents, they never managed to create a broad-based coalition with labor or other social sectors. The student strike was called off, and many of the leaders were imprisoned, not to be released until the next *sexenio*. During the 1970s Mexican universities were a mix of anarchism and passive retreat. Some students joined urban guerrilla movements, which were violently squelched. Other potential dissidents found a niche in the burgeoning higher-education system that flourished under Echeverría.

In 1987 a new student movement, the Congress of University Students (CEU), emerged. This time the issues were limited to academic policy and reform measures described by some critics as "elitist." The movement was triggered by a report issued by Jorge Carpizo, then rector of UNAM, the largest and traditionally most important university in the nation. Carpizo's report addressed what had become common knowledge: the high percentage of UNAM's more than 300,000 students who never completed their degrees, the high percentage of professors who failed to show up for classes, and the disturbing lack of planning and coordination—in one department 87 professors were assigned to 74 students.[14]

The report recommended the elimination of the "automatic pass" and automatic matriculation for graduates of UNAM's preparatory schools. It also recommended the implementation of departmental examinations and an increase in the university's minimal fees, which at the time were the equivalent of two subway tickets. Initially government officials and political commentators praised the report. But students, many of whom were working and came from families with limited income, rejected Carpizo's conclusions. Faced with few job prospects after graduation, they saw the reforms as a threat to their right to a "piece of the national patrimony . . . the right to UNAM."[15]

A student strike developed with some of the flavor of 1968. Students occupied university facilities and marched to the Zócalo. But unlike 1968 the movement focused on issues of academic policy, and student leaders prohibited placards reflecting peripheral issues. After a 19-day strike the university administration and students negotiated a settlement. The reforms were called off and a university congress was promised. Several student leaders later became involved in the Cardenista campaign of 1988 and the founding of the PRD.

By 1991, however, there was little evidence of a student movement in Mexico; and once again officials were sounding the alarm, warning that Mexico's higher-education system needed overhauling. A report prepared by the International Council on Educational Development suggested that universities reduce enrollment, limit their autonomy, control fiscal procedures, and do away with the automatic pass. The current system is "a caricature of what a university ought to be," the report warned. The prevailing practice of relying on adjunct faculty paid by the hour had resulted in a teaching staff that was "not prepared to carry out research and whose pedagogical capabilities are very limited."[16]

Communications Media

The level of press freedom in Mexico is a topic of continuing, hot debate. The constitution guarantees freedom of expression, and the government sets aside June 7 as "Freedom of Expression Day," at which time the president hands out journalism awards. Critical journalists shun the celebration because they consider the official act a farce and one of many ways the state co-opts the media. Other members of the media take the event seriously, demonstrating a high level of consensus with the government.

Self-censorship is the most prevalent form of media control, preempting government need for prepublication or prebroadcast supervision. For instance, there exists an unwritten rule that the Mexican president should not be openly criticized. But this self-censorship is triggered by a series of economic and political levers set in motion by the state. Editors and reporters claim they are accustomed to government pressure. More often than not, the influence is wielded through government manipulation rather than outright assertion of authority. Although government pressure is the main instrument of control over the Mexican media, many media outlets, especially those outside Mexico City, are constrained in what they publish or broadcast by the power of local *caciques* (bosses) and drug traffickers.

Print Media

A handful of outstanding publications and journalists practice aggressive, accurate, and comprehensive reporting. In the 1970s and 1980s the print media increasingly showed signs of becoming more responsive to issues and arguments that challenged government policy. For the most part, however, the Mexican press remains docile and collusive. Although the state exercises no direct control, proprietors, editors, and reporters tend to respond positively to the interests and projects of the government.[1] This tendency is fostered by the fact that 20-30 percent of newspaper revenue is derived from government advertising. For some individual newspapers, government advertising may provide up to 100 percent of their income. The possibility that such revenue might be withdrawn because of critical reporting undermines aggressive journalism. In fact, the state withdrew all its advertising from the weekly newsmagazine *Proceso* in 1982 because of the periodical's criticisms of President López Portillo's politics.

The government practice of secretly paying reporters to write the stories it desires has diminished since President Miguel de la Madrid ordered a "moral renovation" program aimed at quelling corruption in the bureaucracy. But many journalists still depend on under-the-table payments to supplement inadequate wages that can be as low as $200 a month for a daily news writer.

Low salaries have spurred a movement to establish a minimum, professional wage for journalists. Meanwhile reporters and editors commonly look for more money in the pernicious form of an open payoff called the *gacetilla*, a paid political announcement placed in a newspaper and disguised as a genuine news article. In the country's biggest media market, Mexico City, most major dailies average one fully paid front-page story a day. The *gacetillas* are paid at 2 to 3 times the regular advertising rate, and reporters receive an average 15-percent commission for paid stories printed on their beats. Businesses and society-climbers buy *gacetillas*, but the prime clients are PRI and the government.[2]

The government also subtly controls newspapers through loans from its development banks to finance publishing companies. In addition, it was long accused of coercing the press by holding the sole newsprint supply in its parastatal company PIPSA, created in 1935. Although much of the printing industry liked the supply system because it kept paper prices down, three magazines—*Política*, *¿Por Qué?*, and *Proceso*—were subjected to selective paper shortages in the 1960s and 1970s. The controversy over PIPSA's role subsided when the government announced it was selling 60 percent of its interest in the company in 1990, although the government continues to manage the paper supply company.

Currently the most serious complaint is that the government cannot maintain a system of law and order that guarantees journalists safety on the job. In fact, government officials themselves are a threat to journalists. Some 60 Mexican journalists were killed at work between 1970 and 1990—two-thirds of them between 1982 and 1990. During the first two and a half years of the Salinas administration, 21 media workers were killed.[3] Another 366 reporters were attacked while on the job from 1971 to 1990.[4] A substantial number of assaults have been attributed to police, local political bosses, and drug traffickers.

The government has yet to conclude legal proceedings in the May 30, 1984, murder of muckraking columnist Manuel Buendía, whose death has become a symbol of the insecure conditions facing enterprising journalists. Buendía, author of a column called *Red Privada* (Private Network) in the Mexico City daily *Excélsior*, was gunned down outside his office in the prestigious Zona Rosa. The Mexican government maintains that Buendía was on the verge of exposing the corrupt dealings of former Federal Security Directorate chief José Antonio Zorrilla, who is in jail on charges that he masterminded the killing. Among the other theories as to why Buendía was assassinated is the one put forth by syndicated columnist Jack Anderson. The U.S. journalist claimed that Buendía was murdered just as he was about to disclose the complicity of Mexican authorities in an international drug-trafficking ring that the CIA used to run arms to the Nicaraguan contras.[5] The Democratic Journalists Guild, representing 1,500 members in 10 states, have organized demonstrations accusing the government of a cover-up and filed a lawsuit demanding justice and a complete investigation of the Buendía case.

Several of Mexico City's top academic journalists—Jorge Castañeda, Adolfo Aguilar Zinser, and Lorenzo Meyer—received death threats in 1990. But risks for journalists are statistically higher outside the capital. Hector Felix Miranda, "El Gato," an advocacy journalist and co-editor of the Tijuana daily paper *Zeta*, was killed by three bullets on April 20, 1988. Two men have been given jail sentences of nearly 30 years each in the case. But the son of cabinet minister Carlos Hank González, who was also linked to the slaying, escaped prosecution.

Adding to the difficulties faced by journalists is the absence of a shield law that would assure them the right to protect the confidentiality of their sources. Likewise, there is no sunshine law requiring the government to provide them access to information. The government's unresponsiveness to the press has generated a media culture in which reporters often rely on a handful of informed but unofficial sources known as "oracles." The government promotes its version of the news through its official wire service, Notimex, and its own daily newspaper, *El Nacional*.

Foreign influence is marked in the print media, with 90 percent of international news coming from the Associated Press, United Press International, and Agence France Presse.[6] As much as 75 percent comes from the two U.S. wire services.[7] The Hearst corporation distributes 2 million copies a month of its Spanish-language versions of *Cosmopolitan*, *Good Housekeeping*, and *Popular Mechanics* magazines. At one point the Spanish-language version of *Reader's Digest (Selecciones)* enjoyed a higher circulation than all seven of the largest Mexican magazines. Hearst's King Features Syndicate is the largest producer and seller of comic strips in Mexico.

Print media does not suffer much from monopoly strangleholds. In fact, international comparisons show that Mexico is one of the developing countries where the concentration of press ownership is lowest. But important groups do exist. Four families hold the locks and keys of the major media chains. The largest chain, Organización Editorial Mexicana (OEM), is owned by the Vázquez Rana family, which bought and briefly ran UPI in the late 1980s. The Alemán and O'Farrill families own the second largest, *Novedades*, with eight publications in five cities, including Mexico City's English-language daily *The News*. *El Heraldo de México* is part of the diversified enterprises of the Alarcón family, based in the south-central state of Puebla.

These family empires are offset by a plethora of small, independent publishing companies. New magazines and newspapers are born and die every month. Over the past 30 years the number of periodicals has been on the rise. Circulation figures are highly unreliable because these publications go largely unaudited and figures tend to be wildly inflated. Excluding the sports daily *Esto* (400,000 circulation), Mexico City has about thirty dailies with a total circulation of half a million.[8]

Although the northern and Pacific states have more than half of the country's dailies, the three largest cities—Mexico City, Guadalajara, and Monterrey—have the largest number of newspapers and the most distribution. More than 56 percent of national circulation has been registered in the big three. Nearly 48 percent of that is in Mexico City (10 percent of the nation's total) are available on the stands and are shipped out across the country.[9] This cornucopia provides a wide range of political perspectives in editorials, commentary, and basic news coverage.

Among the biggest sellers are the sports daily *Esto*, the middle-of-the-road *Excélsior*, the popular tabloid *La Prensa*, and two conservative publications, *El Heraldo* and *Novedades*. The government's *El Nacional* and the small *El Día* are publishers of establishment and status quo perspectives. *El Financiero* and *El Economista* specialize in finance news. *El Universal* and *Uno más Uno* have broad appeal. OEM's *El Sol* leans toward the conservative, while *La Jornada* takes a progressive slant. The most widely read newsmagazines are—from political left to right—*Proceso*, *Siempre*, and *Impacto*.

The impact of this wealth of print media is deadened by the fact that most people cannot or do not read what is written there. In the post-World War II period, the growth of illiteracy paralleled the growth of the press, with 10 percent increments annually from 1940 through 1960. Officially, Mexico enjoys a 92 percent literacy rate. But unofficial estimates are that as many as 6 million might be unable to read a newspaper. For yet others, comic books are the reading material of preference, with 800,000 read annually. Most people get their news from television. An independent survey in 1982 showed that 66 percent rely on television as their primary news source.

The economic crisis that has gripped the country since 1982 has been a disaster for the book-publishing industry. More than 400 publishers closed their doors between 1982 and 1988. In 1987 4,000 new titles were published, compared with 5,000 to 6,000 published annually in pre-crisis times. Books are now a luxury item, costing at least the equivalent of two days' worth of minimum wage. Book sales have dropped 20-30 percent at some publishing companies. Many have reduced first runs from 5,000 copies to 3,000.

Electronic Communications Media

Unlike the government-massaged and variegated field of print journalism, television and radio are mostly monopolized by large companies and scantily supervised by the state, which they support with little prodding.

For instance, more than 83 percent of electoral news coverage went to PRI in the 1988 presidential election year.[10] The government has its censors, broadcast regulations, and its own television and radio networks. But public programming has collided head-on with an overall policy of privatization of parastatal industries. Government networks are being offered for sale a chunk at a time. As public ownership is whittled away, the private ownership of the electronic media has become increasingly concentrated.

Private radio and television developed before public broadcasting, with the state originally devising broadcast regulations based on those of the United States. The government levies taxes on the private broadcasters and requires that private stations reserve 12.5 percent of air time for public programming. It sends "literary supervisors" to private networks periodically to make sure that nudity, violence, drugs, and offensive language are limited on the airwaves. But its regulations have never been clear or consistently enforced.

Listenership has grown for the approximately 1,000 AM and FM radio stations to which the state has granted concessions. In 1971 an industry chamber estimated that radio reached some 38 million listeners in 6 million residences. About 95 percent of Mexico City residences had radios in the 1980 census. Radio is the only media that reaches the country's numerous isolated rural areas.

The government's Instituto Mexicano de la Radio runs about 60 radio stations, and government programming mushroomed 11,000 percent from 1982 to 1988. However, these enterprises have been limited financially and technologically, as authorities have channeled many resources into private industry.[11] The federal Communications and Transportation Department provided $150 million in credits to small and midsize television and radio stations in 1991.[12]

Private radio got its start in 1921, about 50 years before the government entered the field. A shoe salesman named Emilio Azcarraga, who studied the radio industry in the United States, and his brother Raúl were its first promoters, building a diversified media empire based on the radio business. Through Televisa, the Azcarraga family had major holdings in 136 stations by 1982. Televisa is the largest radio operator of the 10 companies that own more than 77 percent of all commercial stations. Five companies own half of the private stations: Televisa with about 15 percent of them, ACIR with some 13 percent; RAVEPSA with about 10 percent, Radiorama with more than 8 percent, and RASA with nearly 8 percent.

Concentration of power over the airwaves is even more pronounced in private television, which is synonymous with Televisa.[13] The monopoly controls several national stations and runs a cable network. It also owns some 45 companies, including radio, newspaper, videocassette, record, publishing house, aviation, mining, tourism, and sports properties. Many artists and their audiences complain about Televisa's strangling grip on media industries. It has been dubbed the Fifth Estate, providing television coverage in 52 cities and 927 towns to an estimated 25 million Mexican viewers.[14] The Spanish-language chains in the United States depend heavily on Televisa, with Univisión and Telemundo relying on Televisa for about half of their programming. After being forced to sell Spanish International Network to Hallmark Cards in 1986 in a $620 million monopoly lawsuit, Televisa still controlled 80 percent of U.S. Spanish-language broadcasting.[15]

The Azcarragas, who own the majority of Televisa shares, and the O'Farrill family, who owned the second-largest portion until selling theirs to the Azcarragas in 1990, were the pioneers in private television. Rómulo O'Farrill, Jr., ranks 25th among Mexico's wealthiest businessmen. Miguel Alemán Velasco, son of former president Miguel Alemán, is the third partner in the business and one of the country's most prosperous businessmen. Because of family ties, political persuasions, and economic power, Televisa is an outright supporter of government policy. Jacobo Zabludovsky, Televisa's top news director, has been nicknamed "journalist of the regime," "PRI's secretary of information and propaganda," and "minister of information without credentials."[16]

Meanwhile the government is losing money on public broadcasting and is gradually participating less in the market. In 1990 the government announced plans to dismantle its Imevisión network and sell channels 7 and 22, maintaining only channel 13 in its national network. An outcry from hundreds of influential intellectuals convinced the government to reverse the decision to sell Channel 22. Public television suffers from policy swings between presidential administrations. The only project to survive every administration since its inception is one that provides public school courses by television to rural areas. Cable television, marketed by such companies as Multivisión, is steadily gaining in the television market.[17]

Church and Religion

Mexican tradition holds that in 1531 the Virgin Mary appeared three times to a poor Aztec named Juan Diego. She asked that a church be built in her honor at Tepeyac where the Aztec goddess Tonantzín was worshipped. Today, images of the Virgin of Guadalupe are seen everywhere in Mexico, and the basilica is visited annually by a more than a million pilgrims.

The Virgin's appearance to an Aztec Indian eased the incorporation of the Spanish colonial church into the Indian and *mestizo* society. Not just a symbol of faith, the Virgin of Guadalupe became a symbol of Mexican nationality. Few other nations are as Catholic as Mexico. From the national cathedral to the village church, the Catholic religion stands at the center of Mexican society. Catholicism is the heart of the nation's culture and the foundation for many of its traditions.

Church-State Relations

From independence to the Reform movement of Benito Juárez to the Mexican Revolution itself, the church hierarchy has regularly sided with the more conservative social forces. Catholic leaders point out that the early independence movement was led by Father Miguel Hidalgo and other liberal-minded priests like Father José María Morelos but often fail to mention that the enlightened Father Hidalgo was excommunicated and his head left to rot outside the village church. This division between the church hierarchy and the grassroots church has continued into the present. After independence in 1821 the Catholic church began to lose its privileged place in Mexican society. Citizens were no longer obligated to pay tithes or to work for the church. However, the Catholic church did maintain its monopoly on religion as affirmed by the 1824 constitution, which declared that religion "will perpetually be Catholic, apostolic, and Roman."

As the liberal movement took root and Freemasonry gained popularity among the elite in Mexico, relations between the church and the state became increasingly conflictive. In the mid-19th century the Catholic hierarchy joined the conservatives to block the reformist movement led by Juárez. The church, together with the conservatives, welcomed the French occupiers in 1862 and applauded when the Mexican crown was offered to Maximilian of Hapsburg. The imperial venture met stiff resistance, however, and Juárez soon returned to the presidency, once again throwing church-state relations into bitter conflict.

Although diplomatic relations with the Vatican were not renewed, tensions eased considerably during the conservative regime of Porfirio Díaz (1876-1910), but they flared up again with the revolution. The framers of the 1917 constitution set out to define clearly the separation of church from state. Never again would the church be permitted to regain its privileged position in the economy and government. The new constitution denied the church any juridical presence, guaranteed that public education would be secular and humanistic, and prohibited the clergy from participating in political life and from owning property.

It was not until 1925 when President Calles began to enforce strictly the constitutional provisions that the threatened church took the offensive. For nearly four years the country, particularly the central region, was caught up in a religious war. Bands of Catholic peasants—the *cristeros*—fought government troops and militia, while the Catholic clergy were forced into hiding—a historic period fictionalized by Graham Greene in his novel *The Power and the Glory*. A defeated Catholic church asked for a truce in 1929, and the government relaxed its anticlerical restrictions.

During the next three decades the church gradually recovered its prominent position in the country's social and religious life while maintaining an alliance of convenience with the ruling PRI. Relations were not warm but neither did they devolve into open hostility. The Second Vatican Council (1962-65) and especially the Latin American Bishops' Conference in Medellín (1968) opened the way for a more outspoken and aggressive church. Although not to the extent seen in Central and South America, a more socially conscious and committed church arose in Mexico. A network of Christian base communities was formally organized in 1971, and several Mexican bishops vigorously pursued the church's "preferential option for the poor." Most notable was the "Red Bishop" of Cuernavaca, Sergio Méndez Arceo.

It was not until the 1980s, however, that the modus vivendi that had evolved since 1929 between church and state began to deteriorate. Once again sectors of the church became associated with the antigovernment opposition. In the northern states, particularly in Chihuahua, the church became increasingly identified with the rise of PAN, while in the southern Pacific states of Chiapas and Oaxaca the church hierarchy became important supporters of the increasingly militant popular movement. Meanwhile, the Christian base communities began to spread throughout the country and were joining with the socialist left and poor-peoples' organizations to form the backbone of a new grassroots popular movement in rural and urban Mexico. The country also experienced the resurgence of a moralist lay movement with rightist convictions that clashed with the social policies of the PRI government. The differences between the government and the church could also be seen in the rise in the number of pastoral letters that addressed political and economic issues.

The Restoration of the Catholic Church

At a time when the stability of the Mexican state was weakening and PRI's credibility was fading, the church hierarchy, spurred on by the Vatican's apostolic delegate in Mexico, deftly began to maneuver for the restoration of its legal place in Mexican society and the renewal of diplomatic relations with the Holy See. While this effort to remove legal restrictions on church activity has had a strong national base, the restoration movement in Mexico has also been part of a worldwide campaign led by Pope John Paul II to create the conditions necessary for the flourishing of the "one, true church." Local observers have pointed out the close similarities between the papal initiatives seen in Poland during the 1980s and the current efforts in Mexico. For the past several years the church hierarchy has been quietly negotiating to remove the constitution's anticlerical restrictions and to reformulate church-state relations.

The presence of five bishops and Apostolic Delegate Jerónimo Prigione at the inauguration of Carlos Salinas de Gortari in June 1988 indicated the seriousness of PRI's initiatives to incorporate the church into a new alliance with the state. President Salinas declared that church-state relations must be modernized, and as part of this modernization he appointed a personal representative to the Vatican. As yet, however, full diplomatic relations with the Holy See, broken since 1867, have not been renewed.

It was the use of government resources to aid the Pope's visit to Mexico in May 1990 that provided the clearest sign that the historic separation of church and state was being radically modified. Underlying these new government initiatives and overtures was PRI's own political crisis. As the traditional forms of political control broke down, the government was apparently seeking new allies to substitute for its withered corporatist structures. It was commonly speculated that the government and the church were negotiating some type of quid pro quo deal whereby the church hierarchy would give its blessing to the Salinas government in return for the reform of church-state relations.

The church hierarchy has been pleased but hardly satisfied with the government's initiatives. Catholic prelates have called for changes in five articles (3, 5, 24, 27, and 130) of the constitution. Although they remain formally committed to the separation of church and state, they contend that the severe restrictions imposed by the constitution are unnecessary and archaic. They demand that the church be given a legal presence, that clerics be allowed to vote and own property, and that the church be given a role in the formulation of educational principles.[1] Explaining the type of church-state alliance desired by the church, Apostolic Delegate Prigione said, "We don't want the state to see us as its rival, but rather as its ally for all that is good and beautiful."[2]

Proposals to modify the constitution and to renew diplomatic relations with the Vatican face opposition within the ruling party, from the intellectual community, and, on some counts, from the non-Catholic churches and progressive sectors within the Catholic church itself. While many favored modernizing the constitution, they opposed the renewal of diplomatic relations with the Vatican. Many feared that the Catholic church was pushing for constitutional changes to bolster its position as the country's semi-official religious denomination. Leaders of the Methodist, Baptist, and Presbyterian churches met with Salinas in 1990 to express opposition to the constitutional changes proposed by the Catholic bishops. They felt that any changes would disproportionately benefit the Catholic church and expressed the opinion that the prohibition on property ownership by clerics encouraged an exclusive focus on their religious duties. Together with Jewish leaders, the protestant ministers were concerned that constitutional reform would serve to increase the influence of the Catholic church while increasing voter support for PRI. Rather than increasing the freedom of worship, they feared that religious freedom was endangered after the realignment of church-state relations of the Vatican.[3]

The Structure and Divisions of the Catholic Church

Yellow and white paper bunting decorated the streets of Mexico during John Paul II's May 1990 visit to Mexico. Televisa, the country's privately owned media giant, seemed to be serving as the pope's publicity agent, filling the airwaves with images and words of the supreme and infallible leader of the Roman Catholic Church. The euphoria that surrounded the pope's visit boosted the bargaining power of the church hierarchy and Delegate Prigione with respect to their initiatives to formalize the Mexican government's relations with the Vatican. At the same time, however, the church's bargaining position before the state is weakened by extensive popular disagreement with many of the church's social positions on such issues as education, family planning, and political participation.[4] After the 1991 midterm elections, President Salinas introduced constitutional amendments that officially recognize churches, allow them to own property, authorize the teaching of religion in private schools, and permit the clergy to participate in political life. The constitutional reforms, opposed only by the Popular Socialist Party, cleared the path for the diplomatic recognition of the Vatican.

In considering the place of the Catholic church within Mexican society, it is worth remembering that the church is not a monolithic body. Within the church there exist many conflicting ideas of the institution's mission. Because religion can be a powerful force in politics, differences within the church often take on strong political dimensions. Some of these differences are played out between the church hierarchy and what is often called "the church of the people." Within the hierarchy itself, however, there are also many divisions and political and theological tendencies. Although the bishops and priests largely define the institution, lay members have gained new influence in the church's positions on social issues and markedly increased their participation in liturgical functions. This rising involvement of the lay church reflects the steady decline in the clergy. Whereas overall population growth between 1980 and 1990 was close to 18 percent, the clergy expanded by a little more than 1 percent.[5]

Unlike smaller Latin American countries where the church is dependent on foreign funding and clergy, the Catholic church in Mexico is strong and largely self-sufficient. About 70 percent of the priests are diocesan priests, with the balance coming from religious orders.[6] All but a few of the country's 109 bishops are also diocesan, meaning that they pass through the national seminaries. All the country's dioceses are considered equal and autonomous, a structure that gives rise to strong regional differences.[7] Representing the church on a national level is the Mexico Bishops' Conference. Standing outside the national structure is the apostolic delegate from the Vatican, who is mainly concerned with the status of church-state relations, on both a national and international level. Apostolic Delegate Prigione has also used his influence to promote the appointments of centrist and conservative bishops, while isolating the more progressive elements within the church.

There exist several major currents or tendencies within the institutional church. Probably the most important of these is the hegemonic tendency led by the Vatican's Prigione which seeks mutual alliances with the state, the juridical recognition of the church, and the renewal of state relations with the Vatican. Although not part of bishops' conference, Prigione exerts much influence in the internal affairs of the Mexican church. The spiritual or traditional current based in the central states of México, Toluca, Puebla, and Morelos is distinguished by its concern for doctrinal and moral issues—the church's religious faith rather than social issues. Although these bishops are not political activists themselves, they vigorously support moralist and spiritualist initiatives by lay organizations. In the north the church hierarchy became closely associated with the electoral campaigns of the conservative PAN during the 1980s. The political and economic positions of these bishops largely reflect those of business organizations like Coparmex and Concanaco and other conservative organizations like Provida and the Integral Human Development Civil Association (DHIAC).

While bishops in northern cities such as Chihuahua and Hermosillo were expressing their concern about electoral fraud, the bishops of the southern states of Oaxaca and Chiapas have been more concerned with deteriorating socioeconomic conditions and government repression of poor people's struggles. The bishops of this southern current within the hierarchy actively promote base communities and have sought to dismantle the paternalistic structures of the church. In between the conservative and progressive activists is a substantial group of moderates who identify with the principles of Vatican II. Especially among the progressives and moderates there exists a certain nationalist resentment and political reaction against the meddling of the apostolic delegate. As a whole, the church hierarchy is one of the more conservative in Latin America.

The Lay Church: On the Left and Right

The Mexican church, more than most of its counterparts in Latin America, has resisted the inroads of liberation theology and liberalization of liturgical practices. Its conservative feudal traditions were reinforced by its confrontations with the reform and revolutionary governments. This fundamental conservatism has given rise to a long succession of reactionary organizations associated with the church, while at the same time making it difficult for a more socially progressive sector to emerge.[8]

When progressive elements within the church gathered to condemn the government repression of the student movement in 1968, they were silenced by the hierarchy. Nonetheless, a small but influential progressive sector has emerged since the late 1960s. By the 1990s thousands of base communities committed to social justice were found throughout the country, particularly in rural areas and in poor barrios surrounding the major cities. Every week between 150,000 and 250,000 members of these study/action groups gather to discuss their role as Christians in society while also developing new forms of spirituality.[9] Although numerically small, these study and action groups have been crucial in the development of the popular movement.[10] Like the urban movement, most of the base community activists are women, many of whom serve as the main leaders and organizers.

In contrast to the base communities, which are largely independent of clerical control, most other Catholic lay organizations either function as dependencies of the church or count on the public support of the hierarchy. Beginning with the Knights of Columbus, founded in 1882 to spread the Catholic faith, there have been numerous lay organizations created as instruments of the church hierarchy. Most important has been Mexican Catholic Action, which was founded in 1929 for the purpose of strengthening the church after the repressive *cristeros* period.

Also part of the lay church are organizations dedicated solely to spiritual objectives, including such groups as the Legion of Mary and Christian Renewal. Recently the church has given increased support to charismatic ministries as part of its new evangelization efforts to counteract the influence of the non-Catholic evangelicals.

Beginning with the *cristeros* there has been a close connection between Catholic organizations and the right wing in Mexico. One of the earliest of these political groups was the Catholic Legión, which was created by Catholics dissatisfied with the church-state accords reached in 1929. Later splits gave rise to the National Sinarquista Union (UNS) as well as establishing a social base for the creation of PAN and the Mexican branch of Opus Dei, a conservative and highly secretive Catholic organization.[11] Opus Dei continues to exercise strong influence in the church's financial, political, and educational matters.

During the 1980s Mexico experienced a resurgence of Catholic lay organizations with conservative agendas.[12] The close correspondence between the church's social doctrine and the platform of PAN, as well as the influence of Catholic activists within the party, represented an updated partnership of religion and politics, especially in northern Mexico. Rightwing Catholic populists are prominent in the Mexican Democratic Party (PDM), a conservative populist party based in the Bajío region with strong *sinarquista* roots.

The 1980s also gave rise to numerous Catholic organizations concerned with moral issues. Holding high the moralist banner of the church was the National Pro-Life Committee, or Provida, which was founded in 1978 to oppose the government's family planning efforts and to counter a proposal by the leftist parties to legalize abortion. It was not until 1988, however, that Provida became a visible social force. Although abortion is widely practiced and surveys have indicated that most Mexicans favor legalization, Provida has succeeded in building a vociferous and powerful opposition to all attempts to decriminalize abortion. Not confining itself to this one issue, Provida activists have also called for the penalization of homosexuality and for strict moral standards in education and in the arts. Echoing the long-held stance of the Catholic church, Provida organizers call the government-produced textbooks "marxist manuals."[13]

Flexing their muscles, Provida and other conservative groups closely associated with the Catholic church, such as the National Union of Parents, National Sinarquista Union, Knights of Columbus, and the Testimony and Hope Movement, have mounted successful campaigns to shut down art exhibits and cultural events they have considered offensive. One art show at the National Institute of Fine Arts was canceled after having been accused of "insulting the Virgin and the Fatherland." After a march of over 100,000 Catholics in February 1988 to protest a piece of art considered offensive to "the Virgin of Guadalupe and the National Flag," the Museum of Modern Art closed a show. This moralist campaign has received strong support from rightist groups associated with the Autonomous University of Guadalajara and the Autonomous Popular University of Puebla.

For many Mexicans the moral offensive of the Catholic church and the government's increasing willingness to accede to the wishes of the church hierarchy created new concerns about censorship and the social control of the Catholic church. This concern was reinforced by official church pronouncements linking church opinion with government policy, not only with respect to culture and education but also concerning religious freedom. Auxiliary Bishop Genaro Alamilla Arteaga of Mexico City, for example, called for increased government regulation of non-Catholic evangelization activities, noting that "the sects are attacking our cultural values, and the government should also take notice and put the brakes on this threat to our national sovereignty."[14] Rarely does the church distinguish between the historical protestant churches and the more recent evangelical organizations.

The Evangelical Challenge

Even after Vatican II ecumenism never took hold in the Catholic church in Mexico. Instead non-Catholic churches are routinely condemned by the church hierarchy and are often the targets of violent attacks by Catholic fanatics. Not being Catholic in Mexico means being an outsider and a threat to the established order. Academics, reporters, and church officials use a common language of paranoia and bigotry to refer to the "sects." They are called "CIA agents," "antinationalist" intruders, the "Protestant plague," and "attack troops of imperialism."[15]

The "invasion of the sects" is raising alarm throughout Mexico. In early 1990 a Catholic mob proclaiming their allegiance to the Virgin of Guadalupe attacked an evangelical retreat on a Mexico City hillside with clubs and machetes, injuring some 160 congregants. According to the Mexican Fellowship of Evangelicals, five evangelicals were killed in 1989 as a result of religious hatred and fear.[16] In Chiapas, Catholic *caciques* (traditional bosses or elders) have driven hundreds of evangelicals out of their communities because they have refused to participate in and pay for ritual Catholic celebrations.[17]

Reacting to the increased persecution, the evangelical community in Mexico City published a declaration in the daily newspapers declaring that a "climate of intolerance" was being fueled by the country's publishing houses, the academic community, and the Catholic church.[18] The evangelical churches fear that this intolerance will deepen as the church solidifies a new alliance with the government and increases its own evangelization campaigns.

In regular usage, the term "evangelical" and "protestant" are virtually synonymous, although "evangelical" is the more common term to refer to all non-Catholic christians. The term "protestant" is used mainly in reference to the historical churches, such as the Methodists. Mexican evangelicals reject the term "sects," arguing that only such religious institutions as the Jehovah's Witnesses and the Church of Jesus Christ of Latter Day Saints (Mormons), which rely on sources of revelation other than the Bible, should be defined as sects.

Mexican evangelicals readily acknowledge that their churches came to the country by way of the United States, but they are quick to note that Catholicism came from Spain and that the Catholic church in Mexico is still a foreign dependency of the Vatican. The earliest protestant denominations in Mexico—Methodists, Presbyterians, Baptists, and Anglicans—are known as the historical churches. The result of U.S. missionary activity, these historical churches date back to the 1860s. In contrast to the Catholic church, these early protestant churches strongly backed the anticlerical provisions of the liberal reform movements of the 19th century and of the Mexican

Revolution itself.[19] Educational systems pioneered by the Methodist church served as a model for Mexico's own progressive educational system following the revolution.[20]

Following a surge in religious fundamentalism in the United States, nondenominational faith missions began arriving in Mexico in the 1920s and 1930s, including the controversial Wycliffe Bible Translators (also known as the Summer Institute of Linguistics).[21] Whereas the first protestant missionaries had settled in communities of miners and railroad and textile workers, the fundamentalist missionaries began to seek converts among rural and indigenous communities, particularly in the southeast. Beginning in the 1950s pentecostal churches began appearing around the country, and today such pentecostal churches as Assembly of God and Church of God account for over 70 percent of the country's evangelical population. Distinguished by their emotional spirituality, the pentecostals discourage popular organizing around material issues.

Although the protestant churches did not suffer from the anticlerical repression of the 1920s, they did find themselves constrained by the emphasis on socialist education and the prohibition of foreign clergy. As society stabilized, the historical churches expanded steadily between 1940 and 1960, but then protestantism in Mexico ruptured as the fundamentalist and pentecostal churches gained supremacy. Breaking with the bureaucratism and conservative theology of historical protestantism, the new evangelicals stressed emotionalism as a religious response and encouraged the uneducated to become preachers. They sought converts in the squatter communities rising around the cities and in isolated rural areas. In large part this dramatic expansion of the pentecostal groups has been the main cause of new nationalist reaction against and persecution of non-Catholics.

The Religious Future of Mexico

The Catholic church does have cause for concern. Whereas protestant congregations were once limited to small geographical pockets, evangelical churches are now appearing throughout the country. There is no reliable count of non-Catholics in Mexico, but current estimates range from 8 to 12 percent. Although still a small minority, evangelicals have been increasing at a rapid rate since 1980, when the census registered that 3.3 percent of the population was protestant. The most rapid evangelical growth has been in the southeastern states of Tabasco, Chiapas, and Quintana Roo, which are among the poorest and most isolated states in Mexico. If growth rates continue, some Mexican states may have an evangelical majority by early in the next century. "I am not certain that the Catholic church is the religious future of this country," observed religious historian Jean Meyer.[22]

Where the Catholic church is firmly established it has been difficult for evangelicals to gain a foothold. But in the new *colonias* mushrooming on urban peripheries, in border regions, and in isolated rural communities, non-Catholics have had more success. To a large extent, evangelicals in Mexico are associated with the door-knocking pairs of Jehovah's Witnesses and Mormons. But for the most part there is little similarity either in their beliefs or methods of evangelism. Whereas the Jehovah's Witnesses reject all symbols of patriotism, most evangelicals are as nationalistic as any other Mexicans. And while the Mormons tend to target middle-class communities, particularly along the border, the evangelical boom is found largely among the poorest sectors of society. Rather than knocking on doors, Mexican evangelicals tend to win converts more through personal contact and by attracting the curious to retreats, services, and religious rallies.

There is considerable U.S. influence behind evangelical growth in Mexico, but the reasons behind this growth are nonetheless largely internal. The historical churches are for the most part independent of the U.S. denominations, while many fundamentalist and pentecostal churches still maintain organizational links and sponsor missionaries from the United States. For many U.S. missionary organizations, Mexico is a new world to conquer. WEC International compares its evangelical crusade in Mexico to the successful campaign of Hernán Cortez. "He won his prize—a great prize—but it was only of temporary value." Instead, WEC International encourages its missionaries to grasp "an eternal prize for Jesus in Mexico."[23]

The U.S. evangelical crusades have set their eyes on the booming *colonias* that surround the major metropolises. Combining food handouts with spirited preaching, Christian Advance International (CAI) teams visit the major garbage dumps in Mexico City, where they minister to the most desperate of the urban poor. CAI's Reverend Chris Jones talks of Mexico City being "taken for God."[24] Perhaps the most serious evangelical crusade has been coordinated by the Latin America Mission, which selected Mexico City as the main target in 1990 for its "Christ for the City" program.

Catholic officials frequently charge that the evangelical churches are buying converts with money and charity. Although there is evidently some truth in these accusations, the rapid advance of evangelical churches is due more to internal factors. In times of deteriorating economic conditions, poor Mexicans are looking for new answers and solutions. And caught up in a modernizing society, they are questioning religious traditions.

Catholic officials charge that the "*sectas*" are sowing divisions within rural communities. In this country where Catholic traditions seep into most aspects of life, there is no doubt that the rise of the evangelical churches contributes to social divisions. But many divisions already existed in even the most tight-knit rural communities—class divisions, conflicts over land ownership, and leadership splits. In at least some cases the turn to evangelical religion by portions of a community has reflected these pre-existing divisions. It is difficult to predict the long-term social and political impact of the evangelical conversion in Mexico. Support for birth control, anti-alcoholism, the rejection of oppressive tradition, and the encouragement of individual achievement are among the immediately observable positive contributions of this religious reformation in Mexico. Although constituting a major social phenomenon, the evangelical churches, which are not unified on a national or regional level, have thus far had little impact on political trends and the government's social policies.

PART FIVE

E nvironment

"It's ridiculous to think one could die of those poisons that are just for using on the fields. After all, I was there in the camps in Culiacán one time when I was a small child, and I didn't die."

> —Catalina, a Mixtec Indian in Tijuana, quoted in Angus Wright, *The Death of Ramón González, 1990*[1]

© Amy Zuckerman/Impact Visuals

Environment in Figures[2]

Land

Erosion	50% of land surface affected
	371,000 acres rendered useless per year
Desertification	556,000 acres per year
Deforestation	1.5 million acres per year,
	98% of tropical jungles lost by 1991
Reforestation	25,000 to 99,000 acres per year
Protected Areas	1.6% of national territory (84 areas)

Water

Aquifers	50% are overexploited
Water contamination	90% of manufacturing industry origin

Flora and Fauna

Biodiversity	16% of flora and fauna unique to Mexico
Plants	20,000 to 30,000 plant species, 477 threatened
Mammals	439 species, 32 threatened
Reptiles	717 species, 35 threatened
Amphibians	284 species, 4 threatened
Birds	961 species, 123 threatened

Mexico City

Air	80% of days hazardous to lungs due to ozone
	5 million tons contaminants emitted per year
	600 tons of fecal dust each day
Water	30% of population without sewage system
Food	25% of vegetables contaminated with heavy metals

U.S.-Mexico Border

Maquiladoras	20 million tons of waste per year
Illegal toxic waste	8 million tons per year sent from United States to Mexico
Raw sewage in Tijuana River	12 million gallons per day
Chemical analysis of New River, Sonora	100 toxic substances (estimated)
Water supply in El Paso/Juarez	Estimated to run out in 9 years

Pesticides

42% domestically produced are chlorinated compounds such as BHC, DDT and endrin, prohibited or severely restricted in the United States. All the "dirty dozen" (identified by Pesticide Action Network as the most dangerous to human health and the environment) are used.

The Environment and the Ecology Movement

Environmental crisis has descended upon Mexico at a time of economic and political restructuring. Just as Mexico is attempting to modernize its economic and political systems, the country is confronting the rapid deterioration of its natural environment.

The signs of the crisis are unavoidable. Hospital waiting rooms are jammed with patients complaining of respiratory ailments. Waterways are clogged with sewage, and the disposable cans, bottles, and packaging of modern society are strewn throughout the countryside. In the cities, commuters on the metro and buses attempt to ward off smog attacks with throat lozenges and eye drops. The assault on the health of city residents constitutes just one part of the urbanization crisis. Housing scarcity, poor transportation, and the lack of sanitation and water service make living in major metropolitan areas a survival test for the urban poor.

As catastrophic as urban life has become, the urbanization of Mexico continues as peasant families head for the cities to escape the environmental devastation and misery of rural Mexico. Matching the rapid pace of urbanization is the rate of erosion and deforestation, forcing Mexicans to make the hard choice between the urban jungle and rural desertification. By favoring export and single-crop (monoculture) production by agribusiness operations over small-farm production for the domestic market, the government is doing little to halt the decline of sustainable agricultural practices.

Environmental disaster in Mexico is not simply a matter of the loss of natural beauty and a decline in the quality of life. The disruption of the environmental balance also has serious economic repercussions. Watersheds are threatened, farm production declines, worker illness increases, reservoirs for hydroelectric plants dry up, fishing yields fall, and business efficiency and productivity drop.

Mexico, of course, is not alone with these problems. In large part the mounting environmental catastrophe in Mexico is the inevitable result of a model of development that stresses production at the expense of nature and social justice. In that, at least, Mexico has had plenty of company, both in the capitalist and socialist worlds.

Government and the private sector have conspired since the 1940s to push the economy forward in Mexico. For the most part they have been quite successful. But the social and environmental costs of unbalanced development have been routinely ignored in the search for high growth rates and profits. It was not until the early 1980s that environmental consciousness and activism took hold in the country. Ironically this new understanding of the downside of unbalanced economic development came just when the economy was falling apart. The country's model of import-substitution industrialization was exhausted, the oil boom went bust, the farm sector was in crisis, and Mexico could no longer pay its debts. Paralleling this economic turmoil was the crisis of political credibility facing the one-party state.

Since 1982 the Mexican government has established new agencies and adopted new regulations to protect the environment, especially in Mexico City. Overshadowing this incipient environmentalism, however, are the government's own stabilization and modernization programs. To stabilize government finances, the public-sector budget has been slashed, which means that there is little money to enforce the new environmental regulations and still less for waste-treatment facilities. The financial adjustment measures undertaken by the government have reduced the government's capacity to respond adequately to environmental deterioration.

The new model of economic modernization chosen by the country's political elite does not incorporate a more balanced concept of economic development. Rather, the neoliberal model tosses aside the old populist and nationalist rhetoric while giving free rein to market forces and private capital accumulation. Economic growth, foreign investment, and export production are the newly installed idols of the state's economic planners. As in the past, the "externalities" or social and environmental costs of economic growth are being ignored in the single-minded drive for economic recovery. The renewed emphasis on private-sector solutions places new limits on the capacity to regulate and guide economic development in ways that protect the common good.[3]

There exists in Mexico an increasing recognition that economic development without environmental and social safeguards is untenable over the long term. Mexico City, the country's political and economic center, is a harsh reminder of this principle. No longer is environmentalism an exotic concept espoused by an intellectual elite. Environmentalism has found a central place in the national political debate in Mexico. Nonetheless, the country is still far from finding a viable development alternative that would permit it to grow without undermining its natural resources and jeopardizing its future.

Deforestation and Desertification

Mexico has one of the largest forest reserves in the world and the largest remaining tropical rainforest in North America. Yet the country also suffers from one of the world's highest rates of deforestation, losing more than one million acres annually. The most dramatic devastation in recent years has been the clearing of the nation's tropical jungles—only 2 percent of which remain.[4] Expanded cattle ranching, the lumber business, and subsistence farming are responsible for most deforestation. Since the 1940s the Mexican government has considered its tropical forests a "safety valve" to siphon off peasant demands for land and work. Although some officials hoped the tropical lowlands would become the nation's bread basket, the poor forest soils have instead been converted to low-grade pastures for expanding cattle ranches.[5]

Since 1980 the southern states of Chiapas and Tabasco have lost more than half of their remaining jungles to cattle ranching and the extraction of precious woods. The spectacular Lacandon tropical forest, once one of the richest ecosystems in the New World, has been reduced by half since the 1970s when the government launched its peasant colonization programs to diffuse peasant unrest. In an attempt to reduce its foreign debt and at the same time protect its forests, Mexico in 1991 arranged its first "debt-for-nature" swap with the U.S.-based Conservation International with a focus on protecting the Lacandon forest. If the initiative fails and current trends continue, however, by the year 2010 the Lacandon forest will be but a memory.[6]

Reforestation—between 25,000 and 99,000 acres annually—has been grossly inadequate. Not only has reforestation fallen far behind the pace of deforestation, but the various tree-planting programs have also been qualitatively deficient. As yet, reforestation programs have made little effort to recover the biodiversity and ecological complexity of deforested terrain. For the most part these areas are protected in name only.[7] The government issues decrees announcing that endangered lands will be protected, but there is little or no enforcement. In the hills outlying Mexico City, the government has even allowed the landless to settle in protected areas in return for their support of PRI.[8]

Erosion is in great measure the consequence of deforestation and subsequent exploitation either by intensive agriculture or extensive cattle grazing. Mexico is losing fertile topsoil at an annual rate of 560 million tons. Along with continuing drought, this loss is helping to transform some 556,000 acres of Mexican land into desert every year. Already one-third of the nation is desertified. Lakes and rivers are visibly drying up, and hundreds of thousands of acres of land are rendered useless each year, making subsistence farming a desperate proposition.[9]

If the Mexican government is caught in the dilemma of trying to survive economically at the expense of destroying itself environmentally, no Mexican suffers this contradiction more directly than the peasant. Not only are *campesinos* losing their land to capitalist agroindustry, they are also losing it to the processes of erosion and desertification. The peasantry's own need to deforest marginal lands for subsistence agricultural production further aggravates this destruction of Mexico's soil resources. Because of overcultivation of the Mixtec region in Oaxaca, arable land has been reduced by

90 percent, forcing thousands of Indian families into the migrant labor stream.[10]

The Loss of Biodiversity

With its 30,000 plant species, nearly 1,000 bird species, and 1,500 mammals, reptiles, and amphibians, Mexico is among the world's most biodiverse nations. Mexico has at least as many plants as the continental United States, and 15 percent more vertebrates. Scientists estimate that some 15 percent of Mexico's plant and animal species are found nowhere else on earth.[11]

Terrestrial species are not the only ones being threatened by the destruction of Mexican forests. Degradation and overexploitation of marine environments are also taking their toll on such species as the marine turtle. Six of the world's seven marine turtle species nest on Mexican shores. The high value of turtle eggs, their reputation as aphrodisiacs, and Japan's world-leading consumer demand all fuel the contraband business in turtle eggs. Pressure from national and international environmentalist groups caused the government in 1990 to announce a permanent ban on the hunting and exploitation of marine turtles. Local programs have also resulted in a decline in turtle-egg contraband and improved marine turtle protection.

Another major concern is the netting of dolphins during tuna fishing. An estimated 84,000 dolphins died in tuna nets in 1989. Concerted protests resulted in a halt to U.S. tuna imports from Mexico in 1990. In Mexico, the announcement was greeted by charges of "protectionism disguised as ecology," which led some U.S. environmental groups to give more attention to what some call "environmental imperialism."

Petroleum exploitation is seriously threatening the largest wetlands in Mesoamerica, on the coast of the Gulf of Mexico. While this area is designated a sanctuary for species threatened with extinction, under its surface lie enormous oil fields, where the daily production of half a million barrels of crude is causing severe environmental damage. Mexico's petrochemical and mineral resources are increasingly open to investment and large-scale exploitation by foreign investors under the country's liberalized trade regime. Foreign contracts for oil exploration have already expanded and might well increase dramatically after the signing of a free trade accord.

The Chemical Threat

Overexploitation of natural resources in Mexico is compounded by chemical contamination. Of particular concern in rural areas is the overuse and careless application of chemical pesticides and defoliants. The coming of the "green revolution" to Mexico in the 1940s and the increasing focus on export production have been the main factors encouraging the widespread use of chemical inputs. Extensive reliance on these chemical agents has, in turn, led to monoculture farming and a corresponding shift away from more traditional multicrop production. As elsewhere where monoculture farming and extensive chemical spraying are common, natural biological resistance to pests has declined, while the pests themselves become resistant to pesticides, requiring farmers to depend on ever-increasing doses of biocides.[12]

Most of the pesticides used in Mexico are manufactured within the country either by foreign firms—including Bayer, Du Pont, and Stauffer— or by the government's own Fertimex company (now in the process of being privatized).[13] For those pesticides not produced under patent in Mexico, there is a thriving import business.

Public pressure in the United States has resulted in stricter regulations for the use of chemical inputs in domestic agriculture. But the U.S. government and U.S. manufacturers have done little to limit the types of pesticides exported from the United States, including those to Mexico. According to the U.S. General Accounting Office (GAO), U.S. pesticide exports account for about one-fourth of the international trade in pesticides. About one-quarter of those pesticides cannot be sold within the United States.[14]

The "circle of poison" that results from the export of domestically banned pesticides and the subsequent import into the United States of produce grown with these pesticides has consequences for the health of U.S. consumers. Imports account for one-fourth of the produce consumed in the United States, but according to a 1986 study by the GAO, less than 1 percent are tested for pesticides. Moreover, many pesticides are not detectable with current methods of testing. These facts are particularly relevant when considering U.S. imports of Mexican agricultural commodities. About 90 percent of Mexico's fresh fruit and vegetable exports go to the United States, and Mexico supplies more than half of the vegetables eaten by U.S. consumers between December and March.[15]

Mexican growers use at least one-third of the 90 pesticides that have been restricted or whose registration has been canceled or suspended by the U.S. Environmental Protection Agency. Among these are the "dirty dozen" that the Pesticide Action Network in San Francisco has identified as the most dangerous pesticides to human health and the environment. Mexico continues using the organochlorides DDT and BHC, 20 years after their patents were revoked worldwide. Also of common use in Mexico are methyl- and ethylmercuric fungicides, which cause irreversible lesions in the human central nervous system. Mexican agribusinesses also rely on the herbicide paraquat, which causes pulmonary fibrosis in humans.

Perhaps the most serious problem among agricultural workers is the use of parathion, which is up to 60 times as toxic to humans as DDT. According to the director of the Social Security clinic in San Quintín, Baja California, the Mixtec Indian farmworkers applying parathion "come in presenting difficulties in breathing or with symptoms of paralysis, and some go into comas."[16] Mexican agricultural and health experts report that the indiscriminate use of pesticides in Mexico severely poisons thousands of workers each year, resulting in hundreds of deaths.[17]

Urban Pollution

Migration either to the city or to the United States has been a traditional alternative to the hardships of subsistence farming in the countryside. Urbanization has created new forms of misery and its own set of environmental problems, however. Although all Mexico's cities share the fate of smothering smog and deteriorating services, Mexico City is the bleakest example of this spreading urban blight.

Trapped by mountains that prevent the escape of contaminated air and hosting 45 percent of the nation's industry and 22 percent of the nation's population, the Mexico City metropolitan area is an environmental nightmare. The most contaminated city in the world, Mexico City has an unequaled collection of atmospheric poisons derived from industrial emissions, vehicle exhaust, smoke, and human waste. Every day 12,000 tons of contaminants are emitted into the deadening smog that covers the city. More than three-quarters of this pollution comes from the nearly three million cars that circulate daily in the city's clogged corridors. National and international norms of sulfur dioxide, nitrogen dioxide, ozone, and suspended particles are regularly surpassed. Blood lead levels of Mexico City inhabitants are more than twice as high as the levels registered in the world's other major metropolitan areas. So bad were the levels of poisonous ozone gas in 1990 that, according to official levels of tolerance, the air was unbreathable 80 percent of the time. Because of the lack of sanitation facilities, city residents inhale so much fecal dust that infectious diseases such as salmonella and hepatitis can be contracted simply by inhaling the suspended bacteria.[18]

Statistics from the Children's Hospital of Mexico and the National Institute of Pediatrics show that respiratory illnesses such as bronchial asthma, bronchial pneumonia, sinus problems, and chronic colds have surpassed gastrointestinal infections as the number one problem. In the face of rising health problems, the government in the late 1980s finally began to implement a serious environmental action program. One measure is the "Hoy No Circula" (No Driving Today) program, which each day prohibits the use of vehicles with certain license plate numbers. Although the program did help, at least at first, it also prompted the buying of second and third cars.

About 30 percent of Mexico City families live without sewage facilities.[19] One result is that sewage flows into area waterways. The most polluted of these, the Panuco River, receives some 690,000 tons a year of untreated sewage. Every day 11,000 tons of solid waste are produced in the metropolitan area—only 75 percent of which is collected.[20]

A putrid mixture of untreated sewage and industrial wastes flows out of the city to such farming areas as the Mezquital valley. Here, some 50 miles to the city's north, the fields are verdant with alfalfa, beans, cucumbers, and chiles to be trucked to Mexico City. The result has been a domestic "circle of poison." One test showed that vegetables in Mexico City contained lead levels twice as high as the maximum allowable in the United States. Other surveys revealed that at least 25 percent of the vegetables sold in the city were contaminated with heavy metals.[21]

The U.S.-Mexico Border Region

The nearly 2,000-mile demarcation between Mexico and the United States is another environmental disaster zone. Many of the problems are directly related to the economic disparities between the underdeveloped south and industrialized north.

The contamination and overexploitation of the border region's groundwater is perhaps the most critical environmental problem. The use and control of water, the most precious resource of the arid border region, is a source of rising border tensions. The groundwater reserves that span the international boundary represent the future of the mushrooming border communities and the agribusiness operations on either side of the border line.

Five of the six Mexican border states are among the top ten irrigated states in Mexico. Most of the increased pressure on scarce water resources comes, however, from exploding urbanization. From Brownsville and Matamoros to San Diego and Tijuana, rapid development of the borderlands threatens ground and surface water supplies with contamination and depletion.

Pollution has been so severe and infectious disease so conspicuous along the U.S.-Mexico border that the American Medical Association called the border a "virtual cesspool and breeding ground for infectious disease."[22] About 12 million gallons of raw sewage flows daily into the Tijuana River before emptying into the ocean off San Diego. This has cost San Diego, according to one estimate, more than $100 million annually in lost tourism.[23] The Nogales Wash, only a muddy creek at its source in northern Sonora, flows by factories, industrial parks, and shantytowns. By the time it crosses the U.S. border, it has accumulated vast amounts of toxic industrial pollutants and untreated sewage, contributing to the abnormally high incidence of hepatitis along the Arizona border. Pollution is also a major problem in the Rio Grande. More than 100 million gallons of raw sewage laced with pesticides and heavy metals empty into the river each day, making some stretches along the border so contaminated with fecal material that the water is unsafe to touch.

Probably the most egregious example of water contamination along the border is the New River, which flows through Mexicali into the Imperial Valley of California. With approximately 100 toxic substances—including mercury and cancer-causing PCBs, 28 varieties of virus and an unknown number of bacterial strains capable of causing typhoid, cholera, hepatitis, meningitis, dysentery, and polio—the New River is probably the filthiest waterway in the United States. Although no one uses the water for drinking or even irrigation, some fear that epidemic disease is inevitable unless the contamination is curtailed. Probably most at risk are those illegal immigrants who wade through the disease-infested water when crossing the border.

How to clean these rivers is no mystery. "Everybody knows how to stop pollution in the river," said Sergio Reyes Luján, undersecretary for ecology at the Ministry of Urban Development and Ecology (SEDUE). "You construct a treatment plant for sewage." However, for financial reasons, this solution is out of reach for many Mexican cities. What funds these cities have for such matters are not earmarked for sewage treatment plants but are used simply to get raw sewage out of the city streets and neighborhoods. With water contamination spreading north across the border, the U.S. border cities and states face the hard reality of either living with this pollution or entering into joint solutions with their southern counterparts. Besides water problems of its own creation, Mexico also faces the specter of the salinization of its water supplies as a result of extensive irrigation on the U.S. side. Some consider salinity the most pervasive and important water quality problem threatening the border region today.[24]

Wastes on the Border

Just as the United States faces contamination problems deriving largely from the poverty of its southern neighbor, Mexico confronts environmental dangers arising from U.S. industrialization. Hazardous wastes, the lethal byproducts of industrialization, are moved both legally and illegally across the border.

The rapid expansion of the export-oriented assembly plants called *maquiladoras* is one of the main reasons for the tremendous growth of Mexico's border cities. Some 2,000 plants owned by such manufacturing giants as General Motors, Ford, RCA, Zenith, and General Electric employ cheap Mexican labor and take advantage of slack environmental regulations.

Despite a binational pact requiring all toxic wastes to be returned to the country of origin, U.S. government records in 1988 indicated that only 1 percent of the *maquiladoras* operating in Baja California and Sonora requested shipment of hazardous waste back to the United States.[25] Instead of sending their wastes back across the border, many firms stockpile wastes at plant sites, sell them to questionable Mexican "recyclers," flush wastes down sewers, or dump them in the desert.[26] The *maquila* industry generates some 20 million tons of waste annually. Because of inadequate disposal facilities, an estimated 100 million tons of accumulated waste are improperly stored.[27] The National Toxic Campaign Fund in Boston reported in 1991 that there are toxic discharges at 75 percent of the *maquiladora* sites, with severe contamination at one-third of them. The environmental group found chemicals that cause birth defects, cancer, and lung, liver, kidney, and brain damage in open ditches running through worker settlements outside the factories. The toxins were sometimes in concentrations thousands of times higher than U.S. environmental standards for ambient water.[28]

According to SEDUE, the Mexican government's environmental protection agency, most illegal wastes come not from the *maquila* industry but from U.S. companies transporting their toxic wastes across the border. Mexico has had only five commercial sites approved by SEDUE for the disposal of hazardous wastes. Between 1986 and 1989 Mexican authorities intercepted about 500,000 tons of hazardous wastes intended to be dumped along the border by U.S. companies.[29] According to Roberto Sánchez, director of environmental studies at El Colegio de la Frontera Norte in Tijuana, part of the reason for this contraband is the enormous difference between Mexico and the United States in the cost of legal toxic-waste disposal.[30] It is estimated that every year 8 million tons of hazardous wastes are illegally transported from the United States into Mexico, where they are dumped without any concern for the environment.[31]

The Response of the Government

Largely as a result of international environmental initiatives promoted by the United Nations, Mexico began to develop its own environmental policies in the 1970s. A 1971 decree set out a series of general environmental principles but failed to stipulate the norms and standards necessary for enforcement. Formal responsibility for environmental protection was relegated to a low level in the Ministry of Health. In 1978 the term "ecology" was for the first time used in government planning documents, but government commitment to environmental protection remained mostly symbolic.[32]

With news of the environmental damage associated with the country's oil industry, the worsening smog in Mexico City, and concerns about nuclear power development, environmentalism quickly gained ground in the early 1980s. Reacting to this expanding public consciousness, the López Portillo administration in late 1981 formulated a more forceful environmental law. Announced in early 1982, the law transformed what were basically the stated good intentions of the federal government into an official commitment to confront environmental degradation. Upon taking office in December 1982, President de la Madrid created a new cabinet-level ministry, SEDUE.

Although the creation of SEDUE did reflect rising government concern with the deterioration of the Mexican environment, the government's newfound environmentalism was also a product of its traditional practice of cooptive and preemptive policymaking. Starting with his presidential campaign and continuing throughout his presidency, de la Madrid sought to capitalize on rising public concern with the environment and to incorporate new ecology groups into the expansive government bureaucracy.[33]

The government was only partially successful, however, in containing and manipulating the rapidly expanding environmental movement. International disasters at Chernobyl and Bhopal, together with domestic calamities such as that of the 1984 San Juan Ixhuatepec gas explosion, raised environmental awareness while at the same time highlighting the Mexican government's policy failures. Although the de la Madrid administration did much to promote its declared environmentalism, it steadily reduced its financial commitment to SEDUE and environmental protection, and regulatory enforcement remained sporadic and largely nonpunitive.[34]

Like de la Madrid, Carlos Salinas declared himself an environmentalist in his early campaign speeches. One of his closest associates, Manuel Camacho Solís, resigned as SEDUE director to manage the Salinas campaign. Camacho Solís was later appointed regent of the Federal District, while a close associate of Salinas in the Ministry of Planning and Budget became the new head of SEDUE. During his first three years as president, Salinas did step up the pace of environmental protection under the authority of a 1988 statute, the General Law of Ecological Equilibrium and Environmental Protection, which gave SEDUE greater coordination and enforcement powers.

Nonetheless the commitment of the Salinas administration to environmental protection was questionable. The budgetary resources of SEDUE remained minimal, and the agency's industrial enforcement department, charged with monitoring over 30,000 industries, had only nine investigators in 1990.[35] The main thrust of environmental policy was what the Salinas government called *concertación*, or social accord, placing the burden of environmental improvement on voluntary collaboration.[36] Nonbinding industry and interagency agreements were the preferred model of environmental protection, although the government also began fining some Mexico City industries that were in blatant violation of environmental standards.

The 1991 closure of the ancient Azapotzalco refinery in Mexico City seemed more of a public-relations maneuver aimed at securing U.S. support for free trade than part of a comprehensive environmental plan. Whereas the government did formulate an extensive new set of environmental standards, enforcement was lax and focused almost exclusively on Mexico City. Despite the No Driving Today program, contamination indices climbed through 1991. More dramatic steps have been avoided for fear of angering business interests and vehicle owners. And in shameless contradiction to its efforts to reduce vehicular emissions, the government worked closely with the auto industry to increase vehicle production and sales.[37] The pollution disaster in Mexico City would be lessened if the metropolis were not the hub of the country's economic and political life. Although publicly committed to decentralizing the nation's political and business activities away from the capital city, the Salinas administration is doing little to make it happen.

Organizing for a Better Environment

The rapid deterioration of Mexico's environment and the failure of the Mexican government to protect the country's natural resources sparked an expanding environmental movement. This movement ranges from newly founded ecology organizations, composed mostly of the urban middle-class sectors concerned about uncontrolled urbanization and industrial development, to rural peasant communities organizing to keep their land and protect their way of life.

The ecology movement, which began in the early 1980s, includes some two dozen organizations, most of which operate on a local level with small memberships. Although the environmental movement did not catch hold in Mexico until after 1982, there were a few environmental organizations in the 1970s. Probably most important were the Centro de Ecodesarrollo and the various coalitions formed to stop a nuclear-research center at Lake Pátzcuaro.

In the early 1980s rising public concern, together with the government's own promotion of environmental issues, sparked the formation of such groups as the Mexican Ecological Movement (MEM) and the Mexican Ecologist Alliance (AEM). Two major environmental coalitions that formed in the mid-1980s were the Group of 100, a collection of some of Mexico's foremost intellectuals and artists, and the Coalition (Pacto) of Ecologist Groups (PGE). At about the same time, the antinuclear movement was regrouping to protest the opening of the Laguna Verde nuclear power plant in Veracruz, and the National Coordinator against Laguna Verde (Conclave) was founded. Unlike other parts of the national environmental movement, the antinuclear protests brought together local community activists and urban intellectuals. Predating these environmentalist groups were more traditional conservation groups such as Pronatura, most of which are affiliated with international conservation organizations and which have a narrower, more apolitical orientation.[38]

Mexico's Green Party was formed in 1987 as an outgrowth of the Ecologist Alliance, in anticipation of the upcoming 1988 presidential election. It joined the National Democratic Front (FDN) coalition headed by Cuauhtémoc Cárdenas for that election but ran independently under its new name, Mexican Ecological Party (PEM), for the 1991 midterm elections.

The environmental movement, like other branches of the country's popular movement, has frequently fallen victim to the government's political manipulation. Government initiatives to bring environmental activists into the policymaking process and into the government bureaucracy have led to splits in the movement. MEM, for example, has been criticized for its lack of militancy and for being a showcase organization used by the Mexican government in order to legitimize the administration's actions. Other groups have also been criticized for succumbing to the patronage and clientelism of SEDUE and other government agencies. According to Group of 100 spokesperson Homero Aridjis, "The problem of pollution in Mexico reflects the pollution of the political system."[39]

The deepening environmental crisis has also catalyzed rural communities to organize and make demands for democratic participation in the use and management of natural resources.[40] In the 1970s Indian and *ejido* communities began struggling to protect the dwindling forests and to benefit from timber operations. At least in some cases, these communities have succeeded in establishing protected zones and plans to regenerate lost forest lands. A recent example of this continuing battle is that of the Tres Garantías *ejido*, in southern Quintana Roo. After the *ejido* pressured the state governor in 1984 to grant the forest rights to the *ejido* rather than to a lumber company, Tres Garantías experienced a complete reversal in its economic condition. Moving beyond its former condition of deprivation, the peasant community by 1990 had electricity, a clinic, a post office, primary and secondary schools, drinking water, and a soon-to-be-installed telephone service.[41]

Despite the traditional gulf between the concerns of urban middle-class environmentalists and those of the rural peasantry, there are signs that these different perspectives might be coming together in innovative ways. The Union of Homeless, Renters, and Poor Neighborhood Residents of Veracruz (UCISV-VER), a self-declared "popular, ecological, neighborhood coalition," was founded in 1984. A joint project of homeless families, community organizers, and university students, UCISV-VER formed six new communities for 950 families through collective land purchases. Flushless composting toilets and roof-top rain collection projects protect the families from the 500 tons of industrial waste and sewage that the Papaluapan River each day carries through the community as it drains one of the country's seven industrial corridors. The founding charters of the new communities mandate that at least 50 percent of the land be reserved for community gardens, playgrounds, and schools, and that residents commit themselves to plant five trees for every one they fell. An openly activist community coalition, UCISV-VER has regularly filed complaints against factories dumping waste into the river and has stood in opposition to the nearby nuclear power plant. Despite government efforts to undermine UCISV-VER by cutting off funds and arresting leaders, this multiclass coalition continues to strengthen and expand.[42]

Small grassroots groups with environmental agendas exist throughout Mexico, but most do not consider themselves to be environmental organizations. These community groups range from parent associations with concerns about the quality of the school environment to farm associations worried about the destruction of their croplands. Although a national network of these grassroots environmentalist organizations does not yet exist, some activists in Mexico's popular movement say that such a network could go a long way to setting an effective environmental development agenda in Mexico.[43]

In the United States, numerous environmental organizations have taken a new interest in Mexico, mostly because of the quickening pace of economic integration between the two nations. These include Friends of the Earth, Texas Center for Policy Studies, and the Natural Resources Defense

Council. The Border Ecology Project (BEP), founded in 1983 in Bisbee, Arizona, focuses on the environmental issues of the border region. It was instrumental in formulating and implementing a 1987 Mexico-U.S. treaty regulating air pollution from smelters along the border region, which resulted in the shutdown of the highly contaminating Phelps Dodge smelter in Douglas, Arizona. BEP was also active in the 1987 transboundary hazardous-material control agreement, signed by the United States and Mexico to regulate the movement of hazardous materials across the border.[44] Increasingly, environmental organizations on both sides of the border have begun to work cooperatively on issues of mutual concern.

PART SIX

Foreign Influence

"The United States is bigger, stronger, and richer than Mexico . . . . Under these conditions bargaining tends to be unequal; such discrepancies pervade the entire relationship."

—Report of the Bilateral Commission on the Future of United States-Mexican Relations, 1989.[1]

© Debra Preusch/Resource Center

U.S. Foreign Policy

For Washington, Mexico is the third piece of a Northern Hemisphere economic alliance dominated by the United States. Formalized in a North American Free Trade Agreement, the alliance will combine the capital, technology, and cheap labor of the area to compete with other regional economic blocs, such as the European Community (EC). To make such a partnership work, Washington is supporting the Mexican government's adoption of conservative economic policies that open the door for increased U.S. trade and investment. At the same time it is enlisting Mexico in an all-out war on drugs that complements domestic priorities in the United States.

In exchange Washington offers the Mexican government three crucial inducements—its stamp of approval, promises of increased trade and investment, and much-needed economic assistance. These supports provide essential underpinnings for Mexico's economic reforms. In addition they offer the Mexican government important political currency to use against rising popular demands for a democratic opening in the country. By funneling drug control assistance to Mexico's law enforcement agencies and armed forces, the United States is strengthening the repressive arms of Mexico's authoritarian regime.

Washington's policies toward Mexico spring from the special features of the association and U.S. national interests. Bound by a nearly 2000-mile border and a web of cultural and economic ties, the United States and Mexico share a unique relationship.[2] The boundary that both divides and links the two countries marks the only instance in the world where an advanced industrialized country shares such a lengthy border with a major country of the third world. The disparity sparks an asymmetrical relationship dominated by the United States. With 3 times the population, 25 times the GDP, technological superiority, and overwhelming military supremacy, the United States holds the upper hand in most conflicts with its southern neighbor. The predominance of U.S. trade and investment in the Mexican economy—and Mexico's dependence on Washington's help in debt negotiations—lend even more weight to the U.S. position.

The proximity of the two countries gives rise to two other features of the relationship: interpenetration and interdependence. By the year 2000, if current trends continue, Mexico will have the world's largest Spanish-speaking population; the United States will have the second largest.[3] From trade to pollution, what happens on one side of the border affects the other. Even policies chosen for domestic reasons in one country affect internal circumstances in the other. *Peso* devaluations, for instance, clamp off Mexican consumer purchases in U.S. border towns. The cost of dental care in the United States spurs a flourishing community of dentists on the Mexican side of the border. At the macro level, when the United States hikes domestic interest rates to help finance its national debt, Mexico's interest payments rise as well.

A variety of interests drive official U.S. relations with Mexico.[4] One of the most compelling is geostrategic. The United States government prefers to think of the entire country of Mexico as its southern border. For Washington, Mexico is the "ultimate domino," observed one noted analyst.[5] A Mexico identified with northern interests, unhinged from the traditional radicalism and third world perspectives of much of Latin America, is a Mexico more firmly planted in the U.S. sphere of influence. Washington wants a stable Mexico headed by a government that shares its economic and political world view and that will act as a buffer between the United States and the poverty and turmoil of countries farther south. Mexico's stability, peaceableness, and predictability make it easy for the United States to protect its southern flank and, simultaneously, to project its power around the world.

Other interests are economic and social. Their importance skyrocketed during the 1980s, not only because Mexico's near economic collapse in 1982 brought them to the fore, but also because the independent needs of the United States gave these interests greater significance in Washington. Increased flows of illegal drugs into the United States, for instance, coincided with the coming into office of a conservative administration and epidemic levels of drug use in U.S. communities.

More important were the structural problems faced by the U.S. economy. Despite steady rates of growth, the United States in recent years has experienced a persistent recession complicated by vigorous competition from overseas. Much of the growth of the U.S. economy in the postwar period was based on the expansion of exports. Both Latin America in general and Mexico in particular contributed to that growth. Given this history and the consequent export orientation of much of the U.S. economy, beefing up exports to a U.S.-dominated market such as Mexico's has been an essential component of U.S. strategies to climb out of its economic doldrums. Such a relationship, however, depends on a Mexican economy capable of making the purchases, paying the dividends, and making good on the loans generated by trade and investment transactions. Thus promoting a solvent, open Mexican economy is one of Washington's top concerns in its policies toward Mexico.

From Annexation to Integration

Historically, U.S.-Mexican relations featured a pattern of outright U.S. intervention and territorial and economic expansion at Mexico's expense. From the annexation of Texas in 1845, through the "war of the North American invasion," which cost Mexico half its territory, until the interference of the United States in the Mexican Revolution, Washington took a "hands-on" approach to manipulating Mexican politics and economic structures. In so doing, Washington acted no differently than it did in many other developing countries. In Mexico's case, however, the flagrant intervention subsided after the revolutionary government became institutionalized and stable.

The discovery of massive Mexican oil reserves in the 1970s rekindled U.S. strategic interest in Mexico. President Jimmy Carter initiated a sweeping, top-level review of U.S. policy toward the country. Hoping to give U.S. policy better focus and more careful attention, he created a new office of coordinator for Mexican affairs in the U.S. Department of State. But with the coming into office of the interventionist administration of Ronald Reagan, the United States aggressively reasserted itself in Mexico.

One of the "innovations" of the Reagan administration was the institution of a plain-talking style when it came to Mexican issues. After the oil nationalizations of the 1930s and the onset of World War II, most U.S. administrations moderated public criticisms and outspokenness about Mexican affairs. They were deferring to prevailing diplomatic and scholarly opinions that Mexico had to be treated carefully because of its sensitivity to U.S. dominance and its importance to the United States. Under Reagan, however, a resurgent United States confronted a progressively weakened Mexico. As Cathryn Thorup, a specialist on Mexican affairs then at the Overseas Development Council, observed, "A heightened sense of invincibility and moral superiority on the part of the United States contrasted sharply with a deepening sense of vulnerability and social decay in Mexico."[6]

At the same time, several U.S. interests were being threatened with regard to Mexico. Mexico was once again becoming a major supplier of foreign drugs to the U.S. market, for instance, and the famed Mexican stability was reportedly being undermined by economic crisis and political repression under the Mexican government.[7] Moreover, Mexico was making friendly gestures toward revolutionary movements in Central America and nationalizing its banks, all under the disapproving eye of a Washington administration whose two messianic objectives were to rid the world of communism and substitute the free market.

These factors interacted to Mexico's detriment. They gave extra weight to U.S. attempts to influence Mexican policies and fueled a heat wave of rhetoric directed against the country from the United States. By the time George Bush took office in 1988, the abrasive quality of the new plain-spokenness about Mexico had dropped away, replaced by a businesslike determination to advance U.S. policy initiatives.

Given Washington's new expectation that the United States will be involved in decisionmaking about Mexican affairs—and the apparent acquiescence of the Mexican government to that position—many important issues have become "binationalized," in the words of one Mexican observer.[8] Matters that once would have been considered national are now decided in tandem with the United States. These include drug trafficking, environmental protection, commercial and investment policies, tourism, and the prosecution of financial crimes. They join issues such as water rights and boundary questions that have long been subject to joint review and negotiation.

Moving into the 1990s, U.S. influence on Mexican affairs is the greatest it has been since the Mexican Revolution. In addition, there are more arenas opened for U.S. influence. A spiraling bilateral agenda is drawing ever more attention from the two governments. As the governments rush to solve these problems, their solutions are helping to transform Mexico's economy and other aspects of its social system in ways compatible with current U.S. needs. This fact is not only due to U.S. pressure and the added weight U.S. demands carry. It also reflects the dominance of neoliberal technocrats in the ruling PRI government and the belief on both sides of the border that there is a convergence of national interests pulling the two sides together. Whatever the reasons, Washington is promoting a process of integration in which Mexico is encouraged to adopt laws and socioeconomic structures that dovetail with those of the United States.

From Fragmentation to Coherence

Historically, U.S. policy toward Mexico has been fragmented and incoherent. Experts on U.S.-Mexico relations have described Washington's Mexico policy as an "ad hoc collection of incremental and disorganized decisions," characterized by "chronic confusion and inconsistency."[9] In part this is a reflection of the U.S. policymaking system. Decisionmaking in the U.S. bureaucracy is decentralized among executive branch agencies, Congress, and state and local governments. Competition among these elements—each of which has its own bureaucratic interests, field of expertise, and constituency—traditionally results in a fair amount of diversity and inconsistency in Washington's overall stance toward Mexico.

This interagency morass is complicated even more by the fact that Mexico is the target of initiatives of U.S. state and local governments and an array of private organizations. Many of the states, for instance, devise their own goals and enact laws regarding trade, investment, and technology transfer. Likewise private organizations ranging from the AFL-CIO to the American Friends Service Committee attempt to influence U.S. relations with Mexico through congressional lobbying, media campaigns, personal contacts, and other means. As an example, when U.S. manufacturers accused Mexico of unfair trading practices during the 1980s, the U.S. International Trade Commission upheld the charges and required Mexico to limit its steel exports to the United States.

Although there are still different interests attempting to influence U.S. policy, there has been more single-mindedness in Washington's relationship with Mexico in recent years. The Bush administration came into office at the same time that Carlos Salinas took over in Mexico, a coincidence with profound implications for U.S. policy. Both presidents, and the economic planners who surround them, believe strongly in neoliberal economic principles. Salinas thus is a natural ally on many economic policies desired by Washington. His need for U.S. backing on debt relief and trade enhancement makes him flexible on other points as well. Bush took over after nearly a decade of "Reaganomics" and social conservatism had filled the U.S. government with policymakers likely to choose free market solutions for social and economic problems. As a result, U.S. policy toward Mexico is more focused and coherent at the beginning of the 1990s than has generally been the case. These factors combined to put the United States in an even better position to wrest concessions from Mexico during negotiations over sticky matters such as free trade and drug control.

Moving toward Integration

Washington's rediscovered interest in Mexico and concerns about its own economic and social needs stimulated a flurry of initiatives during the early and mid-1980s. Designed at first to stabilize the Mexican economy, discourage foreign policy independence, and reward the Mexican government's halting moves to liberalize the economy, U.S. actions later shifted both in focus and momentum. By the time Salinas took office, Washington and Mexico were barreling toward joint positions on foreign policy, drug control, trade, investment, and debt. At the top of Washington's concerns were the scope and pace of Mexico's economic restructuring and enlisting the country's cooperation in U.S. anti-narcotics activities. Because of the potential effect on the success of these endeavors, ensuring the hold on power of neoliberals within PRI also became an objective of the U.S. government.

Resolving Mexico's foreign debt and jump-starting its economy are top priorities for the U.S. government. Several dynamics propel the United States with respect to economic relations with Mexico. On the one hand, the position of the United States in the global economic arena is slipping. A number of U.S. shortcomings are becoming entrenched structural problems. These include diminished competitiveness, a deteriorating productive sector, burgeoning deficits, and a rising national debt. Such problems have intersected with the growth and enhanced competitiveness of other economic blocs to threaten long-term U.S. economic potential.

On the other hand, Mexico's economic difficulties directly menace the U.S. economy. Mexico has owed up to one-third of its foreign commercial debt to U.S. banks. Even more of a concern is the fact that major U.S. banks have had such a high level of exposure in Mexico. During the height of Mexico's economic crisis, for example, leading financial institutions such as J.P. Morgan and Citibank had about one-third of their primary equity capital exposed in Mexican loans. That level of exposure has been declining, as banks pump up their reserves or limit lending to better cushion the shock of a Mexican default. Still, if Mexico decided it could not pay back its loans, or if its economy fell apart under the strain, the tremors would rock the U.S. banking community.

Moreover a default or a collapse would disrupt trade relations, threaten U.S. investments, and likely increase the migration of displaced workers northward. Mexico would almost surely suffer levels of political upheaval that would menace the stability Washington counts on along its southern border. Finally, if Mexico—a major third world power with a sizable cache of political prestige—defaulted on its debt, it might set off a string of such actions in other countries around the world.

To avoid such catastrophes, Washington actively intervenes to help Mexico keep its identity as a "model debtor" while satisfying the needs of the country's creditors and stimulating U.S. exports. As a consequence, Washington supports the Mexican economy through a complicated and ever-changing package of measures. Over the years these instruments have included emergency bridge loans, food aid, easy credit terms and loan guarantees for Mexican purchases of U.S. goods, and special purchases of large quantities of Mexican oil for the U.S. Strategic Petroleum Reserve to provide badly needed hard currency. Through the Federal Reserve Board and the U.S. Treasury Department, Washington also spearheads debt-relief and economic-assistance agreements involving government agencies, multilateral financial institutions, and commercial banks. While these measures directly support what Washington defines as U.S. interests in Mexico, they also aid the Mexican government's own efforts to stabilize and restructure its economy.

Aside from propping up the Mexican economy, Washington encourages efforts to integrate Mexico's economy with that of the United States. For example in exchange for debt assistance and other types of economic support, Washington insists on Mexico's following through with economic restructuring designed to liberalize the economy and make it more permeable to U.S. trade and investment. A variety of other mechanisms, ranging from the creation of new binational decision-making bodies to the formulation of fresh agreements on trade and investment, also support economic integration. One new entity is the United States-Mexico Binational Commission, a ministry-level government-to-government forum that meets periodically to work out difficult problems. Headed by the U.S. secretary of state and Mexican foreign minister, the commission includes cabinet members and top bureaucrats from each country. In addition to economic issues, the commission deals with a variety of concerns, including tourism, the environment, and migration.

The free trade agreement (FTA) as well as other measures dealing with trade and investment are fundamental to the process of integration now under way. As with other initiatives, the FTA built on and enforced the liberalization process under way in Mexico, to U.S. advantage. Although the Mexican government has its own strong commitments to neoliberal economic strategies, U.S. influence on Mexico's economic reforms—in the form of conditions attached to aid programs, for instance—is significant. In the words of Riordan Roett, a specialist on Mexico and former head of the Latin American Studies Association, the United States "drives the dialogue" on issues of trade and protectionism, interest rates, and debt management.[10]

Ironically, however, as Washington is encouraging Mexico to open up its economy, the United States is raising many of its own trade barriers. In many ways Washington engages in a rhetoric of free trade against a backdrop of protectionism as necessary, with expectations of truly free trading policies aimed primarily at U.S. trading partners. By prodding Mexico to adopt economic policies compatible with those of the United States, Washington is hoping to increase investment opportunities and boost U.S. sales of goods and services to the country. Other interests are ideological. As Senator Steve Symms of Idaho observed, a free trade agreement with Mexico "could be one of the very best mechanisms . . . to spread capitalism to that part of the world."[11]

Keeping Friends in High Places

In times of economic and political stability, Washington has paid little attention to the character of Mexico's political system. For the most part it has been equally indifferent to dictatorial regimes and to democratization movements in the country. This pattern has been the unhappy reality since the mid-1800s. Responding to upheaval south of the border, the United States backed the reform movement of Benito Juárez, not to promote democracy but to exclude European influence from the country. Later Washington allied itself with the pro-U.S. dictatorship of Porfirio Díaz, holding true to this alliance even as the reformist *maderistas* ousted the dictator in pursuit of constitutionalist rule.[12] When a change of administrations in Washington brought Woodrow Wilson into the presidency, the United States briefly supported constitutionalist forces through diplomatic means and moral pressure. But these moderate efforts soon deteriorated into U.S. military interventionism, such as the occupation of Veracruz, and were abandoned. When Mexico's one-party government stabilized in the late 1920s, Washington regained its generally impassive attitude toward the country's political character, a stance shaken only when U.S. interests were threatened, as with the petroleum expropriations undertaken by Lázaro Cárdenas.

Throughout most of the postwar period, Washington took little notice of Mexico's political system outside of occasional rhetorical exhortations. In the 1980s, however, Washington began a short-lived push for political reform in the one-party state, prompted by the Mexican government's opposition to U.S. Central American policies, Mexico's near economic collapse, and the rise of a vigorous conservative opposition movement led by the National Action Party (PAN).

By late 1980s, however, that effort had been abandoned. With the adoption of neoliberalism by the country's political elites and the PRI government's apparent control of the "democratization" process, U.S. initiatives toward the country once again lost anything other than rhetorical references to democracy. The rise of populist and nationalist movements spearheaded by the Party of the Democratic Revolution reinforced Washington's decision. Seeing its interests best advanced by PRI's centralized power structures, the U.S. government reverted to its acceptance of Mexico's "perfect dictatorship."

U.S.-Mexico Trade

Trade with the United States has long dominated Mexico's external sector, and in recent years U.S. dominance has steadily increased. The U.S. market in 1990 absorbed 70 percent of Mexico's exports, and 65 percent of the country's imports came from the United States.[1] Accounting for 6 percent of total U.S. imports and 7 percent of exports, Mexico is also an important trading partner for the United States. Mexico is in fact the third largest U.S. trading partner, ranking after Canada and Japan, and accounts for approximately half of all U.S. trade with Latin America.

Bilateral U.S.-Mexico trade is considerably more important for Mexico than for the United States. It accounts for two-thirds of Mexico's total international trade, with Mexico's exports to the United States contributing an estimated 13 percent of the country's GDP. During the 1980s it was to a large degree the trade surplus that Mexico enjoyed with the United States— averaging almost 60 percent of its global trade surplus during 1985-88—that allowed it to meet its debt-service obligations.[2]

Before the 1982 economic crisis hit it was the United States, not Mexico, that experienced annual trade surpluses in bilateral trade. But the ensuing devaluation of the *peso* and the shrinking of Mexico's domestic market caused U.S. exports to Mexico to plummet, and the U.S. trade balance with Mexico turned sharply negative. With the renewal of economic growth and as a result of the increasing liberalization of Mexican trade, however, U.S. exports shot up again in 1988. Between 1986 and 1990 U.S. exports to Mexico increased 130 percent. Mexico's exports to the United States have also been rising since 1987 but at a slower pace (up by a third). As a result of the faster pace of U.S. exports, the U.S. trade deficit substantially narrowed. By year end 1990, trade between the two nations had evened out, and there will be a U.S. surplus in 1992 (Table 6a).

An important stimulus to U.S.-Mexico trade in recent years has been the *maquiladora* program, which encourages cross-border production sharing. *Maquiladora* trade dominates U.S. imports from Mexico, accounting for about 45 percent of total U.S. imports. Virtually all this *maquila* trade is in manufactures, especially in the automotive and electrical-equipment sectors. Nearly one-third of U.S. exports to Mexico go to *maquila* operations.[3]

Another distinguishing feature of U.S.-Mexico trade has been the large degree of intrafirm dealings. According to the U.S. Commerce Department, nearly 40 percent of the total bilateral trade in manufactured goods is between U.S. firms and their affiliates in Mexico, while the U.S. International Trade Commission estimated that more than half of U.S. imports from Mexico are from intracompany or related-party sales.[4] About 70 percent of all U.S.-Mexico trade occurs within the same industry, meaning that exports and imports are generally in the same product category—motor vehicle parts, for example.[5]

Composition of Trade

Manufactured goods comprise more than 80 percent of U.S. exports and about 75 percent of U.S. imports from Mexico. During the 1980s U.S. imports of manufactures increased dramatically, rising from just 35 percent of total imports in 1980. By 1990 the United States, however, was still enjoying a trade surplus of $2.8 billion in manufactured goods. Nine out of the top ten U.S. exports to Mexico were manufactures, with motor vehicle parts, telecommunications equipment, and electronic equipment leading the list. Motor vehicle parts were the largest U.S. export item to Mexico and the fourth largest import item. Mexico's main exports of manufactured goods to the United States—electronic equipment, automobiles and vehicle parts, and telecommunications equipment—presented nearly a mirror image of Canada's imports from the United States. This dominance of manufactured goods in bilateral trade is due mainly to the large *maquiladora*, or export-processing, sector in Mexico, which assembles imported parts and exports them as finished products back to the United States. The other leading element in U.S.-Mexico trade is the rapidly expanding auto and auto-parts industries (Table 6b).

After manufactures, petroleum is the single largest import item from Mexico, representing more than 15 percent of total imports and making Mexico the fourth largest supplier of petroleum to the United States. With the rise of trade in manufactured goods in the 1980s, the share represented by petroleum has dropped sharply.

Mexico is the third largest export market (after the Soviet Union and Japan) for U.S. agricultural commodities, and it is the second largest supplier of U.S. agricultural imports. Approximately 10 percent of total bilateral trade is in agricultural products. The leading U.S. agricultural exports to Mexico are corn, sorghum, soybeans, dairy products, seeds, and animal fats, while the U.S. imports tropical products and specialty crops, including coffee, vegetables, fruits and nuts, and cattle.

Free Trade Initiatives

Washington has long advocated that Mexico liberalize its economy and create more opportunity for U.S. trade and investment. Mexico's 1980 decision to stay out of the General Agreement on Tariffs and Trade (GATT) angered the U.S. embassy, which at that time regarded the GATT multilateral trade accord as the best instrument for liberalizing the Mexican economy. In subsequent years the United States escalated its pressure by erecting new, mainly nontariff barriers to Mexican exports. Pressure to liberalize also came into play as part of the debt negotiations of the 1980s. In exchange for new loans and lending terms, Mexico began restructuring its economy, especially after 1986.

Reversing its previous decision, Mexico joined GATT in 1986—a major sign that the country was indeed serious about opening up its economy. The rapidity with which the government then began moving to dismantle trade barriers, eliminate import licenses, and remove subsidies indicated that a kind of conservative economic revolution was under way in Mexico. A series of sectoral accords negotiated with the United States after 1986 further accelerated trade liberalization.[6] By 1989 the two countries agreed to move quickly to liberalize bilateral trade by negotiating such issues as nontariff barriers, intellectual property rights, technology transfer, the marketing of services, and obstacles to investment—issues that in 1991 became main topics of the discussions leading toward a free trade agreement.

Even before the free trade negotiations began, liberalized trade was at the top of the economic agenda between the United States and Mexico.

Table 6a

U.S.-Mexico Trade Balance, 1970-91

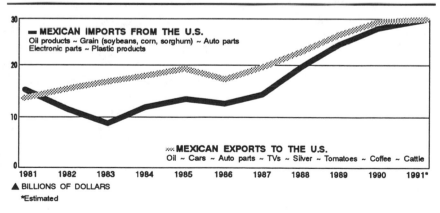

SOURCES: U.S. Bureau of the Census, *Highlights of the U.S. Export and Import Trade, Report FT 990*, 1981, 1982, 1983; International Monetary Fund, *Direction of Trade Statistics Yearbook 1991*; U.S. Department of State, *Economic Trends Report: Mexico*, August 1991.

Mexico's liberalization reforms combined with changing corporate production strategies served to spur what has been called the "silent integration" of the U.S. and Mexican economies during the late 1980s. Between 1982 and 1990 U.S. exports to Mexico rose 240 percent; during the same eight years, U.S. investment in Mexico increased nearly 70 percent.[7] In 1990 the U.S. International Trade Commission (ITC) praised Mexico for having made the transition from "one of the world's most protected economies into one of the most open systems in just a few years."

Although the United States never abandoned bilateral trade and investment frameworks, Washington's preferred postwar instrument for liberalizing world trade and ensuring itself a place in foreign markets was GATT. But in the late 1980s, Washington began to see the potential for bilateral and regional trade negotiations that would complement multilateral initiatives. The formation of European- and Japanese-led economic blocs particularly worried U.S. economic strategists. Washington had also grown increasingly frustrated at the slow progress of the Uruguay Round of GATT negotiations.

The United States, although not abandoning multilateral initiatives, began placing new emphasis on bilateral and regional trade accords. Free trade agreements were signed with Israel (1985) and Canada (1989), and the Bush administration even started talking about forming a hemispheric free trade zone. In 1991, the Bush administration announced its Initiative for the Americas, conveying Washington's intent to seek bilateral free trade agreements with all nations of the hemisphere except Cuba. In its own free trade initiatives with other Latin American nations, Mexico is assisting Washington's drive to liberalize trade throughout the hemisphere.

The United States and Mexico formally declared their commitment to enter into free trade negotiations in mid-1990, and by early 1991 it was announced that Canada would join the talks to formulate a North American Free Trade Agreement (NAFTA). Initially, all sides were optimistic that an accord could be signed quickly, as early as May 1992. But a stagnant U.S. economy, rising protectionist sentiment, and President Bush's declining popularity raised the possibility that President Bush might postpone the negotiations until after the November 1992 presidential election. Such a postponement would represent a sharp setback for President Salinas. A long delay would give free trade opponents a chance to strengthen their ranks and win new allies. Early fast-track approval of a NAFTA could also be obstructed by differences among negotiating partners on such contentious issues as "rules of origin" and phase-out periods for tariffs.

A free trade accord will not mean that bilateral trade will immediately be free of all tariff and nontariff barriers. The NAFTA will be replete with special provisions covering everything from avocados to motor vehicles. Reductions in tariffs and the elimination of quotas will be phased in over ten years or more.

From the beginning Washington has insisted that Mexico will be treated as an equal partner in the negotiations, not meriting unilateral concessions simply because it is a poor nation. Any arrangement to protect a certain economic sector, the peasantry for example, will be matched by exemptions benefiting U.S. producers. Rather than granting Mexico preferential treatment because of its status as a less-developed country, the negotiations are based on the principle of reciprocity (see Trade Imbalances, Part 2). But given the disadvantaged position of Mexico and the fact that President Salinas felt that he must have a free trade agreement with the United States even at a high cost, Mexico did not come to the bargaining table from a position of strength. This unequal status will increase its vulnerability to the "aggressive reciprocity" of the U.S. negotiating strategy.

The NAFTA negotiations began at a time when the United States was struggling to prevent its global market share and its economic competitiveness from slipping any further. As noted in the president's 1991 economic report, "By lowering overall costs of U.S. manufacturing firms, a free trade agreement would make U.S. firms more competitive against imports in the United States and against other countries' exports in the world market."[8] Mexico's cheap labor and its advantages as a production-sharing center are the main reasons why the United States wants to solidify and expand bilateral economic relations.

Also a consideration is the country's own market potential. For the United States, Mexico represents one of the fastest-growing export markets (standing at $28 billion in 1990). Between 1986 and 1990 exports of consumer goods to Mexico tripled, while capital-goods exports nearly doubled. By 1991 per capita Mexico imports amounted to about $295 annually from

Table 6b

U.S.-Mexico Exports and Imports, 1990

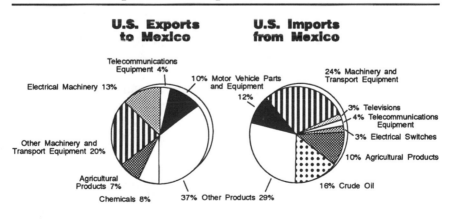

SOURCE: U.S. Department of Commerce, Office of Mexico, 1991.

the United States, compared with $266 from the European Community. The U.S. Commerce Department has been quick to point out that increased exports mean more U.S. jobs. It estimates that a billion dollars in exports to Mexico create 19,600 jobs.[9] At a time when the U.S. trade balance is becoming more critical to the economic health of the United States, a rapidly expanding export market in Mexico is a prominent goal of U.S. trade policy. Washington is betting that a free trade agreement with Mexico will ensure a U.S. trade surplus with that country, while at the same time Mexico is hoping that free trade will boost its own export position.

According to the ITC, a free trade agreement will benefit the U.S. economy by expanding trade opportunities, lowering prices, increasing U.S. competitiveness, and improving the ability of U.S. firms to exploit economies of scale. It predicts that since "gains are likely to outweigh costs, the U.S. economy will probably gain on the net."[10]

The free trade agreement is an instrument to guarantee that Mexico sticks to its policy of economic liberalization and to ensure that U.S. firms obtain a privileged place in the new economic regime. NAFTA would serve to lock in the neoliberal reforms of the Salinas government, while establishing a major obstacle to future policy changes. "We will pry open the Mexican economy even more," explained U.S. Ambassador John Negroponte in a "confidential" cable to Washington. "From a foreign policy perspective, a free trade agreement would institutionalize acceptance of a North American orientation to Mexico's foreign relations."[11]

In the negotiations the United States will seek the greatest possible liberalization for U.S. traders and investors. At the top of U.S. negotiating objectives are intellectual property rules, sweeping changes in foreign investment law, increased access to U.S. services, cross-border harmonization of product standards and certification, and a rules-of-origin provision giving preference to U.S. investors. Another objective is gaining expanded access to Mexico's oil industry.

NAFTA will not create a common market in the sense of a region with a common external tariff and common economic policies. In other words Mexico, Canada, and the United States will maintain their own tariff rates regarding imports from nonmember countries. From the start the negotiations were set up to deal with the flow of goods, services, and investment among trading partners. Much larger than a simple trade agreement, the NAFTA negotiations have extended to such issues as intellectual property protection, banking regulations, and, to a certain extent, health and environmental safeguards. Initially Mexico had wanted to include labor mobility within the framework of the negotiations but later withdrew that proposal fearing that its insistence would jeopardize the progress of fast-track negotiations. For its part, Washington rejected the inclusion of labor mobility and most other matters not strictly related to trade and investment.

Free Trade, Fair Trade

At first the Bush Administration and the business community rejected outright all suggestions that free trade negotiations directly include discussion of the total social cost of economic integration, particularly with respect to environmental conditions and labor disruption. Such issues were termed "externalities" and dismissed as special-interest "politics" that interfered with the issue at hand. Stephen Diamond, in a paper presented at the Center for U.S.-Mexican Studies, said that the limited nature of the free trade negotiations represented "what might be called the neutron bomb approach to economic integration. It secures a safe and level playing field for capital, but it ignores the general human and social cost of the agreement."[12]

Because of mounting opposition to "fast track" negotiations in Congress and among the labor and environmental communities, the Bush administration in May 1991 agreed that, at least to some extent, environmental and health standards would be discussed.[13] It promised to work with Congress to ensure a worker-adjustment program that would provide a safety net for those workers displaced by free trade. Furthermore Washington said that the United States would maintain the right to exclude Mexican products not meeting U.S. health and safety standards. The Bush administration did not agree to put environmental issues directly on the negotiating table but promised to pursue parallel talks on environmental regulations. The subsequent failure by the administration and U.S. trade negotiators to push labor and environmental concerns forward increased the skepticism among NAFTA critics that any substantial progress would be made on these issues.

On the right side of the political spectrum, the administration received strong support for its free trade position from such groups as the Heritage Foundation and the Council for Inter-American Security. These conservative organizations promote economic liberalization as one of the best weapons of U.S. capitalism against statism, socialism, and populism.

Whereas the right jumped in to provide the ideological justification for free trade with Mexico, the business community argues that free trade is in the best interests of U.S. corporations. Although there were pockets of opposition among such affected industrial and agricultural sectors as textiles and many fruit and vegetable growers, the country's leading business organizations (including such groups as the Chamber of Commerce, The Business Roundtable, and the National Association of Manufacturers) strongly support the free trade initiatives. Coordinating the pro-NAFTA campaign was the Mexico-U.S. Business Committee, jointly sponsored by the Chamber of Commerce and the Council of the Americas.[14] As a rule, support for free trade is virtually unanimous among U.S.-based transnational corporations, while less support is found among small- and medium-size businesses. From the point of view of the transnational corporations, NAFTA makes good economic sense. They argue that the removal of trade barriers will allow them to fine tune the production process by increasing production sharing and by using more efficient plant sizes.

In large part the U.S. academic community backed the fast track toward a free trade agreement with Mexico. A prestigious group of U.S. scholars, including Wayne Cornelius, Richard Feinberg, Robert Pastor, Susan Kaufman Purcell, and Clark Reynolds, sent a widely publicized letter to Congress in support of fast-track negotiations, arguing that U.S. national interests would be served by a free trade agreement. Furthermore, the scholars warned that "the political and economic fallout in Mexico would be unpredictable" if the U.S. Congress decided to spurn Mexico's free trade initiatives.[15]

On the left, various coalitions of labor, anti-intervention, church, consumer, and environmental activists formed to lobby against fast track legislation. Active in opposition were such groups as the American Friends Service Committee; American Agricultural Movement; Mobilization on Development, Trade, Labor, and the Environment; and Fair Trade Campaign. Consumer groups such as Public Citizen, Public Voice for Food and Health Policy, and the Community Nutrition Institution also adamantly opposed fast track negotiations, as have such public policy institutes as the Economic Policy Institute in Washington and the Texas Center for Policy Studies in Austin. In general these groups argue that Mexico and the United States should be working more for "fair" trade than for a free trade agreement that will ignore development issues. One of the groups pushing for "fair trade" was the Chicago-based Federation for Industrial Retention and Renewal, which said that "communities, standards of living, and whole value systems are at stake" in the free trade discussions.[16]

According to NAFTA opponents, free trade without an accompanying social charter will lead to the downward harmonization of labor, environmental, and other regulatory standards. These groups voiced concern about job flight, probable environmental damage, and increased worker exploitation. A major preoccupation was that NAFTA, like the multilateral GATT accord, would be used to preempt state and local initiatives on the environment and human health. Rejecting the notion that free trade deals only with traditional trade issues such as tariffs, opponents argued that a free trade agreement with Mexico would have broad and lasting effects on social welfare. This was also the position of many of the Canadian groups that initially formed to oppose the U.S.-Canada free trade accord and then joined the fight against NAFTA. NAFTA negotiations began against a background of falling growth and rising unemployment in Canada since the U.S.-Canada FTA took effect in 1988.

Jobs on the Move

Unions have been the harshest critics of the proposed free trade agreement, claiming that NAFTA will accelerate the decline in manufacturing jobs in the United States. For the AFL-CIO, free trade means runaway plants, lower wages, and the eventual demise of unionism in the manufacturing sector.

Yet the union movement in the United States has not always been against the principle of free trade. On the contrary the U.S. labor hierarchy has a long history of pinning the fortunes of U.S. labor to the ability of U.S. corporations to push into new foreign markets. Until the late 1960s, organized labor strongly supported U.S. initiatives to lower tariff barriers in the framework of international trade negotiations.[17] As U.S. trade surpluses declined and imports of labor-intensive goods increased, U.S. labor changed its tune, moving into the protectionist camp. When free trade meant more U.S. union jobs because of increased exports of manufactured goods, the labor movement was in favor of free trade. But once the tables were turned—with manufactured exports declining and foreign imports increasing—liberalized trade was being strongly opposed.

The U.S. labor movement has good reason to be concerned. Increasing global integration and the decay of the U.S. industrial base has hit the U.S. working class hard since the late 1970s. Overall employment has increased, but mostly in the low-paying service sector. More than 2 million jobs have been lost in the U.S. manufacturing sector. This helps explain why U.S. workers saw a 14-percent decline in their average weekly earnings (in real terms) between 1978 and 1990.[18] Not since the 1920s has union representation been so low. The anti-union climate of the 1980s only partially explains the decline of unionism. Probably more significant in the drop in union membership are the structural changes in global capitalism that have given risen to a new international division of labor, which has resulted in a shift of labor-intensive jobs to low-cost foreign locations.[19]

In their opposition to a free trade agreement U.S. unions see NAFTA as a threat to U.S. manufacturing jobs and to unions in general. But they also realize that even without a free trade agreement, U.S. companies are relocating at least part of their production to Mexico and other places with large pools of cheap labor. As Steve Beckman, an economist for the United Auto Workers (UAW), has argued, Mexican free trade "is an extension of the southern strategy," a reference to the movement of U.S. manufacturing businesses to the low-wage, nonunion Sunbelt.[20] A dramatic case of this north-south flow is the automobile industry. According to James P. Womack of MIT, "By the end of the century, the entry-level products for the entire North American region will be manufactured in northern Mexico in top-to-bottom assemblers—American, European, and Japanese—and their first-tier suppliers."[21]

For the most part, however, union strategies to stop this drain of manufacturing jobs have proved ineffective. Rather than emphasizing fair trade, organized labor has mostly rallied around protectionist positions in an effort to preserve high-paid manufacturing jobs. The "Buy America" and protectionist policies of organized labor have found little support among consumers looking for low-cost, high-quality goods, which often means buying Japanese and other foreign-made items. As a result, unions have been seen as a drag on productivity rather than as allies in the search for new technology and economic organization.[22] It has become increasingly difficult to determine what is "American-made" when so much of industrial production is distributed between two or more countries and shared by various corporations. Protectionist and nationalist responses to free trade have also tended to pit U.S. workers against foreign workers.

Critics both within and outside the union sector have charged that union policymakers need to adopt new strategies that respond to global economic restructuring rather than struggling fruitlessly to block its way. Similarly, these critics argue that unions need to fight to incorporate tough and enforceable labor standards within international trade agreements rather than simply dismissing all free trade initiatives as attacks on U.S. workers. Expanding labor law to cover international investment is another possible avenue that is being tested to fight "downward harmonization." Also slowly gaining ground within the labor community are strategies to build multinational unionism and solidarity. These new efforts contrast sharply with the traditional overseas initiatives by the AFL-CIO and its international institutes, which have closely reflected U.S. foreign policy interests.[23]

The concept of "unionism without borders" was seen at work in the support U.S. Ford workers offered their counterparts in Mexico following a violent 1990 crackdown on rank-and-file workers in the Ford plant in Hermosillo. "Mexicans aren't taking our jobs," said a UAW spokesperson in Kansas City. "Multinationals are taking jobs out of the United States and exploiting workers on both sides of the border."[24] Union solidarity extends to the farm sector, where organizations like the Farm Labor Organizing Committee (FLOC) in Ohio have joined hands with farmworkers in Sinaloa employed by the same transnational companies. In their cross-border organizing campaigns against Campbell's and other agribusiness operations, FLOC declared: "We aren't citizens of two different countries—we are citizens of one giant business. We must struggle together."

Including labor and human rights provisions in U.S. trade legislation is not without precedent, and the AFL-CIO has supported such measures. Among the U.S. trade laws that include worker rights provisions are the Generalized System of Preferences (GSP), Section 301 of the 1974 Trade Act, and the Caribbean Basin Initiative (CBI). The GSP legislation, for example, states that a country will be denied trade benefits if that country "has not taken or is not taking steps to afford internationally recognized worker rights." Washington has, however, tended to ignore these labor rights standards except when they can be used to discriminate against countries opposed by the U.S. government, such as Nicaragua under the Sandinistas. The AFL-CIO has generally cooperated with this political use of labor rights regulations, as seen most clearly in Central America during the 1980s.

The question about the magnitude of job losses in the United States as the result of a free trade agreement with Mexico has sparked heated debate. The International Trade Commission concluded that a free trade agreement "is likely to have little or no effect on employment levels in the United

States. . . . Real income for U.S. skilled workers and capital service owners is expected to rise. Real income for unskilled workers is likely to decline slightly." According to the ITC, total real income in the United States will increase and the incentive for migration from Mexico will decline as the wage differential between the two countries narrows. In the United States, any impact will fall disproportionately on unskilled workers and on those employed in certain industries, including textiles, automobile manufacturing, glassware, and winter fruits and vegetables.[25] Some economists who have supported free trade claim that NAFTA will lead to heightened levels of economic efficiency in both nations, which could mean as much as a 2-percent gain in the national income in both Mexico and the United States.[26]

Supporters of NAFTA regularly point out that the United States is a giant compared to Mexico and could therefore easily absorb the impact on the U.S. job market. Even so, not everybody agrees with the assessment that the job loss will be minimal. According to Jeff Faux, president of the Economic Policy Institute, even ITC's own figures show that nearly three-quarters of the U.S. work force could potentially experience income decline.[27] Critics of the proposed NAFTA argue that even under optimal circumstances Mexican wages will not rise to compete with U.S. wage levels—meaning that U.S. jobs will continue to head south at a frightening pace and that high illegal immigration rates from Mexico will not diminish. It is the position of the Economic Policy Institute that "both Bush and Salinas would be well advised to pay more attention to the benefits of higher wages in both nations, and less attention to short-term profits gained from competitive impoverishment."[28]

In a broad economic sense, the concern that U.S. jobs will be lost to Mexico reflects a failure of U.S. economic policy. According to Sidney Weintraub of the University of Texas, "The United States should not at this stage of its economic history be concerned about protecting low-wage jobs, but rather about moving on to higher value-added occupations."[29] This argument is used by free trade advocates to justify increased production-sharing operations in Mexico. It is argued that these operations would not only keep U.S. firms competitive with Japan and other industrial nations but would also contribute to the maintenance and upgrading of the U.S. industrial base, especially the higher value-added production. But U.S. unions and others against fast-track negotiations contend that the U.S. manufacturing base is in decline and that free trade will accelerate the disintegration of U.S. industry. They fear that wage levels will continue to fall as companies step up threats to leave for Mexico unless wage cuts are accepted and unions broken. Another related issue raised during the fast-track debate was the question of whether the United States had the training programs or education systems in place to retrain or turn out workers for the "high-value" jobs that supposedly will remain in the U.S. economy.

In the face of the juggernaut of global integration, U.S. union critics of free trade are being forced to develop new global strategies. Primitivo

Rodríguez, director of the Mexico-U.S. Border Program of the American
Friends Service Committee, summarized this position:

> As the world becomes a global factory, where national borders are
> replaced by economic blocs and production zones, working people
> and trade unions are beginning to realize that an internationalist
> perspective is a fundamental requirement in defending their rights
> and promoting their empowerment. *Maquiladoras* and immigration,
> for instance, cannot be examined under the narrow (and ineffective)
> perspective of this union's or that nation's interest, but rather, under the
> framework of an internationalized economy where human, labor, and
> democratic rights need to be redefined through new ways of coopera-
> tion and organizing among peoples affected.[30]

The Environmental Critique

Environmentalists have been one of the major constituencies opposing
an unconditioned free trade accord with Mexico. They point out that the
maquiladora industries, dominated by U.S. investors, have been the source
of widespread air and water pollution and that these assembly plants have
overloaded the U.S.-Mexico border infrastructure. Increased U.S. investment
taking advantage of Mexico's cheap labor would aggravate these problems.

Furthermore, U.S. environmentalists note that the Mexican environmental
agency, SEDUE, is severely underfunded and that enforcement of Mexico's relatively new environmental laws is quite weak. Environmental groups argue
that any free trade agreement should be accompanied by mechanisms to fund
environmental regulatory needs and basic potable water and wastewater infrastructure.[31] Two of the mechanisms suggested are the setting of user fees for
U.S. firms operating in Mexico and "debt-for-environment" swaps, in
which a portion of Mexico's foreign debt would be canceled and the money
used for environmental regulation or infrastructure.

The overdevelopment of Mexico's natural resources, including water,
timber, and oil and gas, is another primary concern. In both the United
States and Mexico, environmentalists argue that a free trade agreement
must include specific provisions to ensure that development of these resources, particularly by U.S. companies, would be restricted to sustainable
levels. In the case of oil and gas, many environmentalists favor keeping this
issue off the negotiating table.

The environmental opposition also raises the issue that free trade
would create pressure to harmonize health and environmental standards at
the "lowest common denominator." Opponents claim that, in effect, the
trade agreement could be used to begin to challenge environmental and
health laws as being "nontariff trade barriers." The observable results of the
U.S.-Canada FTA underscore this concern. Following that agreement, U.S.
industries accused the Canadian government of unfairly aiding the competitiveness of Canadian smelters through government incentives for install-

ing pollution-control devices.[32] In turn, the Canadian government used the FTA as a base for challenging U.S. regulations restricting asbestos use.

Finally, environmental groups argue that NAFTA, like the multilateral GATT, might be used as part of an effort to preempt health and environmental regulations imposed by state and local governments that are more stringent than federal laws. If those laws had the effect of discriminating against products from Mexico, they could be challenged as unfair barriers to trade. As groups such as the Texas Center for Policy Studies and the Border Ecology Project note, state and local laws have often been sources of innovative environmental protection.

To win fast-track authorization from Congress, the Bush administration in May 1991 put forth a plan to deal with the environmental implications of NAFTA. However, there remained considerable doubt among environmental critics about the seriousness of this initiative, especially given the opposition of U.S. trade negotiators to adding such "externalities" to the agenda. The measures proposed by Bush are also seen as overly narrow and lacking in legal force and the commitment of financial resources necessary to address the severe environmental problems.

The Farm Community

Views about NAFTA in the agricultural sector range from highly positive to extremely negative, depending on the crop involved. Those farmers and agribusinesses involved in grain and oilseed production look eagerly to a free trade agreement that will eliminate tariff and nontariff barriers to agricultural trade. Mexican growers are simply unable to compete with their more productive counterparts in the United States. Unless the two countries agree to allow certain protectionist policies to remain in place, the Mexican market will be flooded by cheaper U.S. commodities, including corn, wheat, beans, and sorghum. Enthusiasm in the grain sector is somewhat modified, however, by fear that Canadian growers will successfully compete with the United States for an increased market share, especially in the wheat trade.

From the point of view of many fruit and vegetable growers, particularly those unable to transfer their production to Mexico, the proposed NAFTA is greatly feared. The entry of Mexican fruits and vegetables into the U.S. market is a long-running concern of affected growers. With increased trade liberalization in the 1980s, these preoccupations deepened. Ironically, however, this increase of nontraditional agricultural exports from Mexico came largely from U.S. agribusiness operations that had begun contracting crop production in Mexico. A free trade agreement will accelerate this trend and likely increase the presence of direct, 100-percent U.S.-owned agribusiness operations in Mexico.

In Mexico, horticultural crops benefit not only from cheap land and labor but also a more propitious climate (no threat of freezes). Organizations like the Western Growers Association complain that because of

Mexico's cheap wages and less-stringent pesticide laws, almost any crop is cheaper to grow there. A free trade agreement is likely to facilitate the removal of many nontariff barriers (including overly strict sanitary restrictions) imposed to protect U.S. growers.[33] But rules concerning seasonal entry of agricultural products and other complex formulas designed to provide some protection to growers on both sides of the border are likely to be part of a negotiated agreement. If bilateral agricultural trade is to increase substantially, major improvements will be needed at border crossings and in border facilities for checking agricultural imports and exports, both of which consistently result in long queues at the border.

The Role of Foreign Investment

Foreign investors are being warmly welcomed into Mexico, with U.S. investors at the forefront of the new investment boom. Historically, the United States has accounted for the majority of direct foreign investment in Mexico. About 63 percent of cumulative foreign investment is currently held by U.S. investors (Table 6c). Since the late 1980s an even larger proportion (as much as 70 percent) of new foreign investment has come from the United States.

Investment from the United States outweighs that of the second largest source of investments, the United Kingdom, by nearly 10 times. This U.S. domination might become still stronger if a free trade agreement is signed because of proposed "rules of origin" designed to benefit North American investors and traders. Hoping to use Mexico as a duty-free springboard into the U.S. market, investors from other foreign countries will likely also increase their investments in Mexico. According to the U.S. embassy, about 9,000 foreign firms have direct foreign investment in Mexico.[1]

Foreign investment accounts for about 10 percent of total fixed investment and less than 6 percent of the GDP. These figures, however, probably understate the economic impact of foreign firms. In Mexico foreign corporations are among the largest companies and are the leaders in the export sector. According to one report, 60 percent of the U.S. Fortune 500 firms have offices in Mexico.[2] A 1990 survey by the Mexico City business magazine *Expansión* found that companies controlled by foreign investors were the most dynamic, in terms of increases in sales and employment.[3] General Motors is Mexico's largest private-sector employer. Another measure of foreign economic influence in Mexico is that 93 percent of the technology patents registered in Mexico over the past two decades belong to foreign firms, 54 percent of which are U.S. companies.[4]

The composition of direct foreign investment in Mexico has changed dramatically since the *porfiriato* and the early years of the revolution. No longer is foreign investment concentrated in the extractive industries—oil, mining, and agriculture—and in public utilities and transportation. Instead foreign investment is found mostly in the industrial sector.

The post-revolutionary government gradually moved to assume control over the country's natural resources and its communications and transportation infrastructure. Attracted by the expanding and protected domestic market, foreign investors began investing in the country's new industrial sector, coming to dominate the food-processing, pharmaceutical, and other manufacturing industries. By 1990 manufacturing investment accounted for more than 60 percent of cumulative direct foreign investment, whereas mining and agriculture held only 1.6 percent and 0.3 percent shares, respectively. Services represented 29 percent of total investment, and commerce just 6.8 percent.

New investment flowing into Mexico in recent years has not followed these same patterns. Whereas direct investment in agriculture and mining remained minimal, the service sector, mainly tourism, bulged with new foreign investment. Reversing the proportions of cumulative foreign investment, the service sector was the largest recipient of foreign investment, averaging 50 percent of total new investment from 1986 to 1990 and about 60 percent of the total in 1990. Less than one-third of new investment flowed into the manufacturing sector in 1990. In contrast, ten years before, in 1979, 78 percent of new investment went to the manufacturing sector and only 8.5 percent into services.

The rate of return from U.S. investment in Mexico is much higher than that in any other Latin American country. In 1989 the rate of return in Mexico was 21 percent, far above the Latin American average of 13 percent or the world average of 14 percent.[5] Direct investment from the United States in Mexico represents about 12 percent of total U.S. direct investment in Latin America and the Caribbean. Nearly 80 percent of U.S. investment in Mexico is found in the manufacturing sector.[6]

As mentioned previously (see Investing in Mexico, Part 2), foreign investment tends to parallel the ups and downs of the two economies. An accelerating economy indicates a healthy domestic market for goods produced by new investment capital. Increasingly, however, foreign investors, particularly in the manufacturing sector, have their eye more on the global market. This outward orientation and the rise of the *maquila* industry partially explain the fact that during the economic downturn of the 1980s (1983-88) foreign investment more than doubled.[7] At the same time that the local market was shrinking, foreign investment in export-oriented manufacturing and the tourism industry was steadily rising. Sharp increases in foreign investment beginning in 1986 were also the result of changes in the country's foreign-investment regulations and its trade-liberalization initiatives as well as of the government's debt-equity swap initiative and its privatization program.[8]

Mexico has also attracted much indirect or speculative foreign investment. An increasing share of Mexico's foreign investment has been channeled into the stock market. In 1990 about 45 percent of new foreign investment was of the portfolio variety, with a marked upward trend in stock investments visible in 1991.[9] The country's stock market recovered quickly from the spectacular October 4, 1987, crash and by 1989 was outperforming every other market in the world.[10] Beginning in the late 1980s an growing number of U.S. institutional investors, including those managing U.S. pension funds, began increasing their exposure in the Mexican market. In fact, foreigners increased their stock holdings faster than Mexican citizens. The danger, of course, is that since portfolio investment is highly volatile, it could leave Mexico just as quickly as it entered. Although it helps the country's balance of payments, it is less valuable as a base for economic development.

About two-thirds of the foreign investment in the Mexican stock market in 1990 was found among the offerings of just five leading companies: Alfa, Kimberly Clark (Mexico), Apasco, Telmex, and Cifra. Such companies as Cemex, Ericsson, Vitro, and Peñoles also attracted foreign investors.[11] For each $1.32 that entered Mexico as productive investment in 1989-90, $1.00

Table 6c
Foreign Investment in Mexico, 1990

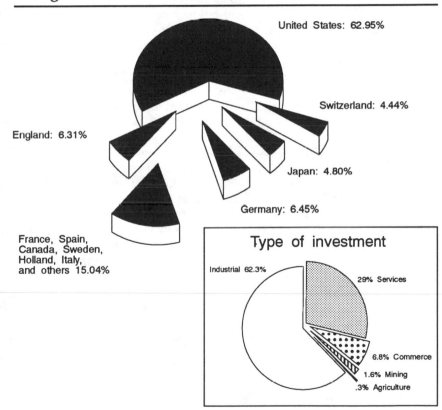

United States: 62.95%

Switzerland: 4.44%

England: 6.31%

Japan: 4.80%

Germany: 6.45%

France, Spain, Canada, Sweden, Holland, Italy, and others 15.04%

Type of investment

Industrial 62.3%

29% Services

6.8% Commerce

1.6% Mining

.3% Agriculture

SOURCE: Banamex, *Review of the Economic Situation of Mexico*, July 1991.

entered as portfolio investment.[12] By 1991 a full 51 percent of the offerings on the Mexican stock exchange had some foreign ownership.[13]

Foreign investment does not necessarily mean new investment in Mexico. In some cases it simply results in the transfer of assets from local to foreign hands. This is frequently the case with foreign investment in the debt-for-equity swaps and in the government's privatization program. But even outside the perimeter of the public sector there is a surge of foreign investment in pre-existing companies. The sale in 1990 of Gamesa, one of Mexico's largest food-processing companies, to PepsiCo raised the alarm that the country was being sold out to foreign investors.

Companies such PepsiCo are interested not only in the Mexican market but also in using Mexico as a low-cost production base for the U.S. market. As many as 40 economic sectors might disappear in the face of foreign competition, according to the Center of Economic Development in Mexico City.[14] Part of the problem is that Mexican companies simply will be unable to compete against highly capitalized and more efficient foreign firms, most of which have well-established global marketing networks. Many Mexican companies might also decide to sell out to foreign investors because of the lower profit margins resulting from foreign competition. Accustomed to a protected market, Mexican businesses have come to expect profit rates in the range of 30-40 percent.[15]

Trade liberalization and the threat of being bought out by foreign firms have been among the main factors pushing the largest Mexican conglomerates to consolidate operations. In the past the country's leading industrial groups tended to diversify their business activities through a wide variety of economic sectors. Lately, however, there has been a marked trend to concentrate investment in one or two areas. Joint-venture agreements between foreign firms and the country's industrial giants have been increasing in line with the accelerating pace of economic integration between the United States and Mexico. Such major U.S. firms as General Electric, Corning, and Whirlpool, for example, found local partners in new manufacturing operations. Whether considering firms as partners or as buy-out targets, U.S. and other foreign investors are primarily looking for large companies with a strong potential to produce for export. But foreign investors are also eager to gain a dominant hold in the domestic market. Such retail firms as Price Club and Wal-Mart have joined hands with Mexican conglomerates to open large commercial outlets. Mexican shoppers are now able to stroll down the aisles of Price Club de México and buy a full range of U.S. imported merchandise. Even the door-to-door sales company Amway has recently set up operations in Mexico.

Controlling the Export Business

In Mexico, as throughout the third world, new emphasis is being placed on the export market. "*Exportar es bueno*," is one export-promotion slogan receiving wide circulation. "Exporting is good" because it brings in desperately needed foreign exchange and helps pay for rising import bills. Not all export production, however, is equally beneficial to the economy. Exports that rely on a high degree of local content obviously have a greater positive impact on the economy than those composed largely of foreign inputs. Similarly, a company that is locally owned tends to have a greater economic impact than a foreign-owned firm.

Exports have been on the rise since 1983, but this increase has been driven almost exclusively by foreign investment. Foreign participation in non-oil exports jumped from 26 percent in 1981 to more than 53 percent by 1987.[16] Just ten firms controlled 60 percent of the country's export income in 1989: Pemex, Chrysler, Ford, General Motors, Mexicana Airlines, Teléfonos de México, Met-Mex Peñoles, Volkswagen, IBM, and Celanese Mexicana.[17] Of these only Pemex and Met-Mex Peñoles are free of direct foreign-investment capital.

As foreign participation in Mexico's export sector has increased, the local content of the country's exports has declined. In the *maquiladora* sector, less than 2 percent of the inputs come from local suppliers. Outside the *maquiladoras* the proportion of local content among the most dynamic export industries is also distressingly low. The domestic content of Mexico's leading computer exports (dominated by such firms as IBM, Data General, and Wang) is generally under 10 percent.[18] When IBM launched new export-production operations in 1987, the domestic content in its microcomputers dropped from 24 percent in 1986 to 6 percent the following year.[19] The same story of low and often declining local content is repeated in other dynamic export industries, including engine, automobile, chemical, and machine production.

Rather than purchasing from local suppliers, transnational corporations (TNCs) are frequently supplied by their own affiliates and subsidiaries. This is especially true in the case of the high-tech industries that dominate Mexico's export sector. Resource-based exports (including coffee, beer, shrimp, wooden furniture, silver, and oil derivatives) usually involve transactions between independent parties. In contrast, the majority of the country's most dynamic export manufactures are traded between related parties. Estimates of intrafirm trade as a proportion of Mexico's total manufactured trade have ranged 40-60 percent.

The main trade usually takes place with the country where the TNC is based. The large degree of U.S. foreign investment in Mexico along with the preponderance of intrafirm trade help to explain why Mexican trade is so heavily dependent on the United States. Not all intrafirm trade is with the country of origin, however. In the case of photographic film, the industry is dominated by Eastman Kodak through its subsidiary Industria Fotográfica Interamericana, which supplies all Latin America as well as the United States. A large part of Mexico's exports of computers and business machines goes to IBM and Xerox dealers in Europe.

The Mexican government has since the 1940s directed foreign investment toward the manufacturing sector and away from extractive industries
and public utilities. During the decades when the import-substitution strategy of industrialization prevailed, new foreign investment came to dominate
the most dynamic and profitable sectors of domestic market. More recently,
foreign investment in manufacturing has flowed predominantly into export-
oriented production. For the most part, however, this investment has been in
what are essentially screwdriver industries, which rely largely on foreign-
made inputs to make goods that are traded back to company affiliates,
thereby limiting the benefits of foreign investment. Unlike other countries
that it is trying to emulate, Mexico has as yet failed to use export-processing
manufacturing as a foundation for broader industrialization.

The Move to Mexico

To increase their global competitiveness, TNCs now consider Mexico
one of their best options. Cost and location lead the list of reasons why
TNCs prefer Mexico as the site for production-sharing operations. The recent liberalization of trade and investment rules and the prospect of a North
American Free Trade Agreement are also drawing foreign corporations to
Mexico. Although TNCs primarily view Mexico as a source of cheap labor
and a platform for exports, the country's large population (rising to 100 million by the year 2000) is an attractive market.

Companies transferring operations to Mexico have become so common
that a network of consulting and financial service firms has emerged to help
relocate manufacturing plants. Companies such as Ventana Growth of San
Diego, in which the Mexican government's development bank Nafinsa has
a substantial interest, search out Rust Belt companies to buy and transplant.
"If 30 percent of their costs are labor, either they find us or we find them,"
boasted a Ventana spokesperson.[20] The Mexican bank Serfin and Inter-
American Holding of San Diego have established a fund to finance runaway plants—a move company representatives say will save U.S. firms an
average of $20,000 per worker. Responding to union critics, a spokesperson
for InterAmerican said, "People say we are raiding U.S. companies and
moving U.S. jobs. We're investing in companies so they can become competitive globally."[21]

The most likely targets for such corporate raiding are labor-intensive
plants such as metal-working, automotive-supply, furniture, small-appli-
ance, and plumbing-fixture factories. Companies with unions and above-
average pay scales in the manufacturing sector have been among the first to
relocate at least part of their production to Mexico. Despite years of concessions and "teamwork" cooperation with management, the United Auto
Workers estimates that 75,000 jobs have been lost to Mexico over the past 15
years.[22] As advocates of the free trade agreement with Mexico would be
quick to point out, however, U.S. jobs have also been saved because of the

increased global competitiveness resulting from production-sharing operations in Mexico.

Just one of the now hundreds of examples of U.S. workers seeing their jobs moving to Mexico is that of Kohler, Wisconsin, a company town whose heart is the Kohler manufacturing complex. Kohler, one of the world's top manufacturers of bathroom fixtures, is opening a highly automated factory outside of Monterrey in Mexico's industrial heartland. In the 1960s the company was the successful target of one of longest strikes in U.S. history, when the UAW organized the plant.[23] Now union workers will be losing their jobs to robots and cheap labor in Mexico.

But it is not just unionized and high-pay workplaces that are being affected. In 1990 AT&T moved an assembly plant in Bradford, Virginia, where workers were taking in $8.50 an hour, to Matamoros, across the border from Brownsville, Texas. And there is the case of the Green Giant broccoli plant in Watsonville, California. The company, a subsidiary of Pillsbury Foods (itself owned by Great Britain's Grand Metropolitan), decided to move operations to Irapuato, where it could pay workers less than $1 an hour rather than the $5 average back in Watsonville.

When one company relocates to Mexico, others often follow. Large manufacturing firms that have established a base in Mexico frequently encourage their suppliers to join them. That way supply delays are avoided and the supplies themselves become cheaper. Clustered around the new computer, engine, and automobile factories in Mexico are other U.S.-based firms that supply companies like Hewlett-Packard and Ford. For many manufacturers and suppliers, Mexico has replaced Singapore and other locations in Asia as the lowest cost, top-quality production site for companies like Black & Decker.[24] Yet even in the case of U.S. firms supplying other U.S. firms with plants in Mexico, dependence on imports remains high.

The rising presence of foreign capital in Mexico extends far beyond the manufacturing sector. Of increasing importance are agro-*maquilas,* which are foreign-controlled food-processing plants that bring together cheap Mexican labor and agricultural components from both Mexico and the United States to produce for the export market. The financing, technical assistance, and management come from the country where the agribusiness firm is based, usually the United States. In the past few years the number of agro-*maquilas* has doubled to more than 40.[25] The California-based Basic Vegetable Products "assembles" a finished onion from imported seed, then re-exports onion flakes and onion powder for distribution in the United States. One of the larger agro-*maquilas* is an operation by Tyson Foods which, along with the Japanese trading company C. Itoh and Mexican chicken grower Trasgo, is exporting chickens on skewers to Japan.[26]

More common are contractual deals with Mexican landowners, where the U.S. firm provides financing for crop cultivation, supplies technical assistance, and then buys all the produce. It has been estimated, for example, that 90 percent of the commercial crops in Baja California are produced with financing. These cross-border contracts are often managed by local growers in the U.S. Southwest but also involve such transnationals as Del Monte and Castle & Cooke.

Opportunities in Services

Beginning in the latter half of the 1980s, an increasing proportion of new foreign investment flowed into the service sector. As noted above, three-fifths of new investment in 1990 was in services. The investment boom in services has been led by investment in the tourism industry, much of which has taken the form of debt-equity swaps. As the Mexican economy opens up and key industries are deregulated, this business interest in the service sector is likely to continue.

The service sector is increasingly critical to the United States economy, accounting for two-thirds of the U.S. GDP and a rising share of U.S. global exports. Worldwide the United States enjoys a heady surplus in services (which includes such industries as banking, insurance, construction, tele-communications, and tourism). With Mexico, however, the United States suffers a deficit in current-account services, mainly because Mexico is a fa-vored vacation spot for U.S. tourists.

The barriers to the extension into Mexico of U.S. service industries are rapidly being pushed aside. Unlike trade in goods, trade in services re-quires a commercial presence in Mexico. In other words, companies that want to sell banking, communications, or food services to the Mexican pop-ulation must establish their own marketing operations in Mexico. With the partial deregulation of the trucking industry, Roadway and Ryder opened Mexican subsidiaries to be in a good position to fight for a share of the country's transportation business. Although the main growth in services has been in the increased commercial presence of foreign investors in ser-vice industries, the cross-border provision of services is also an important growth area. Along the U.S. border, construction companies and other busi-nesses are eager to jump into the Mexican market. The same is true, of course, of Mexican businesses that because of cheap labor can offer U.S. consumers an array of cheap services, such as housecleaning, construction, or lawn maintenance.

An important element in the investment boom in services is the fran-chising business. Franchises, which are neither independent nor wholly owned by parent companies, were deregulated in 1988. In Mexico, business observers call franchising "the business trend of the 1990s," and the Mexi-can Franchise Association predicts that franchising agreements will double annually throughout the decade, while more conservative observers predict a steady 20-percent growth in franchises. In 1990 there were 46 new U.S. franchises registered—more in one year than the combined total through 1988 when the liberalization of franchising licenses began.[27] For the most part franchises are a foreign phenomenon, with parent companies based mainly in the United States and secondarily in Europe and Brazil.

Most of the growth in franchises has been in the fast-food business. The owner of a new Arby's outlet, one of the largest U.S. fast-food chains to move to Mexico, called franchises the wave of the future. This may be an exaggeration, but one has only to look around any Mexican city to see new branches of McDonald's, Kentucky Fried Chicken, and Pizza Huts opening up. Kentucky Fried Chicken (owned by PepsiCo) sells more than 30 million pieces of chicken in Mexico each year and plans to more than triple its outlets to 180 stores in coming years. More fast-food outlets mean less business for Mexican restaurateurs, 30 percent of whom might be forced to close down mainly because of the "savage competition" of U.S. chains, according to Mexico's national chamber of restaurant owners.[28]

Although franchising is most popular in the food business, it is also a common practice in the hotel industry and other tourism services. Once the free trade agreement kicks into gear, many other service industries will be certain to expand to Mexico. One of the first in this new wave of franchises was Coverall, a commercial cleaning business that told one business magazine that it would be pulling in profits by the end of its first year in Mexico.[29] Foreign franchises are leading the way toward new employment practices that stress job flexibility, part-time work, and variable work hours.

Between 1982 and 1991 multiservice banking in Mexico was in government hands, although after 1987 domestic private investors were permitted up to 34 percent ownership. Foreign-owned banks fell outside the reach of the bank nationalization decree of 1982, although they were prohibited from opening commercial deposit banks. Operating under a "grandfather" clause, Citibank has since the 1920s been the only foreign bank with offices and full-service banking operations in Mexico. There are, however, about four dozen other foreign banks with offices in Mexico. These bank offices are active in corporate merger and acquisition operations, and are a foot in the door in the country's banking industry, which might eventually be opened to full foreign participation.

Besides maintaining offices in Mexico City, foreign banks play a major role in private and public financing. At the height of the debt crisis, major U.S. commercial banks had as much as one-third of their primary equity capital at risk in Mexico. Today about a quarter of the total debt remains in the hands of U.S. banks. Beginning in the late 1980s U.S. financial institutions once again began to increase their lending and financing activity in Mexico, both in the private and public sectors. Companies such as J.P. Morgan became the major sources of credit for newly privatized corporations, and First Interstate entered into a trade financing agreement directly with the government.

Investment Projections

Attracting foreign investment is the key to the success of Mexico's chosen path of modernization and restructuring. The government has counted on foreign investors to drive the export sector, which occupies the central place in the restructured economy. As imports increase, continuing flows of foreign investment are also critical in offsetting shortfalls in the current account (mainly international trade). With the current account projected to rise as high as $10 billion by the end of 1991 and much higher in 1992, the government must maintain high inflows of foreign investment. It must be remembered, too, that foreign investment is counterbalanced by outflows in profits, royalties, and intercompany settlements remitted abroad, which together often leave only a slight surplus or even a deficit in the total currency flow.[30]

According to the National Development Plan 1989-94, the target is to capture $25 billion in new foreign investment by the end of the Salinas *sexenio*—more than double the 1983-88 total. If achieved, foreign investment would represent 20-25 percent of total investment by 1994. Thus far, the projections seem overly optimistic. Instead of rising, as predicted, new foreign investment actually dropped substantially in 1990 and continued at a slow pace in 1991. If these trends of expanding trade deficits and a slower than expected pace of foreign investment continue, Mexico's experiment in neoliberal modernization would be seriously at risk.

U.S. Economic Programs

After Mexico's economy ground to a halt in 1982, U.S. economic programs proliferated. This increased assistance to Mexico aims to keep the country solvent and to ensure U.S. businesses maximum access to Mexican labor, investment opportunities, and markets. To meet these two interrelated objectives, Washington is relying on a variety of programs, including food aid, credit guarantees, development assistance, loans, and debt-management support. The principal U.S. agencies involved are the U.S. Department of Agriculture (USDA), Agency for International Development (AID), U.S. Export-Import Bank (Eximbank), U.S. Treasury and Commerce departments, and the National Endowment for Democracy (NED). The different aid mechanisms target specific problems in the Mexican economy, providing critical support for the Mexican government's radical restructuring process and underpinning Mexican purchases of U.S. goods and services.

Some programs, for instance, are designed to ease social tensions by providing temporary compensation for government policies such as social service cutbacks, public-sector layoffs, and other austerity measures. Others serve to relieve debt pressures—albeit without solving the country's mounting debt burden. In line with the push to bolster the private sector, U.S. agencies are funneling assistance to businesses and nongovernmental organizations. This assistance helps the recipients increase their purchases of U.S. goods and services while at the same time bolstering proponents of the government's conservative economic policies. The U.S. aid package serves as a lever to pressure the government to push forward with the economic restructuring process. Notably absent, however, are aid packages or associated U.S. pressure designed to encourage the democratization of Mexico's one-party state.

Confronting the Debt

Since the 1970s the United States has taken a leadership role in helping Mexico squeeze out of the worst of its debt crunches. The alternative was to risk a Mexican default that could undermine both the U.S. banking community and the international financial system. On four occasions—in 1976,

1982, 1986, and 1989—Washington spearheaded major debt-relief and debt-management initiatives involving commercial banks, multilateral lending institutions, U.S. government agencies, and foreign governments.[1] Working through the U.S. Treasury Department and the Federal Reserve Board, the Republican administrations of Gerald Ford, Ronald Reagan, and George Bush coordinated debt packages that provided Mexico with a combination of new money, credits, and lengthier repayment periods on old loans.

Although the bulk of the loans being renegotiated were with U.S. and foreign commercial banks, the U.S. government put money up front as well, in effect subsidizing the transactions with taxpayer support. The Ford administration, for instance, provided a $600 million emergency stabilization loan to underwrite the *peso*. In 1982 President Reagan's negotiators arranged for the U.S. Department of Energy to make an advance payment of $1 billion to purchase Mexican oil for the Strategic Petroleum Reserve. The U.S. Commodity Credit Corporation also joined in the effort, advancing a total of $1.7 billion to pay for Mexican imports of U.S. grain.[2]

In addition to these full-fledged rescue operations, Washington helped out with smaller-scale packages. The Bond Debt Relief Program, for example, was worked out in 1987 by Mexico, the U.S. government, and Morgan Guaranty Trust Co.[3] Mexico would purchase 20-year bonds put up by the U.S. Treasury to hold as collateral for Mexican government bonds that were to be swapped for debt held by commercial banks. Up to $10 billion in debt could have been retired through the program, but Mexico purchased a much smaller quantity than expected, in the end retiring only about $1 billion of its foreign debt.[4] In another effort, the Reagan administration propped up the incoming Salinas government with a $3.5 billion bridge loan at the end of 1988.

An Evolving Strategy

In general, Washington's strategy regarding Mexico's external debt placed responsibility for the bulk of rescheduling and refinancing on private creditors—both U.S. and foreign—because they held the largest portion of Mexico's debt.[5] The U.S. government also promoted international financial institutions (IFIs) as the main vehicles for official intervention in debt-relief efforts. Adhering to the approach taken by other developed industrial countries, Washington insisted that Mexico's case be considered individually and not as a member of a group of developing countries facing similar pressures from the international economic system.

These strategies allowed Washington to play an active and coordinating role in debt negotiations. But they also made it easier for Washington to avoid forgiving Mexico's official debts to the United States or to increase substantially its own contributions of new money to the Mexican government. Most important, by dealing with Mexico's case individually, Washington sidestepped the collective bargaining that might have occurred if

Mexico had been evaluated as a member of a group of indebted developing nations. This fact was even more significant because major third world debtors such as Brazil and Peru were fielding strategies feared by their creditors, including debt moratoriums and repayment terms based on a percentage of export earnings. Mexico's value as a "test case" or model for dealing with the debt was therefore heightened.

Although this general pattern held throughout the 1980s, important novel aspects of Washington's approach to Mexico's debt problems did evolve in recognition of the intransigence of the crisis. Two major shifts occurred, typically identified by the names of the U.S. Treasury secretaries who formulated them.

Treasury Secretary James Baker proposed the "Program for Sustained Growth" in 1985.[6] Whereas previous U.S. and IFI debt-reduction measures called for economic contraction (carried out through austerity and stabilization measures), the "Baker Plan" emphasized the need for growth in the economies of third world debtors. Baker recommended that Western industrialized countries and the IFIs increase loans to debtor nations if they adopted free market strategies, such as liberalized trade, flexible exchange-rate policies, and privatization, which theoretically lead to economic expansion. The Baker Plan assumed that third world debtors could grow out of their problems through a combination of increased short-term financing and long-term economic restructuring. For various reasons, the plan was unsuccessful in reducing Mexico's debt. It did, however, institutionalize free market reforms as conditions for the economic assistance programs of the U.S. government and U.S.-dominated IFIs such as the International Monetary Fund and the World Bank.

The "Brady Plan," advanced by Treasury Secretary Nicholas Brady in 1989, resulted from the recognition that growth alone would not solve third world debt.[7] Like the Baker Plan, Brady's initiative was based on the notion that the debt must be resolved through a market approach and that growth is important. However, it called for a combination of debt forgiveness—something that Baker did not envision—and new money. Brady urged commercial banks to forgive a portion of their loans to countries that put free market reforms in place. He also recommended that the IFIs put part of their funds into debt-reduction devices and encouraged trade-surplus countries like Japan to contribute funds for that purpose.

Mexico was the first country to work out an agreement under the auspices of the Brady Plan. The July 1989 program resulted in a combination of debt forgiveness, reduced interest rates, and new loans. Especially significant was the arrangement worked out with commercial creditors in early 1990, which resulted in a substantial reduction of the commercial foreign debt (see The Debt Crisis, 1982-91, Part 2). But as observed by Susan Kaufman Purcell, a specialist on Mexico with the Americas Society, Mexico got too little, too late, and too slowly.[8]

Besides offering Mexico critical support needed to keep its economy afloat, U.S. assistance was conditioned on the Mexican government moving forward with economic policies desired by Washington. As a consequence, the United States and other foreign entities gained influence over Mexico's monetary, investment, and trade policies. John Saxe-Fernandez, a commentator for the Mexican newspaper *Excélsior*, described the effect on Mexico as a "dizzying process of denationalization of the decisionmaking apparatus for economic policy."[9]

In the end, Washington's intervention in debt negotiations did forestall a debt moratorium in Mexico while slightly easing the burden of debt service. However, with their reliance on new money and resistance to debt forgiveness, U.S.-led strategies actually increased Mexico's foreign debt over the years. Ten years after Mexico first announced it could not meet its debt-payment schedule, the country's foreign debt was actually about $16 billion higher, although because of economic growth and inflation did not represent as heavy a burden.

Promoting U.S. Trade and Investment

Aside from assisting in managing the foreign debt, Washington's major economic programs in Mexico are designed to stimulate U.S. trade and investment in the country. Reflecting the increased cooperation between the United States and Mexico, new bilateral entities have also been created to expand economic interchanges. The Joint Committee for Investment and Trade (JCIT), for instance, was established in 1989 by the U.S. Commerce Department and its counterpart in Mexico. Designed to identify trade and investment opportunities in each country, the JCIT conducts conferences, sponsors business missions, and carries out other activities to encourage commercial relations and investment.

Washington offers various types of export financing arrangements to help promote U.S. exports to Mexico. Available from institutions such as the Export-Import Bank (Eximbank), Commodity Credit Corporation (CCC), and Small Business Administration, these funds are used both for pre-export development operations (such as inventory build-up and market research) and as loans, credits, insurance, and credit guarantees to promote sales of U.S. goods and services to Mexican buyers.[10] Designed to keep U.S. businesses competitive in the face of similar programs sponsored by other industrialized countries, these programs essentially amount to a subsidy for U.S. exporters as they open up new markets or expand old ones in Mexico. By financing export transactions and guaranteeing repayment with taxpayer dollars in case the buyer defaults, the U.S. government assumes many of the risks that are normal byproducts of doing business. As Eximbank describes its mission, "By neutralizing the effect of export credit subsidies from other governments and by absorbing risks that the private sector will not accept, Eximbank enables U.S. exporters to compete effectively in overseas markets."[11]

Export Financing

As the principal export financing arm of the U.S. government, Eximbank is heavily involved in helping U.S. businesses compete in Mexico. According to the bank's president, in fact, Mexico receives more Eximbank credit than any other country.[12] Put another way, in 1989 Eximbank supported more than $3 billion in U.S. exports to Latin America; Mexico purchased nearly one-third of these exports, making it Eximbank's largest market.[13] The bank supports U.S. exports to Mexico under all its programs: direct loans to foreign buyers, intermediate credits to U.S. lending institutions, loan guarantees, and export credit insurance. These services can be used by both public and private buyers, and the loan programs offer the lowest interest rates permitted under international agreements.[14]

From 1946 to 1990 Mexico received more than $3 billion in Eximbank loans and credits.[15] When loan guarantees and insurance are figured in, Eximbank's total authorizations for Mexico over the years exceeds $15.5 billion.[16] In recent years the amount designated for Mexico in any given year reflects the state of Mexico's economy, peaking during the years of oil-backed expansion and plunging when Mexico's economy crashed.[17]

The loans and guarantees provided during the latter years of the 1980s were targeted for projects to improve Mexico's infrastructure and to support the country's restructuring. In one such effort Eximbank worked with the National Finance Company (Nafinsa), Mexico's national credit institution, to develop a special guarantee facility to back a six-year project to privatize and modernize the country's agroindustry and electronics sectors.[18]

One of the most controversial of recent Eximbank programs among Mexicans was a 1990 loan guarantee for $1.5 billion to finance the development of Mexico's oil industry.[19] The loan—guaranteed by Eximbank in case of a Mexican default—was designated for Pemex for offshore projects in the Bay of Campeche.[20] One of the loan's conditions was that Pemex use U.S. firms to conduct the oil exploration and development projects it had planned. Although the head of Pemex said that dozens of U.S. firms were already involved in similar activities and that they would have no share of the oil or gas discovered, the agreement set off a storm of criticism in Mexico.[21]

Fears revolved around suspicions that the agreement would provide a back door into the Mexican oil industry for the United States and would be the first step toward including oil in negotiations of a free trade accord (see Pemex and the Oil Industry, Part 2). Whatever the outcome on those issues, other U.S. interests were served by the loan agreement. Political instability and the possibility of war-related production declines in the Middle East pose both immediate and long-term threats to U.S. strategic needs for reliable sources of oil. Mexico's proximity and the quantity of its reserves make it especially valuable to the United States in this regard. As it is, the country is already the largest supplier to the U.S. Strategic Petroleum Reserve, a trend starting in 1982 as a result of the U.S.-sponsored debt bailout.[22] Steady production of oil in Mexico—which ships more than half its annual petroleum exports to the United States—fits well with U.S. wishes for dependable suppliers.

Through its insurance facilities, Eximbank protects U.S. businesses from political and commercial risks of nonpayment. In addition to its regular insurance programs, Eximbank set up a special insurance facility for Mexico designed to overcome the reluctance of U.S. sellers to do business in the country. From 1983 to 1991 the facility supported more than $350 million in U.S. exports to the country.[23] The insurance covered up to 100 percent of the principal amounts on loans extended by Bancomex and Nafinsa to Mexican companies—both public and private—that wanted to purchase U.S. products.[24]

As with other Eximbank programs, the insurance facility serves the dual purpose of cranking up the Mexican economy and opening the door for U.S. business involvement. The concessionary terms offered by the bank allow Mexican buyers to purchase U.S. goods and services at rates they can afford. Similarly, the fact that major commercial and political risks are assumed by Eximbank encourages U.S. businesses to extend themselves in the country. The economic links that are forged in these transactions tie Mexico more closely to its northern neighbor, simultaneously advancing and entrenching the economic reforms being instituted by the Mexican government.

Expanding the U.S. Food Market

The U.S. Department of Agriculture (USDA) offers an assortment of services and financing programs to benefit U.S. growers and to help the United States maintain its dominant position in Mexico's agricultural market. These programs are carried out through two USDA agencies—the Foreign Agricultural Service (FAS) and the Commodity Credit Corporation (CCC). FAS, for instance, provides profiles on Mexico that outline the U.S. market position for particular products, competition, trends, regulations, and other information useful to U.S. exporters. More important, however, are the export-financing mechanisms used by the two agencies to back commercial exports of U.S. agricultural commodities.

Working through the CCC's credit-guarantee programs, several FAS programs directly subsidize U.S. growers who wish to export their products to Mexico. One of these is the Market Promotion Program (MPP), which provides support to U.S. agricultural organizations wishing to expand into other countries, including Mexico. The MPP was inaugurated in June 1991 to replace the Target Export Assistance (TEA) program, but each operates in similar ways.[25] Funding or commodity certificates from the CCC are provided to reimburse U.S. traders in part for certain market development projects for their eligible products.[26] In 1990 some $1.5 million was spent on TEA projects in Mexico, providing assistance to U.S. trade organizations such as the National Sunflower Association, Northwest Cherry

Growers, and U.S. Meat Export Federation.[27] Projects supported ranged from market research studies to promotional campaigns.

The Export Enhancement Program (EEP) is another FAS service that is backed by credits from the CCC. Its stated purpose is to challenge unfair trade practices, and it allows U.S. exporters of certain products to receive subsidies so that they can meet prevailing world prices. In Mexico, wheat is the crop most subsidized under the EEP; some 1.4 million tons of wheat for export to Mexico were covered under the program in 1987-88.[28] In combination with other credit programs of the CCC, the Export Enhancement Program allowed U.S. producers to corner the Mexican wheat market. In the market year 1989-90, for example, U.S. subsidies from the EEP plus credit guarantees from other government programs helped the United States to take a 95-percent share of the Mexican market for wheat.[29] Vegetable oil has also been subsidized under the program, which backed the export of 600,000 tons of the commodity in 1988.[30] Because both wheat and vegetable oil are produced in Mexico, these programs help U.S. producers and exporters to compete against locally produced commodities.

Both U.S. exporters and the Mexican government benefit under the EEP. The largest U.S. grain producers have been the major participants, among them Cargill, Continental Grain, and Louis Dreyfus Corporation.[31] In Mexico these producers traditionally have worked with Conasupo, the basic-foods distributor of the Mexican government. As Mexico's "food gap" grows worse, Washington's export-promotion efforts and commodity programs are helping the Mexican government provide inexpensive food to its people. At the same time, markets for U.S. commodities such as wheat are developed or expanded with Washington's assistance. These markets will be available even as Conasupo components are privatized, a process begun under Salinas.

Commodities and Credit Guarantees

Washington also underwrites Mexico's commercial imports of U.S. commodities through the GSM (General Sales Manager) credit-guarantee programs of the USDA's Foreign Agricultural Service. These programs allow foreign buyers to purchase U.S. farm commodities from private U.S. exporters with financing from U.S. banks at commercial rates of interest.

Because the loans are guaranteed by the U.S. government, lenders willingly support transactions that they might otherwise avoid due to the risk of nonpayment. As a consequence both the Mexican government and commercial importers get access to the ready cash they need to buy U.S. agricultural products.

In recent years Mexico ranked first in the world among the users of GSM credit guarantees. The country's use of these guarantees skyrocketed from $38 million in 1982 to $1.2 billion in 1988.[32] Most of these transactions occur under the GSM-102 program, which has repayment terms of six months to three years. (Repayment terms for GSM-103 range from three to ten years.) Out of $5 billion in credit guarantees authorized for worldwide GSM-102 programs in 1989, Mexico used $1.1 billion, or over one-fifth.[33] Roughly 65 percent of all Mexico's bulk agricultural commodity imports from the United States are covered under GSM-102.[34] In other words, the U.S. government is using the U.S. Treasury to support Mexico's increasing food imports from commercial U.S. exporters. This relationship is especially significant given the trends in U.S. agricultural exports to Mexico, which rose from $1.9 billion in 1983 to $2.7 billion in 1990—an increase of 42 percent. During the same period Mexico's trade account fell from a $13.8 billion surplus to a $4.1 billion deficit.

The concessionary terms and loan guarantees provided by the United States facilitate the Mexican government's decision to support large, export-oriented agricultural enterprises over small farms that produce basic grains for the domestic market. Mexico can pursue such policies yet continue its "cheap-food policy" by importing ever larger amounts of food products and animal feed from the United States.[35]

Another boon to the Mexican government is the fact that these imports are often simply added to the long-term international debt. The Salinas government need not worry about repayments during the immediate future. Instead, by selling the food to the public, the government actually receives needed income, subsidized, ultimately, by the Mexican poor and the U.S. taxpayer. And by reducing potential popular opposition to the government's economic reforms, these measures also satisfy two of Washington's most favored objectives: keeping Mexico stable and on track toward economic liberalization. At the same time they have benefit U.S. exporters by opening up a market that looks to the United States for its food supplies.

In the long run, however, these credit programs increase Mexico's dependency on food imports from the United States. As that dependency increases, Mexico will need to spend larger amounts of foreign exchange to purchase foodstuffs that it could produce at home. By adding to the foreign debt and institutionalizing food dependency on the United States, these credit guarantees undermine Mexico's long-term economic health.

Compensating for Cutbacks with U.S. Food

In addition to support for commercial exports of U.S. commodities, U.S. food aid programs from 1983 to the early 1990s provided support to the Mexican government.[36] At the same time Mexico's economic reforms were resulting in cutbacks in social programs, U.S. food aid allowed the Mexican government to continue its patronage and welfare programs. Moreover by providing food items that Mexico can and does produce—but in decreasing quantities—the programs help compensate for government policies favoring agricultural production for export.

Food aid in Mexico comes mainly through the Section 416 program, using agricultural products donated by the CCC, a branch of the USDA.[37] In Mexico's case, the 416 donations began in 1983 and coincided with the worst years of the economic crisis. They have also helped to counteract the disruptions of the economic restructuring. From 1983 to 1991 Mexico received more than $284 million in Section 416 food assistance.[38] Historically a major recipient of 416 aid, in 1989 Mexico was the second largest recipient, following India.[39] Due to be phased out by 1993, the program will have undergirded the Mexican government's structural reforms for nearly a decade. By the time the U.S. feeding programs wither away, the liberalization Washington has applauded under de la Madrid and Salinas will be institutionalized and difficult to reverse.

About half of the commodities were funneled to several Mexican nongovernmental organizations and their U.S. counterparts, including CARE, Christian Outreach Appeal, and World SHARE. The rest, however, went to the National System for the Integral Development of the Family (DIF), the Mexican government's social welfare agency. The commodities delivered to these organizations—including powdered milk, cheese, butter, oil, corn, rice, wheat flour, and sorghum—were distributed to poor populations or sold to create revenue for other social welfare activities.

As an AID-contracted evaluation team described it in 1988, "The Mexico Section 416 Program constitutes a limited, though effective vehicle for compensating those most affected by economic crisis and structural adjustment."[40] But the vital assistance offered to those in need was only one payoff of the programs. Big political gains were realized by PRI because the assistance allowed the government's social welfare arm to continue or expand operations that would otherwise have been cut back due to austerity measures and other conservative economic policies backed by Washington.

Over the years DIF has received about 40 percent of the commodities provided under the program.[41] Section 416 allowed the social welfare agency to double its two existing food programs and to create three more: PASAF (for low-income families), PREPAN (for needy children), and FIOSCER (for families of sugar workers).[42] According to the evaluation team mentioned above, by 1987 Section 416 commodities were used in all five feeding programs and accounted for about 65 percent of all the food distributed by DIF.[43]

Whether channeled through DIF or local private charitable organizations, the food aid gave a powerful boost to the Mexican government's economic reforms. An AID evaluation team estimated that some 33 million people were helped through such programs, at an average annual cost of $2 per person. Despite the low economic cost to the United States, the team noted, the political compensation was substantial: "[416 programs] have allowed DIF and private agencies to 'show the flag' of both Mexico and the United States among groups who are suffering most economically and are potentially active politically." Because the economic crisis and the restructuring "limit governmental response to needs of the poor," the team observed, the program was necessary to compensate for structural adjustment and fulfill U.S. desires for Mexican stability.

Development Aid

Washington wants a compatible and stable neighbor along its southern border, and its development assistance programs reflect that desire. From population control to narcotics demand reduction, from border health programs to microenterprise development, U.S. aid serves Washington's agenda at least as much as it serves Mexico's. Washington has been limited, however, by Mexico's nationalist sensibilities and by the fact that U.S. foreign aid priorities have generally rested in countries other than its usually stable southern neighbor. But Mexico's economic crisis and consequent restructuring have revitalized bilateral aid relations, opening new opportunities for Washington to encourage the Mexican government's reforms and ensure a role in the economy for the United States.

Traditionally, Mexico has received little in the way of development assistance from the United States. By mutual agreement most new aid was cut off in 1966 because Mexico refused to sign a provision under the Alliance for Progress guaranteeing U.S. private investment and because the United States did not consider Mexico poor enough to continue operations.[44] Some aid programs did continue, however. The Inter-American Foundation (IAF), for instance, stayed active in Mexico after 1972, when most other U.S. aid programs tapered off. Supporting everything from marketing cooperatives to legal aid for low-income neighborhood associations, IAF projects tend to be more empowering and less self-interested than assistance provided by other arms of the government, such as AID.

After agreeing in 1966 to terminate bilateral aid programs, AID, a branch of the State Department that administers economic assistance, closed its Mexico City mission. Programs that were already funded by AID were allowed to complete their funding cycle, but these ended in the early 1970s. After the mission closed, the United States funneled aid through international organizations such as the World Bank and the United Nation's World Food Program or through channels such as IAF and nongovernmental organizations. Such procedures permitted continued, though limited, U.S. involvement while meeting Mexico's needs for discretion because of nationalist sensitivities.[45]

Renewed AID involvement in Mexico was a gradual process. In 1977— at Mexico's invitation, according to an AID project officer—the agency began supporting population control programs in the country.[46] But it was not until 1983 that significant U.S. assistance through AID began to "fade in again," according to Gerard Bowers, AID's representative in Mexico City. Because it classifies Mexico as an Advanced Developing Country, the agency opened only an office and not a full-fledged mission.[47] In contrast to a bustling and highly visible AID presence in many developing countries, AID's office in Mexico is low-profile and minimally staffed. Running its operations out of the U.S. embassy, the agency has one AID representative and a small cadre of contract workers to carry out its projects.

Far from indicating a lack of interest in Mexico on Washington's part, the low profile of official U.S. programs in Mexico suits both governments by minimizing nationalist reaction against the United States. Moreover, Washington and the Mexican government have devised many other routes by which the United States funnels aid to Mexico. According to Samuel Taylor, head of AID's Mexico City office in 1989, Mexico has the "largest non-mission program" in the world. Taylor explained that "hundreds of projects" are funded by U.S. government agencies ranging from the Commerce Department to the U.S. Information Agency. Like AID, the programs of these other U.S. agencies are often designed to support private-sector organizations on both sides of the border.

From the mid-1980s to the early 1990s, AID's major projects in Mexico fell into four main categories: health, population control, narcotics-demand reduction, and private-sector support.[48] AID keeps pretty much behind the scenes in all this work. Most of the grants are implemented by Mexican non-governmental organizations (NGOs)—the Mexican Federation of Private Family Planning Associations, for instance—or other Mexican institutions such as universities. Likewise, U.S. NGOs participate, but not to the extent seen in areas such as Central America or the Caribbean, where AID relies heavily on U.S. organizations. Rotary International and Northwest Medical Teams, as well as U.S. contractors such as Development Associates Inc., are among the U.S. participants. Some agencies of the Mexican government, including the Ministry of Health and DIF, also help carry out AID grants.

Because Mexico is classified as an Advanced Developing Country, traditional resource transfers are not considered "appropriate" by AID. Instead, projects are designed to "acquaint potential leaders with [U.S.] societal and cultural values, develop trade and investment relations between the United States and [the Mexican] private sector, and increase the utilization of U.S. technology."[49] Assistance from AID, therefore, goes primarily to projects already receiving contributions from the Mexican government or private sector, and most of it is used to pay for U.S. goods and services that would otherwise be too expensive for Mexico to buy.

In keeping with AID's objectives for Advanced Developing Countries, many grants aim to create links between U.S. and Mexican institutions and to improve Mexico's technological infrastructure using U.S. resources. One grant, for instance, funded work with two U.S. universities to apply computer-integrated manufacturing in two manufacturing facilities in Mexicali. AID-funded training, scholarships, and research also build bridges between U.S. and Mexican organizations. For instance, AID pays for a yearly six-week training course for members of the official Mexican union CTM. Sponsored by the AFL-CIO's American Institute for Free Labor Development (AIFLD), up to 20 CTM unionists a year are sent to the United States for training at the George Meany Center in Maryland.[50]

Many AID projects are close reflections of specific U.S. interests. The programs in narcotics-demand reduction, for instance, dovetail with U.S. anti-drug efforts. A project to study employee attrition in the *maquilas*—mostly U.S.-owned—also received AID funding.

AID's work in Mexico helps the government implement projects—often with sophisticated U.S. technology—that would likely have to be cut back if U.S. assistance were not available. In addition, AID grants are directed at areas of top concern for U.S. policymakers. But U.S. assistance is also designed to support elements of Mexico's private sector and to encourage linkages among U.S. and Mexican organizations that will lead to exports of U.S. products and know-how. According to AID's project officer for Mexico, however, the agency's long absence from the country was detrimental to this objective. Reflecting on the agency's interest in stimulating trade with the United States, Robert Kahn of AID's Washington office said, "We don't have the 'ins,' the connections we need," because AID lacks a solid presence in Mexico. Active AID operations, he continued, "help us to keep our foot in the door."[51]

Democracy and Double Standards

More concerned with Mexico's stability than with its movement toward democracy, the United States offered virtually no assistance for democratization in the country. This is a historical pattern, but it has been especially evident since the early 1980s. Washington's tepid and intermittent support for Mexican democracy over the past few years stands in striking contrast to the upsurge of indigenous movements in Mexico demanding democratic change—both from the left and the right. In fact, in the words of El Colegio de México historian Lorenzo Meyer, Washington has been "conspicuous by its absence" in Mexico's recent efforts to create democratic political structures and processes.[52]

For a few years after 1983 the U.S. government appeared to be backing movements to open up Mexico's political system. This policy shift was spurred by several factors. In addition to undermining U.S. trade and investment opportunities, Mexico's economic crash and subsequent depression threatened another of Washington's vital interests in the country: political stability. Moreover the Mexican government under López Portillo and de la Madrid staunchly opposed U.S. militarism in Central America—the "backyard" where President Ronald Reagan was drawing a line in the sand against third world revolutionary advances. Fearful of an eruption of popular unrest and rankled by the Mexican government's stance on Central America, the Reagan administration was prompted to seek ways to transform the Mexican regime politically, as well as economically.[53]

But one more factor was absolutely essential in influencing Washington's decision to press for political change in Mexico. The National Action Party (PAN)—a longtime conservative opponent of PRI—suddenly looked as if it might be a viable contender against the ruling party, at least at the regional level. As PAN's views on economic policies and Central America dovetailed with Washington's, U.S. pressure for openings favoring that party served Washington's interests.

Even so, Washington's pressure on the Mexican government to democratize mostly took the form of rhetoric and admonitions, and was contradicted by the spiraling network of interactions and joint committees linking the two governments. Various forces in the United States—in the executive branch, Congress, academia, and the press—called on the Mexican government to allow effective electoral competition. Diplomatic initiatives favoring the opposition also increased slightly. But in contrast to its policy in countries such as Nicaragua, where U.S. pressures for internal political reforms were increased to full throttle, Washington did not make Mexico's movement toward democracy a condition of other assistance or of further relationships. This fact is especially striking when compared to the conditions that *were* attached to offers of economic aid regarding Washington's insistence that Mexico continue to liberalize the economy.

Washington's official and semi-official aid programs to Mexico offer no real assistance for democratization. This is true despite the fact that aid for democratic development is now one of the major foundations of U.S. foreign-assistance programs. AID, for example, has completely restructured its bureaucracy in order to establish "Democracy Initiatives" (DI) offices within the various regional divisions. Yet according to the DI office for Latin America and the Caribbean, there are no such programs in Mexico.[54]

Since 1985 the U.S. government has funneled grant money to a few Mexican organizations through the National Endowment for Democracy (NED). Established in 1983, NED is a privately incorporated grantmaking agency funded by Congress, purportedly to enhance the democracy-building efforts of private groups overseas. In reality, NED's primary concern is to bolster pro-U.S. organizations that are shaping political, social, and economic structures beneficial to the United States.[55] This is particularly clear in Mexico, where the bulk of NED's grant money has gone to business organizations promoting free market economies and advocating economic liberalization.[56] Nearly half of NED's total grants to Mexico from 1985 to 1991 went to these organizations.

One NED grantee, for example, is the "Young Entrepreneur Training Project," a program of the Mexican affiliate of Junior Achievement, the Desarrollo Empresarial Mexicano (Desem). Designed to "promote the adoption of free market practices" among high-school and university students, Desem receives grants from AID. NED also backed the Monterrey-based Center for Economic and Education Studies, which funds seminars for journalists and op-ed pieces on economics to "counteract socialist media writers."

Other NED grants were split among three institutions whose activities enhanced either traditional PRI structures or the conservative opposition. In 1985 for instance, Mexico's official union, the CTM, received a grant for training activities. Most of the funding, however, went to an organization of social christians, libertarians, and conservatives known as the Democracy, Solidarity, and Social Peace Association (Demos Paz). Grants to the organization are funneled through the National Republican Institute for International Affairs, the international arm of the U.S. Republican Party and one of NED's four "core grantees."

Demos Paz sponsors conferences, seminars, and other special events purportedly designed to educate the public about democracy. The topics often overlap economic issues, however. One cycle of conferences, for instance, called the "Libertarian Hurricane," discussed economic reforms and free market themes, stressing the importance of the "Libertarian message and how it can be used to build a new, modernized society."[57] Not very active in monitoring elections or in other prodemocracy activities Mexico might find useful, Demos Paz in 1990 began sponsoring a monthly public-opinion poll in anticipation of the 1994 presidential election.[58] It did not, however, take much of a role in crucial midterm elections in 1991.

Another NED grant, also funneled through the Republican institute, funded a 1989 conference for conservative political parties from Latin America. Held in Mexico City, the conference took place in July 1989, coinciding with the 50th anniversary celebration of its Mexican sponsor, the National Action Party.[59] PAN also hosted NED-funded seminars in Mexico in conjunction with the Central American Political Academy, another NED grantee.[60]

Although NED grants to business organizations and Demos Paz continued past 1988, U.S. pressure to broaden Mexican democracy ended with the rise of Cuauhtémoc Cárdenas and the National Democratic Front (FDN).[61] The Mexican government's appropriation of free market economic policies took the wind out of PAN's ideological sails and undermined its position as the leading opposition party in the 1988-91 period.[62] And when the FDN rapidly accumulated proponents in Mexico and became the most likely beneficiary of democratic openings, Washington responded by throwing its weight behind the government and its allies in PRI's conservative wing.

Reagan telegraphed congratulations to Salinas on his 1988 election "victory" even before the fraud-riddled election process was concluded. He followed that up with a $3.5 billion bridge loan to the Salinas administration at the end of 1988. Similarly in 1990, following fraudulent local elections in the state of Mexico, in which Cárdenas forces were the probable winners, U.S. President George Bush ignored press reports and popular criticisms to hold a congenial summit meeting with Salinas in Monterrey.[63] A $1.5 billion loan guarantee from the U.S. Export-Import Bank for Mexico's petroleum sector was announced immediately thereafter.

The same pattern held after critical midterm elections in 1991, in which six governorships, half the Senate, and all national congressional seats were at stake. The *Washington Post, New York Times,* and other U.S. newspapers, as well as Mexican observers and U.S. analysts, pointed out widespread fraud on the government's part during the elections. In Washington, however, the U.S. executive branch moved full speed ahead on issues such as the free trade agreement despite the questionable legitimacy of its negotiating partner.

Long-Term Prospects

Mexico exemplifies the double standard Washington holds when measuring the political systems of "friendly" and "unfriendly" states. In Nicaragua's 1990 elections, for example, the U.S. government pulled no punches. Through the National Endowment for Democracy and AID, Washington funded coalition-building activities, infrastructure support, get-out-the-vote drives, international and civic election monitoring teams, media campaigns, and other activities designed to put its candidate over the top and ensure the country's "democratic transition."[64] It insisted on Nicaragua's acceptance of these activities as a quid pro quo for Washington's recognition that democracy had been served in the elections.

As a whole, the Mexican political opposition is not advocating U.S. direct intervention in the country's internal political affairs, even if this intervention were disguised as "democracy aid." What it does want is international pressure to guarantee that the electoral process is fair and free—something that at this point only the presence of foreign observers from multilateral organizations could ensure. But Washington has not even endorsed this idea of nonpartisan observers from the United Nations or some other multilateral organizations such as the Organization of American States—despite the fact that the two major opposition parties (PRD and PAN)—both to the left and right—have requested such observation. Sponsored by organizations such as the United Nations, international observer teams have a solid background of monitoring elections in such sensitive political contexts as Nicaragua, Namibia, and Haiti. The careful observations made by such teams could help advance Mexico's progress toward democracy—although they might also pull the rug out from under the PRI and hamper Washington's moves to promote a Mexican economy complementary to U.S. needs.

Washington's blithe indifference to Mexico's political character does not serve the long-term interests of either country. By ignoring issues of democratization, fraud, and repression, the United States is helping to postpone needed political reforms even as sweeping economic changes dislocate major segments of the Mexican population. If, as is likely, such dislocations continue and popular dissatisfaction rises, the social forces that would be unleashed could mount a serious challenge to Mexican stability.

Even if such a challenge does not to come to pass, the questions raised by allegations of electoral fraud undermine the PRI government's legitimacy at a time when popular support—or the lack of it—is most crucial. Instead of truly resolving stubborn problems such as the foreign debt or stimulating equitable development in the country, U.S. aid increases Mexican dependence on U.S. markets and U.S. resources. It also locks Mexico into the role of being chiefly a source of cheap labor for the regional trade alliance headed by the United States. Such policies increase U.S. dominance over its southern neighbor, while leaving Mexico's long-term economic and political health in question.

U.S. Security Assistance

When the U.S. government looks south in military terms, it sees a budding friendship where once it knew cautious cooperation. As Mexico moves closer to the United States in economic and foreign policy spheres, security linkages between the two countries multiply. Historically low levels of U.S. security assistance to Mexico gave way in the mid-1980s to increased sales of defense items and services, as well as additional training for military personnel and their civilian counterparts (Table 6d). Split between programs designed to modernize the Mexican armed forces on the one hand and bolster narcotics control activities on the other, U.S. aid benefits both the Mexican military and the country's law-enforcement agencies.

As with U.S. economic aid programs, Washington's security assistance to Mexico increasingly aims at integrating Mexico into U.S. strategic visions and at developing binational approaches to issues deemed important by Washington. For example, two new law-enforcement agreements, the Mutual Legal Assistance Treaty and an accord facilitating the exchange of tax information, satisfy Washington's needs for instruments to use against suspected drug traffickers.

Aside from its interests in maintaining Mexico's quiet presence along the U.S. southern flank, Washington has other reasons for wanting to develop friendly relations with Mexican military and security forces. The country is the second most important source of strategic raw materials for the United States, supplying petroleum, strontium, fluorspar, and antimony.[1] In addition, the U.S.-Mexico border is the primary entry point for drugs coming into the United States. According to the State Department, Mexico is "the transit country of principal concern" in terms of drug traffic into the United States.[2] Anti-narcotics programs sponsored by Washington rely heavily on Mexican military and law-enforcement agencies to act as U.S. surrogates in combating drug traffickers and producers whose market is primarily in the United States.

In the event of a threat to its interests, amicable relations with U.S.-trained military officers dependent on U.S.-made equipment could offer Washington important allies. To this end, U.S. military programs are designed to develop ties between armed forces in the two countries with a goal of "expanding U.S. influence in the [Mexican] military."[3] Likewise,

U.S. security-assistance programs support the "modernization" of Mexico's armed forces and law-enforcement agencies in order to assure the "development of a professional military able to guarantee internal security and stability."[4]

Much of the U.S. aid to Mexico's military and law-enforcement forces has gone into the country under the auspices of anti-drug programs. Fighting the war against drugs on Mexican soil has preoccupied the U.S. government since the 1960s, when Mexico became a major supplier of marijuana and heroin to the United States. Ironically, however, widespread cultivation of Mexican opium poppies—and, to a lesser extent, marijuana—began during World War II, at the request of the U.S. government, which was seeking supplies of pain-reducing medications such as morphine.[5] Since then Mexico has been caught up in a U.S.-driven spiral of drug demand and drug control.

To give some idea of the extent of U.S. interest in this matter, of 132 formal agreements and treaties signed between the United States and Mexico as of 1985, 46 pertained to narcotics.[6] Looking at it from another angle, the largest foreign operation of the U.S. Drug Enforcement Administration (DEA) is conducted on Mexican territory. And—on one side of the border or another—more than a dozen U.S. federal government agencies, ranging from the Marine Corps, to the U.S. Information Agency, to the CIA, have been mobilized in anti-drug efforts.[7]

Anti-drug rationales were cited for the two times in recent history that the United States virtually closed the border between the two countries. Known as Operation Intercept, the actions occurred in 1969 and 1985 and consisted of intensive searches of all persons and vehicles crossing into the United States. Designed to coerce Mexico into finding and prosecuting drug traffickers, the second closure resulted from U.S. anger over the torture and killing of DEA agent Enrique Camarena. It was modeled on the 1969 operation conducted under the administration of Richard Nixon. That operation aimed at forcing Mexico to use chemicals to destroy narcotics crops, a procedure then illegal in the United States. A comment by Nixon aide G. Gordon Liddy, one of the designers of the 1969 operation and a culprit in the Watergate scandal, illustrates the coercive intentions of the closure: "It was an exercise in international extortion, pure and simple and effective, designed to bend Mexico to our will. We figured Mexico could hold out for a month; in fact, they caved in after two weeks, and we got what we wanted."[8]

Liddy's boast exposes with rare clarity the sad truth underlying many U.S. policies regarding Mexico, including security assistance. What the United States wants from Mexico in this respect is a "secure, stable, and friendly" neighbor that will look northward for cues on international policies.[9] Remarking on Mexican initiatives that supported U.S. objectives, the U.S. government's 1992 budget submission to Congress on security assistance applauded the fact that Mexico increased its oil production after Iraq's 1990 invasion of Kuwait, in order "to assist the United States and Latin American countries."[10] When Mexico's own interests conflict with those of the United States—as in the diversion of resources and personnel to the drug war or the militarization of Central American conflicts—it is the Mexican interests that are to take the back seat.

Security assistance to Mexico's military and law-enforcement agencies encourages the country's turn toward the United States. Increased training programs, for instance, are designed to inculcate Mexico's security forces with national and regional security perspectives held by their U.S. counterparts, as well as to impart technical skills and tactical guidelines. Similarly, Mexico's acquisition of U.S. defense equipment and services creates a future need for spare parts and technical assistance that will link together the security establishments of the two countries into the 21st century.

Modernizing the Military

Both the dollar value of U.S. military aid to Mexico and the size of the U.S. military presence there have traditionally been low in comparison to the case of other Latin American countries.[11] Even so, the United States, more than any other country, has influenced the Mexican armed forces.[12] Through training and the provision of defense equipment and services, the United States has maintained a steady involvement with the Mexican military. Moreover by the end of the 1980s, as the economic liberalization progressed and as Mexico and the United States amplified their anti-drug activities, direct aid to Mexico's military soared.

U.S. Military Assistance to Mexico, 1981-91

	(in millions $)					
	1981-86	1987	1988	1989	1990	1991
IMET	1.0	0.2	0.2	0.2	0.3	0.4
FMS Sales	133.9	21.0	6.1	12.5	12.7	10.0
Commercial Sales	26.4	207.5	32.0	51.2	2.4	245.9
Excess Defense Sales	0	0	0	0.4	1.5	na
TOTAL	161.3	228.7	38.3	64.3	16.9	256.3

IMET: International Military Education and Training Program
FMS Sales: Foreign Military Sales and Construction Sales Agreements
Commercial Sales: Commercial Exports licensed or approved under the Arms Export Control Act
Excess Defense Sales: Excess defense articles sold under foreign military sales

SOURCE: Department of Defense, *Congressional Presentation for Security Assistance Programs*, FY83, FY84, FY85, FY86, FY87, FY88, FY89, FY90, FY91, FY92.

U.S.-Mexico military relationships until recently followed the pattern developed during World War II and the early postwar years. Issues of hemispheric security and a sense of a common threat to the region from European fascism resulted in closer ties between the armed forces of the two countries.[13] Washington increased its aid to the Mexican military at the time, and the two countries set up a Joint Mexico-U.S. Defense Commission.[14] The ties forged during wartime persisted, although in weakened forms, after the war. The joint defense commission, for example, became inactive, and Mexico refused to accede to U.S. initiatives such as the Rio Treaty (a hemisphere-wide mutual defense treaty concluded in 1951), designed to create formal links among U.S. and Latin American militaries. Mexico received virtually no support under the Military Assistance Program (MAP), a major U.S. grant program that funds the purchase of defense articles and services, training, and technical assistance.[15] Similarly, the United States has not had a Military Assistance Advisory Group (MAAG) based on Mexican soil since the 1960s.[16] Aside from tiny Caribbean nations, Cuba is the only other Latin American country to share this distinction.

Through U.S. government credit initiatives such as the Foreign Military Sales Financing Program (FMS), Mexico received a small amount of financing to purchase U.S. equipment, spare parts, and technical assistance until the 1970s. FMS funding then fell off until 1981, when it jumped back into the millions annually. From 1946 to 1989, for example, Mexico received more than $45 million in loans and grants under both FMS and other credit programs. More than two-thirds of the total was provided through FMS after 1987.[17]

In addition to credit-financing programs such as FMS, Washington licenses commercial exports of defense materials and services to Mexico that enhance linkages between the Mexican military and the U.S. armed forces or commercial suppliers. The United States also transfers excess supplies of defense-related equipment to Mexico. As with FMS there was a jump in sales, leases, and transfers of such equipment and services in the 1980s through these other programs. As a matter of fact, between 1982 and 1990 Mexico leased or purchased more military goods and services from the United States under all categories of assistance (FMS, commercial sales, and excess transfers) than it did in the previous thirty years. Such transactions totaled only $29.5 million from 1950 to 1978; in contrast the United States provided more than $500 million in defense materials and services to Mexico from 1982 to 1990.[18]

Foreign military sales and leases to Mexico—both commercial and government-financed—have provided important backing for the modernization of the armed forces undertaken in the late 1980s. The country's air force has been a major beneficiary, both in terms of its squadron of F-5E aircraft and in terms of its new purchases of Bell 212 helicopters, C-130 transport planes, and other aircraft.[19] Mexico has also leased U.S. UH-1H helicopters and purchased excess U.S. Army jeeps and light trucks. Other material provided by the United States includes communications equipment, some weapons, and spare parts for U.S. origin vehicles, aircraft, and ships.[20]

Given the dearth of other direct U.S. military aid to Mexico, the International Military Education and Training Program (IMET) has traditionally been a key to increasing U.S. access to leadership levels of the Mexican military. One of the cornerstones of U.S. military assistance to foreign countries, IMET grants provide professional military training for selected foreign military personnel and their civilian associates both in the United States and at overseas facilities. Mexico sends more military personnel to U.S. training programs than to those of any other country, a factor which enhances U.S. influence.[21] Elliott Abrams, assistant secretary of state for inter-American affairs under the Reagan administration, observed that Mexico was a country "where our access to the military results from and depends to a large degree on IMET."[22]

In Mexico, IMET has been the major source of direct U.S. military assistance during most of the postwar period, with the exception of funding for narcotics control activities. From 1946 to 1989 the United States provided $4.4 million for training under IMET, with more than one-third of the funding supplied during the 1980s.[23] In recent years IMET grants financed professional military education, maintenance courses at U.S. schools, and training for Mexican personnel to operate and maintain equipment used in anti-drug activities.[24] The students also learn English and develop collegial relationships with their U.S. counterparts.

As with other military programs, IMET training sessions increased dramatically during the 1980s. From 1984 to 1991 the United States trained some 442 Mexican military personnel, and plans included training for another 70 students in 1992.[25] In contrast, during the nearly three decades from 1950 to 1978, only 906 Mexicans participated in U.S. military training programs.[26] Throughout Latin America such relationships have been crucial to U.S. foreign policy. In his widely quoted observation, former Secretary of Defense Robert McNamara explained that training "selected officers and key specialists" of foreign countries provided "probably the greatest return" on U.S. investment in military aid. As McNamara told Congress in 1962: "I need not dwell upon the value of having in positions of leadership men who have the first-hand knowledge of how Americans do things and how they think. It is beyond price to make friends of such men."[27] More recently, the Pentagon justified its assistance in the interests of keeping Mexico "friendly" and "secure," and its troops "apolitical."[28]

Fighting the Drug War

During the 1970s and 1980s the majority of U.S. security assistance to Mexico was funneled into the country under the auspices of anti-narcotics programs. Mexico in fact traditionally receives the largest amount of U.S. annual expenditures for foreign drug control. From 1978 to 1990 the United

States provided $150.3 million to Mexico as assistance for drug-control activities.[29] Nearly half of these funds were allocated following a 1986 National Security Decision Directive—prepared with the help of then Vice-President George Bush—elevating the fight against foreign traffickers to a matter of U.S. national security. Moreover the trend of such assistance is upward. From 1980 to 1985 the United States provided an average of $8.4 million per year for the programs. During the latter years of the 1980s, however, that figure had climbed to $14 million, and the administration planned to request another $26 million in bilateral drug-control assistance for Mexico in 1992 alone.[30]

Mexico's Office of the Attorney General coordinates the drug-control efforts in the country, and the bulk of U.S. aid is granted through that office. The Mexican armed forces also participate in the programs. Like the police agencies, Mexico's military also receives support for equipment purchases, training, and other aspects of force modernization under the anti-drug programs.[31]

Used for all aspects of the drug war, including detection, eradication, intelligence, and interdiction, U.S. anti-drug assistance has boosted the technological capabilities and professional skills of Mexican law-enforcement and military forces.[32] This has been the case since the 1960s, when U.S. agents were sent to the country as advisers.[33] The programs expanded during the 1970s to include support for Mexico's eradication activities. By the 1980s the United States was backing a full spectrum of projects aimed at training and equipping Mexico's police and military forces, under the auspices of narcotics control. For instance armed Huey UH-1H helicopters—and the training to fly them—were provided through a U.S. assistance package in 1990 designed to support Mexico's interdiction efforts.[34] Likewise, the U.S. Air Force has provided computer software, installation, and training in its use.

United States support for Mexico's program of aerial eradication of marijuana and opium-poppy crops began in the 1970s.[35] Initially, Washington's financing enabled Mexico to buy or lease fixed-wing aircraft and helicopters from the United States, construct field air bases, train pilots, and install communications systems. The aircraft, used both for spraying herbicides and transporting troops, are maintained largely with U.S. funding, with maintenance and advisory services provided in part by U.S. corporations such as E-Systems, Inc., of Texas.

Over the years the U.S. program expanded to include several components besides procurement and maintenance of aircraft. By the late 1980s the State Department's Bureau of International Narcotics Matters (INM) was also providing funds to purchase herbicides and fuel for the Mexican air fleet. Salary supplements for Mexican pilots, mechanics, and other technicians are also paid through the INM, the U.S. office that administers foreign drug-control assistance. In addition, according to its 1991 budget submission to Congress, the State Department planned to sponsor an aerial survey project to evaluate eradication efforts. If the project is funded, the

INM will finance training programs for pilots, photo-interpreters, and computer operators, as well as other aspects of the endeavor.[36]

According to U.S. legislation, aid cannot be provided to police or law-enforcement officials in foreign countries in order to support or train them in programs involving internal intelligence or surveillance.[37] The DEA and the Federal Bureau of Investigation (FBI) are exempt from these restrictions if they are helping foreign law-enforcement officials to fight drug trafficking.[38] Despite restrictions, Mexico's police forces have received support from various U.S. agencies, including the U.S. military. The U.S. Army, for instance, has provided helicopters and technical assistance teams to the Mexican Office of the Attorney General and publications to the Mexican National Police.[39] Similarly, Mexican law-enforcement and military personnel participated in training sessions sponsored by the DEA, FBI, Customs Service, and Coast Guard in 1990. Customs, for instance, conducted a course in financial-enforcement programs for investigators from the Mexican Treasury and Central Bank, while the Coast Guard trained Mexican Navy personnel in interdiction and vessel-boarding procedures.[40]

Another example is U.S. aid to Mexico's Northern Border Response Force (NBRF). Established to enhance Mexico's interdiction capability in northern border regions, the NBRF is a rapid response team composed of agents from the Mexican Federal Judicial Police. A U.S. Customs program has trained NBRF pilots to fly, use the radar, and repair fixed-wing aircraft obtained from the United States for use in tracking planes smuggling drugs from South America.[41] Similarly, the U.S. embassy in Mexico City set up a counternarcotics Tactical Analysis Team to relay U.S. Air Force intelligence to Mexican drug authorities about trafficking activities.[42]

In the past, the fact that post-revolutionary Mexico had no significant external enemies meant that it had little need for sophisticated military equipment obtained from foreign sources. As a result both U.S. influence and that of other major arms-supplying countries was minimized. With the advent of the drug war as a matter of U.S. national security policy, however, Mexico was increasingly drawn into U.S. initiatives requiring technologically advanced equipment and training, especially in the fields of communications and detection and tracking devices. For example Mexico purchased specially outfitted tracker aircraft that work in conjunction with U.S. radar facilities located in international airspace.[43]

Aside from providing a channel for Washington's assistance to Mexico's law-enforcement agencies and armed forces, these U.S. aid programs enhance U.S. influence over Mexico's decisions about law-enforcement priorities. The counternarcotics team at the U.S. embassy, for example, helps plan the activities of the Northern Border strike force, as well as gather intelligence.[44] Through actions such as these the United States is becoming a primary actor in Mexican security programs, for the first time in history.

Both U.S. and Mexican government officials describe the programs as the result of cooperation and shared interests. But the history of the drug war has demonstrated Mexico's increasing commitment of resources and trained personnel to cutting off the supply of drugs bound for U.S. consumers, while the United States increasingly turns the screws on its southern neighbor, threatening aid cutoffs, tourist advisories, and border closings if Mexico does not "do more." Mexican critics decry the "coercive character of a U.S.-imposed and futile anti-drug policy."[45] Similarly the PRD's Cuauhtémoc Cárdenas criticized Washington's "troubling tendency to judge Mexico's performance not so much by the results achieved but on the basis of Mexico's willingness to follow U.S. criteria and guidelines and to allow American drug enforcement authorities to operate inside Mexico exempt from reasonable jurisdictional limits."[46]

Given the dismal record of Mexican police and military forces with respect to human rights violations, U.S. assistance to them serves to strengthen and stabilize institutions widely known as corrupt and repressive. Under Salinas moreover, the military has been called out more frequently to act as a police force to deal with political and labor problems, as well as drug control.[47] Washington is thus bolstering the strong arm of a government that has for decades turned to authoritarian measures to silence dissent when other solutions—such as co-option—have been unsuccessful.

Other Foreign Interests

Not since the *porfiriato*, when English was the language of the Mexican railway and French the language of the concert hall and drawing room, has the Mexican government expended so much effort in search of foreign investment.[1] In his first three years of office President Salinas and his economic cabinet criss-crossed the globe in search of new sources of foreign investment and trade, positioning Mexico as an export platform to the world, the key to U.S. markets under the proposed NAFTA. So far the results have been mixed, with both Asian and European Community countries expressing increased interest in Mexico, but with reservations, pending the signing of an agreement that would lock in the Salinas economic program for the next century. Nevertheless, 1991 marked Mexico's entrance into the Pacific Economic Cooperation Conference and provided a new framework for ties to the EC through a new Framework Agreement of Cooperation, the most extensive agreement between the EC and any Latin American country.

After the United States, the leading foreign investors in Mexico are Germany, Great Britain, Japan, Switzerland, France, and Spain.[2] German investment is concentrated primarily in the automotive and pharmaceutical industries. British influence dates from the nineteenth century when British firms dominated the petroleum, mining, and railroad industries. But in recent years it is Japan—Mexico's second most important overall trading partner—and the industrialized nations of the Far East that Mexican officials have courted most aggressively.

The modern Japanese-Mexican relationship dates back over 100 years. The Mexican embassy in Tokyo is located on land donated by the emperor in 1892 in recognition of the fact that Mexico was the first country to sign a treaty of friendship, trade, and navigation on terms of equality with Japan.[3] When much of Tokyo and Yokohama were destroyed by an earthquake in 1923, Mexico donated money for their reconstruction, a gesture returned by Japan in 1985. The signing of the friendship treaty brought several waves of Japanese immigrants to Mexico, beginning with a group of agricultural workers sent to Chiapas. Later immigrants came to work copper and coal mines in Baja California Sur and Coahuila.

Nissan, the leading Japanese corporation in Mexico, first set up operations there in the 1960s, beginning as a producer of automobiles for the domestic market, then as a producer of automobiles and parts for export. In 1986 President de la Madrid visited Japan, followed soon after by Carlos Salinas de Gortari, then minister of planning and the budget. Salinas's fascination with Japan is legendary. While Peru's President Fujimori can rely on his heritage when approaching Japanese business and political leaders, Salinas has had an extra advantage—his Japanese-speaking children, who attend the Japanese bilingual school in Mexico City.

Oil dominates Mexican exports to Japan and has historically accounted for Japanese interest in Mexico. In addition Mexico exports salt, meat, abalone, coffee, vegetables, silver, and other metals to Japan and imports petrochemicals, refined steel, auto parts, household electrical appliances, and heavy machinery. Although Japan is still keenly interested in oil, its Mexico policy is now directed by its interest in greater access to U.S. markets at lower tariffs, possibly through a manufacturing base south of the border.

The Japanese External Trade Organization reported that more than 160 Japanese companies were operating in Mexico in 1990. Leading the list was Nissan, with four plants and a total investment of $500 million, with a projected $1 billion dollars in new investments in Aguascalientes, in north-central Mexico. The *maquiladora* industry represents the greatest increase in Japanese investment in Mexico, concentrated in the electronics and automotive industries in the states of Baja California and Chihuahua. "It's a question of survival," Yasuo Sasaki, vice-president of Sanyo of America, told a German reporter in 1988. "We have to move at least part of our production to stay in the American market.[4]

In less than a decade Japanese *maquiladoras* became a major force along the U.S.-Mexico border, particularly in Tijuana, where the San Diego Economic Development Corporation estimated that by 1988 they employed a quarter of all *maquiladora* workers in the region. Japanese *maquiladoras* represent only 4 percent of the nearly 2,000 *maquiladoras* in Mexico. But they tend to involve larger plants and work forces and are estimated to employ 10 percent of the nation's *maquiladora* workers. Mexican policymakers are courting Japanese investment primarily as a means of reducing their economy's dependence on the United States. A second benefit is access to the advanced manufacturing techniques—including work teams, quality circles, and enhanced training for production workers—that Japanese firms have made famous. A recent study by a leading scholar on labor relations concluded, however, that Japanese manufacturers differ very little from those of other countries in their training and work organization.[5] An even later phenomenon is the presence of South Korea's Goldstar and Hyundai and other Far East Asian manufacturers.

In the 1980s the Japanese government extended a series of loans to Mexico to restructure the steel industry, to build petroleum-related infrastructure (including a pipeline from the Gulf Coast oil fields to the Pacific Coast port of Salina Cruz), and to promote non-oil exports to Japan and other markets. In 1990 the Japanese government authorized a loan of nearly a billion dollars for air and water cleanup projects in Mexico City, in which Japanese, U.S., and French firms will provide the technology.[6] As with other types of official investment in developing countries, the environmental loan was channeled through the Japanese Export-Import Bank and its Overseas Economic Cooperation Fund, resulting in heavy dependence on Japanese firms and technology.[7]

By investing in Mexico, Japan seeks to strengthen Mexico's ability to compete in low- and middle-technology industries that will seek markets in the United States and in areas where the United States is struggling to maintain its share of the market.[8] Nevertheless the debt crisis tempered the interest of Japanese private lenders and government agencies. Business and political leaders have been fairly open in their complaints about the problems of doing business in Mexico and in explanations of Japan's reluctance to invest at a more substantial rate there; total Japanese investment in Mexico still represents less than 2 percent of all Japanese foreign investment. The former ambassador said Mexico would be the ideal country for investment, if it made real structural reforms and modified "an extremely slow bureaucracy."[9]

Most recently Kochio Ejiri, head of a government trade mission, announced that he was "very impressed" with Mexico's "notable economic improvement," but cautioned that new flows of investment would depend on the extent to which Japanese companies receive higher profits on investment.[10] He also complained about union problems and noted that Japan had already suffered losses in the Mexican steel industry.

NAFTA Increases Foreign Interest

Like their Japanese counterparts, European businesses and governments have expressed an increased interest in Mexico with the prospect of NAFTA. European investment and trade has received less media attention in the United States, compared to the amount of media attention devoted to Asian *maquiladoras* along the border. When considered as a group, however, the EC nations are Mexico's second-largest trading partner after the United States.

Petroleum accounts for more than 80 percent of Mexican exports to the EC. Other leading exports include basic foods or raw materials such as cotton, cacao, coffee, honey, tobacco, tin, lead, and zinc. Mexico imports machinery engines, electric generators, and capital goods from the EC.[11] Accords signed by the EC and Mexico in 1991 provide for a center of distribution of Mexican products in Europe, provisions for joint ventures, the development of the furniture industry and its export potential, and improved mechanisms for settling antidumping disputes. Mexico's current exports to the EC represents 15 percent of total exports, down from more than 20 percent in 1982.[12]

Compared to trade and investment with its northern neighbor, the Far East, and the EC, Mexico's economic relationships with Latin America and the Caribbean are minimal—less than 6 percent of total trade. At their January 1991 summit in Tuxtla Gutiérrez, Chiapas, Salinas and five Central American presidents agreed to establish a free trade zone before 1997. In September 1991, Mexico signed a free trade agreement with Chile.

Canada's 1988 free trade agreement with the United States generated fierce controversy; a recent Gallup poll found that a majority of Canadians believe that a Mexico-U.S.-Canada agreement will have harmful effects on the Canadian economy because of the wage disparity with Mexico. The sentiment was expressed by a columnist for *MacLean's* as "Canadians who hated free trade with the United States are going to loathe free trade with Mexico."[13]

The 1990 announcement by the United States and Mexico of plans to pursue a free trade agreement inevitably prompted Canada's request for the negotiations to become trilateral. Until recently Mexico has been a less than significant market for Canada, with bilateral trade registering less than 2 percent of total trade in 1990. But even so, Mexico is Canada's most important Latin American trading partner.[14] Canada has expressed little interest in Mexico's *maquiladora* industry and currently ranks eighth in terms of overall foreign investment in Mexico. That is expected to change with NAFTA.

Reference Notes

Part One: Government and Politics

The Legacy of Revolution

1. Lorenzo Meyer, "La democracia, solo un horizonte," *Excélsior*, August 14, 1991.
2. Daniel Levy and Gabriel Székely, *Mexico: Paradoxes of Stability and Change* (Boulder: Westview Press, 1987), p. 28. The following section on the revolution's early years drew largely on the above and on the following works: Lorenzo Meyer, *Historia de la revolución mexicana* (Mexico City: El Colegio de México, 1971); Daniel Cosio Villegas, ed., *Historia moderna de México* (Mexico City: El Colegio de México, 1977); Alan Riding, *Distant Neighbors: A Portrait of the Mexicans* (New York: Alfred A. Knopf, 1985), pp. 41-65. The most comprehensive history available in Spanish is the two-volume edited set, *Historia general de México* (Mexico City: El Colegio de México, 1977, 1981). A comprehensive English-language account of this period is Alan Knight's two volumes entitled *The Mexican Revolution* (London: Cambridge University Press, 1986).
3. See Peter Smith, "The Making of the Mexican Constitution," in William Aydelotte, ed., *The History of Parliamentary Behavior* (Princeton: Princeton University Press, 1977).
4. In the 1928-34 period there were three presidents who were largely controlled by Calles. There were Emilio Portes Gil, Pascual Ortiz Rubio, and Abelardo Rodríquez.
5. Stephen Haber, *Industry and Underdevelopment: The Industrialization of Mexico* (Stanford: Stanford University Press, 1988).
6. For an examination of the roles of competing coalitions (the bankers' alliance and the progressive Cárdenas coalition) in establishing the direction of the Mexican state, see Sylvia Maxfield, *Governing Capital: International Finance and Mexican Politics* (Ithaca: Cornell University Press, 1990).
7. "Cárdenas represented a coalition of forces that was progressive but not committed to destroying the foundations of Mexican capitalism," concluded Wayne Cornelius and Ann L. Craig, *The Mexican Political System in Transition* (San Diego: Center for U.S.-Mexican Studies, 1991), p. 13.
8. For an excellent analysis of this period, see Nora Hamilton, *The Limits of State Autonomy: Post-Revolutionary Mexico* (Princeton: Princeton University Press, 1982).
9. Wayne A. Cornelius and Ann L. Craig, *Politics in Mexico: An Introduction and Overview* (San Diego: Center for U.S.-Mexican Studies, 1988), p. 81.
10. In an interview with *Newsweek*, President Salinas addressed this issue of the relative pace of economic and political modernization. He acknowledged that a full-tilt movement toward democratization would have to await the success of his economic policies: "In some countries it has been demonstrated that because economic change has failed, the long-awaited hour of democratic change hasn't materialized. [We will] respond to the call of Mexicans for improved well-being. It's a matter of the two reforms going at different rhythms, but the priority is economics." "Reform at Two Different Rhythms," *Newsweek*, December 3, 1990.

11. John Bailey, *Governing Mexico: The Statecraft of Management* (New York: St. Martins Press, 1988), p. 3.
12. During the 1988 presidential campaign, the government's Imevisión television network ignored the opposition altogether, while the private Televisa network, which is run by prominent *priistas*, dedicated some 90 percent of its election coverage to Carlos Salinas. "La televisión, órgano de propaganda del PRI," *Proceso*, February 2, 1988.
13. See Nuri Pimentel González and Francisco Rueda Castillo, "Reforma del PRI: entre la apertura económica y el proteccionismo político," *El Cotidiano*, January-February 1991.

Structure of Government

1. Levy and Székely, *Paradoxes of Stability*, p. 29.
2. Amendments are incorporated directly into the constitution, without notation of the changes or the date when they were made. López Portillo, for example, had the national banking system inserted in the clause about government control of strategic institutions in the constitution, a phrase that was removed in 1990, to make way for the privatization of the nationalized banks.
3. The legislature meets from November 1 to December 31 and from April 15 to July 15. Since the 1970s, however, special sessions called by the president have become routine.
4. In 1977 the Chamber of Deputies was increased from 300 to 400 to accommodate opposition party deputies selected as a result of political reform, and another reform in 1986 increased the number of deputies to 500.
5. In 1987 the constitution was amended so that half of the Senate changes every three years.
6. The 50.7-percent figure ascribed to Salinas excludes the tally of annulled ballots and votes for unregistered presidential candidates. For a good description of the widespread election fraud in the 1988 election, see Andrew Reding, "Mexico at a Crossroads: The 1988 Election and Beyond," *World Policy Journal*, Fall 1988. One of the most convincing studies of the 1988 fraud is by José Berberán et al. *Radiografía del fraude: Análisis de los datos oficiales del 6 de julio* (Mexico City: Editorial Nuestro Tiempo, 1988).
7. PAN won its first governorship in 1989, after the government recognized the PRI election victory as fraudulent. Immediately following the 1991 midterm elections, the PRI candidate resigned, allowing a PAN leader to assume the role as interim governor. Vehement protests by the opposition parties (PAN, the PRD, and the PDM, joined together in the Frente Cívico Potosiano) in San Luis Potosí raised the possibility that PRI would release a third governorship to the opposition.
8. *Proceso*, September 10, 1990.
9. Perhaps the most comprehensive historical study of PRI is by Luis Javier Garrido, *El partido de la revolución institucionalizada: Medio siglo de poder político en México* (Mexico City: Siglo Veintiuno Editores, 1982).
10. Cornelius and Craig, *Politics in Mexico*, 1988, p. 16.
11. Miguel Angel Centeno, "The New Científicos: Technocratic Politics in Mexico, 1970-1990," Ph.D dissertation, Yale University, 1990.
12. Cornelius and Craig, *The Mexican Political System*, 1991, p. 28.
13. Andrew Reding, "Mexico: The Crumbling of the 'Perfect Dictatorship,'" *World Policy Journal*, Spring 1991, p. 256.
14. Cornelius and Craig, *The Mexican Political System*, 1991, p. 46.
15. Stephen D. Morris, "Salinas at the Brink: The Challenge from the Left and Political Reformism in Mexico," paper presented at Latin American Studies Association XVI International Congress, April 4-6, 1991, Washington, D.C. Morris describes this concentration of power as a noteworthy element in the reformist initiatives of Salinas.
16. Roderic Camp, quoted in *New York Times*, July 5, 1990.
17. Recent studies of the pendulum effect in Mexican policymaking include: Dale Story, "Policy Cycles in Mexican Politics," *Latin American Research Review* 3, 1985; and Steven Sanderson, "Presidential Succession and Political Rationality in Mexico," *World Politics* 35, April 1983. Cornelius and Craig, *The Politics in Mexico*, p. 20, place in the conservative category Calles, Alemán, Díaz Ordaz, and de la Madrid; the progressives or reformists, at least rhetorically, include Cárdenas, López Mateos, and Echeverría.

Avila Camacho, Ruiz Cortines, and López Portillo are described as transitional figures and consolidators of the status quo.

18. For a helpful discussion of Mexico's unusual political system, see Levy and Székely, *Paradoxes of Stability*, pp. 121-125.

19. Levy and Székely, *Paradoxes of Stability*, p. 54, citing Phillipe Schmitter, "Still the Century of Corporatism," in Frederick Pike and Thomas Stritch, eds., *The New Corporatism: Social-Political Structures in the Iberian World* (Notre Dame: Notre Dame University Press, 1974).

20. For more discussion of corporatism and its limits in Mexico, see: John Sloan, "The Mexican Variant of Corporatism," *Comparative Political Studies,* July 1981; Rose Spalding, "State Power and Its Limits: Corporatism in Mexico," *Inter-American Economic Affairs* 38, no. 4, 1985. Sergio Zermeño, in "Crisis, Neoliberalism, and Disorder," in Joe Foweraker and Ann L. Craig eds., *Popular Movements and Political Change in Mexico* (Boulder: Lynne Reinner, 1990), argues that Mexico is not a corporatist state at all, because there is no organic link between corporatist leaders and their bases. Instead, the idea of corporatism should be substituted by that of bureaupolitics.

21. The National Federation of Popular Organizations (CNOP), established in 1946 as a counterweight to the official peasant and labor organizations, has mainly served to represent those, like cab drivers, vendors, and bureaucrats, who depend on the PRI for their jobs, concessions, or business licenses. The CNOP was an outgrowth of the Federation of State Employee Unions (FSTSE), organized by President Cárdenas in 1937.

22. Cornelius and Craig, *Politics in Mexico,* 1988, pp. 20-23.

23. Levy and Székely, *Paradoxes of Stability*, p. 118.

24. For an excellent study of how *camarillas* and political elites in Mexico function, see Roderic A. Camp, "Camarillas in Mexican Politics: The Case of the Salinas Cabinet," *Mexican Studies/Estudios Mexicanos* 6, no.1, Winter 1990.

25. For an analysis of Mexico's social welfare system, see Peter Ward, *Welfare Politics in Mexico: Papering over the Cracks* (London: Allen & Unwin, 1986). Ward makes the point that since the revolution, land distribution has been the primary medium for political mediation, but with urbanization and the decrease of available land, the government is now winning loyalty through the distribution of urban plots to squatters and the allocation of property titles.

26. See: Merille S. Grindle, "Power, Expertise and the 'Técnico,'" *Journal of Politics* 36, May 1977; Roderic A. Camp, "The Political Technocrat and the Survival of the Political System," *Latin American Research Review* 20, no.1, 1985.

27. Levy and Székely, *Paradoxes of Stability*, pp. 119-120.

28. Cornelius and Craig, *Politics in Mexico,* 1988, p. 26.

29. Ibid.

Political Parties and Elections

1. What PRI apologists fail to note is that in Japan there is an opposition-run senate, and the political opposition in parliament has occasionally forced the president to resign—something inconceivable in Mexico.

2. One of the first major critiques within Mexico was by Pablo González Casanova, *La democracia en México* (Mexico City: ERA, 1965). Recent important works in English examining the political system in Mexico include: Judith Hellman, *Mexico in Crisis* (New York: Holmes and Meier, 1978); Roderic A. Camp ed., *Mexican Political Stability: The Next Five Years* (Boulder: Westview Press, 1986).

3. Enrique Krauze, *Democracia sin adjetivos* (Mexico City: Joaquín Mortiz/Planeta, 1986).

4. For a history of PRI reform movements, see: John Bailey, *Governing Mexico: The Statecraft of Management* (New York: St. Martin's Press, 1988); and Bailey, "Can the PRI Be Reformed?" in Gentleman et al. eds., *Mexican Politics in Transition* (Boulder: Westview Press, 1987).

5. Reding, "'Perfect Dictatorship,'" p. 259.

6. The governability clause increases the overrepresentation of the dominant party in the range of 35-60 percent of the vote. Under the terms of the 1989 reform, the distribution

of chamber seats is proportionate from 0-35 percent and from 60-70 percent. A first place party receives 251 of the 500 seats if it gets a minimum of 35 percent of the vote, and two seats for every percentage point over 35.

7. Reding, "'Perfect Dictatorship,'" p. 261.
8. *Informe Especial* (Mexico City), November 30, 1990, citing a phrase used by Jesús Reyes Heroles in 1979 to describe the role of opposition parties in Mexico.
9. Demetrio Sodi de la Tijera, "¿Por qué ganó el PRI?" *La Jornada*, August 23, 1991.
10. Among those mentioned as being part of the Democratic Current (the name used by Uno más Uno to describe this faction) were: Porfirio Muñoz Ledo, Ifigenia Martínez, Rodolfo González Guevara, Gonzalo Martínez, Cuauhtémoc Cárdenas, and Carlos Tello.
11. The phrase is from Juan Molinar Horcasitas, *El tiempo de la legitimidad: Elecciones, autoritarismo, y democracia en México* (Mexico City: Cal y Arena, 1991), p. 63., cited in Cornelius and Craig, *The Mexican Political System*, 1991, p. 73.
12. Lorenzo Meyer, "Personalidad dividida," *Excélsior*, December 24, 1982.
13. For an analysis of internal party reform prospects, see Lorenzo Meyer, "Democratization of the PRI: Mission Impossible," in Wayne A. Cornelius, Judith Gentleman, and Peter Smith eds., *Mexico's Alternative Political Futures* (La Jolla: Center for U.S.-Mexican Studies, 1989), pp. 26-36. González Guevara later left the PRI to form the Renovation Party and then joined the PRD as a precandidate for the 1991 elections.
14. *La Jornada*, June 2, 1990. In general, the MCD has accepted that the PRI leadership is willing to implement reforms, but as post-party congress events demonstrated, reforms in party statutes are not translated into effective change unless pushed forward by leading party militants.
15. Cornelius, Gentleman, and Smith eds., *Mexico's Alternative*, pp. 26-33.
16. Elaine Burns, "Mexico's PRI Wins Bid to Ensure That 'Change Continues,'" *Guardian*, September 18, 1991.
17. PRI won 70 percent percent of the vote in the 1989 state elections in all but two states: Baja California and Michoacán. In 1990 all state elections produced majorities of 70 percent or more for PRI.
18. Televised victory speech by Carlos Salinas, July 7, 1988.
19. PAN is a member of the International Democratic Union, an international confederation of conservative parties that was founded in 1983 with then Vice-President George Bush in attendance. Some of its members in Latin America and the Caribbean have received funding for travel and other expenses from the National Endowment for Democracy (NED), a U.S.-government-funded organization formed during the first Reagan administration.
20. Besides the Democratic Current, among the first members of the new political coalition that was to become the PRD were the Organization of the Revolutionary Left-Mass Tendency (OIR-LM), the Movement toward Socialism (MAS), and the Punto Crítico revolutionary organization. The Mexican Socialist Party merged into the PRD later in 1989.
21. Andrew Reding, "The Democratic Current: A New Era in Mexican Politics," *World Policy Journal*, Spring 1988, p. 325.
22. For a good overview of what is known as the "social left" in Mexico, see: *Informe Especial* (Mexico City), August 24, 1990; see also Foweraker and Craig eds., *Popular Movements*.
23. *Llamamiento al pueblo de México* (A PRD founding document), October 21, 1988.
24. Oscar Hinojosa, "El PRD: Contendiente en la disputa por la Revolución," *Proceso*, June 5, 1989.
25. "Denuncia Jorge Alcocer: Cuauhtémoc, intolerante y autoritario," *Proceso*, January 7, 1991.
26. Morris, *"Salinas at the Brink,"* p. 31.
27. Oscar Hinojosa, "El Frente Democrático Nacional no se rompe, pero tampoco se integra," *Proceso*, February 6, 1989.
28. Sources for these profiles of fringe parties include: Election news from SIPRO (Mexico City), August 14, 1991; and *Informe Especial* (Mexico City), June 1, 1990, August 24, 1990, and January 4, 1991.
29. *Sinarquismo* is a populist variation of social-christian philosophy that, among other things, advocates the disappearance of social classes by spreading property ownership throughout the entire society.

30. Analogy used by Louis Rubio in "Hacia el ethos democrático," *Vuelta* (Mexico City), November 1988.
31. For a clear expression of the views of President Salinas on the relative pace of economic and political modernization, see his interview in *New Perspectives Quarterly*, Winter 1991, pp. 4-10.
32. See Juan Tamayo, "Neoliberalism and *Neocardenismo,*" in Foweraker and Craig, *Popular Movements*, pp. 130-135. Tamayo offered the observation that starting in 1988 political crisis in Mexico "was deepened by the emergence of a vast social movement (*neocardenismo*) that extends well beyond the electoral arena but is constrained by the political system itself, which is unable to cede it a place."
33. See Paco Ignacio Taibo, "*Cardenismo* in Mexico," *The Nation*, December 17, 1990.
34. Quoted in Tamayo, in Foweraker and Craig, *Popular Movements*, p. 130.
35. Cited in Americas Watch, *Human Rights in Mexico: A Policy of Impunity*, (New York: Americas Watch, 1991) p. 41.
36. Jorge Alcocer, "Salinas y su Pronasol," *Proceso*, August 13, 1990.
37. Morris, "*Salinas at the Brink,*" p. 16.
38. Cuauhtémoc Cárdenas,"Misunderstanding Mexico," *Foreign Policy*, Spring 1989, p. 115.
39. Ibid.
40. See, for example: Ilán Bizberg, "El México neocorporativo," *Nexos* (Mexico City), December 1989; and Nuri Pimental González and Francisco Rueda Castillo, "Reforma del PRI," *El Cotidiano* (Mexico City), January-February 1991.
41. Elías Chávez, "Exhorta la Corriente Crítica a desconocer dirigentes," *Proceso* (Mexico City), February 26, 1990.
42. *Proceso* (Mexico City), September 10, 1990.
43. It was the opinion of the PRD's Cárdenas, as expressed in his article in *Foreign Policy*, Spring 1989, that "The Government hopes to manage the dilemma of separating political and economic reform by relying on U.S. financing and on Washington's political support. The regime is gambling that it can buy off the country's middle classes and neutralize popular discontent with the help of American resources."

Security Forces

1. Riding, *Distant Neighbors*, p. 91.
2. Although the army's corporatist place in the government ended during the Camacho presidency, army generals continued to serve in the largely symbolic role as party presidents until 1964, which served to ensure military support of the government and its official party.
3. Stephen J. Wager, "A Repoliticized Military," *Hemisphere*, Winter 1989.
4. The three main armed leftist groups were those led, respectively, by Genaro Vásquez Rojas, and Lucio Cabañas, and the urban terrorist group 23rd of September Communist League. The PROCUP-PDLP (Partido Revolucionario Obrero Clandestino Unión del Pueblo y el Partido de los Pobres) was the only armed leftist revolutionary organization active in the early 1990s.
5. There exist, in English, only two book-length studies of the Mexican military: the seminal work by Edwin Lieuwen, *Mexican Militarism: The Rise and Fall of the Revolutionary Army 1910-1940* (Albuquerque: University of New Mexico Press, 1968), and an enlightening collection of essays edited by David Ronfeldt, *The Modern Mexican Military: A Reassessment* (San Diego: Center for U.S.-Mexican Studies, 1984). Also see Roderic A. Camp, *Generals in the Palacio: The Military in Modern Mexico* (London: Oxford University Press, forthcoming 1992). Books in Spanish include: Jorge Alberto Lozoya, *El ejército mexicano* (Mexico City: El Colegio de México, 1970), and Guillermo Boils, *Los militares y la política en México* (Mexico City: El Caballito, 1975). The armed forces chapter in *Mexico: A Country Study* (Washington: Department of the Army, 1983) remains an important source for details on internal military functions. Two other important studies are José Luis Piñeyro, "The Modernization of the Mexican Armed Forces," in Augusto Varas, ed., *Democracy Under Siege: New Military Power in Latin America* (Westport: Greenwood Press, 1989); Franklin D. Margiotta, "Civilian Control

and the Mexican Military," in Claude E. Welch, ed., *Civilian Control of the Military: Theories and Cases from Developing Countries* (Albany: State University of New York Press, 1976); and Roderic A. Camp, "Mexican Military Leadership in Statistical Perspective since the 1930s," in James W. Wilkie and Peter Reich, eds., *Statistical Abstract on Latin America* No. 20 (Los Angeles: University of California, 1980).

6. Camp, *Generals in the Palacio.*
7. *World Military Expenditures and Arms Transfers 1989* (Washington: United States Arms Control and Disarmament Agency, 1990), p. 99.
8. Economist Intelligence Unit, *Mexico Country Profile 1990-91* (1991).
9. Phyllis Greene Walker, "The Modern Mexican Military," Unpublished thesis in International Affairs (American University, 1987), cited by Camp, *Generals in the Palacio.*
10. The 36 zonal garrisons in 1991 included 24 motorized calvary units, eight artillery regiments, and 80 infantry battalions. In addition, the army comprised two infantry brigades, a mechanized brigade (the presidential guard), three armed regiments, and an airborne brigade.
11. International Institute for Strategic Studies, *The Military Balance 1990-1991* (1990), p. 199.
12. Economist Intelligence Unit, *Mexico Country Profile* (1991), p. 93.
13. Ibid., p. 94.
14. James H. Street, "Can Mexico Break the Vicious Circle of 'Stop-Go' Policy? An Institutional Overview," *Southwest Journal of Business and Economics*, Spring 1990. According to Alan Riding, "it became government policy to corrupt the army. Senior officers were encouraged to enrich themselves with assorted business opportunities, sinecures, and favors, and even illicit activities, such as contraband, drug trafficking, and prostitution, were tolerated." Riding, *Distant Neighbors*, p. 94.
15. Ronfeldt, *The Modern Mexican* Military, p. 1.
16. Levy and Székely, *Paradoxes of Stability*, p. 53.
17. Wager, "A Repoliticized Military."
18. Ibid.
19. For the role of the military in elections see Lyle McAlister, *The Military in Latin American Socio-political Evolution: Four Case Studies* (Washington: Center for Research in Social Systems, 1970), p. 243.
20. See Larry Rohter, "Mexican President's Use of Army Draws Concern," *New York Times*, November 5, 1989.
21. Among the most sensational reports of human rights violations by the army was the 1989 testimony by a former Mexican soldier, who told the Canadian Immigration Board that he was part of a secret military unit that murdered at least sixty political dissidents in the late 1970s and early 1980s. At the time of these killings, the two Mexican officials in charge of internal security were Fernando Gutiérrez Barrios (interior minister as of 1991) and Miguel Nazar Haro (chief of police intelligence in Federal District). See Larry Rohter, "Former Mexican Soldier Describes Executions," *New York Times*, February 19, 1989.
22. In the early 1980s, "The army's manpower and other resources may be strained to the breaking point if it should have to mobilize in both the capital and provincial areas simultaneously"; Ronfeldt, *The Modern Mexican Military*, p. 12. Subsequent reports, however, indicated that the military had achieved this capacity.
23. Camp, *Generals in the Palacio.*
24. The first public discussion of the term was in Olga Pellicer de Brody, "La seguridad nacional de México: Preocupaciones nuevas y nociones tradicionales," in Carlos Tello and Clark Reynolds, eds., *Las relaciones México-Estados Unidos* (Mexico City: Fondo de Cultura Económica, 1981). Further examination is found in Ronfeldt, *The Modern Mexican* Military. For the most complete investigation of the subject, see Sergio Aguayo Quezada and Bruce Michael Bagley, eds., *En busca de la seguridad perdida: Aproximaciones a la seguridad nacional mexicana* (Mexico City: Siglo Veintiuno Editores, 1990).
25. The term made its first appearance, however, during the Echeverría administration, when the Ministry of the Interior (Secretaría de Gobernación) assigned the Dirección Federal

de Seguridad (DFS) to "analyze and report on those situations related to the security of the nation"; cited in Sergio Aguayo Quezada, "Usos, abusos y retos de la seguridad nacional, 1946-1990," in Aguayo and Bagley, eds., *En busca de la seguridad perdida*, p. 115. The DFS was disbanded in 1985 and replaced with the Dirección General de Investigación y Seguridad Nacional, which was transformed, in 1989, by presidential decree into the Centro de Investigación y Seguridad Nacional, which, among other functions, has the responsibility to "establish and operate an information and investigative system for the security of the country"; "Reglamento interior de la Secretaría de Gobernación," *Diario Official*, February 13, 1989.

26. The Reagan administration repeatedly attempted, eventually successfully, to have Mexico change its foreign policy regarding Central America, claiming that Mexico's own national security was threatened by the spread of revolution in Central America.

27. Roberto Vizcaíno, "La seguridad del país, fin primordial del Estado," *Proceso* (Mexico City), September 22, 1980.

28. Aguayo, "Usos, abusos y retos," pp. 116-117.

29. Ibid., and Luis Herrera-Lasso and Guadalupe González, "Balance y perspectivas en el uso del concepto de la seguridad nacional en el caso de México," in Aquayo and Bagley, *En busca de la seguridad perdida*, pp. 391-410.

30. The Ministry of the Interior, in late 1990, released a report from its Citizen Protection Services department that found that more than 70 percent of the population surveyed had no confidence in the police.

31. Americas Watch, *Human Rights in Mexico*, p. 6.

Human Rights

1. Ibid., p. 1.

2. PRD Human Rights Secretariat, "Saldo de la represión politica," December 31, 1990.

3. Americas Watch, *Human Rights in Mexico*; prepared statement of Ronna Weitz, Deputy Director, Washington Office; Amnesty International, Current Developments in Mexico, Hearing before the subcommittees on Human Rights and International Organizations of Western Hemisphere Affairs of the Committee on Foreign Affairs, House of Representatives, September 12, 1990.

4. Americas Watch, *Human Rights in Mexico*, p. 3, and *Proceso* (Mexico City), July 9, 1990, p. 22.

5. *Miami Herald*, September 13, 1990.

6. U.S. law prohibits military and economic assistance to countries that engage in "consistent patterns of gross violations of internationally recognized human rights"; Americas Watch, *Human Rights in Mexico*, p. 83.

7. Ibid., p. 1.

8. Americas Watch, *Prison Conditions in Mexico* (New York: Americas Watch, 1991), p. 1. The report did commend the Salinas administration for implementing social rehabilitation programs, an amnesty program, and an early release program, as well as for authorizing new prison construction.

9. Ibid., p. 9.

10. Víctor Clark Alfaro, "La tortura: una práctica institucionalizada en México," Informe del Centro Binacional de Derechos Humanos, 1991, p. 4.

11. Mariclaire Acosta, "The Democratization Process in Mexico: A Human Rights Issue," *Resist*, January 1991, p. 7.

12. Americas Watch, *Human Rights in Mexico*, p. 9; Victor Clark Alfaro, "La Tortura."

13. The most active organization in confronting the issue of political prisoners and the disappeared was founded by Rosario Ibarra de Piedra; it is known as EUREKA, or the Committee for the Defense of Prisoners, the Persecuted, Disappeared Persons, and Political Exiles. Ibarra de Piedra's fight is documented in Elena Poniatowska, Fuerte es el silencio.

14. Americas Watch, *Human Rights in Mexico*, p. 12.

15. Ibid., pp. 16-19.

16. Ibid., p. 17.

17. Ibid., pp. 35-39; Cindy Anders, "Freeing the Mexico 400," *Mexico Journal* 11, no. 23., pp. 16-20.
18. Americas Watch, *Human Rights in Mexico*, p. 35.
19. PRD Secretaría de Derechos Humanos; Amnesty International, *Mexico: Human Rights in Rural Areas* (London, 1986).
20. Jorge Luis Sierra, "'Yo soy él que anda moviendo todos los problemas': Testimonios de la violencia agraria," *Pueblo* (Mexico City), no. 149, April- May, 1990, p. 11.
21. Americas Watch, *Human Rights in Mexico*.
22. Ibid., p. 53.
23. Including the UN "Declaration against Torture and Other Inhuman, Degrading or Cruel Treatment" and the "Interamerican Convention to Prevent and Punish Torture" of the OAS.
24. John Ross, "Behind Bars," *Mexico Journal* 11, no. 47, September 4, 1989, p. 21.; Americas Watch, *Human Rights in Mexico*, p. 27.
25. As of the end of August, 1990, there were 938 foreigners, representing 44 nations, in Mexico's prisons. The United States was at the head of this list with 400 citizens, followed by Colombia, with 161; El Salvador, 87; Guatemala, 54; Belize, 30; Honduras, 28; Ecuador, 23; and Peru, 18. The remaining countries each had 15 or fewer citizens held. *Uno más Uno*, August 31, 1990.
26. *El Financiero*, May 6, 1991.
27. Ibid.; *La Jornada*, March 25, 1991, p. 13.
28. Although Mexican law requires that translators be provided for the trials of non-Spanish speakers, this requirement is rarely met in the cases of indigenous people; Americas Watch, *Human Rights in Mexico*, p. 28.
29. Sierra, "Testimonios."
30. To head the organization, Salinas appointed Jorge Carpizo, the former rector of the National Autonomous University of Mexico. Other important and highly respected members of the commission were Rosario Green, Jorge Madraxo Cuellar, and Luis Ortiz Monasterio. The commission is made up of Héctor Aguilar Camín, Guillermo Bonfil Batalla, Carlos Escandón Domínguez, Carlos Fuentes, Javier Gil Castañeda, Oscar González César, Carlos Payán Velver, César Sepúlveda, Rodolfo Stavenhagen and Salvador Valencia Carmona.
31. Americas Watch, *Unceasing Abuse: Human Rights in Mexico One Year after the Introduction of Reform* (September 1991).
32. Ignacio Ramírez, "Las recomendaciones de la comisión de derechos humanos no se acatan," *Proceso*, March 1, 1991, p.17. According to the PGR, it has complied with the majority of the 16 recommendations pertaining strictly to its office. However, the public accounting (published in all the major national dailies on May 17, 1991), revealed that none of the agents who had been accused of "abuse of authority" (in each case, torture resulting in death) had actually been arrested. All disappeared.
33. Following the earthquake, the tortured and mutilated bodies of several Colombian prisoners and a Colombian lawyer were found in the trunks of cars buried beneath the rubble of the PGR. A photographer from a French press agency was there, and the incident received wide international attention. See Acosta, "The Democratization Process," p. 5.

Foreign Policy

1. Standard works on Mexican foreign policy include: Jorge Castañeda, "Revolution and Foreign Policy," *Political Science Quarterly*, September 1963, which relates Mexican's foreign policy to the goals of the revolutionary period; Susan Kaufman Purcell, *Mexico-U.S. Relations* (New York: Academy of Political Science, 1981); Mario Ojeda, *Alcances y límites de la política exterior de México* (Mexico City: El Colegio de México, 1976); Josefina Zoraida Vázquez and Lorenzo Meyer, *The United States and Mexico* (Chicago: University of Chicago Press, 1985); and Humberto Garza, ed., *Fundamentos y prioridades de la política exterior de México* (Mexico City: El Colegio de México, 1986). More recently, see: Blanca Torres, ed., *Interdependencia: ¿Un enfoque útil para el*

análisis de las relaciones México-Estados Unidos (Mexico City: El Colegio de México, 1990); Rosario Green and Peter H. Smith, eds., *Foreign Policy in U.S.-Mexican Relations*, volume 5 of papers prepared for the Bilateral Commission on the Future of United States-Mexican Relations (La Jolla: Center for U.S.-Mexican Studies, 1989); Robert A. Pastor and Jorge G. Castañeda, *Limits to Friendship: The United States and Mexico* (New York: Vintage Books, 1989). The journal published by El Colegio de México, Foro Internacional, is also an excellent source.

2. Rosario Green and Peter H. Smith explain this emphasis on reason over force and international law as a reflection of "the conviction that respect for the international juridical order is the most effective means of defending the sovereignty and integrity of Mexico and other nations, especially the weaker countries of the world." See Smith and Green, "Foreign Policy in U.S.-Mexican Relations: Introduction," in Smith and Green, *Foreign Policy in U.S.-Mexico Relations.*

3. This principle of "universalism" was first proclaimed in 1930, in the Estrada Doctrine, named after Minister of Foreign Relations Genaro Estrada. The companion policy of nonintervention is known as the Carranza Doctrine.

4. Levy and Székely, *Paradoxes of Stability*, pp. 189-190.

5. See Rosario Green, "México: La política exterior del nuevo régimen," *Foro Internacional* (Mexico City) 18, no. 1, 1977.

6. Levy and Székely, *Paradoxes of Stability*, p. 191. Among the possible reasons for this new assertiveness were the decline of bipolar international dominance, the sense that domestic development required changes in the world order, a growing disenchantment with new U.S. protectionist policies, and a crisis of political legitimacy that could be eased by emphasizing independence from the United States. Also see Olga Pellicer de Brody, "Cambios recientes en la política exterior mexicana," *Foro Internacional* (Mexico City) 13, no. 2, 1972.

7. Levy and Székely, *Paradoxes of Stability*, p.191. Mexico's support for third world causes, as shown by its sponsorship of the Charter of Economic Rights, led U.S. officials to conclude that Mexico was openly hostile to the United States and that it was advocating a "tyranny of the majority" within the United Nations. See Smith and Green, *Foreign Policy*, pp. 10-11.

8. Smith and Green, *Foreign Policy*, p. 7.

9. Ibid.

10. Fernando Solana, "Preservar la soberanía primero: Objetivo de la política exterior," *México Internacional* (Mexico City), August-September 1989.

11. *Mexico Journal* (Mexico City), May 29, 1989.

12. *Proceso* (Mexico City), May 13, 1991 and May 20, 1991, citing a "confidential" cable from the U.S. embassy in Mexico City to Bernard Aronson, Assistant Secretary of State for Interamerican Affairs; author's translation.

13. *The Mexican Agenda* (Mexico City: Presidencia de la República, 1991), p. 19.

14. Ibid.

15. See, for example, articles in *Proceso* (Mexico City), March 4, 1991.

Part Two: The Economy

Restructuring and Modernization

1. Quoted in David Goldman, "A Revolution You Can Invest In," *Forbes*, July 9, 1990.

2. Economic liberalism is a doctrine that took form in the late 18th and early 19th centuries and that was given new attention by the neoclassical economists of the late 19th century. See James M. Cypher, *State and Capital in Mexico: Development Policy Since 1940* (Boulder: Westview Press, 1990) pp. 13-14.

3. Despite the pronounced neoliberal direction of government economic policy in the 1988-91 period, the political right and some members of the business community in Mexico, as well as foreign investors, worried that the quirky turns that have traditionally

characterized Mexican policymaking would once again turn the country back toward a more populist and nationalist approach, particularly if social unrest were to threaten political stability. Salinas was accused of "financial pragmatism," implying that neither he nor his cabinet was irrevocably committed to the economic opening and neoliberalism.

4. Rolando Cordera and Carlos Tello, *México: La disputa por la nación* (Mexico City: Siglo Veintiuno Editores, 1981).

5. For an examination of this conflict, see Sylvia Maxfield, *Governing Capital: International Finance and Mexican Politics* (Ithaca: Cornell University Press, 1990).

6. The concern of the *científicos* for facilitating capitalist accumulation did not rule out an important role for an interventionist state, especially in contracting foreign loans for infrastructure projects conducive to private investment.

7. The nationalist-populist state in Mexico has, according to James O'Connor, fulfilled both an accumulation and a legitimation function. It has facilitated private and public accumulation of wealth while at the same time legitimizing the economy to peasants and workers, through such measures as agrarian reforms and labor laws. See: James O'Connor, *The Fiscal Crisis of the States* (New York: St. Martin's, 1973) p. 6; and Cypher, *State and Capital in Mexico*, p. 11.

8. Gary Gereffi and Donald L. Wyman, eds., *Manufacturing Miracles: Paths of Industrialization in Latin America and East Asia* (Princeton: Princeton University Press, 1990) p. 308.

9. For a critique of the "debt-centered" explanation of the 1982 crisis see: Cypher, *State and Capital in Mexico*, pp. 155-64; and David Barkin, *Distorted Development: Mexico in the World Economy* (Boulder: Westview Press, 1990) pp. 57-75.

10. For a good summation of Mexico's debt crisis before the 1989-90 restructuring, see: Sidney Weintraub, *A Marriage of Convenience: Relations between Mexico and the United States* (New York: Oxford University Press, 1990) pp. 133-53.

11. Ibid., p. 136.

12. Holding most of this debt were the following six U.S. banks: Citibank, Bank of America, Chase Manhattan, Manufacturers Hanover Trust, Morgan Guaranty Trust, and Continental Illinois. See Roberto Gutiérrez, "El endeudamiento externo del sector privado de México," *Comercio Exterior* (Mexico City), April 1986.

13. Daniel Levy and Gabriel Székely, *Mexico: Paradoxes of Stability and Change* (Boulder: Westview Press, 1987) pp. 232-33.

14. Weintraub, *A Marriage of Convenience*, p.140, citing David Feliz and Juana Sánchez, "Capital Flight Aspect of the Latin American Debt Crisis," Working Paper no. 106, Department of Economics, Washington University, St. Louis, February 1987. Morgan Guaranty Trust estimated that capital flight totaled $53 billion in the 1975-81 period. Other more conservative estimates show capital flight equaling one-third to one-half of the increased debt during that period. In 1987 Banamex estimated capital flight to be $40 billion, while less conservative estimates that same year placed capital flight as high as $70 billion or even $84 billion. See: *El Cotidiano* (Mexico City), July-August 1988; and *Development Forum*, January-February 1990.

15. At the end of 1983 these nine industrial groups, in order of size, were Alfa, Visa, Mexicana de Cobre, Vitro, Tubos de Acero de México, Cydsa, Celanese Mexicana, Cervecería Moctezuma, and Asesores de Finanzas. Alfa had more than 10 percent of the private-sector debt. See Roberto Gutiérrez, "El endeudamiento externo," p. 339.

16. This agency is the Trust Fund for the Coverage of Foreign Exchange Risks (FICORCA).

17. Norman Bailey, "La inversión extranjera en México," in Riordan Roett, ed., *México y Estados Unidos: El manejo de la relación* (Mexico City: Siglo Veintiuno Editores, 1989) p. 59.

18. But this time around the government attempted to counter the inflationary effects by regulating the discount rate and controlling the destination of the debt-for-equity funds. The new program's most important feature, however, was that it targeted local, not foreign, investors.

19. There were actually two agreements, one with the Paris Club of governments and multilateral creditors signed in May 1989, and another more dramatic agreement with commercial creditors signed the following month.

20. State Department, *Economic Trends Report: Mexico* (Mexico City: August 1991).
21. *El Financiero*, January 8, 1991.
22. Shafique Islam, "It's a Bad Deal for the Model Debtor," *New York Times*, August 6, 1989.
23. Quoted in *El Financiero*, January 10, 1991.
24. The domestic burden in the 1990-91 period, however, was eased by decreased interest rates, which meant that despite nominal increases the overall burden was declining in real terms.
25. The following analysis of modernization comes largely from David Barkin, *Distorted Development*, pp. 77-97.
26. Ibid.
27. World Bank, *World Development Report 1980* (1980) p. 50.
28. See David Felix, "Income Distribution Trends in Mexico and the Kuznets Curve," in Sylvia Hewlett and Richard Weinert, eds., *Brazil and Mexico: Patterns in Late Development*(Philadelphia: Institute for the Study of Human Issues, 1982).
29. Weintraub, *A Marriage of Convenience*, p. 35, citing Salvador Kalifa-Assad, "Income Distribution in Mexico: A Reconsideration of the Distribution Problem," Ph.D. dissertation, Cornell University, 1977. Similar trends in income distribution are reported by the Secretaría de Agricultura y Recursos Hidráulicos, *Estadísticas básicas 1960-1986 para la planeación del desarrollo rural integral* (1986).
30. Consejo Consultivo del Pronasol, "El combate a la pobreza: Lineamientos programáticos," cited in *La Jornada*, September 1, 1990.
31. According to the Mexican government definition, those living in extreme poverty cannot afford to pay for 60 percent of their basic needs.
32. World Bank, *México, propuesta de estrategia para el desarrollo regional/rural en los estados en situación desventajosa* (1989), cited in *El Financiero*, October 26, 1989.
33. John Ross, "Hunger: The Grumbles Grow Louder," *Mexico Journal*, February 27, 1989, quoting Dr. Adolfo Chavez of the National Nutrition Institute in Mexico City.
34. *El Cotidiano* (Mexico City), no. 19, September-October 1987.
35. Study by the Economic Analysis Workshop (TAE) of the National Autonomous University, August 1991.
36. ECLA, *Notas sobre la economía y el desarrollo* (1990). Of the countries surveyed, only Ecuador and Peru had lower minimum wages.
37. Statement by the president of the National Minimum Wage Commission, April 29, 1990. A 1991 report by the National Institute of Statistics, Geography, and Information (INEGI) indicated that 45 percent of the labor force earned between one and two minimum wages, 28.4 percent earned between two and five minimum wages, and 11 percent earned less than the minimum, with the balance either earning no income or not specified. See: *El Financiero*, April 30, 1991; and *El Universal*, April 30, 1991.
38. INEGI, *Sistema de Cuentas Nacionales*.
39. Weintraub, *A Marriage of Convenience*, pp. 36, 214.
40. *El Financiero*, April 3, 1990.
41. For a fine overview of the problems of economic and population growth, see Lorenzo Moreno, "The Linkage between Population and Economic Growth in Mexico," *Latin American Research Review* 26, no. 3, 1991.
42. Leopoldo Solís, "Social Impact of the Economic Crisis," in Dwight Brothers and Adele Wick, eds., *Mexico's Search for a New Development Strategy* (Boulder: Westview Press, 1990), p. 46.
43. Article 3 of the constitution stipulates that "elementary education shall be compulsory" and "all education given by the state shall be free." Article 4 guarantees the right to health care and "the right to enjoy appropriate and decent housing." Furthermore the constitution requires that the state "organize a system of democratic planning and national development that imparts strength, dynamism, permanence, and equity to the growth of the economy."
44. IMF, *Government Finance Statistics Yearbook 1990* (1991).
45. "Los empresarios al rescate," *Expansión* (Mexico City), August 15, 1990.

46. Julio Moguel, "Programs de Solidaridad, ¿para quién?," *El Cotidiano* (Mexico City), November-December 1990, and "Pronasol: Solidaridad en entredicho," *Informe Especial* (Mexico City), November 9, 1990.

47. According to official figures, Pronasol operated with an estimated budget of $680 million in 1989, $950 million in 1990, and $1.7 billion in 1991. *Gaceta de Solidaridad*, April 15, 1991. As Dresser notes, the parallel institutional network created by Salinas keeps Pronasol out of the direct scrutiny by Congress. The pervasive presence of Pronasol suggested that the presidential program was relying on a larger pool of resources than presented in the Public Account. Dresser, ""Neopopulist Solutions," p. 16.

48. State Department, *Economic Trends Report: Mexico* (Mexico City: August 1991).

49. Office of the Presidency, *Solidaridad en México*.

50. Pascual Beltrán del Río, "Solidaridad, oxígeno para el PRI en el rescate de votos," *Proceso* (Mexico City), August 6, 1990.

51. Phrasing from Denise Dresser, "Neopopulist Solutions to Neoliberal Problems: Mexico's National Solidarity Program," Paper presented at XVIth Congress of Latin American Studies Association (Washington: April 4-6, 1991), p. 1.

52. Armando Bartra, "Modernidad, miseria extrema, y productores organizados," *El Cotidiano* (Mexico City), July-August 1990.

53. In Mexico the World Bank funds development programs that are directly incorporated into the solidarity campaign while AID contributes indirectly through its food aid program and social-service projects tied to the government.

54. Dresser, "Neopopulist Solutions," pp. 32, 35.

55. Ibid., p. 41.

56. Ibid., p. 51.

57. The above analysis is largely drawn from Dresser's excellent study of Pronasol.

58. The Private-Sector Center for Economic Studies (CEESP) in Mexico City reports that the informal sector's activity adds up to 25-33 percent of the GDP. For other estimates, see: *El Financiero*, April 3, 1990; and Louis Uchitelle, "Untaxed Vendors Thrive in Mexico City," *New York Times*, August 27, 1990.

59. Study by Banco Nacional, cited in William Neuman, "Mexico's Informal Sector Gains Political Clout," *Business Latin America*, February 25, 1991.

60. See Raúl Monge and Fernando Ortega, "El comercio informal explosivo," *Proceso* (Mexico City), December 31, 1990.

61. Neuman, "Mexico's Informal Sector."

62. Private investment was equivalent to 18.9 percent of the GDP in 1990, compared with 26.5 percent in 1981.

63. In 1983 private-sector investment accounted for 60.5 percent of total investment, increasing to 72.1 percent in 1990. See *El Financiero*, January 8, 1991.

64. Jeffery T. Brannon et al., "An Evaluation of Mexican Policy toward Foreign Direct Investment," *Southwest Journal of Business and Economics*, Spring 1990.

65. As of March 1991 the government reported $7 billion in new direct foreign investment during the course of Salinas's term.

66. In 1987 Mexico devoted just 0.60 percent of its GDP to research and technology, more than half of which was to pay for imported technology. In contrast Korea, whose export economy is a model for the restructured Mexico, devoted 2 percent. James Cypher, in *State and Capital in Mexico*, pp. 7-9, observed that a high share of Mexico's expenditures on research and technology has been allocated to a "small army of clerks, functionaries, and other 'unproductive' personnel, especially when compared with more developed nations."

67. Lindajoy Fenley, "Keeping Tabs on the Commercial Opening," *Business Mexico*, June 1990.

68. Juanita Darling, "Consumer Goods Imports," *Los Angeles Times*, May 27, 1990.

69. "Terms of trade" refers to the relative position of the weighted average price of main exports versus the weighted average of imports.

70. The United Nation's Economic Commission for Latin America (ECLA) issued a report in late 1990 stating that between 1981 and 1988 Mexico suffered a 33.1-percent deterioration in its commercial standing with respect to terms of trade. Report cited in *El Financiero*, January 9, 1991.

71. U.S.-Mexico trade figures for 1990 from *Comercio Exterior* (Mexico City), April 1991. Other Western Hemisphere nations absorb 8 percent of Mexico's exports and account for nearly 7 percent of its imports. The member countries of the European Community purchase 13 percent of Mexico's exports and account for nearly 19 percent of its imports.

72. This was the case after the 1974 and 1982 recessions in the United States; the effects of the 1990-91 recession were still not clear at the time of writing.

73. In 1990 Mexico's top five trading partners, other than the United States, accounted for only 16 percent of the country's trade.

74. During the 1970s, instead of participating in the multilateralism sponsored by the developed nations—embodied, for instance, in GATT trading standards—Mexico placed its allegiances with the United Nations Conference on Trade and Development (UNCTAD) and the Group of 77. In contrast to GATT's commitment to free trade and reciprocity, both UNCTAD and the Group of 77 called for trading concessions on the part of the industrialized countries (North) in recognition of the unequal status of the poorer nations (South). See Gustavo del Castillo, "Política exterior y seguridad nacional en México," *Frontera Norte* (Tijuana), January-June 1989.

75. Between 1977 and 1982 Mexico also regarded Washington's pressure to join GATT as a ploy for the United States to gain greater access to Mexican oil. In the end, however, oil was excluded from Mexico's 1986 GATT accord.

76. Tariff barriers were lowered from 100 percent in some cases to a maximum of 20 percent, although the trade-weighted average tariff in 1990 was about 10 percent—not too different from Canada's level of protection when it signed the Free Trade Agreement (FTA) with the United States. Quotas and licenses have been removed in all but a few sectors. For an excellent discussion of GATT and U.S. FTA initiatives, see Sidney Weintraub, "Regionalism and the GATT: The North American Initiative," *SAIS Review*, Winter-Spring 1991.

77. United States International Trade Commission, *Review of Trade and Investment Liberalization Measures by Mexico and Prospects for Future United States-Mexico Relations* (Washington, 1990).

78. It was Mexico's hope that it could remain a "free rider" in having good access to the U.S. market and receiving favorable treatment because of its special status as a developing nation. In this arrangement it would attempt to defend its access to the U.S. market through specific bilateral accords while not risking loss of ownership of its strategic resources (mostly oil). This "free rider" argument was basically the same one used against joining GATT. See Sidney Weintraub, "The North American Free Trade Debate," *The Washington Quarterly* 13, no. 14, 1990.

79. Also driving Mexico toward an FTA were the escalating trade conflicts with the United States, following Mexico's initial decision not to join GATT. According to Weintraub, an "open season" was declared on Mexican imports. Weintraub also makes the interesting observation that Mexico's decision to distance itself from GATT and multilateralism in 1980 eventually led to increased bilateralism with the United States. See Weintraub, *A Marriage of Convenience*, p. 89.

80. According to one survey, the Mexican public stood strongly behind the government's effort to enter into a free trade agreement. The survey found that 80 percent of Mexicans were in favor of the trilateral agreement without conditions, 40 percent thought that Mexico should have much closer relations with Canada and the United States, and two-thirds were in favor of forming a single North American country if it would mean an improved standard of living. See *Este País* (Mexico City), April 1991.

81. In November 1987 Mexico and the United States signed a framework agreement on trade and investment. The agreement, the first of its type between the two countries, instituted a mechanism for addressing disputes and established an action agenda for future consultations on textiles, agriculture, steel, investment, technology transfer, protection of intellectual property, electronics, and the service sector. As a result of the 1987 agreement, the two countries signed subsequent accords for liberalized trade in steel, textiles, alcoholic beverages, and other items. In October 1989 another broad

trade and investment agreement was signed, paving the way for a new series of bilateral agreements on specific sectors.

82. Bruce Campbell, "Beggar Thy Neighbor," *NACLA Report on the Americas*, May 1991, p. 22.

83. To remain consistent with GATT rules, the FTA will have to meet two conditions. Virtually all trade restrictions between the parties to the accord will need to be removed, and any duties and restrictions placed against non-bloc countries must not be more restrictive than before the bloc was formed. See Lenore Sek, "Mexico-U.S. Free-Trade Agreement?" *CRS Issue Brief*, November 7, 1990.

84. Other Mexican exports frequently cited as being discriminated against by nontariff barriers are potatoes, cement, tuna, mangos, poultry, and beef.

85. Lawrence Kootnicoff, "Coming Together," *Business Mexico*, March 1991. To grant Mexico special status would not be unprecedented. When Spain and Portugal joined the European Community in 1986, they benefited from a phase-in period and special compensation arrangements.

86. Campbell, "Beggar Thy Neighbor," p. 26.

87. Kurt Unger, *Mexican Manufactured Exports and U.S. Transnational Corporations: Industrial Structuring Strategies, Intrafirm Trade, and New Elements of Comparative Advantage* (Washington: Commission for the Study of International Migration and Cooperative Economic Development, 1990) p. 12.

88. The Mexican government introduced in 1991 a comprehensive bill for the protection of intellectual property, including biotechnology, computer software, literary works, and industrial design that should satisfy most of Washington's demands in this area.

89. *Business Week*, November 12, 1990.

90. Edward P. Neufield, "Three-Way Trade Gains," *Journal of Commerce*, February 14, 1991. Neufield, executive vice-president of the Royal Bank of Canada, said, "The Mexican relationship would give Canadian companies the option of continuing labor-intensive operations there."

91. Cited in Campbell, "Beggar Thy Neighbor," p. 28.

92. Cuauhtémoc Cárdenas, "The Continental Development and Trade Initiative," speech delivered in New York, February 8, 1991.

93. "Platform of the Mexican Action Network on Free Trade," *The Other Side of Mexico*, March-April 1991.

94. Oscar Humberto Vera Ferrer, "The Political Economy of Privatization in Mexico," in William Glade, ed., *Privatization of Public Enterprises in Latin America* (San Diego: Institute of the Americas, 1990) p. 37.

95. Banamex, "Privatization: Goals and Achievements," *Review of the Economic Situation*, June 1991, p. 232.

96. Vera Ferrer, "Political Economy of Privatization," p. 52.

97. Ibid. Also see Oscar Humberto Vera Ferrer, "La privatización en México: Causas y alcanzes," in *Privatización: El inevitable sendero del gigante decreciente* (Mexico City: Centro de Estudios en Economía y Educación, 1988).

98. Estimates of the number of state enterprises vary widely. One of the main reasons for the different figures cited in journalistic accounts of the disincorporation process is that there is no single official registry, and different state agencies report different numbers. In addition the government often includes among companies that have been sold or transferred those that are only in the process of being disincorporated. When calculating the number of state enterprises, observers commonly refer to de la Madrid's inaugural address, in which he cited 1,155 parastatals. Of these the state had majority control in 759 and a minority interest in 75, along with 103 decentralized institutions and 223 *fideicomisos*, or special trust funds. See Ben Schneider, "Party for Sale: Privatization and State Strength in Brazil and Mexico," *Journal of Interamerican Studies and World Affairs*, Winter 1988-89, p. 102.

99. Vera Ferrer, "The Political Economy of Privatization," p. 53.

100. María Amparo Casar and Wilson Peres, *El estado empresario en México: Agotamiento o renovación* (Mexico City: Siglo Veintiuno Editores, 1988) p. 31.

101. Barbara Belejack, "Chipping Away at Government Ownership," *Business Mexico*, March 1990. Many businesses were also acquired as a result of the 1982 bank nationalization, when the state became the owner of the sundry bank holdings.
102. Secretaría de Programación y Presupuesto, *Cuentas de producción del sector público* (1984); "Las finanzas públicas: 1982-1988," *CIEN 100* (Mexico City) 9, no.2., September 1988.
103. Vera Ferrer, "The Political Economy of Privatization," pp. 41-42.
104. The sale of public entities to the private sector is only one part of the disincorporation process. The program has also included the transfer of ownership title to a state or local government, the extinction or liquidation of bankrupt companies (whose components are then generally purchased by private businesses), and the disappearance of companies through merger with other parastatals.
105. Cited in *U.S. News & World Report*, October 16, 1989.
106. From a 1990 speech delivered in Switzerland, cited in *Latin America Weekly Report*, March 7, 1991.
107. *Plan nacional de desarrollo 1989-1994* (Mexico City: 1989).
108. Vera Ferrer, "The Political Economy of Privatization," pp. 56-57.
109. The amendment to Article 28 of the national constitution that authorized the nationalization of the country's banks actually gave the state control over a multiple financial system that integrated banking, real estate, brokerage services, and insurance. During the de la Madrid *sexenio* most of the nonbanking functions were returned to their former owners.
110. The government's majority interest in Telmex was sold for $1.8 billion in 1990 to a consortium composed of Grupo Carso, Southwestern Bell, and France Radio et Cable. The reprivatization of the banks could bring the government as much as $8.7 billion in new revenues, although a more conservative estimate put the value of the national banking system at $6 billion. Besides this injection of funds, the sale will erase the government's responsibility for more than $5 billion in foreign debt held by these banks.
111. Among the most important companies privatized were Aeroméxico, Teléfonos de México, Mexicana de Aviación, Compañía Minera de Cananea, Constructora Nacional de Carros de Ferrocarril, Diesel Nacional, Compañía de Manufacturas Metálicas Pesadas, Grupo Industrial NKS, Turalmex, Turbinas y Equipos Industriales, and Productora Mexicana de Tubería. Besides the banking system, other major firms up for sale included Instituto Mexicano de Televisión (a partial sell-off of sixty stations), the iron and steel conglomerate Sidermex (includes AHMSA and SIRCARTSA), the Tabamex tobacco commercialization corporation, the Inmecafe coffee company, the Asemex insurance conglomerate, and the Fertimex fertilizer company.
112. According to one report, between 1983 and 1991 the federal government closed down 48 percent of its parastatals, sold 32 percent to the private sector, merged 9 percent with existing companies, cut all federal subsidies to 7 percent, and transferred 3 percent to the state governments. See *El Financiero*, September 6, 1991.
113. Prepared by the Disincorporation Unit for Parastate Entities of the Ministry of Finance and Public Credit, *El proceso de enajenación de entidades paraestatales* (1991).
114. *El Financiero*, May 7, 1991.
115. Other areas defined as "strategic" by the constitution are the national mint, post office, telecommunications, central banking, basic petrochemicals, radioactive minerals, and nuclear energy. In privatizing Telmex the government ostensibly violated the constitution, but to ward off critics it retained a minority share and declared its right to retain a "normative rectorship" over telecommunications. The same stipulation was utilized in outlining the terms of sale of the national banks.
116. The 11 strategic and decentralized industries are: Compañia de Luz y Fuerza del Centro, Comisión Federal de Electricidad, Ferrocarriles Nacionales de México, Servicio Postal Mexicano, Petróleos Mexicanos, Banco de México, Casa de Moneda de México, Instituto de Investigaciones Eléctricas, Instituto Mexicano de Petróleo, Instituto Nacional de Investigaciones Nucleares, and Telégrafos Nacionales.

117. The four largest public-sector corporations were Pemex, the CFE, Sidermex, and Fertimex, the last two of which are slated for privatization by 1991. See *El Financiero*, February 4, 1991.
118. Schneider, "Party for Sale," p. 104.
119. *El Financiero*, May 7, 1990, citing a 1990 Concamin report, "Gasto público destinado a la inversión." According to Concamin, public-sector expenditures for investment dropped from 5.7 percent to 2.9 percent of the GDP between 1983 and 1989.
120. Figures from the Secretaría de Programación y Presupuesto, as cited in *El Financiero*, October 16, 1990.
121. *El Financiero*, May 14, 1991.
122. *El Financiero*, March 22, 1991.
123. For a good summary and analysis of privatization from a rightwing perspective, see "Privatization in Mexico: Good But Not Enough," *The Heritage Foundation Backgrounder*, November 15, 1990. Information for the report came largely from the Center for Free Enterprise Research (CISLE) in Mexico.
124. Among the parastatals bought in whole or in part by the country's major investor groups are: Grupo Diesel Nacional-DINA (bought by Grupo G, including the Consorcio Arago of Guadalajara); Telmex (Grupo Carso); Mexicana de Cobre and Compañia Minera Cananea (Jorge Larrea and STMMS); Aserradores Técnicos Nacionales, Envases y Empaques Nacionales, Industrias Forestales Integrales (Grupo Durango); eight industrial and domestic appliance manufacturers, including Aceros Esmaltados (Grupo Vitro); and 13 companies, most of which are in the sugar industry (Grupo Xabre).
125. José Gasca Zamora, "Sources for the Study of Privatized Mexican State-Run Industries, 1983-1988"; and Noel Cruz Serrano, "Privatization Enhances Monopoly and Oligopoly in Mexican Market," *El Financiero*, May 7, 1991.
126. *El Financiero*, May 7, 1991.
127. It has been estimated that prior to the bank nationalization, in 1981, just nine companies controlled 85 percent of the banking system and that just two—Bancomer and Banamex—controlled approximately 50 percent of the system's capital and profits. See Angel Tello, *La nacionalización de la banca en México* (Mexico City: Siglo Veintiuno Editores, 1984).
128. For a good summary of bank privatization, see articles in *Business Mexico*, April 1991.
129. Cited in Roberto Salinas, "Pushing Privatization," *Business Mexico*, June 1990.
130. By May 1991 only 12 of the 138 state enterprises privatized during the Salinas administration were sold to the "social sector," mainly unions and producers organizations. *Business Mexico*, June 1991.
131. Among the major privatization deals involving foreign investors have been Mexicana Airlines (bought in part by Chase Manhattan Bank), Conasupo (Unilever), Dina (Cummins), and Telmex (Southwestern Bell and France Radio et Cable).
132. A 1991 report by the U.S. International Trade Commission called for an open and fully competitive financial system in Mexico, asserting that total liberalization of the financial system would result in the return of flight capital and more foreign investment. It also acknowledged that this would probably cause the failure of certain banks, insurance companies, and stock-brokerage firms. See *El Financiero*, January 30, 1991.
133. Cypher, *State and Capital in Mexico*, p. 152.
134. In his study of Mexico's industrial parastatal firms, Benito Rey Romay, a former Nafinsa official, observed that "state firms . . . never engage in profit making for their own purposes; rather they transfer such profits to the private sector, allowing them to have levels of profitability in the last decade that are without precedent." See Benito Rey Romay, *La ofensiva empresarial contra la intervención del estado* (Mexico City: Siglo Veintiuno Editores, 1984) p. 88.
135. Ibid., p. 148.
136. Statement by Michel Camdessus, managing director of the IMF, at the Seminar on the Mexican Debt Agreement, January 25, 1990, Washington, DC.
137. Between 1985 and 1990 the value of exports increased 22 percent while the value of imports increased 123 percent. The trade balance for 1990 was a negative $2.9 billion. Preliminary figures from Banco de México.

138. Economist Intelligence Unit, *Mexico Country Profile 1990-91* (1991) pp. 25-26.
139. Comment by Jorge Castañeda in *Proceso*, May 21, 1990.

Structure of the Economy

1. Sidney Weintraub, *Transforming the Mexican Economy: The Salinas Sexenio* (Washington: National Planning Association, 1990), pp. 64-65.
2. Banamex, "General Population and Housing Census 1990," *Review of the Economic Situation in Mexico*, September 1990.
3. *El Financiero*, September 9 and 10, 1991.
4. For an examination of the changing patterns of industrialization in Mexico, see Michel Husson, "Maquiladorización de la industria mexicana," *El Cotidiano* (Mexico City), May-June 1991.
5. Figures from SECOFI, August 1991.
6. The world's five largest oil companies are: 1) Aramco, 2) Royal/Dutch Shell, 3) Exxon, 4) Pemex, and 5) Petróleos de Venezuela. Of the 65 largest oil companies, 29 are state-owned. *Petroleum Energy Intelligence Weekly*, March 17, 1991.
7. In 1990 Pemex paid the federal government $11.6 billion in taxes and fees, corresponding to 30 percent of total federal revenue and equal to 63 percent of the government's operational budget. *El Financiero*, March 15, 1991. According to Pemex's own *Memoria de labores 1990* (Mexico City, March 1991), the agency accounted for 33 percent of the government's tax revenues in 1990.
8. In 1990 oil exports accounted for 37.7 percent of total exports, up about four percentage points from the previous year largely because of the windfall profits resulting from the Persian Gulf war.
9. Between 1982 and 1990, exploration and development operations dropped 75 percent, and as a consequence production fell from 3 million barrels daily in 1982 to about 2.5 million currently. Pemex, *Informe* 43 (Mexico City), 1991.
10. Luis Angeles, "El futuro de la industria petrolera mexicana," in Pablo González Casanova, ed., *México hacia el 2000: Desafíos* (Caracas: Nueva Sociedad, 1989), p. 98. Unless new reserves are discovered and developed, annual crude oil production is projected to drop to 1.6 million barrels per day (bpd) by 2005, down from the current production of 2.5 million bpd. Some project that Mexico will become a net petroleum importer as early as 1997.
11. Quoted in Damian Fraser, "Mexican Oil Reforms Still Have a Long Way to Go," *Financial Times*, May 31, 1991.
12. Gabriel Székely, "Dilemmas of Export Diversification in a Developing Economy: Mexican Oil in the 1980s," *World Development* 17, no. 11, 1989, p. 1783.
13. This modernization process is well under way. Pemex has formed a new worldwide marketing arm, Petróleos Mexicanos Internacionales, which is negotiating strategic alliances with foreign governments and companies. Pemex has entered joint ventures for refining operations overseas and has purchased new distribution channels in the United States and Europe. Within Mexico, Japanese investors have been particularly active in developing new refining and production operations. See Juanita Darling, "Mexico's Giant Takes Big Steps into a New Era," *Los Angeles Times*, July 29, 1990.
14. Fernando Ortega Pizarro, "Se puso en operación Laguna Verde," *Proceso* (Mexico City), August 20, 1990.
15. Before the major discoveries of the 1970s, proven hydrocarbon reserves totaled only 5.7 billion barrels. Known reserves peaked in 1983 at 72.5 billion barrels and have since been declining. Of the approximately 65 billion barrels in current hydrocarbon reserves, 44.5 billion are crude oil reserves, 6.7 billion are condensates, and 14.2 billion are associated gas. Pemex, *Memoria de labores 1990* (Mexico City, March 1991). Reserve estimates are, however, the subject of much debate. A Congressional Research Service report, "Mexican Oil Less Than Meets the Eye" (Washington), July 3, 1991, concluded that true oil reserves were 26.4 billion barrels. A 1990 study by UNAM professor Carlos Castillo Tejero also indicated that true proven reserves were less than 60 percent of what Pemex claimed. Cited in *El Financiero*, November 14, 1990. In

mid-1991 Pemex claimed that oil discoveries in the Bay of Campeche and in Chiapas could boost proven reserves by a third. With extensive exploration, something that Pemex has been unable to do on its own, Mexico may prove to be the proprietor of a vast sea of oil, as much as or more than the Saudi Arabian reserves, according to the most optimistic projections.

16. In its 1990-94 energy program, the government predicted that exports will fall to just over 1 million bpd, down from the 1.25 million bpd of recent years.

17. *Mexico Update* (Mexico City), February 15, 1991. In 1990, Campeche Sound, located in the Gulf of Mexico, accounted for 71 percent of total production, and the Mesozoico Chiapas-Tabasco field accounted for 22 percent. The Mexican Association of Petroleum Engineers estimates that the Campeche Sound has an undiscovered potential of 26 billion barrels.

18. Quoted in Darling, "Mexico's Giant Takes Big Steps."

19. Mexico is the fourth largest oil supplier to the United States, following Saudi Arabia, Canada, and Venezuela.

20. According to Pemex, Mexico exported crude oil to 22 countries in 1990, with the United States receiving 56.2 percent of total exports, followed by Spain (16.7 percent), Japan (11.4 percent), France (4.4 percent), and Israel (2.3 percent). Pemex, *Memoria de labores 1990* (Mexico City, March 1991). Because of different pricing and accounting practices, there exist differences in export estimates. Other official figures show the United States receiving 58.2 percent of total 1990 exports, up from 57 percent in 1989. Pemex has also reported that the United States received 60.5 percent of Mexico's exports in 1990. Agence France Presse, January 14, 1991, reporting statements of Pemex chairman Francisco Rojas. See also: *El Financiero*, February 26, 1991.

21. For a valuable examination of the historical links between oil and foreign policy in Mexico, see: George Grayson, *Oil and Mexican Foreign Policy* (Pittsburgh: University of Pittsburgh Press, 1988).

22. *Business Latin America*, March 18, 1991.

23. Two of these new holding companies are Petróleos Mexicanos Internacionales, called Grupo PMI, and Mexpetrol. Since 1989 Grupo PMI, in which Pemex has a 35-percent stake, has handled crude oil marketing and trade in refined products and petrochemicals. For more information see Daniel Molina, "Pemex: La reprivatización de facto," *El Cotidiano* (Mexico City), November-December 1989.

24. Victoria Novelo, "Las fuentes de poder de la dirigencia sindical en Pemex," *El Cotidiano* (Mexico City), March-April 1989.

25. *El Financiero*, February 5, 1991. See U.S. General Accounting Office (GAO), *U.S.-Mexico Energy: The U.S. Reaction to Recent Reforms in Mexico's Petrochemical Industry* (Washington, 1991). The GAO noted that according to the U.S. Department of Commerce the Mexican government could reduce its monopoly list of 20 basic chemicals by 50 percent or more and still maintain its control over major raw materials in the petrochemical industry. Following the publication of the report, Mexico reduced this list to 19 basic petrochemicals.

26. According to analyst Adolfo Aguilar Zínser, "What remains to be defined is not whether oil will be negotiated but the form of those negotiations.... In any case, without oil, the society that Carlos Salinas de Gortari wants to create with the free trade agreement with the United States would be simply impossible." *El Financiero*, February 21, 1991.

27. For an interesting look at the different ways the state oil companies in Mexico and Venezuela are approaching privatization, see Kimm Fuad, "More in Mexico, Venezuela than Meets the Eye," *Hemisphere*, March 1991.

28. National Institute for Statistics, Geography, and Information (INEGI), *Mexico: Economic and Social Information* (Mexico City: 1990), pp. 56-59.

29. The 1990 petrochemical deficit was $282 million.

30. U.S. International Trade Commission (ITC), *The Likely Impact on the United States of a Free Trade Agreement with Mexico* (Washington, 1991), p. xiv.

31. In 1985, 70 "basic" petrochemicals were reserved for exclusive production by Pemex. By 1991 this number had been cut to 19. At the same time, the number of "secondary" petrochemical products was reduced to 66 from the previous 700 or more, thus freeing

the remainder from all government controls over production. George Baker, "Deregulate or Else," *Business Mexico*, April 1991.

32. Good sources on U.S. tariff regulations are: ITC, *The Use and Economic Impact of TSUS Items 806.30 and 807.00* (Washington, 1988); and Joseph Grunwald and Kenneth Flamm, *The Global Factory: Foreign Assembly in International Trade* (Washington: The Brookings Institution, 1985), pp. 34-37.

33. Labor costs account for more than 50 percent of this "value-added," with overhead costs and non-U.S. materials constituting the balance of the value added. As labor costs have dropped because of the *peso* devaluation so has the value-added or taxable portion of the finished product, thereby making *maquila* manufacturing even more profitable.

34. The term "*maquiladora*" or "*maquila*" originates from the verb "*maquilar*," which refers to the practice of millers to collect a portion of the grain which they grind for customers.

35. In December 1989, 78 percent of the country's 1,795 registered maquilas were located in the U.S.-Mexico border zone. Committee for the Promotion of Investment in Mexico, *An Overview of the Maquiladora Industry in Mexico* (January 1990).

36. Banamex, "In-Bond Industry," *Review of the Economic Situation in Mexico*, September 1990.

37. Joseph Grunwald, "Opportunity Missed: Mexico and Maquiladoras," *The Brookings Review*, Winter 1990-91.

38. Value-added by activity for 1989 were the following: electric and electronic goods (41.0 percent), transport equipment (24.0 percent), wood and metal furniture (5.1 percent), food processing (1 percent), chemicals (0.7 percent), equipment and tools (1.5 percent), and all other activities (20.7 percent). Employment largely follows this same proportional breakdown, with the high-tech electric and electronics sector providing 38 percent of *maquila* employment and the low-tech textiles and apparel sector accounting for 9 percent of total employment. Committee for the Promotion of Investment in Mexico, *An Overview of the Maquiladora Industry in Mexico* (January 1990).

39. "Las maquiladoras más importantes de México," *Expansión* (Mexico City), October 24, 1990.

40. Eilwyn R. Stoddard, *Maquila Assembly Plants in Northern Mexico* (El Paso: University of Texas, 1987), p. 46.

41. Sandy Tolan, "The Border Boom: Hope and Heartbreak," *New York Times*, July 1, 1990.

42. David Bacon, "Maquiladoras Menace Workers on Both Sides of the Border," *Political Affairs*, May 1988, p. 21.

43. University of Lowell Work Environment Program, *Back to the Future: Sweatshop Conditions on the Mexico-U.S. Border* (Lowell, 1991).

44. David Ehrenthal and Joseph Newman, "Explaining Mexico's *Maquila* Boom," *SAIS Review*, Winter-Spring 1988, p. 192.

45. Thomas Rohan, "Mexico Border Boom," *Industry Week*, August 15, 1988.

46. Stoddard, *Maquila Assembly Plants*, p. 31.

47. Joseph Grunwald blames both the Mexican government and U.S. investors for this failure to expand the linkages with the Mexican economy. The Mexican government has until recently insisted that the *maquiladora* sector remain a restricted enclave, and U.S. companies have been "hesitant to share ownership of plants and vital technology with Mexican firms." He points to the industrialization process followed by the "four tigers" (Hong Kong, Singapore, South Korea, and Taiwan). "By making shrewd use of assembly plants, the 'four tigers' moved up the ladder of technology and upgraded their labor force, allowing initially abysmally low wages to increase as technology rose through education, training, and improved job skills." To follow that model, Grunwald advocates the application of temporary national content agreements that would require foreign companies to purchase a minimum proportion of inputs from a Mexican supplier network. Grunwald, "Opportunity Missed."

48. *Mexico Update* (Mexico City), March 15, 1990. Tax codes now exempt domestic sales to *maquiladoras* from the 15-percent sales tax.

49. Ibid.

50. William Neuman, "Mexico's *Maquilas* Foresee Limited Effect of FTA," *Business Latin America*, January 2, 1991. In the case of Sanyo, 80 percent of its supplies came from Japan in the early 1980s while currently 80 percent comes from the United States.

51. For an excellent study of the transnationalization of the automotive industry and the role of the Mexican state in this process, see Douglas C. Bennett and Kenneth E. Sharpe, *Transnational Corporations versus the State: The Political Economy of the Mexican Auto Industry* (Princeton: Princeton University Press, 1985).

52. General Motors established its first *maquiladora* in 1978, with Ford and Chrysler close on its heels. By 1990 there were more than 160 in-bond plants assembling automobile parts.

53. Pablo Wong-González, "International Integration and Locational Change in Mexico's Motor Industry: Regional Concentration and Deconcentration," paper presented at the Third British-Mexican Geography Seminar in Mexico City, September 18-22, 1989.

54. Harley Shaiken, "High Tech Goes Third World," *Technology Review*, January 1988, p. 39.

55. For a revealing examination of advanced production processes in Mexico, see Harley Shaiken, *Mexico in the Global Economy: High Technology and Work Organization in Export Industries* (San Diego: Center for U.S.-Mexican Studies, 1990). An earlier study by Shaiken found that advanced production processes can be successfully located in Mexico and similar countries in a relatively short time frame. Harley Shaiken and Stephen Herzenberg, *Automation and Global Production: Automobile Engine Production in Mexico, the United States, and Canada* (San Diego: Center for U.S.-Mexican Studies, 1987).

56. Shaiken, *Mexico in the Global Economy*, pp.31-32.

57. Luis Uchitelle, "Mexico's Plan for Industrial Might," *New York Times*, September 25, 1990.

58. See, for example, the studies of James P. Womack, which show that new industrialization in Mexico is demonstrating extraordinary flexibility. James P. Womack, "North American Integration in the Motor Vehicle Sector: Logic and Consequences," prepared for a forum sponsored by the Universidad Tecnológica de México, June 13, 1990.

59. Between 1981 and 1990 auto sales in Mexico grew at an average annual rate of nearly 6 percent, whereas U.S. auto sales averaged only 2-percent growth in the same period. The ratio of cars to people in Mexico is one to 11, compared to the one to 1.4 ratio in the United States.

60. In 1990, 77 percent of the tourism income came from foreigners visiting Mexico, and 23 percent came from visits by Mexican nationals living abroad, primarily in the United States.

61. Notimex, April 6, 1991.

62. The external balance in the tourism sector was a positive $1.6 billion for 1990, but curbs on the *peso* devaluation since 1988 have encouraged an increased flow abroad of Mexican tourists. In 1990 6.4 million tourists came to Mexico while 4.5 million Mexicans traveled abroad.

63. *Comercio Exterior* (Mexico City), July 1991.

64. Bob Shacochis, "In Deepest Gringolandia," *Harper's Magazine*, July 1989, p. 45.

65. Ibid.

66. These are Marina Ixtapa (Ixtapa-Zihuatanejo, Guerrero), Punta Ixtapa (Guerrero), Santa María del Obraje (San Miguel de Allende), Bahía de Cacaluta (Oaxaca), Punta Bono (Baja California Sur), Puerto Bello (Cozumel), Soldado de Cortez (Guaymas-San Carlos), La Pesca (Marina, Tamaulipas), Rancho Majagua (Manzanillo, Colima), San Buenaventura (Cancún, Quintana Roo), Puerto Chahué (Huatulco), Puerto Escondido (Loreto, Baja California Sur), and Puerto Cancún (Quintana Roo). Another megaproject sometimes mentioned is El Alcortete (San Cristóbal de las Casas). Banamex, "Tourism Megaprojects," *Review of the Economic Situation in Mexico*, July 1991.

67. According to one report, tourism currently accounts for about 30 percent of the total foreign investment dollars in Mexico. *Journal of Commerce*, November 26, 1990.

68. Mexico is not, however, self-sufficient in minerals. It remains heavily dependent on imports of iron ore, nickel, potash, metallurgical-grade coke, asbestos, tin, and certain sands and clays.

69. In 1991 foreign investment was still limited to 49 percent for most mining ventures and 34 percent for the mining of strategic minerals (sulphur, phosphate, potassium, and coal). Foreign firms are, however, permitted to invest up to 100 percent for a 12-year period through a special trust arrangement.

70. Lindajoy Fenley, "Mining Industry Explores Prospects," *Business Mexico*, September 1989.

71. The government faces serious liquidity and operational problems in the most important mining firms it still controls. These include Pan-American Sulphur, Isthmus Exploration Company, Mexican Phosphate Rock, Mining Development Commission, Rio Escondido Coal Mine, and the Benito Juárez-Peña Colorada Mining.

72. *El Financiero*, June 27, 1990.

73. Two instructive articles examining the sale of Cananea are: Joaquín Ortiz, "¿Cobre por liebre?" *Expansión* (Mexico City), November 21, 1990; and Carlos Acosta, "Jorge Larrea, casi seguro dueño de Cananea," *Proceso* (Mexico City), August 8, 1990.

74. The *ejidos* are a community with rights to communally held land, worked collectively or distributed to individual peasant families. *Ejido* lands are inheritable, but legally cannot be sold, although renting is common.

75. Philip Russell, *Mexico in Transition* (Austin: Colorado River Press, 1977), p. 73.

76. One hectare equals 2.47 acres.

77. For information on SAM, see Mario Montanari, "The Conception of SAM," in James Austin and Gustavo Esteva, eds., *Food Policy in Mexico: The Search for Self-Sufficiency* (Ithaca: Cornell University Press, 1987).

78. Quoted in Alan Riding, *Distant Neighbors: A Portrait of the Mexicans* (New York: Alfred A. Knopf, 1985), p. 191.

79. In 1985 Mexico required import licenses on 317 different agricultural commodities. By 1990 only 57 commodities required such licenses. U. S. General Accounting Office (GAO), *U.S.-Mexico Trade Liberalization* (Washington, 1991). Throughout 1990 and 1991 Mexico continued to eliminate import licenses, removing at least a dozen more. *El Financiero*, August 20, 1991.

80. Quoted in Rosario Robles and Julio Moguel, "Agricultura y proyecto neoliberal," *El Cotidiano* 34 (Mexico City), March-April 1990, p. 3.

81. Gray Newman, "Mexico Agricultural Reforms Promise Future Openings for Agribusiness Firms," *Business International*, February 11, 1991.

82. Ibid.

83. Quoted in Laura Carlsen, "New Products, New Markets," *Business Mexico*, July 1991.

84. Economic Commission on Latin America and the Caribbean, *Statistical Yearbook for Latin America and the Caribbean* (Santiago, Chile: 1989), pp. 600-605.

85. Carlos Salinas de Gortari, *Primer informe de gobierno 1989* (Mexico City: Estados Unidos Mexicanos, Poder Ejecutivo Federal, 1989).

86. Cited in David Barkin and Billie R. DeWalt, "Sorghum and the Mexican Food Crisis," *Latin American Research Review* 23, no. 3, 1988, pp. 30-59.

87. *Informe Especial* 1 (Mexico City), no. 24, October 19, 1990, p. 19.

88. Agency for International Development (AID), *Action Plan for Fiscal Years 1985 and 1986* (Mexico City: U.S. Embassy, 1984), p. 30.

89. Arturo Warman, *Los campesinos: Los hijos predilectos del régimen* (Mexico City: Nuestro Tiempo, 1972). Quoted in *Informe Especial* 1 (Mexico City), no. 24, October 19, 1990.

90. *El Financiero*, July 30, 1991, citing a 1991 Banrural report.

91. Gerardo Otero, "The New Agrarian Movement: Self-Managed, Democratic Production," *Latin American Perspectives* 16, no. 4, 1989, pp. 28-59.

92. Banamex, "Agrofood Trade Balance," *Review of the Economic Situation*, September 1991. This agrofood trade balance includes agricultural commodities, forestry, livestock, and processed foodstuffs. The largest deficit was in processed foodstuffs, and there was a $200 million surplus in livestock.

93. Kenneth Shwedel, "Will the Countryside Modernize?" *Business Mexico*, July 1991, citing government figures.

94. Michael Foley, "Agenda for Mobilization: The Agrarian Question and Popular Mobilization in Contemporary Mexico," *Latin American Research Review* 26, no. 2, 1991, pp. 39-74.

95. David Winder and Deborah Eade, "Agricultural Issues in the U.S. and Mexico: Views from a Third Country," in Bruce F. Johnston, Cassio Luiselli, Celso Cartas Contreras, and Roger D. Norton, eds., *US-Mexico Relations: Agriculture and Rural Development* (Stanford: Stanford University Press, 1987), pp. 361-78.

96. See, for example, Barkin and DeWalt, "Sorghum and the Mexican Food Crisis," pp. 30-59.

97. AID, *Action Plan for Fiscal Years 1985 and 1986*, p. 30.

98. Emilio Romero Polanco, "La crisis y la alimentación nacional: Opciones de desarrollo," *Comercio Exterior* 40 (Mexico City), no. 9, September 1990, pp. 859-67.
99. *Anexo estadístico del primer informe de gobierno 1989*, cited in *El Financiero*, July 13, 1990.
100. Cited in *La Jornada*, September 13, 1991.
101. Barkin and DeWalt, "Sorghum and the Mexican Food Crisis," pp. 30-59.
102. Amado Ramírez Leyva, Marcos Portillo Vásquez, and Cecilia Sánchez Solano, "Mexican Agriculture: The Potential for Export Production and Employment Generation in Rural Areas," paper no. 49 (Washington: Commission for the Study of International Migration and Cooperative Economic Development, July 1990).
103. Martine Vanackere, "Conditions of Agricultural Day Laborers in Mexico," *International Labor Review* 127, no. 1, 1988, pp. 91-110.
104. Kjell I. Enge and Scott Whiteford, *The Keepers of Water and Earth: Mexican Rural Social Organization and Irrigation* (Austin: University of Texas Press, 1989), p. 5.
105. David Brooks, "Mexico: Whose Crisis, Whose Future?" *NACLA Report on the Americas*, September-December 1987, p. 32.
106. Ursula Oswald, *La agricultura en México ante la integración comercial*, Manuscript (Mexico City: CRIM-UNAM, 1991), p. 5.
107. Economist Intelligence Unit, *Mexico Country Profile* (London: Business International Limited, 1990).
108. Linda Wilcox Young, "Economic Development and Employment: Agroindustrialization in Mexico's El Bajío," *Journal of Economic Issues* 22, no. 2, June 1988, pp. 389-96.
109. Robles and Moguel, "Agricultura y proyecto neoliberal," p. 10.
110. Laura Carlsen, "Changes Brewing," *Business Mexico*, April 1991.
111. U.S. International Trade Commission (ITC), *The Likely Impact on the United States of a Free Trade Agreement with Mexico* (Washington, 1991), pp. 4-13.
112. GAO, *US-Mexico Agricultural Trade* (Washington, 1990), pp. 29-31.
113. Steve Sanderson, *The Transformation of Mexican Agriculture* (Princeton: Princeton University Press, 1986), p. 117. The backbone of horticultural exports is cheap migrant labor. Frequently these workers, who are employed on a day-to-day basis, are not even paid the minimum wage. Farm contractors often do not allow them the legally mandated rest period of one-half hour, and these farmworkers rarely receive the Sunday bonus or double-time benefits to which they are legally entitled. Vanackere, "Conditions of Agricultural Day Laborers," pp. 101-3.
114. Testimony by the U.S. General Accounting Office before the House Committee on Agriculture, *U.S.-Mexico Agricultural Trade Liberalization*, April 24, 1991.
115. Romero Polanco, "La crisis y la alimentación nacional," pp. 859-67.
116. Joel Millman, "There's Your Solution," *Forbes*, January 7, 1991.
117. Research by UNAM agricultural economist José Luis Calva, cited in a series in *El Financiero* on the effect of free trade on the agricultural sector. See Francisco Gómez Maza, "La agricultura mexicana y el Tratado de Libre Comercio," *El Financiero*, August 20 and 21, 1991.
118. Ibid.
119. Foley, "Agenda for Mobilization," p. 65.
120. See: Blanca Rubio, *Resistencia campesina y explotación rural en México* (Mexico City: Era, 1987); Michael Foley, "Agrarian Conflict Reconsidered: Popular Mobilization and Peasant Politics in Mexico and Central America," *Latin American Research Review* 26, no. 1, 1991; and Foley, "Agenda for Mobilization."
121. For an insightful examination of agricultural modernization and its effect on food production in Mexico, as well a proposal as to how Mexico could achieve food self-sufficiency, see David Barkin, *Distorted Development: Mexico in the World Economy* (Boulder: Westview Press, 1990).
122. Michael Foley, "Structural Adjustment and Political Adaptation: The Politics of Neoliberal Reform in Mexican Agriculture," *Governance: An International Journal of Policy and Administration* 4, no. 4, October 1991.

Part Three: Social Forces

The Private Sector and Its Organizations

1. Peter Baird and Ed McCaughan, *Beyond the Border* (New York: NACLA, 1979), p.27.
2. Recent articles on the subject include: "La IP en busca de rumbo político," *Informe Especial* (Mexico City), June 20, 1990; Luis Alberto Rodríguez, "The Top Level Management Group in Mexican Business," *Voices*, 1990; and Francisco Valdés, "The Quest for Business Survival," *Hemisphere*, Winter 1989.
3. Roderic Camp, *Entrepreneurs and Politics in Twentieth Century Mexico* (Oxford: Oxford University Press, 1989), p. 84.
4. Luis Felipe Bravo Mena, "Coparmex and Mexican Politics," in Sylvia Maxfield, ed., *Government and Private Sector in Contemporary Mexico* (San Diego: Center for U.S.-Mexican Studies, 1987), p. 93.
5. See Rolando Cordera, "Estado y economía en México," in Nora Lustig, ed., *Panorama y perspectivas de la economía mexicana* (Mexico City: El Colegio de México, 1980), p. 449.
6. For further discussion of this view about the influences on state autonomy, see: Nora Hamilton, *The Limits of State Autonomy* (Princeton: Princeton University Press, 1982); Rolando Cordera and Carlos Tello, *Disputa por la nación* (Mexico City: Siglo Veintiuno Editores, 1979); Sylvia Maxfield, *Governing Capital: International Finance and Mexican Politics* (Ithaca: Cornell University Press, 1990).
7. Maxfield, *Governing Capital*, p. 15.
8. Cordera and Tello, *Disputa por la nación*.
9. For a discussion of this "progressive subordination" of the state, see Carlos Pereyra, "Estado y sociedad," in Pablo González and Enrique Florescano, eds., *México, Hoy* (Mexico City: Siglo Veintiuno Editores, 1979).
10. Juan Martínez Nava, *Conflicto estado-empresarios* (Mexico City: Editores Nueva Imagen, 1982), p. 170.
11. See Elvira Conchiero, Antonio González, and Juan Manuel Fragosa, *El poder de la gran burguesía* (Mexico City: Ediciones de Cultura Popular, 1979), pp. 37-49.
12. CCE was considered the supreme business association, or the *cúpula de cúpulas*. Its member groups, each of which has one vote, include Coparmex, Concamin, Concanaco, National Agricultural Council (CNA), Mexican Council of Businessmen (CMHN), Mexican Investors Association (AMCB), and the Mexican Association of Insurance Institutions (AMIS).
13. James M. Cypher, *State and Capital in Mexico: Development Strategy Since 1940* (Boulder: Westview Press, 1990), p. 32.
14. See Coparmex, "Propuestas preliminares que la Coparmex presenta para la discusión del anteproyecto de una nueva ley federal del trabajo" (Mexico City), 1990.
15. Roderic Camp, "Attitudes and Images of the Mexican Entrepreneur: Political Consequences," in Sylvia Maxfield, ed., *Government and Private Sector in Contemporary Mexico* (San Diego: Center for U.S.-Mexican Studies, 1987), pp. 127-44.
16. See, for example, María Rosas, "Pugnas empresariales," *Expansión* (Mexico City), June 20, 1990.
17. The term *"charro"* is most frequently used to refer to official unionists, used by the government to keep the rank and file under tight control.
18. Celso Garrido and Cristina Puga, "Transformaciones recientes del empresariado mexicano," *Revista Mexicana de Sociología*, April-June 1990, p. 60.
19. For a description of the government's role in industrial restructuring, export promotion, and its sector programs *(programas de rama)*, see Cypher, *State and Capital*, p. 184.
20. See Angela Delli Sante, "La cámara americana de comercio en la lucha ideológica en México," *Ideologies & Literature* 3, no. 2, Fall 1988.
21. Alicia Ortiz Rivera, "Un grupo muy cómodo negoció el pacto," *Uno más Uno*, May 19, 1988.
22. Enrique Quintana, "Los nombres detrás de los pesos," *El Cotidiano* (Mexico City), July-August 1988.
23. Ibid.

24. See Camp, *Entrepreneurs and Politics*, p. 14. Camp concluded that the banking industry offered the most significant channel for the "exchange of private and public-sector leadership."
25. Cypher, *State and Capital*, p. 163.
26. The PAN leader here is José Angel Conchello. He was referring to members of a *neopanista* group called Integral Human Development Civil Association (DIHAC), who raised the possibility of forming a new probusiness political party. *Informe Especial* (Mexico City), July 20, 1990.

Mexican Labor and Unions

1. As in many countries, public employees are excluded from the right to strike under federal labor law.
2. Ilan Bizberg, *Estado y sindicalismo en México* (Mexico City: Colegio de México, 1990).
3. Lorenzo Meyer, in Graciela Bersusan and Carlos García, *Estado y sindicatos: Crisis de una relación* (Mexico City: Fundación Friedrich Ebert, 1989), p. 25.
4. One of the most notable exceptions is the National Garment Workers Union "19 de Septiembre," which won its registration with the massive mobilizations following the 1985 earthquake in Mexico City.
5. Kevin Middlebrook, "The Sounds of Silence: Organized Labor's Response to Economic Crisis in Mexico," *Journal of Latin American Studies* 21, May 1989.
6. For statistics on the contraction of production and employment, and the cutbacks in social spending, see Rosa Albina Garavito and Augusto Bolívar, eds., *Mexico en la década de los ochenta: La modernización en cifras* (Mexico City: Universidad Autónoma Metropolitana, 1990). The Banco de México reported that manufacturing employment in December 1990 was down 22.5 percent from its level in 1980.
7. Middlebrook, "The Sounds of Silence," p. 200.
8. In an internal document, the leading business organization Coparmex made the following distinctions: "negotiators" (CROM, CTR), "dinosaurs" (CTM, FSTSE), "modernizers" (STRM, SME, SNTE, Association of Pilots), and "left" (COR, SUNTU, STUNAM, SITUAM, COTRASE).
9. The authenticity of the letter cannot be proved but was widely publicized by the Mexican press, generally believed by the public, and Secretary Farrell waited nearly three days to deny having written it.
10. *The Other Side of Mexico* (Mexico City), March-April 1990.
11. See for example, Laura Carlsen, "Testimonies of Mexican Garment Workers," manuscript, 1988.
12. *La Jornada*, August 6, 1990.
13. *La Jornada*, August 23, 1990.
14. Luis Méndez, "Productivity, Wages and Business' Response," *The Other Side of Mexico* (Mexico City), no. 18, September-December 1990.
15. For a brief history of Mexican unionism, see George Grayson, *The Mexican Labor Machine: Power, Politics and Patronage* (Washington: Center for Strategic Studies, 1989).
16. The CTM estimates the figure at nearly one-third, while other estimates are closer to 20 percent. Kevin Middlebrook (in "Sounds of Silence") estimates it at 15-20 percent of the economically active population (EAP). According to Luis Guaida, a private-sector labor relations attorney, social security figures also indicate that around 20 percent of the EAP is unionized.
17. Laura Carlsen, "From the Many to the Few," *Multinational Monitor*, June 1991.
18. Bersusan and Garcia, *Estado y sindicatos*, p. 28.
19. *La Jornada*, May 27, 1991.
20. Enrique de la Garza in Bersusan and García, *Estado y sindicatos*.
21. Bersusan and García, *Estado y sindicatos*, p. 40.
22. Interview with José Antonio Pérez, director of the *maquiladora* program, American Chamber of Commerce, Mexico, May 1991.
23. *Los Angeles Times*, March 4, 1990.
24. Regarding the garment industry, see for example, Laura Carlsen, "Business Mexico Coming Apart at the Seams?" *Business Mexico*, December 1990.

Popular Organizing

1. See Peter Baird and Ed McCaughan, *Beyond the Border* (New York: North American Congress on Latin America, 1979), on the electrical workers' movement and other social movements in the 1970s.
2. See Jeffrey Rubin's fine work on the COCEI, including "Popular Mobilization and the Myth of State Corporatism," in Joe Foweraker and Ann Craig, eds., *Popular Movements and Political Change in Mexico* (Boulder: Lynne Rienner Publishers, 1990).
3. Important sources on the CNTE include: Maria Lorena Cook, "Organizing Opposition in the Teachers' Movement in Oaxaca," in Foweraker and Craig, eds., *Popular Movements*; Luis Hernández, "Diez años de trincheras," Julio Moguel, "Las coordinadoras de masas," and "¿Que es la CNTE?" all in *Hojas* (Mexico City), no. 1, March 1990. Also see Luis Hernández, "The SNTE and the Teachers' Movement, 1982-1984," in Barry Carr and Ricardo Anzaldua Montoya, eds., *The Mexican Left, the Popular Movements and the Politics of Austerity* (La Jolla: Center for U.S.-Mexican Studies, 1986).
4. Ana Maria Prieto, "Mexico's National Coordinadoras in a Context of Economic Crisis," in Carr and Anzaldua, *The Mexican Left*; and Emilio Garcia, "La disyuntiva real de la CNPA en la coyuntura actual," *Hojas* (Mexico City), no. 1, March 1990.
5. Arturo Warman, "La fuerza del pasado," *Nexos* (Mexico City), no. 100, April 1986.
6. See, for example: Hernández, "Diez años de trincheras," and "The SNTE and the Teachers' Movement," and Moguel, "Las coordinadoras de masas." Other useful sources are: Gerardo Bohórquez, "Tendencias actuales del movimiento urbano popular en México," *El Cotidiano* (Mexico City), September-October 1989; Ricardo Hernández, "La coordinadora nacional del movimiento urbano popular," *Hojas* (Mexico City), no. 1, March 1990; and Daniel Rodríguez Velázquez, "From Neighborhood to Nation," *NACLA Report on the Americas*, November-December 1989.
7. In some cases activists put together organizations that could act as broad popular fronts in opposition to government policies. One example was the *Frente en Defensa del Salario Contra la Austeridad y la Carestía* (FNDSCAC). A broad front of union, peasant, and community organizations, the FNDSCAC called "civic strikes" in 1983-84.
8. On the Asamblea de Barrios and Super Barrio, see: Equipo Pueblo, "Asamblea de barrios," *Historias del Movimiento Urbano 2* (pamphlet). Super Barrio's quotations are from an interview by David Brooks: "We Are All Super Barrio," *Z Magazine*, April 1989.
9. Victor M. Quintana, "XIII National Gathering of Christian Base Communities," *The Other Side of Mexico* (Mexico City), no. 7, October-December 1988.
10. Among Mexico's most respected political cartoonists are El Fisgón, Magú, Helguera, and others at *La Jornada*; and Naranjo, who publishes in *Proceso*. Almost everyone opens magazines or newspapers to the cartoons first, to get the "real story." These cartoonists continue a tradition that is more than a century old. Their immediate forefathers were Rius and Abel Quezada.
11. Crime fiction writer (as well as historian and cultural critic) Paco Ignacio Taibo II is well-known for his "independent (not private) detective" character, among others. Two of his novels have been translated and published by Viking Penguin: *An Easy Thing* (1990) and *Shadow of the Shadow* (1991).
12. José Berberán et al., *Radiografía de un fraude: Análisis de los datos oficiales del 6 de julio* (Mexico City: Editorial Nuestro Tiempo, 1988); and Andrew Reding, "Mexico at a Crossroads: The 1988 Election and Beyond," *World Policy Journal*, Fall 1988 provide useful descriptions of the election process. On the *cardenista* campaign, see Equipo Pueblo, *Crónica del nuevo México*, (Mexico City, 1989). On the nature of the *cardenista* movement, see Paco Ignacio Taibo II, "A New Politics with Deep Roots," *The Nation*, December 17, 1990.
13. Warman, "La fuerza del pasado."
14. Among the resources available on these expanding popular linkages are: Jonathan Fox, "Time to Cross the Border," *Radical America* 22, no. 4, September 1989; and summary reports, Mexico-U.S. Diálogos, *Binational and Trinational Exchanges on Popular Perspectives*. Also see press reports on Super Barrio's California trip in: *People*, April

10, 1989; *San Diego Union*, February 21, 1989; *Los Angeles Times*, February 25, 1989. Farmers' exchanges have been fostered by the Institute for Agricultural and Trade Policy in Minneapolis. Labor exchanges have been facilitated by the Mexico-U.S. Border Program at the American Friends Service Committee, Mexico-U.S. Diálogos, and various unions (including locals of ACTWU, ILGWU, and the UAW). Environmental exchanges have occurred via the Texas Center for Policy Studies. In addition, opposition to NAFTA has spurred the creation of various coalitions throughout the United States, many of which have invited Mexican counterparts to join them in their initiatives.

15. Carlos Monsivais, *Entrada libre* (Mexico City: Ediciones Era, 1987).

Nongovernmental Organizations

1. Several directories of Mexican NGOs exist, although none is comprehensive or up-to-date: Luis Lopezllera Méndez, *Sociedad civil y pueblos emergentes, Mexico City: promoción de instituciones filantrópicas* (Mexico City: Directorio de Instituciones Filantrópicas, 1990); and Programa Interdisciplinario de Estudios de la Mujer, "Organizaciones no gubernamentales que trabajan en beneficio de la mujer," *Documentos de trabajo* (Mexico City), no. 2, (Mexico City: El Colegio de México, n.d.).

2. Two histories that trace the evolution of NGOs from church-based components for community action to some of the newer types of organizations are: Luis Hernández and Gabriel Torres, *Lá busqueda del nuevo sujeto social* (Mexico City: Equipo Pueblo, 1987); and Praxis, *Nosotros también nacemos la historia con el movimiento popular*, presented at Gestión y Políticas Institucionales para ONGD de América Latina, August 1987, Rio de Janeiro, Monograph 22.

Part Four: Social Sectors and Institutions

Women and Feminism

1. Cited in Office of the Presidency, *Mexican Agenda*, April 1991.

2. The term *Malinche* is a derogatory reference to the name of the woman given to Hernando Cortez by an Indian leader in the 1500s. Malintzin, who acted as a translator for Cortez, was also expected to serve the *conquistador* sexually. The epithet is used to describe someone who sells out her own people on behalf of the interests of outsiders.

3. The quote is from *Memoria del primer encuentro de mujeres de la coordinadora única de damnificados* (Mexico City: CUD, 1986).

Native People

1. See, for example, Alfredo Lopez, *Los mitos del Tlacuache* (Austin: Alianza Editorial, 1990); and Ramón Vera, "El descuartizado resusita," *México Indígena* (Mexico City), no. 14.

2. Instituto Nacional Indigenista, "Programa nacional de desarrollo de los pueblos indios 1991-1994" (Mexico City, 1991), p. 11. The preliminary results of the 1990 census indicate an indigenous population of 7.3 million. Like INI, the census only counts Indians over the age of five. According to sociologist Rosa del Campo y María, a consultant to the United Nations, such a counting method drastically undercounts the Indian population. "If we were only to consider two children under five for each Indian included in the census," she explained, "the native population would treble." *Latin American Weekly Report*, February 7, 1991.

3. Philip Russel, *Mexico in Transition* (Austin: Colorado River Press, 1977), p. 110; and *Third World Guide 89/90* (Argentina: Third World Editors, 1988).

4. Luz María Valdés, *El perfil demográfico de los indios mexicanos* (Mexico City: Siglo Veintiuno, 1988).

5. Alan Riding, *Distant Neighbors: A Portrait of the Mexicans* (New York: Alfred A. Knopf, 1985), pp. 199-218, provides a useful and lively overview of the history of Mexico's Indian populations and their current positions in the country.

6. See, for example, the special issues of *México Indígena* on migration to the United States (no. 4), and migration to the cities (no. 21).

7. Riding, *Distant Neighbors*, p. 208.

8. An interesting discussion of the particular features of poverty in indigenous zones can be found in Consejo Consultivo del Programa Nacional de Solidaridad, *El combate contra la pobreza* (Mexico City, 1990): "The mechanisms to maintain indigenous poverty have been diverse, just as the interests behind these actions have been diverse. The poverty of Indian peoples, although shared with other groups in society, has its own history and peculiar characteristics that must be taken into account to resolve the conditions of subordination, overcome the historic backwardness that has inhibited their healthy development, and understand the necessity for differentiated treatment."

9. Laura Carlsen, "One Hundred Years of Solitude," *The Other Side of Mexico* (Mexico City), July 1989.

10. Luis Hernández, "One Hundred Years of Solitude," *Cafetaleros*, 1991.

11. José Reveles and Heriberto Rodríguez, "Cultivos de la ira," *México Indígena* (Mexico City), July 1990.

12. For more detailed information on rural violence and human rights violations among indigenous populations, see Americas Watch, *Human Rights in Mexico: A Policy of Impunity* (New York, June 1990), pp. 53-65.

13. Laura Carlsen, "12 de octubre . . . ," *Pueblo* (Mexico City), September-October 1989.

14. See Andrew Friendly, "Lighthawk," *Business Mexico*, August 1991.

15. Marco Barrera Bassols, "De pueblos espejos y reflejos: La Unión Comunal de Museos Comunitarios del Estado de Oaxaca," *México Indígena* (Mexico City), no. 24, September 1991.

Immigration and Refugees

1. For a lengthier discussion on the factors that "push" migrants out of Mexico and "pull" them into the United States, see: Wayne Cornelius, "The U.S. Demand for Mexican Labor," in Jorge Bustamante and Wayne Cornelius, eds., *Mexican Migration to the United States: Origins, Consequences, and Policy Options*, vol. 3 of papers prepared for the Bilateral Commission on the Future of United States-Mexican Relations (San Diego: Center for U.S.-Mexican Studies, 1989); Daniel Levy and Gabriel Székely, *Mexico: Paradoxes of Stability and Change* (Boulder: Westview Press, 1987), pp. 211-18; Sidney Weintraub, "Implications of Mexican Demographic Developments for the United States," in Frank D. Bean, Jurgen Schmandt, and Sidney Weintraub, eds., *Mexican and Central American Population and U.S. Immigration Policy* (Austin: Center for Mexican American Studies, 1989), pp. 179-99.

2. The following sources offer excellent descriptions of the history of Mexican migration to the United States and U.S. policy regarding it: Bilateral Commission on the Future of United States-Mexican Relations, *The Challenge of Interdependence: Mexico and the United States* (Lanham, MD: University Press of America, 1989); Wayne Cornelius and Ann Craig, *The Mexican Political System in Transition* (San Diego: Center for U.S.-Mexican Studies, 1991), especially the chapter on the "International Environment"; Georges Vernez and David Ronfeldt, "The Current Situation in Mexican Immigration," *Science*, March 8, 1991, pp 1189-90; Alan Riding, *Distant Neighbors: A Portrait of the Mexicans* (New York: Alfred A. Knopf, 1985), pp. 329-33; and Abraham F. Lowenthal, "The United States and Mexico: Uneasy Neighbors," in *Partners in Conflict: The United States and Latin America in the 1990s* (Baltimore: Johns Hopkins University Press, 1990).

3. Immigration and Naturalization Service, *1989 Statistical Yearbook of the Immigration and Naturalization Service* (Washington, September 1990); and figures drawn from INS annual reports given by Wayne Cornelius, "One-Way Travel to US on the Rise," *Hemisfile 2*, no. 2 (La Jolla, CA), March 1991.

4. A discussion of some of the methods used to calculate estimates of undocumented migrant flows is given in: Keith Crane, Beth J. Asch, Joanna Zorn Heilbrunn, and Danielle C. Cullinane, *The Effect of Employer Sanctions on the Flow of Undocumented Immigrants to the United States* (Santa Monica, CA: The RAND Corporation, April 1990); and Jorge A. Bustamante, "Measuring the Flow of Undocumented Immigrants," in Cornelius and Bustamante, *Mexican Migration*, pp. 95-106.

5. General Accounting Office (GAO), *Immigration: Studies of the Immigration and Control Act's Impact on Mexico* (Washington, February 1988), p. 15.

6. Manuel García y Griego, "The Mexican Labor Supply, 1990-2010" in Cornelius and Bustamante, *Mexican Migration*, pp. 49-93.

7. Elvia Gutiérrez, "Creciente discriminación a indocumentados en Estados Unidos," *El Financiero*, February 6, 1991; and Leo R. Chávez, Estevan T. Flores, and Marta López-Garza, "Migrants and Settlers: A Comparison of Undocumented Mexicans and Central Americans in the United States," *Frontera Norte* 1, no. 1, January-June, 1989, pp. 49-75.

8. Cindy Anders, "Migrant Money," *Mexico Journal*, October 17, 1988.

9. See, for example, the following sources: Ashley Dunn, "Nationwide Arrests of Illegal Immigrants Rise," *Los Angeles Times*, February 16, 1991; Edward Cody, "New Tide of Mexicans Crossing U.S. Border"; Bustamante, "Measuring the Flow"; and Crane, et al., *The Effect of Employer Sanctions*.

10. GAO, *Immigration Reform: Employer Sanctions and the Question of Discrimination* (Washington, March 1990).

11. Francisco Alba, "The Mexican Demographic Situation," in *Mexican and Central American Population and U.S. Immigration Policy*, pp. 5-32.

12. José Luis Pérez Canchola, "Violations of Human and Labor Rights of Migrant Workers in the United States," *The Other Side of Mexico* (Mexico City), January-February 1991.

13. Gutiérrez, "Creciente discriminación."

14. Chávez, Flores, and López-Garza, "Migrants and Settlers," Table 5, pp. 67-69. The sample size in this study was limited; the researchers interviewed 266 Mexican men and women, most of whom had left Mexico for economic reasons and who planned eventually to return to their homeland. They were not, however, planning a rapid return to Mexico; that is, they were not part of the migrant ebb-and-flow characteristic of those who cross for a few months to help with seasonal agriculture.

15. In her comments on the manuscript, Claudia Isaac, assistant professor of community and regional planning at the University of New Mexico, observed that the absence of men for long periods of time has not had a universally negative effect on these communities. In her research on rural communities in Mexico, Isaac found that there is a much greater mobilization of women (in cooperatives and other alternative forms of income generation, as well as in political and social activities) in communities with large populations of male migrants. She also found that the same process of increased community mobilization and collective action seemed to reduce the power of entrenched elites and provided openings for broad-based, popular mobilization.

16. Anders, "Migrant Money."

17. Ibid.

18. Alba, "The Mexican Demographic Situation."

19. Emilio Vázquez Pérez, "Son explotados 85.5 porciento de los refugiados centroamericanos," *Uno más Uno*, January 3, 1991.

20. "Atención a refugiados," *Excélsior* news service, April 19, 1991.

21. Fredy López Arévalo, "Refugiados guatemaltecos: Un largo retorno," *México Indígena* (Mexico City), August 1990. See also Luis Raúl Salvado, *The Other Refugees: A Study of Nonrecognized Guatemalan Refugees in Chiapas, Mexico* (Washington: Center for Immigration Policy and Refugee Assistance, 1988).

22. Elliot Spagat, "The Other Illegal Aliens," *Mexico Journal*, April 18, 1988.

23. Victor Clark, "The Human Rights Situation of Central American Refugees in Mexico at the Tijuana Border," *Basta!* (National Journal of the Chicago Religious Task Force on Central America), December 1989, p. 48.

24. Quoted in ibid.

25. See, for example, the testimony in Bill Frelick, U.S. Committee for Refugees, "Running the Gauntlet: The Central American Journey through Mexico" (Washington, January 1991).
26. Ibid.
27. Ibid.
28. "México dejó de ser opción para inmigrantes de Centro América," *El Financiero*, April 16, 1990.
29. José Luis Castillejos, "Frenan éxodo centro americano a EEUU," March 14, 1991, manuscript.
30. Bill Frelick, U.S. Committee on Refugees, "Update on Interdiction of Central Americans in Mexico" (Washington), July 16, 1991.
31. INS, "Enhancement Plan for the Southern Border," February 16, 1989; and INS Memoranda SITREP No. 1, 2, and 2.1, Project 091, E.M. Trominski, INS district director (Mexico City), February 22, 1989 and February 23, 1989. These INS documents were cited in Frelick, "Running the Gauntlet."
32. Janelle Jones and Lisa Roney, "Operation Hold the Line Succeeds in Cutting Flow of Illegals into South Texas," *Commissioner's Communique*, June 1989.
33. Bill Frelick, "No Central Americans Need Apply," *Los Angeles Times*, June 25, 1991.
34. "Autorizo la secretaria de gobernación," *Excélsior* news service, April 21, 1991.
35. Tracy Wilkinson, "Mexico Consulate Speaks Out," *Los Angeles Times*, January 11, 1991.
36. "Mexico Seeks to Protect Migrants' Pay," *Financial Times* (London), August 9, 1990.
37. Article 42 of the new law defines refugees as persons who "have been threatened by general violence, foreign aggression, internal conflicts, massive human rights violations, or other circumstances that have greatly upset public order in their nation of origin." *Ley General de Población*, as amended July 17, 1990.
38. Ibid.
39. José Luis Pérez Canchola, "Salinas y los indocumentados," *El Universal*, December 22, 1990.

Health and Welfare

1. From 1980 to 1986 published reports indicated that cardiovascular illnesses were the leading cause of death. Accidents occupied second place. Malignant tumors and infectious diseases were the third- and fourth-leading causes of death in 1986. This profile indicates that Mexico straddles the developed and developing worlds in terms of health conditions, stress levels, infrastructure development, and other factors. See *Comércio Exterior* (Mexico City), February 1991, p. 146.
2. Interview by author, September 29, 1991.
3. National Health Plan, 1990-1994.
4. President Salinas, "State of the Nation Report, Annex" (Mexico City), November 1, 1990.
5. Ibid.
6. Julio Frenk, National Institute of Public Health, "Los futuros de la salud."
7. See Peter Ward, *Welfare Politics in Mexico: Papering Over the Cracks* (London: Allen and Unwin, 1986), pp. 120-26, for a discussion of these ideas.
8. John Borrell, "Psst, You Wanna Plastic Surgeon?" *Time*, June 15, 1987, p. 60.
9. Harry Nelson, "Pinpointing the Culprits," *World Health*, June 1989, p. 13.
10. Ibid.
11. Program Committee for the United Nations Childrens Fund, March 23, 1989, p. 3.
12. Asa Cristina Laurell and María Elena Ortega, "Privatización de los servicios de salud," *El Cotidiano* 39 (Mexico City), January-February 1991.
13. Ibid.
14. José Luis Calva, "El estigma de la desnutrición," *Demos* 3 (Mexico City), 1990, p. 27.
15. See the articles in *La Jornada*, February 13, 1990; February 14, 1990; and March 26, 1990.
16. José Luis Castillejos, "Epidemia de sarampión en Chiapas," *El Universal*, April 9, 1986.
17. Ibid.
18. Elaine Burns, "Poder copular fights Mexico AIDS," *Guardian*, June 20, 1990.
19. Figures given by Grupo de Investigación Social sobre el SIDA y Derechos Humanos (GISSIDA) in *El Nacional*, October 9, 1990.
20. Jesús Belmont Vásquez, "Aumenta la incidencia de bronquitis crónica y otras," *El Financiero*, March 12, 1991.

21. Jesús H. Guadarrama, "Tiene problemas visuales 70% de los habitantes del D.F.," *El Financiero*, December 18, 1990.
22. Ward, *Welfare Politics*, p. 110.
23. Laurell and Ortega, "Privatización de los servicios." The privatization argument is frequently stated by researchers from the Autonomous University of Mexico's Xochimilco School of Social Medicine. Others disagree, pointing out that there have always been some privately funded medical insurance programs.
24. Ibid.
25. Frenk, "Los futuros."
26. Laurell and Ortega, "Privatización de los servicios."

Education and Student Organizing

1. Juan Prawda, *Logros, inequidades y retos del sistema educativo mexicano* (Mexico City: 1988).
2. Karen Kovacs, "The Quest for Changes in Mexican Education," *Current History* 86, no. 518, March 1987.
3. Carlos Monsivais, "El magisterio y la modernidad," *Hojas* (Mexico City), March 1990.
4. Consejo Nacional Técnico de la Educación, "Hacia un nuevo modelo educativo" (Mexico City), July 31, 1991.
5. Kovacs, "The Quest for Changes."
6. Daniel Morales-Gomez and Carlos Alberto Torres, *The State, Corporatist Politics and Educational Policy-Making in Mexico* (New York: Praeger, 1986).
7. Kovacs, "The Quest for Changes."
8. *Proceso* (Mexico City), February 5, 1990.
9. Secretaria de Educación Pública de México, "Average Public Expenditure on Education in Mexico (1980-1990)" (Mexico City), 1990.
10. *Proceso* (Mexico City), December 17, 1990.
11. Morales-Gómez and Torres, *The State, Corporatist Politics.*
12. Patricia de Leonardo Ramírez, "Los cuadros de la derecha," *El Cotidiano* (Mexico City), 1988.
13. Quoted in *Mexico Journal* (Mexico City), October 10, 1988.
14. Carlos Monsiváis, "Duro, duro, duro! El CEU," in *Entrada libre* (Mexico City: Ediciones Era, 1987).
15. Ibid.
16. Homero Campo, "Exigencia a las universidades públicas," *Proceso* (Mexico City), July 8, 1991.

Communications Media

1. Pablo Arredondo Ramírez and Enrique Sánchez Ruiz, *Comunicación social, poder, y democracia en México* (Guadalajara: Universidad de Guadalajara, 1986).
2. For a thorough examination of the *gacetilla* or *desplegado*, see Joe Keenan, "Gacetilla," *Mexico Journal* (Mexico City), November 25, 1987.
3. "El control: Clave de la relación prensa-poder," *Informe Especial* (Mexico City), August 9, 1991.
4. *Uno más Uno*, May 31, 1990, quoting the former director of the government news agency Notimex, Raymundo Riva Palacio.
5. *The Washington Post*, August 21, 1990. Jack Anderson also reported that the CIA denied any role in the Buendía killing.
6. Luis Ramiro Beltrán and Elizabeth Fox de Cardona, *Comunicación dominada: Estados Unidos en los medios de América Latina* (Mexico City: Instituto Latinoamericano de Estudios Transnacionales, 1980).
7. Fátima Fernández Christlieb, *Los medios de difusión masiva en México* (Mexico City: Juan Pablo Editores, 1985).
8. Medios Publicitarios Mexicanos, "Medios Impresos," (Mexico City), February 1990.
9. Ramírez and Ruiz, *Comunicación social, poder, y democracia.*
10. Data from Centro de Estudios de la Información y la Comunicación de la Universidad de Guadalajara.

11. "Crisis de identidad y de recursos en el IMER," *Informe Especial* (Mexico City), November 16, 1990.
12. *Notimex*, February 3, 1991.
13. See María del Carmen Merodio, *Televisa, el quinto poder* (Mexico City: Claves Latinoamericanos, 1989).
14. "Televisa: Un imperio traslado a la pantalla," *Informe Especial* (Mexico City), November 2, 1990.
15. The most profitable Televisa programming is its production of soap operas, or "telenovelas." See Joaquín Ortiz de Echeverría, "Televisa: La industria del melodrama," *Expansión* (Mexico City), October 10, 1990.
16. *Informe Especial* (Mexico City), November 2, 1990.
17. See Carola García Calderón, *Para conectarse a cablevisión* (Mexico City: Ediciones El Caballito, 1987).

Church and Religion

1. The position of the Catholic bishops with respect to changes in the constitution was presented in a June 5, 1989 letter to President Salinas. See *Informe Especial* (Mexico City), May 1990.
2. Cited in José Díaz, "La relación Iglesia-Estado en México," *Estudios Ecuménicos*, June 1989.
3. Guadelupe Baéz, "El motivo de las demandas de católicos," *Uno más Uno*, March 24, 1990.
4. See, for example, Roberto Blancarte, "Fortalecimiento del México secular," *Este País* (Mexico City), June 1991, pp. 3-10.
5. Mexican Bishops Conference (CEM), *Anuarius Statisticus Ecclesias 1979*, and *Anuario Pontifico 1990*.
6. Manuel Carrillo Poblano, "Jerarquía católica mexicana," *Este País* (Mexico City), June 1991, p. 14. According to statistics from the *Anuario Pontifico 1990*, 1 percent of the clergy are bishops, 71 percent are diocesan priests, and 28 percent belong to religious orders.
7. Roderic Camp, "Religious Elites in Mexico: Some Preliminary Observations," paper presented at the Latin American Studies conference, December 1989, citing Archdiocese of Mexico, *Directorio Eclesiástico de la República Mexicana* (Mexico City: Archdiocese of Mexico, 1985).
8. For an overview of the progressive Catholic movement, see: Miguel Concha Malo et al., *La participación de los cristianos en el proceso popular de liberación en México*, (Mexico City: Siglo Veintiuno Editores, 1986).
9. Mario Monroy and Enrique Valencia, "Las CEBs: Su crecimiento, caracterización y participación en el movimiento popular," *Estudios Ecuménicos*, September 1988, p.21. According to Monroy and Valencia, there are about 15 members in each of the 8,000 to 10,000 base communities, and all but four states (Aguascalientes, Baja California Sur, Durango, and Tamaulipas) have active base communities.
10. Rogelio Gómez-Hermosillo, "El compromiso político de las CEBs," *Estudios Ecuménicos*, June 1989.
11. Estela Sánchez Albarrán, "El quehacer de los laicos católicos," *El Cotidiano* (Mexico City), May-June 1990, p. 25.
12. Ibid. Also see: Manuel Canto and Javier Rojas, "Iglesia y derecha en México," *El Cotidiano* (Mexico City), July-August 1988, pp. 83-88.
13. Bernando Barranco Villafán and Raquel Pastor Escobar, *Jerarquía católica y modernización en México* (Mexico City: CAM Palabra Ediciones, 1989), pp. 53-66.
14. "Evangelicals in Mexico," *The Christian Century*, January 17, 1990.
15. Without any documentation, Mexican newspapers (particularly *El Universal*) and scholarly studies report that the evangelical churches form part of an imperialist conspiracy.
16. Chris Woehr, "Catholic-Protestant Tensions Rise," *Christianity Today*, March 19, 1990, p. 44.
17. Enrique Marroquín, "El campo religioso en las comunidades indígenas de Oaxaca," *Cristianismo y sociedad*, no. 101, 1989; Jean Pierre Bastian, *Protestantismo y sociedad en México* (Mexico City: Casa Unida de Publicaciones, 1983), pp. 230-35.
18. "Declaración protestante al pueblo de México," *Excélsior*, March 3, 1990.
19. Jean-Pierre Bastian, *Los disidentes: Sociedades protestantes y revolución en México 1872-1911* (Mexico City: Colegio de México, 1988).

20. Ibid.
21. The Summer Institute of Linguistics has been the main target of those whose claim that the evangelicals are imperialist agents whose goal is to acculturate and divide Mexican society. Because of its translation work, the institute previously worked closely with the government's National Indian Institute, but this collaboration was terminated in 1979. See Carlos Garma Navarro, "Los estudios antropológicos sobre el protestantismo en México," *Cristianismo y Sociedad*, no. 101, 1989.
22. Daniel Moreno Chávez, "Las sectas religiosas en México," *Uno más Uno*, March 24, 1990.
23. (WEC International) *Worldwide Thrust*, January-February 1991, p. 4.
24. Peter K. Johnson, "Sunday School at a Garbage Dump," *Saturday Evening Post*, September 1988.

Part Five: Environment

1. Angus Wright, The Death of Ramón González: The Modern Agricultural Dilemma (Austin, University of Texas Press, 1990), p. 299.
2. Lilia Albert, Enrique Aranda, J. Fernando Rincón Valdez and Rogelio Loera, "Situación de los plaguicidas en México y sus efectos en la salud y el medio ambiente," *Dossier 2*, no. 5, 1987, pp. 11-19; Conservation International, *Mexico's Living Environment: An Overview of Biological Diversity* (Mexico City, 1989); Testimony by Leslie Kochan of the AFL-CIO before the Subcommittee on Trade of the Committee on Ways and Means, House of Representatives, *The Maquiladoras and Toxics: The Hidden Costs of Production South of the Border*, June 28, 1990; Fernando Ortiz Monasterio, *Tierra profanada: Historia ambiental de México*, Colección Divulgación (Mexico City, SEDUE, 1987); Michael Redclift, "Agriculture and the Environment: The Mexican Experience," in George Philip, ed., *The Mexican Economy* (New York, Routledge Publishers, 1988) pp. 164-82; Philip Russel, *Mexico in Transition* (Austin, Colorado River Press, 1977); SEDUE, "Informe sobre el estado del medio ambiente en México," (Mexico City, 1986); Víctor Manuel Toledo, "La crisis ecológica," *México ante la crisis*, 3a. edición (Mexico City, Siglo Veintiuno Editores, 1987).
3. Stephen P. Mumme, *Preemptive Environmental Reform under Salinas* (Boulder, Colorado State University, 1991), p. 3; see also Carlos Ballesteros, "Políticas ecológicas y procesos de modernización en México," Manuscript, (Mexico City), 1990.
4. Estimate by Dr. Gonzalo Halfter, chairperson of the World Association for the Biosphere, and director general of Mexico's Institute of Ecology.
5. Marilyn Gates, "Institutionalizing Dependency: The Impact of Two Decades of Planned Agricultural Modernization on Peasants in the Mexican State of Campeche," *Journal of Developing Areas*, April 22, 1988, pp. 293-320.
6. Michael Redclift, "Agriculture and the Environment: The Mexican Experience," in George Philip, ed., *The Mexican Economy* (New York: Routledge Publishers, 1988), p. 171.
7. SEDUE, "Informe sobre el estado del medio ambiente en México" (Mexico City, 1986), p. 11-12.
8. For further discussion of the planning of the Ajusco area, see Keith Pezzoli, "Land Use Conflicts at Mexico City's Ecological Frontier: The Ajusco Case," paper presented at the 1990 meeting of the Western Political Science Association, Newport Beach, California, March 24, 1990.
9. Juan Carabia and Victor M. Toledo, eds., *Ecología y recursos naturales: Hacia una política ecológica del PSUM* (Mexico City, 1982), cited in Fernando Ortiz Monasterio et al., *Tierra profanada: Historia ambiental de México* (Mexico City: Colección Divulgación, 1987), p. 274. See also Redclift, "Agriculture and the Environment," p. 172.
10. Mumme, *Preemptive Environmental Reform*, p. 2.
11. Knowledge of Mexico's biodiversity is highly incomplete. The Mexico-based National Research Institute for Biotic Resources (INREB) and Conservation International in the United States have begun working together to narrow this gap. See Conservation International and INREB, *Mexico's Living Environment: An Overview of Biological*

Diversity/ Patrimonio vivo de México: Un diagnóstico de la diversidad biológica(Mexico City, 1989).

12. See Iván Restrepo, *Naturaleza muerta: Los plaguicidas en México* (Mexico City: Océana Ediciones, S.A., 1988).

13. Angus Wright, "Rethinking the Circle of Poison," *Latin American Perspectives* 13, no. 4, pp. 43-44.

14. Chris Bright, "Shipping unto Others," *E Magazine*, July-August, 1990.

15. General Accounting Office, *Trends and Impediments in Agricultural Trade* (Washington, 1990), p. 31; General Accounting Office, *Food Safety and Quality* (Washington, 1990), p. 71. Also see Barry Meier, "Poison Produce," *Wall Street Journal*, March 26, 1987.

16. Lilia Albert et al., "Situación de los plaguicidas en México y sus efectos en la salud y el medio ambiente," *Dossier* 2, no. 5, pp. 11-19; *El Financiero*, January 11, 1991, p. 34; and William Kistner, "Scrutiny of the Bounty," *Mother Jones*, December 1986, pp. 28, 58.

17. Kistner, "Scrutiny of the Bounty," pp. 28, 58. For an excellent study of the pesticide problem among Mexican peasants, see Angus Wright, *The Death of Ramón González: The Modern Agricultural Dilemma* (Austin: University of Texas Press, 1990).

18. Enrique Leff, "Población y medio ambiente," *Demos*, no. 3, 1990, pp. 25-26; "La ciudad," *El Nacional*, February 7, 1991; and Philip Russel, "Environment," in Philip Russel, ed., *Mexico in Transition*.

19. *New York Times International*, May 12, 1991.

20. Redclift, "Agriculture and the Environment," p. 166.

21. Cited in *Christian Science Monitor*, October 16, 1990.

22. *San Jose Mercury News*, April 16, 1991.

23. *US News and World Report*, May 6, 1991, pp. 32-41.

24. Albert E. Utton, "Transboundary Water Quality: Institutional Alternatives," in Paul Ganster and H. Walter, eds., *Environmental Hazards and Bioresource Management in the United States-Mexico Borderlands* (Los Angeles: UCLA Latin American Center Publications, 1990).

25. Diane M. Perry et al., "Binational Management of Hazardous Waste: The Maquiladora Industry at the US-Mexico Border," *Environmental Management* 14, no. 4, 1990, pp. 441-50.

26. Bruce Tomaso and Richard Alm, *Transboundary Resources Report* 4, no. 1, Spring 1990.

27. Testimony by Leslie Kochan of the AFL-CIO before the Subcommittee on Trade of the Committee on Ways and Means, House of Representatives, *The Maquiladoras and Toxics: The Hidden Costs of Production South of the Border*, June 28, 1990, p. 3.

28. Marco Kaltofen and Sanford J. Lewis, *Border Trouble: Rivers in Peril* (Boston: National Toxic Campaign Fund, 1991).

29. *Sun Diego Union*, November 10, 1989.

30. Roberto Sánchez Rodríguez, *El medio ambiente como fuente de conflicto en la relación binacional México-Estados Unidos* (Tijuana: El Colegio de la Frontera Norte, 1990), p. 46.

31. *US-Mexico Report*, July 1990, p. 15.

32. L. Cabrera Acevedo, "Legal Protection of the Environment in Mexico," *California Western International Law Journal*, Winter 1978, pp. 22-24; Mumme, *Preemptive Environmental Reform*, pp. 6-7. For additional analysis of government environmental policy, see: David Barkin, "Environmental Degradation and Productive Transformation in Mexico: The Contradictions of Crisis Management," *Yearbook of the Conference of Latin American Geographers* 15, 1990; Ballesteros, "Políticas ecológicas"; and Stephen P. Mumme, C. Richard Bath, and Valerie Assetto, "Political Developments and Environmental Policy in Mexico," *Latin American Research Review*, no. 22, 1988.

33. L. Cabrera Acevedo, "Administrative and Judicial Protection of the Environment in Mexico: Problems in Enforcing the Law," in Garth Hanse, ed., *Proceedings of the 1986 Meeting of the Rocky Mountain Council on Latin American Studies* (Las Cruces: New Mexico State University, 1986).

34. Mumme, *Preemptive Environmental Reform*, p. 11.

35. *Excélsior*, February 12, 1990.

36. Mumme, *Preemptive Environmental Reform*, p. 20.

37. Among other programs, the government provided incentives to Volkswagen to produce low-cost Beetles. According to one newspaper report, a government study showed that Mexico City realized a net gain of 67,554 vehicles in 1989; *Excélsior*, February 17, 1990, cited in Mumme, *Preemptive Environmental Reform*, p. 33.
38. Mumme, *Preemptive Environmental Reform*, p. 31.
39. *In These Times*, October 7, 1987.
40. See Patricia Gérez-Fernández, "Movimientos y luchas ecologistas en México," manuscript (Mexico City).
41. Mary Farquharson, "The Business of Rain Forests," *Business Mexico*, March, 1990, pp. 54-58.
42. Elaine Burns, "Mexican Villagers Forge Sustainable Society," *The Guardian*, April 25, 1990.
43. See, for example, Victor M. Toledo, "Los campesinos y la questión ecológica," *Pueblo* (Mexico City), no. 144-45, 1989.
44. Dick Kamp, "Maquilas and Hazardous Materials: Some Arizona-Sonora Experiences," manuscript (Naco, Arizona: Border Ecology Project).

Part Six: Foreign Influence

U.S. Foreign Policy

1. Bilateral Commission on the Future of United States-Mexican Relations, "The Challenge of Interdependence: Mexico and the United States," (Lanham, MD: University Press of America, 1989), p. 26.
2. For a few interesting and thoughtful overviews of U.S.-Mexico relations, see: Alan Riding, *Distant Neighbors: A Portrait of the Mexicans* (New York: Alfred A. Knopf, 1985), especially the chapter entitled, ". . . And So Close to the United States"; William D. Rogers, "Approaching Mexico," *Foreign Policy*, no. 72, Fall 1988, pp. 196-209; Peter H. Smith, "Uneasy Neighbors: Mexico and the United States," *Current History* 86, no. 518, March 1987; Paul Ganster and Alan Sweedler, *The United States-Mexican Border Region: Security and Interdependence*, reprinted from David Lorey, ed., *United States-Mexico Border Statistics Since 1900* (Los Angeles: UCLA Latin American Center Publications, 1990); and Abraham F. Lowenthal, "The United States and Mexico: Uneasy Neighbors," in *Partners in Conflict: The United States and Latin America in the 1990s* (Baltimore: Johns Hopkins University Press, 1990).
3. *Department of State Bulletin*, October 1989.
4. There is nothing sinister or conspiratorial about the fact that the U.S. government plans and carries out its foreign policy with Mexico on the basis of national interests defined by Washington. Idealistic notions aside, all governments—including Mexico's—construct and implement foreign policy with reference to interests defined by the national government and powerful elites. It is important when evaluating foreign policy, however, to pick through the rhetoric that is often used to justify particular policy choices to discover which interests are motivating policy and who will benefit or suffer as a result of given policies.
5. Smith, "Uneasy Neighbors," p. 98.
6. Cathryn L. Thorup, "U.S. Policymaking toward Mexico: Prospects for Administrative Reform," in Rosario Green and Peter H. Smith, eds., *Foreign Policy in U.S.-Mexican Relations* (San Diego: Center for U.S.-Mexican Studies, 1989), p. 150.
7. Bob Woodward, *Veil: The Secret Wars of the CIA 1981-1987* (New York: Simon and Schuster, 1987) discusses the manipulation of CIA intelligence reports on Mexico to accentuate the level of domestic unrest and consequent threat to Mexican stability.
8. Luis González Souza, "Lo deseable y lo posible en las relaciones México-EU: Democracia," *Mexico International*, July 1990.
9. The quotations are from, respectively, Smith, "Uneasy Neighbors," p. 131; and Peter H. Smith and Rosario Green, "Foreign Policy in U.S. Mexican Relations: Introduction," in Green and Smith, *Foreign Policy in U.S.-Mexican Relations*, p. 4.

10. Riordan Roett, "Mexico and the United States: Managing the Relationship," in Riordan Roett, ed., *Mexico and the United States: Managing the Relationship* (Boulder: Westview Press, 1988), p. 5.
11. Statement in "American Economic Policies toward Mexico and Latin America," hearing before the Joint Economic Committee of the Congress of the United States, September 17, 1990, p. 42.
12. See: Lorenzo Meyer, "Mexico: The Exception and the Rule," in Abraham F. Lowenthal, ed., *Exporting Democracy: The United States and Latin America* (Baltimore: John Hopkins University Press, 1991), pp. 215-32; and Fred R. Harris, "Mexico: Historical Foundations," in Jan Knippers Black, ed., *Latin America: Its Problems and Its Promise* (Boulder: Westview Press, 1984) for a discussion of these years.

U.S.-Mexico Trade

1.. Department of State, "Economic Trends Report," August 1991. Calculations include exports and imports of the *maquila* sector.
2. Gary Teske, "U.S. Trade with Mexico in Perspective," *Business America*, June 18, 1990.
3. U.S. Department of Commerce, *North American Free Trade Agreement: Generating Jobs for Americans* (Washington, 1991), p. 50.
4. *Business America*, June 18, 1990; U.S. International Trade Commission, *Background Study of the Economies and International Trade Patterns of the Countries of North America, Central America, and the Caribbean* (Washington, 1981), p. 163.
5. Ibid. Mexican economist Kurt Unger estimated that more than 60 percent of Mexican exports of manufactured goods are produced by subsidiaries of multinational firms. See Kurt Unger, *Competencia monopólica y tecnología en la industria mexicana* (Mexico City: El Colegio de México, 1985).
6. In 1950 the United States and Mexico terminated the Reciprocal Trade Agreement that had governed trade relations since 1943. It was not until the 1980s that the two countries moved to devise new formal mechanisms covering trade relations. Two major agreements were worked out. The Framework Understanding on Trade and Investment signed in 1987 opened the doors to separate agreements on different trade items (ranging from beer to steel). It was the most comprehensive and flexible trade agreement ever negotiated between the two nations and established a thorough consultative mechanism for trade disputes. Going beyond the 1987 framework agreement, the 1989 Trade and Investment Facilitation Understanding created a mandate to broaden trade and investment relations and established action plans for reaching desired goals. These agreements set up a mechanism for the resolution of trade disputes and are now being used as models for trade negotiations under the auspices of the Initiative for the Americas.
7. U.S. Department of Commerce, *Survey of Current Business*, August 1983, August 1990, and June 1991. The book value of direct U.S. investment increased from $5.6 billion in 1982 to $9.4 billion in 1990. Investment figures from the Commerce Department do not correspond with those recorded by the Mexican government, nor do they portray the full extent of U.S. direct investment, mainly because they report only the book value or historical costs of U.S. investment. They are based on a $500,000 minimum-investment standard and identify direct investment as having at least 10 percent of voting securities. These figures do not include the value of management, licensing, or technology contracts. They include only direct investment, not the assets of foreign affiliates.
8. *1991 Economic Report of the President* (Washington, 1991).
9. *North American Free Trade Agreement*, p. 25; Sara Melton, "U.S.-Mexico Business Experience," *Business America*, April 8, 1991, p. 11.
10. "Summary of Views on Prospects for Future United States-Mexico Relations," USITC Publication no. 2326, October 1990; "The Likely Impact on the United States of a Free Trade Agreement with Mexico," USITC Publication no. 2353, February 1991.
11. *Proceso* (Mexico City), May 13, 1991; May 20, 1991.

12. Stephen Fielding Diamond, "Labor and the North American Free Trade Agreement: Toward a Constructive Critique," paper presented at the Center for U.S.-Mexican Studies, University of California, San Diego, February 20, 1991, p. 24.

13. Under the fast-track authority Congress approves or disapproves the final text of the agreement and its implementing legislation without amendment within 90 legislative days. In exchange for this expedited process, the executive branch agrees to consult with Congress throughout the negotiating process. As a practical matter, without fast-track authority few countries would enter negotiations on such matters, knowing that the agreement could subsequently be revised by Congress.

14. The Mexico-U.S. Business Committee regularly contracts studies to support its free trade position. See, for example, Policy Economics Group of KPMG Peat Marwick, *The Effects of a Free Trade Agreement between the U.S. and Mexico* (Washington, 1991). The study concludes that real income, the real wage rate, and the real rate of return to capital in the United States would be lower in the United States without a free trade agreement with Mexico.

15. Letter reprinted in *Mexico Policy News*, Spring 1991.

16. *Business Week*, November 12, 1990, quoting Center director James B. Benn.

17. Daniel Mitchell, "The Impact of International Trade on U.S. Employment," in Ward Morehouse, ed., *American Labor in a Changing World Economy* (New York: Praeger Publishers, 1978); Diamond, "Labor and the North America Free Trade Agreement," pp. 20-21.

18. Calculated by authors. Information taken from Economic Indicators, August 1991. Prepared for the Joint Economic Committee by the Council of Economic Advisers. U.S. Government Printing Office, Washington: 1991. See also Economic Indicators, July 1985. Prepared by the Joint Economic Committee by the Council of Economic Advisers. U.S. Government Printing Office, Washington: 1985.

19. See, for example: Joseph Grunwald and Kenneth Flamm, *The Global Factory: Foreign Assembly in International Trade* (Washington: Brookings Institution, 1985); and Joyce Kolko, *Restructuring the World Economy* (New York: Pantheon Books, 1988).

20. Quoted in Stephen Baker, "Mexico: A New Economic Era," *Business Week*, November 12, 1990.

21. Quoted in Willaim A. Orme, Jr., "The Sunbelt Moves South," *NACLA Report on the Americas*, May 1991, p. 15.

22. Diamond, "Labor and the North American Free Trade Agreement," p. 21.

23. See Beth Sims, *Workers of the World Undermined: American Labor's Role in U.S. Foreign Policy* (Boston: South End Press, forthcoming 1992).

24. *Christian Science Monitor*, July 11, 1991.

25. USITC, *Likely Impact of a Free Trade Agreement*.

26. See, for example, Clark W. Reynolds, "Integrating the U.S. and Mexican Economies," *Business Mexico*, December 1990.

27. Jeff Faux, "No: The Biggest Export Will Be U.S. Jobs," *Washington Post*, April 14, 1991.

28. Richard Rothstein, "A Hand for Mexico, a Slap for Us," *Los Angeles Times*, November 23, 1990. Rothstein is a research associate at the Economic Policy Institute.

29. Sidney Weintraub, "Jobs on the Line," *Business Mexico*, March 1991.

30. Cited in Jeremy Brecher and Tim Costello, "Labor Goes Global: Global Village vs. Global Pillage," *Z Magazine*, January 1991.

31. See: Staff Subcommittee on International Policy and Trade (U.S. Congress), "A North American Free Trade Agreement: Too Fast a Track," (Washington), May 20, 1991; and Texas Center for Policy Studies and Border Ecology Project, "Mexico-U.S. Free Trade Negotiations and Environment: Exploring the Issues" (Austin), January 1991.

32. For an excellent assessment of the results of the Canada-U.S. FTA and an analysis of the impact of the proposed NAFTA on Canada, see Bruce Campbell, "Beggar Thy Neighbor," *NACLA Report on the Americas*, May 1991.

33. An obvious case of such overly restrictive sanitary regulations is the prohibition of the import of Mexican avocados to protect U.S. growers. See United States General Accounting Office, *U.S.-Mexico Trade: Impact of Liberalization in the Agricultural Sector* (Washington, 1991).

The Role of Foreign Investment

1. John V. Sweeney, "Foreign Investment Issues Facing Mexico," *Business Mexico*, September 1991. Sweeney is the U.S. financial attaché at the U.S. embassy in Mexico City.
2. Lawrence Kootnikoff, "Coming Together," *Business Mexico*, March 1991.
3. "Las empresas más importantes de México," in a special issue of *Expansión* (Mexico City), August 15, 1990. According to the article, 15 of the top 50 companies in Mexico were foreign firms. Although this survey is a good indicator of the importance of foreign investment in Mexico, it failed to include those companies that did not respond to the magazine's questionnaire. As a result, dozens of foreign firms were not included, including such major firms as Bayer, Becton Dickinson, Black & Decker, Chrysler, General Foods, Ralston Purina, Kimberly-Clark, NCR, Borden, Union Carbide, and Upjohn.
4. *El Financiero*, January 11, 1991, and August 23, 1991, citing figures from SECOFI's Technological Development Department.
5. U.S. Department of Commerce, *Survey of Current Business*, August 1990, p. 95. Rate of return is calculated by dividing income by that year's direct investment.
6. U.S. Department of Commerce, *Survey of Current Business*, June 1991, p. 29.
7. Cumulative foreign investment, as approved by the Foreign Investment Commission of SECOFI, jumped from $11.5 billion in 1982 to $24 billion by 1988. Total cumulative investment by the end of 1990 was $30.3 billion.
8. Between 1986 and 1988 debt-equity swaps accounted for 16 percent of the new direct foreign investment.
9. During the first half of 1991, foreign investment in the stock exchange was up 100 percent over 1990, with an estimated $9.4 billion in total foreign funds invested.
10. David Goldman, "A Revolution You Can Invest In," *Forbes*, July 9, 1990.
11. *El Financiero*, June 27, 1990.
12. Banamex, *Review of the Economic Situation of Mexico*, July 1991. The main vehicles of foreign portfolio investment were temporary investment trusts, which allowed foreign corporations to invest in restricted activities such as mining and secondary petrochemicals. The second most commonly used instruments were neutral investment trusts, which offer a share of profits but no rights to the corporation.
13. *El Financiero*, March 21, 1991.
14. According to Luis Rubio of the Center of Economic Development in Mexico City, "A country the size of Mexico should have only about half the sectors it does." Quoted in Christine MacDonald, "Gamesa Heat," *Business Mexico*, March 1991.
15. This is according to Jonathan Health of Macro Asesoría Económica in Mexico City. And according to a recent study by Operadora de Bolsa in Mexico City, the average operating margin in 1990 was 13.4 percent, down nearly 6 percentage points from the 1987 average, and substantially below the average 22.8-percent operating margin in 1984.
16. Kurt Unger, "Mexican Manufactured Exports and U.S. Transnational Corporations: Industrial Structuring Strategies, Intrafirm Trade and New Elements of Comparative Advantage," in Commission for the Study of International Migration and Cooperative Economic Development, *Unauthorized Migration: Addressing the Root Causes* (Washington, 1987-1990), p. 1103. Another study indicates that 59.2 percent of the increase in exports between 1982 and 1987 came from firms that were either partially or wholly owned by foreign investors. See Eduardo Gitli and Juan Rocha, "La inversión extranjera directa (IED) y el modelo exportador mexicano de los ochenta," (Mexico City: Universidad Autónoma Metropolitana, 1989).
17. Figures from the National Foreign Trade Bank.
18. Unger, "Mexican Manufactured Exports," p. 1112.
19. Ibid.
20. *Business Week*, November 12, 1990.
21. Juanita Darling, "Fund to Buy U.S. Factories, Relocate Them to Mexico," *Los Angeles Times*, May 24, 1990.
22. Kim Moody, "Free Trade Threatens Jobs and Income," *Labor Notes*, July 1991.
23. Chris Kraul, "Kohler Building Big Fixtures Plant in Mexico," *Los Angeles Times*, January 26, 1990.

24. The challenges and problems of foreign investment in the rapidly changing Mexican market are examined in Business International, *Succeeding in the New Mexico: Corporate Strategy, Globalization, and the Free Trade Agreement* (New York, 1991).
25. Joel Millman, "There's Your Solution," *Forbes*, January 7, 1991.
26. Juanita Darling, "Hungry Mexico Takes Reforms out to the Farm," *Los Angeles Times*, November 26, 1990.
27. Juanita Darling, "Mexican Franchise Effort is Having Its Growing Pains," *Los Angeles Times*, May 12, 1991.
28. *El Financiero*, citing the National Restaurant and Food Industry Chamber (CANICRAC).
29. Brendan J. Hudson, "The Fast Growth of Franchising," *Business Mexico*, June 1990.
30. The Banco de México in 1989 showed a surplus of only $57 million in the total balance of payments of foreign investment when the inflow of foreign investment was about $2 billion.

U.S. Economic Programs

1. For a more detailed summary of these U.S. rescue efforts, see James H. Street, "Mexico's Development Crisis," *Current History* 86, no. 518, March 1987.
2. Ibid.
3. Sidney Weintraub, *A Marriage of Convenience: Relations between Mexico and the United States* (Oxford: Oxford University Press, 1990), p. 149.
4. K. Larry Storrs, *Mexico-U.S. Relations: Issues for Congress* (Washington: Congressional Research Service, 1990), p. 8.
5. This summary of U.S. strategies comes largely from Bilateral Commission on the Future of United States-Mexican Relations, *The Challenge of Interdependence: Mexico and the United States*, (Lanham, MD: University Press of America, 1989), pp. 53-54.
6. For discussions see: Weintraub, *A Marriage of Convenience*, pp. 144-48; and Street, "Mexico's Development Crisis," pp. 75-76.
7. Overviews of the Brady Plan and its impacts on Mexico are given in: Weintraub, *A Marriage of Convenience*, p. 149; Abraham F. Lowenthal, *Partners in Conflict: The United States and Latin America in the 1990s* (Baltimore: John Hopkins University Press, 1990), p. 90; K. Larry Storrs, *Mexico-U.S. Relations*; Testimony by Sally Shelton-Colby before the Subcommittee on Western Hemisphere Affairs, U.S. House of Representatives, June 7, 1989; and U.S. Department of State, *Dispatch*, September 24, 1990.
8. Testimony before the Subcommittee on Western Hemisphere Affairs, U.S. House of Representatives, June 7, 1989, p. 59.
9. From a commentary by John Saxe-Fernandez in *Excélsior*, cited in *Latin America News Update*, November 1990.
10. In contrast to its participation in these other programs, Mexico is one of only four Latin American countries that do not have operations supported by the Overseas Private Investment Corporation (OPIC). Created by the U.S. Congress, OPIC provides insurance and loans to U.S. transnational corporations to support their overseas activities. Because Mexico refuses to sign a bilateral investment guarantee agreement, OPIC cannot extend its services to U.S. TNCs in that country. Interview with John Gurr, OPIC, April 15, 1991.
11. Export-Import Bank, *Export-Import Bank of the United States: An Independent Government Agency that Assists the Financing of U.S. Exports*, pamphlet, November 1990.
12. *El Financiero*, April 25, 1991; *The Mexico City News*, April 26, 1991.
13. U.S. Export-Import Bank, *1989 Annual Report* (1990).
14. Eximbank categorizes countries under terms of an agreement worked out among members of the Organization for Economic Cooperation and Development. Mexico is classified as an "intermediate" country in terms of income level. This designation qualifies Mexican buyers for rates of interest lower than those assigned to "rich" countries but higher than those for "poor" countries.
15. U.S. Export-Import Bank, *1987 Annual Report* (Washington) and interview with Quang Phung, Eximbank, August 26, 1991.

16. "Eximbank in Mexico," *Business America,* December 4, 1989, p. 17.
17. From 1978 to 1982—the years of heady oil-backed expansion—the bank loaned more than $1.5 billion to Mexican buyers to purchase U.S. exports. In 1983, however, Eximbank loans crashed along with Mexico's economy. Throughout the rest of the 1980s, the value of Eximbank loans to the country crept up and down, reaching a high of $66.5 million in 1984, dropping to zero in 1986, and climbing back to $38.8 million in 1989. Loans awarded for Mexican projects nearly doubled the following year, reflecting renewed business interest in the country and a growing sense that the economic liberalization was really going to go forward. But in recognition of continued economic uncertainty, the 1990 total of $73.6 million in loans came nowhere near the yearly totals for the late 1970s and early 1980s.
18. *Business America,* December 4, 1989.
19. About the same time as the $1.5 billion loan guarantee was announced—November 1990—a flurry of press reports in both the United States and Mexico suggested that a $5.6 billion loan or loan guarantee was also being put together for Pemex. The figure came up at discussions held by presidents Bush and Salinas in Monterrey that same month and referred to the amount Pemex said it needed for its development projects. According to Marian Hinchman, senior loan officer for Mexico at the Export-Import Bank, Eximbank was not considering making such a commitment. Interview with Marian Hinchman, Eximbank, August 23, 1991.
20. Ibid.
21. Edward Cody, "Oil Loan Touches a Mexican Nerve," *Washington Post*, December 7, 1990.
22. By 1986, Mexico was contributing more than one-third of the annual deposits of oil to the U.S. reserve. See U.S. Department of Energy, "Strategic Petroleum Reserve Annual Report" (Washington), February 1987, p. 10.
23. Interview with Daniel Dowd, Eximbank, August 23, 1991.
24. Export-Import Bank, "1990-91 Eximbank/FCIA Trade Credit Insurance Facility for Mexico," August 9, 1990.
25. Under the TEA program, U.S. exporters had to show that Mexico was engaging in unfair trade practices that made it difficult for U.S. exports of a given commodity to enter the Mexican market. As Mexico liberalizes, however, this rationalization for Washington's own subsidies to U.S. growers is being undermined. The justification will likely prove even less viable as the two countries move toward a free trade pact. At any rate, under the MPP, the requirement was abandoned, and Washington may now pay toward these activities without alleging unfair trade practices on Mexico's part. Interview with Kent Sisson, FAS, August 22, 1991.
26. Foreign Agricultural Service, "Fact Sheet" (Washington), December 1989.
27. TEA, "Budget Report by Country" (Washington), October 2, 1990, pp. 181-83.
28. Interview with Kevin Bernhardt, FAS, August 13, 1991.
29. Agricultural Affairs Office, "Grain and Feed Annual Narrative" (Mexico City), 1990.
30. Interview with Kevin Bernhardt, FAS, August 13, 1991.
31. Ibid.; and FAS, "Report PR 320-88" (Washington), June 2, 1988.
32. U.S. General Accounting Office, *U.S.-Mexico Trade: Trends and Impediments in Agricultural Trade* (Washington, 1990), p. 34.
33. Ibid.; interview with Max Bowser, FAS, November 18, 1990; and U.S. Department of Agriculture, *Desk Reference Guide to U.S. Agricultural Trade* (Washington, 1990), p. 10.
34. Agricultural Affairs Office, "Grain and Feed," pp. 10-11.
35. See the discussion by economist David Barkin in his book, *Distorted Development: Mexico in the World Economy* (Boulder: Westview Press, 1990), p. 5.
36. Until 1972 Mexico received modest levels of support under three PL480 programs. This included a total of $24.6 million in PL480's Title I commodities. Under Title I, U.S. commodities are sold at concessionary rates with long pay-back terms in order to shore up currency-poor recipients. The recipient government sells the commodities to national processors in order to generate local currency. The local currency is then added to government coffers and can be used for other government programs. Also until 1972, Mexico received some $53.5 million in Title II commodities and another $19.7 million under a third program for barter contracts. Although quite extensive in

many less developed countries, the use of PL480 Title II commodities in Mexico is minimal and intermittent. Title II is the main U.S. government food-donation program, with commodities meant to be distributed free to poor populations. Small amounts of food were distributed through PL480 Title II programs in the 1980s. Commodities such as wheat flour, nonfat dry milk, corn, and vegetable oil were distributed by multilateral entities such as the World Food Program and its International Emergency Food Reserve. The food was used for special populations such as refugees. See Food for Peace, "1972 Annual Report on Public Law 480" (Washington), pp. 88, 113, and 115; interview with Mary Chambliss, FAS, August 30, 1991; Food for Peace, "Annual Reports on Public Law 480," (Washington), 1985-87; and interview with Skip Brown, PL480 Title II office, August 29, 1991.

37. The title of the program refers to Section 416(b) of the Agricultural Act of 1949, which, in its amended version, authorizes the food donation activities carried out under 416 auspices. Donations under 416 had occurred in the 1950s and 1960s but were cut off in 1966 in favor of PL480 programs. Section 416 food distribution programs were reinstated by congressional amendment in 1983. Foreign Agricultural Service summary, "Section 416(b) of the Agricultural Act of 1949, As Amended," February 14, 1990.

38. FAS, "U.S.G. Section 416(b) Assistance to Mexico," August 26, 1991.

39. FAS, "Section 416(b) of the Agricultural Act of 1949, As Amended," p. 7.

40. Barton R. Burkhalter, Janet W. Lowenthal, and James M. Pines, "Evaluation Report: The Section 416 Program in Mexico," report of an AID-contracted evaluation by Development Assistance Corp., August 1987, p. 91.

41. Percentage generated from figures given in: Burkhalter et al., "Evaluation Report," ibid.; AID, "Mexico: Project Assistance (Projects Active as of March 1991)," May 1991, p. 38; and interview with Gerard Bowers, AID/Mexico, July 26, 1990.

42. The new programs were the Program for Social and Food Assistance to Families (PASAF), the Program for Providing Food to Needy Children (PREPAN), and the Program of Food Assistance to Families of Sugar Workers (FIOSCER). See Burkhalter et al., "Evaluation Report," p. 12.

43. Ibid.

44. Alan Riding, *Distant Neighbors*, p. 344; and interview with Gerard Bowers, AID/Mexico, July 26, 1990.

45. AID's departure was not a big loss for Mexico. From the mid-1940s until 1961, the United States provided an assortment of loans, grants, and food-assistance programs in Mexico. But AID programs in the country never assumed the proportions of similar U.S. assistance elsewhere in Latin America. From 1962 to 1971, for instance, loans and grants from AID to Mexico totaled only $70 million, the lowest on a per capita basis of any Latin American country. Moreover, most of AID's assistance was in the form of loans, thus obligating repayment on Mexico's part. See Riding, *Distant Neighbors*, p. 344; and AID, *U.S. Economic Assistance Programs Administered by the Agency for International Development and Predecessor Agencies*, (Washington), 1971, p. 35.

46. Interview with Robert Kahn, AID/Washington, August 27, 1991.

47. AID has missions in countries that it classifies as underdeveloped or poor. In Latin America, this category includes Bolivia, Ecuador, Peru, and the Central American countries except for Belize. Each of these countries has AID missions. Advanced Developing Countries, according to AID, include Argentina, Belize, Brazil, Chile, Colombia, Mexico, Paraguay, and Uruguay. AID maintains offices in all these countries. Ibid.

48. These categories are developed from a reading of AID grants in AID, "Mexico: Project Assistance." In two cases, they represent a composite of AID grant categories with similar focuses. Grants for "health" projects, for example, include the following AID categories: Child Survival, AIDS, and Health, while "private sector support" includes AID's grants for Private Sector, Energy, and Environment; and Education and Human Services.

49. AID, –Congressional Presentation Fiscal Year 1989" (Washington), 1990, p. 283.

50. Interview with Mike Verdu, AIFLD representative in Mexico, January 1991; and Burkhalter et al., "Evaluation Report," p. 40

51. Interview with Robert Kahn, AID/Washington, August 27, 1991.

52. Lorenzo Meyer, "Mexico: The Exception and the Rule," p. 218.

53. See the discussion by Claude Heller, "U.S. and Mexican Policies Toward Central America," in Green and Smith, *Foreign Policy in U.S.-Mexican Relations*, pp. 171-213, for a description of U.S.-Mexico regional foreign-policy conflicts. See also Cathryn L. Thorup, "U.S. Policymaking toward Mexico: Prospects for Administrative Reform," in the same volume, pp. 150-52, for a statement on the Reagan administration's belief that the best way to protect U.S. interests under the circumstances of the early 1980s was to "weigh in on the issues of political reform in Mexico."

54. Interview with LAC Democracy Initiatives project officer, February 21, 1991.

55. Beth Sims, "National Endowment for Democracy: A Foreign Policy Branch Gone Awry" (Albuquerque: Inter-Hemispheric Education Resource Center, 1990), critiques NED and its activities, especially its assertion that it is a democracy-building institution.

56. National Endowment for Democracy, "Annual reports" (Washington), 1985-89; Board meeting minutes of the National Endowment for Democracy, 1990; various proposals and grant evaluations submitted by NED grantees; and interview with Scott Day, public information officer at NED, September 6, 1991. The business associations that received NED funding were the Centro de Estudios en Economía y Educación (CEEE), Confederación Patronal de la República Mexicana (Coparmex), Desarrollo Mexicano (DESEM/DEMAC), Confederation of National Chambers of Commerce, Services, and Tourism (Concanaco), and the Latin American Association of Business Organization Executives (ALEOE).

57. National Republican Institute for International Affairs (NRIIA), third-quarter report, 1990, p. 9; and NRIIA, "Mexico FY90," evaluation summary submitted by the NRIIA to NED, p. 1.

58. NRIIA third-quarter report, p. 9.

59. NRIIA, "Mexico FY89," program proposal; and NRIIA quarterly reports to NED for 1989.

60. Interview with Otto René Quiñónez, director of Academia Política de Centro América, June 29, 1990. The Guatemalan branch of the academy is the Academia para la Libertad y la Justicia; it is closely associated with the Solidarity Action Movement (MAS), the party of Guatemala's president, Jorge Serrano.

61. The following authors look at various aspects of U.S. support for Mexican democratization and the subsequent retreat from that stand: Meyer, pp. 225-29; Andrew Reding, "Mexico Under Salinas: A Facade of Reform," *World Policy Journal*, Fall 1989; Andrew Reding, "Mexico: The Crumbling of the 'Perfect Dictatorship,'" *World Policy Journal*, Spring 1991; Cuauhtémoc Cárdenas, "Misunderstanding Mexico," *Foreign Policy*, Spring 1990; as well as articles by Jorge G. Castañeda in *Proceso* (Mexico City) during 1988 and 1989 and by Adolfo Aguilar Zínser in *Excélsior* (Mexico City) over the same period.

62. Although PAN remained a strong opposition force, especially in the strategically important industrial northern states, at the national level the contest in 1988 was between PRI and the FDN.

63. Reding, "The Crumbling of the 'Perfect Dictatorship.'"

64. A variety of writers have looked at NED's grants regarding Nicaragua's 1990 elections. Among the most useful are: Holly Sklar, "Washington Wants to Buy Nicaragua's Elections Again," *Z Magazine*, December 1989; William Robinson and David MacMichael, "NED Overt Action: Intervention in the Nicaraguan Election," *Covert Action Information Bulletin*, Winter 1990; William I. Robinson, "Nicaraguan Electoral Coup," *Covert Action Information Bulletin*, Summer 1990; and George R. Vickers, "U.S. Funding of the Nicaraguan Opposition: A Preliminary Assessment," paper presented at the Washington Office on Latin America conference on *U.S. Electoral Assistance and Democratic Development: Chile, Nicaragua, Panama*, January 19, 1990. Also see: U.S. Agency for International Development, *Report to Congress on Public Law 101-119*, AID Grant to the National Endowment for Democracy, December 4, 1989; Beth Sims, "National Endowment for Democracy"; and Beth Sims, "Democratization, Political Aid, and Superpower Intervention: The U.S. Role in the 1990 Nicaraguan Election," paper presented at the XVI International Congress of the Latin American Studies Association, April 4, 1991.

U.S. Security Assistance

1. *Department of State Bulletin*, October 1989.
2. U.S. Department of State, *Dispatch*, February 18, 1991.
3. Section on Mexico from the U.S. executive branch's *Congressional Presentation for Security Assistance Programs*, fiscal year 1989, p. 248.
4. Ibid.
5. Robert A. Pastor and Jorge G. Castañeda, *Limits to Friendship: The United States and Mexico* (New York: Alfred A. Knopf, 1988), p. 244; and James Van Wert, "El control de narcóticos en México. Una década de institucionalización y un asunto diplomático," in Gabriel Székely, ed., *México-Estados Unidos 1985* (Mexico City: El Colegio de México, 1986), cited in Samuel I. del Villar, "The Illicit U.S.-Mexico Drug Market: Failure of Policy and an Alternative," in Roett, *Mexico and the United States: Managing the Relationship*, p. 196.
6. Del Villar, p. 191.
7. On the U.S. side of the border, members of U.S. armed forces such as the Marine Corps and the National Guard work under the supervision of the U.S. Army's Joint Task Force Six in anti-drug activities. Other U.S. agencies involved in the effort on the U.S. side of the border include the Customs Service, the Immigration and Naturalization Service, the U.S. Border Patrol, the FBI, the Bureau of Alcohol, Tobacco, and Firearms, and the DEA. They work within frameworks devised by the Office of National Drug Control Policy, based in the White House, as does the State Department's Bureau of International Narcotics Matters, which supervises international aspects of the drug war.
8. Quoted in del Villar, p. 200.
9. Department of Defense, *Congressional Presentation for Security Assistance Programs*, fiscal year 1992 (Washington), 1991, p. 217.
10. Ibid.
11. From 1950 to 1978, only Caribbean microstates and a few small countries such as Costa Rica, Haiti, Panama, and El Salvador received less military aid from the United States than Mexico did. See: Lars Schoultz, *Human Rights and United States Policy toward Latin America* (Princeton: Princeton University Press, 1981), p. 215; and AID, *U.S. Overseas Loans and Grants and Assistance from International Organizations*, Obligations and Loan Authorizations, July 1, 1945-September 30, 1981 (Washington), 1981.
12. David Ronfeldt, ed., *The Modern Mexican Military: A Reassessment* (San Diego: Center for U.S.-Mexican Studies, 1984), p. 100.
13. This discussion of historical U.S.-Mexico military ties draws heavily on Ronfeldt's analysis in *The Modern Mexican Military*, pp. 100-101, but see also Ganster and Sweedler, *The United States-Mexican Border Region*, pp. 420-21.
14. M. Delal Baer, "Mexico: Ambivalent Ally," *The Washington Quarterly*, Summer 1987, p. 105.
15. During the entire postwar period, Mexico received less than $50,000 in support under MAP. See: AID, *U.S. Overseas Loans and Grants and Assistance from International Organizations*.
16. Ronfeldt, *The Modern Mexican Military*, p. 101, citing Center for Advanced International Studies, *The Political and Socioeconomic Role of the Military*, pp. 1-28; and Schoultz, *Human Rights*, p. 238.
17. AID, *U.S. Overseas Loans and Grants and Assistance from International Organizations*, p. 56; *Congressional Presentations for Security Assistance Programs*, 1983-1992; and Hearings before a Subcommittee of the Committee on Appropriations, U.S. House of Representatives, "Foreign Operations, Export Financing, and Related Programs Appropriations for 1991," p. 426.
18. See: Carmen Lira, "Desde 1982, México ha comprado a EU más armas que en los 30 años anteriores," *La Jornada*, June 30, 1989; and *Congressional Presenations for Security Assistance Programs*, 1983-1992.
19. *Congressional Presentation for Security Assistance Programs*, 1989, pp. 248-50.
20. *Congressional Presentation for Security Assistance Programs*, 1992, p. 217.
21. Ronfeldt, *The Modern Mexican Military*, p. 101.
22. Quoted in a commentary by John Saxe-Fernandez, *Excélsior*, April 2, 1991.

23. AID, *U.S. Overseas Loans and Grants and Assistance from International Organizations*, various years.
24. Hearings before a Subcommittee of the Committee on Appropriations, U.S. House of Representatives, "Foreign Operations, Export Financing, and Related Programs Appropriations for 1991," p. 585.
25. These totals are drawn from two sources: Lira, "Desde 1982," who cited a total of 297 Mexican personnel trained from 1984 to 1988; and an interview with Major Michael González, U.S. Department of Defense, Latin America and Africa Division, September 13, 1991.
26. Schoultz, *Human Rights*, p. 215.
27. Hearings before the Subcommittee on Foreign Operations Appropriations, Committee on Appropriations, House of Representatives, "Foreign Operations Appropriations for 1963," 1962, p. 359.
28. The quotes are from Pentagon documents cited in Lira, "Desde 1982."
29. AID, *U.S. Overseas Loans and Grants and Assistance from International Organizations*, various years.
30. Office of National Drug Control Policy, *National Drug Control Strategy* (Washington, 1991), p. 83.
31. Both military and civilian security forces are deeply involved in activities to combat narcotics production and trafficking. U.S. General Accounting Office, *Drug Control: U.S.-Mexico Opium Poppy and Marijuana Aerial Eradication Program* (Washington, 1988), p. 9. As of the mid-1980s, Mexico allocated about one-third of its military budget and more than 60 percent of its attorney general's budget to the drug war. See: Del Villar, "The Illicit U.S.-Mexico Drug Market," p. 199.
32. In many cases, especially with agricultural spray pilots and aircraft mechanics and technicians, the professional boost given by U.S. anti-narcotics aid helped land the personnel lucrative jobs in the private sector. The low salaries offered by the Office of the Attorney General proved unable to hold many of the individuals trained through U.S. programs. See: U.S. General Accounting Office, *Drug Control*, pp. 28-29.
33. Storrs, *Mexico-U.S. Relations*, p. 9.
34. Marjorie Miller, "Mexico Has New General in the War on Narcotics," *Los Angeles Times*, November 13, 1990.
35. The following discussion of U.S. support for Mexico's aerial eradication efforts is drawn largely from U.S. General Accounting Office, *Drug Control*.
36. State Department International Narcotics Control Foreign Assistance Appropriations Act, Fiscal Year 1991 Budget Congressional Submission, in hearings before a Subcommittee of the Committee on Appropriations of the House of Representatives, "Foreign Operations, Export Financing, and Related Programs Appropriations for 1991," 101st Congress, Second Session.
37. The legislation is the Foreign Assistance Act of 1961, as amended.
38. Robert L. Wilhelm, "The Transnational Relations of United States Law Enforcement Agencies with Mexico," *Proceedings of the Pacific Coast Council on Latin American Studies* 14, no. 2, 1987, p. 161.
39. Cable from the U.S. Secretary of Defense to Army Headquarters in Washington DC, No. 221825Z, January 1991; and Cable from the U.S. Secretary of Defense to Army Headquarters in Washington DC, No. 141130Z, October 1990.
40. *International Narcotics Control Strategy Report* (Washington), March 1991.
41. Miller, "Mexico Has New General."
42. *International Narcotics Control Strategy Report*, p. 157; and Edward Cody, "U.S. Congressmen Laud Cooperation of Mexico on Antidrug Campaign," *Washington Post*, December 13, 1990.
43. Office of National Drug Control Policy, *National Drug Control Strategy*, p. 83.
44. Douglas Jehl and Marjorie Miller, "U.S. Military Unit in Mexico Aids Drug War," *Los Angeles Times*, June 7, 1990.
45. Del Villar, "The Illicit U.S.-Mexico Drug Market," p. 205.
46. Cárdenas, "Misunderstanding Mexico," p. 117.

47. See: Larry Rohter, "Use of Troops a Cause of Concern in Mexico: Armed Forces are Sent to Deal with Politics, Labor, and Crime," *New York Times*, November 5, 1989.

Other Foreign Interests

1. Jonathan Kandell, *La Capital* (New York: Random House, 1988), pp. 353-80.
2. Ministry of Trade and Industrial Development (SECOFI), "Accumulated Foreign Investment as of December 1990" (Mexico City).
3. *Business Japan*, November-December 1987.
4. Susanne Grader, "Wirtschaftswoche of Dusseldorf," *World Press Review*, January 1988.
5. Harley Shaiken and Harry Browne, "Japanese Work Organization in Mexico," in Gabriel Székely, ed., *Manufacturing across Borders and Oceans: Japan, the United States and Mexico* (La Jolla: Center for U.S.-Mexican Studies, 1990), p. 26.
6. Ibid., p. 20.
7. Derek Ramsamooj, "Japan in Mexico: Taking the Long View," *Business Mexico*, May 1990.
8. Ibid.
9. *Excélsior*, October 16, 1988.
10. *El Financiero*, April 16, 1991.
11. INEGI, "Mexico: Economic and Social Information," *International Review* II, no. 1, April 1990.
12. Antonio Salinas Chávez, "El comercio de México con la CEE: 15 años de avances y retrocesos" (Mexico: Mexico City, 1991).y
13. *Maclean's*, June 25, 1990.
14. David Winfield, Canadian ambassador to Mexico, press conference, May 30, 1990.

Chronology

1325	Aztecs settle in central Mexico and found their capital at Tenochtitlán, on present-day site of Mexico City.
1519	Aztecs rule most of central and southern Mexico. Hernán Cortez arrives in Mexico from Cuba with a group of Spanish adventurers.
1521	Cortez takes Tenochtitlán, conquering Aztec Empire and initiating three hundred years of Spanish rule over Mexico.
1535	First Spanish Viceroy arrives in Mexico.
1692	Spanish reconquer rebellious Pueblo Indians in present New Mexico.
	Major food riot in Mexico City.
1810	Miguel Hidalgo y Costilla, a priest, proclaims Mexican independence from Spain on September 16th.
1811	Hidalgo captured and executed by Spanish.
1813	Another priest, José María Morelos, leads liberation of much of southern Mexico from Spanish control. Drafts a constitution calling for fair land distribution and racial equality.
1815	Morelos captured and executed by Spanish.
1821	Spain adopts a progressive constitution.
	Conservative forces led by former Spanish officer Agustín de Iturbide secure Mexican independence.
1822	Iturbide crowned Emperor Agustín I.
	Mexico annexes Central America.
	Texan politician Stephen Austin granted permission to settle U.S. colonists in Texas.
1823	Iturbide forced to abdicate. Central America secedes from Mexico.
1824	First constitution drafted. Guadalupe Victoria elected first president of Mexico.
1828	Mexico abolishes slavery in attempt to discourage Anglo settlement of Texas.
1830	Mexican government bans further Anglo settlement of Texas.

1834	Texas secedes from Mexico.

1836   Mexican General Santa Anna arrives in Texas with an army. He storms the Alamo but is defeated and captured at San Jacinto by rebellious Texans. Forced to grant Texas independence.

1845   United States annexes Texas.

1846   Border skirmishes lead to United States declaration of war on Mexico.

1847   General Zachary Taylor decisively defeats Mexican forces at Angostura.

A U.S. army under Winfield Scott lands at Veracruz and then takes Mexico City.

1848   Mexico signs Treaty of Guadalupe Hidalgo. In exchange for $15 million, Mexico cedes California, Nevada, Arizona, New Mexico, Utah, and part of Colorado to United States.

1853   United States purchases large tract of southern New Mexico and Arizona from Mexico for railroad expansion. Known as the Gadsen Purchase.

1857   Mexico's Liberal government adopts a new constitution, limiting church power and broadening individual freedoms.

Conservatives stage a revolt and take Mexico City.

Benito Juárez leads Liberal forces.

1860   Juárez recaptures Mexico City and becomes first full-blooded Indian president of Mexico.

1861   Spanish, British, and French forces occupy Veracruz demanding repayment of debts. British and Spanish appeased, but French stay with goal of making Mexico a colony.

1862   French forces badly defeated at Puebla.

1863   French install Maximilian, Austrian Emperor's brother, as Mexico's emperor.

Juárez flees to north.

1867   Juárez captures and executes Maximilian.

1876   Juárez's successor, Lerdo de Tejada, overthrown by General Porfirio Díaz.

1906   The U.S. owner of Cananea copper mine in Sonora calls in Arizona Rangers to bloodily put down a strike.

Mexican Liberals in St. Louis, Missouri, issue proclamation against Díaz.

1910   Moderate Francisco Madero proclaims Plan of San Luis Potosí, calling for revolt against Díaz and free elections. Beginning of Mexican Revolution as rebellions break out in the north and in Puebla.

1911   After thirty-five years of rule, Díaz resigns in the face of expanding rebellions and is exiled to France.

Madero returns from exile in the United States and is elected president in October.

Emiliano Zapata, in south, declares Madero a traitor and drafts Plan of Ayala, calling for land redistribution.

1913   U.S. Ambassador Henry Lane Wilson negotiates alliance between General Victoriano Huerta and Felix Díaz, Porfirio's nephew.

Huerta has Madero killed and assumes presidency.

Pancho Villa and Venustiano Carranza, in north, and Emiliano Zapata, in south, all take up arms against Huerta.

1914   U.S. troops occupy Veracruz to deprive Huerta of arms shipments.

Huerta flees Mexico, and Carranza's forces under General Alvaro Obregón take Mexico City.

Revolutionary convention at Aguascalientes adopts Plan of Ayala.

Carranza openly splits with Villa and Zapata, and is forced to abandon Mexico City. United States throws its support behind Carranza.

U.S. soldiers withdraw from Veracruz.

1915   Obregón defeats Villa at Celaya, but Villa continues to fight.

Carranza recognized by the United States as chief of government forces.

1916   Villa raids town of Columbus, New Mexico. U.S. army under General John Pershing immediately invades Mexico in search of Villa.

Carranza's forces invade Morelos, center of Zapata's support.

1917   Pershing withdraws from Mexico, failing to find Villa.

Carranza's government adopts the Constitution of 1917, providing for labor and land reform. Carranza elected constitutional president.

1919   Carranza uses treachery to have Zapata murdered.

1920   Obregón overthrows Carranza, who is killed. Villa ends his rebellion.

1921   José Vasconcelos becomes Minister of Education and starts literacy campaign.

1923   United States and Mexico sign Bucareli Agreements, guaranteeing sanctity of U.S. property in Mexico in exchange for United States recognition of Obregón's government.

Villa assassinated.

1924   United States gives Obregón arms to suppress a coup.

Mexico recognizes Soviet Union.

Plutarco Elías Calles elected president.

1926   Calles's anticlerical policies leads to Cristero Rebellion, an uprising of priests and peasants.

1928   Calles succeeded by Obregón, who is assassinated in July.

1929	Founding of National Revolutionary Party (PNR), and Cristero Rebellion suppressed. Calles, who remains political strongman through 1935, chooses Emilio Portes Gil as president.
1934	Lázaro Cárdenas assumes presidency, with support of workers, peasants, and leading elements of military.
1936	Cárdenas sends Calles into exile. The president arms 60,000 peasants to support his sweeping land reforms.
1938	Cárdenas nationalizes oil industry. United States responds with economic sanctions.
1940	Manuel Avilo Camacho succeeds Cárdenas.
1942	United States and Mexico initiate Bracero Program, allowing Americans to contract Mexican agricultural labor.
1943	Mexico declares Texas off-limits to Bracero Program because of racism.
1946	Miguel Alemán elected President.
	Ruling party renamed Institutional Revolutionary Party, or PRI.
1952	Adolfo Ruiz Cortines succeeds Alemán.
	United States begins deporting illegal Mexican workers as part of "Operation Wetback."
1954	Women granted right to vote.
1958	López Mateos elected president.
1963	Mexico and United States settle Chamizal boundary dispute, which arose in 1864 when the Rio Grande changed its course and passed 440 acres of Mexican territory to the U.S. side of the river.
1964	Gustavo Díaz Ordaz assumes presidency.
	Bracero Program suspended.
1965	Border Industrialization Program (BIP) created by Mexican government.
1968	Prior to Mexico City's hosting of Olympics, government brutally cracks down on leftist student demonstrations; hundreds of demonstrators massacred at Tlatelolco.
1970	Luis Echeverría elected president. The foreign policy activism and "Mexicanization" investment policies of the Echeverría government stimulates a significant downturn in U.S. relations with Mexico.
1976	José López Portillo assumes presidency. During his term, high oil revenues bring record growth to Mexican economy and stimulate massive borrowing by government.
1977	The government launches electoral reform in face of growing voter apathy and criticism about the country's "one-party democracy." Chamber of Deputies increased to 400 seats to make room for opposition parties.

1979   Mexico breaks off relations with Nicaraguan dictator Anastasio Somoza and refuses to admit the Shah of Iran following his ouster by fundamentalist Islamic forces. The two actions rankle the U.S. administration of President Jimmy Carter.

1980   President López Portillo decides that Mexico will not joint the General Agreement on Tariffs and Trade (GATT)

1981   Oil prices plummet late in year.

   Mexico and United States establish the U.S.-Mexico Joint Commission on Commerce and Trade for government-to-government consultations.

1982   Mexico forced to suspend payments on principal of foreign debt. Mexico's economic crisis, coupled with the global assertion of U.S. hegemony under the Reagan administration, weakens Mexico's position vis-a-vis the United States and reduces Mexico's freedom to differ with Washington over economic and international issues.

   President López Portillo nationalizes banking system.

   Miguel de la Madrid elected president. Mexico's massive foreign debt forces him to implement an economic stabilization program with austerity measures and to begin a neoliberal restructuring program by midterm.

1983   A wave of local victories by the center-right PAN raises new questions about the invincibility of the PRI government.

1985   Mexico City hit by devastating earthquake on September 19; prompts upsurge of popular organizing.

   Founding of EUREKA and other grassroots human rights organizations.

   Slaying of DEA agent Enrique Camarena in Mexico strains U.S.-Mexican relations.

1986   Another electoral reform, again designed to increase the government's credibility, increases the number of Chamber seats to 500, but conditions for effective multiparty democracy still do not exist.

   Mexico joins the multilateral trade agreement GATT, ushering in a new period of trade liberalization.

1987   Mexico and United States sign the bilateral framework agreement for trade and investment.

   A PRI faction called the Democratic Current leaves the party after the selection of technocrat Carlos Salinas de Gortari as presidential candidate. The Democratic Current, led by Cuauhtémoc Cárdenas, goes on to form the National Democratic Front (FDN) to contest the 1988 presidential elections.

1988   Carlos Salinas de Gortari defeats opposition candidate Cuauhtémoc Cárdenas in presidential elections. Accusations of fraud lead to massive protests.

1989   The Party of the Democratic Revolution (PRD) formally founded, succeeding the FDN electoral coalition led by Cuauhtémoc Cárdenas.

Mexico and United States undertake bilateral Trade and Investment Facilitation Talks (TIFTS).

PAN wins first governorship in Baja California (Norte).

A constitutional amendment paves the way for another electoral reform which is later approved by most opposition party members with the exception of those belonging to the PRD.

Carlos Jonguitud, *cacique*-style leader of national teachers union (SNTE) removed from office as result of grassroots protests.

Year-end agreements with multilateral lenders and commercial banks reduce Mexico's commercial debt and ease debt-service schedule.

1990   President Bush and President Salinas issue joint statement in June in support of negotiations for free trade agreement.

1991   Canada joins free trade negotiations for the establishment of a North American Free Trade Agreement (NAFTA) in February.

Congress allows fast-track trade NAFTA negotiations to proceed in June.

Large PRI plurality in 1991 midterm elections restores official party's strong hold in Congress. Next presidential election scheduled for 1994.

Abbreviations

AID	U.S. Agency for International Development
CBDH	Binational Human Rights Center
Canacintra	National Chamber of Manufacturing Industries
CCC	Commodity Credit Corporation
CCE	Businessmen's Coordinating Council
CD	Democratic Current
CDP	Popular Defense Committees
CEMAI	National Foreign Trade Council
CFE	Federal Electricity Commission
CMHN	Mexico Council of Businessmen
CNC	National Peasant Confederation
CNDH	National Human Rights Commission
CNOP	National Federation of Popular Organizations
CNPA	National Coordinator/Plan of Ayala
CNPI	National Coordinator of Indian Peoples
CNTE	National Coordinator of Education Workers
COCEI	Student-Worker-Peasant Coalition of the Isthmus
COECE	Coordinator of Foreign Trade Groups
Conamup	National Coordinator of Urban Popular Movements
Conasupo	National Staple Products Company
Concamin	Confederation of Industrial Chambers
Concanaco	Confederation of Chambers of Commerce
Coparmex	Mexican Employers Confederation
CROC	Revolutionary Confederation of Workers and Peasants
CROM	Revolutionary Confederation of Mexican Workers
CT	Labor Congress
CTM	Mexican Workers Confederation
DEA	Drug Enforcement Administration
DFS	Directorate of Federal Security
DIF	National System for the Integral Development of the Family
ECLA	Economic Commission for Latin America and the Caribbean
EC	European Community

FDN	National Democratic Front
FTA	Free Trade Agreement
GAO	U.S. General Accounting Office
GATT	General Agreement on Tariffs and Trade
GDP	Gross Domestic Product
GNP	Gross National Product
IFI	International Financial Institutions
IMF	International Monetary Fund
IMSS	Mexican Institute of Social Security
INEGI	National Institute of Statistics, Geography, and Information
INS	U.S. Immigration and Naturalization Service
ITC	U.S. International Trade Commission
Nafinsa	National Finance Company
NAFTA	North American Free Trade Agreement
NED	National Endowment for Democracy
NGO	Nongovernmental Organization
PAN	National Action Party
PARM	Authentic Party of the Mexican Revolution
PDM	Mexican Democratic Party
PEM	Mexican Ecologist Party
Pemex	Mexican Petroleum Company
PFCRN	Party of Cárdenas Front for National Reconstruction
PGR	Office of the Attorney General
PJF	Federal Judicial Police
PMS	Mexican Socialist Party
PPS	Popular Socialist Party
PRD	Party of the Democratic Revolution
PRI	Institutional Revolutionary Party
PRM	Party of the Mexican Revolution
Pronasol	National Solidarity Program
Provida	National Pro-Life Committee
PRT	Revolutionary Workers Party
SAM	Mexican Food System
SECOFI	Ministry of Trade and Industrial Development
SEDUE	Ministry of Urban Development and Ecology
SEP	Ministry of Public Education
SNTE	National Union of Education Workers
SPP	Ministry of Planning and the Budget
STPRM	Petroleum Workers Union of the Mexican Republic
Telmex	Mexican Telephone Company
TNC	Transnational Corporation
UNAM	National Autonomous University of Mexico
USDA	U.S. Department of Agriculture

Index

Extraños No Más

This pocket-size booklet answers questions that Spanish-speaking immigrants have about life in the United States. Extraños No Más provides vital information in Spanish about deportation, amnesty, temporary work permits, and legal rights. Also included is basic information about living in the United States and an extensive list of immigrant aid organizations, farmworker associations, consulates, and legal aid centers.

48-page booklet
isbn 0-911213-37-6. First edition, November 1991

1-10 copies   **$2.00 each (postpaid)**
11-99 copies   **$ .60 each (postpaid)**
100+ copies   **$ .25 each (postpaid)**

Cross-Border Links

Canada–United States–Mexico

This invaluable and timely directory provides an English/Spanish annotated listing of all educational, social justice, labor organizations, and scholarly and business groups with a special interest in relations between Mexico, Canada, and the United States. Cross-Border Links lists organization name, description of activity, key contact, address, phone, and publications.

50 pages
isbn 0-911213-38-4, First edition, April 1992.

$6.95

Mexico PUBLICATIONS

ORDERS

When calculating charges, include $2.50 postage for the first item you order; add 50¢ for each additional item. Subscriptions to the quarterly Resource Center **Bulletin** are $5.00 annually ($7.50 foreign). Send orders and correspondence to:

R E S O U R C E   C E N T E R
PO Box 4506 • Albuquerque, NM 87196
Phone: (505) 842-8288 • Fax: (505) 246-1601

Please call or write for a complete catalog of Resource Center publications!

COUNTRY GUIDE SERIES ◆

The Country Guide Series

"The Country Guides fill a serious need. Executed with care and accuracy, they provide an invaluable guide to understanding the Central American region."

— Noam Chomsky

Each book in the Country Guide series gives you the most up-to-date, comprehensive information available on one of the most rapidly changing regions in the world. Ideal for educators, students, travelers, and activists.

$9.95 each

Belize: A Country Guide
by Tom Barry
paperback, 115 pages
isbn 0-911213-32-5, Third edition, March 1992

Guatemala: A Country Guide
by Tom Barry
Paperback, 190 pages
isbn 0-911213-33-3, Third edition, April 1992

El Salvador : A Country Guide
by Tom Barry
paperback, 193 pages
isbn 0-911213-30-9, Second edition, January 1991

Honduras: A Country Guide
by Tom Barry and Kent Norsworthy
paperback, 160 pages
isbn 0-911213-22-8, May 1990

Nicaragua: A Country Guide
by Kent Norsworthy with Tom Barry
paperback, 226 pages
isbn 0-911213-29-5, Second edition, December 1990

Costa Rica: A Country Guide
by Tom Barry
paperback, 108 pages
isbn 0-911213-36-8, Third edition, June 1991

Panama: A Country Guide
by Tom Barry
paperback, 154 pages
isbn 0-911213-24-4, April 1990

Other **P U B L I C A T I O N S**

ORDERS

When calculating charges, include $2.50 postage for the first item you order; add 50¢ for each additional item. Subscriptions to the quarterly Resource Center *Bulletin* are $5.00 annually ($7.50 foreign). Send orders and correspondence to:

R E S O U R C E   C E N T E R
PO Box 4506 • Albuquerque, NM 87196
Phone: (505) 842-8288 • Fax: (505) 246-1601

Please call or write for a complete catalog of Resource Center publications!